SOURCEBOOK

FOR SUNDAYS, SEASONS, AND WEEKDAYS 2021 • YEAR B–I

THE ALMANAC FOR PASTORAL LITURGY

Leisa Anslinger, Eric Bermani, Michael Cameron, Paul H. Colloton, OSFS, Kate Cousino, Mary Katharine Deeley, Ann Dickinson Degenhard, Mary A. Ehle, Edrianne Ezell, Christopher J. Ferraro, Mary Frances Fleischaker, OP, Patrick J. Hartin, Kathy Hendricks, J. Philip Horrigan, Patricia Hughes, Timothy A. Johnston, Maggie Kast, Ed Langlois, Corinna Laughlin, Maria Leonard, John Marquez, Anne C. McGuire, Mary O'Neill McManus, Michael McManus, Jill Maria Murdy, Michael R. Prendergast, Paul Radkowski, Jakob Rinderknecht, Tanya Rybarvzyk, Daniel J. Scholz, Anne Elizabeth Sweet, OSCO

Nihil Obstat
Rev. Mr. Daniel G. Welter, JD
Chancellor
Archdiocese of Chicago
December 23, 2019

Imprimatur
Most Rev. Ronald A. Hicks
Vicar General
Archdiocese of Chicago
December 23, 2019

The *Nihil Obstat* and *Imprimatur* are declarations that the material is free from doctrinal or moral error, and thus is granted permission to publish in accordance with c. 827. No legal responsibility is assumed by the grant of this permission. No implication is contained herein that those who have granted the *Nihil Obstat* and *Imprimatur* agree with the content, opinions, or statements expressed.

LTP is grateful to the many authors and publishers who have given permission to include their work in this resource. LTP is especially grateful for contributing authors of past editions of *At Home with the Word; Children's Liturgy of the Word*; *Pastoral Liturgy*® Magazine; and *Sourcebook for Sundays, Seasons, and Weekdays* for providing additional material. Every effort has been made to determine the ownership of all texts to make proper arrangements for their use. Any oversight that may have occurred, if brought to our attention, will gladly be corrected in future editions.

This book was edited by Danielle A. Noe. Christian Rocha was the production editor, Anna Manhart was the designer, and Kari Nicholls was the production artist.

Cover art by Cody F. Miller. Interior art by Martin Erspamer, OSB.

Printed in the United States of America

ISBN: 978-1-61671-549-6

SSS21

Contents

Abbreviations

The following terms are used throughout the Daily Calendar in this *Sourcebook* and are abbreviated as noted below. This file is available as a free supplemental PDF download on www.ltp.org.

Book of Blessings	BB
Ceremonial of Bishops	CB
Collection of Masses for the Blessed Virgin Mary: Missal	CMMM
Collection of Masses for the Blessed Virgin Mary: Lectionary	CMML
Common of Apostles	CA
Common of the Dedication of a Church	CDCh
Common of the Blessed Virgin Mary	CBVM
Common of Martyrs	CM
Common of Pastors	CP
Common of Doctors of the Church	CDC
Common of Saints	CS
Common of Virgins	CV
Common of Holy Men and Women	CHMW
Constitution on the Sacred Liturgy	CSL
Dies Domini	DD
Eucharistic Prayer	EP
Eucharistic Prayer for use in Masses for Various Needs	EPVN
Eucharistic Prayer for Reconciliation	EPR
Foundations for Preaching and Teaching	FPT
Gaudium et spes	GS
Gregorian Institute of America, Inc.	GIA
Gospel	G
Lectionary for Mass	LM
Lectionary for Masses with Children	LMC
Lectionary for Mass: Introduction	LMI
Lectionary Supplement	LS
Liturgy of the Hours	LH
Liturgy Training Publications	LTP
Lumen gentium	LG
Masses and Prayers for Various Needs	MPVN
Order of Baptism of Children	OBC
Order of Christian Funerals	OCF
Order of Confirmation	OC
Order of Celebrating Matrimony	OCM
Oregon Catholic Press	OCP
Ordinary Time	OT
Paschale Solemnitatis	PSol
Pastoral Care of the Sick: Rites of Anointing and Viaticum	PCS
Preface	P
Penitential Act	PA
Prayer over the People	PP
Proper of Saints	PS
Proper of Time	PT
Rite of Christian Initiation of Adults	RCIA
Rite of Penance	RP
The Roman Missal	RM
Seasonal Weekday	SW
Solemn Blessing	SB
Sourcebook for Sundays, Seasons, and Weekdays	SSS21
Universal Norms on the Liturgical Year and the General Roman Calendar	UNLY
Universal Prayer	UP
World Library Publications	WLP

How to Use *Sourcebook for Sundays, Seasons, and Weekdays*

WELCOME to *Sourcebook* 2021! *Sourcebook* has been a trusted resource for priests, deacons, parish musicians, and liturgy coordinators for decades. *Sourcebook* has been redesigned and reenvisioned to make it as useful as possible for your whole liturgy team. This introduction provides an overview of what you'll find inside and some ideas for how to use it.

Use *Sourcebook* to Prepare Masses for Sundays, Solemnities, and Feasts of the Lord

Gathering for Mass on Sunday is the heart of parish life, and the pages dedicated to each Sunday of the year are the heart of this *Sourcebook*. For every Sunday, as well as for every solemnity and feast of the Lord, you'll find a wealth of material to help you prepare the parish liturgy.

The entry for each Sunday, solemnity, and feast of the Lord begins with the basics: the full name of the liturgical observance, the date in the civil calendar, and the Lectionary numbers both for the *Lectionary for Mass* (LM) and the *Lectionary for Masses with Children* (LMC), and vestment colors. A brief introduction provides context and background for special feasts and observances. Under "Scripture Insights" you will find a thoughtful commentary on the readings of the day. This section does not summarize but rather synthesizes the readings, making connections between the readings and the season. "Preaching Points" are provided for each Sunday for parish Masses (intergenerational) and for children's Liturgy of the Word. These features will be helpful not only for preachers, but also for readers, adult initiation dismissal leaders, and those who prepare homilies and reflections for the Liturgy of the Word with children.

Sourcebook also serves as an indispensable companion to the Missal, helping you navigate the sometimes bewildering array of options the Missal offers. Under "Missal Options" you'll find a bulleted list, indicating the prayers and Prefaces that may (or must) be used, as well as highlighting other possibilities (Gloria, Creed, sprinkling rite, and so on) and suggesting a Eucharistic Prayer. Under "Other Rites and Customs," you'll find another bulleted list, which indicates special rites associated with a particular day or season. You'll be reminded of how many candles to light on the Advent wreath, and when rites like Baptisms could (or shouldn't) be celebrated in the context of the Mass. For parish musicians, there is a bulleted list of "Music Preparation" and "Music Suggestions" which includes reminders of Church guidelines on music for the feast or season, helpful tips for parish musicians, and concrete suggestions of appropriate music, ranging from hymns, to psalm settings, to Mass parts, along with details about where you can find them.

This edition of *Sourcebook* will also help you keep track of the complex and overlapping civic and liturgical calendars. For every Sunday, solemnity, and feast of the Lord you'll find a bulleted list that notes upcoming civic observances and liturgical observances—special holidays or days of remembrance like Labor Day and Mother's Day, as well as holydays of obligation or feast days. This information can prompt ideas for the intercessions and the parish announcements as well and is listed under the heading "Taking Place this Week."

The entries for each Sunday include original texts for use in the liturgy. There are newly composed invocations for the Penitential Act, form III, which draw inspiration from the readings of the day and the themes of the liturgical season. You'll also find full texts for three dismissals that may be used during the Mass: the Dismissal for the Children's Liturgy of the Word, the Dismissal of Catechumens and Elect, and the Dismissal of Extraordinary Ministers of Holy Communion who are sent forth to bring Communion to the homebound or to those in hospitals at the end of Mass. In addition, a complete text for the Universal Prayer is provided for each Sunday, solemnity, and feast of the Lord. All of these texts can be used as they are, or they can be freely adapted or simply used to inspire the texts composed for your own parish community.

Finally, the section "Liturgy and Life" invites all who are involved in preparing the liturgy to reflect on the meaning of each liturgical celebration, and find ways to pray more deeply in the seasons of the year and through our liturgical ministry as well as become committed to Gospel acts of charity and justice.

Use *Sourcebook* to Prepare Weekday Masses

Sourcebook is unique among the resources currently available in providing substantial guidance not only for Sunday, but for every day of the liturgical year. You will find brief "Scripture Insights" on the weekday readings and preaching points for parish Masses, with additional preaching points for Masses with children (whether taking place at school or in the parish). For those days in which those who preside, preach, and prepare the liturgy have the option of selecting readings from the Proper of Saints instead of the seasonal weekday, Scripture Insights and Preaching Points have been provided for these days!

This resource also includes short theological reflections on the charism of the saint, which should be more helpful to both preachers and catechists in getting to the heart of the celebration in their preaching and teaching. You'll also find a summary of "Missal Options," with reminders of texts that should be used, as well as suggestions for appropriate optional texts. The segment on "Other Rites and Customs" offers reminders of seasonally appropriate rites and suggests ways to weave traditions or observances into the community's prayer. The daily "Song of Day" segment features hymn suggestions drawn from a range of sources, ancient and contemporary, based on the liturgy of the day, for every single day of the year. The weekday calendar entries also include the full name of the liturgical observance, the date in the civil calendar, and the Lectionary numbers both for the *Lectionary for Mass* (LM) and the *Lectionary for Masses with Children* (LMC), and vestment colors. This resource also includes references to the other options from the Proper of Saints and the Commons.

Use *Sourcebook* to Prepare for the Liturgical Year

For each of the seasons of the liturgical year—Advent, Christmas Time, Lent, Triduum, Easter Time, and Ordinary Time—an extensive introduction offers a detailed overview. Regular users of this resource will find a fresh approach to the seasonal introductions in *Sourcebook 2021.* There are four major sections to each of the introductions:

- **The Meaning of the Season** provides theological and historical reflection on each season of the year in a clear and accessible way. The commentary draws on Scripture and on Church documents to give all who prepare the liturgy a sound understanding of what each season is—and what it isn't!
- **The Sounds of the Season** is full of wisdom for parish musicians. There are specific suggestions of appropriate music for each season of the year, as well as ideas for how we can keep the seasons *through* the music, from the waiting and expectation of Advent, to the festive joy of Christmas Time, the penitential simplicity of Lent, and the exuberance of Easter.
- **The Look of the Season** offers ideas for arranging the liturgical environment throughout the year. You'll find a summary of what the documents have to say about the arrangement and decoration of the worship space for each season of the year, as well as an abundance of ideas to consider for your own parish community.

- **Evangelizing the Parish through the Season** is a brand-new feature in this year's *Sourcebook.* This segment includes ideas for reaching out to the parish community and beyond through the liturgy throughout the year.

Use the *Sourcebook* Online Supplement to Prepare for Special Rites

In the online supplement of *Sourcebook* you'll find pages dedicated to each of the rites that form such an important part of the parish's liturgical life, from Baptism and Confirmation to Marriage, Anointing of the Sick, funerals, and many others. There are also pages dedicated to rites that a parish may celebrate less frequently or even once in a lifetime—the Liturgy of the Hours, Sunday celebrations in the absence of a priest, Ordination and religious profession, and the Dedication of a Church and Altar. You'll also find guidance on other devotions and prayers, like Worship of the Eucharist outside of Mass, the saints, and devotions and sacramentals. Each of these sections includes an overview of the rite, a bulleted list of seasonal considerations (when can or should these rites be celebrated? When should they not be celebrated?), and a list of recommended reading that will point you to key passages in Church documents. Liturgy committees will find the questions for discussion and reflection especially helpful as they prepare and evaluate the celebrations of the rites in the parish community. The supplement is available for free download at: https://ltp.org/sss.

Use *Sourcebook* to Prepare, Enrich, and Evaluate Liturgy in Your Parish

Sourcebook can help with long-term preparation in your parish. If you're in a rut, or if the liturgy in the parish feels stale or uninspired, assign "homework"—have each member of your liturgy committee and environment team read the seasonal introduction and reflect on it. Ask people to find something they love and something that rubs them the wrong way. Talk about why. You'll be on your way to a fresh approach to the liturgical season.

To help you use *Sourcebook* for preparation, a sample agenda for a liturgy committee meeting has been included at the end of each seasonal introduction. The agenda includes questions that can help get a conversation started on the season, and help open up new ideas for everything from liturgical environment to liturgical evangelization.

Use *Sourcebook* to become Familiar with the Evangelist for Year B

It is Year B in the Sunday Lectionary cycle and Week I in the weekday cycle. The primary evangelist for Year B is Mark. Understanding the order and flow of the Lectionary (and the season and special days that occur during the liturgical year) should guide your liturgical preparations—music selection, prayer texts (where there are options and when texts need to be composed), homily and reflection preparation, and catechesis. *Sourcebook* will help you become more familiar with the Scripture readings, providing valuable insights for preparation purposes. What follows is an overview of the Gospel according to Mark.

In the late 60s of the first century, nearly forty years since the Resurrection and Ascension of the Lord, he had not yet returned. Jerusalem was under siege by the Romans, and the persecution of Christians in Rome itself was intensifying after the fire of 64. Peter and Paul had died, and few eye witnesses to Jesus' ministry were left. Christians had told and retold the stories of Jesus' ministry, Death, and Resurrection over the years, but Christians began to feel the need for written instruction.

In these years, Mark, leaning on the teachings of Peter and others, wrote his Gospel, the earliest one we have. It is likely that he wrote for his suffering community in the environs of Rome. His main concern was to record the basic facts and stay faithful to the tradition, and Mark wrote with a flair for the dramatic and a rich theological sense.

Suffering had thrown Mark's community into a spiritual crisis. The crisis came not because of weak faith, but through a strong faith too focused on the privileges and glory of being the community of the Resurrection: Being disciples meant enjoying the benefits of Jesus' victory (see 10:35–45). As a counterweight to this, Mark refocused on Jesus' Death as the foundation of discipleship (8:31–35).

Mark's primary themes of the Kingdom of God, the identity of Jesus, and the call to discipleship each undergo dramatic development in the Gospel in light of the Cross. For Mark, everything, even Jesus' glorious return, stands in the shadow of his Crucifixion. The German New Testament scholar Martin Kähler aptly called the Gospel according to Mark "a passion narrative with an extended introduction."

In Mark's first chapters, Jesus is a messianic figure on the move, proclaiming the nearness of God's Kingdom in his words and works. As the Spirit "drove" Jesus into the wilderness after his baptism (1:12), so Jesus charges the early pages of Mark with divine power and urgency. The synagogue exorcism in 1:21–28 demonstrates Jesus' mastery of the spiritual world; the healings that follow in 1:29—2:10 reveal that the Kingdom's power lies in redemptive service. Jesus never defines the Kingdom of God, but the parables of chapter 4 describe its characteristics. Irresistibly it comes, grows, changes everything, feeds everyone. It heals bodies, repairs hearts, defeats evil, creates community. Nothing stops its relentless coming; not sin (2:7), disease (1:40–45), calamity (4:35–41), or demonic forces (3:22–27). The Kingdom emerges as a result of God's action, not humanity's.

The unfeeling religious leaders fail to receive the message (3:1–6). They lack the spiritual eyes and ears to perceive the new in-breaking of God's love in Jesus' ministry and the new turning to God's love that this requires. Paradoxically Jesus does find this among tax collectors (2:15–17), the sick (1:29–34), and the wretched (5:1–20).

Initial faith through the miracles is only a first step. The disciples struggle to fulfill the Master's hopes for them. "Do you not yet have faith?" Jesus asks early on (4:40). After Jesus feeds the five thousand, he cares for the disciples by walking to them on the water during their midnight struggle. They merely become frightened, Mark comments, "They had not understood the incident of the loaves. On the contrary, their hearts were hardened" (6:52). Jesus tries again by feeding the four thousand, but their minds are fixed on literal bread. "Do you still not understand?" Jesus asks (8:21).

Peter confesses that Jesus is the Messiah (8:29). But his awareness is only partial, for he needs Jesus to fit his expectations, which definitively exclude suffering. Jesus calls the idea satanic (8:33). Eventually one disciple betrays him, another denies him, and all desert him. Some readers think that Mark's telling of the disciples' failures is his way of disparaging "official" Christian leadership. But the disciples were later reconciled to the Lord after his Resurrection and lived to prove their faith. It is more likely that Mark is encouraging Jesus' followers to take heart from the disciples' example of recovery from failure. With Peter's martyrdom still a recent memory, the story of him denying the Lord would have special power.

The Son of God has a rich, deep humanity in this Gospel. Mark's Greek word for Jesus' reaction to the plight of the leper in 1:41 might be translated "his heart melted with compassion," the same word used for Jesus' compassion on the crowds.

Jesus insists that his divinity should not be made known (1:44; 3:12; 5:43; 7:36; 8:26, 30), a motif known as the messianic secret. He refuses to be the political messiah that people expected. He reinterpreted honors in terms of his mission as suffering servant, processing into Jerusalem on a humble little donkey (11:1–10), not a horse, as a conquering king would. He is anointed by an anonymous woman, not for enthronement but for burial (14:3–9). He wears royal attire and receives homage from the Gentiles, but in mockery (15:16–20). Jesus establishes the new covenant of Jeremiah 31 by becoming the Suffering Servant of Isaiah 53: "This is my blood of the covenant poured out for many" (14:24).

From the beginning the reader knows that Jesus is the Son of God (1:1). Throughout the Gospel the only voices to confess his true identity come from God (1:11; 9:7) and demons (1:24; 3:11; 5:7). Meanwhile, religious leaders call him demon-possessed (3:22), his family thinks he's a lunatic (3:21), and village neighbors complain he's pretentious (6:2–3). To their credit the disciples do begin to wonder, "Who then is this?" (4:41). But no human lips confess his true identity—until the end. Stripped of his dignity, his disciples, his life, destitute and utterly alone, Jesus draws his last breath. But at this precise moment the long-awaited confession comes from a Roman centurion: "Truly this man was the Son of God!" (15:39). Jesus' Death reveals the identity of God's Son, a living tableau of the disciples' calling to live the Way of the Cross. The Resurrection is proclaimed by disciples who have received a new life after they have lost their lives "for my sake and that of the gospel" (8:35).

Sourcebook is for the Whole Liturgy Team

Sourcebook is a useful resource for everyone involved in the liturgy.

- **Preachers:** Use the "Preaching Points" for Sundays and weekdays. Explore the reflections on the readings for every day of the year and the "Meaning of the Season" at the beginning of each seasonal introduction.
- **Presiders:** Consult the "Missal Options" provided for each day of the year, which suggest prayers for weekdays in Ordinary Time so you can open up more of the riches of *The Roman Missal* for your parish community. Use the texts provided for the Penitential Act, the dismissals, and the Universal Prayer.
- **Liturgy Coordinators:** Use the sample agendas to prepare for meetings of your liturgy team. Use the online supplement to incorporate other rites into the parish's liturgical life. Use the seasonal introductions and the overviews of each Sunday to enhance your understanding of the liturgy and share it with parish liturgical ministers.
- **Dismissal Leaders, Catechists, and Teachers:** Read the commentaries on the readings and use the "Preaching Points" for exploring the Liturgy of the Word with catechumens or with children at a separate Liturgy of the Word. Use the brief reflections on the saints to teach about the many gifts of the Spirit and the many paths to Christian holiness.
- **Parish Musicians:** Look at the "Music Preparation" and "Music Suggestions" for each Sunday and at the "Song of the Day" for weekdays. Reflect on "The Sound of the Season" in each seasonal introduction. Try something new in each season of the year.
- **Sacristans:** Use *Sourcebook* along with your *Ordo* to mark the Lectionary and the Missal and to prepare the vestments for each day. Look ahead to Sundays for a reminder of special ritual elements that need to be prepared.

It is LTP's hope that *Sourcebook 2021* will be an indispensable resource for preparing the liturgy in your parish, something to keep on the counter in the sacristy all year round and to bring to every meeting of the liturgy committee, a book that will help you carry out your important ministry in service of the liturgy of the Church. If you have questions or concerns please contact LTP: orders@ltp.org.

Sample Preparation Calendar

The following calendar may be used in conjunction with *Sourcebook* and your seasonal preparation. This calendar indicates at what point in the year liturgy committees should meet to discuss and prepare a particular season or feast. It also includes a proposed time for evaluating how the liturgies took place in your parish.

Season or Feast	Initial Preparation	Final Preparation	Evaluation
Advent	mid-September	mid-October	following the season
Christmas (Vigil through Day)	mid-September	mid-October	following the season
Christmas Time (Holy Family—Baptism of the Lord)	early October	early November	following the season
Ordinary Time during Winter	mid-November	mid-December	following the season
Lent	late December	mid-January	following the season
Sacred Paschal Triduum	early January	early February	following the season
Easter Time	late January	late February	following the season
Ordinary Time (weeks 9 to 15)	late March	late April	following the weeks
Ordinary Time (weeks 16 to 26)	late May	late June	following the weeks
Ordinary Time (weeks 27 to 34)	late July	late August	following the weeks
Patronal Feast or Anniversary	Three months before	Two months before	Two weeks after liturgy
Special Observance (i.e. Confirmation, etc.)	Three months before	Two months before	Two weeks after liturgy

This table was adapted from *Groundwork: Planning Liturgical Seasons* by Yvonne Cassa and Joanne Sanders © 1988, Liturgy Training Publications, Archdiocese of Chicago.

Advent

Grant your faithful, we pray, almighty God, the resolve to run forth to meet your Christ with righteous deeds at his coming.

—Collect, First Sunday of Advent

The Meaning of the Season

DURING every Mass, immediately after the Our Father, the priest says a short prayer known as the embolism: "Deliver us, Lord, we pray, from every evil, graciously grant peace in our days, that, by the help of your mercy, we may be always free from sin and safe from all distress, as we await the blessed hope and the coming of our Savior, Jesus Christ."

This prayer is particularly meaningful during Advent, the season when we consciously "await the blessed hope and the coming of our Savior, Jesus Christ" with joyful expectation. This kind of waiting is often difficult, as joy and expectation do not generally characterize our everyday experiences of waiting. Few of us are filled with hope as we sit in a traffic jam, stand at a bus stop, or experience delays when traveling by plane or train. We shop online and are willing to pay for guaranteed two-day (or overnight) delivery. We assume that Wi-Fi access will be fast and omnipresent—and we grow less patient when we have to wait for websites, audio, or video to load. Amid these everyday experiences, the Advent liturgies play a crucial role in teaching and reminding us how we ought to wait with joyful expectation.

First, we do not wait alone or in isolation. We wait with others, as Christians have waited for two millennia. Msgr. Pierre Jounel notes that in early Advent—the three-week period dating back as far as the late fourth century—Catholics in Spain and Gaul together prepared for Epiphany and the celebration of baptism together with "asceticism, prayer, and more frequent assemblies" ("The Year," in *The Liturgy and Time*, vol. 4, ed. Martimort, pp. 91–92). In subsequent centuries, Advent celebrations with varying scriptural, ascetic, and eschatological dimensions developed in communities throughout the Christian world (see M. Connell, "The Origins and Evolution of Advent in the West," in *Between Memory and Hope*, ed. Johnson, 349–371). Eventually, these practices converged in what we now experience as a four-week season with a twofold emphasis, one in which we await both the Christmas feast of Christ's Incarnation and his Second Coming at the end of time.

For us, it can be easier to focus on the celebration of Jesus' birth than on his Second Coming. After all, many people have experiences of waiting expectantly for the birth of a child—and celebrating the birth of a baby is generally more appealing than envisioning that same baby having grown up and returning in glory to judge us. But the Advent liturgies insist that the two cannot be separated and that we should wait for both of them with equal confidence and equal joy. "Creator of the Stars of Night," a traditional chant hymn, reminds us that the same God who was born of the Virgin is also the majestic Judge to whom "all knees must bend, all hearts must bow." Preface I for Advent also directly connects the two comings: Christ "assumed at his first coming / the lowliness of human flesh" and, eventually, "when he comes again in glory and majesty . . . / we who watch for that day / may inherit the great promise / in which now we dare to hope." This year, the Second Reading for the Second Sunday of Advent offers perhaps the season's most vivid reminder that we need not wait in fear or anxiety: even though "the heavens will pass away with a mighty roar."

Advent teaches us that we are to wait actively. The season's Sunday readings leave no room for passivity. They demand action. The readings bear the same message: we are not to wait in a state of apathy or indifference. Rather, as disciples of Christ, we must make our entire lives a time of active waiting, of undergoing continual conversion and transformation. We must both heed and emulate the call of John the Baptist, who leapt for joy in the womb and who preached repentance to all whom he encountered. We must focus our lives on God.

Advent reminds us that we ought to model our waiting on Mary, the Holy Mother of God. For Catholics in the United States, both Marian observances during Advent are patronal feasts: the Immaculate Conception is the patroness of the United States, and Our Lady of Guadalupe is patroness of America (both continents). The Gospel reading for the Immaculate Conception—and, this year, for the Fourth Sunday of Advent—is Gabriel's announcement to Mary (Luke 1:26–38), when she affirms that she is and will be God's handmaid. That same Gospel passage is one of two options for Our Lady of Guadalupe, the other being the passage that follows it immediately (Luke 1:39–47), when Mary visits Elizabeth.

Waiting can be a time of great uncertainty, but these Gospel passages remind us that, for Mary, even that uncertainty was a time of great joy. Her song of praise, the Magnificat (Luke 1:46–55), extols God's saving action and presence throughout all time. This song of praise reflects that, for Mary, her *fiat*—her yes, her "may it be done to me according to your Word"—was truly a great act of trust. Even as she awaited the birth of her Son, she waited in joyful hope because she knew all that God had done for those who came before her: how he had humbled the mighty and fulfilled his promise to Abraham. As Christians who know that Jesus has already been born, has died, and has risen to save us, we too should be able to echo Mary's yes in our own lives, to trust in God and to wait in joyful hope.

This season of Advent, then, is a season that invites us to deeper conversion. As disciples of Christ, we learn anew what it means to wait as Christians. We light the candles on our wreaths, place the ornaments on our Jesse trees, and sing our Advent hymns. We pray, "Come quickly, King of kings," with the entire Church. We wait actively, trimming the hearth and setting the table. Finally, we "Rejoice! Rejoice!" in knowing that the promised Key of David, Rod of Jesse's Stem, and Emmanuel of the O Antiphons has come . . . and will come again.

The Sounds of the Season

The ongoing liturgical renewal has brought along with it a welcome awareness, and much needed reminder, that the Advent season is very distinct from that of Christmas. An important season and the beginning of the Church's liturgical year, Advent is one of the shortest seasons of the liturgical year (never having more than twenty-eight days and sometimes having as few as twenty-two). It is a rich, complex season with great potential to lead the faithful into a deeper and fuller understanding of the Christian mysteries through its ritual, liturgy, and music.

At its root source, Advent (*Adventus* is Latin for "coming") is very much about preparing for the coming of the Lord. Both terms—"preparing" and "coming"—are important and indeed synonymous with the season. As with all music chosen for liturgy, Advent selections must be both intentional and purposeful.

It is important that we keep our Advent texts faithful to the Advent season. If you have not investigated or researched incorporating the use of the *introits*, perhaps this may be the year to do so. The texts for the introits are like a rich theological tapestry: don't be afraid of approaching them and thinking of creating ways of adding them to your parish's repertoire. The best source to look at is the *Graduale Romanum*. Both the *Graduale Romanum* and the *Liber Usualis* should be on everyone's bookshelf.

Recognizing that we are all ministering with different communities, there are some other excellent resources you should be familiar with: Columba Kelly's *Saint Meinrad Entrance and Communion Antiphons for the Church Year* (OCP, 30130174), Norman Gouin's "Entrance Antiphon for Advent" (GIA, G-7992), Paul Tate's *Radiant Light: Introits for Advent and Christmas* (GIA, 7994), Russel Weismann's *Advent Communion Antiphons* (GIA, G-8520), Richard J. Clark's *Communion Antiphons for Advent* (WLP, 005309), and James Biery's *Communion Antiphons for the Advent Season* (Morning Star Music, 80-005) are but a few of the gems available.

Christoph Tietze has compiled a wonderful resource that takes the texts of the introit and pairs it with several hymn tunes, thus enabling parish music ministers to select a hymn format based solidly on the introit text. Check out *Introit Hymns for the Church Year* (WLP 017291). Richard Rice has very accessible choral settings titled *Simple Choral Gradual* (published by the Church Music Association of America). In these recent years, the restoration of the introit has caught on in many locations. Some parishes utilize the introit as a call to worship followed by a processional hymn. Other communities utilize the introit in its entirety. Some use the official Latin chant, and some use more contemporary settings. Options do exist to fit every community. Please keep it as an option as you go about preparing the music for Advent this year!

The Look of the Season

Winter comes with cold and darkness, prompting us to seek the warmth of shelter and the lights that illuminate and sparkle. In the midst of winter, on one of the shortest days of the year, we celebrate Christmas, a wonderful mixture of sacred and secular. Well, sometimes it is a confusing mixture of sacred and secular! And Advent, which is the season of promise leading us to Christmas, is often lost in family plans and school programs and singing carols for neighbors or shut-ins. How can we celebrate both seasons, which are really the two halves of an Incarnation season, with integrity and beauty?

These seasons of the Incarnation evoke a wonderful mix of sights, sounds, and smells, both sacred and secular. It seems obvious that our environment will have an Advent wreath during Advent, or that the Christmas season dictates a Nativity scene and some evergreen trees. From the First Sunday of Advent to the Baptism of the Lord, there is a natural relationship between dark and light that becomes manifest explicitly on Epiphany. This natural relationship is rooted in the timing of the seasons themselves, especially the farther north one lives. During Advent, the days get shorter and shorter, and Christmas is marked by the first lengthening of days—a peek at what the meaning of Son-Sun means for us in the English-speaking world.

Advent: violet vestments and an Advent wreath. Done. Okay, let's reconsider: the Advent wreath is clearly a strong symbol for today's Catholic and is understood for its connection to the colors of the season, purple and rose; to the four Sundays, four candles; as well as to the evergreen wreath itself, the "ever" green and the never-ending nature of a circle both reminding us of God's never-ending love, the eternal nature of the promise fulfilled with the coming of the Messiah. If the Advent wreath is to indeed be a strong symbol, however, it must clearly be an integral part of the liturgical environment and not a visual distraction. Since the candles themselves are the primary symbol, and are a primary symbol of the entire Incarnation season as well as a response to the darkening days of winter, then the candles should be prominent. The placement of the Advent wreath should not "argue" visibly with the primary liturgical focal areas, though, whether it is freestanding, on a table, or hung from the rafters. Any of these can work. Consider the following alternative, which responds to the question: how can the liturgical assembly be drawn into the ritual of the Advent wreath, as each week one more candle is lit and the circle of the wreath and the candles is somehow completed?

Over the main aisle, from the ceiling or even directly below a central light fixture, hang a very large evergreen wreath. It should be substantial and visible. One possibility is to have very large candles, also substantial and visible, so that the flames lit each week are equally visible and prominent. An alternative, however, is to have four spaces on the exterior walls of the worship area to locate the "prominent" candles. They may even be existing sconces, or they may be large freestanding candle stands. Drape deep violet, rich fabric from the sconce or the candle space to the wreath above the main aisle. The length of the fabric will be extensive, but the entire assembly will be enveloped by the semblance of a wreath, drawn together by light surrounding them and the fabric pulling them in. The purple fabric should complement the vestments and other uses of violet.

The light of the candles and the stronger visibility of the wreath without clashing with the liturgical action and liturgical focal areas speak to the Incarnation itself—Word made visible. Underscoring the entire twofold season is Christ entering our lives, and so the visible elements of the liturgical space require integrity, prominence, and beauty.

Evangelizing the Parish through the Season

Advent is one of the two preparatory seasons of the liturgical year. During this season, the Church looks back, reflecting on the promises of the coming Messiah that were filled in the Incarnation, and looks forward to the promised Day of the Lord and the fulfillment of all things. Meanwhile, most people are at their busiest, running around preparing for and already celebrating the Christmas holiday. The simple offer of a place of quiet, of retreat, and of prayer may be appreciated by many.

During this season, consider adding a weeknight public prayer service, perhaps paired with a simple dinner of soup and bread with time for conversation. Such an event need not add to the busy-ness of the season but might offer a place of retreat for already busy people. It also needn't overburden the parish staff, as the Liturgy of the Hours can be celebrated with little preparation. The Liturgy of the Hours are liturgical celebrations that can cut against peoples' expectations of Catholic prayer. The Hours may be led by properly trained laypersons and provide significant time for reflection on Scripture. The Magnificat, the canticle for Evening Prayer, provides Mary's strong words of hope in God's work for his people, and in these words the Church prophecies against the unjust structures of our world. Consider inviting those in your area who work for justice to join in these times of prayer. It might be a chance to renew an old collaboration or to build a new bridge.

The Liturgy of the Hours can also be celebrated ecumenically and so might offer opportunities for cooperation and fellowship between churches in your area. Many Protestant churches already have soup suppers with prayer during the Advent and Lenten seasons. Perhaps different congregations could host on different weeks of Advent and welcome each other into their spaces and their ways of praying Evening Prayer. Not only does this kind of cooperation strengthen bridges between churches, but it is itself a witness to the world. When Christians pray together, they enact God's love that binds all Christians to Christ and therefore to God. In the Gospel according to John, it is this unity that Jesus says is necessary if the world is to believe.

Worship Committee Agenda for Advent

Meeting Time

Consider any members who wish to discern off the committee in August, after a parish staff retreat which includes the worship committee. Invite new member(s) and celebrate informally with a picnic lunch in late August or early fall. The first official meeting to discuss Advent should be in mid-September.

Goal for Meeting

- Consider Lectionary Year B, using *Sourcebook 2021* as introduction, and decide on the scriptural emphasis for Advent
- The Advent wreath: what does it mean, what is needed (a replacement or renewal), where should it be placed?
- Commit to using Invocations I, spoken or chanted, found in appendix VI of *The Roman Missal*, throughout the season of Advent.
- Consider and decide what seasonal catechesis to provide, in the bulletin or on the parish website, made available in late November. Post an article or two from the archive of *Pastoral Liturgy*, https://www.pastoralliturgy.org. Also, locate, select, and publish several bulletin inserts that may provide helpful liturgical catechesis for the parish.
- December 25 falls on Friday; determine the Vigil of Christmas, Christmas, and January 1 Mass times; advertise early and often.
- Liturgically, gently restrain the musical instrumentation and hymn choices to build a prayerful sense of joyful anticipation of Christmas. Agree to emphasize psalmody, perhaps even during the Communion procession.

Opening Prayer

- Set up four Advent candles and use Luke 1:1–56 as a scriptural reflection to focus on the season of Advent.
- Pray the Liturgy of the Hours together, either Morning or Evening Prayer. Invite a parish musician to accompany an opening song and an accessible version of the Benedictus or the Canticle of Mary.

Seasonal Questions and Initiatives

- Which team will organize the smooth liturgical environment transition(s) from the conclusion of Ordinary Time to beginning Advent to the season of Christmas? Who will schedule this, find volunteers, and assess after the season?
- Attend early to storage concerns and budget considerations regarding what is needed and what may need to be replaced, anticipating Advent and the season of Christmas.
- What liturgical catechesis should happen with the People of God during the season of Advent? How can "joyful anticipation" be part of Advent homilies? How will this catechesis be communicated to the catechists for children and for youth ministry? How will "occasional worshipers" who visit your parish know about the topics you selected for catechesis?
- Should extra, or more convenient, occasions be scheduled for the Sacrament of Penance? If so, ask someone to gauge the numbers of persons taking advantage of a renewed (or new) schedule for reconciliation. Make certain that this schedule is widely known. "Test" the newly gained information during Lent to schedule the Sacrament of Penance for the parish.
- Is there a quiet or contemplative liturgical activity that can welcome or involve the parish during Advent, i.e., Evening Lessons and Carols, Evening Prayer (Liturgy of the Hours, with beautiful music), Parish Rosary for Peace (or Calm, or Hope, or for Those Who Are Lonely in Our World)? Follow the rosary with (daytime) donuts, fruit, and coffee or (evening) warm beverages and Christmas pastries.
- Organize the Christmas season Mass schedule, making sure to include the Baptism of the Lord as the ending day. This solemnity "punctuates" the season of Christmas for the parish's liturgical calendar
- Support and encourage any planned service-type activities to begin with a simple prayer this Advent. Think of decorating the "angel tree," for example, setting up the outdoor shrine, wrapping gifts, or loading a truck with food for the food pantry.

Liturgical Catechesis for Worship Committee

- Familiarize the worship committee with the liturgical expectations for a ministry, during each liturgical season. Provide a booklet for each member to read and reflect on before Advent begins.

Liturgical Catechesis for the Assembly

- What resources are available for catechizing the assembly: what can we reprint, what can be published electronically? How will these resources be accessible to all? Remember to consider all "audiences" in the parish: youth, young adults, single persons, those who are in nursing homes and unable to attend Mass with the assembly, newlyweds, visitors, college students, or "snowbirds" who may not attend the same church every Sunday.

Closing Prayer

- Anticipating Advent, read reflectively the Preface from the Eucharistic Prayers for Reconciliation (I or II) as prayer, reciting the Holy, Holy, Holy together as a group.

S U N **29** LM #2B / LMC #2B / violet
First Sunday of Advent

Scripture Insights

Isaiah 63 dates from a time after the honeymoon period that followed the return from exile. The people are beginning to face the harsh difficulties of reestablishing their spiritual identity as God's people, caught in the crush between soaring hopes and paltry performance. They question and recall glories that the Lord once performed for the nation. They repent. They surrender themselves anew and, despite the possibility of rejection, plead longingly for God to appear.

Paul writes to a Church that needs that perspective. Considering itself ready for the Lord's coming, the Corinthian Church will learn in this letter how woefully unprepared the apostle thinks it is: theological errors, unethical practices, misplaced priorities, forgetting the poor, constant infighting, interest in self-advancement. But at the letter's beginning, Paul celebrates the fact that for all their faults the Corinthians are nevertheless a true Christian community. He reminds them that God alone keeps them faithful.

Mark's account of the Gospel stresses the need for constant watchfulness among the disciple-servants who must account for their actions. A subtle move by the evangelist should not be missed. Note how Mark deliberately juxtaposes these words of Jesus on the Mount of Olives with the disciples' failure in the Garden of Gethsemane in the very next chapter (14:26–41). On the mount Jesus suddenly turns to the reader directly and says, "Keep awake!" (13:37); in the garden Jesus again warns the disciples, "Keep awake" (14:34). On the mount he warns the disciples lest the Lord come and find them sleeping; in the garden he returns after prayer and finds them asleep (14:36–41). On the mount they do not know the time that the Lord "will come" (13:35); in the garden he declares "the hour has come" (14:41). Mark portrays these sorrowful events as a warning to disciples of every generation.

Preaching Points

Parish Masses

- All people fall short of God's expectations of them. In love, our Lord does not harden his heart against us but makes possible a way for us to gain his presence again. Jesus will return to his people as promised.
- Despite our imperfections, our sin, and our weaknesses, we are unified in our Christian community through Christ. We grow in him and are strengthened by him.
- Though God understands our weaknesses, we are called to overcome those weaknesses in Christ.
- Through Christ we will be found blameless on the last day. We will not know when the last day shall occur, because only God knows that day and hour.

Children's Liturgy of the Word

- Our families, parishes, classrooms, and groups of friends are imperfect. None of us behave as we ought to behave all the time. Despite that imperfection, we are still Christ's family.
- Though we commit sins, we are forgiven and transformed in Christ. When he returns again, we can be found worthy of heaven through him and in him.
- Sometimes we may hear that people predict the end of time. Nobody but the Father knows when the Son will return. We wait for Jesus in joyful hope, because we are happy he has promised to return to us.

Missal Options

- Consider using Form II of the PA.
- The Gloria is not sung (or said).
- The Creed is said or sung.
- Use an Advent Collect to conclude the UP.
- P-I of Advent is said or sung through December 16.
- You might use EP-III and the SB for Advent.

Music Preparation

- The musical choices you make today set the tone for the entire experience your parish will have of Advent. Choose wisely.
- If you are using a song throughout the season, take the time to introduce it, explain it, and rehearse it before the liturgies.
- "In Advent the use of the organ and other music instruments should be marked by a moderation suited to the character of this time of year, without expressing in anticipation the full joy of the Nativity of the Lord" (GIRM, 313). Keep this important instruction in mind! Save using the festival trumpet and pedal bassoon for Christmastime! Try to sing a cappella music or with less instrumentation and simpler organ stops. Use a gentler Mass setting throughout Advent.

Music Suggestions

- Gathering: "The Advent of Our God" (POTSDAM; various publishers)
- Communion: "Wait for the Lord" by Jacques Berthier (Taizé/GIA)
- "*Missa Simplex*" by Richard Proulx and adapted by Michael O'Connor, OP (WLP)

Mass Texts

Introduction to Mass

We may sometimes feel as withered as the autumn leaves that are carried away by the wind, but in truth we are the work of the hands of God who never forgets us. As we begin this season of Advent, let us be mindful of him, that at the coming of his Christ we will be found doing good. Let us keep watch, and, fortified by this Eucharist, let us run forth to meet him. *My brothers and sisters, let us acknowledge our sins, and so prepare ourselves to celebrate the sacred mysteries.*

Tropes for Penitential Act, Form III

Lord Jesus, to you we lift up our soul: Lord, have mercy.

Rend the heavens, O Lord, and come to us: Christ, have mercy.

You will not let us be put to shame: Lord, have mercy.

Dismissal for Children's Liturgy of the Word

My dear children, Christmas is less than a month away, but today's Gospel tells us that we do not know when Jesus will come. We do know, however, that he loves us very much and that he longs to be with us. In fact, he is already with us in the sacraments, in the love of our family and friends, in the ministers of the Church, and in the Scriptures. Go now and listen to him speaking to you in the Word of God.

Dismissal of Catechumens

My friends, God has called you each by name. Having listened to his Word, we now send you forth to reflect on it and to watch for the revelation of Jesus Christ in your own hearts. Be alert! Call on his name, and we will keep you in prayer until the day when you can join us in receiving him in the Eucharist. Go in peace.

Dismissal of Extraordinary Ministers of Holy Communion

Dear ministers, we are mindful of our brothers and sisters who cannot join us because of illness or infirmity, and so we send you to them bearing the life-giving Body of Christ. Remind them that he has not hidden his face from them and that they are one with us in praising our God who is Father, Son, and Holy Spirit. Go in Christ's peace.

Universal Prayer

My brothers and sisters in Christ, the Lord calls us to be watchful and to be alert. We do not know when he will return and so we turn to him in prayer for the needs of our world.

1. For the Church, that we may be awake to receive the Lord when he comes, we pray:
2. For peace in our world, that leaders of nations seek together the way of peace, we pray:
3. For those trapped in the darkness of sin and addiction, that they may be freed, we pray:
4. For our community of faith, that we may be a people of charity and justice, we pray:
5. For our beloved dead, that those who have gone before us may await the Lord's return, we pray:

Loving God of power and might,
you alone are the source of our peace.
We wait in hope for the coming of
your Kingdom.
Keep us watchful and ready as we await
the glorious coming of your Son,
Jesus Christ, our Lord,
who lives and reigns with you in the unity
of the Holy Spirit,
one God, for ever and ever.
Amen.

Other Rites and Customs

- Bless the Advent Wreath at the conclusion of the Universal Prayer of Mass or during Evening Prayer. This is done at the first Mass of Advent (Saturday evening Mass). The blessing is not repeated at subsequent Masses; instead light the first candle on the wreath before Mass begins.
- Have an Advent sale offering advent wreaths and candles, religious Christmas cards, copies of *At Home with the Word 2021,* and other spiritually related items.
- Celebrate Advent Lessons and Carols.
- Contrary to popular practice, don't celebrate the Rite of Acceptance into the Order of Catechumens today—save it for another Sunday in Ordinary Time when the inquirers are ready.
- Invite a local Scripture scholar to give a workshop on the Gospel according to Mark.
- Consider chanting the appointed Entrance and/or Communion Antiphons from the Missal, particularly if your parish does not do this regularly.
- Hang greenery in the church with violet bows.

Liturgy and Life

The First Sunday of Advent is the Church's official "New Year's Day." Today's reading from the Gospel suggests a good new year's resolution: develop one good habit for keeping alert to God's saving action. When we look around, what do we see? Lights, tinsel, carols, frantic holiday shopping. How can we find a center in this distracting world? Perhaps keeping a spiritual journal could help. Make time each day to write your thoughts and questions about where God is leading you at this moment.

Growth in the spiritual life depends not on occasional inspirations and good feelings but on ingrained practices that see us through the hard times. Jesus says, "Be watchful! Be alert!" By paying attention to the quiet, hidden things God is already doing in your life every day, you will see that you already live as God's beloved. Happy new year!

Taking Place This Week . . .

Consider what can be done liturgically, catechetically, and ministerially to respond to these important needs.

- World Solidarity with Palestinian People (11/29)
- World AIDS Day (12/1)
- World Day for Slavery Abolition (12/2)
- World Day for Persons with Disabilities (12/3)
- International Volunteer Day and World Soil Day (12/5)

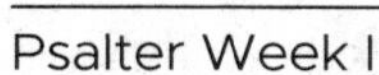

MON 30 LM #684 / LMC #423 / red
Feast of St. Andrew, Apostle

Today's Saint

In John's Gospel account, Andrew is first to follow Jesus, then he brings his brother, Simon Peter, to Jesus. The Letter to the Romans asks how people can hear the Good News without someone to preach and how they can preach without being sent. Like the Apostles, our Baptism calls us to Christ and to live Jesus in concrete ways so that others see and follow him. How will we live Jesus clearly this Advent feast day for people to see Christ and hear his call to follow him?

Scripture Insights *(PS)*

"How can people preach unless they are sent?" The word *apostle* means "one who is sent"—sent to preach that we might believe and live according to God's ways. What was it about Christ that made people leave their belongings, their livelihoods, and their families to follow him? They were sent *"to the ends of the world,"* and most paid with their lives, so that we may believe.

Preaching Points

Parish Masses

- "*How beautiful are the feet of those who bring the good news*!" We are hearing these words today because of the Apostles and many, many others who spread the Gospel.
- Fishermen, in Jesus' day, were not necessarily poor. The fact that those men had boats and nets meant that they were doing well, yet they left all behind to be fishers of men and women.

Masses with Children

- We believe, in part, because we heard the Gospel preached. Reflect with the children on how the Word and those who tell it to us helped shape our faith. Have them consider: Which stories are your favorites? Who told them to you? Who is it in your life that really loves God and shares that love with you?
- Jesus called Peter and Andrew and James, John, and Mary Magdalene and countless others to spread his Word. Many left their old lives behind. Others stayed right where they were but lived profoundly differently after encountering Jesus.

Missal Options

- The prayers are proper and found in the PS.
- Sing (or recite) the Gloria; the Creed is omitted.
- Use either of the prefaces for the Apostles and consider using EP-I.
- The SB for Apostles may be used as well.

Song of the Day

"By All Your Saints Still Striving" (various publishers)

Other Rites and Customs

- Light the first candle on the Advent wreath before Mass begins.
- If your parish has an icon or statue of St. Andrew, consider highlighting it with décor.
- Does your parish celebrate Evening Prayer as a community? The high seasons present a wonderful opportunity to explore the rich tradition of praying the Hours. Sunday Vespers are, of course, a popular option for introducing this ritual, but consider also the celebrations of the saints during this season! Provide an Advent gathering afterward for parishioners.
- To help parishioners understand the meaning of this new liturgical season, share this free video on your parish website, social media page, or email to liturgical ministers and other parish volunteers: https://vimeo.com/303377978.
- Hours: Use the Proper Psalter from the PS today.

TUE 1 LM #176 / LMC 172–175 / violet
Advent Weekday

Scripture Insights

Isaiah gives us a vision of the coming of the Lord. Luke's account of the Gospel furthers this by reminding us that the Father is fully revealed in the Son. We get images of the "Peaceable Kingdom," followed by Jesus telling the disciples that he is the fullness of God.

Preaching Points

Parish Masses

- The prophet reveals numerous images of the peace and abundant life brought by God's emergence among us.
- Christ reveals the Father. Christ reveals the love that the Father and the Son have for each other. Jesus is the fullness, revealed to the disciples and to us.

Masses with Children

- Isaiah paints a picture of a world where "a little child" guides the calf and the young lion. This world brought about by God's presence among us has no danger, not even for children.
- Jesus tells that "the childlike" people are the ones who will better understand the love between him and the Father.

Missal Options

- Use the same form of the PA prayed on the Sundays of Advent.
- The Gospel from the LMC is proper. The other readings may be from the CA.
- The prayer texts are for the Tuesday of the First Week of Advent found in the PT.
- Use an Advent Collect to conclude the UP.
- Continue to pray P-I of Advent.
- Consider using EPVN-I.

Song of the Day

"On That Holy Mountain" by Joe Mattingly (WLP)

Other Rites and Customs

Light the first candle on the Advent wreath before Mass begins.

LM #177 / LMC #172–175 / violet

Advent Weekday

Scripture Insights

Once again, here at the start of Advent, Isaiah gives us a rich vision of the Kingdom as a lush feast for all peoples on God's Holy Mountain. Jesus enacts this vision in his life, as he too ascends a mountain. He gathers the people, even the blind and the deformed, and they are healed. Then he feeds them with such generosity that seven baskets are left over after everyone has their fill.

Preaching Points

Parish Masses

- Isaiah gives us a glimpse of God's plans for all of us: a rich feast, the removal of all that separates us, a wiping away of all tears, the end of death itself.
- Jesus begins his Kingdom by drawing the people to him, healing the mute and the lame, and feeding them. We carry on Christ's mission. We feed his people. He feeds us.

Masses with Children

- Isaiah shows us that heaven may well be like a huge, delicious meal. Everyone will get along there, and all sadness and death will disappear.
- Jesus saw that his people were sick and hungry, so he healed them and fed them.

Missal Options

- Use the same form of the PA prayed on the Sundays of Advent.
- The prayer texts are for the Wednesday of the First Week of Advent found in the PT.
- Use an Advent Collect to conclude the UP.
- Continue to pray P-I of Advent.
- Consider using EPR-I.

Song of the Day

"Come, My Way, My Truth, My Light" (various publishers)

Other Rites and Customs

- Light the first candle on the Advent wreath before Mass begins.
- Does your Advent environment extend past the worship space? How does your local community know that Catholics are celebrating this sacred time? Purchase weatherproof fabric and create an Advent banner to hang outside the church and parish center, parish office, rectory, or school.

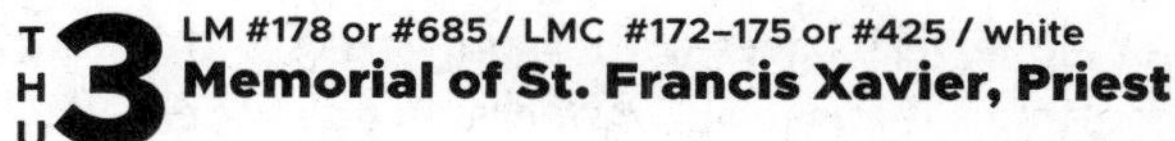

LM #178 or #685 / LMC #172–175 or #425 / white

Memorial of St. Francis Xavier, Priest

Today's Saint

St. Francis Xavier (1506–1552) built his house on the strong foundation and rock of faith in, and love for, Jesus Christ. While a Jesuit missionary in Japan, Francis discovered that he needed to connect faith in Christ with the strengths and virtues of the culture. In so doing, he opened doors that might divide people and united them through Jesus Christ. By the way you live, do you proclaim the Gospel in ways that unite people? Can you affirm the strengths and virtues of others to open doors, connect differences, and allow Christ to affirm unity in diversity?

Scripture Insights

Where do we live? How do we build our city? What is the foundation of our house? The City of God, according to Isaiah, is a stronghold, yet open to all people who long for faith and peace and justice for the poor. Christ reminds us that our dwelling must not be on the shifting sands of our world but on the Rock that is his Word and his life.

Preaching Points

Parish Masses

- The Word of God, spoken by the prophet and revealed in Jesus, impels us to act in this world, to build cities of peace and trust in the Lord, to build houses anchored in Christ.
- "Everybody talking 'bout Heaven ain't going there," says the old Spiritual, but only the one who does the will of the Father.

Masses with Children

- Another image of heaven that we get from the Bible is a city filled with faith and peace.
- Build your life on the Rock that is God, not things that fade away or fall apart over time.

Scripture Insights *(From PS)*

The task of an Apostle is to proclaim the Gospel to the whole world, tirelessly seeking the salvation of all.

Preaching Points

Parish Masses

- What does St. Paul mean when he says he became "all things to all"? The Gospel message remains the same, but St. Paul didn't preach it exactly the same way everywhere he went. Instead, he adapted himself to the circumstances and attitudes of those to whom he preached. He used creativity and insight in the proclamation of the Gospel.
- Jesus sends the Apostles out to proclaim the Gospel, but not alone: Jesus goes with them, works with them, and continues to perform wonders through them. It is no different in the Church today. Amazing things happen when we let Jesus work through us.

Masses with Children

- Jesus is always with us. We are never alone. He helps us to spread his message to everyone. We don't just talk about Jesus, but we show our friends and family who Jesus is by how we act.

Missal Options

- Use the same form of the PA prayed on the Sundays of Advent.
- The prayers are proper and are from the PS.
- Use the seasonal Collect to conclude the UP.
- Any of the readings from the CP (For Missionaries) may also be used.
- Continue to pray P-I of Advent or P-I or P-II of Saints.
- Consider using the EPVN-II.

Song of the Day

"Arise, Stand on the Height" by Genevieve Glen, OSB (OCP)

Other Rites and Customs

Light the first candle on the Advent wreath before Mass begins.

Optional Memorial of St. John Damascene, Priest and Doctor of the Church / white

---

Scripture Insights

The God of Jacob, the God revealed in Jesus Christ, is forever healing us and leading us to the fullness of life. The deaf hear, the blind see, and the poor rejoice. Even when Christ commands the once-blind men to keep quiet about the healing, such is their joy that they cannot keep silent.

Preaching Points

Parish Masses

- Isaiah tells us that "the lowly will ever find joy in the LORD" but "the arrogant will have gone." The God of Jacob cuts down the tyrant but lifts up the poor and heals the sick.
- The two blind men followed Jesus. How did they know him? When Jesus asked if they believed he could heal them, they said yes. What is it inside us that impels us to follow Christ before we know him? Before he heals us?

Masses with Children

- Jesus was able to heal the blind men because of their faith. He tells them to tell no one, but they were so excited they told everyone throughout the land about him.
- Jesus "touched their eyes," and their eyes were opened. These men had likely been beggars and outcasts due to their blindness. Think how they must have felt to be touched by someone instead of being scorned and avoided.

Missal Options

- Use the same form of the PA prayed on the Sundays of Advent.
- The prayer texts are for the Friday of the First Week of Advent found in the PT.
- Use an Advent Collect to conclude the UP.
- Continue to pray P-I of Advent.
- Consider using EPR-I.

Song of the Day

"Open My Eyes" by Jesse Manibusan (OCP)

Other Rites and Customs

Light the first candle on the Advent wreath before Mass begins.

Optional Memorial

St. John Damascene was a Syrian monk. He authored the Fountain of Wisdom, a summary of the teachings of the Greek Fathers, and is honored as a Doctor of the Church for his theological writing on the Assumption and his defense of the veneration of images.

- The readings may be taken from the SW, #686, any reading from the CP or CDC, or LMC #426.
- The Collect is from the PS; the other texts are taken from the CP (For One Pastor) or from the CDC.
- You may use the seasonal Collect to conclude the UP.
- Continue to use P-I for Advent, or P-I or P-II of Saints, or the Preface of Holy Pastors.
- Consider using EPVN-IV.

SAT 5 LM #180 / LMC #172–175 / violet
Advent Weekday

Scripture Insights

In the Gospel, Christ proclaims "the Kingdom," and his Kingdom starts in this world, here and now. Isaiah assures us that the Lord will give us actual bread and water, actual soil for our crops, and real food for our livestock. Jesus chooses us as disciples to go out and heal and proclaim. The Kingdom is real, here and now, among us.

Preaching Points

Parish Masses

- "[The Lord God] will be gracious when you cry out," Isaiah assures us. He will answer us in our world, through our world, with gifts as simple and necessary as rain and wheat.
- Christ was "moved with pity" at the sight of his people, for they were "like sheep without a shepherd." Who does he send to proclaim the Good News? To heal his people? Us, his disciples.

Masses with Children

- God comes to us in the world through the things of this world. All the gifts of Creation—food, water, animals, friends, plants, and trees—are ways in which God is being generous to us.
- Christ proclaimed the Kingdom of Heaven, which began on earth with his presence. He uses us, his disciples, to heal his people and proclaim the Good News.

Missal Options

- Use the same form of the PA prayed on the Sundays of Advent.
- The prayer texts are for the Saturday of the First Week of Advent found in the PT.
- Use an Advent Collect to conclude the UP.
- Continue to pray P-I of Advent.
- Consider using EP-III.

Song of the Day

"Savior of the Nations, Come" (various publishers)

Other Rites and Customs

- Light the first candle on the Advent wreath before Mass begins.
- Tomorrow is the Second Sunday of Advent, which falls on December 6. Because of the importance of this Sunday, St. Nicholas is not celebrated liturgically. This is a good opportunity to catechize parishioners about the centrality of Sundays during the high seasons. BUT: This does not mean that families cannot celebrate the wonderful traditions associated with St. Nicholas. Does your parish bulletin include helpful hints for honoring the saints at home?
- LTP's *Blessings and Prayers Through the Year* includes an order of prayer for St. Nicholas that could easily be used by families and parish communities.

SUN 6 LM #5B / LMC #5B / violet

Second Sunday of Advent

Scripture Insights

Early in the sixth century before Jesus, the kingdom of Judah was overrun and its people carried into exile in Babylon. The Temple was destroyed and Jerusalem was leveled. Into this mournful situation came an anonymous disciple of the prophetic school of Isaiah preaching a scintillating message of hope. The poet-prophet recalled God's first "coming" to the people at the time of the Exodus (see Isaiah 41:17–18; 42:16; 43:16–17; 48:21; 50:2). Then, God had come to the people Israel through one of their own, Moses. But this time, the prophet proclaimed, God would come through a pagan, Cyrus, the Persian king and conqueror of the Babylonians. This second "coming" ("Here is your God!" [40:9]) confronted the doubt of the exiles with a trumpet call of good news, "Comfort, give comfort to my people" (40:1).

Mark used this picture of God's "second" Old Testament coming to speak of God's New Testament "coming" in the Gospel. John the Baptist's appearance and thunderous preaching prepared the people for "one mightier than I" (1:7). John seems to have expected the day of judgment that had been announced by the old prophets. But in the rest of his account of the Gospel Mark unfolded the unlikely story of God's anointed who came to teach, heal, suffer, and finally give his life as a ransom for others (Mark 10:45).

Peter's second letter refers to a future coming of Christ. By the time the letter was written by an anonymous representative of Peter in the second century, Christ's final coming was long delayed. But the writer rekindles anticipation by speaking like John the Baptist and the Old Testament prophets. He warns that Christ delayed his Second Coming only to give people time to prepare and calls for urgent and active obedience. Such obedience not only prepares for but even "hastens" God's final coming.

Preaching Points

Parish Masses

- *Preparation!* This one word describes the journey that Advent is for the Church. John the Baptist prepared the way for Jesus' First Coming. We are called to prepare for the Second Coming of our Lord. He will return to us again, and we recall that reality in the peace of Christ himself.
- Jesus desires for his beloved Church to be prepared to greet him. How we prepare ourselves individually matters; are we brave and dedicated, like John the Baptist?
- Through Christ we are brought into union with the Father and the Holy Spirit. Our Baptism with water and the other sacraments of initiation unite us with Christ and his Church.
- We must prepare ourselves for the coming of the Lord; what does such a task look like in this day and age? How will you make ready the way of the Lord?

Children's Liturgy of the Word

- People spend time getting ready for important events. The Church's important event is the coming of Christ. She doesn't know when he will come, so the faithful are called to be ready to greet Jesus.
- We must prepare ourselves for the coming of the Lord; what does such a task look like for young children, school-aged children, and preteens?

Missal Options

- Consider using Form II of the PA.
- The Gloria is not sung or said.
- The Creed is said or sung.
- Use an Advent Collect to conclude the UP.
- P-I of Advent is said or sung through December 16.
- You might use EPRI or EPRII and the SB for Advent.

Music Preparation

- Sometimes as musicians and liturgists we are torn between trying to experience Advent and "preparing the way" for Christmas. It is essential for liturgical ministers to take moments for prayer and reflection—even with a big "to-do list."
- We all have our favorite seasonal songs, and there are many beautiful traditional seasonal hymns from which to choose, but don't be afraid to try something new. Lovely contemporary pieces have been composed for this season that work well with a congregation. Consider the options from WLP, GIA, and OCP.

Music Suggestions

- Gathering: "Raw the Voice and Fierce the Message" by Michael Joncas (OCP)
- Preparation or Sending Forth: "On Jordan's Bank" (various publishers)
- Communion: "Prepare the Way of the Lord" by Jacques Berthier (Taizé/GIA)
- Sending Forth: "Ready the Way" by Curtis Stephan (OCP)

Mass Texts

Introduction to Mass

We have come together to listen to God speaking tenderly to us of the coming of the Lord and the fulfillment of his Kingdom. Trusting in his kindness and the promise of salvation, let us prepare his way by acknowledging our sins, so that we may receive Christ's Body and Blood with joyful hearts. *My brothers and sisters, let us acknowledge our sins, and so prepare ourselves to celebrate the sacred mysteries.*

Tropes for Penitential Act, Form III

All people, O Lord, shall see the revelation of your glory:
Lord, have mercy.

You wish that all people should come to repentance:
Christ, have mercy.

You, yourself, will gather your sheep and feed your flock,
have mercy.

Dismissal for Children's Liturgy of the Word

Children, whom God holds so dear, we hear John the Baptist calling out to us today, helping us to prepare for Jesus' coming. As we wait, remember what St. Peter tells us, that a thousand years are like one day for God. The day will come soon. Until then, go and listen to the Word of God. It promises you joy and peace.

Dismissal of Catechumens

My friends, you have listened with us to the message and promise of salvation. Let it take root in your hearts, that the glory of the Lord will not only dwell in our land and be revealed in new heavens and a new earth but also shine forth in your very selves. Go with our prayers for the hastening of that day when will you join us at the Lord's table. Go now in peace.

Dismissal of Extraordinary Ministers of Holy Communion

My dear ministers, the Lord makes provision for the feeding of his flock, and so we give you his Word and the Body of Christ to take to his sick and homebound sheep, that they may be one with us in the eager anticipation of his coming. Go in peace.

Universal Prayer

John the Baptist prepared the way of the Lord as a great messenger. As baptized disciples in the Lord, we too are his messengers on behalf of those who suffer and are burdened. Let us bring their needs to our Lord.

1. For the Church, that she may faithfully prepare the way for the Lord's return in glory, we pray:
2. For all civic leaders, that they may respect and honor all those they govern, we pray:
3. For all catechumens, that they may hear the preaching of the Gospel and follow Christ with joy, we pray:
4. For the outcasts of our society and for those in prison, that they may hope for release, we pray:
5. For all our beloved dead [*especially* **N.** *and* **N.**], that they may know eternal light, rest, and peace, we pray:

Almighty God,
you sent John the Baptist into the world
to prepare the way for your Son.
May the testimony of the Baptist's
preaching and the example of his life
continue to draw the world
into the mystery of your Kingdom.
Open our hearts to your wonders this day.
Through Christ our Lord.
Amen.

Other Rites and Customs

- Consider having a communal Reconciliation service during the week using Form II of the *Rite of Penance*. Reach out to other priests in the area to help with hearing confessions.
- Announce the Mass schedule for the Solemnity of the Immaculate Conception of the Blessed Virgin Mary.
- Light the first and second candles on the Advent wreath before Mass begins.

Liturgy and Life

Today's Scriptures continue the Advent theme of preparing to welcome the Lord—this Christmas and at the Second Coming. The Second Reading tells us to "be eager to be found without spot or blemish," and John the Baptist calls us to repentance. Make plans to celebrate the Sacrament of Reconciliation as part of your personal spiritual preparation for Christmas, at a parish penance service, or at another time. Sending holiday cards can be an act of prayer. Write a brief, handwritten note on each card and offer a prayer for each recipient as you seal the envelope. Bless your cards prior to mailing.

Taking Place This Week . . .

Consider what can be done liturgically, catechetically, and ministerially to respond to these important needs.

- Pearl Harbor Remembrance Day (12/7)
- Immaculate Conception (12/8)
- World Genocide Commemoration Day (12/9)
- Human Rights Day (12/10)
- Chanukah begins (12/11)
- International Mountain Day (12/11)
- Our Lady of Guadalupe (12/12)
- Catholics honor the Divine Infancy during December.
- December is AIDS Awareness Month, National Drunk and Drugged Driving Prevention Month, Human Rights Month, Spiritual Literacy Month, National Car Donation Month, and Worldwide Food Service Safety Month.
- Animal shelters and adoption awareness groups host Operation Santa Paws during this month to increase awareness about pet adoption.

M O N 7 LM #181 or #688 / LMC #172–175 or #428 / white
Memorial of St. Ambrose, Bishop and Doctor of the Church

Today's Saint

St. Ambrose (340–397) was baptized and ordained both presbyter and bishop in one week. He let nothing get in his way. His way of settling conflict brought him to be elected a bishop. He cared for his people as did the friends of the paralytic and Jesus, who cured body and soul. Can we live Christ today, even if opposition and disbelief try to dissuade us?

Scripture Insights

Isaiah describes, in beautiful detail, how the earth exults and proclaims "the splendor of our God." Our God will heal the broken and ransom the captives. This happens both worldwide and in the life of a paralyzed man who gets up and walks.

Preaching Points

Parish Masses

- Creation itself is among God's gifts to us—flowing waters, abundant flowers, the life he breathed into us. Grace builds on that, as streams burst forth in deserts, and the lame leap like a stag.
- In the time of Jesus, the sick and the lame were ostracized—partly for fear of contagion, but mostly because it was believed that their sickness or injury was part of divine punishment. When Jesus healed, or forgave sin, he both cured the people and allowed them to rejoin the community.

Masses with Children

- Look at the beauty of our world! It is part of God's gift to us.
- Christ healed everyone he could, and people came from all over for this healing power. Think how desperate those men must have been to help their friend, such that they cut a hole in the roof to lower him down! And their friend was restored to wholeness, and walked away, rejoicing!

Scripture Insights *(PS)*

The task of the shepherd is to proclaim the mysteries of Christ, free of charge.

Preaching Points

Parish Masses

- St. Ambrose, like St. Augustine—whom he baptized—immeasurably enriched the Church with his teaching of the mysteries of Christ. That is why he is given the title "Doctor." Faith must constantly seek understanding, so that we can love God with heart, soul, and mind.
- The Church has had its false shepherds, people who seek their own gain, power, and pleasure at all costs. We need to pray for good shepherds, shepherds like Jesus, who seek the good of the other, not themselves.

Masses with Children

- Saints are known by the ways they live their lives. They loved Jesus so much that they wanted to be like him and show others how to be like him. St. Ambrose was a bishop in the fourth century. He tried to help people understand Jesus so that others could love him with their whole heart, soul, and mind.
- People who follow Jesus do so not for themselves but for the good of other people. They are not selfish. They love others just as much as they love God.

Missal Options

- Use the same form of the PA prayed on the Sundays of Advent.
- The prayers are proper and are found in the PS.
- Use an Advent Collect to conclude the UP.
- The readings may also be from the CP or CDC.
- Continue to pray P-I of Advent or P-I or P-II of the Saints, or the Preface of Holy Pastors. Consider using EP-I.

Song of the Day

"Ready the Way" by Bob Hurd (OCP)

Other Rites and Customs

Light the first and second candles on the Advent wreath before Mass begins.

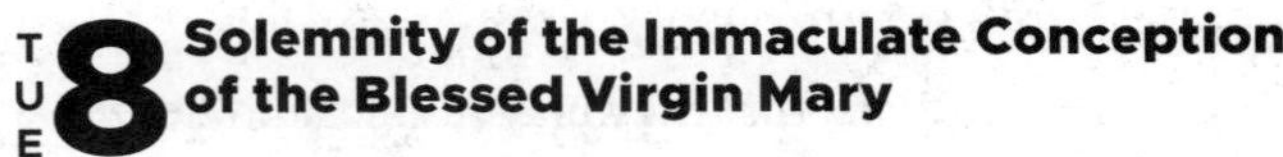

See page 18.

Optional Memorial of St. Juan Diego Cuauhtlatoatzin / white

Scripture Insights

The Lord, who created the world with power, shares that power with us when we are weak. When we hope in the Lord we "soar as with eagles' wings." Christ himself draws us in when we are weary and burdened.

Preaching Points

Parish Masses

- Though we get worn down with life's burdens, the Lord renews our strength.
- Christ is "meek and humble of heart." In him we find rest.

Masses with Children

- God is full of life and energy, even when we aren't. When we hope in the Lord, we can soar like eagles.
- Jesus is forever humble and gentle. Whenever you feel tired or hopeless, you can go to him for comfort.

Missal Options

- Use the same form of the PA prayed on the Sundays of Advent.
- The prayer texts are for the Wednesday of the Second Week of Advent found in the PT.
- Use an Advent Collect to conclude the UP.
- Continue to pray P-I of Advent.
- Consider using EPVN-IV.

Song of the Day

"Come to Me" by J. Michael Joncas (GIA)

Other Rites and Customs

- Light the first and second candles on the Advent wreath before Mass begins.
- Advent is a time to think about peace, justice, unity, and the hope that is Christ. How does your parish connect liturgy to Catholic Social Teaching? How does your parish integrate the needs of the world into the liturgy? How does your parish send the assembly into the world to reflect the Gospel by the way they live? What opportunities are provided to adults, teens, and children for serving the poor, helping the local community, and thinking beyond their "self" and being conscious of the "other"? How do the members of your community see God's presence in every human person and in every created being? How are we called to love?

Optional Memorial

It is legend that in December 1531, Mary appeared to the peasant Juan Diego on the hillside of Tepeyac, once the site of an Aztec temple dedicated to human sacrifice, now on the outskirts of Mexico City. A popular rendition of the legend suggests that Guadalupe instructed Juan Diego to ask the bishop to build a shrine on that spot. To provide evidence of her intervention, she inscribed her image on Juan Diego's tilma and filled it with roses gathered from the desolate Tepeyac. This tilma is a twofold symbol of hospitality and hope: hospitality, in being the holy object that welcomes millions of pilgrims each year, and hope, in reminding the Mexican people of Mary's choice of the poor, lowly Juan Diego to spread her message of peace. God loves to choose the "Juan Diegos" of this world to do his will—he can certainly choose you.

- The readings may be from the SW, #689A (LS), LMC #430, or from the CHMW. The Collect is from the PS; the other texts are taken from the CP (For One Pastor) or from the CHMW (For One Saint).
- You may use the seasonal Collect to conclude the UP.
- Continue to use P-I for Advent or P-I or P-II of Saints.
- Consider using EP-III.

THU 10

LM #184 / LMC #172–175 / violet

Advent Weekday

Scripture Insights

During Advent, we delve deep into the prophets, from Isaiah to the Baptist, and at times they appropriately disturb us. Isaiah tells us not to be afraid but then tells us we will grind the mountains to dust. Jesus warns us that the Kingdom of Heaven will suffer violence, yet the least in the Kingdom will be greater even than John the Baptist. Great things are on the horizon, but not without looming threats.

Preaching Points

Parish Masses

- Our Lord, when he speaks through the prophets, speaks of upheaval and tumult. Yet our Lord also brings comfort to the poor and the suffering. God's own earth rises to help them.
- John the Baptist is the last of the Old Testament prophets and the first of the New. All prophecy leads to Christ, but the journey has its jolts.
- "Fear not" and "be not afraid" are commonly spoken by the prophets; they lead us into the violence we will suffer as we build the Kingdom of Heaven.

Masses with Children

- God promises to take us by the hand as he guides us to build a world where all are comforted and healed.
- Jesus invites us to be citizens in the Kingdom of Heaven. We may have problems, but we will share in his victory.

Missal Options

- Use the same form of the PA prayed on the Sundays of Advent.
- The prayer texts are for the Thursday of the Second Week of Advent found in the PT.
- Use an Advent Collect to conclude the UP.
- Continue to pray P-I of Advent.
- Consider using EP-II.

Song of the Day

"Come, Thou Long-Expected Jesus" (various publishers)

Other Rites and Customs

Light the first and second candles on the Advent wreath before Mass begins.

FRI 11 LM #185 / LMC #172–175 / violet

Advent Weekday

Optional Memorial of St. Damasus I, Pope / white

Scripture Insights

This Gospel is hard on "this generation," which certainly includes today's hearers as well. We dismiss the Baptist for fasting, then turn around and reject Jesus for allegedly overindulging in food and wine. Far from hearkening to God's commandments, as Isaiah impels us to do, we look for reasons to shirk the costs of discipleship.

Preaching Points

Parish Masses

- Jesus' final comment is intriguing: "But wisdom is vindicated by her works." There seems to be a threat softened by the promise of the power of wisdom.
- Today's word from the prophet contains the promise of being taught and led by the Lord. If we listen, our descendants will be as numerous as the grains of sand. But if not, our lives become insignificant, "blotted out from my presence."

Masses with Children

- God leads us and guides us, teaches us and loves us. If we follow God's teaching, our families will prosper for ages and ages.
- John the Baptist and Jesus take different approaches to lead us to God. We try to ignore and avoid God, but God's wisdom wins in the end.

Missal Options

- Use the same form of the PA prayed on the Sundays of Advent.
- The prayer texts are for the Friday of the Second Week of Advent found in the PT.
- Use an Advent Collect to conclude the UP.
- Continue to pray P-I of Advent.
- Consider using EP-III.

Song of the Day

"Peace Is Flowing Like a River" (various publishers)

Other Rites and Customs

Light the first and second candles on the Advent wreath before Mass begins.

Optional Memorial

Pope Damasus presided over the Council of Rome, which codified the canon of Scripture and commissioned the Vulgate translation of the Bible from St. Jerome. His vision and patronage helped preserve and transmit the Word of God to later generations.

- The readings may be taken from the SW, #690, the CP (For a Pope), or LMC #431.
- The Collect is from the PS; other prayers may be taken from the CP (For a Pope).
- You may use the seasonal Collect to conclude the UP.
- Continue to pray P-I of Advent or use P-I or P-II of Saints or Holy Pastors and consider using EP-III.
- Consider using EPVN-IV.

SAT 12 LM #690A or #707–712 / LMC #432 / white

Feast of Our Lady of Guadalupe

Patronal Feastday of the Americas

About Today's Feast

Today the Church throughout America (North, Central, and South) celebrates Our Lady of Guadalupe, Patroness of the Americas. Today is a feast in the United States of America, but in many Hispanic countries, such as Mexico, it is raised to a solemnity. The story of the origins of the miraculous image of Our Lady of Guadalupe is well known. Juan Diego Cuauhtlatoatzin was a quiet, humble man, a poor peasant. When the Blessed Virgin Mary appeared to him and asked him to tell the local bishop to build a church in her honor, Juan Diego became a very reluctant messenger. The bishop would not believe him. So Mary filled Juan Diego's tilma, or cloak, with roses in December, and when he emptied out these beautiful flowers at the bishop's feet, there, imprinted on his tilma, was a wonderful image of the Virgin, dressed like a young Aztec woman.

Scripture Insights

God entering humanity and being among us is startling, yet we've become numb to its shock. In Christ, God "stirs forth from his holy dwelling." In the second option for the First Reading, the Book of Revelation recounts the cosmic showdown between the dragon and the woman clothed with the sun. An archangel asks a teenager to bear God's son. An unborn prophet leaps in his aged mother's womb to hail the unborn messiah inside Mary, whose soul proclaims the greatness of the Lord.

Preaching Points

Parish Masses

- We humans tend to want to confine God—to keep God inside the box, the temple, the heavens. God constantly bursts forth, pitches his tent among us as we wander, becomes one of us.
- Only Christ garners more of our imagination and devotion than Mary. Mary's faith, courage, and joy at bringing God into our world are unmatched.

Masses with Children

- Zechariah tells a story of God stirring forth from his holy dwelling. Why is it important that God comes to share our life? Revelation tells a scary story, where God emerges victorious. Why did the dragon want to destroy the child?
- We tend to think of Mary as quiet and somber, staring up into heaven adoringly. What if we thought of the young girl who was just visited by an angel? How about this young woman running to tell her cousin the story?

Missal Options

- The prayers are proper and are found in the PS.
- Use the same form of the PA prayed on the Sundays of Advent.
- The Gloria is sung or said; the Creed is omitted.
- Use an Advent Collect (or a Collect from the CBVM) to conclude the UP.
- The readings may also be from the CBVM or the CMMM.
- Use P-I or P-II of the Blessed Virgin Mary.
- Consider using the EPVN-I.

Music Preparation

- If your parish does not have a custom of *Las Mananitas* or *Las Posadas*, it may be time to start. Seek the insights of the Latino community.
- If this is an early morning celebration, you may want to pitch things lower, and if members of the community are going to help with the music, they often play by ear, so D, C, G, and A are keys friendly to the guitar.
- Make sure that introducing Spanish music for a Hispanic feast isn't perceived as "tokenism." If there are Hispanic members in your community, Spanish music should be integrated consistently throughout the year.

Music Suggestions

- Gathering: "*Mañanitas a la Virgen de Guadalupe*" (various publishers)
- Preparation: "Mary's Song" by Millie Reith (OCP) or "*O Sanctissima*" (various publishers)
- Sending Forth: "*Adiós, Oh Virgen de Guadalupe*" (various publishers)

Other Rites and Customs

- Light the first and second candles on the Advent wreath before Mass begins.
- Display images of the Blessed Virgin Mary and adorn with candles and flowers. In Mexico, this feast begins with the Mass of the Roses (note the reference to St. Juan Diego's tilma).
- Add the needs of pregnant women to the UP (see ideas from this past Sunday). Encourage parishioners to volunteer at shelters for battered women, mothers, and children. Donate funds to a pregnancy help center. Consider how your community can help women with crisis pregnancies and unplanned pregnancies.
- Consider ways you can celebrate and honor the Hispanic heritage of the United States.
- Invite the community to remain after Mass and pray the Rosary for peace, justice, and asylum for Hispanic peoples.
- Follow Mass and prayer with a fiesta party with an assortment of Hispanic foods. Donate a portion of food to battered women's shelters.
- Share this free video about Our Lady of Guadalupe with parishioners. Post on social media or a parish blog or website or email to parish ministers and volunteers. It is available in English (https://vimeo.com/304654352) and Spanish (https://vimeo.com/305532657).
- Hours: Use the Proper Psalter from the PS today.

TUE 8 LM #689 / LMC #429 / white

Solemnity of the Immaculate Conception of the Blessed Virgin Mary

Patronal Feastday of the United States of America
Holyday of Obligation

About Today's Solemnity

God has endowed us with the gift of freedom. True, multiple conditions influence how that freedom is exercised. But, nonetheless, the gift is ours. Today's Scripture reminds us that human beings have a choice to cooperate with evil or blessing. Furthermore, the consequences of these choices have incredible ramifications. We honor Mary because God favored her with a special grace and her decision to cooperate with it has blessed humankind. Are we aware of the graces showered on us in Christ? How are we saying yes to God's will for our lives?

Scripture Insights

God's miraculous powers are evident in the announcement Gabriel makes to Mary. She who is full of grace will become the mother of God's Son, and her elderly kinswoman has also conceived. Miracle upon miracle appears.

Today's solemnity concerns the earliest miracle of the series: the Immaculate Conception of Mary. From the moment her parents conceived her, Mary was preserved from all sin. We believe this in part because of the way Gabriel greets her: "full of grace." Gabriel announces that Mary, though a virgin, will become a mother. We commonly call this second miracle of the series the virgin birth of Christ. The words "Immaculate Conception" refer to Mary, not to Jesus. The miracle of Jesus' virginal conception was preceded by the miracle of Mary's Immaculate Conception.

As if that were not enough, Gabriel announces yet another miracle. Elizabeth, Mary's relative, a woman advanced in years was to reassure Mary that "nothing will be impossible for God." Mary first found the angel's announcement preposterous. How can a virgin conceive? But she had to rethink the news in light of another miracle. How can an elderly woman conceive? Nothing is impossible for God.

This solemnity celebrates the triumph of God's power. It consoles us in our weakness and sin, in our misfortune and misjudgment. God is more powerful than we are, and God has proven it throughout the course of time, miracle upon miracle.

Preaching Points

Parish Masses

- From the events of Genesis arose the division between God and his creation. In Luke's account of the Gospel we find that division beginning to heal. After Eve's disobedience came Mary's glad obedience. Her assent to God's will brought forth our Lord Jesus Christ.
- Adam blamed Eve for his choice to eat from the tree; we must be responsible for our own actions.
- The fall has left all of us with Original Sin. Original Sin resolves with Baptism, but we are left with concupiscence. The Blessed Virgin Mary is "full of grace" and lacks concupiscence. She was uniquely filled with grace and able to cooperate with God. How do we become a vessel for God's grace?
- The Virgin Mary gave her assent to God's great plan; she was not selfish or absorbed in others' opinions. She used her free will to serve God. How do we use our free will to serve God?

Children's Liturgy of the Word

- All people sin, and we must always be honest about our sins. We should not lie to our teachers, parents, God, or ourselves about our shortcomings.
- The Virgin Mary was the first person to know that God's promised savior was coming to earth. She had no sin and was very happy to serve God.
- The Virgin Mary wasn't worried about being popular and didn't base her decision on others' opinions. She served God freely and gladly.

Missal Options

- The Missal texts are found in the PS for December 8.
- Because today is a solemnity, it is appropriate to include more festive music, incense, and a more formal Gospel procession.
- You might replace the PA with a sprinkling rite. However, if the PA is prayed, continue to use the same form as on the Sundays of Advent.
- Even though it is Advent, the Gloria is sung today.
- The Creed is sung or said.
- Use an Advent Collect (or texts from the CBVM) to conclude the UP.
- The Preface is proper and found on the pages for the Immaculate Conception.
- Consider using EPR-II and SB #15 ("The Blessed Virgin Mary").

Music Preparation

- Because today is a solemnity the Gloria is sung. Consider singing the version from the same simpler and gentler Mass setting you've been using for Advent or a more robust setting.
- Parishioners often love to hear instrumental version of Marian hymns such as the "Salve Regina" and the "Ave Maria." Consider doing so for an extended prelude or postlude or during the Preparation of the Gifts.

Music Suggestions

- Gathering: "Blessed One" by Aaron Thompson (OCP)
- Preparation: "The Angel Gabriel" (various publishers)
- Thanksgiving or Prelude: "Let It Be Done" by Chris Muglia (OCP)
- Sending Forth: "Immaculate Mary" (various publishers)

Mass Texts

Introduction to Mass

In his goodness God has chosen us for adoption in Christ, and to prepare us for this gift he preserved Mary from the stain of sin from before the foundation of the world. As we celebrate that mystery and this Eucharist, let us praise the glory of God's grace. *My brothers and sisters, let us acknowledge our sins, and so prepare ourselves to celebrate the sacred mysteries.*

Tropes for Penitential Act, Form III

Lord, you have clothed the Virgin Mary with a robe of salvation: Lord, have mercy.

You have filled Mary with grace and made her the new Eve: Christ, have mercy.

You give Mary to us as our spiritual Mother: Lord, have mercy.

Dismissal for Children's Liturgy of the Word

My dear children, you will now go to hear God's Word and to think about how you, like the Blessed Mother, can prepare your hearts to be ready for Jesus' coming. May God help you to understand and live the Good News. Go now in peace.

Dismissal of Catechumens

My dear catechumens, the Word of God can do all things. It took flesh in the womb of the Blessed Virgin. It now seeks a home in your own hearts. We send you forth to ponder this Word, and we pray that, as with Mary, the Lord's will may be done in you. Go in peace.

Dismissal of Extraordinary Ministers of Holy Communion

Friends, ministers of the Lord, we give you the glorified Word and Body of the Son of the Most High and Son of Mary. Take him to our sick brothers and sisters, nourish them, and remind them that, with us, they are adopted children of God. Go in peace.

Universal Prayer

My brothers and sisters, Mary found favor with God and was protected from sin from the moment of her conception. Let us too find favor with God as we pray for the needs of the Church and the world.

1. That the Church might always seek to reveal God's grace in our world, we pray:
2. That all nations might strive to promote peace and justice, especially where there is war and civil unrest, we pray:
3. That all pregnant women may be blessed with the faith to believe fully in the life they are sustaining, we pray:
4. That all newborn infants may be welcomed into households of love, we pray:
5. That the souls of the faithful departed may be raised to glory in the Lord's Resurrection, we pray:

Lord God of heaven and earth,
you made the Virgin Mary sinless
from the moment of her conception,
and so prepared a pure vessel of grace
for the coming of your Son into our world.
Through the faith of the beautiful Virgin,
you renew the world and call us to holiness.
May we imitate her faith and thus inherit eternal life.
Through Christ our Lord.
Amen.

Other Rites and Customs

- Offer a blessing for expectant parents. It is found in the BB, chapter I, part VII, or the Rite of Blessing a Child in the Womb (this order of blessing is not found in the BB: it is available as a single ritual text from the USCCB).
- Celebrate the National Night of Prayer for Life uniting the Solemnity of the Immaculate Conception with the Memorial of St. Juan Diego.
- In the Universal Prayer, mention couples struggling to conceive or those who have lost a child through miscarriage, stillbirth, or death. These parents may also receive a blessing. Explore the many options found in the BB, chapter I.
- Invite people to pray the Rosary for a few minutes after the conclusion of Mass.
- Light the first and second candles on the Advent wreath before Mass begins.
- If your parish has a Marian shrine outside, today is a good day to decorate it. Use Advent colors, evergreens, and other "winter" foliage indigenous to your area. Consider using luminaries and solar lights to highlight Our Lady to the neighboring community.
- Share this free video about the Immaculate Conception with parishioners. Post on social media or a parish blog or website or email to parish ministers and volunteers: https://vimeo.com/303377978.

Liturgy and Life

Mary's child is our hope, the one who came in history, comes daily in mystery, and will come again to complete what he has begun. Whatever happens this week, we can call on Mary, who hoped through shame, poverty, confusion, and grief "that what was spoken to you by the Lord would be fulfilled" (Luke 1:45).

S U N **13** LM #8B / LMC #8B / violet or rose
Third Sunday of Advent

Scripture Insights

Catholic Christians traditionally call this "Gaudete Sunday" (Latin *gaudere*, "to rejoice," from the Entrance Antiphon) to stress the joy of anticipating the Lord's coming. Today's texts express the joy of the watcher who heralds the dawn while standing between darkness and light.

The prophet of the school of Isaiah was one returning from exile in Babylon. Our passage appears in a magnificent series of salvation proclamations (chapters 60–62) that bolstered the courage of the exiles. The prophet exults in his call as bearer of God's good tidings: "I will greatly rejoice in the Lord . . . for God has clothed me with the garments of salvation" (61:10).

New Testament readers know this text from the time Jesus stood in his home synagogue at Nazareth announcing his messianic mission (Luke 4:18–19). Here on Gaudete Sunday it characterizes John the Baptist's joy as the herald of Christ.

John is a dour man in a camel-hair tunic who eats a ghastly diet foraged from the wilderness. But a distinct joy infuses the New Testament texts about him, springing from his privileged position as forerunner and friend of Jesus. His mother Elizabeth hears the greeting of Mary and says, "the child in my womb leaped for joy" (Luke 1:44). In the fourth Gospel account, John came "to testify to the light" (John 1:7), saw Christ's glory, "full of grace and truth," and cried out in witness to his majesty (1:14). Later, when Jesus first came to him, John exclaimed, "Here is the Lamb of God" (1:29). He then surrendered his disciples to Jesus and described his joy with a vivid metaphor: "The best man rejoices greatly at the bridegroom's voice. So this joy of mine has been made complete. He must increase; but I must decrease" (3:29–30). This is the joy in the Isaiah text applied to John today, all the more striking for the contrast between the prophet's "garments of salvation" and John's rough clothing.

Paul's letter to the Thessalonians strongly anticipates the Lord's coming, while also reminding readers to "rejoice always" (5:16). How would you describe the character of joy in a time of waiting?

Preaching Points

Parish Masses

- This day—*Gaudete* Sunday—is named for a Latin word that means "rejoice." We remember today that the wait for the Christ-child is nearly over and that he will soon be among us.
- Prophets are sent to help the people return to God's ways. Throughout the Old Testament, God's people strayed from his ways and were pulled back by a truth-telling prophet. John the Baptist was the last of the prophets, and he made ready the way of the Lord.
- John the Baptist made the way ready for Jesus. He spoke about Jesus and helped people be ready for his message.

Children's Liturgy of the Word

- *Gaudete* is derived from a Latin word that means "rejoice." We rejoice because our wait for Jesus, the Christ-child, is nearly finished.
- Jesus' preaching and teaching ministry brought a lot of surprises and new ideas to God's people. John the Baptist prepared the people and helped them to be ready for Jesus' ministry.

Missal Options

- Consider using Form II of the PA.
- The Gloria is not sung or said.
- The Creed is said or sung.
- Use an Advent Collect to conclude the UP.
- P-I of Advent is said or sung through December 16.
- You might use EP-III and the SB for Advent.

Music Preparation

- Knowing where to look for planning and preparation can greatly reduce one's agita (Italian for "heartburn"). Check out http://www1.cpdl.org /wiki/index.php/Category: Sacred_music_by_season to help find appropriate choral music for the right occasion, *including* Gaudete Sunday!
- Be sure one can sense rejoicing in your music as we near Advent's end.
- Though it is hard to resist, use "O Come, Emmanuel" only as a prelude or instrumental piece until December 17. This hymn is based on the "O Antiphons," which serve as the antiphons for the Magnificat at Evening Prayer and the verses for the Gospel Acclamation at Mass December 17–23; a different verse is sung each day. You may need to explain this to parishioners. Here is a reproducible text you can use: http://www.pastoralliturgy.org/resources /0709ReproRsrc.pdf.

Music Suggestions

- Gathering or Communion: "Jesus, Hope of the World" by Deanna Light and Paul A. Tate (WLP)
- Preparation: "Creator of the Stars of Night" (various publishers)
- Communion: "Come, Lord Jesus" by Chris de Silva (GIA)
- Sending Forth: "You Have Anointed Me" by Mike Balhoff, Gary Daigle, and Darryl Ducote (GIA)

Mass Texts

Introduction to Mass

We gather as God's people, trusting in the fulfillment of his promises. As testimony to the coming of the light of Christ, he sends us John the Baptist, to make the Lord's paths straight before him. With great rejoicing and longing for Christ' return, let us take John's words to heart and prepare ourselves to celebrate these sacred mysteries. *My brothers and sisters, let us acknowledge our sins, and so prepare ourselves to celebrate the sacred mysteries.*

Tropes for Penitential Act, Form III

Lord Jesus, you baptize us with fire and the Holy Spirit:
Lord, have mercy.

Christ Jesus, you are God's anointed, faithful and true:
Christ, have mercy.

Lord Jesus, you clothe us with the robe of salvation:
Lord, have mercy.

Dismissal for Children's Liturgy of the Word

My dear children, there are many references to rejoicing at today's Mass. That is because we are getting closer to Christmas and the celebration of God becoming human. As you listen to God's Word, remember that his Son is the source of all our joy and that it is he himself who speaks to you in today's readings. Go in peace.

Dismissal of Catechumens

My dear catechumens, this community is eagerly awaiting the celebration of the Lord's Nativity. We also look forward to the day when you will join us in the celebration of the Eucharist. Until then, reflect on his Word and know that you are in our prayers. Go in peace.

Dismissal of Extraordinary Ministers of Holy Communion

My friends, go to our sick and homebound sisters and brothers. Assure them of our prayers that, together with us, God will make them perfect in holiness, even as they share with us in the one Body of Christ. Go in peace.

Universal Prayer

Preparing the way for the Lord's return, we turn to him in prayer for the needs of our Church and of our world.

1. For Church leaders to guide us in the way of humility, we pray:
2. For governments to act with humility, we pray:
3. For those seeking to enter the Church, we pray:
4. For all who are married to put the needs of their spouses before themselves, we pray;
5. For patience and hope this Advent season, we pray:
   For those who have died, we pray

King of Kings and Lord of Lords,
we look forward to your coming at the
end of time.
Help us to prepare your way
by straightening our hearts and purifying
our desires.
Give us the humility of John the Baptist.
You live and reign with the Father in the
unity of the Holy Spirit,
one God, for ever and ever.
Amen.

Other Rites and Customs

- Highlight the arrival of the O Antiphons this week.
- Light the first, second, and third candles on the Advent wreath before Mass begins.
- Post a brief thought or reflection on each of the O Antiphons on the parish's social media sites.
- Have parishioners write Christmas cards to the homebound and those in prisons.
- As we get deeper into the Advent season and closer to Christmas, consider providing additional catechetical resources about the season to help parishioners "prepare their hearts for Jesus." Here is a link to a free video that you may share on social media, a parish website, or by email: https://vimeo.com/304228001.
- Rejoice!

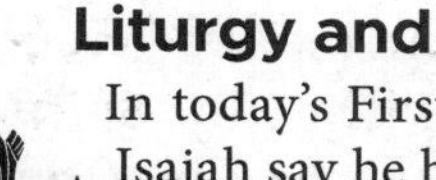

Liturgy and Life

In today's First Reading, we hear the prophet Isaiah say he has been sent "to bring glad tidings to the poor, to heal the brokenhearted, to proclaim liberty." Reflect this week on the different ways the Gospel, or "glad tidings," can be proclaimed. How could you help to do this? The Committee on Evangelization and Catechesis of the United States Conference of Catholic Bishops provides descriptions of programs that parishes have used, both to evangelize the parish and to share the Good News outside the parish. Get a sense of how Catholics are evangelizing and consider how you might find a role for yourself. Visit http://www.nccbuscc.org/evangelization/programs.shtml. Wherever the Gospel is preached, hope grows.

Taking Place This Week . . .

Consider what can be done liturgically, catechetically, and ministerially to respond to these important needs.

- The O Antiphons begin at Evening Prayer (12/17).
- Last day of Chanukah (12/18)
- International Migrants Day (12/18)

MON 14 LM #187 or #693 / LMC #172–175 or #434 / white
Memorial of St. John of the Cross, Priest and Doctor of the Church

Today's Saint

St. John of the Cross was a Carmelite priest, spiritual director, writer, mystic, and reformer who lived during the early years of the Counter-Reformation. His prose and poetry express a deep wisdom learned from his personal experience of the Paschal Mystery. His efforts at reform met with opposition, misunderstanding, and even imprisonment—the fate of so many prophets, including John the Baptist. Advent reminds us of the paradox of light revealed in the darkness. Our journey of faith always includes both.

Scripture Insights

The readings come from early in the Old Testament and from Jesus' last days in Jerusalem. The Spirit of God speaks through Balaam, who sees greatness coming out of the tribes of Israel; "a star shall advance." Jesus has a run-in with the priests who will command his death. They must either declare him to be God or face the crowds, who already know it.

Preaching Points *(PS)*

Parish Masses

- Where does Jesus' authority come from? We know it now. Did the crowds? Did the powerful of his day know?
- Balaam saw the tribes of Israel living in tents, yet saw a king rising from their midst. The slaves who fled Egypt, living in tents en route to the Promised Land, gave birth to the Messiah.

Masses with Children

- The Jews lived as slaves in Egypt until Moses led them out. They lived in tents as they fled, but soon this people gave rise to Jesus, the king, heralded by a star.
- The chief priests and elders tried to trick Jesus. Though he was just from humble origins, Jesus turned the tables on them and trapped them with their own words.

Scripture Insights *(PS)*

Following Christ in radical poverty opens us up in a special way to the mysterious wisdom of God.

Preaching Points

Parish Masses

- St. John of the Cross, with St. Teresa of Avila, reformed the Carmelite order, bringing it back to its Gospel roots. Through his simple, ascetic life, detached from possessions, and his countless hours of prayer, St. John came close to the heart of Christ. In his writings, he shared what he learned through this profound prayer life.
- St. John of the Cross is famous for his writing about the "dark night." For John, the "dark night" is not a place of doubt but a holy darkness in which the soul is purged of illusions, trusting only in the light that burns within the soul, a light that leads surely toward God.

Masses with Children

- St. John of the Cross was a priest during the Middle Ages. He reformed the Carmelites (to be the Discalced Carmelites) and wrote about his personal experiences with God. He helped people understand that God is always with us, even during the darkest times.
- Today's Scriptures teach us that, like St. John of the Cross, when we live a simple life we are more focused on the ways of God and open to his wisdom.

Missal Options

- Use the same form of the PA prayed on the Sundays of Advent.
- The prayers are proper and are found in the PS.
- The readings may also be taken from the CP or the CDC.
- Use the seasonal Collect to conclude the UP.
- Continue to pray P-I of Advent or use P-I or P-II of Saints, or the Preface of Holy Pastors and consider using EP II.

Song of the Day

"Making Their Way" by Dolores Dufner, OSB (GIA)

Other Rites and Customs

Light the first, second, and third candles on the Advent wreath before Mass begins.

TUE 15 LM #188 / LMC #172–175 / violet
Advent Weekday

Scripture Insights

Zephaniah tells of us God's holy remnant—"a people humble and lowly" who will keep God's message alive despite the corruption of the world. Jesus gives us the parable of the two sons. The chosen people did not accept the message of John the Baptist. The sinners, scorned by the world, embraced the message.

Preaching Points

Parish Masses

- Are we God's remnant? "They shall do no wrong and speak no lies." How are we keeping alive God's wisdom and love?
- The parable of the two sons impels us to look deeper—which son are we? Do we claim God's name but do nothing to live it out? What of those who seemed to have rejected God but live with great love and joy?

Masses with Children

- One way of looking at the Church is to see ourselves as a "remnant"—a small part of a larger community. As this "small part," we keep God's love and truth alive in this world.
- Jesus tells of two sons: one says he'll follow God but doesn't. The other refuses the Father's commands at first but in the end does God's will. Which one are you?

Missal Options

- Use the same form of the PA prayed on the Sundays of Advent.
- The prayer texts are for the Tuesday of the Third Week of Advent found in the PT.
- Use an Advent Collect to conclude the UP.
- Continue to pray P-I of Advent.
- Consider using EPR-I.

Song of the Day

"The Time Has Come When from the Past" by John L. Bell (GIA)

Other Rites and Customs

Light the first, second, and third candles on the Advent wreath before Mass begins.

WED 16 LM #189 / LMC #172–175 / violet
Advent Weekday

Scripture Insights

The Lord's words from Isaiah are bold and beautiful: "Let the earth open and salvation bud forth." God gives the beauty and abundance of the world, and justice besides. The culmination comes in the person of Christ. How do we know? The blind see, the lame walk, and the poor get the good news.

Preaching Points

Parish Masses

- "I am the LORD, there is no other." God, speaking through Isaiah, expounds on the beauty of creation, made for its own beauty, but also made for us "to be lived in."
- John is in prison, never to emerge alive. He asks if Jesus is the one. Jesus responds by proclaiming the healing accomplished through him.

Masses with Children

- Many find proof of God's existence in the beauty of nature. Yes, and so much more, like God's justice and mercy and care for us.
- John proclaimed Jesus coming but still wondered if Jesus was the one. What did Jesus tell the followers of John?

Missal Options

- Use the same form of the PA prayed on the Sundays of Advent.
- The prayer texts are for the Wednesday of the Third Week of Advent, found in the PT.
- Use an Advent Collect to conclude the UP.
- Continue to pray P-I of Advent.
- Consider using EPVN-I.

Song of the Day

"O Heavens, Send Your Rain" or "Drop Down Dew" (various publishers)

Other Rites and Customs

Light the first, second, and third candles on the Advent wreath before Mass begins.

THU 17 LM #193 / LMC #172–175 / violet
Advent Weekday

Scripture Insights

Today's readings delineate, in both vivid and tedious detail, the Old Testament roots of Jesus. The passage from Genesis tells of Jacob passing the scepter to Judah (think Lion of Judah). Both names are mentioned as Jesus' forefathers, as in Jesse (recall the root of Jesse) from Isaiah. Five women are mentioned along the way, the key one being Mary.

Preaching Points

Parish Masses

- The antiphon for the psalm gives us some messianic insights: "Justice shall flourish in his time, / and fullness of peace for ever." The psalm speaks of how the king should act, though they seldom did, thus our need for a messiah in the form of Christ.
- The lineage leads to Joseph, not Mary. Further, many of the men mentioned are far from upstanding examples of faith and justice. The fatherhood of Joseph gives to Jesus the richness and greatness of Hebrew history, plus a few blemishes. The best comes from Mary and God.

Masses with Children

- God changed Jacob's name to Israel, and his sons became the Twelve Tribes of Israel, and Jesus later was born in the tribe of Judah. Many great people are mentioned—Abraham, Ruth, David. The greatest was Mary, Jesus' mother. Joseph brought all the greatness of Jewish history to Jesus.

Missal Options

- Use the same form of the PA prayed on the Sundays of Advent.
- The prayer texts are for December 17.
- Use an Advent Collect to conclude the UP.
- Begin to use P-II of Advent today.
- Consider using EP-II.

Song of the Day

"O Come, O Come, Emmanuel" (various publishers) or "Holy Wisdom, Lamp of Learning" by Ruth C. Duck (The Pilgrim Press)

Other Rites and Customs

- Light the first, second, and third candles on the Advent wreath before Mass begins.
- The O Antiphons begin at Evening Prayer.
- Tonight's antiphon is: "Wisdom, O holy Word of God, you govern all creation with your strong yet tender care. Come and show your people the way to salvation."

FRI 18 LM #194 / LMC #172–175 / violet
Advent Weekday

Scripture Insights

These readings are stacked with names and titles for Jesus. "The Lord our justice" brings the Jewish nation back together. The angel of the Lord tells Joseph to name the boy Jesus (*Yeshua*, Joshua), which means "God saves" ("because he will save his people from their sins"). And last, Emmanuel—"God with us." God our justice. God who saves us. God forever with us.

Preaching Points

Parish Masses

- The name "God with us" can be simultaneously jarring and comforting. Why would God stoop and humble himself to be with us? What comfort that in Christ we have God with us, for us, eternally saving us!
- The story of Mary and Joseph has become so familiar that we fail to "hear" it, since we (think we) know it too well. Put yourself into the shoes of Mary or Joseph. Feel what they felt—the fear, the awe, the shock, the joy!

Masses with Children

- We have heard the story of Jesus' birth again and again. Think how nervous and confused Joseph must have been. He reveals himself to be kind, brave, and faithful in many ways.
- What does the name "Jesus" mean? Why is that important? How about "Emmanuel"? Flesh out these questions with the children.

Missal Options

- Use the same form of the PA prayed on the Sundays of Advent.
- The prayer texts are for December 18.
- Use an Advent Collect to conclude the UP.
- Use P-II of Advent today.
- Consider using EP-II.

Song of the Day

"O Come, O Come, Emmanuel" (various publishers)

Other Rites and Customs

- Light the first, second, and third candles on the Advent wreath before Mass begins.
- Tonight's O Antiphon at Evening Prayer is: "O sacred Lord of ancient Israel, who showed yourself to Moses in the burning bush, who gave him the holy law on Sinai mountain: come, stretch out your mighty hand to set us free."

SAT 19

LM #195 / LMC #172–175 / violet

Advent Weekday

Scripture Insights

As we approach the birth of Jesus, we hear two stories of unexpected births to women thought to be unable to bear children. An angel appears to the unnamed mother of Samson and to Zechariah, the father of John the Baptist. Samson went on to help the Jews triumph over the Philistines, and John the Baptist prepared the way of the Lord.

Preaching Points

Parish Masses

- Throughout salvation history, God brings life where there was none, quite often out of unexpected places and people.
- Just as illness was seen as a punishment from God, so "barrenness" was seen as a shame on women. Elizabeth said the Lord "has seen fit to take away my disgrace." God not only heals but restores people in the community.

Masses with Children

- Many children's Bibles have the story of Samson and his famous hair. Here we hear the story of the angel appearing to his mother and giving her life inside her.
- John the Baptist had holy, famous parents just like Jesus. We hear the story of how the angel Gabriel appeared to Zechariah and told him how his wife Elizabeth, who was old just like him, would soon become pregnant for the first time.

Missal Options

- Use the same form of the PA prayed on the Sundays of Advent.
- The prayer texts are for December 19.
- Use an Advent Collect to conclude the UP.
- Use P-II of Advent today.
- Consider using EPR-I.

Song of the Day

"O Come, O Come, Emmanuel" (various publishers) or "Lo, How a Rose E're Blooming" (various publishers)

Other Rites and Customs

- Light the first, second, and third candles on the Advent wreath before Mass begins.
- Tonight's O Antiphon at Evening Prayer is: "O Flower of Jesse's stem, you have been raised up as a sign for all peoples; kings stand silent in your presence; the nations bow down in worship before you. Come, let nothing keep you from coming to our aid."

Something to Consider...

- ◈ With the liturgy committee, assess in discussion, then plan: what does your assembly know about Christmas?
- ◈ What resources are available for catechizing the assembly about Christmas?

S U N 20 LM #11B / LMC #11B / violet
Fourth Sunday of Advent

Scripture Insights

The dynamic of prophetic promise and fulfillment is deeply embedded in the Christian understanding of the Bible. Four peak moments unify the sweeping story of salvation in the Jewish Bible, our Christian Old Testament. These are represented by the election of Abraham, the deliverance through Moses, the kingship of David, and the restoration after the Babylonian exile. Christianity affirms the continuing potency and reality of these events for both synagogue and church and adds a fifth, culminating moment in the person and Paschal Mystery of our Lord Jesus Christ. We believe that this final moment of salvation history was figuratively anticipated by "types" that are found in the previous four Old Testament moments and many others. These interrelationships of "typology" continue to shape Christian liturgy, prayer, theology, and practice.

The third of these moments and its fulfillment in Jesus are in view today. The promise given to King David in today's 2 Samuel text assured that his royal line would never fail. Israel's king would call God "father" and be called God's "son." This promise originated the Jewish hope of a coming Messiah (see Isaiah 9:5–6; 11:1–9). But when David's royal line was broken following the Babylonian exile, this promise became problematic (see Psalm 89, used in today's liturgy). Christians found its new and deeper fulfillment in Jesus. Many New Testament texts recall Jesus' royal heritage as the "son of David" (Matthew 1:1; Acts 2:25–36; Romans 1:3). But nowhere is the fulfillment of promise of the "sure love for David" (Isaiah 55:3) more strongly invoked than in Luke's story of the annunciation, where the angel Gabriel's words to the Messiah's mother, Mary, are modeled on the promise given to David.

Preaching Points

Parish Masses

- Our Blessed Mother was born of David's line, the ancient and great king of Israel. God's promise to David was fulfilled in the Virgin Mary. Mary responded to God's call with faith, love, and bravery.
- The Virgin Mary is often depicted as being meek and mild. It takes great strength, however, to follow God. Mary selflessly and bravely looked to serve God and cooperate with his salvific plan for his people.
- God's promises are always kept; he honors his people with truth and goodness. The promise he made to David is echoed in the words spoken to the Virgin Mary, as God kept the promise he made to David.

Children's Liturgy of the Word

- In the Bible many people are said to have similar characteristics. Esther, an ancient Jewish queen, saved her people by interceding for them. The Virgin Mary assisted her people by agreeing to be the mother of the savior.
- A promise is a person saying they will do something for sure, and promises are meant to be kept. God always keeps his promises, and he promised David favor, a kingdom, and the future Son. God kept his promise when Mary agreed to become the Mother of God, and Jesus was made incarnate in her womb.

Missal Options

- Consider using Form II of the PA.
- The Gloria is not sung or said.
- The Creed is said or sung.
- Although the Missal provides prayer texts proper to December 20, use the prayer texts for the Fourth Sunday of Advent.
- Use an Advent Collect to conclude the UP.
- P-II for Advent is used.
- You might use EP-III and the SB for Advent.

Music Preparation

- As we enter these final days of Advent, try to resist the temptation to use Christmas music! Advent has so many rich and appropriate texts: various settings of the "Ave Maria," "Alma redemptoris mater," "The Angel Gabriel," "Magnificat," and "Rorate caeli" are appropriate and effective for today.

Music Suggestions

- Gathering: " O Come, O Come, Emmanuel" (various publishers): begin with "O Key of David" today.
- Responsorial Psalm 89: "Forever I Will Sing" by Ed Bolduc (Kat Shak Productions)
- Recessional: "O Come, Divine Messiah" (various publishers)
- Postlude: "Soon and Very Soon" by Andre Crouch (various publishers)

Mass Texts

Introduction to Mass

We gather in God's house, reminded of the humility of the Lord. Long ago he chose to pitch his tent with us, taking flesh in the womb of the Virgin Mary. Today he seeks to make his dwelling in our community and find a home in our hearts. Let us make room for him, removing everything from our lives that is contrary to love, and prepare ourselves for the coming celebration of his birth. *My brothers and sisters, let us acknowledge our sins, and so prepare ourselves to celebrate the sacred mysteries.*

Tropes for Penitential Act, Form III

Your Kingdom, O Lord, shall endure for ever:
Lord, have mercy.

We have sinned against you, yet you are faithful:
Christ, have mercy.

You are our rock, our savior: Lord, have mercy.

Dismissal for Children's Liturgy of the Word

Dear children, King David had big plans for building a house for God, but God promised to make a home not just for him but for all of us, and that home will last forever. Jesus is our home, and in a few short days we will celebrate the day of his birth, when he came to us and took us to himself. Go now and listen to how much he loves you.

Dismissal of Catechumens

Dear friends, St. Paul speaks of "the mystery kept secret for long ages but now manifested" in Jesus Christ. That mystery is being revealed in your own lives as you walk this path of initiation. We give you time now to reflect further on this revelation, and we pray for your increasing enlightenment until the day when you join us at the Lord's table. Go in peace.

Dismissal of Extraordinary Ministers of Holy Communion

Dear ministers of the Lord, Christ longs to dwell among all his people. Mindful of the ill and infirm among us, we send you to them with the Eucharist, that he may make his dwelling with them through his Sacred Body. Give them our love and God's blessing of peace.

Universal Prayer

O Come, O Key of David, come, and open wide our heavenly home, make safe the way that leads on high, and close the path to misery. Hear now, O Lord, the prayers we hold in our hearts.

1. For the people, our local bishop, and all who lead, that they may follow the example of Mary's fiat, we pray:
2. For all civic leaders and all who share in the responsibilities of enacting laws for the common good, we pray:
3. For our world, that all places where violence reigns may be healed by the Lord's gift of peace, we pray:
4. For all students and teachers who prepare for Christmas break, we pray:
5. For all modern-day prophets who challenge society to read the signs of the times, we pray:
6. For all those who find this time of year difficult, especially those who are mourning the death of a loved one, we pray:
7. For our parish, that together we may wholeheartedly respond to God's invitation to serve the poor and the needy among us, we pray:
8. For those who have died, that they may be embraced by God at the heavenly banquet, we pray:

God of all goodness,
you provide the key that unlocks the way to salvation,
the gift of your Son.
Through him you destroy the prison walls
of death for all those who dwell in fear and darkness.
As we await his return in glory,
may we see in our world your desire
to free all who are burdened with heavy chains.
Through Christ our Lord.
Amen.

Other Rites and Customs

- Light all the candles on the Advent wreath before Mass begins.
- These final days before Christmas are a great time for Christmas pageants and concerts. These should be scheduled outside of liturgical prayer.
- Have a carol-sing followed by a bonfire with hot chocolate and cookies on the church plaza.
- Invite parishioners to bring the infant Jesus from their home nativity scene to be blessed at Sunday Mass.
- Provide a brief prayer service for parishioners to bless their Christmas tree or Nativity scene at home (see *Catholic Household Blessings & Prayers*).
- Bless engaged couples after Masses (see the *Order of Celebrating Matrimony*).
- Sing "O Come, O Come, Emmanuel" a cappella as the closing hymn, leaving parishioners in anticipation of the celebration of the Nativity to come.
- Tonight's O Antiphon at Evening Prayer is: "O Key of David, O royal Power of Israel controlling at your will the gate of heaven: come, break down the prison walls of death for those who dwell in darkness and the shadow of death; and lead your captive people into freedom."

Liturgy and Life

Our time of preparation draws to a close. As the Solemnity of the Nativity nears, there is always much to do and many demands on our time. In the midst of the busyness, stay true to the call of Advent. The Scriptures invite us to remember God's fulfillment of promises made long ago by the prophets. Set aside time to read and reflect on chapters 1 and 2 of Luke's account of the Gospel. Ponder the work of the Holy Spirit in the story of Jesus' birth: Mary's openness to the annunciation, the visitation of Mary to Elizabeth, the humble birth, the adoration of the shepherds, the presentation of the infant Jesus in the Temple, and much more. Like Mary, ponder these miraculous events deeply in your heart.

Taking Place this Week . . .

Consider what can be done liturgically, catechetically, and ministerially to respond to these important needs.

- International Human Solidarity Day (12/20)
- December/Winter Solstice (12/21)
- Christmas Eve (12/24)
- Christmas Day (12/25)
- Boxing Day (12/26)

MON 21 LM #197 / LMC #172–175 / violet
Advent Weekday

Optional Memorial of St. Peter Canisius, Priest and Doctor of the Church / violet

Scripture Insights

Two options are given for the First Reading, one from Song of Songs, with the "lover" springing across the mountains to the beloved, the other with Zephaniah extolling us to shout for joy and sing joyfully. Both set the stage where one pregnant woman hurried to be with her pregnant cousin and for the visitation, where the unborn John "leaped for joy" at the arrival of the unborn Jesus.

Preaching Points

Parish Masses

- The reading from Song of Songs is an expression of the delight of the lover for the Beloved—such is God's love for us. The reading from Zephaniah tells of how the Lord sings "joyfully" because of us.
- At the core of what we call the visitation is one young woman hurrying to share the good news (and Good News) of her pregnancy with her older pregnant cousin. The Divine Plan begins with, and builds on, human relationship.

Masses with Children

- God loves you—loves all of us. We know that, but how do we feel it? Do you ever feel God's love? The joy God has for you?
- Mary can't wait to visit her cousin Elizabeth and hurries across the hills to do so. Two women who said yes to be a huge part of God's salvation of the world.

Missal Options

- Use the same form of the PA prayed on the Sundays of Advent.
- The prayer texts are for December 21.
- Use an Advent Collect to conclude the UP.
- Use P-II of Advent today.
- Consider using EP-II.

Song of the Day

"O Come, O Come, Emmanuel" (various publishers) or "Treasures Out of Darkness/*Tesoros Ocultos*" by Alan Revering (WLP)

Other Rites and Customs

Light all the candles on the Advent wreath before Mass begins.

- Tonight's O Antiphon at Evening Prayer is: "O Radiant Dawn, splendor of eternal light, sun of justice; come, shine on those who dwell in darkness and the shadow of death."

Optional Memorial

St. Peter Canisius wrote a German-language catechism and founded the Jesuit College in Fribourg, Switzerland, as a response to Protestant Reformation. He avoided polemics and direct debate with Protestant theologians and believed that it was better to attract people with solid orthodox teaching and let the truth speak for itself.

- Use the same form of the PA prayed on the Sundays of Advent.
- Today's readings and Missal texts are proper to December 21. There are two options for the First Reading. For the readings for children, use the Advent seasonal weekday readings.
- You may use the Collect from the saint's day to conclude the UP.
- Continue to pray P-II of Advent and consider using EP-II.

TUE 22 LM #198 / LMC #172–175 / violet
Advent Weekday

Scripture Insights

Hannah herself had been childless and had prayed fervently for a child. Eli, one of the priests, had heard her praying in the Temple, as had God. As God gave her the child, so she returned the child to God and delivered her own Song of Praise to God. Mary's Magnificat is a foreshadowing of the upheaval her son would bring. The proud are scattered, the mighty are cast down, and the hungry are filled.

Preaching Points

Parish Masses

- Mary is often portrayed as meek and mild. Her hymn of praise to God shows quite a bold side as she audaciously proclaims what her son will do to fulfill God's promises.
- "My soul proclaims the greatness of the Lord," says Mary. How many of us can say that? What would that look like?

Masses with Children

- Mary gracefully accepted the task of being mother to Jesus. Here she proclaims her love of God and rejoices that God chose her.

- Mary also tells of the great changes that Jesus will bring. The powerful will fall, the lowly will be lifted up, the hungry will be filled, and the rich will go away empty.

Missal Options

- Use the same form of the PA prayed on the Sundays of Advent.
- The prayer texts are for December 22.
- Use an Advent Collect to conclude the UP.
- Use P-II of Advent today.
- Consider using EPVN-IV.

Song of the Day

"O Come, O Come, Emmanuel" (various publishers) or "The King of Glory Comes" by Willard F. Jabusch (WLP)

Other Rites and Customs

- Light all the candles on the Advent wreath before Mass begins.
- Today's O Antiphon is: "O King of all the nations, the only joy of every human heart; O Keystone of the mighty arch of man, come and save the creature you fashioned from the dust."

WED 23

LM #199 / LMC #172–175 / violet

Advent Weekday

Optional Memorial of St. John of Kanty, Priest / violet

Scripture Insights

These are the last lines of the last prophet, Malachi. The last word: doom. We shouldn't forget that "the Day of the Lord," the coming of the messiah, was both eagerly awaited and feared for the destruction and upheaval to come. Then comes John, the last of the Old Testament prophets, the first of the New Testament prophets. Elizabeth gave birth, John was named, and fear came upon the neighbors. "What, then, will this child be? For surely the hand of the Lord was with him."

Preaching Points

Parish Masses

- Malachi recounts the prophetic foretelling of Jesus' coming: a messenger prepares the way, Elijah will come, the day of the Lord will burn us all with a fire like that of the refiner's. How was Jesus' coming like this? How was or is it different?
- Elizabeth was clearly loved and revered by all around her, and all rejoiced at the baby's birth. Suddenly Zechariah declares the name—John—though no one in his family has had the name. This is the subtlest of signs that things are changing.

Masses with Children

- The prophet Malachi uses the possibly disturbing imagery of fire, like a fire that burns away our impurities. Yet that which remains afterward is precious, like gold and silver.
- John's birth brought great excitement to his town and his family, but also a bit of surprise and changes. Just like John himself and the one he proclaimed brought.

Missal Options

- Use the same form of the PA prayed on the Sundays of Advent.
- The prayer texts and readings are for December 23. Use the seasonal weekday readings for children's liturgies.
- Use an Advent Collect to conclude the UP.
- Use P-II of Advent today.
- Consider using EP-II.

Song of the Day

"O Come, O Come, Emmanuel" (various publishers) or "Emmanuel" by Steve Angrisano (OCP)

Other Rites and Customs

- Light all the candles on the Advent wreath before Mass begins.
- Tonight's O Antiphon is: "O Emmanuel, king and lawgiver, desire of the nations, Savior of all people, come and set us free, Lord our God."

Optional Memorial

St. John of Kanty was a Polish theologian and physicist who taught at the University of Krakow. Although his head was in the heavens, both theologically and astronomically, his heart was with the poor of Krakow, to whom he devoted most of his university salary.

- The readings are taken from the SW.
- Use the prayer texts for December 23. The Collect from the saint's day may conclude the UP.
- Continue to pray P-II of Advent.
- Consider using EP-I.
- Continue to use the same form of the PA.

THU **24** LM #200 / LMC #172–175 / violet
Advent Weekday

Scripture Insights

David wants to build a temple to house the Ark of the Covenant, which dwells in a tent, as it did during the flight from Egypt. God told Nathan to tell David, "Should you build me a house to dwell in?" God recounted all that he had done for his people and one-upped all of that. God promised to raise up an heir from David's lineage "and make his Kingdom firm." Zechariah continues and confirms the prophecy. His Son will prepare the way for the Son of God, who will "guide our feet in the way of peace."

Preaching Points

Parish Masses

- King David wants to build a temple for the Ark. God reminds him who takes care of whom and promises far more and far better to the House of David.
- Zechariah prophesies about his son John, who will "give his people knowledge of salvation." Ultimately Zechariah's proclamations are about "the tender compassion of our God."

Masses with Children

- King David loved God greatly and wanted to build him a great temple. God essentially said, "Thanks, but it is I who take care of you and your people."
- Zechariah was father to John the Baptist. God spoke to Zechariah and assured him that his son would play a part in the salvation of all the people of Israel and prepare the way for Jesus.

Missal Options

- Use the same form of the PA prayed on the Sundays of Advent.
- The prayer texts are for December 24.
- Use an Advent Collect to conclude the UP.
- Use P-II of Advent today.
- Consider using EP-III.

Song of the Day

"Gospel Canticle: Luke 1:68–79" by Ruth Duck (GIA)

Other Rites and Customs

Light all the candles on the Advent wreath before Mass begins.

Christmas Time

For us, God has become a gift. He has given himself. He has entered time for us. He who is the Eternal One, above time, he has assumed our time and raised it to himself on high. Christmas has become the Feast of gifts in imitation of God who has given himself to us. Let us allow our heart, our soul and our mind to be touched by this fact!

—Pope Benedict XVI, Christmas Homily, December 24, 2006

The Meaning of the Season

H*ODIE Christus natus est*! Today, Christ is born! During our Christmas celebration of the Nativity of the Lord, the Church rejoices in the Incarnation of Christ, when the Word became flesh. This moment inspires such awe that, during the recitation of the Creed at the Christmas Masses, we adoringly genuflect at the *et incarnatus est*—the line that affirms that Christ "by the Holy Spirit was incarnate of the Virgin Mary / and became man" (see GIRM, 137).

The Mass readings for each of the liturgies for the Nativity of the Lord offer the fullness of the story of the Incarnation. As Adolf Adam explores in his seminal book *The Liturgical Year* (p. 126–30), each set highlights a particular aspect of the Incarnation. With its prophetic First Reading (Isaiah 62:1–5), the appearance of John the Baptist in the Second Reading (Acts of the Apostles 13:16–17, 22–25), and the Gospel's genealogy of Jesus and the account of Joseph's dream (Matthew 1:1–25), the Vigil Mass marks the transition from Advent to Christmas. Its Gospel Acclamation verse is anticipatory: "Tomorrow the wickedness of the earth will be destroyed: the Savior of the world will reign over us."

The Mass during the Night can be preceded by the chanting of the Christmas Proclamation, which situates the birth of Christ in light of all of salvation history. During this Mass, the "tomorrow" of the Vigil yields to "today" in the Responsorial Psalm and Gospel Acclamation verse, while the prophetic tone of the Vigil's Isaiah reading yields to another Isaiah text (9:1–6), this one in the present tense: "a child is born to us, a son is given us." The Mass at Dawn is filled with light imagery, from the Entrance Antiphon and Responsorial Psalm ("A light will shine on us this day: the Lord is born for us") to the Collect. Finally, the Mass during the Day reminds us that the Christ who was born as a baby is the one whose "saving power" (Psalm 98) has spoken to us, who is seated "at the right hand of the Majesty on high" (Hebrews 1:1–6), and who is the true "Word made flesh" (John 1:1–18). For these three Christmas Masses only the Lectionary permits using any of the three sets of readings at any Mass (rubric at 13ABC).

Taken as a whole, the readings for the Masses of the Nativity of the Lord do not simply focus on the birth of a child; they invite us to recall that the same baby who was born in a manger is the man who came to redeem creation. As Pierre Jounel notes, Christmas "prepares us to understand Easter better by showing the Redeemer to be the very Son of God made man. In addition, Christmas helps us to live the paschal mystery" ("The Year" in *The Liturgy and Time,* vol. 4, ed. Martimort, p. 82).

While we may not often think of Christmas in this way, our musical texts reflect this twofold meaning. In "O Little Town of Bethlehem," we pray that the "holy child of Bethlehem" will "descend to us" and "cast out our sin," while John Neale's translation of "Of the Father's Love Begotten" reminds us that the Virgin "bore the Savior of our race . . . the Babe, the world's redeemer." This connection also forms the foundation for more recent compositions, such as Andrew Everson's "Heaven and Earth Are Wed" (WLP) and Francis Patrick O'Brien's "Wood of the Cradle" (GIA), the latter of which begins with an explicit statement of the connection between birth and death: "Wood of the cradle, wood of the cross."

This deep mystery of the Incarnation is worthy of extended reflection, so we are challenged to ensure that our Christmas celebration extends throughout the entire season. Even after the carols have stopped playing on the radio, the commercial decorations have started to be taken down, and the "after-Christmas" sales have begun—and sometimes even ended (!)—the Christmas season includes a number of observances that invite us to a deeper reflection on the meaning of Christ's birth.

The Octave of Christmas makes this invitation explicit. December 26 is the Feast of St. Stephen, the First Martyr. This feast can be traced to the fourth century. The account of his stoning (Acts of the Apostles 6:8–10; 7:54–59) is followed by Psalm 31 with the antiphon, "Into your hands, O Lord, I commend my spirit." This is a direct echo of Good Friday, when we sing, "Father, into your hands I commend my spirit." Matthew's Gospel account (10:17–22) is the warning that men will "hate" and "hand over" Christians, even to the point of parents, siblings, and children betraying each other to death.

On December 28 we are faced yet again with martyrdom with the Feast of the Holy Innocents. This story is recounted in the Gospel for the day (Matthew 2:13–18), in which the Holy Innocents are murdered by Herod. This feast extends as far back as the sixth century.

For the remaining Christmas weekdays through the Feast of the Baptism of the Lord, the First Readings are taken from 1 John, with "antichrists" (December 31, 2:18–21, and January 2, 2:22–28) and warnings about sin playing a prominent role.

Such readings are not meant to temper our Christmas joy, but they do remind us that even during Christmas Time we must be prepared to undergo hardships as we await the next coming of the newborn king. If we are to come and adore him in the manger, we must also be willing to follow him to the point of death on the cross.

Ultimately, then, Christmas Time reminds us of our call as Christians in the world. The way that we celebrate Christmas marks us as different from those for whom it is simply a pleasant holiday, an occasion for giving gifts and gathering with loved ones. We do those things too, but we do so with the knowledge that the newborn Christ whom we are celebrating eventually suffered and died to save all of creation—and, consequently, so too must we be prepared die to self and live for him and for all of creation. When the shepherds found the manger and told Mary of the angels' proclamation of the birth of her son, she "kept all these things, reflecting on them in her heart" (Luke 2:16–21). The Christmas season is a time for us to do the same, to pray that "we may be numbered among those who belong to him, in whom is the fullness of human salvation" (Collect for December 31).

On the final day of Christmas Time, the Feast of the Baptism of the Lord, we receive one final message from our Second Reading (1 John 5:1–9). We are reminded that we show our love for God by keeping his commandments and that our Savior is "the one who came through water and blood." It then continues: "Whoever is begotten by God conquers the world. And the victory that conquers the world is our faith. Who indeed is the victor over the world but the one who believes that Jesus is the Son of God?"

The Christmas season is a time for us to remember that we if believe in the Son of God, we too will ultimately share in his triumph over death. Indeed, that promise should inspire us to make sure that our hearts "prepare him room" and to raise our voices in jubilant song: "Glory to the newborn king!"

The Sounds of the Season

"Today is born our Savior: Christ the Lord!" From the very first notes of the first Mass on Christmas Eve, the assembly should know just by the sounds that something is completely different. Now is the time to let the carols ring out in their full glory! Liturgical music should be "intentional" and "purposeful" so, in Christmas Time, the festal joy of the Nativity needs to be sustained throughout the entire season—from Christmas Eve straight through to the Feast of the Baptism of the Lord. Utilize those Christmas carols throughout the next few weeks.

This is probably not the most opportune time to introduce new settings of the Gloria or Eucharistic Prayer acclamations. Use something the assembly knows well and settings that visitors will be able to join without too much difficulty. Many parishes use ordinaries based on familiar Christmas carols. Some resources include Daniel Laginya's *Christmas Gloria* (GIA, G-7800), Richard Proulx's *Gloria for Christmastime* (GIA, G-3485), Paul Gibson's *A Christmas Mass* (OCP, 30106749), James Chepponis's *w*In Advent, it was suggested that music directors incorporate the use of the proper Introit. You can maintain this practice throughout Christmas Time as well! Use of the Introits and Communion Antiphons should not be seen as being relegated to a particular season but, rather, part of the parish repertoire.

Seasonal favorite solos such as Adolph Adam's *Cantique de Noël*, Handel's *Rejoice, Greatly*, and Pietro Yon's *Gesu, Bambino* can certainly be utilized provided they are placed appropriately and do not cause an interruption to the flow of the liturgy.

The various liturgies in Christmas Time have rich and beautiful texts, which can be creatively highlighted and illuminated by choosing correlating sacred, liturgical and ritual music.

The Second Vatican Council teaches that the "treasury of sacred music is to be preserved and fostered with great care" (CSL, 114). If your choir accesses this great repertory of motets and choral music, let *The Roman Missal*, *Roman Gradual*, and Lectionary be your guide as what to use and where. Sit down with these liturgical books in order to immerse yourself in these great texts: allow yourself to pray with them and let them speak to you, stir your soul, and spark your imagination. The assembly just may notice the texts—either those spoken or sung—as they never have before.

Utilizing some of the great musical settings of *"Hodie Christus Natus Est"* or *"O Magnum Mysterium"* may enhance—or illuminate—a particular reading or presidential prayer in a way like nothing else. These pieces, and a host of others like them, are part of our tradition and should be used wherever the resources allow. Don't be overwhelmed in searching for material: check out www.cpdl.org/wiki for scores in the public domain.

The Look of the Season

The environment for the Christmas season requires the same principles addressed in the Advent environment section (see page 3). It is not enough to simply place a Nativity scene somewhere and trot out as many poinsettias as can be delivered by the local florist. Nor is it enough to fill in every corner with evergreen trees. All of these elements have legitimacy in our Christmas liturgical spaces, but placement can either distract or enhance the liturgy itself. And more is not always better or more beautiful.

If you are able to have large candles during Advent, then place the same or similar floor candles near the Nativity scene, a way of seaming the two seasons together. Like the Advent wreath, the location for the Nativity scene is critical. It should not be visually competing with the liturgical prayer or the liturgical furnishings, but it does not have to be hidden either. Each worship space is set up differently: for some, a large gathering space provides a perfect setting for children's oohs and aahs; for others, a side altar or side statue area might frame the Nativity scene well. The celebration of the Eucharist, as for any liturgical season, is the primary prayer, and so altar and ambo need to remain dominant visually.

This same principle underscores the placement—and amount—of poinsettias. The color of the season is white, and while red is a perfect complement visually, neither the flowers themselves should block the liturgical action visually or physically nor should their color dictate all else in the space. Use the flowers to accent the various focal points, especially the altar and the ambo. There is no need to bank the flowers in any area, which tends to give them a kind of visual power to overtake all else.

Christmas trees can have a similar effect, but because they are trees, they are usually in the background and are less obtrusive. The dark green actually makes them recede into the background visually. As the season is one of light, however, placing small white lights on them can extend the lights of the candles in the liturgical space, the lights in the darkness of the world, and connect—even if indirectly—to the candles of the Advent wreath, which were part of the season of promise. As the season of fulfillment of the promise, Christmas should be well lit. White cloths trimmed in gold can deck the ambo, the altar, and even the "halls" of the church.

Arranging cloth, candles, Christmas flowers, and evergreen can make the magic of the secular world move into the arena of holiness in our worship spaces. We are not imitating the secular world; rather, what we have been anticipating for weeks on our streets and in our malls has now found its home in the liturgical space and this most appropriate time to be visible. The Word became flesh, became visible, and we find the beauty of God in the lights and colors of this wonderful season of the Incarnation.

Evangelizing the Parish through the Season

Of the seasons of the liturgical year, Christmas is perhaps the best known and the most celebrated in our society, even if the liturgical celebration of the Incarnation is far from most people's minds. Despite this distance, however, the season is one in which many congregations will host many people whom they do not usually see. When considering the season in light of evangelization, it is important to remember that the liturgy—the public work of the Church—is the Church at her most transparent. Here we speak and sing about our hope and our gratitude. Here we gather as the Body of Christ, "a body at the same time holy and always in need of being purified" (LG, 8). Here we also often live out the sins of which Pope Francis has regularly called the Church to repent, including self-righteousness and a lack of mercy. In the United States, the fruit of our national shame is also often on display as we worship in assemblies divided by race or ethnicity, operating often as if we were members of different Christs (see 1 Corinthians 1:13; 11:29).

The Solemnity of the Nativity of the Lord celebrates the unique moment of God's condescension to all of humanity. The Word who was with the Father from before all ages, creator of all things, "did not regard equality with God something to be grasped. Rather he emptied himself, taking the form of a slave, coming in human likeness" (Philippians 2:7).

In preparing the liturgies of Christmas, it is easy to get wrapped up in the to-do lists. Certainly, the beauty of these liturgies is important and is itself an opportunity to preach the Gospel of the Incarnate Word. The tangible things of this world also matter; beauty can reveal truth about the God become flesh. But it is important to remember also that the Word appeared among travelers, was announced to shepherds, and immediately became a refugee. This Word is spoken to all in the midst of the winter's darkness. God-with-us shines in the darkness. The Christian community gathers to gaze in wonder at the simplicity of this poor child and his road-weary parents. How does the beauty of the liturgy welcome people to share in this wonder? Does it invite them to sit and be received by this child and his Church? Does the Body of Christ welcome the stranger, the unexpected, and those angry at the Church and make it easier for them to hear the welcome that is Christ's welcome?

Holidays are fraught for many families, including the Church. We gather to gaze at the beauty of the Incarnation, to hear the familiar stories, and to sing the old songs. But we also can forget that this is not our feast and that the welcome comes from God. The best we can do is to echo the shepherds: "Let us go, then, to Bethlehem to see this thing that has taken place, which the Lord has made known to us" (Luke 2:15).

Worship Committee Agenda for Christmas Time

Meeting Time

The meetings need to take place early in the fall (mid-September and early November) so that Christmas information can be conveyed to all those involved in aspects of liturgy in a timely fashion.

Goal for Meeting

Consider and review the ritual elements and rubrics of Christmas Time:

- Placement of the creche
- Chanting the Announcement of the Birth of Christ at Christmas Night Mass and the Announcement of the Date of Easter and the Movable Feasts at Epiphany Masses
- Chalking and blessing of the doors at Epiphany Masses
- Keeping the Christmas season alive when the secular world has moved on

Opening Prayer

- Pray the Liturgy of the Hours
- Read the Gospel of John for Christmas Day (John 1:1–18)
- Sing a favorite Christmas hymn

Seasonal Questions

- Are there any issues or pitfalls from last year that need to be avoided?
- How will we demonstrate hospitality? More greeters? Details in worship aid? Providing overflow seating? Will there be multicultural elements?
- Are there any safety procedures that need to be discussed? Is the parish equipped with an external defibrillator?
- How will we address the difficulty of getting all the ministry volunteers we need for Christmas Masses? Consider after-Mass signups.
- Should we include the text of the Creed in the worship aid with notations on when to kneel?
- How can we recruit additional choir members and musicians? Have there been any thoughts about a seasonal choir?
- How do we invite new members to the art and environment committee?
- Who determines the Scriptures and prayers to be used? Who conveys the appropriate information to liturgical ministers?
- When will incense be used during Christmas Time? Passing this information on to musicians in advance is appreciated so they can plan offertory music.
- Are there any special needs for environment or music that need to be budgeted for?
- Are all proper copyrights secured for any printing, podcasts, or livestreams?
- Does the fire marshal need to be contacted about live trees? Has there been a consideration to spraying trees and liturgical cloths with flame retardant?

Liturgical Catechesis for the Worship Committee

- Review the Christmas section of this *Sourcebook* as an overview of the season and an opportunity to bring up additional ideas and questions.
- Study the four principles mentioned in *To Crown the Year* (LTP) and review the Christmas chapter.
- Read seasonal excerpts from *La Navidad Hispana at Home and at Church* (LTP)

Liturgical Catechesis for the Assembly

- *Keeping the Seasons* (LTP)

Closing Prayer

- Read the Gospel from Midnight Mass (Luke 2:1–14)
- Sing "Silent Night"

FRI 25 LM #13, 14, 15, and 16ABC / LMC #13ABC / white

Solemnity of the Nativity of the Lord (Christmas)

Holyday of Obligation

About Today's Solemnity

The Nativity of the Lord (Christmas Day) carries such importance within the life of the Church that it is an entire period of liturgical time lasting nearly three weeks. The doctrine of the Incarnation states a fundamental Christian belief that God's divine nature assumed a human nature. In other words, the unseen God became human. Both human and divine natures come together in the person of Jesus Christ. This became known as the "holy exchange," which tells us that the divine became a human being so that humans could become divine.

Scripture Insights: Vigil

In our First Reading, the prophet speaks in beautiful and compelling imagery about God's forthcoming salvation, but his words are as much a prayer as a promise. He will keep speaking about this beautiful transformation of Jerusalem and Israel until God makes it happen. At that time the Jews were recovering from a devastating invasion decades earlier in which it seemed as if God had forsaken them. The prophet declares that God will give the city a new name to signify his new relationship with them, a relationship so intimate it's as if God has married his people.

The God of Israel may have seemed absent at times, but he was working steadily through the history of his chosen people to bring salvation not only to them but to the whole world. The passage from the Acts of the Apostles offers a brief reminder of the ways in which has God already saved his people. He led them out of Egypt into a homeland of their own, protected them from their enemies under the reign of King David, and sent a herald in John the Baptist to prepare them for the radical new way in which he would act within history.

In his genealogy, Matthew zeroes in on part of the history of God's chosen people. He presents the lineage of Joseph, who faithfully takes Mary and her unborn child into his home, thereby grafting them onto his family tree and fulfilling ancient promises. Salvation history has come to a climax with the Incarnation. God has come among his people in the flesh. Today we speak of Jesus as the bridegroom of the Church. Isaiah's glorious vision has been fulfilled.

Preaching Points

Parish Masses

- God has been steadfast and faithful to his people, Israel. His plan was to reconcile his human creation to himself, and in the Incarnation we see the bud of salvation.
- *Emmanuel* is the name of Jesus and it means "God with us." In the person of Jesus, God is truly with his people.
- When we say that God is with his people, we are realizing that he is with us because he became one of us; fully human and fully divine, our Lord is one of us.
- The generations of names listed in the reading are meant to help the reader understand the connection and completion between Jesus and the House of David.

Children's Liturgy of the Word

- When you hear "-el" at the end of a biblical name, it is a reference to the name "El-Shaddai," which is a name of God in the Old Testament. *Emmanuel* means "God with us," and it is one of Jesus' names.
- We believe that God is with his people through Jesus because Jesus is fully human and fully God—Jesus is one of us.
- The Jewish people waited a long time for the Messiah—Jesus—to come to earth. He had been promised to the Jewish people, and his family tree could be traced to David.

Scripture Insights: Mass during the Night

At the Mass during the Night celebrating Christ's coming into human history, the Scriptures once again call us to reflect upon past, present, and future. Titus bids Christians to live today as Christ taught us when he was on earth, while we wait, stretching toward a final "appearance" of Christ. Luke announces that God fulfills human hopes in ways that both complete and exceed our expectations.

Isaiah proclaimed God's Word at a time of fear and upheaval, when Judah's very survival was threatened by the superpower of his day, Assyria. In Isaiah's time, God's people needed a leader to rescue them from this military juggernaut. God responded by promising a ruler who would meet all the expectations of an Israelite king: not only a political and military leader, but a champion of God's ways of justice. The child to be born would fulfill the divine promise of a "sign," a son of David who would reassure Judah that "God is with us" (7:14).

At the beginning of the Gospel, Luke describes the situation of God's people some seven centuries later: they live in occupied territory, under control of that era's dominant power, Rome. The evangelist indicates God's definitive fulfillment of all prophecy by referring to Bethlehem, "the city of David" (Luke 2:11). The child born here begins the final act of God's plan of salvation, and this son of David exceeds all Israelite hopes and expectations.

The angel of the Lord tells of "Good News" that will break even the power of mighty Rome. Public proclamations called "good news" among the Romans announced success of military feats, political campaigns, and the glories of Caesar, often called "savior of the people" and "lord." But Luke announces divine Good News: "a savior . . . who is Christ and Lord" (Luke 2:11).

Preaching Points

Parish Masses

- God, who once commanded Gideon to reduce his army and blow horns to achieve victory, sent a savior to his people. Instead of a mighty grown man, God sent a helpless baby who was born in the poorest of places. God's ways surprise his people!
- In his goodness, God prepared to send his Son, whose awe-inspiring titles include "Wonderful Counselor" and "Prince of Peace." What goodness that we are sent this holy child!
- We are called to be "zealous for good deeds" just like our Lord had such zeal. How do we sustain such zeal outside Christmas Time?
- An occupied land, a poor couple who traveled at the whim of the emperor—this plain and ordinary scene of ancient, poor Jewish life was the scene of God's human birth.

Children's Liturgy of the Word

- When Jesus was born, his country was ruled by a distant emperor, and he was born to poor and common parents. God could have chosen for Jesus to be born into a royal home, but instead chose for him to be born into poverty.
- Long before Jesus was born, Israel awaited their savior who would be called "Wonderful Counselor" and "Prince of Peace." Jesus filled these roles and was much more to God's people.
- Like Jesus, we are called to be "zealous for good deeds." How do we create zeal and how do we sustain it?

Scritpure Insights: Mass at Dawn

In the First Reading, the prophet declares that God will come to overturn the hardship that his people have endured. At the time of this prophecy, the Jews were recovering from a devastating invasion in which it seemed as if God had forsaken them. The prophet tells how God will give the city a new name to signify his new relationship with them. This new name indicates that people all over the world will come to visit and worship God in the sacred city.

In our Gospel passage, a chorus of angels have just announced to shepherds that a savior has been born. The shepherds dash off to see what has happened. St. Luke twice notes that the shepherds declare what they had seen and heard. Like the prophet in the First Reading, the shepherds become witnesses of God's salvation: they proclaim "to the ends of the earth" that a savior has come (Isaiah 62:11).

The love and excitement that permeates the First Reading and the Gospel passage is also evident in the passage to Titus where again we hear that a savior has appeared. This time we're reminded that Jesus came because of God's love for his people. God wanted to deliver us from sin, suffering, and death. We have done nothing to deserve such deliverance, but we actively participate in it by being baptized and welcoming the presence of the Holy Spirit in our lives.

As we become part of Christ's saving work through Baptism, we become part of a new era. We are no longer beholden to sin with its dark end. Rather, we are made heirs of eternal life. A new day dawns for us, a day without end.

Preaching Points

Parish Masses

- Love is the great driver of the Gospel, and indeed of all salvation history. God's great love for his people is seen in the person Jesus; this love is seen at his mother's assent, at the Incarnation, and in the birth of our Lord. Love was incarnate, and love came to earth.
- Through Jesus, we are given the gift of rebirth; we recall our rebirths as we celebrate the Incarnation of Jesus, the dawn of salvation.
- How joy-filled the shepherds were as they proclaimed the heavenly message they received! We too are filled with joy knowing that God has come to us, and has been born one of us.
- The Virgin Mary, a young mother with a newly born baby, pondered all that happened —she witnessed God's word coming to fruition.

Children's Liturgy of the Word

- Through our Baptism, we are reborn. Today we celebrate the birthday of Jesus, Emmanuel, God-with-us, who has brought us our rebirth.
- The shepherds were filled with joy because Jesus was born! We too can be filled with joy about Jesus.
- The Virgin Mary was the first person to know about Jesus coming to earth. She treasured all events around Jesus' birth and understood that God's word had come to pass.

Scripture Insight: Mass during the Day

In the First Reading, heralds hasten to Jerusalem to announce God's victory over Israel's enemies. The men keeping watch over the city echo the good news, which reverberates throughout the city until everyone is singing for joy. God has liberated his holy city, once besieged and destroyed by Babylon, for all to see. God's people no longer need to lament their circumstances nor feel ashamed of past misdeeds.

Those times when God's people experienced his saving power all ultimately point to the advent of God's Son, who brought about a salvation beyond anything they had ever experienced. As the author of our Second Reading explains, the prophets of the Old Testament testified for God, but they did so incompletely. Only God's Son, who is himself divine, speaks perfectly and completely for God. Even the angels, despite their closeness to God, do not share the status of the Son.

The Second Reading complements the prologue of John's account of the Gospel, which presents Jesus in exalted, cosmic language. Just as in the beginning God created by the power of his Word, so Jesus, the embodiment of God's Word, finally and forever saves people from the sin that endangers creation. Jesus is the light that defeats the uncomprehending darkness. Those who believe that Jesus is God's Son belong to God. Just as Jesus came from above, so now those who believe in this Word and turn to this light are joined to what is above.

John the Baptist, as well as the author and community of the fourth account of the Gospel, have testified that God's Son came among us, as did the author of Hebrews. Today we raise our voices in joyful song at all that God has done, and we pray that our jubilant cries will reverberate to the ends of the earth.

Preaching Points

Parish Masses

- We are a people called to the light of Christ. Through Christ's Incarnation, death, and Resurrection we are called to participate in the life of the trinity, in the light of Christ, and through the light of Christ.
- The Lord is faithful to his people, and brings them into communion with himself; he has brought salvation to his people.
- The Son of God is of God himself; he is not angel or pure spirit simply inhabiting a body. God the Son became incarnate, and after the Resurrection he ascended to heaven and is now with the Father.
- In darkness, Christ is our light. In his light, we can become the children of God.
- We are a people called to the light of Christ. Through Christ's Incarnation, death, and Resurrection we are called to participate in the life of the trinity, in the light of Christ, and through the light of Christ.
- The Lord is faithful to his people, and brings them into communion with himself; he has brought salvation to his people.
- The Son of God is of God himself; he is not angel or pure spirit simply inhabiting a body. God the Son became incarnate, and after the Resurrection he ascended to heaven and is now with the Father.
- In darkness, Christ is our light. In his light, we can become the children of God.

Children's Liturgy of the Word

- God is always faithful to his people and wants to be in relationship with them.
- Jesus came from the Father when he became incarnate, and returned to the Father at the Ascension. He is with the Father now.
- In darkness, Christ is our light. In his light, we can become the children of God.

Missal Options

- Vigil Masses should not take place before 4 PM on Christmas Eve (unless otherwise stipulated by your diocese). However, the Vigil may be celebrated before or after Evening Prayer.
- The Christmas Proclamation should be sung before the Mass during the Night begins. The text is found in appendix I of the Missal. The entrance song immediately follows the chant.
- Consider the sprinkling rite in lieu of the PA.
- The Gloria is sung or said; use a magnificent setting.
- In the worship aid, remind the assembly that during the Creed all kneel when the Incarnation is mentioned. Because this is out of the normal routine, it is easy to forget and not understand the gesture.
- To highlight the festivity of these Christmas days, presiders might consider chanting the introductory dialogue and the Preface to the EP.
- Presiders may choose to use P-I, P-II, or P-III of the Nativity of the Lord.
- If using EP-I, the proper form of the Communicantes should be used.
- Pull out the stops for this great feast of the Incarnation—use the best vestments, linens, and vessels (be sure to clean them before the season) and include a more elaborate Gospel procession.
- The SB for the Nativity of the Lord may be used.

Music Preparation: Vigil

- For the Christmas season, change the Mass setting to something joyful, but distinctive from Advent and other seasons of the year.
- The parish Vigil Mass too often becomes a Christmas pageant with and for young children. If there is to be a pageant, it should take place before or after the celebration of the sacred liturgy. Sacred Liturgy (see Introduction to the LMC, 52).

Music Suggestions

- Gathering: "A Child is Born in Bethlehem" translated by R. Wright, OSB (WLP)
- Preparation: "Peace Child" by B. Farrell and S. E. Murray (OCP)
- Communion: "Love Has Come" by M. Maher (OCP)

Music Preparation: Night

- Traditionally, the proclamation of the birth of Christ is sung during the Liturgy of the Hours, but for most communities it is sung before the beginning of Christmas Mass during the Night. Because of the range, choose a cantor carefully and spend time rehearsing in the church at a microphone. The music and text is found in appendix I of *The Roman Missal.*
- Music ministry might invite the priest/deacon to sing the Gospel at this liturgy.
- Music ministry should avoid non-liturgical carols during Mass.

Music Suggestions

- Gathering: "O Come, All Ye Faithful" (various publishers)
- Gloria: "Gloria of the Bells" by C. Alexander Peloquin (GIA)
- Communion: "Of the Father's Love Begotten" (various publishers)

Music Preparation: Dawn

- Ensure that music ministry is present to maintain the festive and joyful nature of this solemnity. Recruit either a small schola, a children's group, or a cantor and accompanist for this Mass.
- The psalm assigned to the Mass at Dawn is Psalm 97, and it invites the assembly to make the connection between the rising sun and the birth of Jesus, the Light of the World. Set these two verses to a psalm tone.
- Be attentive when choosing music that it is not too devotional or saccharin. Use the three judgments from *Sing to the Lord* to evaluate a piece if a question or doubt arises.

Music Suggestions

- Call to Worship: "Rejoice, O Daughter Sion" by C. Walker (OCP)
- Communion: "Love is His Word" by C. Hampton and L. Connaughton (WLP)
- Sending Forth: "Joy to the World" (various publishers)

Music Preparation: Day

- The worship aid should also include common responses. This is a gesture of hospitality.
- Similar to the Mass in the Night, today's liturgies are festive. For the Mass during the Day, invite brass and other instruments to help the Gloria and other parts of the Mass speak the joy of the Nativity.

Music Suggestions

- Gathering: "Cry Out with Joy and Gladness" by J. Marchionda (WLP)
- Responsorial Psalm 98: "All the Ends of the Earth" by J. Schiavone (OCP)

Mass Texts

Introduction to Mass

The Lord does not leave us orphans. Whatever griefs or sorrows we carry, whatever sins we have committed, God does not abandon us, but comes to us, giving us his only Son whose birth we celebrate this very day, whose birth is the dawning of our hope, joy, healing, and salvation. Let us lift up our hearts in praise and thanksgiving as we enter into this Christmas Eucharist. *My brothers and sisters, let us acknowledge our sins, and so prepare ourselves to celebrate the sacred mysteries.*

Tropes for Penitential Act, Form III

You are the eternal Word of God, in unapproachable light:
Lord, have mercy.

You took flesh in the womb of the Virgin:
Christ, have mercy.

You reconcile us to the Father and to one another:
Lord, have mercy.

Dismissal for Children's Liturgy of the Word

The birth of the Lord is announced to shepherds, those whose job it is to keep watch over their flocks. God's message of peace falls upon the hearts of the world. May you go forth to hear about the love of God. Go in peace.

Dismissal of Catechumens

My friends, this mystery we celebrate, the mystery of God becoming a human being in Jesus, is one that can only be accepted with faith, which itself is a gift from God. As we dismiss you, we pray for the deepening of your faith and we eagerly await the day when you will remain with us to receive the mystery of the Eucharist. Go now in the peace of the Son of God.

Dismissal of Extraordinary Ministers of Holy Communion

My dear friends, as we conclude this glorious celebration, we remember our sick and homebound brothers and sisters. Take the Lord to them in his Word and his Body, give them our Christmas blessing, and assure them of our continued prayers.

Universal Prayer

A holy *[night/day]* has dawned upon us! With wonder and spiritual joy, let us bring to our Lord our needs.

1. For our Holy Father, **N.**, for all the bishops and all the clergy who proclaim the Good News of the Lord throughout the world, we pray:
2. For peace on earth, that the song of the angels may inspire those who govern nations and guide armies to seek peaceful resolutions to global and domestic conflicts, we pray:
3. For the sick and the homebound, especially for those who have no family by their side this Christmas, we pray:

4. For the poor and for those who struggle to provide the basic needs of food, clothing, and shelter for their families, that they may be surrounded by people who see in them the light of Christ, we pray:
5. For our parish family, that we might announce the Good News of salvation in our wider community through our charitable actions and our words of hope, we pray:

O Lord Jesus, our Christ,
as at your birth as a helpless infant,
you melted every stony heart,
draw us into the mystery of God,
who saves us through weakness and vulnerability.
You live and reign for ever and ever.
Amen.

Other Rites and Customs

- Be sure to be extra hospitable to the many guests that will attend Mass today.
- Offer a special bulletin for Christmas that highlights the varied ministries and activities of the parish.
- Contact the local high school band to have them play Christmas Carols on the plaza as people arrive for Mass.
- In addition to traditional Christmas Carols, sing some contemporary carols that highlight some of the social justice issues of our time.

Liturgy and Life

"The word *today* is key to entering into the mystery of Christmastime, for if Christ is born today that means we can see and touch and hold Christ. It also means that we must feed, clothe and protect Christ, no, today. If Christ is alive in our midst, then truly the reign of God has begun, the reign in which the very rocks of the earth cry out for justice and compassion, acclaiming the coming of the Lord. And that is the only intelligent way to interpret the authentic customs and decorations of Christmas—not as signs of a birthday anniversary of God's reign, emblems of eternity, of health, and wholesomeness and the endless design of heaven itself" (Peter Scagnelli). In today's divided and polarized political and religious nature of our country, we often hear complaints about the so-called "war against Christmas." The only war against Christmas is to fail to act as Christ taught us to act through the glory of his Incarnation. If we are truly to put "Christ" back in Christmas we must love God and love each other—*all* people and *all* of God's beautiful creation. Today is born our Savior, Christ the Lord!

SAT 26 LM #696 / LMC #437 / red
St. Stephen, The First Martyr

Today's Saint

St. Stephen was one of the first seven deacons of the Church and is remembered as the first martyr. The faith that led him to devote himself to serve God's people as a deacon also inspired his courageous testimony and martyrdom.

Scripture Insights *(PS)*

The day after we celebrate the birth of our Savior, we commemorate the death of this first martyr, the first of thousands and thousands. Something in the dark side of humanity recoils at the "grace and power" given to Stephen, which is also available to us. The Gospel promises that the Spirit of the Father will speak during these times of trial. "Whoever endures to the end will be saved," Jesus tells us, but he doesn't protect us from experiencing the persecution.

Preaching Points

Parish Masses

- As Stephen described his vision of Jesus at the Father's right hand, the crowd "covered their ears, and rushed upon him." Yet present in the crowd was Saul, who took the name Paul and became a fearless preacher of the Gospel.
- The word martyr is the Greek word for "witness." Jesus tells us that, for his sake, we will be called before governors and kings "as a witness before them and the pagans." Perhaps we are called to provoke the world more, even if it means trouble with the authorities, in order to be witnesses to Christ.

Masses with Children

- St. Stephen loved Christ and spread his message with "grace and power." Even the smartest people of his time couldn't beat him in a debate.
- At times, following Christ and speaking his Word will get us into trouble with the authorities. Don't worry, Christ tells us; the Spirit will be there with us, speaking through us.

Missal Options

- The prayer texts are in the PS for December 26.
- Continue to sing (or recite) the Gloria.
- If you are using the LMC, the First Reading is proper and is found in the PS (#437). The other readings are from the CM.
- Presiders may use any of the three Prefaces for the Nativity of the Lord.
- Consider using EP-I.
- Conclude with the SB for the Nativity of the Lord to unify the days of the Octave.

Song of the Day

"Good Kind Wenceslaus" (various publishers) or "Into Your Hands, Lord" by Greyson Warren Brown (OCP)

Other Rites and Customs

Boxing Day originated in the United Kingdom and is always celebrated on the Feast of St. Stephen, the second day of Christmas. St. Stephen was known for his outreach to the poor. During the year, the British would collect money for the poor. The money would be stored in little clay boxes. On Boxing Day, the boxes would be broken and the money given to the poor. Parish families in the United States could be invited to do the same! Set aside a box in the family home. This could be used as an Advent calendar. Throughout the days of Advent, as the families count down toward Christmas, change, clothing, nonperishable foodstuff, and other needed items can be added to the family box (one item per day). On this day, the box can be distributed to the poor. Consider adding this to your own Christmas traditions.

S U N **27** LM #17B / LMC #14ABC / white
Feast of the Holy Family of Jesus, Mary, and Joseph

About today's feast

Today is the Feast of the Holy Family. The ordinary events of the Holy Family should not blind us from seeing that God is truly in our midst and only God brings us to the fullness of life. The full Gospel text for today is the account of the Presentation of Jesus in the Temple. This includes the encounter between Jesus' parents and Simeon and Anna. It is worth reading the complete story. The presentation allows us to recognize that the event of Jesus' birth is greater than a simple family moment. His Nativity is intended to change the course of history, as represented in the beautiful prayer of Simeon. This change will begin with Jesus' family life, but will eventually affect our lives. We will all become his family, his beloved, and his disciples.

Scripture Insights

"The word of the Lord came to Abram in a vision." The Bible never explains the mechanics of God's communication with the patriarchs, matriarchs, prophets, and apostles. But God's Word was a vivid reality to its hearers, and it caused them to act decisively, even if to outsiders that obedience appeared strange or even insane.

Abraham and Sarah set out to receive an unseen inheritance, sure of nothing except the word that had burned itself into their souls. They went out, not knowing where they were going, *the Lord* prompting them in vague but unmistakable ways. Most translations of Hebrews 11:11 say that Abraham received the power to father Isaac by faith. Some manuscripts, followed by the *New Jerusalem Bible,* say that it was Sarah who received this word: "It was equally by faith that Sarah, in spite of being past the age, was made able to conceive, because she believed that he who had made the promise was faithful to it." Whether or not this is the original reading, her pregnancy shows that Sarah shared Abraham's habit of trusting the Word of the Lord.

Venerable Simeon and Anna represent Old Testament piety at its best, very much like Abraham and Sarah. Their hidden source of life was their expectant trust in the Word given by the Lord. Simeon was "awaiting the consolation of Israel" (2:25); Anna was counted among those "awaiting the redemption of Jerusalem" (2:38). From long experience they knew and lived *the Word* and its prophetic fulfillment as if it already existed. Because they loved and lived it, they sensed its near approach and instantly recognized the reality when it arrived.

Preaching Points

Parish Masses

- Trusting in God's Word, Abraham, Sarah, Mary, Joseph, Simeon, and Anna witnessed the Word of God coming to fruition in their own lives and before their eyes.
- The Word of God inspires us to fortitude in our faith lives. A relationship with God doesn't mean constant assurance or never being scared in our lives.
- The Word of God in Scripture promised the coming of a Savior, and, in the person Jesus, the Word of God became a person, flesh, dwelling on Earth.
- Simeon recognized the Savior, knowing God's Word was true.

Children's Liturgy of the Word

- Fortitude is a virtue of courage or bravery. In the reading, we hear about the faithful fortitude that Abraham, Sarah, Mary, Joseph, Simeon, and Anna all exhibited in their wait for the Lord. We too are called to faithful fortitude.
- Fortitude doesn't mean eternal comfort; it means that we have the character that can abide through difficult times.
- Simeon was joyful because he saw God's promise in little Jesus. We too are joyful because we behold salvation.

Missal Options

- Use the Missal texts for the Holy Family instead of those in the PT for December 27.
- If you did the sprinkling rite instead of the PA on Christmas, continue to do so today to unify the season ritually.
- Continue to sing (or recite) the Gloria and the Creed.
- To highlight the festivity of these Christmas days, presiders might consider chanting the introductory dialogue and the Preface to the EP.
- You may use P-I, P-II, or P-III of the Nativity of the Lord. Consider P-II since it declares Christ restoring unity to all creation and calling humanity back to itself, a theme to be embraced by all families.
- EPVN-I is a good option for today; however, if EP-I is used, use the proper form of the Communicantes.
- Although the Missal doesn't note the use of a SB, the SB for the Nativity of the Lord may be used today.

Music Preparation

- The Church's celebration of Christmas continues through the Baptism of the Lord. Retain the same settings of liturgical music used a few days ago on the Solemnity of the Nativity of the Lord and keep singing those Christmas carols! It is okay to utilize some contemporary Christmas carol texts, but, as with all things, it is important to retain a balance with the familiar. A serious question you should ponder: will the assembly gathering today on December 27 really know and own a text that may have been recently published?
- Even though Christmas Time is one of the most glorious parts of the year, you will likely be working with a lighter crew of musicians as many choirs take off the week after Christmas; however, make sure that things are rich and lively.

Music Suggestions

- Gathering: "Come, Sing a Home and Family" by Alan J. Hommerding (WLP)
- Preparation of the Gifts: "Christmas Hymn" by Paul A. Tate (WLP)
- Sending Forth: "Once in Royal David's City" (various publishers)

Mass Texts

Introduction to Mass

In a particular way today we celebrate the Holy Family of Jesus, Mary, and Joseph, but we also remember that we are all God's family and called to holiness. With gratitude for the many exemplars of faith, hope, and love that God gives us, and in the joy of the Incarnation, let us prepare to celebrate these mysteries of our salvation. *My brothers and sisters, let us acknowledge our sins, and so prepare ourselves to celebrate the sacred mysteries.*

Tropes for Penitential Act, Form III

Lord Jesus, you became human for us and developed and were formed in a human family: Lord, have mercy.

You surround us with the bonds of love: Christ, have mercy.

You are our brother and the one who saves us: Lord, have mercy.

Dismissal for Children's Liturgy of the Word

My dear children, Jesus was once as old as you are now, and he had parents who loved him very much. Whatever your family looks like, know that it is a sign of God's love for you. As an extension of your family, this faith community is here for you, and we give you this time together now to listen to the Scriptures and to praise God for his love. Go now in peace and love.

Dismissal of Catechumens

My friends, this community, this family of faith, sends you forth to reflect on God's Word and on how it is forming you to grow in wisdom and knowledge. We look forward to the day when you will join us in the celebration of the Eucharist. Go in peace.

Dismissal of Extraordinary Ministers of Holy Communion

Dear ministers, we give you the Word and Body of Christ to take to those in our community who are ailing and confined to home. Remind them that they are one with us as beloved children of God. Go in peace.

Universal Prayer

Our God has appeared on earth and lived among us within a holy family. We turn to him now in prayer.

1. For the Church, that she will continue to advocate for displaced families and those seeking refuge, we pray:
2. For world leaders, that the laws they pass will protect and support the family, we pray:
3. For the obedience to God's Word that creates true families, we pray:
4. For those who have not known parental love or the affection of their siblings, we pray:
5. For immigrant and refugee families, that they will find welcome in new lands, we pray:
6. For the ability to withhold judgment against families who are not traditional, we pray:

Eternal Father,
through the Incarnation of Christ and the Sacrament of Baptism,
you have made us your adopted sons and daughters.
Help us, like the Holy Family,
to deepen our relationship through faith, hope, and charity.
Through Christ our Lord.
Amen.

Other Rites and Customs

- Offer a blessing of families today from the BB.
- Include music that mentions the plight of refugees.
- Give the parish choir a needed rest and invite young people home from college to lead the music.

Liturgy and Life

What parent has not at some point felt that a sword has pierced their heart? We pray that, like Christ, each family member will grow in strength, wisdom, and grace. This week, as a family, tell stories of your best and hardest moments together. Reach out to someone who has lost a family member or has no living family.

Taking Place This Week . . .

Consider what can be done liturgically, catechetically, and ministerially to respond to these important needs.

- New Year's Eve (12/31/20)
- New Year's Day (1/1/21)
- World Day of Prayer for Peace (1/1/21)
- Solemnity of Mary, the Holy Mother of God (1/1/21)
- First Friday (1/1/21) and First Saturday (1/2/21)

MON 28 LM #698 / LMC #439 / red
Feast of the Holy Innocents, Martyrs

Scripture Insights/Today's Feast

On the Fourth Day of Christmas, we mourn the Holy Innocents. Herod had told the Magi to return to him, but they were warned in a dream not to go back to him. He slaughtered all the boys simply because they might one day have threatened his power. The Gospel remembers the murdered children and the grief of their mothers.

Preaching Points

Parish Masses

- This is not the first or the last story of innocent people being destroyed by wicked leaders in their lust for power. Christ had been prophesied to be "the rise and fall of many" (Luke 2:34). The tumult and chaos started before he could even walk.
- Rachel weeping for her children has become a potent symbol for all of us who grieve loved ones lost to violence.

Masses with Children

- All during Christmas Time we hear about the infant Jesus and the visit of the Magi, or the Three Kings. This is the sad story of what happens afterward. Sometimes innocent people peoples suffer, through no fault of their own.
- Rachel represents all mothers who mourn children lost to violence. We join her in her lamentations and are reminded to do all we can to comfort the present day "Rachels" in our neighborhoods and our world.

Missal Options

- The prayer texts are found in the PS for December 28.
- Continue to sing (or recite) the Gloria.
- If you are using the LMC, the Gospel is proper (#439) and the other readings are from the CM.
- Presiders may use any of the three Prefaces for the Nativity of the Lord.
- Consider using EP-II.
- Conclude with the SB for the Nativity of the Lord to unify the days of the Octave.

Song of the Day

"A Hymn for Martyrs Sweetly Sing" (various publishers) or "Coventry Carol" (various publishers)

TUE 29 LM #202 / white
Fifth Day within the Octave of the Nativity of the Lord

Optional Memorial of St. Thomas Becket, Bishop and Martyr / white

Scripture Insights

The darkness and waiting of Advent is over, "and the true light is already shining," so John tells us. John also lays down the integral relationship between the commandments and love of God. Speaking of light, Mary and Joseph present their child in the Temple, only to be surprised by Simeon, who recognizes Jesus as "a light to reveal [God] to the nations."

Preaching Points

Parish Masses

- John's words are inspiring ("whoever keeps his word, the love of God is truly perfected in him") and challenging ("whoever says he is in the light, yet hates his brother, is still in darkness").
- Though the light has come into the world, the challenge is far from over. Simeon calls Jesus "a sign that will be contradicted" and tells Mary, "you yourself a sword will pierce."

Masses with Children

- Which is more important: loving God or keeping God's commandments? John tells us that these are one and the same, that either one brings forth the other.
- What happened when his parents brought Jesus to the Temple? How do you think they felt when an old man they'd never met took their boy and called him "the salvation which [God] prepared in the sight of every people"?

Missal Options

- There are no Christmas weekday readings in the LMC.
- The prayer texts are found in the PT for December 29.
- Because today is within the Octave of the Nativity of the Lord, the Gloria is sung.
- P-I, P-II, or P-III of the Nativity of the Lord may be used.
- If EP-I is prayed, use the proper form of the Communicantes; however, EP-III is also a good option for today.
- Conclude with the SB for the Nativity of the Lord to unify the days of the Octave.

Song of the Day

"Luke 2:29/*Nunc Dimittis*" by Jacques Berthier (Taizé/GIA) or "Now Let Your Servant Go in Peace" by Ruth C. Duck (GIA)

Optional Memorial

St. Thomas Becket was the archbishop of Canterbury in the mid-twelfth century. He was murdered in his own cathedral by followers of King Henry II due to conflict between the saint and the king. He is recognized as a saint by the Roman Catholic and Anglican Churches.

- The Collect is proper and found in the PS for December 29. The other prayers are from the Mass of the day because this memorial falls within the Octave.
- Continue to sing the Gloria because it is within the Octave.
- The Collect from the SW may be used to conclude the UP.
- P-I, P-II, or P-III of the Nativity of the Lord may be used.
- If EP-I is prayed, use the proper form of the Communicantes; however, EP-III is also a good option for today.
- Conclude with the SB for the Nativity of the Lord to unify the days of the Octave.
- The readings may be from the SW, #699, LMC #440, the CM, or CP.

WED 30

LM #203 / white

Sixth Day within the Octave of the Nativity of the Lord

Scripture Insights

The First Letter of John reminds us not to be lured in by love of the things of this world. These things pass away; those who do the will of God do not. Like Simeon, Anna too has been waiting in the Temple of the Lord and told all who would listen about the child Jesus.

Preaching Points

Parish Masses

- John is writing to his fellow Christians about being detached from the things of this world. For him, it is very much either/or—either you do the will of God, "who is from the beginning," or you fall to the world's enticements.
- "The child grew and became strong" with his parents in Nazareth and Egypt. We hear about nothing of this part of his life, but we can gather a lot about what Mary and Joseph taught him, based on all we have heard about them.

Masses with Children

- We must be careful not to let the frivolous things of this world distract us from the will of God.
- We hear very little about Jesus' childhood, but today we hear that he was "filled with wisdom, and the favor of God was upon him." Ask the children: what do you think Jesus was like as a child?

Missal Options

- The prayer texts are found in the PT for December 30.
- Because today is within the Octave of the Nativity of the Lord, the Gloria is sung.
- There are no Christmas weekday readings in the LMC.
- P-I, P-II, or P-III of the Nativity of the Lord may be used.
- If EP-I is prayed, use the proper form of the Communicantes; however, EP-III is also a good option for today.
- Conclude with the SB for the Nativity of the Lord to unify the days of the Octave.

Song of the Day

"See Amid the Winter's Snow" by Edward Caswell (various publishers)

Other Rites and Customs

As we near the end of the Octave of the Nativity of the Lord, it is good to remind parishioners that Christmas is a season and extends to the Feast of the Baptism of the Lord. Help them unpack this aspect of the Paschal Mystery by making available this short (and free!) video. You may share on Facebook, Twitter, or Instagram; post on your parish website; or send the link via email: https://vimeo.com/305125035.

THU 31

LM #204 / white

Seventh Day within the Octave of the Nativity of the Lord

Optional Memorial of St. Sylvester I, Pope / white

Scripture Insights

The Gospel according to John does not include a Nativity story—there is no birth narrative, no Mary and Joseph, no baby Jesus, no shepherds or wise men. Instead, we boldly get: "In the beginning was the Word." These words echo the first verse of Genesis and go beyond. "The Word became flesh and made his dwelling among us." Yet here on the seventh day of Christmas we also get rumblings of grave problems in the early Church: "the antichrist." There is an urgency too: "we know this is the last hour." Yet, two thousand years later, we know truly that "the Light shines in the darkness."

Preaching Points

Parish Masses

- The Gospel according to Matthew and Luke provide us with the narratives of Jesus' birth. John's account of the Gospel reveals the heavenly and eternal existence of Christ and his oneness with the Father, "full of grace and truth."
- "What came to be through him was life, and this life was the light of the human race." The words *life* and *light* resound through these descriptions of Christ. Life to the fullest. Light that reveals the truth.

Masses with Children

- Today's Gospel gives a different look at Christ's beginnings, beginnings that go back before "in the beginning" since Christ was always with God and always one with God. God became flesh in Jesus.
- What is stronger, light or darkness? Light: light always conquers darkness. Jesus is the Light of the World. The light shines, and the darkness cannot overcome it.

Missal Options

- There are no Christmas weekday readings in the LMC.
- The prayer texts are found in the PT for December 31.
- Continue to sing (or recite) the Gloria.
- You may use P-I, P-II, or P-III of the Nativity of the Lord.
- If EP-I is prayed, use the proper form of the Communicantes. Consider also EPR-I.
- Conclude with the SB for the Nativity of the Lord to unify the days of the Octave.

Song of the Day

"Of the Father's Love Begotten" (various publishers)

Optional Memorial

Pope Sylvester's papacy began after the conversion of Constantine ended persecutions against Christians. St. Sylvester built churches in Rome and presided over the First Council of Nicaea, providing structures, both physical and theological, for the growing Christian community.

- The readings may be taken from the SW, #700, or the CP (For a Pope), or LMC #431.
- The Collect is from the PS for December 31. The remaining prayers are from the seasonal weekday because we are still within the Octave.
- The seasonal Collect may be used to conclude the UP.
- P-I or P-II of the Saints, or of Holy Pastors, or any of the three Christmas Prefaces may be used.
- Use EP-I with the Communicantes for the Nativity.

Solemnity of Mary, the Holy Mother of God

See page 46.

LM #205 or #510 / LMC #235 / white

SAT 2

Memorial of Sts. Basil the Great and Gregory Nazianzen, Bishops and Doctors of the Church

Today's Saints

Sts. Basil (329–379) and Gregory (329–390) were close friends. They fought against Arianism, a fourth-century heresy that denied the full divinity of Christ. Their voices prepared the way of the Lord. Basil challenged people to live simply and care for the poor and dying. Though shy, Gregory became a great preacher.

Scripture Insights

All true prophets speak God's Word and proclaim God's Kingdom. John the Baptist carries on this tradition. All true disciples point to Christ, and John is a true disciple. The First Letter of John confirms this: "whoever confesses the Son has the Father as well."

Preaching Points

Parish Masses

- "Remain in him" we hear again and again in the First Reading. The writer's community is being threatened by forces inside and out. What should we do when this happens? Remain in the Son and in the Father. What is promised us? Eternal life. Remain in him.
- John the Baptist is repeatedly questioned as to who he is and rejects all suggestion. When pressed, he cites Isaiah, "I am the voice of one crying in the desert." When asked why he baptizes, he dodges the question, makes reference to Christ, and keeps on baptizing.

Masses with Children

- The First Reading gives us great simple advice—remain in God. Remind the children that when they were baptized they were "immersed" in God (the word *baptism* comes from the Greek word for "immerse"). The Christian life is to remain where you were immersed—in the Father and the Son and Holy Spirit.
- Speaking of Baptism, it's what John the Baptist does. The people can't quite figure out who he is. They make suggestions, he denies them. He points to Christ, in whom he baptizes, and keeps on baptizing.

Scripture Insights (PW)

- Each person in every vocation is called to live out Christ's love. If everyone had the same vocation and role in life, our tradition would not have its depth or effective ministry. The discernment processes helps people discover their vocations.

Preaching Points

Parish Masses

- We are called to live holy lives appropriate to each vocation or place in life that is our own. Each of us has a calling, and in that calling we must act as Christ to one another.

Masses with Children

- All of God's people are called to goodness and holiness. Each person is part of the Body of Christ, and must function for good in the way Christ intended.

Missal Options

- There are no Christmas weekday readings in the LMC.
- The readings may also be from the CP or CDC.
- The prayers are found in the PS for January 2.
- There is no *Gloria* since the Octave concluded yesterday.
- Use the seasonal Collect to conclude the UP.
- Use P-I or P-II of the Saints, the Preface of Holy Pastors, or any of the Prefaces for the Nativity of the Lord.
- Consider using EP-I.

Song of the Day

"On Jordan's Bank" (various publishers)

Other Ideas

Hours: Psalter Week I begins today.

Something to Consider...

◈ In what ways can you help members of the assembly perpetuate the Christmas season in their home life?

◈ Organize an outing for volunteers willing to visit those in nursing homes. Christmas can be a very lonely time for people.

◈ Encourage family members to bless their homes on Epiphany.

F R I **1** LM #18ABC / LMC #15ABC / white

Solemnity of Mary, the Holy Mother of God

The Octave Day of the Nativity of the Lord / Holyday of Obligation

About Today's Solemnity

Today, the Church celebrates Mary as the Mother of God. She is called *Theotokos* (God-bearer), for "God sent his Son born of a woman." Because Mary found favor with God, his Son took the flesh of Mary—it is thanks to her that Jesus is *fully* human, with flesh like ours, except for sin, and also fully divine. As the child grew in her womb, he dispensed blessings and graces to all who came into contact with Mary—Elizabeth and John the Baptist. In this, Mary is the ultimate sign of the Christian, for what is a Christian if not one who bears Christ within our world and brings him to people?

Scripture Insights

In the First Reading, we recognize familiar words of blessing, asking that the Lord let his face shine upon us. The Responsorial Psalm also speaks of God's face shining upon us. A radiant face is a sign of favor, so God's face shining on us means grace. God's blessing is no mere external help but an inner force that both supports and enriches our human willing and doing. May this blessing be with us this new year!

The Second Reading celebrates our identity as beloved children of God. In the verses leading up to this text, Paul argues that it is through faith and not by the law that one becomes a true child of Abraham and so inherits the blessing promised to him—that through him all his families of the earth will be blessed (see Genesis 12:3). The law acted as a sort of guardian, guiding people as if they were minors until they came of age. That coming of age occurred when God sent us the Son. With this sending, God also changed the guardian—instead of the law, God sent us the Spirit of his Son. It is this Spirit who makes us children of God and teaches us to relate to God as "*Abba*" (Father), thus, allowing us to share in Jesus' intimacy with his Father.

Luke's account of the Annunciation bears some echoes to the First Reading. The woman Eve is chastised by God, but Mary is greeted with a pronouncement of grace and told she has "found favor with God." Her offspring will bring salvation to the people, not shame. The whole event gives witness to how God will bring about salvation. It is God who sends the messenger, it is God who names the child to be born, and it is God who will continue overcome all human boundaries, "for nothing will be impossible for God."

Preaching Points

Parish Masses

- The Virgin Mary carried Jesus in her womb as any mother carries a child in her womb, and she birthed her holy child and mothered her holy child. She was a mother who lived under the Jewish law and raised her son in that same law.
- When the Virgin Mary heard the words of the shepherds, she reflected on their words in her heart. What must have gone through her heart and mind with this joy-filled visit?
- God chose for Jesus to be born into a poor family and to be greeted by poor shepherds. If God had chosen otherwise, Jesus could have been born in a palace to a queen or to a rich merchant. Instead, God chose poverty. We are reminded who we are and who Christ is.
- Jesus came to us, lived among us, and indeed became one of us; it is through him and his humanity that we are called into greater unity with our Lord. Through Christ we are adopted into God's family. Mary is the one who brought Christ into the world; she is the *Theotokos*, the God-bearer.

Children's Liturgy of the Word

The preaching points for adult Masses may also be used for children's Liturgy of the Word.

Missal Options

- Today is also the Octave Day of the Nativity of the Lord.
- The prayer texts are found in the PT for January 1.
- Although today is New Year's Day, the solemnity may not be replaced with the Mass for Civil Needs: At the Beginning of the Civil Year.
- Since today honors motherhood (new life), offer the sprinkling rite instead of the PA.
- The Gloria and the Creed are sung or recited today.
- If the Preface and introductory dialogue was chanted on Christmas and Holy Family, continue to do so today.
- P-I of the Blessed Virgin Mary is used.
- If EP-I is prayed, use the proper form of the Communicantes. EP-III is a good option for today.
- Conclude today's liturgy with the SB for the Blessed Virgin Mary.

Music Preparation

- Today is a Marian day, the World Day of Prayer for Peace, and New Year's Day. How do your musical choices reflect all of these important elements? Try to incorporate all of these needs into the liturgy. It takes thought.
- There are beautiful contemporary Marian hymns that are available from Catholic publishers. Don't be afraid to use them and start a new tradition. Liturgy is always a delicate balance between new and old.
- For Marian music, include Christmas carols that focus on Mary's role as the Mother of God.

Music Suggestions

- Gathering: "Daily, Daily, Sing to Mary" (various publishers)
- Preparation of the Gifts: "Prayer of Peace" by David Haas based on Navajo prayer (GIA)
- Song of Thanksgiving: "We Adore" by Sarah Hart and Scott Krippayne (OCP)
- Sending Forth: "She Will Show Us the Promised One" by Willard F. Jabusch (WLP)

Mass Texts

Introduction to Mass

Our God, who is without beginning, who transcends all space and time, chose to be born on earth of the Virgin Mary, and so we rightly honor her as Mother of God. Through her our salvation dawns. This Eucharist is our thanksgiving—for Mary, for the mystery of the Incarnation, and for all the blessings God has bestowed on us. Let us ask for his continued blessing in the coming new year. *My brothers and sisters, let us acknowledge our sins, and so prepare ourselves to celebrate the sacred mysteries.*

Tropes for Penitential Act, Form III

Lord, you are the author of life and redeemer of the fallen:
Lord, have mercy.
You were sent by the Father, that we might receive adoption as God's children: Christ, have mercy.
You are the Prince of Peace for the whole world:
Lord, have mercy.

Dismissal for Children's Liturgy of the Word

My dear children, go forth to hear God's Word, to praise God in song, and to reflect on Mary's faith. May God the Father, and the Son, and the Holy Spirit help you to understand and live the Good News. Go in peace.

Dismissal of Catechumens

My friends, Mary is a model of faith. She was open to God's Word before she ever became his mother. As you go now to reflect on today's Scriptures, I encourage you to look to her for guidance in your own journeys of discipleship. Go in peace.

Dismissal of Extraordinary Ministers of Holy Communion

Ministers of the Lord, go to our brothers and sisters who cannot be with us due to sickness or injury and share with them God's Word and the Sacred Body of his Son. Assure them of Jesus' love and that through his Spirit they are one with us in prayer. Go in peace.

Universal Prayer

Today a light shines on us, for the Lord is born to us. We now turn to him with the needs of our world.

1. For the Church, that she may shine with the light of faith, sharing the Good News of Christ with others, we pray:
2. For the blessings of peace and justice upon this new year for all peoples of the world, especially those seeking refuge and asylum, we pray:
3. For new parents, as they prepare for the birth of a new child, we pray:
4. For mothers and fathers, who, like Mary and Joseph, reflect with hope on the future of their children, we pray:
5. For children and infants who will be baptized this year, we pray:
6. For the sick, the chronically ill, and those in hospitals and institutions of care, we pray:

Lord Jesus,
may your name be praised.
May heads bow and knees bend
as we understand that you came to save us from our sins.
Draw us ever closer to you,
where you live and reign for ever and ever.
Amen.

Other Rites and Customs

- Offer a Mass, holy hour with Exposition and Benediction, or a prayer service close to midnight on New Year's Eve for those who choose to ring in the new year in a spiritual way.
- A "New Year's resolution" might be to encourage your parishioners to pray the Office of Readings. Make this available in your chapel or church. Provide a small lectern in your chapel (or another suitable place), where the Office of Readings is placed each day. Someone will need to take the responsibility of making sure the pages are turned to the appropriate day. This might encourage those who pray in the presence of the Blessed Sacrament to see and pray the Office of Readings.

Liturgy and Life

Today's solemnity, Mary, the Holy Mother of God, is the oldest Marian feast in the liturgical calendar, on which we celebrate the Incarnation of Christ, born from the fruitful Virgin Mary. Since Pope Paul VI established the practice in 1968, the popes have used the first day of the new year to pray for world peace. Consider reflecting on the words of Pope Benedict XVI's homily from the 2010 celebration of this day. He calls for respect for each human person, care for the environment, and a willingness to lay down weapons and "convert" to peacemaking. Through the intercession of Blessed Mary, may our faith be strong so that we can bear peace into the world.

SUN 3 LM #20ABC / LMC #16ABC / white

Solemnity of the Epiphany of the Lord

About Today's Solemnity

Today's solemnity continues the celebration of the astonishing mystery of God's manifestation to the very ends of the earth. The visitors from the east symbolize the extent of God's salvation as it unfolds for peoples of every land. As they offer gifts, as would be fitting a king, they announce to the world that an astonishing event has taken place; all peoples will know the glory of God.

Scripture Insights

The anonymous disciple of Isaiah wrote just after the exile, when the prophet spoke to the shrinking hope of those who had returned to the desolate land. To them he proclaimed a lyrical vision of Jerusalem's future splendor. The opulence pictured is less striking than who it is that bears it: It is a long column of Gentiles lined up to do homage in Jerusalem. The image reflects God's glory and recalls Isaiah's prophecy that many nations will one day stream to Mount Zion to learn God's ways (Isaiah 2:1–4).

Casual readers of Matthew's Gospel might focus on the exotic visitors from the east, or on Herod's anger against them. But in Matthew's account of the Gospel the appearance of the Magi represents an almost liturgical introduction of the Gentiles into the court of the Messiah-King. This is the message of today's three readings as well as the Responsorial Psalm.

It is difficult to overstate the complexity and importance of the question that faced the first generation of Christians, virtually all of whom were Jews. Must Gentiles become Jews in order to become Christians? A strong conservative group on one side said yes, this was the way of salvation revealed to Moses. A more liberal group said no, Jesus offered salvation freely to everyone who responded to him, even to Gentiles.

Matthew seems to represent a middle group that insists on the integrity of Torah and includes the Gentiles by the mercy of God. In his Gospel, on the one hand, Jesus insists that "not the smallest letter or the smallest part of a letter will pass from the law, until all things have taken place" (5:18). But on the other hand, "many will come from the east and the west, and will recline with Abraham, Isaac, and Jacob at the banquet in the kingdom of heaven, but the children of the kingdom will be driven out into the outer darkness" (8:11–12).

Preaching Points

Parish Masses

- God desires relationship with his entire human creation; he has promised love and devotion to his people Israel, and gentiles were grafted onto the vine that is Israel. The arrival of the Magi reminds us that Jesus came for all humanity.
- Jesus came for all people, freely giving salvation. The early Church struggled with understanding how people would approach Jesus, and concluded that new converts did not need to become Jewish before becoming Christians.
- Gold and frankincense were expensive gifts, reserved for royalty or the very wealthy; they were gifts meant for a king. In these gifts we see that Jesus' kingship isn't limited to Israel.

Children's Liturgy of the Word

- Jesus' mission was one for all the world, not exclusively for the ancient Jewish people. The early Church struggled with the formation of Gentile converts but ultimately decided that new converts did not need to become Jewish in order to become Christian.
- The Magi were Gentiles, and their gifts show us that they respected Jesus as a king; Jesus' kingship is for the world, not for Israel alone.

Missal Options

- A Vigil Mass is celebrated before or after First Vespers of the Epiphany. The same readings for the Mass of the Day are used; however, prayer texts are proper to the Vigil.
- Although the prayer texts are different, the same rubrics apply to both the Vigil and the Mass during the Day.
- If you did the sprinkling rite on Christmas, continue to do so today.
- Sing the Gloria in full splendor (it may be recited), and say or sing the Creed.
- To highlight the festivity of these Christmas days, presiders might consider chanting the introductory dialogue and the Preface to the Eucharistic Prayer. Use the Preface of the Epiphany of the Lord.
- If EP-I is prayed, use the proper form of the Communicantes.
- Presiders may offer the SB for the Epiphany of the Lord.
- Continue to pull out all the stops: incense, fine linens, vessels, and vestments, as well as a more elaborate Gospel procession.

Music Preparation

- The Announcement of Easter and the Moveable Feasts is an option that may be sung on the Solemnity of the Epiphany after the proclamation of the Gospel. The GIRM gives direction that the Announcement of Easter is sung from the ambo by either a deacon or a cantor. Music for the Announcement may be found in appendix I of *The Roman Missal.*

Music Suggestions

- Gathering: "Songs of Thankfulness and Praise " (various publishers)
- Preparation: "Arise, O Jerusalem" by Bob Hurd (OCP)
- Communion: "The First Nowell" (various publishers) or "What Child Is This" (various publishers)
- Sending Forth: "We Three Kings of Orient Are" (various publishers)

Mass Texts

Introduction to Mass

We were once in darkness, ignorant of God and under the power of sin and death, but the Lord has shone his face on us, calling us here, to new life, by the light of a star, the light of his Christ. Jesus offers himself for the life of the world. Let us turn from the ways of darkness and receive him with joy in this Eucharist. *My brothers and sisters, let us acknowledge our sins, and so prepare ourselves to celebrate the sacred mysteries.*

Tropes for Penitential Act, Form III

You saved us from the valley of the shadow of death:
Lord, have mercy.
You reveal to us the Good News of
salvation: Christ, have mercy.
All the nations on earth shall walk by
your light: Lord, have mercy.

Dismissal for Children's Liturgy of the Word

My dear children, the Magi gave the newborn Jesus precious gifts, though he was only a baby. Now Jesus gives us the gift of everlasting life, so much does he love us. Remember his love as you go now and listen to him speaking to you in the Scriptures.

Dismissal of Catechumens

My friends, God has revealed to us his Only Begotten Son and called all peoples to follow him. As you continue your pilgrimage to communion with him and with his Church, we give you time now to reflect on today's readings and to marvel at the light of Christ shining in your own life. Go in peace.

Dismissal of Extraordinary Ministers of Holy Communion

My dear ministers, go to our friends who are suffering from illness or injury and cannot gather here with us. Share with them the gift of God's Word and the Body of Christ. Share with them too the gift of our love and prayers and the assurance that they are one with us in the Spirit. Go in peace.

Universal Prayer

Kings bow down before our Lord. All nations serve him! He has enriched us with a diverse world. Let us turn to him in prayer for its needs.

1. For the Church, that she may be a light to all nations, leading all to the Good News of Christ, we pray:
2. For all nations of the earth, that they come to know the greatness of God's providence, we pray:
3. For those entrusted with governance of peoples and nations, we pray:
4. For a return to seeking wisdom as a holy and human pursuit, we pray:

5. For those who live in fear of strangers and others whom they have never encountered, we pray:
6. For all those whose journey is difficult and whose spirits are weary, we pray:
7. For astronomers, astronauts, and others who study the skies to improve our lives and understanding, we pray:
8. For the gift of hospitality toward people of every language, culture, creed, and way of life, we pray:

Lord Jesus Christ,
as we celebrate the mystery of your Incarnation
and witness how you drew to yourself the high and the low,
the shepherd and the king,
the wise and the unlearned,
we pray that you might draw us also to you
and make us true disciples.
You live and reign for ever and ever.
Amen.

Other Rites and Customs

- Bless and distribute chalk for the families to take home to bless their doors and inscribe the year and the initials of the three Magi (20+C+M+B+21)
- Use incense today in the Entrance Procession, the Gospel, and at the Preparation of the Gifts.

Liturgy and Life

As the foreigners from the East are led to the infant Christ in today's Gospel, we see the mysterious ways in which God arranges for an "epiphany" (or manifestation, showing) of Christ to the world. The love of God's glory shines forth in Christ our Light, through whom we are renewed and remade in God's image and likeness. How can you be a light of love for all nations and all peoples?

Taking Place This Week . . .

Consider what can be done liturgically, catechetically, and ministerially to respond to these important needs.

- World Braille Day (1/4)
- Traditional date for the Epiphany of the Lord, which is maintained in many other countries (1/6)
- Twelfth Day of Christmas (1/6)
- Orthodox Christmas Day (1/7)
- January is National Mentoring Month and Slavery and Human Tracking Month
- For Catholics, January is traditionally celebrated as the Month of the Holy Name (this optional memorial usually takes place on 1/3)

MON 4 LM #212 / LMC #236 / white
Memorial of St. Elizabeth Ann Seton, Religious

Today's Saint

Elizabeth Ann Bayley, born during the Revolutionary War, grew up in comfort on Wall Street. The big story is her role in founding the Sisters of Charity and her work in establishing orphanages, hospitals, and Catholic schools. The undertold story is her personal struggle: motherless at age three, a good marriage with children shortened by bankruptcy and the death of her husband, loss of friends as she converted to Catholicism, anti-Catholic persecution, the death of two daughters, and the heartache of a wayward son. Persevering faith is the road to sanctity.

Scripture Insights

Believe in Jesus, love one another, but "test the spirits to see whether they belong to God." This community is clearly working hard to discern false prophets from the ones that are of God. Jesus begins his ministry of teaching and healing, and the crowds are beginning to gather. He cures all who come to him.

Preaching Points

Parish Masses

- "*The people who sit in darkness / have seen a great light.*" Jesus fulfills this prophecy among the people of Galilee and Syria.
- Numerous ailments are cured by Jesus—physical, psychological, and spiritual—as though the evangelist wanted to give many details of how Jesus cured everything that could affect humanity.

Masses with Children

- Those who acknowledge Christ in the flesh belong to God. Those who reject him and don't love each other belong to the world. When we love God and love each other, we remain in God.
- Jesus was teaching and "curing every disease and illness among the people." Everybody was gathering around him because he healed them and made them whole again.

Missal Options

- There are no Christmas weekday readings in the LMC, however, the readings may also be from the CS (For Religious) or the SW.
- For parish Masses, the readings may be from the SW, #510A, or the CHMW (For Religious; LM).
- The texts for the memorial are proper and found in the PS for January 4.
- Use the seasonal Collect to conclude the UP.
- Presiders may use P-I or P-II of Saints, the Preface of Holy Virgins and Religious, or any of the three Prefaces for the Nativity of the Lord.
- Consider using the EPVN-IV.

Song of the Day

"For All the Faithful Women" by Herman G. Stuempfle, Jr. (GIA)

TUE 5 LM #213 / LMC #237 / white
Memorial of St. John Neumann, Bishop

Today's Saint

John Neumann, a Bohemian who could not find a pastoral assignment in his own country, left for America. Ordained in New York and later named bishop of Philadelphia, Neumann immediately responded to pastoral needs by inviting religious from various European countries to serve in his diocese. Likewise, he became fluent in several languages. The American Catholic community is built on the strength and courage of men and women like St. John Neumann—pastors, teachers, and builders.

Scripture Insights

In this passage from the First Letter of John, the writer focuses on how to separate the true followers from the false: those who love are of God, and those who don't are not. Yet it is not our love of God but rather God's love for us that is most important. Jesus, deeply moved with love for his people, not only taught them but fed all of them with just five loaves and two fish.

Preaching Points

Parish Masses

- Love is the sure sign of God's presence, and the fullest expression of love is God sending his Son to us.
- The disciples wanted to send the hungry people away. Jesus replied, "Give them some food yourselves." Christ performs miracles but asks something of us in the process.

Masses with Children

- The Bible tells us to love each other again and again and again. When we love, we are truly God's children.
- Jesus not only fed all the people but was so generous that there were twelve baskets left over. God will not be outdone in generosity.

Missal Options

- There are no Christmas weekday readings in the LMC.
- The readings may also be from the CP.
- The prayers are proper and found in the PS for January 5.
- Use the seasonal Collect to conclude the UP and EP-I or II.
- Presiders may use P-I or P-II of Saints, the Preface of Holy Virgins and Religious, or any of the three Prefaces for the Nativity of the Lord.

Song of the Day

"Love Divine, All Love's Excelling" (various publishers)

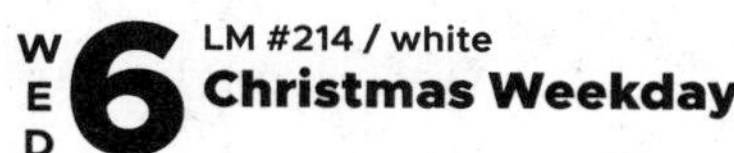

LM #214 / white

Christmas Weekday

Optional Memorial of St. André Bessette, Religious / white

Scripture Insights

God is love. God, whom we don't see, lives in us when we live in love. Jesus had just fed the five thousand, yet the disciples still didn't quite grasp who he was. The wind was howling, the waves were crashing, and they were terrified. "I am," he says, literally (the text gives "It is I"), "do not be afraid."

Preaching Points

Parish Masses

- The First Letter of John strives to figure out what separates Christians from the rest of the world. Here it is. God is love, and love drives out fear.
- Jesus walks on the water, calms his disciples, then calms the storm. The key may be that they were headed to "the other side." Jesus always pushes us toward the "others" and walks alongside us. And the storm is always raging.

Masses with Children

- Who is God? How do we know who God is? God is love; where love is, God is. When we love one another, we are participating in the very life of God.
- The disciples were stuck in the boat as the storm was raging, and they were scared to death. Jesus walked on the water, told them they had nothing to fear since he was with them, then calmed the storm. Don't be afraid.

Missal Options

- There are no Christmas weekday readings in the LMC.
- For the optional memorial, the readings may be from LMC #238 or the CS/PS (For Religious)
- Use the prayer texts in the PT for the Weekdays of Christmas Time occurring from January 2 to the Saturday before the Feast of the Baptism of the Lord.
- For today, use those specific to days after Epiphany.
- Presiders may select any Preface for the Nativity of the Lord or of the Epiphany.
- Consider using EP-II.

Song of the Day

"We Watch for You, O Lord, Till Break of Day" by Genevieve Glen, OSB (OCP)

Optional Memorial

St. André Bessette was an uneducated doorkeeper for the Congregation of the Holy Cross in Montreal, but he attracted so many visitors with his counsel and healings that he needed a church to shelter them: the Oratory of St. Joseph. He was so well loved for his humility and kindness that a million people came to mourn the "simple doorkeeper" when he passed.

- The readings may be taken from the SW, #510C (LS), the CHMW (For Religious), or LMC #238 or CS (For Religious)
- The Collect is from the PS. Other texts are from the CHMW (For Religious).
- Use the seasonal Collect as the conclusion to the EP.
- Consider the seasonal Prefaces, or P-I or P-II of Saints, or the Preface of Holy Virgins and Religious.

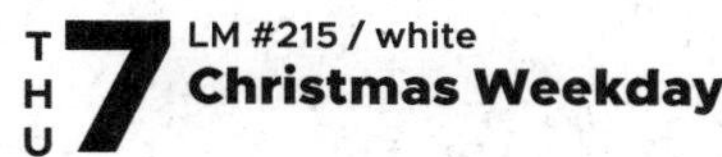

LM #215 / white

Christmas Weekday

Optional Memorial of St. Raymond of Penyafort, Priest / white

Scripture Insights

Jesus reads the prophecy from the scroll about how the anointed one will bring glad tidings to the poor, freedom to the oppressed, and healing to the broken. When? Now, in your midst. The First Letter of John had asked how you could love God, who you can't see, when you don't love your brother, who you can see. Jesus is asking: what is the good news? You're hearing it. You're looking at it.

Preaching Points

Parish Masses

- Be very careful not to be proud because you love God. We are able to love God only because God loved us first. And be careful: If you claim to love God without loving your brothers and sisters, you are a liar.
- We stand during the reading of the Gospel because the Gospel "is fulfilled in our hearing." Christ is here! Jesus is saying and living out the same things in today's reading. He reads the prophecy of the anointed one, the Messiah, and tells the crowd that what the prophet foretold is alive in front of them.

Masses with Children

- Whoever loves Jesus, loves God who sent him. Whoever loves God and Jesus must love their brothers and sisters. We are able to do all this because God loved us first.
- Jesus read a reading from a prophet and was telling his people what the Messiah will do: the poor will hear the good news, the blind will see, and the oppressed will be freed.

Missal Options

- There are no Christmas weekday readings in the LMC.
- For the OM, the readings may be from LMC #239 or the CP.
- Use the prayer texts in the PT for the Weekdays of Christmas Time occurring from January 2 to the Saturday before the Feast of the Baptism of the Lord.
- For today, use those specific to days after Epiphany.
- Presiders may select any Preface for the Nativity of the Lord or of the Epiphany.
- Consider using EP-II.

Song of the Day

"We Praise You, God" translated by Louis Blecnkner, OSB, and composed by Henry Brian Hays, OSB (Liturgical Press)

Optional Memorial

St. Raymond put his law education to work collecting and codifying papal and council documents into a canon law collection that would be consulted by the Church for the next seven centuries. Although his keen mind made him rise to prominence, his heart burned to bring the Gospel to non-Christians, evangelizing the Jews and Muslims of Spain.

- The readings may be taken from the SW, #511, the CP, or LMC #239.
- The Collect is from the PS; other texts are from the CP (For One Pastor).
- Use the seasonal Collect to conclude the UP.
- Presiders may use P-I or P-II of Saints, the Preface of Holy Pastors, or any of the three Prefaces for the Nativity of the Lord.
- Consider using EP-I.

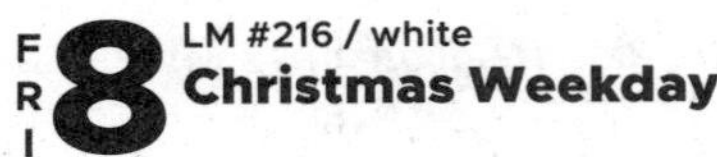

Scripture Insights

The First Letter of John gives us a great imagery and detail. Clearly, this must come out of the community's Baptism rituals, and thus the language is rich with symbols, which attempt to describe a reality that is ultimately beyond words. Jesus takes Baptism a step further, as it were, by cleansing a leper. All who needed cleansing and healing began to flock to him.

Preaching Points

Parish Masses

- The letter from John is likely from a baptismal liturgy practiced in the community. We are immersed into life with God through Baptism.
- Jesus' healings are filled with mystery. "If you wish, you can make me clean," says the leper. Jesus does will it and does cleanse him. Others flock to him, yet he withdraws to pray.

Masses with Children

- What happens in Baptism? On earth? In heaven? How does this earthly ritual change us forever?
- The man with leprosy was cleansed by Jesus. What would you ask Jesus to cleanse you of? How might that happen? What if it doesn't happen?

Missal Options

- There are no prayer texts for the weekdays of Christmas in the LMC.
- Use the prayer texts in the PT for the Weekdays of Christmas Time occurring from January 2 to the Saturday before the Feast of the Baptism of the Lord. For today, use those specific to days after Epiphany.
- Presiders may select any Preface for the Nativity of the Lord or of the Epiphany.
- Consider using EP-II.

Song of the Day

"The Spirit Sends Us Forth to Serve" by Dolores Duffner, OSB (OCP)

LM #217 / white
Christmas Weekday

Scripture Insights

Today's Gospel has both Jesus and John baptizing in the same region. John, who had baptized Jesus, kept on baptizing. One of John's disciples essentially complained to him that the people were flocking to Jesus. As always, John decreases so Jesus may increase, noting that with Christ among us "this joy of mine has been made complete." John the Baptist clearly had the gift of discernment mentioned in the First Reading, "to know the one who is true."

Preaching Points

Parish Masses

- The First Letter of John exhorts us to pray for our brother or sister who is sinning and even warns us that "there is such a thing as deadly sin," yet that's not the final word. The final word is that Jesus Christ "is the true God and eternal life."
- John the Baptist was sent to prepare the way for Christ. He did, always being vehemently clear that he was not the Christ. We should imitate John and, like John, rejoice when we hear Christ's voice.

Masses with Children

- The First Reading assures us that God hears us when we ask for things. It also assures us that Christ is True God, and eternal life, and that we are "in him."
- John the Baptist always points to Christ, never to himself. He always does God's will as well, but never to make himself look good. Only to bring people to Christ.

Missal Options

- There are no Christmas weekday readings in the LMC.
- Use the prayer texts in the PT for the Weekdays of Christmas Time occurring from January 2 to the Saturday before the Feast of the Baptism of the Lord. For today, use those specific to days after Epiphany.
- Presiders may select any Preface for the Nativity of the Lord or of the Epiphany.
- Consider using EP-II.

Song of the Day

"Baptized in Water" by Michael Saward (Hope Publishing Company)

Something to Consider...

◈ As a parish staff, read *The Liturgy and Catholic Social Teaching: Participation in Worship and the World* from LTP and consider the important ways parish life reflects Catholic social teaching.

S U N 10 LM #21B / LMC #17ABC / white

Feast of the Baptism of the lord

Scripture Insights

The verses from Isaiah culminate the poetic proclamation of the prophet who preached about 550 years before the birth of Christ, in the dark days after Jerusalem's destruction and the exile to Babylon.

The prophet announces that these events were not the end; they were an astonishing new beginning in the story of salvation. "I am doing something new!" declares the Lord (43:19). This prophet revels in the riches of a new version of the Davidic covenant. As David's royal line was lost during the exile, the prophet announced that the spectacular "sure love for David" was now the property of the entire people of God. He imitated the vendors' cries in the marketplace of Babylon as they sold necessities like water and bread and luxuries like wine and milk. But this vendor was offering—for free—the blessings of the God of Israel!

Five hundred years later, a man like the ancient prophets came proclaiming God's impending judgment. John preached that his baptism would prepare people for God's rending of the heavens to mete out justice. But his word was fulfilled in a way he did not expect. The one mightier than John did indeed appear when he "was baptized in the Jordan by John." The heavens were indeed "torn apart": Mark's use of the Greek word *schizo*, "splitting," carries a threatening, apocalyptic image of judgment (Mark 1:10). But what emerged from the opening in the heavens was a dove, the Spirit of God in the form of the ancient symbol of God's peace following divine judgment (Genesis 8:8–12). The Gospel changed the template of salvation: Now salvation is offered *before* rather than *after* judgment. This remarkable change marks the "beginning of the good news of Jesus Christ, the Son of God" (1:1). "By water and blood" (1 John 5:6) links Jesus' baptism with his death. Jesus himself likened his death to a baptism (Mark 10:38–39). How is death like a baptism?

Preaching Points

Parish Masses

- Baptism and death are uniquely contrasted in the faith as they are reflections of one another. Through Baptism we are brought into union with Christ and his Church, and through this sacrament we are reborn. Likewise, death can bring us to union with Christ in the afterlife, and death is a birth into eternal life.
- Jesus' baptism in the River Jordan signified the beginning of his preaching and teaching ministry on earth.
- When the Holy Spirit descends as a dove, we witness the Father's blessing on his Son's ministry, and we see the foreshadowing of the Trinitarian baptism that was to come.
- We are called to seek the Lord always. Our minds and hearts do not match that of God, so we must strive for greater understanding of God and his ways.

Children's Liturgy of the Word

- Jesus lived his life with his parents; he would have grown up in a community, attended synagogue and learned St. Joseph's trade. When he began his preaching and teaching ministry, his life changed. His baptism in the Jordan River is the beginning of that change.
- We can see an image of the Trinity in the baptism of Jesus: the Father's voice approving his Son's ministry, the Holy Spirit descending like a dove, and the Son humbly approaching his cousin John for baptism.
- Because we are human, our ways are not God's ways. We are called to seek God and grow in understanding of him.

Missal Options

- It's tempting for music ministry to peak on December 24 and 25 and fade a bit for the rest of Christmas Time. While the choir has probably earned a well-deserved break, other musicians could step up and continue the beauty and fullness of Christmas music. Tap into the energy of students home from college, cantors who may be willing to put in a little extra time singing as an ensemble, and middle and high school students on school breaks. Since today marks the end of the Christmas season, the liturgies will benefit from fresh musical energy.

Music Preparation

- Today is the last day of the Christmas season. Continue to use the same musical settings for the sprinkling rite and the Mass parts to unify today's liturgy with the rest of the season.
- Hopefully, you kept the Christmas decorations up and the Christmas music going despite the culture's opposite signal. "Joy to the World" is quite appropriate for today's celebration.

Music Suggestions

- "Gathering: "When John Baptized by Jordan's River" by Timothy Dudley-Smith (Hope Publishing Company)
- Sprinkling Rite: "Streams of Living Water" by Cyprian Consiglio, OSB (OCP)
- Sending Forth: "To Jordan Jesus Humbly Came" by Alan J. Hommerding (WLP) or "Joy to the World" (various publishers)

Mass Texts

Introduction to Mass

We thirst for eternal life and for the love of God. Through Jesus Christ our thirst is quenched. Let us call to mind the grace of our Baptism, by which we were cleansed of sin and made adopted daughters and sons of God. In answer to the thundering voice of the Father, let us raise our voices today in praise and thanksgiving. *My brothers and sisters, let us acknowledge our sins, and so prepare ourselves to celebrate the sacred mysteries.*

Tropes for Penitential Act, Form III

You, Lord, are generous in forgiving: Lord, have mercy.

You, Lord, wash us clean in the bath of rebirth: Christ, have mercy.

You, Lord, make us beloved children of your heavenly Father: Lord, have mercy.

Dismissal for Children's Liturgy of the Word

Dear children, Jesus is God's beloved Son. You are adopted sons and daughters of God. That means that you can consider Jesus your brother. He is with you to teach you, to protect you, to comfort you, to be your companion for the rest of your life. He now speaks to you in today's readings. Go and listen to him.

Dismissal of Catechumens

My dear catechumens, as the prophet Isaiah says, seek the Lord, call to him, and turn to him for mercy. For our part, we pray for your continuing and deepening growth in grace, and we long for the day when you will be one with us in the celebration of the Eucharist. Go now in peace.

Dismissal of Extraordinary Ministers of Holy Communion

Dear friends, we give you Christ in Word and Sacrament to go to our ailing and infirm brothers and sisters, to remind them of their rebirth in Baptism, and to strengthen them with divine nourishment. Let them know they are one with us in the joy and love of the Spirit. Go in peace.

Universal Prayer

The Lord baptizes us with the Holy Spirit. As his disciples, we are urged to pray for the needs of all peoples. And so we turn to him in prayer.

1. For world leaders, that they will seek to protect populations in regions where water is scarce, polluted, or wasted, we pray:
2. For expectant parents who are preparing to have their child baptized, we pray:
3. For a deeper appreciation of the Baptism that has made us sons and daughters of God, we pray:
4. For a greater awareness of the Christian responsibilities and actions that flow from our common Baptism, we pray:
5. For the progress of evangelization wherever hearts are seeking and expectant, we pray:

Lord Jesus,
you are the Father's beloved Son, his anointed one, our savior.
Inspire us always to act on the grace bestowed on us in Baptism.
Cleans us of our sin, open our eyes to your grace,
and beckon us to drink deeply from the springs of eternal salvation.
You live and reign for ever and ever.
Amen.

Other Rites and Customs

- Continue singing Christmas carols, particularly those that don't focus on the infant Jesus in Bethlehem since the focus of today's celebration is Jesus' baptism as an adult.
- Use the Rite for the Blessing and Sprinkling of Water found in appendix II of *The Roman Missal.*
- Celebrate Solemn Evening Prayer to conclude Christmas Time and then have an undecorating party as the environment returns to Ordinary Time.
- Welcome back families who have had their children baptized in the past year or have infants baptized at today's liturgy.

Liturgy and Life

Rising from the Jordan River, Jesus heard: "You are my beloved," and God has proclaimed these words over everyone baptized since that day. Coming to understand the meaning of Baptism, accepting the grace and responsibility given to us by that encounter with God's love, is the fundamental task of Christian life. The Word of God is a sure guide, and so is the liturgy. When we witness a Baptism, we have an opportunity to savor that sacrament and relive our own Baptism, whether or not we remember it. Make a point of attending a Baptism soon. Observe carefully and listen deeply to the words of the rite. Pray for the newly baptized. Then write in your journal about what you experienced and what insights you gained. What hope does your Baptism give you for acting out your identity as a beloved of God?

Taking Place This Week . . .

Consider what can be done liturgically, catechetically, and ministerially to respond to these important needs.

- Tomorrow is the first day of Ordinary Time.
- Orthodox New Year (1/14)

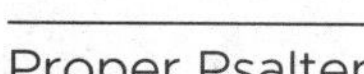

Ordinary Time during Winter

Ordinary Time enables the Church to appreciate more fully the ministry and message of Christ.

—*Sunday Celebrations in the Absence of a Priest*, 106

The Meaning of the Season

This year, there are only five Sundays of Ordinary Time between the Feast of the Baptism of the Lord and Ash Wednesday. Liturgically, such a short period of Ordinary Time can feel like a valley between the Advent/Christmas and Lent/Triduum/Easter cycles. So too can this season feel like a lull in the broader culture, especially in the wintry northern latitudes of the United States. Even when the sun shines, a chill often fills the air. Although the days are lengthening, they can still seem short and dark. At our worst moments during this season, our feelings echo Job's lament from the reading for the Fifth Sunday: "Is not man's life on earth a drudgery? . . . I have been assigned months of misery . . . the night drags on."

When we feel surrounded by darkness, the Eucharistic liturgy is all the more significant because it is where we are drawn into the "compelling love of Christ" who "sets [us] on fire" (CSL, 10). For us who serve as liturgical ministers, we must be especially conscious of ensuring that these Sundays of Ordinary Time pierce the darkness and reflect the radiance of the Lord's Day, the day of the light of Christ and the fire of the Holy Spirit.

During Ordinary Time, we pray that God will "direct our actions" so that "we may abound in good works"

(Collect, Third Sunday). As ever, we turn to the Word of God for such direction—the living Word that is a "lamp for my feet, a light for my path" (Psalm 119:105). On the Second Sunday, the First Reading (Samuel 3:3b–10, 19) and the Responsorial Psalm (40) invite us to pray, "Here I am, Lord," and submit ourselves completely to the will of God. Subsequent Sundays offer a variety of Old Testament readings and semi-continuous readings from St. Paul's First Letter to the Corinthians and chapter 1 of the Gospel according Mark. Mark's account jumps quickly into Jesus' ministry, and on these Sundays, we do as well. We are called to abandon our nets and follow him (Third Sunday; 1:14–20), and, with the Apostles, we witness him driving out unclean spirits (Fourth Sunday; 1:21–28), curing various diseases and driving out demons (Fifth Sunday; 1:29–39), and cleansing a leper (Sixth Sunday; 1:40–45).

Just as the disciples were amazed by these actions, so too are we astonished anew. The same baby boy whose birth we celebrated at Christmas is grown and doing wondrous deeds—fulfilling the prophetic message that we heard throughout the Advent and Christmas seasons. So too, then, are we baptized followers of Christ called to do the same. As the "Introduction" to the *Lectionary for Mass* notes, Baptism and Confirmation "have made all Christ's faithful into messengers of God's word," so we "must therefore be bearers of the same word in the Church and the world, at least by the witness of [our] lives" (7).

In addition to Sundays, this period of Ordinary Time contains other feasts and memorials, through which the Church "opens up to the faithful the riches of her Lord's powers and merits," so that we may "lay hold of them" and be "filled with saving grace" (CSL, 102). The most significant is the Feast of the Presentation of the Lord, or Candlemas, which falls on Tuesday, February 2. Although in the modern United States it has become more popularly associated with the seasonal prognostications of a certain groundhog in Punxsutawney, Pennsylvania, it has long been a significant day in the liturgical year.

In *Eternity Today,* his two-volume tome on the liturgical year, theologian Martin Connell provides an extensive treatment of Candlemas (see volume 1, pp. 199–233). He explains its historical development as a forty-days-after-Epiphany celebration to a forty-days-after-Nativity-of-the-Lord celebration and urges a renewed celebration of the liturgical rites. The most notable element of these rites is a procession with candles. Rooted as far back as Egeria's fourth-century account of Christian celebrations in Jerusalem, this procession begins in a place outside of the sanctuary. All gather for the sprinkling, blessing, and lighting of candles, which are then carried into the church in procession (see RM, Presentation of the Lord, 1–8). As with Palm Sunday, there is also a ritual option for a simpler Solemn Entrance (see RM, Presentation of the Lord, 9–11).

In addition to the symbolism of lit candles—especially in this dark season of the year—Connell emphasizes that this feast can be understood as a "bridge between Christmas and Easter" (p. 226). The lighting of candles and sprinkling with Holy Water evokes the Easter Vigil, and the Gospel for the day (Luke 2:22–40) also links Christmas to Easter: the baby Jesus is presented at the Temple, and Simeon and Anna prophesy of the future that awaits this tiny newborn. With these strong liturgical connections to Easter, robustly celebrating Candlemas is an especially fitting way for communities to emphasize the centrality of the Paschal Mystery.

This period of Ordinary Time also includes other feasts and memorials that, when celebrated, truly "proclaim the wonderful works of Christ in his servants and display to the faithful fitting examples for their imitation" (CSL, 111). One such popular celebration is the blessing of throats for the optional Memorial of St. Blaise (February 3), either on the day itself or moved to the weekend Masses to increase participation.

Speaking of shifting days, UNLY permits some saints' days to be transferred to the Sundays of Ordinary Time if they "fall during the week and that are agreeable to the devotion of the faithful" (58). Most notably, parish patronal feasts are to be celebrated as solemnities. During this period of Ordinary Time, there are many saints who serve as parish patrons and whose celebration could be transferred to Sundays: St. Agnes (January 21), the Conversion of St. Paul (January 25), Sts. Timothy and Titus (January 26), St. Thomas Aquinas (January 28), and St. Agatha (February 5), to name just a few. The dates of two other saints' feasts—St. Francis de Sales (January 24) and St. John Bosco (January 31)—coincidentally happen to fall on Sundays this year. Also falling on a Sunday this year is the memorial of Sts. Cyril and Methodius (February 14). Their memorial is often overshadowed by Valentine's Day, which—for all of its secular popularity—honors a saint whose feast is no longer on the Roman calendar but who is still listed as a saint in the Roman Martyrology.

Even in communities whose patronal celebrations do not fall during these weeks, appropriately honoring the sanctoral cycle is a way of further sanctifying this period of Ordinary Time, one in which we are both "inspired with a new reason for seeking the city which is to come" and "taught to know a most safe path by which . . . we will be able to arrive at perfect union with Christ" (LG, 50).

The Sounds of the Season

Ordinary Time during the winter months can be a good opportunity to introduce new music in the parish community. When choosing a new Mass setting, look for material that is *singable*: melodic, memorable, accessible, and beautiful. This could be a good time to remember that "steps should be taken enabling the faithful to say or sing together in Latin the parts of the Ordinary of the Mass belonging to them" (CSL, 54). *Sing to the Lord* echoes and reinforces this by telling us that "each worshiping community in the United States, including all age groups and all ethnic groups, should, at a minimum, learn *Kyrie XVI, Sanctus XVIII*, and *Agnus Dei XVIII*, all of which are typically included in congregational worship aids" (STL, 75).

Take advantage of these six weeks between the Feast of the Baptism of the Lord and Ash Wednesday to evaluate your parish music ministry. Is there anything that can be augmented, changed, or added? Are there things that your community is doing particularly well? There could be different ways of extending that excellence to other areas that might not be meeting a fuller potential.

Do not be discouraged if introducing new Eucharistic Prayer acclamations or ordinaries are just not possible. Challenge yourself to think adaptively, creatively, and outside the box. Perhaps your readers could chant "The Word of the Lord" following the proclamation of the readings. Or perhaps your deacon could chant the Gospel formulas. These dialogues are simple enough for both liturgical ministers *and* the assembly. Perhaps you can encourage singing "the Lord be with you" at each liturgy. Simple chanting such as these examples can allow the assembly to enter into the sacred mysteries more fully. These important words of praise should be fully exclaimed and not just mumbled by rote. If your assembly can sing a Responsorial Psalm, they will be able to sing these formulas and dialogues.

The Look of the Season

These weeks of Ordinary Time between the Baptism of the Lord and the beginning of Lent—a number determined by the date for Easter—is a good time to allow the liturgical space to breathe. The Christmas displays, often rather lavish in color and elements, should be set aside, and a somewhat less complex environment is called for. The Scriptures during this time usually present the "call" accounts, those texts where Jesus calls the first disciples and begins to prepare them to be his followers.

The liturgical environment needs to be understated for us to concentrate on our response to Jesus' call to be faithful disciples. A visual overabundance of decorations should not become a distraction. In a sense, these first few weeks of Ordinary Time during winter are intended to allow us to stretch into the serious business of the Lenten journey that awaits us in a very short time.

The liturgical space and its portable environment should not need a lot of effort in these weeks. But since the liturgical environment, as always, serves both the liturgical ritual and its message, it deserves careful attention.

In these winter weeks, a darker, warmer green tone for vesture and fabric is warranted rather than the green for the summer weeks of Ordinary Time. The range of green tones that can be used to coordinate with a darker shade of green are practically limitless. Fabrics that have patterns and texture could be nice additions to the liturgical environment.

What to do with all the poinsettias, especially red ones? Because they are so closely associated with Christmas, and the Christmas environment, much like lilies and Easter, they say "Christmas" loud and clear. But they really should be removed after the Christmas season. They might be offered to parishioners or relocated to other parish spaces such as meeting rooms or offices. A few white poinsettias can be incorporated into the Ordinary Time environment as long as they do not appear to be a main element of the decor.

The simple things from winter's palette can be used to create wonderful arrangements. Large earthenware vessels that are filled with tall white branches and bunches of winter berries and fresh evergreen branches can make attractive arrangements. It's helpful to remember that the scale of most churches dictates that these arrangements should be in a few large vases that can be placed in different locations throughout the space. Make a practice of putting some of these in areas that aren't normally used. If all the decorative items are in or near the sanctuary such that they can be seen from only the front half of the space, they tend to make the sanctuary a stage setting for those who sit in the front pews. The assembly occupies the whole space, and that should be a guide for how the space is included in any scheme for seasonal decorations.

Some parishes mark Catholic Schools' Week during this time. If this involves a liturgical celebration in the church, the environment and art committee will want to work with the school staff to add some elements to the liturgical environment, perhaps artwork from students that could be displayed in the gathering area. These items can add some color to the space and serve to recognize the gifts of the younger members of the parish.

The Week of Prayer for Christian Unity is usually marked during the last week of January. This offers an opportunity to recognize the other Christian denominations in the community; even a display of photos of the churches in the neighborhood could draw attention to the intent of this week of prayer. If the parish hosts an ecumenical prayer service, the environment and art committee should see that the liturgical space is also a hospitable space.

A number of memorials are celebrated during these weeks. If one of these saints is also the patron or patroness of the parish, then some attention could be given to the liturgical environment for that day. One suggestion is to place an image (statue, sculpture, or painting) of the particular saint in a prominent place within the church.

The liturgical environment for Ordinary Time during the winter should not require a lot of effort for the environment and art committee once all the Christmas decorations have been put away, so this is a good time to plan for Lent, Holy Week, and Easter Time. It might also be an opportune time for the committee to celebrate their ministry some evening. Recreation should be part of any ministry. Getting to know each other during relaxing events often enhances the prayer and preparation that members of organizations do together as they serve the liturgical life of the Church.

Evangelizing the Parish through the Season

The Church draws her life from the communal worship of God and the sacraments, and she uses this life to gather the world together to participate in this central activity. This means that the work of evangelization also has its source and its goal in the liturgy, but the liturgy is first.

The Church is God's gift, built up in the sacraments and given to the world. But that doesn't let us off the hook! Baptism, Confirmation, and Eucharist call each of us and all of us together to live as a community of the Gospel.

Many people in our world are hungering for community and for communion. Ordinary Time during these winter months provides an opportunity to consider how your community welcomes those who come to the liturgy. Are they welcomed and offered the help that they might need to participate at Mass? Are there adequate explanations of the rites, the postures, the patterns to help someone who is unfamiliar with the Catholic liturgy? Are visitors welcomed individually? Are they welcomed as people, or are they pressured as potential members or converts? Is there an easy way for people to request a follow-up visit with pastoral staff if they wish?

On a more global note, because the liturgy makes a *community*, the presence of a healthy and strong community is itself a powerful demonstration of the work of the Gospel. How does your parish function as a community? How is the Body of Christ visibly present in your place? Would someone walking in off the street be able to tell that this liturgy gathered together a people who were connected to each other, who were somehow different from the crowd gathered at the theater or the library?

Jesus calls his disciples to "come and see" (John 1:39). They encountered a person so startling that they left their old lives behind and followed him on a mission that they didn't understand. The day-to-day life of the parish, as ordinary as it can be, is itself a form of evangelism made possible because the Church is built up by the liturgy. In this low season between the festivals of Christmas and our preparation for Easter, where is the Lord's voice calling your parish to grow? What gifts from sacraments will God give to build up the Body? How are these returned to serve the Church's worship of the God who gave them?

Worship Committee Agenda for Winter Ordinary Time

Meeting Time

Plan to meet in mid-November to prepare for Winter Ordinary Time, which lasts about a month.

Opening Prayer

- Pray the Liturgy of the Hours
- Offer the prayer for the Second Week in Ordinary Time from Celebrating the Lectionary for Primary Grades (LTP)
- Read the one of the Prefaces for Ordinary Time (Roman Missal)

Goal for Meeting

Consider and review the ritual elements and rubrics of this period of Ordinary Time:

- Review final preparations for Advent or Christmas Time
- Create a contrast in environment, sound, and solemnity between Christmas and Ordinary Time
- Prepare for a very short season (Mass settings, environment, other logistics)
- Include preparations for the Day of Prayer for the Legal Protection of Unborn Children
- The Solemn Procession and Blessing of Candles on the Presentation of the Lord
- The Blessing of Throats
- Look ahead to Lent and Easter Time

Seasonal Questions

- What is progressive solemnity and how do we model it in our liturgies? (see *Musicam Sacram* 11, 40, 42–42 and CSL, 12)
- Will the Mass setting reflect the simplicity of Ordinary Time? Consider using through-composed Gloria if the assembly can sing along.
- Beyond daily Mass, how does the parish pray together? Do members pray the Divine Office together?
- How well does our parish celebrate Ordinary Time? Have we had someone from the diocesan worship office or a neighboring parish evaluate our liturgies?
- Are we training new liturgical ministers?
- How do we provide ongoing formation and encouragement for our liturgical ministers?
- Do we wish to bring in an outside presenter or have a time for fellowship and offer appreciation to our liturgical ministers?
- Do we wish to consider offering liturgical ministers the opportunity to attend an LTP Virtual Workshop?
- Do we want to offer explanation of the liturgy in the weekly bulletin or the worship aids? Consider looking to the resource, *Disciples Making Disciples: Print and Digital Resources for Forming the Assembly* from LTP.

Liturgical Catechesis for the Worship Committee

- Study the various books in *The Liturgical Ministry Series* (LTP). These small, affordable, accessible volumes are available for ten different ministries.
- Read *Liturgy with Style and Grace* (LTP).

Liturgical Catechesis for the Assembly

- *From Mass to Mission: Understanding the Mass and Its Significance for Our Christian Life* (LTP)
- *We Learn about Our Parish Church* (LTP) (children's resource)

Closing Prayer

- Pray the Magnificat (spoken or sung)
- Sing the doxology "Praise God from Whom All Blessings Flow"

MON 11 LM #305 / LMC #193–232 / green
Weekday

Scripture Insights

Jesus was obedient to the Father, and the Apostles were obedient to the Son. The word *obey* comes from the Latin term meaning "to hear." How do we listen for the Lord, and how do we respond to his call?

Preaching Points

Parish Masses

- There is only one Jesus Christ, one Son of God. The angels and other people are not the Son. Jesus is unique in his identity.
- We are called to look to the Son and follow his instruction to "repent, and believe in the Gospel." How do we live out this conversion?

Masses with Children

- God the Son is Jesus and is Jesus alone. The angels are not Jesus, and we are not Jesus. God the Son is unique in that he is a person and he is God.
- Jesus has called for us to obey him. How do we repent of things we have done wrong? How do we live our belief in the Gospel?

Missal Options

- The Missal provides a set of prayer texts in the PT that can be used during the First Week in OT.
- Use any of the three forms of the PA and select from the eight Prefaces for OT or the six common Prefaces.
- Consider using EP-I.
- Any OT Collect may conclude the UP.

Song of the Day

"*Pescador de Hombres*" by Cesareo Gabarain; translated by Rev. Willard F. Jabusch (OCP)

TUE 12 LM #306 / LMC #193–232 / green
Weekday

Scripture Insights

Even though our Lord was destined for suffering in his earthly life, while he walked this earth he relieved the suffering of those around him. He used his power and authority to bring wholeness and wellness to others.

Preaching Points

Parish Masses

- Human beings are made in the image and likeness of God; we are the crown of his creation. That is who we are, which is why God is mindful of us.
- Jesus is the Son of God and the second person of the Trinity. He is fully God and fully human; he bore a face like our own and lived like us in all ways except sin. He, however, had authority over nature and the supernatural world.

Masses with Children

- We know that when God created human beings, he made us in his own image and likeness. We are the part of creation made to reflect the creator, and God cares for his human creation.
- Jesus is the Son of God and the second person of the Trinity. He is fully God and fully human. He ate food, suffered childhood injuries, and lived as humans live. Unlike other humans, he had authority over nature and the supernatural world.

Missal Options

- The Missal provides a set of prayer texts in the PT that can be used during the First Week in OT.
- Use any of the three forms of the PA and select from the eight Prefaces for OT or the six common Prefaces.
- Consider using EPVN-IV.
- Any OT Collect may conclude the UP.

Song of the Day

"All My Days" by Daniel L. Schutte and J. Glenn Murry, SJ (OCP)

WED 13 LM #307 / LMC #193–232 / green
Weekday

Optional Memorial of St. Hilary, Bishop and Doctor of the Church / white

Scripture Insights

Rather than let humanity languish in sin, our Lord chose to sacrifice himself for the sake of humanity. He lived in poverty and died in pain. His act was done in service to us.

Preaching Points

Parish Masses

- Because of his human experience being one of suffering, our Lord is more merciful than we can imagine. He intimately understands humanity.
- Simon's mother-in-law was healed from her illness and, in response to Jesus, served him. How is her response to healing Christ-like? How do we respond to Christ's presence in our own lives?

Masses with Children

- Jesus suffered during his life; he lived in poverty and experienced a painful death. Because of his human experience, God the Son can uniquely understand human beings and is merciful to us.
- What is your response to Jesus? Simon's mother-in-law's response to being healed was to serve Jesus. How do you serve Jesus?

Missal Options

- The Missal provides a set of prayer texts in the PT that can be used during the First Week in OT.
- Use any of the three forms of the PA and select from the eight Prefaces for OT or the six common Prefaces.
- Consider using EP-II.
- Any OT Collect may conclude the UP.

Song of the Day

"Loving and Forgiving" by Scott Soper (OCP)

Optional Memorial

St. Hilary wrote theological works that made the Christology developed by Eastern, Greek-speaking theologians accessible in Latin for the West. His defense of persecuted Christians and his preaching against Arianism twice resulted in his exile from Poitiers, but Hilary persisted in his defense of orthodoxy despite division within the Church.

- The readings may be taken from the SW, #512, the CP or CDC, or LMC #240.
- The Collect is from the PS; other texts are from the CP (For a Bishop), or the CDC.
- Use P-I or P-II of Saints or the Preface of Holy Pastors.
- Consider using EP-II.

THU 14 LM #308 / LMC #193–232 / green
Weekday

Scripture Insights

Jesus' heart was oriented toward his people; Jesus was oriented toward tremendous love. We too are called to soften our hearts to those around us and to serve them as Jesus would serve them.

Preaching Points

Parish Masses

- God tells us to have hearts that are softened for him and for his message. We should not harden our hearts toward his message or replace it with other messages.
- Jesus healed the leper out of love for a fellow human person. His heart was softened toward the man's painful plight.

Masses with Children

- Having a hardened heart means that a person has closed off his or her understanding of God's will. We want our hearts to be softened toward God and the goodness he offers us.
- Jesus' heart was softened toward all the people he encountered. When the leper asked for healing, Jesus gladly healed the man. We too must soften our hearts toward the suffering of others.

Missal Options

- The Missal provides a set of prayer texts in the PT that can be used during the First Week in OT.
- Use any of the three forms of the PA and select from the eight Prefaces for OT or the six common Prefaces.
- Consider using EPVN-IV.
- Any OT Collect may conclude the UP.

Song of the Day

"If Today You Hear the Voice of God" by Ed Bolduc (WLP)

FRI 15 Weekday

LM #309 / LMC #193–232 / green

Scripture Insights

To enter into God's rest on the seventh day is to follow God's law. In Christ, we also enter into rest; resting in him we are allowed to rest in the presence of God in heaven, someday.

Preaching Points

Parish Masses

- The paralytic man was able to enter in the rest and relief that Jesus offered to him, but the scribes' hearts were hardened toward the Lord. They were not able to rest in Jesus that day.
- Jesus has the authority to forgive sins, and this authority was shocking to the scribes and was blasphemy to them. They did not yet understand Jesus' identity.

Masses with Children

- Jesus brings rest, relief, and wellness to those who seek his care. The paralytic man found rest and relief in Jesus and his healing, but the scribes could not find that same rest in Jesus.
- Because Jesus is God, he has the authority to forgive the sins of others. The scribes didn't understand who Jesus was so they thought that he was speaking outside the Jewish law.

Missal Options

- The Missal provides a set of prayer texts in the PT that can be used during the First Week in OT.
- Use any of the three forms of the PA and select from the eight Prefaces for OT or the six common Prefaces (except for if EP-IV is used as suggested).
- Consider using EP-IV with its proper Preface.
- Any OT Collect may conclude the UP.

Song of the Day

"Be Forgiven" by Tom Booth (OCP)

Other Rites and Customs

Today begins the Week of Prayer for Christian Unity. Consider using the Mass for Various Needs: For Promoting the Unity of Christians (#17).

SAT 16 Weekday

LM #310 / LMC #193–232 / green

Optional Memorial of the Blessed Virgin Mary / white

Scripture Insights

Our Creator created us in his own image; he intimately knows how our hearts and minds operate and sees deeply inside our spirits. In his omniscience, the Lord knows each of us and sees each of our souls for what it truly is.

Preaching Points

Parish Masses

- God calls to each of us, knowing our shortcomings and imperfections. Like Levi, we are called to follow the Lord.
- Jesus had little concern about others' opinions of him, and he invited socially rejected people into relationship with him.

Masses with Children

- Despite knowing our imperfections, sins, and shortcomings, God desires to be in relationship with us. Levi responded to the Lord's call, and we too are called to respond to God.

Missal Options

- The Missal provides a set of prayer texts in the PT that can be used during the First Week in OT.
- Use any of the three forms of the PA and select from the eight Prefaces for OT or the six common Prefaces.
- Consider using EPR-I.
- Any OT Collect may conclude the UP.

Song of the Day

"Your Words Are Sprit and Life"
by Bernadette Farrell (OCP)

Optional Memorial

- Saturdays in OT that are not assigned an obligatory observance may be celebrated as a Memorial of the Blessed Virgin Mary.
- The readings may be taken from the SW, CBVM, or the CMML. The prayer texts may be taken from the CBVM or the CMML. You may also use the various Votive Masses for the BVM.
- Use either of the Prefaces for the BVM.

Why not make the Lord's Day a more intense time of sharing, encouraging all the inventiveness of which Christian charity is capable? Inviting to a meal people who are alone, visiting the sick, providing food for needy families, spending a few hours in voluntary work and acts of solidarity—these would certainly be ways of bringing into people's lives the love of Christ received at the eucharistic table.

—*Dies Domini*, 72

S U N **17** LM #65B / LMC #60B / green
Second Sunday in Ordinary Time

Scripture Insights

As with many of John's images (light and dark, spirit and flesh), looking and seeing have a deeper meaning than ordinary usage would suggest. One has only to think of the story of the man born blind (John 9:1–41) to know that "seeing" someone implies understanding who they really are, especially in Jesus' interactions. Here in the beginning of the section of John's account of the Gospel known as the "Book of Signs" (John 1:19—12:50), the call of the first disciples challenges both the disciples in the story and the readers to see who Jesus really is and interpret properly the signs that he does.

John the Baptist points to Jesus, saying, "Look, here is the Lamb of God." He calls attention to the true nature of Jesus in the world by inviting his listeners to see him as the Passover lamb whose blood saved the Israelites from the death of the firstborn in Egypt and as the lamb ritually slaughtered as an offering for sin (see Isaiah 53:7, 10). It is up to the would-be disciples to see that nature for themselves. Jesus probes their search for truth by asking: "What are you looking for?" Their response indicates their desire to follow him, and Jesus then invites them to see where he is staying. As with seeing the true nature of Jesus, seeing the place where he stays means more than we think. When Andrew and the other man see where Jesus stays, it becomes their place as well, and they leave John for the new teacher.

It is not only the disciples who look intently to discern their teacher's true nature. Jesus himself looks into Simon, Andrew's brother, and sees his deepest self, renaming him *Cephas* ("rock"), Aramaic for *Peter*. Peter's new name signifies his new identity and bond with the Son of God. Later, Jesus astonishes Nathanael with what he knows of his character from seeing him under the fig tree. John will continue to use "seeing" as a code word for understanding and believing in Jesus. Those who see rightly will believe that Jesus is the one to come.

The invitation to come and see applies to our lives as well. Where might you see Jesus staying today? What does following him as a disciple mean for us?

Preaching Points

Parish Masses

- John the Baptist prepared the way of the Lord; he was the last prophet, and he served God by preparing Jesus' path. In this Johannine reading we hear something else—we hear John identifying Jesus' identity to others. We hear Jesus called the "Lamb of God," which is a reference to his salvific sacrifice on the cross.
- In the Gospel, John clearly identifies the sacrificial role that Jesus will embrace. Moreover, John identifies the salvific role Jesus' sacrifice will entail.
- The disciples begin to follow Jesus; he calls to people, and they respond to his call. Jesus also calls us and asks for our response to his call.
- When we respond to Jesus' call, we can look to the First Reading and Samuel's response, "Speak, for your servant is listening." We listen to God in many different ways.

Children's Liturgy of the Word

- In the Gospel, John the Baptist references the sacrificial role that Jesus will embrace when he is crucified on the cross.
- Jesus called the disciples to follow him, and they chose to follow him. Jesus calls us to follow him, and we make the choice to follow him every day of our lives.
- In the First Reading, when God called Samuel, Samuel responded, "Speak, for your servant is listening." We listen to God in many different ways.

Missal Options

- The Mass texts are found in the "Ordinary Time" section of the PT.
- Although any form of the PA or a rite of sprinkling may take place on the Sundays of OT, consider using the Confiteor followed by the Kyrie throughout the winter months.
- Sing or recite the Gloria and the Creed.
- Any of the eight Prefaces of the Sundays of OT may be used.
- Consider using EP-III.
- Any OT Collect, except for the prayer for today, may conclude the UP.
- There are six SBs for OT from which to choose. You may also use a PP.

Music Preparation

- Reflect on your call to ministry. How did you first hear the call? Likely, someone encouraged you when you were in grade school or as an adult.
- Do you invite new musicians to join you? Do you call others to serve? Do you encourage and mentor them, or have you become set in your ways?

Music Suggestions

- Gathering: "Here I Am, Lord" by Dan Schutte (OCP)
- Responsorial Psalm: "Psalm 40: Here I Am" by Rory Cooney (OCP)
- Communion: "Behold the Lamb" by Martin Willet (OCP)
- Sending Forth: "We Are Called to Serve/*Se Nos Llama a Servir*" by Julie and Tim Smith (OCP)

Mass Texts

Introduction to Mass

The Lord calls each of us by name. Together we are members of Christ's Body, each with a unique role to play. Through us, his Church, Christ accomplishes the will of the Father. In this Eucharist, he gives us the grace we need to answer his call, to fulfill our destiny as his members, and so to give glory to God. *My brothers and sisters, let us acknowledge our sins, and so prepare ourselves to celebrate the sacred mysteries.*

Tropes for Penitential Act, Form III

You call us, Lord, from sin to new life: Lord, have mercy.

We have waited for you, for your saving help:
Christ, have mercy.

You have stooped down to us and heard our cry:
Lord, have mercy.

Dismissal for Children's Liturgy of the Word

Children, today you will hear of God calling to young Samuel. Two times Samuel ignores God's call. But on the third try Samuel replies, "Speak, Lord, for your servant is listening." Only then do we hear that Samuel grew up and that God was with him. God calls to you, too, and you now have an opportunity to listen to him in the Scriptures and to answer him in your hearts. Go in peace.

Dismissal of Catechumens

Friends, the life of faith proceeds with questions and answers and more questions. Jesus asks, "What are you looking for?" and we answer with another question: "Where are you staying?" You are seeking the Lord and you have questions. Let him question you, and listen to the answers arising in your own hearts. Go now to reflect on the mystery of this relationship to which he is calling you.

Dismissal of Extraordinary Ministers of Holy Communion

My friends, we are one spirit with those who are absent from us due to sickness and injury, and so we give you Christ's Body to take to them. Though weak and limited, their bodies, like ours, are temples of the Holy Spirit. With them, we will all sing a song of joy to the Lord. Go in peace.

Universal Prayer

Behold, the Lamb of God! Come to him, he who is the Messiah. Place upon him your fears, your struggles, and your needs.

1. For the Church, may she be steadfast in the call to build communities of faith and healing, we pray:
2. For inclusive structures of government in nations and communities, we pray:
3. For the habit of rejecting all spontaneous prejudices against outward appearances, we pray:
4. For those who are indifferent to Jesus' call to "come and see," we pray:

O Divine Teacher,
grant that we might never hesitate
to follow you and to abide with you.
Help us to know and live
within the sovereignty of your Father's eternal Kingdom.
Who live and reign with God the Father in
the unity of the Holy Spirit,
one God, for ever and ever.
Amen.

Other Rites and Customs

- As Friday is the Day of Prayer for the Legal Protection of Unborn Children, include an appropriate petition in the Universal Prayer.
- In observance of the Week of Prayer for Christian Unity, invite clergy and parishioners from neighboring Christian ecclesial communities for an ecumenical prayer service or Taizé Prayer around the Cross.
- Since today's Gospel reading focuses on the call of the disciples, host a Ministry Fair to expose the parish to the many ways people share their gifts and talents.

Liturgy and Life

After the lights and carols of Christmas, Ordinary Time can seem so, well, ordinary. But it is in the ordinary days of our ordinary lives that God asks us to build his Kingdom. The Lectionary readings during these weeks take us through the life of Christ. Striving to live Jesus' example of love, reconciliation, and healing can transform our most ordinary moments into extraordinary moments of charity. Take time this week to look for God in the ordinary moments of your life.

Taking Place This Week . . .

Consider what can be done liturgically, catechetically, and ministerially to respond to these important needs.

- World Religion Day (1/17)
- The Week of Prayer for Christian Unity begins tomorrow (1/18–1/25).
- Martin Luther King Jr. Day (USA: 1/18)
- The Day of Prayer for the Legal Protection of Unborn Children is Friday.
- The annual March for Life in DC takes place this week.

MON 18 Weekday

LM #311 / LMC #193-232 / green

Scripture Insights

The word *priest* refers to one who "offers sacrifice." Jesus is our priest, and he offered sacrifice for us. During Jesus' ministry, the Apostles were not in a time of sacrifice and did not fast. Even today, our liturgical year reflects the seasons of fast and feast.

Preaching Points

Parish Masses

- *Obedience* is a loaded word in modern society. When we say that Jesus was obedient to the Father, we say it knowing that Jesus' will and the Father's will are united. The two are one and exist in relationship.
- Being with Jesus brought great joy to the disciples and all whose hearts were oriented toward Jesus and the Good News. All people have hearts made to crave God, and in Jesus, their hearts found wholeness.

Masses with Children

- Jesus was obedient to the Father in all things, and his will was one with Father's will. Jesus and the Father live in perfect relationship with one another.
- Brides and (bride)grooms are very happy on their wedding days. When we talk about Jesus and the Church, we call Jesus the (bride)groom, and the Church the bride. When Jesus was on earth, those who loved him were happy to be near him, because their hearts had been aching for God's presence in their lives.

Missal Options

- Consider using the prayers from the Mass for Various Needs and Occasions #20.
- Use any of the three forms of the PA.
- Any of the eight Prefaces for OT or the six common Prefaces may be used (except for if EP-IV is used as suggested).
- You might use EP-IV with its proper Preface.
- Any OT Collect may be used or adapted to conclude the UP.

Song of the Day

"God's Holy Mystery" by Paul A. Tate (WLP)

TUE 19 Weekday

LM #312 / LMC #193-232 / green

Scripture Insights

The Lord created the Sabbath day to be a day of rest. We are meant to engage in the Sabbath, but it isn't meant to saddle us with stressful expectations. The Sabbath is meant to be assistance to us, and we are not meant to serve the Sabbath.

Preaching Points

Parish Masses

- God sees our actions and knows what is at the heart of what we choose to do in our lives. He understands our actions and intent.
- We are called to readily and enthusiastically serve God.
- The Sabbath, or Lord's Day (a day of rest), is meant to be a blessing and not a grim responsibility.

Masses with Children

- God knows and understands our hearts, minds, and souls. He knows and understands what we do and why we do it. We must engage our free will for good in order to grow in God's goodness.
- We are called to serve God in great joy. How do we serve our Lord in joy?

Missal Options

- Consider using the prayers from the Twenty-Ninth Sunday in OT.
- Use any of the three forms of the PA.
- Any of the eight Prefaces for OT or the six Common Prefaces may be used.
- You might use EP-III.
- Any OT Collect may be used or adapted to conclude the UP.

Song of the Day

"We Are Called" by David Haas (GIA)

WED 20 Weekday

LM #313 / LMC #193-232 / green

Optional Memorials of St. Fabian, Pope and Martyr / red; St. Sebastian, Martyr / red

Scripture Insights

The priesthood is an ancient and holy calling. In Jesus' time, priests offered sacrifice and helped people to interpret, understand, and live by God's law. Jesus, our high priest, helped the people understand that we are meant to live in the spirit of the Sabbath, not under the thumb of a ruthless Sabbath.

Preaching Points

Parish Masses

- The priests and scribes described in the Gospel were more concerned about finding fault than finding compassion. Their interpretation of the Sabbath law was one that followed the letter of the law rather than the spirit of the law.
- Priests held an important role in ancient Judaism, and they hold an important role in modern Catholicism. Priests offer sacrifice and are called to preach and teach the faith to the people.

Masses with Children

- In Jesus' time, the priests and scribes often looked for fault in Jesus' ministry. When he healed someone on the Sabbath, they believed that he violated the Sabbath; Sabbath should not stop people from helping one another.
- The law is meant to benefit and serve the people of God. It is not meant to keep them ill when the healing Jesus was present in their midst.

Missal Options

- Consider using the prayers from the Twenty-Fifth Sunday in OT.
- Use any of the three forms of the PA.
- Any of the eight Prefaces for OT or the six Common Prefaces may be used.
- You might use EP-II.
- Any OT Collect may be used or adapted to conclude the UP.

Song of the Day

"As a Chalice Cast of Gold" by Thomas H. Troeger (Oxford University Press)

Optional Memorials

St. Fabian

St. Fabian, pope and martyr, was only a layman when he was named pope by acclamation; it was said that a dove landed on his head to mark him as the future pope. He proved an able choice, founding the minor orders as part of the process for candidates to the priesthood and dividing Rome into seven districts, with secretaries assigned to record the stories of the martyrs in each district.

- The readings may be taken from the SW, #514, or any from the CM or CP (For a Pope), or LMC #242.
- The Collect is proper and is found in the PS. The other texts may be taken from the CM (For One Martyr) or from the CP (For a Pope).
- Use P-I or P-II of the Saints, the Preface of Holy Martyrs, or the Preface of Holy Pastors.
- Consider EP-I.
- One of the OT Collects may conclude the UP.

St. Sebastian

St. Sebastian was a captain of the Praetorian Guard until Diocletian learned of his Christianity. Although he had served both loyally, he would not choose his emperor over his Savior, so Diocletian ordered him shot with arrows and later had him bludgeoned to death.

- The readings may be taken from the SW, #515, the CM, or LMC #243.
- The Collect is proper and is found in the PS.
- The other texts may be taken from the CM (For One Martyr).
- Use P-I or P-II of the Saints, or the Preface of Holy Martyrs.
- Consider EP-I.
- One of the OT Sunday Collects may conclude the UP.

Today's Saint

St. Agnes was killed at the age of twelve or thirteen for rejecting the advances of a would-be rapist; she acclaimed the Lord as her spouse. She is often depicted with a lamb, the symbol of innocence and of being a follower of the Good Shepherd.

Scripture Insights

For centuries, God's people offered lambs for sacrifice. Jesus' sacrifice was the one sacrifice meant to satisfy the need all other sacrifices.

Preaching Points

Parish Masses

- God does not seek sacrifices from us, nor does he want us to bring him burnt offerings. Instead we are called to seek God with all our hearts.
- Jesus' sacrifice is the final and complete sacrifice on which we depend.
- When Jesus traveled, so many people sought him that he was inundated with throngs of people. He healed those who sought him.

Masses with Children

- The ancient Jewish people offered sacrifices and burnt offerings to God. Our Lord no longer asks such things of us, and Jesus' sacrifice is the only sacrifice needed for our salvation.
- Jesus continued to heal people in his years of earthly mission, and they sought his healing with hearts oriented toward him.

Scripture Insights (PS)

God's ways are not our ways. Weakness is strength; foolishness is wisdom. The Kingdom of God is worth everything we have, everything we are.

Preaching Points

Parish Masses

- In the lives of saints and martyrs, we glimpse the paradoxical grace of God, who brings triumph out of seeming failure. What are the weaknesses and failures of our lives? Can we find God in these moments?
- Jesus compares the Kingdom of God to a hidden treasure. It's not always visible from the outside. Do we recognize it and claim it with joy

Masses with Children

- The saints give witness to real struggles and rising above these challenges. They are human just like us and have the same problems and the same joys. How do we find God in our own failures?
- God's Kingdom is a great treasure. But it can be hidden. Help the children to find God's presence in the ordinary days of life.

Missal Options

- Consider using the prayers from the Twenty-Second Sunday in OT.
- The LMC readings may also be from the CM or CS.
- The readings may also be from the CM (For a Virgin Martyr) or the CV (For One Virgin).
- Use any of the three forms of the PA.
- You might use P-I or P-II of Saints, P-I or P-II of Holy Martyrs, or the Preface for Holy Virgins and Religious.
- You might use EP-I.
- Any OT Collect may be used or adapted to conclude the UP.

Song of the Day

"Around the Throne a Glorious Band" (various publishers)

F R I 22 LM #315 / LMC #193-232 / white or violet
Day of Prayer for the Legal Protection of Unborn Children

About Today's Day of Prayer

Today is a day of prayer for the victims of abortion and for those who have had abortions. We also pray that our nation's leaders might be cognizant of the needs of the unborn, establishing laws to protect them. On this day, let us remember that all life is sacred—from womb to tomb.

Scripture Insights

God is a keeper of covenants. He maintains his word always and cares for his people. The new covenant was formed in Jesus, and it is through him that the Gentiles came to know the one God who was first known by Abraham and his descendants.

Preaching Points

Parish Masses

- We are the heirs of the new covenant that God has formed with his human creation. We have been grafted onto the vine that is Israel and adopted into God's family. We live in his mercy and salvation.
- Jesus selected twelve Apostles from among his many disciples. These Twelve are the ones from whom the modern bishops trace their apostolic lineage.

Masses with Children

- We live in the new covenant that, through Christ, God created for humanity. We may not be of the bloodline of Israel, but we are the adopted sons and daughters of the Lord.
- Jesus selected twelve Apostles from among his many disciples. Modern bishops became bishops by ordination; these ordinations can be traced back to ancient times.

Missal Options

- Refer to the LS, #516A. Readings for the Day of Prayer may be taken from the Masses for Various Needs and Occasions, III (In Public Circumstances, #26A), For Giving Thanks to God for the Gift of Human Life (#947A–847E, LS), or For Public Needs: 14. For Peace and Justice (#887–891, LM).
- You might consider using form III of the PA.
- If using the Masses and Prayers for Various Needs and Occasions: For Giving Thanks to God for the Gift of Human Life, wear white vestments.
- Consider EPVN-II and Common P-III, "Praise to God for the creation and restoration of the human race."

- If using the Mass for the Preservation of Peace and Justice, wear violet vestments.

Song of the Day

"Pie Jesu" by Gregory Norbert (OCP) or "Hear Us, Almighty Lord/*Attende Domine*" (various publishers)

SAT 23 LM #316 / LMC #193-232 / violet **Weekday**

Optional Memorials of St. Vincent, Deacon and Martyr / red; St. Marianne Cope, Virgin / white; Blessed Virgin Mary / white

Scripture Insights

Jesus' relatives didn't recognize the Messiah in their midst, yet in this man Jesus was the final sacrifice, which rendered the Temple animal sacrifices unnecessary. The new covenant had begun!

Preaching Points

Parish Masses

- Ancient Judaism required animal sacrifice to worship God and forgive sins. Using Temple architecture and design, the First Reading explains that Jesus' blood is the only sacrifice needed for our salvation.
- Jesus' relatives would have considered him an ordinary child, an ordinary teen, and an ordinary man. When they heard about his ministry, they objected to Jesus' message.

Masses with Children

- Ancient Judaism required animal sacrifice to worship God and forgive sins. Because of Jesus' sacrifice, no more animal sacrifice is needed. Jesus' sacrifice is all that is needed for our salvation.
- Jesus' relatives would have considered him an ordinary child, an ordinary teen, and an ordinary man. When they heard about his ministry, they didn't think that the person they thought was so ordinary should act in such a way, so they didn't believe him.

Missal Options

- Consider using the prayers from the Tenth Sunday in OT.
- Use any of the three forms of the PA.
- Any of the eight Prefaces for OT or the six Common Prefaces may be used.
- You might use EP-II.
- Any OT Collect may be used or adapted to conclude the UP.

Song of the Day

"Praise to the Lord, the Almighty" (various publishers)

Optional Memorials

St. Vincent

St. Vincent was martyred during the Diocletian persecutions after he refused to desecrate a copy of the Scriptures to save himself. While he was imprisoned, Vincent's courage and devotion in the face of torture and impending martyrdom inspired his jailor to convert to Christianity.

- The readings may be taken from the SW, #517 (LS), LMC #245, or the CM.
- The Collect is from the PS; the other texts may be taken from the CM (For One Martyr).
- Choose from P-I or P-II of the Saints, or P-I or P-II of Holy Martyrs.
- Consider EP-I.

St. Marianne Cope

St. Marianne Cope was a Franciscan sister who helped establish hospitals in central New York State to serve the sick of any race or creed. Following the call to love Jesus in "the least of these," St. Marianne later joined St. Damien of Molokai in sheltering and caring for leprosy patients, ensuring that the mission would continue after his death.

- The readings may be taken from the SW, #517A (LS), the CV, or the CHMW (For Those Who Work for the Underprivileged).
- No alternate readings are provided in the LMC; you could use those from the CS.
- Choose from P-I or P-II of the Saints, or the Preface of Holy Virgins and Religious.
- Consider EP-I; other prayers may be from the CHMV (For Religious).

Blessed Virgin Mary

- Saturdays in OT that are not assigned an obligatory observance may be celebrated as a Memorial of the Blessed Virgin Mary.
- The readings may be taken from the SW, CBVM, or CMML. The prayer texts may be taken from the CBVM or the CMML. You may also use the various Votive Masses for the BVM.

S U N 24 LM #68B / LMC #63B / green
Third Sunday in Ordinary Time

Scripture Insights

Written in the period after the exile to Babylon, the Book of Jonah is a prophecy to the Jews returning home. Ancient prophecies were intended to call God's people back to faithfulness. They often contained indictments of neighboring powers that defied God by conquering God's people. So it is not unusual that Jonah would be directed to pronounce doom on Nineveh, capital of Assyria. That nation had conquered the northern kingdom of Israel in an earlier period of Israel's history—722 years before the birth of Christ.

The Book of Jonah is unusual, however, because the Ninevites believe Jonah immediately and repent. No prophet to the Jews had such instantaneous success. Isaiah was warned that the people wouldn't believe (Isaiah 6:8–10); Jeremiah was thrown into a cistern (Jeremiah 38); Ezekiel found the Israelites rebellious (Ezekiel 3:27). But the Ninevites changed their ways. More astounding—God repents of the punishment that was intended.

This had happened before, but rarely (Exodus 32:18 is a notable example). It had never happened with non-Jews and sworn enemies of Israel. If we read further, we find that Jonah becomes very angry with God for this.

How does this story prophesy to Jews after the exile and bring them back to faithfulness? How does it prophesy to us? The story of Jonah speaks eloquently to the constancy of God as one who is "slow to anger and rich in kindness and fidelity" (Exodus 34:6; Jonah 4:2). It also draws on a theology of creation that understands God as Lord of all. Whoever turns to God is gathered in love. Finally, the story cautions against putting boundaries on God's care and concern. Israel cannot claim God exclusively for itself. No nation can. Jonah's story suggests that if God cares for the enemies of Israel so much, then God will care for Israel that much more. (Matthew 6:26 makes a similar point.) The prophecy of Jonah teaches that God is not bound by human notions of judgment and justice and that we do not have exclusive rights to God's mercy and love.

How do we counteract the idea that we are more favored by God than others?

Preaching Points

Parish Masses

- "Repent, and believe in the Gospel" (distribution of ashes, RM). These words remind us of what the Christian life calls us to do each day. Each day, perhaps even each hour, we are called to repent and turn toward the Good News Jesus brings to us.
- When we turn to the Lord, we are turning toward goodness and love; we are greeted with God's open arms.
- Our thoughts and God's thoughts are not the same; God is not impeded by our assumptions about him. None of us can claim that we are more loved by God than others.
- How do we show God's love to one another in our marriages, families, friendships, and workplaces?

Children's Liturgy of the Word

- God always greets his children with open arms when his children turn to him.
- God loves all of his children with a deep and abiding love. We cannot claim to know God's mind and decide he loves certain people more than others.
- How do we show God's love to one another in our families, classrooms, friendships, and activities?

Missal Options

- Use the same form of the PA throughout these winter Sundays of OT.
- Sing or recite the Gloria and the Creed.
- Any of the eight Prefaces of the Sundays of OT may be selected today.
- Consider using EP-III.
- Any OT Collect, except the prayer for today, may conclude the UP.
- There are six SBs for OT from which to choose. You may also select a PP.

Music Preparation

- There is a sense of urgency in all the readings today, followed by the directive "Come after me." Is there a sense of importance or have we become ambivalent?
- Now is a really good time to check out the continuing education opportunities available in your area or nationally. Perhaps you need to revive a drooping spirit.
- Although we have a few weeks to go before the beginning of Lent, we should be thinking about who is singing what during the Easter Triduum, most especially the Exsultet. Make sure the individual charged with this important task has the music and that either you are working with them or they are aware of important resources: NPM, Corpus Christi Watershed, and YouTube have mp3 files. Start practicing this important chant now!

Music Suggestions

- Gathering or Sending Forth: "Fish with Me" by Ken Canedo (OCP)
- Preparation of the Gifts: "Take My Life" by Scott Underwood (Mercy/Vineyard Publishing)
- Communion: "Strength for the Journey" by Michael John Poirier (WLP)
- Sending Forth: "Two Fishermen" by Suzanne Toolan (GIA)

Mass Texts

Introduction to Mass

St. Paul and Jesus himself today encourage us to make the most of the time we are given. We hear too of the Ninevites, who heeded Jonah's warning and turned to the Lord. The Kingdom is at hand, and God, in his mercy, gives us time to repent. He gives us his very own Son as our way back to him. So let us approach this altar with eagerness, gratitude, and joy. *My brothers and sisters, let us acknowledge our sins, and so prepare ourselves to celebrate the sacred mysteries.*

Tropes for Penitential Act, Form III

We are sinners, O Lord, and you show us the way to repentance: Lord, have mercy.

Your compassion and your love are from of old: Christ, have mercy.

You call us to leave all and follow you: Lord, have mercy.

Dismissal for Children's Liturgy of the Word

Today, children, we hear of Jesus calling his very first disciples. Simon and Andrew, James and John, all dropped what they were doing to follow Jesus. He calls each and every one of you too, through your parents and teachers, your siblings and friends; through the beauty of nature and the events of the world; through the sick, the lonely, and the poor. He calls to you in the Scriptures you are about to hear. Go now and listen to him, for he calls to you with the greatest of all love.

Dismissal of Catechumens

My friends, time is God's gift to us. Through it he allows us to change and to grow. He gives you this time now to reflect on what you have heard in today's readings, to consider how God is calling you to change, and to grow closer to him through Jesus Christ. We pray that this will be a fruitful time for you and that it will lead you closer to full communion with us at the Lord's table. Go in peace.

Dismissal of Extraordinary Ministers of Holy Communion

Dear ministers of the Lord, God does not forget his people, but in kindness and compassion he remembers them in their pain and lowliness. Go to our sick and homebound brothers and sisters, bearing Christ to them in Word and Body, and remind them of his love and of our prayers. Go in peace.

Universal Prayer

The Kingdom of God is at hand. His Kingdom reigns among us, among all peoples. Conscious of their needs of our call to service, we turn to God in prayer.

1. For vocations to the priesthood and religious life and that all baptized Christians may serve the Kingdom in love, we pray:
2. For those who follow the call to serve their country in military duty, for their commitment and their safety, we pray:
3. For all who labor on the waters of the sea, especially for fishermen and sailors, we pray:
4. For all those who will pass this day with nothing to eat and no one to care for their needs, especially for the starving children of our world, we pray:
5. For all those for whom we have promised to pray, and for those who have no one to pray for them, we pray:

Lord Jesus,
we often become entangled in our nets,
hesitating to heed your call in our lives.
Help us, like the Apostles,
to respond to you with ready hearts and joyful zeal.
Who live and reign with God the Father in the unity of the Holy Spirit,
one God, for ever and ever.
Amen.

Other Rites and Customs

- In observance of Catholic Schools Week, invite children from the parish or regional Catholic school to be more involved in ministerial roles in the liturgy.
- Today is a good day to celebrate the Rite of Acceptance into the Order of Catechumens if a parish has any inquirers who are ready.

Liturgy and Life

Jesus proclaims, "This is the time of fulfillment. The kingdom of God is at hand." That Kingdom—so long promised by the prophets—is unfolding. And what does this mean? How are we to be part of this unfolding? "Repent, and believe in the Gospel" (distribution of Ashes; RM). Apparently living in the new Kingdom requires us to hope and to change the way we live. Are you purposefully growing your knowledge of the Kingdom of God and all that it requires?

Taking Place This Week . . .

Consider what can be done liturgically, catechetically, and ministerially to respond to these important needs.

- Today the special collection is for the Church in Latin America.
- World Leprosy Day (1/24)
- The Week of Prayer for Christian unity ends tomorrow (1/25).
- International Customs Day (1/26)
- Australia Day (1/26)
- World Holocaust Victims Remembrance Day (1/27)
- Tu Bishvat/Tu B'Shevat (1/28)
- Catholic Schools Week begins today.

MON 25 LM #519 / LMC #247 / white
Feast of the Conversion of St. Paul, Apostle

About Today's Feast

As with Paul, the time or place of conversion cannot be predicted. It can only be recognized and embraced. Each of us needs to be released from the blindness and hardness of heart that causes pain and suffering to our sisters and brothers near and far. Only then can the light of the Gospel shine fully through our lives.

Scripture Insights

Conversion is something that affects our deepest selves so utterly and completely that we are made new. St. Paul's conversion was dramatic and immediate, but other conversions take more time. We are called to be continuously converted to Christ and his ways.

Preaching Points

Parish Masses

- St. Paul was a persecutor of Christians, and his oppression was well known. His conversion to Christ forced him to understand his persecution of others.
- Despite working against Christians for a time, St. Paul became a most ardent follower of Christ and spread the Gospel to many lands. His words continue to spread the Gospel today.

Masses with Children

- St. Paul, known as Saul before his conversion, was a terrible oppressor of Christians. His dramatic conversion on the road to Emmaus changed his heart and mind, and he committed his life to helping others come into the faith.
- Saul's persecution of others didn't make him unable to minister. With Jesus' help and the help of the Apostles, he changed his life and became a great evangelizer.
- St. Paul's letters to the various ancient communities still help people understand the faith today.

Missal Options

- The prayers are proper and found in the PS.
- Use any of the three forms of the PA.
- Sing or recite the Gloria; the Creed is not said or sung.
- Use P-I of the Apostles and consider EP-I.
- Since the SB for Paul also includes Peter, use the SB for All Saints (#18).

Song of the Day

"Go Make of All Disciples" by Leon M. Adkins (various publishers)

Other Rites and Customs

Hours: Use the Proper Psalter from the PS.

TUE 26 LM #520; Gospel #318 / LMC #248 / white
Memorial of Sts. Timothy and Titus, Bishops

Today's Saints

Despite the struggles, arrests, and punishments St. Paul endured, he was blessed with helpers and friends such as Timothy and Titus. His esteem for and trust in them is evident in his epistles. Timothy was a young man who received the faith from his grandmother, Lois. Paul sent him as an ambassador to quell disputes in certain churches. Likewise, Titus undertook difficult missions and was left to organize the church in Crete. These two early bishops became the links between Paul and the developing Church.

Scripture Insights

The First Reading from the PS is proper. The reflections that follow pertain to the Gospel; #318.

Throughout his Gospel account, Mark presents Jesus' ministry as one that establishes a household of followers; they are the ones who accept his teachings and vision of the Kingdom of the Father. Those who do not accept his teaching are "outside" this household. Those outside include the religious leaders, who actually think they are inside, and those who reject the movement of the Spirit. Today's story is an example of Jesus' intent. He is not rejecting his family or the familial relationship. He is stating that a new relationship exists between him and those who do the will of the Father.

Preaching Points

Parish Masses

- What binds us together as followers of Jesus? We are baptized into the faith, and we are also made a family by our willingness to open our hearts to Jesus and his commandments.

Masses with Children

- Jesus recognized that his family are those who do the will of God, not simply those who have blood ties to him. We are Jesus' family, and we are called to follow his commandments.

Scripture Insights (PS)

If the full texts from the PS are used, the following pertains to the Gospel, #520. All of the readings from the PS open up the concept of discipleship. Given today's readings and memorial, it is good to focus on the responsibilities that flow from our Baptism.

Our freedom as disciples in Christ comes with a responsibility—the responsibility to work for the coming of God's Kingdom. Sometimes the difficulties of ordinary life constrain us in fulfilling our responsibility to live as people of God. They lead us to think God no longer accompanies us. When Jesus sends us out to labor for God's Kingdom as he does the seventy-two in the Gospel, we know true joy and peace will be ours for the abundance of God's power in Jesus' reign. Indeed, nothing else matters.

Preaching Points

Parish Masses

- We will come and go in mission our entire lives as disciples. We will return in joy as the seventy-two did. We might also return wearied but hopeful. We could also return dejected or disappointed because it seems we might not have accomplished much, but the message of the Kingdom of God is always a timely message. How people respond to it will lead them to know God's peace and mercy or yearn for it. Either way, the Kingdom of God is near. Be alert for how the Kingdom of God is at hand for you, your family, friends, and neighbors as you are sent forth this week.
- The Lord calls each of us to labor for the harvest of the Kingdom. We will harvest the Kingdom in different ways depending on our gifts and our situation in life. As disciples who labor, each of us will know rejection and acceptance as Jesus did. Each of us will also know joy because we have been given the power of Jesus. Nothing will harm us. Ours is the Kingdom of God.

School Masses

- Discipleship is again the theme of today's Gospel. Jesus sends seventy-two disciples out to announce that the Kingdom of God is at hand. The word *kingdom* does not refer to a location but expresses an adherence to God's rule of love. Jesus is now sending us to be "laborers for his harvest." Remind the children that discipleship is not only challenging but also extremely rewarding. What we are called to do is simply to be faithful.
- Encourage the children to see themselves as Jesus' "laborers for his harvest" who can take up the work of announcing "the kingdom of God is near!"

Missal Options

- The FR from the LMC is proper; the other readings may be from the CP.
- The prayers are proper and are found in the PS for January 26.
- There is no Gloria or Creed.
- Use either Preface for the Saints.
- Consider using EP-II.

Song of the Day

"Seed, Scattered and Sown" by Dan Feiten (OCP)

Optional Memorial of St. Angela Merici, Virgin / white

Scripture Insights

God desires for each of us to live in communion with him; our ultimate goal is to share in the life of God in heaven. On earth, one of the ways we live in communion with our Lord is by cultivating the soil of our hearts to hear and respond to his Word.

Preaching Points

Parish Masses

- God created humans in his own image and likeness; each of us bears this image. He created our hearts and minds to know and understand his law. Our informed consciences have a place in moral theology.
- While our hearts are meant to receive the goodness of God through his law, it is up to each person to make their hearts a fertile ground for growing God's law.

Masses with Children

- God made each human person to know the law of God, and he has made each of our hearts able to receive his Word. A person's conscience helps him or her to process moral decisions.
- A garden grows when a gardener carefully tends the soil and the plants. Like gardeners, we must carefully tend our hearts so that they are ready to grow in understanding of God and his ways.

Missal Options

- Consider using the prayers from the Mass for Various Needs and Occasions #18A and EP-III.
- Use any of the three forms of the PA.
- Any of the eight Prefaces for OT or the six common Prefaces may be used.
- Any OT Collect may be used or adapted as the concluding prayer for the UP.

Song of the Day

"Parable" by M.D. Ridge (OCP)

Optional Memorial

St. Angela Merici's vision of an order of consecrated single women educating girls while living in the world led to the founding of the Ursulines, the first women's teaching order. St. Angela began with a small school for girls in her own home, beginning a legacy that would spread Ursuline schools across the world.

- The readings may be taken from the SW, #521, LMC #249, the CV, the CHMW (For Teachers), or the CS (For Educators; LMC).
- Use the Collect from the PS. The other prayers may be taken from the CV (For One Virgin) or the CHMW (For Educators).
- Chose from P-I or P-II of Saints, or the Preface of Holy Virgins and Religious.
- Consider EP-I.
- An OT Collect may be used or adapted to conclude the UP.

THU 28

LM #320 or #522 / LMC #193–232 / white

Memorial of St. Thomas Aquinas, Priest and Doctor of the Church

Today's Saint

As a Dominican, St. Thomas's study was both a spiritual and an intellectual discipline—a matter of both heart and mind. The rich fruit of Thomas's reflection has enlightened the Church with wisdom expressed through academic writing and sacred poetry. His Eucharistic texts continue to inspire faith, especially on Holy Thursday.

Scripture Insights

God's people are given confidence before God; this gift comes through Christ. We respond to that gift every day of our lives; our response to Christ should be known in our interactions with family, friends, coworkers, and other community members.

Preaching Points

Parish Masses

- How do we inspire one another to do good works, as Jesus has taught us to do? Rather than lecture one another on good works, we ought to inspire one another to do good works.
- The Gospel is for everyone to hear. Jesus' Word is not secret, nor is it special knowledge for only a few people.

Masses with Children

- Jesus wants us to use our free will to help others, be kind to others, and to do what is right and good in our lives. How do we make sure we are doing our best to do those things, and how do we encourage others?
- Some people think that knowing Jesus and understanding his teaching is only for a select few people. We know that Jesus wanted the Good News to be available to all people.

Scripture Insights *(PS)*

To search for wisdom is to search for God, because true Wisdom flows from God. We have just one teacher: Christ.

Preaching Points

Parish Masses

- Wisdom is not about knowing facts—important as those are. Wisdom goes deeper, because Wisdom is an attribute of God himself. No matter our age, are our minds open? Do we seek knowledge of the things of God? God calls us to a lifelong pursuit of wisdom.
- Science is not opposed to God. If we seek the truth in sincerity, we will be drawn closer to God.

Masses with Children

- The preaching points for parish Masses may also be used for Masses with children.

Missal Options

- The readings may also be taken from the CDC or CP.
- Use the Collect from the PS; the other prayers may be taken from the CDC or CP (For One Pastor).
- Use any of the three forms of the PA.
- Choose from P-I or P-II of Saints, or the Preface of Holy Pastors.
- Consider using EP-II.
- Any OT Collect may be used or adapted to conclude the UP.

Song of the Day

"Christ, Be Our Light" by Bernadette Farrell (OCP)

FRI 29 LM #321 / LMC #193–232 / green

Weekday

Scripture Insights

The early Christians bravely faced persecution and the suffering that accompanied it. They kept before them the truth of such suffering lasting only in this life and the knowledge that they had the better portion in Christ.

Preaching Points

Parish Masses

- Suffering for Jesus' sake is not something that is permanent; those who suffer will be relieved. In many places Christians are still persecuted for their faith.
- The Kingdom of God is something that is living and growing. It begins as something absolutely tiny but blossoms forth like lush vegetation.

Masses with Children

- The early Christians were persecuted for their faith, and today people in some parts of the world still face persecution for their faith.
- The Kingdom of God is something that is living and growing. Mustard seeds are some of the very tiniest seeds, yet when they grow, they become big, bushy plants.

Missal Options

- Consider using the prayers from the Mass for Various Needs and Occasions #28 and EP-III.
- Use any of the three forms of the PA.
- Any of the eight Prefaces for OT or the six common Prefaces may be used.
- Any OT Collect may be used or adapted as the concluding prayer for the UP.

Song of the Day

"The Supper of the Lord" by Laurence Rosania (OCP)

SAT 30 LM #322 / LMC #193–232 / green

Weekday

Optional Memorial of the Blessed Virgin Mary / white

Scripture Insights

Jesus has called us to lives of faith—our faith in him touches every aspect of our lives. When we place our faith in him, we are trusting in his deep love and devotion to us. We trust that he will care for us regardless of our life circumstances.

Preaching Points

Parish Masses

- Having faith can be difficult, because we are believing in that which we can't necessarily see. We can see in Scripture how others responded to God's call to faith.
- When Jesus calmed the sea, the Apostles were amazed that he had authority over nature. Jesus desired for the Apostles to have faith in him, instead of living in terror.

Masses with Children

- We believe in Jesus' love for us, and we believe in God's care for his beloved children. We believe these things even though we cannot see God. This is faith!
- When Jesus calmed the sea, the Apostles were amazed that he had authority over nature. Jesus wanted the Apostles to trust in him, and he wants us to trust in him too.

Missal Options

- Consider using the prayers from Eighth Sunday in OT and EP-II.
- Use any of the three forms of the PA.
- Any of the eight Prefaces for OT or the six common Prefaces may be used.
- Any OT Collect may be used or adapted as the concluding prayer for the UP.

Song of the Day

"With Faith Grown in Suffering" by Carey Landry (OCP)

Optional Memorial

- Saturdays in OT that are not assigned an obligatory observance may be celebrated as a Memorial of the Blessed Virgin Mary.
- The readings may be taken from the SW, CBVM, or CMML. The prayer texts may be taken from the CBVM or CMML. You may also use the various Votive Masses for the BVM.
- Use either of the Prefaces for the BVM.

SUN 31 LM #71B / LMC #66B / green

Fourth Sunday in Ordinary Time

Scripture Insights

Jesus' first miracle is an exorcism set in the context of his teaching. Why is this so important? When Jesus entered the synagogue and spoke, the people were amazed at the power and authority with which he taught. The scribes quoted previous experts and authorities for important interpretations of Scripture and the Law. The Greek word used to describe Jesus' teaching, *exousia*, means that he taught "out of himself." In other words, he did not use other authorities to strengthen his arguments.

Into this context wanders the possessed man. The unclean spirit, a demon in other translations, reveals the identity of Jesus as the Holy One of God. In the Old Testament, particularly in the prophecy of Isaiah, God is the Holy One of Israel. In this passage, in Acts 3:14, and in 1 John 2:20, Jesus is the "Holy One." These similar phrases imply a connection between Jesus and God. Jesus silences the demon, not because it is wrong about his identity, but because the time has not yet come for Jesus to be revealed.

With the confidence of authority, he commands the unclean spirit to come out. The crowd watches in amazement —often a signal that they do not understand what is happening. Their remarks about a new teaching are meant for the reader. Jesus' power is greater than any other power. Even the demons obey him.

Throughout Mark's account, Jesus' identity is revealed by demons who are then silenced, while the people with Jesus come to know who he is only slowly, if at all. The remarkable exorcisms and healings of Jesus defeat the powers of evil that oppose God. But they will soon lead to a greater question for both his followers and his detractors: What is the source of Jesus' authority?

In Mark's account, things happen very quickly. Consequently, when Mark slows down enough to tell the details of the story, the readers pay more attention. What do the details have to say about the nature of Jesus or the unclean spirits?

Preaching Points

Parish Masses

- Jesus amazed the people by casting out unclean spirits. This ability begs the question as to where Jesus finds such authority and who he is.
- The prophets stated that the Messiah would come from the Israelite people; he would be one of them. Jesus seemed to be a common Jewish man, although everyone he encountered did not immediately know his identity. Over time, he was clearly identified as the one for whom the prophets spoke.
- We must all set a good example for one another so we may walk into holiness and not into sin.
- Jesus' words and actions destroyed evil. They revealed God's tremendous love for the world and its people—for us, for you. Be open to the ways Jesus seeks to destroy evil in your own life and reveal his love for you. Ponder how you harden your own heart to God's Word.

Children's Liturgy of the Word

- Jesus would have looked like any other Israelite man of his time. Passing him on the street, there was nothing obvious that announced the Messiah walking among the people.
- Jesus was able to cast out unclean spirits because he is the Son of God, with God's own power and authority.
- Christians set a good example for one another by living lives that are honest and striving toward holiness.

Missal Options

- Use the same form of the PA throughout these winter Sundays of OT.
- Sing or recite the Gloria and the Creed.
- Any of the eight Prefaces of the Sundays of OT may be selected today.
- Consider using EP-III.
- Any OT Collect, except the prayer for today, may conclude the UP.

Music Preparation

- It doesn't matter how beautiful the Scriptures were or how powerful the homily, people leave church humming the final hymn. Through your careful preparation, practice, and implementation you and your ensemble may be the voice of God for someone.
- When one plays multiple liturgies a weekend it is easy to fall into autopilot. Be sure that you are listening to God's voice.

Music Suggestions

- Prelude: "If Today" by Trevor Thompson (OCP)
- Gathering: "Introit for Fourth Sunday in Ordinary Time Laetetur cor Psalm 105" by Christoph Tietze (WLP)
- Preparation of the Gifts: "All Will Be Well" from *Revelations of Divine Love, Julian of Norwich* by Steven C. Warner (WLP)
- Communion: "God Is Still Speaking" by Marty Haugen (GIA)

Mass Texts

Introduction to Mass

Something greater than a prophet has been given to us to speak the words of God: Jesus Christ, God's own Son. He teaches with divine authority, with power, and with love. He also gives us something more than teaching, more than words: he gives us his very own self in the Eucharist. Let us not harden our hearts to the life he offers us but receive him with joy and thanksgiving. *My brothers and sisters, let us acknowledge our sins, and so prepare ourselves to celebrate the sacred mysteries.*

Tropes for Penitential Act, Form III

We have tempted and tested you, though we have seen your works: Lord, have mercy.

You are our God, the rock of our salvation: Christ, have mercy.

You make life-giving water well up for us: Lord, have mercy.

Dismissal for Children's Liturgy of the Word

Dear children, God provides for us in our need. He sends us prophets and teachers, people who can help us in our journey of faith. Best of all, he sends us his Son, Jesus, who not only teaches us but is with us always and who will never fail us or lead us astray. He wishes to speak to you now in today's readings, to give you his love and protection. Go and listen to him.

Dismissal of Catechumens

This community now acknowledges those who are on the path of initiation, and we send you forth to reflect further on the message you have heard in the Scriptures. Take these words to heart, let them form you and transform you and lead you closer to Christ, who is your peace and your life. Go with our prayers.

Dismissal of Extraordinary Ministers of Holy Communion

Friends, we send you to our brothers and sisters who are suffering and in pain and alone, that you may share with them the Bread of Life. May he free them from all anxiety and assure them that in him they are never alone. Go in peace.

Universal Prayer

Seeking to be free of all that keeps us from our God, we turn to him in prayer for our needs and the needs of the world.

1. That our Christian assemblies of prayer may truly be open to responding to the challenge of the Gospel, we pray:
2. That our civil and religious authorities may always be attentive to those most troubled in our society, we pray:
3. That all those possessed by demons of any sort, especially demons of addiction, may be freed from their turmoil, we pray:
4. That those seeking change in their lives may face transition with hope for a bright future, we pray:
5. That all our beloved dead, especially [*insert names*], may be mercifully welcomed into eternal life, we pray:

All-powerful and ever-living God,
you sent your Son to be our Savior
and give him authority to cast out demons
and to heal the world in your name.
Grant your Church the compassionate spirit needed
to see those troubled among us
and to reach out with possibilities for transformation.
Make us agents of conversion for our world.
Through Christ our Lord.
Amen.

Other Rites and Customs

- Include a petition in the Universal Prayer for those struggling with various demons in their lives.
- If some new music will be sung during the Triduum this year, consider introducing it to the parish today or on one of the other Sundays of Ordinary Time so folks become familiar with it ahead of time.

Liturgy and Life

Today's psalm refrain challenges us each day, each "today," not to harden our hearts if we hear God's voice. That voice may come through events in our ordinary life, or through a unique situation, or even in the weekday Scripture readings for daily Mass. However the voice of God comes to you, reflect each night before sleep: "What did I hear? Did I harden or open my heart?"

Taking Place This Week . . .

Consider what can be done liturgically, catechetically, and ministerially to respond to these important needs.

- National Freedom Day (2/1)
- World Wetlands Day and Groundhog Day (2/2)
- The Feast of the Presentation of the Lord is 2/2; it is also the World Day for Consecrated Life.
- World Cancer Day (2/4)
- First Friday (2/5) and First Saturday (2/6)
- February is Black History and American Heart month.
- February is also traditionally celebrated by Catholics as the Month of the Passion of Our Lord.

MON 1 LM #323 / LMC #193–232 / green
Weekday

Scripture Insights

The faithful people can know God's comfort. Trusting in God, they can live in the peace of God's presence and guidance. Always caring for the hurting people, our God has tremendous love for us.

Preaching Points

Parish Masses

- God has taken our future in hand. We know that he has prepared a place for us in heaven.
- Every person has struggles in life. Our Lord cares deeply for each of us and is present with us in our struggles. We can take refuge in him, confidently knowing he cares for us.

Masses with Children

- In the Old Testament, we hear a great deal about the conquering of lands and cities. We know that God has a place for us, and that place is heaven. He desires for each of us to be in heaven with him, someday.
- It is normal to have struggles in our lives, and these struggles look different to each of us. We can know that God cares deeply for each of his children and that we can trust in his care.

Missal Options

- Consider using the prayers from the Twenty-Third Sunday in OT and EPR-I.
- Use any of the three forms of the PA.
- Any of the eight Prefaces for OT or the six common Prefaces may be used.

Song of the Day

"Amazing Grace" (traditional); be sure to update the verse, "that saved a wretch like me" to "that saved and set us free."

TUE 2 Feast of the Presentation of the Lord

See page 86.

WED 3 LM #325 / LMC #193–232 / green
Weekday

Optional Memorials of St. Blaise, Bishop and Martyr / red; St. Ansgar, Bishop / white

Scripture Insights

It is said that the opposite of love is not hate but indifference. God loves us very much, and out of love for us, he helps us to learn discipline. Discipline isn't necessarily enjoyable, but it can help us grow into healthier people.

Preaching Points

Parish Masses

- When we strive for peace with others, we look for ways to offer kindness, assistance, and love while maintaining healthy boundaries. We ought to be sure our interpersonal relationships help others to grow in relationship with God.
- In Nazareth, the people did not accept the man that Jesus had become; in a sense, they thought he had reached above his station in life.

Masses with Children

- If life is like a garden, how do we grow peaceful relationships? We can look for ways to offer kindness, assistance, and love while maintaining healthy boundaries.
- In Nazareth, people didn't accept Jesus; they thought that he should be like his parents and neighbors and not like himself.

Missal Options

- Consider using the prayers from the Mass for Various Needs and Occasions #40 and EPR-II.
- Use any of the three forms of the PA.
- Any of the eight Prefaces for OT or the six common Prefaces may be used.

Song of the Day

"Prayer of Peace" by David Haas (GIA)

Optional Memorials

St. Blaise

St. Blaise was one of the early martyrs known as the Fourteen Holy Helpers invoked against various diseases. Although we know very little of St. Blaise's life, he is reputed to have been a doctor who healed a boy choking on a fish bone; accordingly, this healer and martyr is invoked against illnesses of the throat.

- The readings may be taken from the SW, #525, CM, CP, or LMC #253.
- Use the Collect from the PS; the other prayers may be taken from the CM (For One Martyr) or CP (For a Bishop).
- Choose from P-I or P-II of Saints, P-I or P-II of Holy Martyrs, or the Preface of Holy Pastors.
- Consider EP-I.
- An OT Collect may conclude the UP.

St. Ansgar

Motivated by his desire to be reunited with his mother in heaven, St. Ansgar became a missionary in Denmark and Sweden during the tumultuous period following the death of Charlemagne. His piety and devotion impressed local rulers, who allowed him to establish missions, monasteries, and churches across Scandinavia.

- The readings may be taken from the SW, #526, CP (For Missionaries), or LMC #254.
- Use the Collect from the PS; the other prayers may be taken from the CP (For Missionaries or For a Bishop).
- Choose from P-I or P-II of Saints, or the Preface of Holy Pastors.
- Consider EP-I.
- Any OT Collect may conclude the UP.

Other Rites and Customs

There are many options for today's blessing of throats (see BB, ch. 51). It may take place within Mass, within a service of the Word, or as a shorter rite. The blessing itself may be done by a priest or deacon or lay minister. Therefore, busy pastors can encourage a deacon or lay minister to do the blessing. Perhaps a celebration of Morning or Evening Prayer is a good option for your community. If done during Mass, the blessing follows the UP or may take the place of the final blessing. If during the LH, it is given prior to the Gospel canticle.

THU **4** LM #326 / LMC #193–232 / green

Weekday

Scripture Insights

When Moses came down from the mountain, Scripture says that he was "terrified and trembling." We too have fear of the Lord, and we also have trust in the tremendous mercy our Lord has for us.

Preaching Points

Parish Masses

- We are reminded that through Christ we are able to approach God with confidence; Jesus' sacrifice is so complete that it outshines anything else.
- When Jesus sent out his disciples, he sent them to continue his ministry of healing and preaching and his message of repentance and mercy.

Masses with Children

- Sin is a sad part of human life, but through Jesus, our sins are forgiven! If sin is like the darkest time of night, Jesus is the sun who overcomes the darkness.
- Jesus wanted his Apostles to carry on his ministry after he returned to the Father. He taught his Apostles to do this holy work in groups of two. They healed people and preached about repentance and God's mercy.

Missal Options

- Consider using the prayers from the Mass for Various Needs and Occasions #1 and EPVN-III.
- Use any of the three forms of the PA.
- Any of the eight Prefaces for OT or the six common Prefaces may be used.

Song of the Day

"Let All Mortal Flesh Keep Silence" (various publishers)

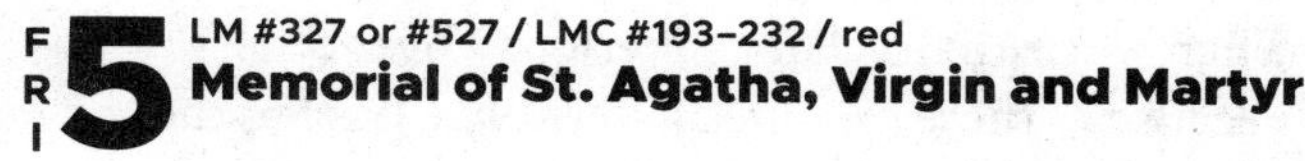

FRI **5** LM #327 or #527 / LMC #193–232 / red

Memorial of St. Agatha, Virgin and Martyr

Today's Saint

St. Agatha was a virgin martyr of the third century whose breasts were cut off by her persecutors. Although she was very beautiful and came from a prominent and privileged family, St. Agatha displayed courage beyond her years when she accepted martyrdom rather than abandon her faith.

Scripture Insights

The Ten Commandments can be reduced to two: love God and love your neighbor. It is up to us to care for one another as Jesus himself would have cared for us. We must live in such a way that others' lives are honored and respected.

Preaching Points

Parish Masses

- Brotherly love is a love that cares for others as if they are brothers and sisters related by blood. Loving others in this way means that we prioritize their needs fairly.

- Marriage is a sacrament, which means it gives grace to the married couple. People should honor marriage, and husbands and wives should honor one another.

Masses with Children

- When we love one another with a brotherly love, it means we are caring for one another like brothers and sisters would care for each other. We are called to give each other's needs priority. If someone is cold, help that person find a sweater. If someone is hungry, find that person some food.
- Marriage is a vocation and a sacrament, and sacraments give grace. Husbands and wives should show love by honoring and respecting one another.
- John the Baptist was a holy man who was killed for preaching truth. We probably won't ever know anyone who faces death for telling the truth like John the Baptist. It is important to always tell the truth, even if it lands you in trouble.

Scripture Insights *(PS)*

The world looks different to God: the marginalized are at the center; those who let go of everything have what really matters in God's Kingdom.

Preaching Points

Parish Masses

- There's nothing intrinsically wrong with being included, respected, or smart. The trouble starts when we begin to claim superiority over others because of these qualities. None of us has anything to boast about—except for the glorious fact that God has called us and loved us.
- These are hard words from Jesus: words about loss, self-denial, and witness in challenging times. There is no way around it: every Christian must carry the cross.

Masses with Children

- There is nothing wrong with being popular. What is important, however, is that we respect others, love others, and care for others. We must never use our popularity over others; instead, we must include others.

Missal Options

- The readings may also be from the CM, CV, or LMC #255 or CS.
- Use the Collect from the PS; the other prayers may be taken from the CM (For a Virgin Martyr) or CV (For One Virgin).
- Use any of the three forms of the PA.
- Consider using EP-I.

Song of the Day

"Psalm 27: The Lord Is My Light" by David Haas (GIA)

SAT 6 LM #328 or #528 / LMC #193–232 / red

Memorial of St. Paul Miki and Companions, Martyrs

Today's Saints

Along with the other twenty-six martyrs of Japan, St. Paul Miki endured the six-hundred-mile march to his crucifixion in Nagasaki by singing the Te Deum. Although this martyrdom was intended as a deterrent to Christian community in Japan, the martyrs' bravery so inspired the persecuted Japanese Christian Church that returning missionaries found communities of secret Christians that had endured in isolation for three centuries.

Scripture Insights

Our faith in the Father, Son, and Holy Spirit is witnessed by the good works we do for others. When we do good for others, God is pleased with us. Jesus expects his followers to do good things for one another.

Preaching Points

Parish Masses

- When Jesus was on earth, he saw how deeply the people craved communion with God and understanding of the Lord. He saw their deep need for him, and he called them "sheep without a shepherd." Jesus is our Good Shepherd.
- Hebrews reminds us that our Good Shepherd hasn't left us without guidance. The Church guides us in our lives, and Jesus is with us in the Eucharist.

Masses with Children

- All people are made to crave God; each of us has a built-in need to know our creator. Jesus saw how much the people needed him when he saw the crowds who were so anxious to see him.
- Jesus knew that we would need to have continued shepherding after he returned to the Father. Jesus is with us in the Eucharist, and the Church helps us follow Jesus' path.

Scripture Insights *(PS)*

The work of the Church is to make disciples, and the call of the baptized is to become more and more one with Christ, even on the cross.

Preaching Points

Parish Masses

- We are called to proclaim the Gospel. It's a daunting task, but we do not do it by ourselves: we do it as part of the Church, in the constant presence of Christ. Together with Christ, there is no limit to what we can accomplish.
- Saints are people who identify with Christ so completely that they can say, "I live, no longer I, but Christ lives in me." Can we make a little more room for Christ in our lives—a little less room for self?

Masses with Children

- Reflect on the life of St. Paul Miki and his companions with the children. Stress how the life of a Christian is to proclaim the Gospel, not necessarily with words, but by our actions. Be sure to include how we don't do it by ourselves: our friends, our families, our teachers, and our parish community help us and support us. And we do so with Jesus by our side.

Missal Options

- The readings may also be taken from the CM.
- Use the Collect from the PS; the other prayers are taken from the CM (For Several Martyrs).
- Use any of the three forms of the PA.
- Choose from P-I or P-II of Saints, or P-I or P-II of Holy Martyrs, and consider using EP-II.
- Any OT Collect may conclude the UP.

Song of the Day

"Come to Me" by Gregory Norbet (OCP)

Something to Consider...

◈ "Liturgical services are not private functions, but are celebrations belonging to the Church, which is the 'sacrament of unity,' namely, the holy people united and ordered under their bishops" (*Sacrosanctum concilium*, 26).

TUE 2 LM #524 / LMC #252 / white

Feast of the Presentation of the Lord

About Today's Feast

Today's feast is an echo of the past Christmas season and the completion of the mystery. Jesus—born, revealed to Israel, manifested to the nations—is now encountered by the Church in the person of Simeon. Indeed, Greek Christians call today's feast "The Meeting" or "The Encountering." The Church embraces Christ, the Light of the World, in her arms. The Mass begins with the blessing of candles for liturgical and home use, reminding the faithful of the Baptism that enlightened them. Hence, the Roman Church calls this Candlemas Day. Let us embrace Christ more tenderly by living our baptismal vocation each day.

Scripture Insights *(From PS)*

Malachi's prophecy tells of a messenger who is like fire purifying the world, preparing it for the coming of the Lord. This description fits the preaching of John the Baptist, who appears in the Gospels calling Israel to repent. Because Malachi names Elijah as the messenger at the end of his prophecy (Malachi 3:23), the New Testament writers take care to identify John as Elijah who has returned to prepare the way. John's clothes and diet are like those of Elijah in the First Book of Kings.

There was little in the prophets or in John's preaching, however, to prepare Israel for the tiny child who made his first public appearance in the Temple for the purification rite prescribed by the law. Jewish custom considered a woman who bore a child to be unclean. A mother of a son spent forty days being purified of her blood (Leviticus 12:1–5), then she presented an offering in the Temple. Only Luke's Gospel relates this story, commemorated in today's feast. The Feast of the Presentation of the Lord was once called the feast of the Purification of Mary. A second command (which Luke mentions in 2:23) says that the firstborn male shall be dedicated to the Lord. Since the earlier form of this law in Exodus 13 does not specify any sacrifice, it seems likely that Luke combined the two laws in his telling.

What is remarkable in this story is the reaction of two old wise people. When they look at the child, they see the salvation of Israel, the Messiah who has come to redeem the world. Simeon confidently describes the child's destiny and the joy and sorrow that Mary will feel. Anna bursts into proclamation about the child to anyone who will listen. Most Jews believed that the Messiah would be a great warrior, bringing God's justice and righteousness to a sinful nation. Even the preaching of John the Baptist pointed to someone greater than he. Could this infant really be the promised one? The Letter to the Hebrews answers the unspoken question. In order to save humankind Jesus had to be human.

"Refiner's fire" is a strong metaphor for the messenger. What does a refiner's fire do? What does that mean when applied to us?

Preaching Points

Parish Masses

- Israel had been prepared for the coming of a messiah over the years. The Presentation, which occurred when John the Baptist was just reaching toddlerhood and young Jesus was beginning to interact with the world around him, marks the recognition of Jesus in a public place—not just any place, but the Temple. Israel would be purified through the Son.
- To obtain specific types of elements, metals were purified in fire. We are purified in Christ.
- Jesus came to earth so that humanity might be redeemed. He became one of us—fully human, while also maintaining full divinity.
- Joseph and Mary were a faithful and observant Jewish couple who brought their child to the Temple as commanded. Their son was recognized by Simeon, who had lived to see the coming of God's promised Messiah.

Children's Liturgy of the Word

- To be pure means to be ritually or spiritually clean. We are made pure through Christ.
- Jesus came to earth specifically for humanity—he became one of us, fully human while also being fully divine.
- Jesus was recognized by Simeon. Simeon knew that he would not die until he saw the Messiah.

Missal Options

- Today's texts are found in the PS.
- The Missal calls for today's Mass to begin with the blessing of candles and a more elaborate procession ("The Procession" or "The Solemn Procession").
- For "The Procession," invite the faithful to gather in a place apart from the worship space, and make sure all have candles, which are lit before it begins. The opening song takes place while everyone's candles are lit (suggested antiphons are found in the Missal). This is followed with the Sign of the Cross, Greeting, and a special introduction. Candles are blessed and the procession into the church takes place while another song is sung (suggested antiphons are found in the Missal).
- "The Solemn Procession" is simpler: the people gather in the church, and the candles are blessed in a place that is visible to the assembly.
- There is no PA.
- Sing or recite the Gloria.
- The Creed is not recited or sung.
- Any OT Collect may conclude the UP.
- The Preface is proper and is found with the other texts in the PS.
- Consider chanting the introductory dialogue and the Preface to highlight today's festivity.
- Consider using the EPVN-II.
- Use one of the six options for the SB for OT.

Music Preparation

- Sing the Nunc Dimittis, the Gospel Canticle of Simeon, used every night at Night Prayer.
- *By Flowing Water*, a resource from Liturgical Press, has set many of the proper chants for feasts like today to simple chant and psalm tones. They are very accessible to the assembly.

Music Suggestions

- Candle Lighting: "Behold, Our Lord Will Come," found in the RM (Chant Mode VIII)
- Procession: "Christ, Be Our Light" by Bernadette Farrell (OCP)
- Preparation of the Gifts: "Song of Simeon" by Janét Sullivan Whitaker (OCP)

Mass Texts

Introduction to Mass

Forty days have passed since our celebration of the Lord's birth. The joy of that feast is not meant only for ourselves. It should be a light of revelation going before us, enlightening everyone we meet. May this Eucharist and the commemoration of the Lord's Presentation purify us to be shining lights of God's glory to the whole world. *My brothers and sisters, let us acknowledge our sins, and so prepare ourselves to celebrate the sacred mysteries.*

Tropes for Penitential Act, Form III

Lord Jesus, you shared our flesh and blood to free us from slavery to sin: Lord, have mercy.

Lord Jesus, through your death you have destroyed the power of death: Christ, have mercy.

Lord Jesus, you are the king of glory, the salvation of all the world: Lord, have mercy.

Dismissal for Children's Liturgy of the Word

Beloved children, we send you now to listen carefully to the Word of God. Think about how you can be more like Jesus. May you open your hearts wide to the truth of the Scriptures and follow his light. Go in peace.

Dismissal of Catechumens

My friends, consider well the mystery you have heard in today's readings. May the Holy Spirit, who led Simeon to recognize Jesus as the Messiah, enlighten you to see in Christ your own salvation. In time, may you be one with us in the celebration of the Eucharist, that we all may praise the King of Glory with joy. Go in peace.

Dismissal of Extraordinary Ministers of Holy Communion

Dear ministers, like Joseph and Mary carrying the infant Jesus into the Temple, bear the Body of Christ to our ailing and injured friends, that his light may give them life and joy, and that they may be one with us in the Holy Spirit. Go in peace.

Universal Prayer

We rejoice, for the Lord is in our midst! Our eyes have seen his salvation, which is prepared for all peoples. Let us bring to him our prayers for the needs of our world.

1. That the Church may continue to embody Christ's presence in all her words and actions, bearing the light of Christ to all the world, we pray:
2. That the light of Christ may burn brightly in the hearts of all entrusted with power, we pray:
3. That all the Simeons and Annas of our world—the elderly, widows, and widowers—may be granted honor and respect, we pray:
4. That we may learn to offer great sacrifices in obedience to the Lord, just as Mary and Joseph, we pray:
5. That all those awaiting death may hope in the Lord's promise of glory, we pray.

Lord our God,
your Son was presented in the Temple,
as Mary and Joseph were obedient to the Law.
Your servant Simeon recognized him
as the long-awaited hope of Israel.
May we, too, recognize his glory shining in our hearts
and in the hearts of those who seem least important
among us.
May your glory enlighten our way.
Through Christ our Lord.
Amen.

Other Rites and Customs

- Mass begins with the blessing of candles using either the Procession or Solemn Procession.
- Encourage people to bring their own candles from home to be blessed.

Liturgy and Life

Simeon sees the love of God revealed in this infant, "a light for revelation to the Gentiles" and the glory of Israel (Luke 2:32). Simeon trusted in God's love. What voices are we listening to? Those who trust in God's love or those who don't? On this feast, also called Candlemas, it is traditional to bless candles. Encourage parishioners to bring candles to Mass today for the blessing and take them home for personal or family prayer. Families may begin their prayers by saying, "Blessed be God, who has brought light into our darkness." Encourage families to light their candles daily and spend a moment reading the words of someone who trusts in God's love. They might use 1 Corinthians 13.

S U N **7** LM #74B / LMC #69B / green

Fifth Sunday in Ordinary Time

Scripture Insights

After the exorcism that is the first of Jesus' miracles, Jesus performs a physical healing on Peter's mother-in-law. Mark shows that Jesus exercises authority over both demonic possession and physical illness. Indeed, Jesus' ability to cast out demons and to heal the sick becomes the way in which the world first knows him.

The difference in the details of the two healings is significant. Jesus orders the demon out; he touches the mother-in-law, and the fever leaves her. For Mark, exorcism is accomplished through verbal authority (demons respond to command), and it is often an instrument for teaching and preaching. By contrast, physical healing is brought about by the touch of one who is holy. In both of these incidents, by command and by touch, Jesus is authoritative. His cure of both victims is total.

In the evening exorcisms that follow, Jesus will not allow the demons to speak, because they know him. Mark will show this many more times as Jesus seeks to be known in the full context of the passion and Resurrection and not just in a handful of miraculous healings. This "messianic secret" of Mark's account of the Gospel places the full revelation at the end of Jesus' public life, not at the beginning.

Night is the traditional time for confrontation with evil, and here the sick and possessed are brought to Jesus at sundown. The power that Jesus wields is not diminished by darkness. In fact, it offers a way to encounter God with no distractions. Jesus seizes the opportunity to pray in a deserted place apart from his disciples and the crowds. Mark connects Jesus' power to his prayer by interrupting the healings to narrate this incident. When the disciples search him out, though, he immediately returns to his work, extending his mission to the neighboring towns, proclaiming the message and exorcising demons. Jesus' fame spreads, but it also attracts the attention of the Jewish leaders who will begin to question him.

Preaching Points

Parish Masses

- Our Lord speaks his commands and illness is cured and unclean spirits are driven away. Jesus' command over nature and the supernatural clearly illustrates his identity.
- After being healed, Simon's mother-in-law served Jesus and his friends. How do we respond to Jesus' healing action in our own lives?
- Jesus' power is identifiable at all times, day and night. His ministry is real and touched actual people.
- Healing can come to God's people in many forms. Sometimes healing comes in unexpected ways.

Children's Liturgy of the Word

- We are called to respond to Jesus in our lives, just as Peter's mother-in-law responded to Jesus' action in her life.
- Jesus was able to speak life into hurting peoples' lives; his word and touch healed them.
- The healings described in the Bible are very specific healings for specific people. God still heals people today, but sometimes healing happens in ways we don't understand or ways we don't expect.

Missal Options

- Use the same form of the PA throughout these winter Sundays of OT.
- Sing or recite the Gloria and the Creed.
- Any of the eight Prefaces of the Sundays of OT may be selected today.
- Consider using EPVN-IV.
- Any OT Collect, except the prayer for today, may conclude the UP.
- There are six SBs for OT from which to choose. You may also select a PP.

Music Preparation

When selecting psalm settings, consider (a) how closely the text matches actual Scripture, and (b) how long the song is. Sometimes a beautiful setting may just be too much to use as the responsorial because it will overpower the other Scripture readings.

Music Suggestions

- Gathering: "Gather Your People" by Bob Hurd (OCP)
- Preparation of the Gifts: "There Is a Balm in Gilead" (various publishers)
- Communion: "Quietly, Peacefully" by Lorie True (GIA)
- Sending Forth: "Christ in Me Arise" by Trevor Thompson (OCP)

Mass Texts

Introduction to Mass

We come before the Lord bearing our many burdens and troubles. If we lay them down here at this altar, Christ will take them upon himself. Indeed, he will bear us in his arms and bind up our broken hearts and wounded souls. For this purpose he has come. Let him be your healing and nourish you with his sacred Body and Blood. *My brothers and sisters, let us acknowledge our sins, and so prepare ourselves to celebrate the sacred mysteries.*

Tropes for Penitential Act, Form III

We suffer, Lord, through our own sins: Lord, have mercy.

You are the physician of our souls: Christ, have mercy.

Your love cleanses us of all impurity: Lord, have mercy.

Dismissal for Children's Liturgy of the Word

My children, we hear in today's psalm that God has numbered all the stars and calls each of them by name. How much more does he know each of you and all the things that make you happy and sad? He speaks to each of you now in the Scriptures in ways that only he knows you need to hear. His love for you is greater than all the stars in the universe! Go now in that love.

Dismissal of Catechumens

Dear friends, we all know some degree of Job's experience: drudgery, restless nights, days that seem to pass without meaning or hope. Christ is God's promise of joy, peace, and the fulfillment of all our hopes. Seek him in the Scriptures and let them reveal to you how he is already present in your lives. We pray that he will bring you to union with us in faith, hope, and love. Go in peace.

Dismissal of Extraordinary Ministers of Holy Communion

My friends, we give you God's Word and Christ's Body to strengthen our sick and homebound brothers and sisters. Remind them that the Lord takes upon himself all their weakness in exchange for new life in the Holy Spirit, in whom they are one with us. Go in peace.

Universal Prayer

We are grateful for all that the Lord has bestowed on us and are cognizant of those who have less. We turn to the Lord with grateful hearts. Please respond, Lord, bless your people.

1. For the gift of the Church and her sacramental life, we pray:
2. For the gift of peace in our world, we pray:
3. For the gift of our families and all that they have done for us, we pray:
4. For the gift of employment and the ability to earn a living wage, we pray:
5. For the gift of healing for all the sick, we pray:
6. For the gift of our education and the ability to teach others, we pray:
7. For the gift of new life for our deceased relatives, we pray:

Loving Father,
you alone are the source of life,
and you abundantly bless your creation with
happiness and joy.
May we always turn to you in thanksgiving
for all that we are and all that we have received.
Through Christ our Lord.
Amen.

Other Rites and Customs

- Remind parishioners to bring their palms from last Palm Sunday to be burned for Ash Wednesday.
- Brush up on the rubrics for Holy Week utilizing LTP's *Guide for Celebrating Holy Week and the Triduum.*
- Since the readings today focus on healing, consider celebrating the Sacrament of Anointing of the Sick at one of the Masses today. Brush up on the rubrics for this ritual in LTP's *Guide for Celebrating the Pastoral Care of the Sick.*

Liturgy and Life

Job's hopelessness in today's First Reading may stir memories of our own moments of darkness or may remind us of so many others who suffer—from illness, poverty, or threat of violence. Jesus, who acted in the world as the Lord who heals the brokenhearted, showed us how he expects his disciples to care for people in need. More than twenty-one million refugees across the world must wonder, as Job did, if they will ever see happiness again. (Find the most current statistics from the United Nations High Commission on Refugees at http://www.unhcr.org/en-us/figures-at-a-glance.html.) Learn more about the plight of displaced people and the Church's response from the United States Conference of Catholic Bishops' Migration & Refugee Services: http://www.usccb.org/about/migration-and-refugee-services/. Become a regular donor to organizations that help refugees and learn how you might assist in resettling a family in your community.

Taking Place This Week . . .

Consider what can be done liturgically, catechetically, and ministerially to respond to these important needs.

- Today is the National Day of Prayer for the African American Family and Boy Scout Sunday.
- World Day of the Sick and International Day of Women and Girls in Science (2/11)
- Chinese or Lunar New Year (2/12)

M O N 8 LM #329 / LMC #193–232 / green
Weekday

Optional Memorials of St. Jerome Emiliani / white; St. Josephine Bakhita, Virgin / white

Scripture Insights

In the beginning, God created out of nothing. When we read from Genesis, we remember that God is the creator, and we are, and everything we see is, his creation. We realize the goodness of God's creation in Genesis; we hear that God found his creation to be good. How wonderful to live in the creation that God found to be good!

Preaching Points

Parish Masses

- When Jesus traveled during his ministry, the throngs of people followed him. People were so moved by faith in him that they touched just the fabric of his garments and were healed.
- The creator of the universe, God the Father, sent his only Son to live among us. When people touched Jesus' garment's edge, they touched the fabric of him who was sent by the creator of the universe. They are part of God's good creation, and God himself was moved to heal them.

Masses with Children

- People followed Jesus because they wanted to be near him and be healed by him. Jesus loved the people and was glad to help them.
- People in Jesus' time had no idea that, when they touched Jesus' garment, they were touching the garment of God himself. They desired to know God, and, in Jesus, they came to know him.

Missal Options

- Consider using the prayers from the Thirty-First Sunday in OT and EPVN-III.
- Use any of the three forms of the PA.
- Any of the eight Prefaces for OT or the six common Prefaces may be used.

Song of the Day

"Canticle of the Sun" by Marten Haugen (GIA)

Optional Memorial

St. Jerome Emiliani

St. Jerome Emiliani responded to famine and plague in his native city of Venice by founding hospitals, orphanages, and hostels. He fell ill and died while tending the sick with the religious community he founded in southern Italy.

- The readings may be taken from the SW, #529, LMC #257, CHMW (For Teachers), or CS (For Educators; LMC).
- Use the Collect from the PS; the other prayers may be taken from the CHMW (For Educators).
- Consider EP-I.
- Choose from P-I or P-II of Saints, or the Preface of Holy Virgins and Religious.

St. Josephine Bakhita

St. Josephine was abducted from her childhood home in Darfur to slavery in the Sudanese capital of Khartoum under a series of cruel owners. Eventually, she came into the keeping of an Italian family and claimed her freedom as a Canossian sister in Italy, where her holiness and kindness as porter endeared her to the local community.

- The readings may be taken from the SW, #529A (LS), or CV.
- There are no options in the LMC, although you could use those from the CS.
- Use the Collect from the PS; the other prayers may be taken from the CV (For One Virgin).
- Select from P-I or P-II of Saints, or the Preface of Holy Virgins and Religious and consider using EP-I.
- Use any OT Collect to conclude the UP.

Scripture Insights

Human beings are made in God's image and likeness yet struggle to treat one another with love and respect. When we treat each other badly, we are disrespecting other people who, like ourselves, are made in the image and likeness of God. When God created, he said that his creation is good, and we are called to recognize that goodness in one another.

Preaching Points

Parish Masses

- Humans are the crowning creation in God's earth. Made in God's own image, we are meant to be like him and be in relationship with him.
- Human beings were given responsibility for the earth. Fish, reptiles, and other mammals cannot care for creation or affect the earth the way humans can affect it. We must take responsibility for all that the creator has given us.
- Jesus taught people to be concerned with character rather than ritual cleanliness.

Masses with Children

- Human beings are the only part of God's creation to be made in his image and likeness and are the only ones meant to be like him.
- When God created the earth and created human beings, he desired for the people to care for his earthly creation.

Missal Options

- Consider using the prayers from the Seventeenth Sunday in OT and EP-IV with its proper preface.
- Use any of the three forms of the PA.
- Any of the eight Prefaces for OT or the six common Prefaces may be used if EP-IV is not prayed.

Song of the Day

"All the Ends of the Earth" by Robert J. Dufford, SJ (OCP)

WED 10

LM #331 or #530 / LMC #193–232 / white

Memorial of St. Scholastica, Virgin

Today's Saint

Knowing that she would die soon, St. Scholastica prayed up a literal storm to extend a visit with her brother, St. Benedict, by another night. St. Gregory wrote that God answered this prayer because, as God is love, "with good reason, she was more powerful who loved more."

Scripture Insights

Free will is a gift that God has given to each of his children. God has asked us to use our free will for obedience to him; we are called to obey his rules for us and to live lives of love and charity. God's rules for us are meant to lift us in goodness; living in this way is meant to bear good fruit.

Preaching Points

Parish Masses

- We are made in God's image and likeness and are made for relationship with him. We are supposed to be obedient to God and to resist sin. How do we help ourselves to grow in virtue so that we can resist sin?
- God has created the earth to serve humankind; the food we need can be grown in the soil, and the air we breathe has oxygen emitted from plants.
- Jesus affirmed the cleanliness of all foods. He taught that we should be concerned about how our behaviors should concern us more than the ritual cleanliness of foods.

Masses with Children

- What does it mean to be obedient to God if we can't hear him talking to us? We are called to be obedient to God's Word and the teachings of the Church.
- God made the earth's systems to serve people; the food we need can be grown in the soil, and the air we breathe has oxygen emitted from plants.
- Jesus taught that eating certain foods would not make people unclean but that what we do and say in life should be a bigger concern.

Scripture Insights *(PS)*

Love is more powerful than death: love comes first.

Preaching Points

Parish Masses

- The Song of Songs is a love song—but this is not sentimental love. This love is an unquenchable fire, more powerful than death, a free gift. This is God's love for us, and the image of how we are to love each other.
- Like Martha, our lives are often full and busy—perhaps too busy. We all need to make time to be Mary, to do nothing but be in the presence of the Lord and bask in the love that is stronger than death itself.

Masses with Children

- Today's First Reading is a love song. It's not about love between husband and wife, though, but about God's love. God's love is so great that it's more powerful than sadness or death. And it's a free, unconditional love! It's his gift to us! How we love others is supposed to model how God loves us.

Missal Options

- The readings may also be from the CV, CHMW (For Religious), LMC #258, or the CS (For Religious; LWC)
- Use the Collect from the PS; the other prayers may be taken from the CV (For One Virgin) or CHMW (For a Nun).
- Use any of the three forms of the PA.
- Select from P-I or P-II of Saints, or the Preface of Holy Virgins and Religious.
- Consider EP-II.
- Use any OT Collect to conclude the UP.

Song of the Day

"Praise, My Soul, the King of Heaven" (various publishers)

THU 11 LM #332 / LMC #193–232 / green
Weekday

Optional Memorial of Our Lady of Lourdes / white

Scripture Insights

The Blessed Trinity is three persons in one God; the members of the Trinity live in relationship with one another. We are made in God's image, and many of us are called to live in a Marriage relationship. Within Marriage, people are called to live out the love of God in relationship to one another.

Preaching Points

Parish Masses

- Two creation accounts are found in Genesis, and both teach different lessons. In today's reading we learn about God's gift of companionship and marriage.
- Jesus' message was not meant only for the Jewish people; those from other lands and even other religions would look to his teaching.

Masses with Children

- There are two creation stories in Genesis, and we can learn different lessons by listening to each story. Today's reading tells us about marriage and people living in relationship to one another.
- Jesus was a Jewish man who grew up in a Jewish family. His coming was promised by God through the Jewish tradition. His words and his mission to earth are events meant for all people, Jewish and Gentile.

Missal Options

- Consider using the prayers from the Mass for Various Needs and Occasions #18 and EPR-II.
- Use any of the three forms of the PA.
- Any of the eight Prefaces for OT or the six common Prefaces may be used.

Song of the Day

"*O Sanctissima*/O Most Holy One" (various publishers)

Optional Memorial

Today's memorial recognizes the apparitions of the Blessed Virgin to St. Bernadette Soubirous, a young peasant girl who, although not known for great intellect, was able to articulate the Virgin as "The Immaculate Conception," thus giving credibility to her experience.

- The readings for Our Lady of Lourdes may be taken from the SW, #531, LMC #259, CBVM, or CMML.
- Use the Collect from the PS; the other prayers may be taken from the CBVM or CMMM.
- Select from P-I or P-II of the BVM.
- You might use the ritual Mass for the Sick.
- Any OT Collect may conclude the UP.
- You might use any SB for OT, a PP, or the SB for the BVM.

FRI 12 LM #333 / LMC #193–232 / green
Weekday

Scripture Insights

Through their sin, Adam's and Eve's eyes were opened to their nakedness, but the deaf man's ears were opened through Jesus' goodness. The deaf man recognized Jesus' holy ability and submitted himself to Jesus. We too are called to follow Jesus.

Preaching Points

Parish Masses

- Sin doesn't always look ugly or distasteful; indeed, Eve found that the fruit appeared attractive, as did the idea of having knowledge. We must be aware of sin that is a wolf in sheep's clothing.
- Adam and Eve had the gift of free will; they were able to choose obedience or disobedience.

Masses with Children

- Sin can be sneaky—it doesn't always look bad. In fact, sometimes sin can look like a lot of fun. God wants us to recognize sin and reject it.
- Free will is something God gives each of us. Having free will means that God doesn't make our choices for us, it means that we make our own choices. God wants us to use our free will for good.

Missal Options

- Consider using the prayers from the Eighteenth Sunday in OT and EP-III.
- Use any of the three forms of the PA.
- Any of the eight Prefaces for OT or the six common Prefaces may be used.

Song of the Day

"Open My Eyes" by Jesse Manibusan (OCP)

SAT 13 LM #334 / LMC #193–232 / green
Weekday

Optional Memorial of the Blessed Virgin Mary / white

Scripture Insights

Through Jesus, we understand the miracle of the loaves and the fish; people ate gladly and fared well as their food came with a blessing. Adam and Eve ate from that which was forbidden and suffered banishment as a result.

Preaching Points

Parish Masses

- The Genesis reading is about the fall of humankind; humans lived in unadulterated relationship with God, but after sin entered the world, the relationship was damaged.
- The loaves and the fishes are a foreshadowing of the Eucharist; in the Eucharist we consume the saving Christ. The Eucharist is that which feeds us, because Christ repairs the rift between humankind and God.

Masses with Children

- Before sin, Adam and Eve lived in happy and close relationship with God. When they sinned, that relationship was damaged.
- The damaged relationship required repair, which is why Jesus would someday come to earth. When we hear about the loaves and the fishes, we are reminded of the Eucharist. By eating the forbidden fruit, Adam and Eve sinned. By consuming Christ in the Eucharist, we are obeying God.

Missal Options

- Consider using the prayers from the Mass for Various Needs and Occasions #18B and EP-II.
- Use any of the three forms of the PA.
- Any of the eight Prefaces for OT or the six common Prefaces may be used.

Song of the Day

"In Every Age" by Janét Sullivan Whitaker (OCP) or "O God, Our Help in Ages Past" (various publishers)

Optional Memorial

- Saturdays in OT that are not assigned an obligatory observance may be celebrated as a Memorial of the Blessed Virgin Mary.
- The readings may be taken from the SW, CBVM, or CMML. The prayer texts may be taken from the CBVM or CMML. You may also use the various Votive Masses for the BVM.
- Use either of the Prefaces for the BVM.

Something to Consider...

◈ The World Day of the Sick occurred this past week. How are you including the sick and homebound in parish life?

◈ What outreach opportunities do you provide?

S U N **14** LM #77B / LMC #72B / green
Sixth Sunday in Ordinary Time

Scripture Insights

For lepers, the law of Leviticus must have seemed very harsh. They could not live in the camp with anyone. They had to warn people that they were coming. Actually, any skin disease was considered leprosy unless proven otherwise. The Book of Leviticus devotes two chapters (13 and 14) to laws requiring a period of separation and examination before anyone with a skin lesion is allowed back into the camp. Leprosy was worse than other ailments because the opening on the skin often exposed blood, the source of life, and any contact with blood made a person unclean.

Every Jew reading Mark's account of the Gospel would have been familiar with the laws regarding leprosy. When Jesus touched the leper to heal him, Jews collectively gasped. Not even the prophet Elisha (2 Kings 5) cured a leper this way. Touching the leper made Jesus unclean, yet neither he nor Mark seem concerned. The encounter with the leper again shows Jesus confronting the conditions that separate people from each other. The possessed man was disturbed and frightening; Peter's mother-in-law could not fulfill her place in the family; the leper is alienated by the unclean nature of his disease. In each case, by word or touch, Jesus restores the person to the family and the community.

Mark adds two interesting details to this story. First, Jesus is "moved with pity" for the man. Mark, who tells the story of Jesus more simply than the other Gospels, describes Jesus' emotional state. This makes Mark's portrayal of Jesus very human. But he also emphasizes the healing power of Jesus to show his divine identity. Second, as he did with the demons, Jesus urges the leper to tell no one. Jesus did not want followers based solely on his ability to heal. If we were to hear all of verse 45 in this reading, we would understand what Jesus feared. He is no longer able to move about openly because people flock to him seeking healing. In the face of their preoccupation with physical healing, his message may well be lost.

Preaching Points

Parish Masses

- We are called to live in imitation of our Lord. What does this mean for our own lives, and how is society transformed when we live this calling?
- Jesus reached out to those on the fringes of society. How do we, in imitation of him, reach out to those on the margins?
- When Jesus healed people, they were able to return to the normal function of family and community lives. What drives people from their communities today?
- Jesus desired for his followers to know him for more than healing and miracles; that is why he would say, "tell nobody."

Children's Liturgy of the Word

- People on the margins are those who don't participate fully in the life of their community. Who are those people today, and how can we reach out to them?
- In Jesus' time, those with leprosy were not allowed near the healthy community. Jesus' healing gave a leper his life back again; the priests would let him return home. Jesus' healing was of body, soul, and community.
- Jesus desired for his followers to know him for more than healing and miracles; that is why he would say, "tell nobody."

Missal Options

- Continue to use the same form of the PA you have been using on these winter Sundays of OT.
- Sing or recite the Gloria and the Creed.
- Any of the eight Prefaces of the Sundays of OT may be selected today.
- Consider using EPR-II.
- There are six SBs for OT from which to choose. You may also select a PP.

Music Preparation

- Musical selections should convey heartfelt humanity and brokenness and the need for God.

Music Suggestions

- Gathering or Sending Forth: "I Heard the Voice of Jesus Say" (various publishers)
- Preparation of the Gifts: "Be with Me Lord" by Tom Booth (OCP)
- Communion: "Create in Me" by Bob Hurd (OCP) or "Be Still, My Soul" (finalandia)

Mass Texts

Introduction to Mass

No matter the extent or the number of our sins, the Lord Jesus wills to make us clean. No matter how much society judges us to be an outcast, repugnant, or simply different, Christ, in his compassion and love, comes close to us and touches us. Let us then proclaim his goodness to the world, finding strength to do so in his Body and Blood, which we receive at this altar. *My brothers and sisters, let us acknowledge our sins, and so prepare ourselves to celebrate the sacred mysteries.*

Tropes for Penitential Act, Form III

To you, O Lord, we acknowledge our sins: Lord, have mercy.

You have power to make us clean: Christ, have mercy.

You fill us with the joy of salvation: Lord, have mercy.

Dismissal for Children's Liturgy of the Word

Dear children, St. Paul tells us, in so many words, to be imitators of Christ. As you listen to today's readings, think how you might be more like Jesus. Who are the people in your life that are in need of a little love, and how might you treat them as Jesus would? Let the Scriptures guide you, and ask Jesus himself to help you imitate him. Go in peace.

Dismissal of Catechumens

Friends, regardless of our past deeds, or perhaps because of them, Christ calls us to himself for healing and new life. As you reflect on today's readings, seek him with boldness and confidence in his mercy. We pray that mercy of his will bring you to full communion with us in the celebration of the Eucharist. Go in peace.

Dismissal of Extraordinary Ministers of Holy Communion

My friends, the Lord is moved with pity for the sick and the weak, the elderly and the infirm. Therefore take to them Christ's Body, that he may touch their souls and be one with them in their suffering. Remind them, too, that they remain one with us in giving glory to God.

Universal Prayer

The Lord has pity on us and makes us clean. We believe that he restores all of creation and so we turn to him with our prayers for the needs of all the world.

1. For the Church, especially in her ministry of Anointing the Sick and reconciling sinners, we pray:
2. For the outcasts of our society, especially those who are afflicted by terminal diseases and those who are poor and homeless, we pray:
3. For the prophets in our midst who call our attention to injustice, we pray:
4. For all the sick and for those who care for the sick, especially for those in hospitals and nursing homes, we pray:
5. For the dying, especially those who face death alone with no one at their side, we pray:

Lord of all kindliness,
your Son, our Lord Jesus Christ,
healed the leper and restored him to relationship
with others.
Turn our attention to those in our midst
in most need of your healing,
and give us the desire to make them one with us again.
Make this world know the power of your gentle care.
Through Christ our Lord.
Amen.

Other Rites and Customs

- Sing lots of Alleluias this weekend too since we won't be hearing them until the Easter Vigil.
- Bid farewell to the Alleluia by burying it after Mass. Although the Church does not provide an "official" ritual for this custom, you might look to LTP's *Guide for Celebrating Holy Week and the Triduum* for guidance on preparing this paraliturgy.
- Be sure to advertise the Ash Wednesday schedule and remind parishioners that Wednesday is a day of fasting and abstinence.
- Have a Mardi Gras celebration and include a palm burning ceremony. Although there is also no "official" ritual for this custom, you may also look to LTP's *Guide for Celebrating Holy Week and the Triduum* for preparing this paraliturgy.

Liturgy and Life

Imagine the feelings of the leper in the Gospel reading—disfigured by his illness, rejected by his family, banished from the community—a physical, social, cultural, and religious outcast. Today throughout the world there are orphaned, abandoned, and neglected children with the same feelings—some handicapped, hearing-impaired, or blind. They too wait for the healing touch of Jesus. In India, Northeast Africa, Eastern Europe, and the Middle East, the Catholic Near East Welfare Association provides the means necessary to shelter, feed, clothe, and school these children. Through a person-to-person child sponsorship program, a benefactor can contribute to the support of an individual child. Visit the Website (www.cnewa.org) to find out how you might become the healing touch of Jesus for a needy child.

Taking Place This Week . . .

Consider what can be done liturgically, catechetically, and ministerially to respond to these important needs.

- Valentine's Day is on 2/14.
- Today is World Marriage Day.
- Presidents' Day, Rose Monday, and National Flag of Canada Day (2/15)
- In preparation for Lent, today is Carnival, Monday is Rose Monday, and Tuesday is Mardis Gras or Shrove Tuesday.
- Ash Wednesday is 2/17; the special collection is for Aid to the Church in Central and Eastern Europe. Catholic Relief Services' Rice Bowl takes place throughout Lent. Check out their app for donations: https://www.crsricebowl.org/.
- World Day of Social Justice (2/20)

MON 15 LM #335 / LMC #193–232 / green
Weekday

Scripture Insights

Murder is an evil that has been in our world since the dawn of humanity. We are called to protect human life from conception to a natural death. Support young single mothers, support women facing violence, and care for the elderly and sick whose lives are coming to an end.

Preaching Points

Parish Masses

- Cain killed Abel in jealousy and anger, and we hear about God's punishment for such an act. We are called to always protect human life, because it is right and good to protect those who cannot protect themselves.
- Jesus preached about people wanting signs. Instead of seeking signs, the people should have looked to Jesus, who was God standing before them.

Masses with Children

- Murder is wrong. God calls his people to protect life and not take lives.
- Sometimes people look for signs of God's presence; sometimes they see what they think are signs and believe that it was from God. Instead of looking for signs, the people could have looked at God standing before them in the person Jesus.

Missal Options

- Consider using the prayers from the Sixteenth Sunday in OT and EP-I.
- Use any of the three forms of the PA.
- Any of the eight Prefaces for OT or the six common Prefaces may be used.

Song of the Day

"There Is a Longing" by Anne Quigley (OCP)

TUE 16 LM #336 / LMC #193–232 / green
Weekday

Scripture Insights

God desires for his people to follow his laws and to live out his teachings. In Genesis, we hear about Noah's ark, which God told him to build in anticipation of the flood. This flood was meant to cleanse the earth of the wrongdoers.

Preaching Points

Parish Masses

- We should not listen to wicked words or teachings such as that which Herod and the Pharisees gave the people. We must look to Jesus and his message to find what is right and good.
- The Apostles did not always understand Jesus' words; frequently the Lord had to explain his ways more clearly. We must look to Jesus' teachings and do our best to follow them.

Masses with Children

- In every age, there are people who share false teaching instead of truth. In Jesus' time, some of these people were Herod and the Pharisees.
- The Apostles did not always understand Jesus' words; frequently the Lord had to explain his ways more clearly. We must look to Jesus' teachings and do our best to follow them.

Missal Options

- Consider using the prayers from the First Week in OT and EP-II.
- Use any of the three forms of the PA.
- Any of the eight Prefaces for OT or the six common Prefaces may be used.

Song of the Day

"'Tis the Gift to Be Simple" by Joyce Merman (various publishers); sing verses 2 and 3.

Lent and Holy Week

For you have given your children a sacred time for the renewing and purifying of their hearts, that, freed from disordered affections, they may so deal with the things of this passing world as to hold rather to the things that eternally endure.

—Preface II of Lent

The Meaning of the Season

As he traces the historical development of Lent, Patrick O'Regan, OSB, notes that, for Christians of the fourth and fifth centuries, Lent's "purpose and character" were "entirely derived from the great festival for which it prepares . . . the yearly reminder of their own incorporation into the paschal event through baptism" ("The Three Days and the Forty Days" in *Between Memory and Hope*, ed. Johnson, p. 129).

Lent cannot be separated from Easter—not then and not now. Just as it was for the early Christians, it is a time for us to prepare our hearts and reflect more deeply on our baptismal call to continuing conversion. This call to conversion is at the forefront of Lent from the first day of the season. On Ash Wednesday, people flock to churches to receive ashes and to be told, "Remember that you are dust and to dust you shall return" or "Repent, and believe in the Gospel." These two formulas for the imposition of ashes offer insight into the meaning of this season. The first formula is a *memento mori*, a remembrance of death. Even in our world, where rituals surrounding death are increasingly sanitized and privatized, this formula reminds that the reality of death is undeniable. The second formula is a call to repentance—urging us to turn away from sin and toward the Good News.

Both of these formulas also invite us to deeper meditation on our Baptism and the Paschal Mystery. The first tells us that we shall die and return to dust, but we already know that we need not fear death. After all, we have already been "buried with Christ in the death of baptism" so that we may "rise also with him to newness of life" (RCIA, 222). The second echoes the message of John the Baptist, who spent his ministry "proclaiming a baptism of repentance for the forgiveness of sins" (Luke 3:3).

The First Reading for Ash Wednesday (Joel 2:12–18) lays out what we are to do to repent of our sins—and the list has not changed much in the intervening millennia. The Book of Joel is not prominent in the Lectionary, as its readings appear only a few times besides Ash Wednesday. On Ash Wednesday, though, its seven verses speak with a prophetic clarity that resounds anew each year. It tells us what to do: to bring all of the people together and return to God with our whole heart, with fasting, weeping, and mourning.

God's grace and mercy are manifest in the Sacrament of Baptism. Immediately following their Baptism, children are told that God "has freed you from sin, / given you new birth by water and the Holy Spirit," (OBC, 62). During the Lenten season, those adults who are preparing for their own Baptism participate in a preparatory period that is "part of the distinctive character of Lent" (RCIA, 126). At the parish level, there is a Rite of Sending on the First Sunday before the diocesan Rite of Election; three Scrutinies on the Third, Fourth, and Fifth Sundays, and the Presentations of the Creed and the Lord's Prayer. Celebrating these rites is essential because they "renew the entire community" by encouraging all—baptized and not yet baptized—to make Lent "a time for spiritual recollection in preparation for the celebration of the paschal mystery" (RCIA, 138). While the elect are preparing for their own Baptism, those who have already been baptized are preparing themselves "through a spirit of repentance for the renewal of their baptismal promises" (CB, 249).

Regardless of whether any adults will be initiated during the Easter Vigil, Lent is a busy season in most communities. The Masses of the season themselves emphasize "the baptismal and penitential aspects of Lent," but parishes do much else to ensure that Lent "disposes the faithful . . . to celebrate the paschal mystery" (CSL, 109). They hold missions, provide daily devotional booklets (or emails or text messages), celebrate the Liturgy of the Hours, offer additional weekday Masses, communally celebrate the Sacrament of Reconciliation, increase the number of other opportunities for individual Reconciliation, pray the Stations of the Cross, sponsor service projects, and share meals from simple soup suppers to elaborate fish fries. All of these practices demonstrate that while we are urged to the three traditional Lenten practices—prayer, fasting, and almsgiving—together we heed the message from the Ash Wednesday Gospel (Matthew 6:1–6, 16–18) by not doing so in an individualistic, self-aggrandizing, or gloomy way. And all of these practices are the ways in which the baptized prepare to renew their baptismal promises at Easter.

With the notable exceptions of the Solemnities of St. Joseph and the Annunciation, Lent is a series of seasonal weekdays, with Gospel readings predominantly from Matthew and Luke early in the season and John later in the season. The season reaches its end with Palm Sunday and the first days of Holy Week.

The Palm Sunday Mass begins in glorious triumph but quickly changes tone and directs our attention to the cross. An exuberant procession with palms yields to a Collect that reminds us that God "as an example of humility . . . caused our Savior to take flesh and submit to the Cross," while the readings and prayers for the Mass emphasize his self-emptying. The Second Reading (Philippians 2:6–11) and the Gospel Acclamation verse recall that he "became obedient to the point of death, even death on a Cross," and the Preface for the Passion of the Lord tells that, "though innocent, he suffered willingly for sinners." The first weekdays of Holy Week—which feature violet vestments, prayers alluding to the passion and the cross, and readings focusing on Christ as Servant—are the final period of preparation for the upcoming mysteries of the Triduum.

In his 2015 Palm Sunday homily, Pope Francis urged us to remember that God's way is humility, "a way which constantly amazes and disturbs us." As disciples of Christ, then, we too must humble ourselves, "making room for God by stripping oneself, emptying oneself." Doing so is essential as we prepare to celebrate Holy Week, because "only in this way will this week be 'holy' for us too." The Lenten season is indeed a time for us to grow in humility. In Preface III of Lent, we praise God in these words: "For you will that our self-denial should give you thanks, humble our sinful pride, contribute to the feeding of the poor, and so help us imitate you in your kindness." Every Lent, as we deny ourselves, repent of our own sinfulness, and recall our Baptism, we open ourselves anew to the power of God's healing, transformative grace.

The Sounds of the Season

One of the guiding musical principles for Lent is the limited use of instrumentation (see GIRM, 313). This can be challenging for many parishes but it can often be rewarding and beautiful. Perhaps this is the time to implement the Introits and Communion Antiphons of the Missal. Resources abound from the Latin *Graduale Simplex* to collections by Columba Kelly, OSB (OCP), Paul Ford (*By Flowing Waters*, Liturgical Press), Adam Bartlett (www.musicasacra.com), Charles Thatcher (*Eleven Communion Chants for Lent, Triduum and the Easter Season*, WLP, #e05286), or Richard Clark (WLP, #005322) to more contemporary settings such as those by Paul Tate ("In the Shadow of God," GIA). "Attende Domine" (Mode V), "Ubi Caritas" (Mode VI) and "Parce, Domine" (Mode I) are annual Lenten favorites with simple refrains that can be sung a cappella. They can be sung either in Latin or in a mix of English and Latin (refrain in Latin, verses in English). Taizé offers gems such as "Domine Deus," "Salvator Mundi" and "Benedictus Qui Venit," which have found their way into many parish repertoires.

Lent encourages each of us to retreat and reflect and bask in silence. This is a good reminder that the liturgy also calls for silence. *Sing to the Lord* reminds us of the importance of incorporating silence in the liturgy:

> Music arises out of silence and returns to silence. God is revealed both in the beauty of song and in the power of silence. The Sacred Liturgy has its rhythm of texts, actions, songs and silence. Silence in the Liturgy allows the community to reflect on what it has heard and experienced, and to open its heart to the mystery celebrated. Ministers and pastoral musicians should take care that the rites unfold with the proper ebb and flow of sound and silence. The importance of silence in the Liturgy cannot be overemphasized. (118)

We have the ability to create beautiful and meaningful music as well as foster moments of silence. Perhaps we can all make an effort to be more purposeful and intentional in when we begin our liturgical and ritual music.

The season of Lent provides opportunities for liturgies other than the celebration of the Eucharist: Stations of the Cross, various Christian initiation rituals, communal Penance (Reconciliation) services, Morning Prayer, Evening Prayer, and Taizé prayer are just a few services and liturgies you may be asked to coordinate. Space does not allow us to tackle each one individually, but keep in mind that we are not reinventing the wheel. Somewhere, someone has been engaged in a liturgy similar to what you have been charged with preparing. Contact your local cathedral or Office for Worship, or refer to ChoralWiki (www.cpdl.org), canticanova.com, the preparing pages of the NPM website (www.npm.org), or Google to get ideas, suggestions, and recommendations. You could even use social media, such as Facebook. An important note is that the Gloria, mostly suspended during Lent, is prescribed for ritual Masses celebrated during Lent. This includes weddings and Confirmations. Keep the settings simple and not overly festive.

The Look of the Season

The whole Church goes on retreat for the forty days of Lent. Within the ecclesial community two groups embark on their Lenten journey: the catechumens who are preparing for the Sacraments of Initiation at Easter and those already baptized who are preparing to renew their baptismal identity at the same time. These two groups are intimately connected in this spiritual journey, walking together with the Lord toward the profound joy of Easter.

The liturgical environment for the season of Lent finds its inspiration in this spiritual character of the Church's tradition. The rich images from the narratives of Scripture, the Lenten devotions and practices of penitence, the rites that accompany the catechumens, the prayer texts of the Eucharist, and the chants of the Sunday celebrations all inform the liturgical environment.

The liturgical environment then becomes one of the texts of the liturgy. Through the use of color and texture, arrangements and objects, the liturgical environment enhances the physical space and helps the community. If the invitation to the waters of Baptism is the central focus for the catechumens, and the renewal of baptismal promises is a primary intention for the baptized, the baptismal font deserves particular attention within the liturgical environment.

To allow the baptized faithful and catechumens preparing for Baptism to reflect on the meaning of the sacrament, keep the font filled with water throughout the days of Lent. The practice of removing the water from the font during Lent is neither advisable nor appropriate. Even less laudable is the trend to turn the font into a sandbox or desert landscape. The font is first and always a font, and its purpose is to hold water. The catechumens are called to the waters of the font, not to an empty vessel. The font contains the water that signifies our dying and rising with Christ. The water of the font invites those already baptized to recall their baptismal identity as followers of Christ; the water of the font is a sacramental symbol. We do not fast from this fundamental act of faith or the gesture that accompanies it. In fact, the baptized should be even more attentive to the gesture of blessing with water from the font during Lent.

By incorporating the font in the arrangement of the liturgical space, and by making frequent references to their significance both for those approaching the sacraments of initiation and for those already baptized, the liturgical environment becomes an important source for the spiritual journey for the whole ecclesial community.

Evangelizing the Parish through the Season

At the beginning of Lent, we receive ashes, the ancient sign of sorrow, and hear one of two calls to repentance: "Remember that you are dust, and to dust you shall return," or "Repent, and believe in the Gospel" (*The Roman Missal*, Distribution of Ashes). This call to self-knowledge, repentance, and belief is the axis around which Lent revolves. We prepare to celebrate the Lord's Paschal Mystery by preparing to receive it as the entirely unearned gift that it is. Our preparations will not change the fact that we will "return to dust." Nor will they let us earn a place in God's Kingdom as something we deserve. The Christian life is a life of repentance.

And yet, precisely because of this, Lent is a season of joy. We are freed from the impossible task of saving ourselves. The English-speaking Church has a unique reason to notice this character of the season. In most other languages, the word used for Lent means something like "the time of fasting" or simply "the forty days." But the etymology of lent comes from a word related to "lengthen." This is the season in which the days are lengthening and light is returning. In a word, spring. But it's more than this. When we come to new honesty about ourselves and repent, we are freed to trust in God's mercy. No longer having to justify ourselves, we are freed for the task of learning to live what God desires for us. In this sense, Lent is the time for stretching out, pushing forward, striving to follow Christ.

And if this is our goal, then we can have nowhere better to look than the epistle to the Philippians. Paul tells that Church to "have among yourselves the same attitude that is also yours in Christ Jesus" (2:5). This attitude does not grasp for glory but empties itself for others. It stretches out to follow Christ in service and shines "like lights in the world" (2:15). The Church's work of evangelization lies precisely in this work. Not only each of the baptized, but parishes, dioceses, and the whole Church need to do the hard work of coming to deeper honesty about themselves and their service of the Gospel. The honest, repentant Church is freed to live out Christ's life because it has given up its own. And Christ's life shines in the darkness, as a beacon of hope and freedom. It is this light that the nations are waiting for and that the Church prepares to receive anew at the Easter Vigil.

Worship Committee Agenda for Lent

Meeting Time

Members of the committee should begin to meet in late December to prepare the parish liturgies for Lent and Holy Week.

Goal for Meeting

- Anticipate Ash Wednesday and prepare for this day and evening in the parish: liturgy, art and environment, Penance services, opportunities for devotional prayer.
- Create a calendar for all Lenten activities.
- Consider, then determine, what time of the day might be convenient for people to attend the Lenten events. Ask: Are there "carpool parents" who might arrive a half-hour early and appreciate praying the Stations of the Cross together? How do you welcome parents of young children who could come in the daytime, if child care was offered, for Lenten Bible study? Is there interest in a one-, two- or three-day parish mission with a guest speaker? Lent is a perfect time to introduce the Liturgy of the Hours to the parish; it can be lay-led and scheduled at a time when people may want to pray intentionally: very early morning en route to the workplace, or in the evening to place the night's rest into the hands of God. Challenge the creative vision of the committee!

Opening Prayer

Sing and pray the text of "Christ, Be Our Light" (©1993, 2000, Bernadette Farrell, OCP) together, using a YouTube accompaniment or a parish musician. This song is published in English and in Spanish.

Seasonal Questions and Initiatives

- Lent is ordered to prepare for Easter and the great Fifty Days. How will the seasonal environment be arranged to reflect the penitential nature of the season? If a wedding occurs during Lent, who will arrange for an alternate place for photos to be taken, without disturbing the signs and symbols of Lent in the worship space?
- Is there signage on the church property and communication on the website so that parish members, visitors, and guests are welcomed to Lenten liturgies (and any Lenten fellowship offered by the parish)?
- In what ways can the RCIA process be supported by the worship committee? Does the RCIA team need an evening off (replaced by a worship committee member) or a simple supper? Make certain that the parish "gets a good look" at those to be fully initiated at the Easter Vigil: make plans to publish photos, ask for extra prayer for them, accompany them (or offer to drive, if a distance) to the Rite of Election.
- Read about the Liturgy of the Hours, in the Lent section of *Sourcebook*. This season is a fine time to introduce a basic celebration of Morning Prayer or Evening Prayer, depending on the time that is convenient to parish members. Encourage families to attend, so perhaps you move Evening Prayer to just after the supper hour.
- Review a copy and consider using *What Am I Doing for Lent?* (LTP, published in both Spanish and in English) as a parish bulletin insert, or mail to families along with the Lenten schedule. Discounts are available for purchasing in quantities.
- Review the archive for *Pastoral Liturgy* magazine https://pastoralliturgy.org and determine which Sundays to use bilingual bulletin inserts. Decide if some articles might be reproduced on the parish website.

Liturgical Catechesis for the Assembly

- This year, publish a "vocabulary list" or glossary for the parish: If the catechumens attend the same Sunday celebration each week, so that not every member of the parish sees or is aware of them, then provide a (perhaps downloadable) file of the key words for the RCIA process so the rest of the parish becomes familiar with it. Many parishioners might not be knowledgeable about the Rite of Election, especially the scrutinies. Guide the parishioners to understand what the Church asks, and accomplishes, in these important rites.
- Use social media to share the Rite of Election and the Scrutinies at your parish.
- As Lent begins, ask the congregation if there are any persons who may have missed receiving the Sacrament of Confirmation, and welcome them to some preparation sessions during Lent. Perhaps they will experience the Stations of the Cross as a group, or do a service project together, allowing time for "basic mystagogy" after the experience. Preparation of this type always presumes that these Catholics are already catechized by regular attendance at the Sunday Mass.
- Put all the catechists and families in touch with Lent and Easter: review Keeping the Seasons for Lent and Easter 2021 (LTP), a bilingual print and digital resource for the entire parish.

Closing Prayer

Use the *Book of Blessings* (1690 and 1691) and pray the Intercessions, reciting together the Litany of St. Joseph (his solemnity takes place in Lent). Have cookies in the center of the table, and conclude with the Prayer of Blessing (1693) before passing the bowl so that each person may select a simple snack as they leave.

WED 17 LM #219 / LMC #176–184 / violet
Ash Wednesday

About Today's Liturgy

"Rend your hearts, not your garments," proclaims the Lord to the assembly gathered before him. As intensely personal as Lent is—with its core disciplines of fasting, prayer, and almsgiving—it is a time of preparing a people worthy of the Lord's special care. As much as we must work on our individual hearts, Lent is also a time when we must work on the heart of the community, calling it to a change of life. How might you make a resolution to change something in the Christian community in which you assemble?

Scripture Insights

Joel prophesied during a terrible crisis: huge swarms of locusts were devouring crops. There was so little food that people couldn't bring their offerings to God in the Temple. The prophet urges people to leave whatever they're doing in order to meet in one great assembly and cry out to God for help. Young and old, rich and poor, priests and laity—all must gather to beg God to deliver them from disaster.

St. Paul also insists that the time to act is now. God reconciled the world to himself through Christ. God sent Paul and others to share the news that God has made people righteous, although, sadly, people can reject this gift. When we accept God's gift of salvation, we not only are saved from sin but also become ministers of reconciliation ourselves. If we have truly embraced God's reconciliation, then we will live it. We will be patient, forgiving, and peaceful.

Jesus likewise assumes that those who follow him will act uprightly and continue the traditional practices of prayer, fasting, and almsgiving. People who turn these private acts into public ones have received a reward in the form of public recognition. Our own prayer, fasting, and almsgiving should be done only for God to see because they express and strengthen our relationship with God. We give alms as a symbol of all that God has given us. We fast because we hunger for God, and we don't look gloomy about it because we aren't gloomy! We are living for God.

These readings send us into Lent mindful of the urgency of strengthening our relationship with God. Although we are to be discreet in our acts of piety, we must be bold in our love for others so that all will know that the day of salvation has come and the time to enter it is now.

Preaching Points

Parish Masses

- We like to be rewarded for our efforts. We exercise to stay fit, and we diet to lose weight. If these do not achieve our goal, we are frustrated. The disciplines of the spiritual life—prayer, fasting, and good works—have a reward too. This reward might be a deeper relationship with God, greater clarity of mind, or an appreciation of the plight of the poor. Self-congratulation or ostentation is not among the intended rewards. There is no spiritual fruit to showy piety. We receive only what we have sought, if that.
- Each year as we begin a season when many make (often public) resolutions to deny themselves of favorite foods or TV programs or to adopt some practice of prayer, we hear this Gospel that warns of the dangers of hypocrisy and of public shows of piety. If that's your motive, you've already got your reward, so don't expect a thing from God. Such dangers are real, and so is the damage they do. But if your motives are pure, keep your goodness to yourself. God will know. And that will be enough.

Masses with Children

- We give up things and spend more time praying or reading the Bible during Lent. By giving up something or spending more time praying with your family, you are following in Jesus' example of loving God and loving others.
- We do not do these things to show off or so that we can say we are better than someone else. Instead, we do them because God asks us to so that we have more room in our lives to love him. By doing them, we become better followers of Jesus.

Missal Options

- Mass texts are found in the PT for Lent.
- The ashes that are blessed and distributed today are "made from olive branches or branches from other trees [palms] that were blessed the previous year" (RM).
- The PA is omitted and replaced with the blessing and distribution of ashes.
- The Gloria and the Creed are not sung (or said).
- The blessing and distribution of ashes takes place after the homily. Use the texts found in the RM rather than the older translation from the BB. Ministers should commit to memory the texts that are used when distributing ashes ("Repent, and believe in the Gospel" and "Remember that you are dust, and to dust you shall return.")
- Music may be sung while people receive ashes.
- The UP is said after ashes have been distributed. Any Lenten Collect (except for today's) may be used to conclude the prayer.
- Use P-III or P-IV of Lent.
- Consider using the EPR-I.
- The PP is found on the pages in the RM for Ash Wednesday.

Music Preparation

- Consider using traditional chant settings from the RM for the Lenten season.
- Are extra ministers necessary to help distribute ashes today? Make sure their instructions are clear for them.
- If you sang music during the ashes, choose silence or instrumental for preparation.
- The music for Ash Wednesday need not be elaborate. Instead, think of ways to simplify the music and strip away the excess. Use the antiphon of the Responsorial Psalm again during the distribution of the ashes or during Holy Communion. Rather than begin with a strophic hymn, use a Taizé-like refrain as the Entrance song to mark the distinctive nature of Lent.

Music Suggestions

- Entrance: "Litany for the Season of Lent" by Richard Proulx (WLP) or "From Ashes to the Living Font" by Alan J. Hommerding (WLP)
- Sending Forth: "Again We Keep This Solemn Fast" (various publishers)
- Placing of Ashes: "Hold Us in Your Mercy: Penitential Litany" by Rory Cooney (GIA)

Other Rites and Customs

- On Ash Wednesday and every Friday during Lent, Catholics are asked to fast from eating meat. In the dioceses of the United States, Catholics are obliged to refrain from eating meat on every Friday of the year unless he or she substitutes this practice with another act of penance (see the 1966 USCCB document, *Pastoral Statement on Penance and Abstinence*).
- Hopefully, a visit can be scheduled to all the sick and homebound on Ash Wednesday to share already-blessed ashes. There is a simple order in the BB, chapter 52. A priest, deacon, or lay minister may distribute ashes, but the lay minister excludes the prayer of blessing. The lay minister should bring already-blessed ashes.
- Distribute the Operation Rice Bowl banks on Ash Wednesday. Each one comes with activities and suggestions to connect what's going on in the liturgical year with what's going on in the world.
- Introduce your parishioners to sacred music that they can take on the go. GIA Publications, Inc. (giamusic.com), Oregon Catholic Press (ocp.org), and World Library Publications (wlp.jspaluch.com) may be the publisher of your parish's hymnal, but they also offer many products to enhance the individual's spiritual life.

Liturgy and Life

Simple things, such as not eating meat once a week, have great implications for the environment, and many environmentalist groups advocate for meatless Mondays (this includes fish). These groups argue that if everyone would fast from eating meat, just one day a week, we would minimize water usage, reduce greenhouse gases, and reduce fuel dependence. As a way of living our baptismal call to care for creation, encourage parishioners to take on the habit of meatless Fridays throughout the year. Refer to this practice as "Fruit and Veggie Friday." This website explores the scientific connection between going meatless and protecting the environment (www.downtoearth.org/go-veggie/environment/top-10-reasons).

THU 18 LM #220 / LMC #176–184 / violet
Thursday after Ash Wednesday

Scripture Insights

Moses sets a choice before the people: follow God and live, or go your own way and perish. Jesus amplifies the options with a twist: want to live? Pick up your cross and follow me. Want to save your life? Lose it. Thus Lent begins: deny your very self.

Preaching Points

Parish Masses

- Almost every day, we face choices between life and death, God or selfishness. In this season of penance and fasting, we strip things down so we see and choose better.
- Christ tells the disciples of his coming suffering, death, and Resurrection. To the crowds, he offers self-denial and the cross and warnings of the emptiness of what the world has to offer.

Masses with Children

- Moses reminds us that we face choices between life and death. Following God leads us to life. Without God, we perish.
- Christ invites us to follow him, but we know his way leads to the cross. To the Resurrection too, but the path goes through Calvary.

Missal Options

- Use the Mass texts for the Thursday after Ash Wednesday.
- Since music ministers may not be available for daily Mass, it might be better to pray form I or II of the PA on weekdays.
- Any Lenten Collect (except for today's) may be used to conclude the UP.
- Any Lenten Preface may be used.
- Consider using EPR-II.
- Consider concluding the Lenten weekday Masses with a PP.

Song of the Day

"Take Up Your Cross" by Charles W. Everst (various publishers)

FRI 19 LM #221 / LMC #176–184 / violet
Friday after Ash Wednesday

Scripture Insights

The stage is set for our Lenten self-denials: the Bridegroom will be taken away, and the fasting and mourning begin. Isaiah guides us on how to fast. Not mere self-mortification, but a rejection of injustice, a breaking of every chain, and letting go of indifference toward our suffering brothers and sisters.

Preaching Points

Parish Masses

- Jesus' disciples came to know him as the Messiah, the promised one, the foretaste of the heavenly banquet. Dark days are coming, Jesus tells us. For these, we fast and mourn.
- There is a place in the spiritual life for asceticism and denial. Isaiah pushes us even deeper: toward fasting from injustice, toward the carrying of others' burdens, and toward comforting the afflicted.

Masses with Children

- Christ is the feast. While he is with us we celebrate. Yet there was a time when he was taken away. To remember this, we fast and prepare for his return.
- How should we fast? How about breaking the chains that bind our fellow humans? Don't just avoid food and the finer things—share them with those who really need them.

Missal Options

- Use the Mass texts for the Friday after Ash Wednesday.
- Since music ministers may not be available for daily Mass, it might be better to pray form I or II of the PA on weekdays.
- Any Lenten Collect (except for today's) may be used to conclude the UP.
- Any Lenten Preface may be used.
- Consider using the EPVN-IV.
- Consider concluding the Lenten weekday Masses with a PP.

Song of the Day

"In These Days of Lenten Journey" by Ricky Manolo, CSP (OCP)

SAT 20 LM #222 / LMC #176–184 / violet

Saturday after Ash Wednesday

Scripture Insights

This Gospel begins with "Follow me" and leads to a feast with unlikely guests—the sinners and the sick. With Isaiah we once again fast from meanness and oppression. The Sabbath becomes a day of removing injustices and sharing all the gifts we've received. "Then light shall rise for you in the darkness."

Preaching Points

Parish Masses

- Here, early in Luke's account of the Gospel, we see the Good News unfolding—sinners are called and invited to the feast. The sick are welcomed by the Healer.
- "If you bestow your bread on the hungry and satisfy the afflicted, then light shall rise for you in the darkness." Here we have (proper) fasting, almsgiving, and a foretelling of resurrection.

Masses with Children

- In Jesus' day, it mattered who you ate with. By eating with sinners, Jesus was making them his family and leading them toward healing.
- The Lord, through Isaiah, is telling us to quit lying and spreading meanness. He's telling us to share our food, to help the afflicted, and to free all those who are in chains. This is how we celebrate the Sabbath—the Lord's Day.

Missal Options

- Use the Mass texts for the Saturday after Ash Wednesday.
- Since music ministers may not be available for daily Mass, it might be better to pray form I or II of the PA on weekdays.
- Any Lenten Collect (except for today's) may be used to conclude the UP.
- Any Lenten Preface may be used.
- Consider using the EPR-II.
- Consider concluding the Lenten weekday Masses with a PP.

Song of the Day

- "This Season Calls Us" by Harry Hagan, OSB (OCP)

Something to Consider...

◈ "In the light of God's word and in a sense in response to it, the congregation of the faithful prays in the universal prayer as a rule for the needs of the universal Church and the local community, for the salvation of the world and those oppressed by any burden, and for special categories of people" (*Lectionary for Mass:* "Introduction," 30).

SUN 21 LM #23B / LMC #19B / violet
First Sunday of Lent

Scripture Insights

The Genesis passage comes from the priestly writer, a postexilic compiler with a special interest in worship and obedience to the law. This writer sees God as all-powerful, creative, transcendent, holy, and orderly. Notice that perspective in the first creation story of Genesis 1:1—2:4a. God creates by the power of the Word, creatures appear in orderly array, and God rests on the seventh day as if the Sabbath were written into the very order of the cosmos.

For this writer, then, the flood represents a mighty tearing of the fabric of creation, which God had originally pronounced "very good" (Genesis 1:31). After sin causes the wrath of God to break forth, God forswears the violence of the flood by making a covenant. This seems to anticipate the unconditional covenant made with Abraham. God promises never to destroy creation and sets a sign of the covenant in the heavens: a rainbow. Alongside the dove, the rainbow becomes a sign of peace. So, despite the terrors of war, the upheavals of nature, the catastrophes of human judgment, God's graciousness ensures stability "for all future generations." The reestablishment of God's orderly rule after the flood would have had a strong impact on the community hoping to regroup after the disaster of the exile.

Mark's account of the Gospel pictures Jesus being tempted in the wilderness following his baptism. But the most striking parallel today is between Jesus' proclamation of the Gospel and God's good news of repudiating vengeance. The "good news of God" (1:13) is thus a message of reconciliation.

The First Letter of Peter tells of Jesus going to make a proclamation to the spirits in prison who had disobeyed in the time of Noah. The precise meaning of this passage is hard to grasp, but the general sense seems clear: Christ's death is a powerful Gospel for all times and people, admitting people into a new spiritual Noah's ark that saves them through the ritual flood of Baptism.

Preaching Points

Parish Masses

- God's order is a good and wonderful reality in creation. In Genesis, God promises not to flood the world again, and in the Gospel reading we hear about further reconciliation between God and his human creation.
- Noah's ark saved people from certain death; likewise, Christ is our ark, protecting the faithful from human sin.
- As Lent begins, we are reminded that these forty days are a time to repent of sin, return to the Gospel, and recommit ourselves to our baptismal promises.
- God's covenants are forever; he never forgets a promise he made to his people.

Children's Liturgy of the Word

- Noah's ark saved people during the flood; the ark kept them save during the deluge. In a similar way, Jesus keeps us safe from sin.
- On Ash Wednesday, we hear the words "repent, and believe in the Gospel." These forty days are a time to turn our backs to sin and embrace God's Good News.
- God never forgets or ignores a promise; his covenants are forever.

Missal Options

- Begin today's Mass in a unique way by chanting the Litany of Saints instead of the traditional Entrance Antiphon or opening song. PSol notes, "In the Mass of this Sunday there should be some distinctive elements which underline this important moment, e.g., the entrance procession with litanies of the saints" (23).
- PA form III is a wonderful option for Lent. Use whatever form is chosen on every Sunday of Lent.
- The Gloria is not sung (or said).
- The Creed is recited or sung. Because of its baptismal significance, consider using the Apostles' Creed throughout Lent and Easter.
- Any Lenten Collect (except for today's) may be used or adapted to conclude the UP.
- The Preface is found in the pages for the First Sunday of Lent ("The Temptation of the Lord").
- Consider EPR-II.
- Lenten Sunday Masses may conclude with a PP.
- Today is the usual date for the Rite of Election (although some dioceses have multiple celebrations starting before and concluding after the First Sunday of Lent). Will your parish be celebrating the Rite of Sending beforehand? Look to RCIA, 106 for guidance.

Music Preparation

- Jesus went to a lonely place to wrestle his demons. Sometimes music ministry is a lonely place with odd hours and little time for family. Yet it can bear much great fruit if we are patient. Use this Lenten season to put a better sense of balance in your life.
- Rehearse octavos for the Triduum early (start them soon!), but leave the psalm settings until later with cantors on the verses (private rehearsals) and the choir on the antiphons.

Music Suggestions

- Gathering: "Return to God" by Marty Haugen (GIA)
- Preparation of the Gifts: "Jesus Walked This Lonesome Valley" (various publishers)
- Communion: "Lord Jesus, as We Turn from Sin" by Ralph Wright, OSB (Liturgical Press)
- Sending Forth: "Jerusalem, My Destiny" by Rory Cooney (GIA)

Mass Texts

Introduction to Mass

God has made a covenant with us to lead us to the fullness of life. Though we may be unfaithful, he is always faithful. He sends his Son to take upon himself the wounds of our infidelities and his Spirit to wash us clean in Baptism. Let us acknowledge and repent of our sins and believe in him who, through his very own Body and Blood, gives us eternal life. *My brothers and sisters, let us acknowledge our sins, and so prepare ourselves to celebrate the sacred mysteries.*

Tropes for Penitential Act, Form III

You show sinners the way and guide the humble in right paths: Lord, have mercy.

You suffered for us, the righteous for the unrighteous: Christ, have mercy.

You rose from the dead and are seated at the right hand of God: Lord, have mercy.

Dismissal for Children's Liturgy of the Word

Dear children, today you will hear of the rainbow that God sent to Noah as a sign of a covenant, a promise of God's mercy and protection. The rainbow can remind you, too, that God is near and that, no matter how difficult or painful some things might be, God will lead you through them to wonderful things. Go now and listen to his Word, and when you return to us we will continue our celebration with great joy.

Dismissal of Catechumens/Elect

My friends, you are now following Jesus to the waters of Baptism and rebirth in his Spirit. Trusting in him, continue boldly on this journey, that you may celebrate the Paschal Mystery with joyful hearts and in communion with us at Easter.

Dismissal of Extraordinary Ministers of Holy Communion

Dear ministers of the Lord, the angels ministered to Jesus in the desert, and we send you to minister to our sick and homebound brothers and sisters in the desert of illness and infirmity. Give them the Bread of Life and assure them of our prayers and love. Go in peace.

Universal Prayer

This is the time of fulfillment, for the Kingdom of God is at hand. If we are to repent and believe in the Gospel, then we must bring to him our prayers for the needs of the world.

1. For the Church, that these days of Lent may be a time of renewal for every Christian believer. In your mercy, we pray:
2. For our nation, that we may find ways to share our abundance with the millions in our world who lack the basic necessities of life. In your mercy, we pray:
3. For all who are experiencing temptation, that they may have the strength to recognize evil in all its forms and to resist it. In your mercy, we pray:
4. We pray for all of us, gathered in this holy place, that the prayer, almsgiving, and fasting we offer this Lent may draw us closer to God and to one another. In your mercy, we pray:
5. For our beloved dead, [*especially* **N.** *and* **N.**], that they may be brought into the light and joy of God's presence with all their sins forgiven. In your mercy, we pray:

Gracious God,
through your Son Jesus Christ,
you have taught us that we do not live by bread alone,
but by your powerful Word.
At the beginning of this holy season of Lent,
help us to ponder our ways,
and walk in your truth.
Through Christ our Lord.
Amen.

Other Rites and Customs

- Utilize the option in *The Roman Missal* of reciting the Apostles' Creed throughout Lent.
- Sing the Litany of the Saints during the Entrance Procession as suggested in PSol and the CB.
- Even if you don't have catechumens going to the Rite of Election, be sure to include prayers for those throughout the world preparing for initiation at the Easter Vigil.
- Consider using EPR-I or EPR-II throughout Lent.
- Keep the organ and other instruments restrained for Lent, using it only to accompany the singing.
- Throughout Lent, consider having complete silence at the Preparation of the Gifts rather than a hymn or anthem sung.
- Sing simple chanted Eucharistic Acclamations a cappella.
- Chant the Penitential Act, or at least the Kyrie, during the Sundays of Lent.

Liturgy and Life

The forty days Jesus spent in the desert was a time of intense focus on his relationship with God. We can follow his lead, stripping away distractions and making ourselves more available to the Father in prayer. Make a plan for this spiritual work. Some people live in a desert-like state of existence all the time, due to poverty or physical or mental illness. What service could you commit to during your forty days?

Taking Place This Week . . .

Consider what can be done liturgically, catechetically, and ministerially to respond to these important needs.

- International Mother Language Day (2/21)
- Purim (evening 2/25)

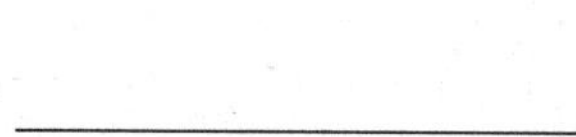

MON 22 LM #535 / LMC #263/ white
Feast of the Chair of St. Peter the Apostle

About Today's Feast

The original Feast of the Chair of St. Peter derives from Antioch, where followers of Jesus were first called Christians and Peter presided. This feast celebrates Peter's pastoral authority over the Church continued through the ministry of the bishop of Rome. The chair, or cathedra, symbolizes authority; it is not an actual chair or antique. The issue of authority has vexed Christianity throughout its history and has caused divisions. Catholics celebrate the unity of faith that the pope both symbolizes and works to secure.

Scripture Insights

The reading from First Peter subtly reminds all presbyters and pastors that they will ultimately need to face "the Chief Shepherd" and thus should tend their flocks accordingly. Peter himself was the first to declare Christ as Messiah and thereby merited the Keys to the Kingdom.

Preaching Points

Parish Masses

- The psalm has us pray "The Lord is my shepherd; there is nothing I shall want." It is ultimately God who shepherds us, but God often does this with the leaders of the community of faith here on earth.
- "Upon this rock I will build my church" probably sounded audacious when first spoken and written yet two millennia later "the gates of the netherworld" have not prevailed against it.

Masses with Children

- Peter was perhaps Christ's best friend, and evidently his most trusted apostle. Jesus called him "the rock" on which he would build his Church.
- Peter was also the first to recognize Jesus as "the Christ, the son of the living God."

Missal Options

- The prayer texts for today are proper and are found in the PS.
- All of the orations include mention of St. Peter, as might be expected, and focus on his teaching and our need to hold fast with integrity to the faith that Peter confessed.
- Since today is a feast, the Gloria is sung—even though it is Lent.
- The Creed is omitted.
- Use P-I of Apostles and consider EP-I.
- It is a good idea to use the SB for the Apostles today.

Song of the Day

"By All Your Saints Still Striving" verse for Chair of Peter (various publishers)

Other Rites and Customs

Hours: Use the Proper Psalter from the PS today.

TUE 23 LM #225 / LMC #176–184 / violet
Lenten Weekday

Optional Memorial of St. Polycarp, Bishop and Martyr / violet

Scripture Insights

Just as the waters fall from the skies to give life to the earth, so does the Lord send his Word to give us life. Intriguing is the fact that God speaks of the Word returning to him. Jesus, God's Word, also teaches us to pray to the Father. Don't babble—God already knows what you need.

Preaching Points

Parish Masses

- The prayer we call the Our Father is remarkably concise—a simple declaration of praise and petition, with a huge emphasis on the act of forgiving and its necessity.
- The Scriptures tell us in a multitude of ways of the Father sending the Son and the Spirit into the world to bring us together and to bring us, together, back to our Father.

Masses with Children

- God sends us the rain to water the earth and bring us life. In a similar, yet more powerful, way, God also sent the Word (Jesus) to bring us life.
- All of us know the Our Father. This is the story of how Jesus gave it to us. We don't need to use a lot of words to pray. God already knows what we need before we say it.

Missal Options

- Use the prayers for Tuesday of the First Week of Lent.
- Since music ministers may not be available for daily Mass, it might be better to pray form I or II of the PA on weekdays.
- You might use the Collect from the saint's day to conclude the UP.
- Any Lenten Preface may be used.
- Consider using the EPR-II.
- Consider concluding the Lenten weekday Masses with a PP.

Song of the Day

"Turn to Me" by John Foley, SJ (OCP)

Optional memorial

St. Polycarp (c. 69–c. 155) was the bishop of Smyrna in the second century. With Clement of Rome and Ignatius of Antioch, he is an apostolic father, one who was converted by the Apostles. He was martyred by beheading. Polycarp is one of the earliest Christians whose writings we still have.

- The readings are from the SW.
- Use the Collect from the PS; the other prayers are from the PT.
- Use any of the Lenten prefaces.
- Consider EP-II.
- Any Lenten Collect may be used to conclude the UP.
- Continue to use the same form of the PA.

WED 24 LM #226 / LMC #176–184 / violet
Lenten Weekday

Scripture Insights

Jonah obeyed God and warned the huge city of Nineveh to repent or be destroyed. They repented, called a fast, and relented. Using blunt language, Jesus warns "an evil generation" that seeks a sign. The sign has already been given by way of Jonah. The wickedness is greater now, Jesus seems to say. So is the messenger, says Jesus, speaking of himself.

Preaching Points

Parish Masses

- Jonah, it turns out, was a bit disappointed that the Ninevites listened to God and repented. He didn't like them and was hoping for God's wrath. Instead, God's power of persuasion won out, as did forgiveness.
- Christ is often described as the fulfillment of all that was foretold by the prophets. Today we hear of a great achievement by a prophet. Christ acknowledges it, and says he himself is greater still.

Masses with Children

- We all know about "Jonah and the whale." This is a story of Jonah at work proclaiming God to a city that has fallen into evil.
- Sometimes we want signs—like "please God give me a sign that tells me what to do." Today Jesus says essentially, "You want a sign? You're looking at him."

Missal Options

- Use the prayers for Wednesday of the First Week of Lent.
- Since music ministers may not be available for daily Mass, it might be better to pray form I or II of the Penitential Act on weekdays.
- Any Lenten Preface may be used.
- Consider using EPR-I.
- Lenten weekday Masses may conclude with a PP.

Song of the Day

"Grant to Us, O Lord" by Lucien Deiss (WLP)

THU 25 LM #227 / LMC #176–184 / violet
Lenten Weekday

Scripture Insights

The Psalmist sets the tone: "Lord, on the day I called for help, you answered me." We hear Esther praying and pleading for deliverance from oppressive enemies. Jesus elucidates all that is available to us if we but call on his Father.

Preaching Points

Parish Masses

- Jesus uses the analogy of human parenting to explain prayer, but the words can feel jarring: "If you then, who are wicked, know how to give good gifts to your children." We don't like to see ourselves this way, but when confronted with the Father's generosity, then the blow is softened.
- Here Jesus gives us what we know of as "The Golden Rule": "Do to others whatever you would have them do to you." Jesus' explanation of this is intriguing: "This is the law and the prophets."

Masses with Children

- Queen Esther was one of the great and powerful women of the Old Testament. Here we hear her, a queen, pleading to God for help. She prayed and God delivered her and her people.
- Jesus teaches us two things. First, God loves you, so ask for what you need and you just might get it. Second, we get the Golden Rule: "Do to others whatever you would have them do to you."

Missal Options

- Use the prayers for Thursday of the First Week of Lent.
- Since music ministers may not be available for daily Mass, it might be better to pray form I or II of the PA on weekdays.
- Any Lenten Collect (except for today's) may be used to conclude the UP.
- Any Lenten Preface may be used.
- Consider using EP-III.
- Consider concluding the Lenten weekday Masses with a PP.

Song of the Day

"Take, O Take Me as I Am" by John L. Bell (GIA)

FRI 26 Lenten Weekday

LM #228 / LMC #176–184 / violet

Scripture Insights

Ezekiel sets the stage: do what is right and just and you will live; commit inequity and you will die. Jesus takes it deeper—it is not enough to follow the law externally. You must change your heart or be liable to judgment. "You shall not kill," of course, but you must also not be angry or derisive.

Preaching Points

Parish Masses

- In Ezekiel, God says, "Do I not rather rejoice when he turns from his evil way that he may live?" God is always inviting us to change and is always joyful when we do.
- Jesus uses the example of secular law (judge, guard, prison) to challenge the Pharisee's adherence to the Law of Moses. Ultimately, either law is punitive. Far better if we change our hearts. Far better if we settle the matter face-to-face with our brother or sister.

Masses with Children

- Sometimes we think of God as the great judge waiting to catch us and punish us. No, not at all, says the Lord through Ezekiel, I rejoice when they turn away from wickedness and toward life.
- Jesus wants us to love and be kind. It is important not to be outwardly mean (like hitting or yelling) but far better if our hearts are so full of love and respect that we don't even feel anger or contempt for our brothers and sisters.

Missal Options

- Use the prayers for Friday of the First Week of Lent.
- Since music ministers may not be available for daily Mass, it might be better to pray form I or II of the PA.
- Any Lenten Collect (except for today's) may be used to conclude the UP.
- Consider using the EPR-II.
- Consider concluding the Lenten weekday Masses with a PP.

Song of the Day

"Out of the Depths" by James O Gerrish (WLP)

SAT 27 Lenten Weekday

LM #229 / LMC #176–184 / violet

Scripture Insights

With this covenant, this people will be God's and they will observe God's commandments "with all your heart and with all your soul." Observing this commandment is more than just an external adherence. Jesus calls us even deeper, to love not just the loveable but our enemies and persecutors as well. In doing this, we are "children of [our] heavenly Father."

Preaching Points

Parish Masses

- Being God's people is not merely following rules. It is much deeper. We are "to walk in his ways . . . to hearken to his voice."
- Without letting ourselves become proud, we can and should ask ourselves what makes us different from "the tax collectors" and "pagans." This love that goes even to those we might see as enemies may be a key difference.

Masses with Children

- Moses is describing the "agreement" between God and the Jewish people. We are uniquely God's, and therefore we keep God's commands.
- Jesus tells us that God shows his goodness to the bad and the unjust by still sending them sunshine and rain. Even more than this, Jesus calls us to love not only our friends but even our enemies.

Missal Options

- Use the prayers for Saturday of the First Week of Lent.
- Since music ministers may not be available for daily Mass, it might be better to pray form I or II of the PA on weekdays.
- You may use the Collect from any OT Sunday to conclude the UP.
- Any Lenten Preface may be used.
- Consider using the EPR-II.
- Consider concluding the Lenten weekday Masses with a PP.

Song of the Day

"The Love of the Lord" by Michael Joncas (GIA)

Something to Consider...

◈ "Liturgical services involve the whole Body of the Church; they manifest it and have effects upon it; but they also concern the individual members of the Church in different ways, according to their different orders, offices, and actual participation" (*Sacrosanctum concilium*, 26).

SUN 28 LM #26B / LMC #22B / violet
Second Sunday of Lent

Scripture Insights

God acts in mysterious ways in many places in the Old Testament: rejecting Cain's sacrifice (Genesis 4:5), choosing Jacob over Esau (Genesis 25:23), sending Job's time of trial (Job 10:1–22), forcing Jeremiah to suffer (Jeremiah 20:7–18), using Babylon to judge Judah (Habakkuk 1:12–13). But the story of Abraham's sacrifice of Isaac renders God almost completely incomprehensible.

The entire story line about Abraham from Genesis 12 to this point has pointed to the birth of an heir to fulfill the astounding promise of descendants as countless as the sands of the seashore (Genesis 15:1–6). But God's frightening demand throws everything into jeopardy. The story-teller seems unconcerned about the picture of God that this episode draws: God putting God's own integrity at risk. Nor does the storyteller take into account the other parts of the Bible that repudiate child sacrifice (see Jeremiah 7:31).

If God is incomprehensible, Abraham's steadfast faith stands out more boldly than ever. Abraham bargained with God about destroying Sodom (Genesis 18:22–33) but not about this. Why? He became the father of the faithful not only by boldly believing in God's promise but by boldly believing despite God's threat. He not only trusted, as Paul taught in his letters (Romans 4:16–22; Galatians 3:6–9), but *acted* on his trusting faith (James 2:18–24).

Put Isaac's sacrifice side-by-side with today's passage in Romans ("He who did not spare his own Son," 8:32). In Jesus' death, God is not the one to demand the sacrifice but the one to make the sacrifice. In the Jesus story, God is more like Abraham than like God in the Isaac story. So what made God believe in us? "God proves his love for us in that *while we still were still sinners* Christ died for us" (Romans 5:8). In this sacrifice, God became the *Abba* of those who believe.

Preaching Points

Parish Masses

- We are called to a steadfast faith in God. Our Lord did not spare his only son from the suffering of his life and death.
- Like Abraham, we are called to faithfully trust in God. He will not ask for the blood of our children, but we are called to believe and act in accordance with God's will.
- As Abraham was faithful to God, God is faithful to us. Despite not understanding God's ways, Abraham trusted in him.

Children's Liturgy of the Word

- Faithfully trusting in God is the central message of the story of Abraham and Isaac.
- Abraham was faithful in a way that resembles God's faithfulness.
- Despite not knowing or understanding God's ways, Abraham was faithful to God.

Missal Options

- PA form III is a wonderful option for Lent. Use whatever form is chosen on every Sunday of Lent.
- The Gloria is not sung (or said).
- The Creed is recited or sung. Because of its baptismal significance, consider using the Apostles' Creed throughout Lent and Easter.
- Any Lenten Collect (except for today's) may be used or adapted to conclude the UP.
- The Preface is found in the pages for the Second Sunday of Lent ("The Transfiguration of the Lord").
- Consider using EP-II.
- Lenten Sunday Masses conclude with a PP.

Music Preparation

The Transfiguration was an "aha moment" where suddenly Jesus was seen in another perspective by Peter, James, and John. Sometimes within liturgy we have these same moments if we are paying attention. When were you last transformed by the liturgy? Perhaps we are so busy working that we miss it. Take time to reflect on what has taken place during the Mass.

Music Suggestions

- Gathering: "Transfiguration" by Brian Wren (Hope Publishing Company)
- Preparation of the Gifts: "Transfiguration" by Carey Landry (OCP) or "'Tis Good, Lord to be Here" (various publishers)

Mass Texts

Introduction to Mass

Our own hearts testify to us of the love of God, that Jesus Christ is his beloved Son, for God dwells in our hearts through his Spirit. So that we may hear this Good News clearly, as we continue our Lenten observance, let us search out all impurity in our hearts, ask the Lord's mercy upon us, and seek his face. *My brothers and sisters, let us acknowledge our sins, and so prepare ourselves to celebrate the sacred mysteries.*

Tropes for Penitential Act, Form III

Against you, you alone, we have sinned: Lord, have mercy.

Remember your compassion and your love,
for they are from old: Christ, have mercy.

We long to see your face in the land of the living:
Lord, have mercy.

Dismissal for Children's Liturgy of the Word

My dear children, St. Paul asks, "If God is for us, who can be against us?" We believe that God is indeed for us, and he shows us that in so many ways: in the love of family and friends, in the beauty of the natural world, in this community of faith, and in giving us his Son, Jesus, who speaks to you now in today's readings. Go and listen to him.

Dismissal of Catechumens/Elect

My friends, continuing your journey to Easter, remember that God has not withheld his own Son. He awaits you on the cross, at the font of new life, and in the feast of eternal life. As you go to reflect on this great mystery, we pray for you and look forward to your union with us in Baptism and the Eucharist. Go in peace.

Dismissal of Extraordinary Ministers of Holy Communion

Dear friends, taking the Body of Christ, go to our sisters and brothers who cannot join us in body due to sickness or injury. Remind them that they are one with us in the Spirit as beloved daughters and sons of God. Go in peace.

Universal Prayer

God plans the transfiguration of the world in his Son. It is only by our prayer and action, guided by his Holy Spirit, that this can happen. And so we turn to the Lord with our needs.

1. That the Church may be a source of transfigured life for the world, we pray:
2. That leaders of nations may persevere in the ways of honesty and integrity, we pray:
3. That travelers may behold the beauty of new lands, we pray:
4. That our hearts may be transfigured by the Spirit to be more like the heart of Jesus, we pray:
5. That our families may enjoy traditions and cherished moments together, we pray:
6. That our deceased relatives and friends may behold the beauty of the Lord in the halls of heaven, we pray:

Lord Jesus,
transfigured in glory,
you are the hope of the world,
and all the faithful look to you.
On the mountain you were recognized
as perfectly obedient to the Father's will,
and from there you beckon us to the way
of transformation.
Teach us to follow in your footsteps,
and so come to share in your glory.
Who live and reign with God the Father in the
unity of the Holy Spirit,
one God, for ever and ever.
Amen.

Other Rites and Customs

- Consider having a communal Reconciliation Service during the week using form II of the RP.
- Be sure to include music that references Baptism as Lent is a season of preparation for Baptism and the renewal of baptismal promises (see CSL, 109).
- Today is the usual date for the Penitential Rite for candidates for full communion. If your community celebrates this optional rite for baptized but uncatechized candidates (see RCIA, 459) the rite may conclude with a song, which transitions into the Liturgy of the Eucharist. The rite provides several options from the psalter (see RCIA, 470). No changes are made to the prayer texts; they are from the Mass of the day. This rite follows a pattern similar to the Scrutinies for the elect; instead of focusing on preparation for Baptism, however, the texts and prayers look to preparation for Reconciliation. The Penitential Rite should not be combined with any of the Scrutinies for the elect (see Third Sunday of Lent). This rite may also take place on a Lenten weekday or at another suitable time.

Liturgy and Life

Today's First Reading, the story of Abraham's willingness to sacrifice his only son, brings us face-to-face with a God who calls us to total trust even as he entrusts his only Son to us. Isaac suffered no harm, but many children in the world are truly in danger. Catholic Relief Services (CRS; www.crs.org) devotes many projects to children, especially concerning child labor and human trafficking. Follow your heart. Whatever you do, pray for children who have no one to speak for them.

Taking Place This Week . . .

Consider what can be done liturgically, catechetically, and ministerially to respond to these important needs.

- Zero Discrimination Day, Self-Injury Awareness Day, and St. David's Day (3/1)
- Read Across America Day (3/2)
- World Wildlife Day (3/3)
- Employee Appreciation Day and the World Day of Prayer (3/5)
- First Friday (3/5) and First Saturday (3/6)
- March is National Social Work, Women's History, Irish-American Heritage, and Youth Art Month.
- March is traditionally set aside by Catholics as the Month of St. Joseph.

MON 1 LM #230 / LMC #176–184 / violet
Lenten Weekday

Scripture Insights

Isaiah, speaking for all the Israelites, is nothing but penitent. Jesus offers mercy and guidance for forgiveness. Jesus gives us four great commands: Stop judging. Stop condemning. Forgive. And give.

Preaching Points

Parish Masses

- Isaiah's confession is stunning in its honesty. He acknowledges God's mercy and our guilt in the same sentence.
- Jesus reminds us that God will not be outdone in generosity.

Masses with Children

- Isaiah does a wonderful job of describing how he and his people have sinned and done wrong, while emphasizing God's mercy and forgiveness.
- Jesus also reminds us of God's mercy but reminds us that we are also to be forgiving. Don't judge and condemn, and you will not get judged and condemned.

Missal Options

- Use the prayers for Monday of the Second Week of Lent.
- Since music ministers may not be available for daily Mass, it might be better to pray form I or II of the PA on weekdays.
- Any Lenten Preface may be used.
- Consider using the EPR-I.
- Consider concluding the Lenten weekday Masses with a PP.

Song of the Day

"The Glory of These Forty Days" (various publishers)

TUE 2 LM #231 / LMC #176–184 / violet
Lenten Weekday

Scripture Insights

This is the beginning of Isaiah's preaching. "Come now, let us set things right." God is always the Lord of new beginnings. Jesus, on the other hand, warns us against empty external displays and against exalting ourselves. The final sentence, "whoever exalts himself," is perhaps more of a statement of natural consequences rather than a description of what God will do. History, especially Church history, is replete with examples.

Preaching Points

Parish Masses

- Isaiah's message is simple: "cease doing evil; learn to do good." The forgiveness of God offers is stunning: "Though your sins be like scarlet, they may become white as snow."
- Jesus lays bare the hypocrisy of the religious leaders of his day. One almost cringes at the harshness. Yet he exhorts us to do and observe whatever they tell us, "but do not follow their example."

Masses with Children

- God tells us, through Isaiah, to "cease doing evil; learn to do good." He also tells us that part of this is helping the widows and orphans—the most vulnerable peoples.
- You might hear someone say to another: Practice what you preach! Jesus is saying this to the religious leaders of his day, and he says it to us today.

Missal Options

- Use the prayers for Tuesday of the Second Week of Lent.
- Since music ministers may not be available for daily Mass, it might be better to pray form I or II of the PA on weekdays.
- Any Lenten Collect (except for today's) may be used to conclude the UP.
- Any Lenten Preface may be used.
- Consider using EP-II.
- Consider concluding the Lenten weekday Masses with a PP.

Song of the Day

"Behold, Before Our Wondering Eyes" by Genevieve Glen, OSB, Barney Walker, and Gael Berberick (OCP)

WED 3 LM #232 / LMC #176–184 / violet
Lenten Weekday

Optional Memorial of St. Katharine Drexel, Virgin / violet

Scripture Insights

Jeremiah is stuck between God and the people God sent him to. These people want to destroy Jeremiah. Jeremiah has spoken on their behalf, to keep away God's wrath. Jesus is in a similar position. He tells his disciples that he is about to be killed by the people he came to save. Even with blunt language like this, the disciples don't get it, until Jesus makes clear the need to be a servant and suffer for it.

Preaching Points

Parish Masses

- Jeremiah epitomizes the tension of the life of the prophets. Sent by God to challenge both religious and state authorities, he is despised by both, even by the people he came to set free.
- Even those who walked with Christ were not immune to jockeying for power and privilege. The power, Christ says, comes only by way of suffering, and the only privilege is that of serving.

Masses with Children

- Jesus seemed to know that going to Jerusalem would lead to his death. He went anyway.
- His disciples seemed unable to hear Jesus' prophecy of suffering and continued to think that following him would lead to glory. It does, but not in the way they thought. Only by way of servanthood and suffering for it.

Missal Options

- Use the prayers for Wednesday of the Second Week of Lent.
- Since music ministers may not be available for daily Mass, it might be better to pray form I or II of the PA on weekdays.
- Any Lenten Collect (except for today's) may be used to conclude the UP.
- Any Lenten Preface may be used.
- Consider using the EPVN-II.
- Consider concluding the Lenten weekday Masses with a PP.

Song of the Day

"Turn to Me" by John Foley, SJ (OCP)

Optional Memorial

St. Katharine Drexel founded the Sisters of the Blessed Sacrament, an order that built elementary and high schools for African American and Native American populations across the United States and established Xavier University to train teachers for those schools. St. Katharine was from a prominent Philadelphia family, but her compassion for marginalized people led her to set aside her desire for contemplative life for five decades while she engaged in active ministry.

- The readings are from the SW.
- Use the Collect from the PS; the other prayers are from the PT.
- Use any of the Lenten Prefaces.
- Consider EP-II.
- Any Lenten Collect may be used to conclude the UP.
- Continue to use the same form of the PA.

THU 4 LM #233 / LMC #176–184 / violet
Lenten Weekday

Optional Memorial of St. Casimir / violet

Scripture Insights

The words of Jeremiah and Jesus should make us quake. Jeremiah describes the arid lifelessness of those who trust in the world, as contrasted with the lush, deep life of those rooted in the hope of the Lord. The unnamed rich man in Jesus' parable starkly shows us what happens when we ignore the commands of Moses and the prophets to care for the least among us. If we don't listen to them, why would we "be persuaded if someone should rise from the dead"?

Preaching Points

Parish Masses

- "I, the LORD, alone probe the mind and test the heart." How would I stand up to such scrutiny? How would you? How do we?
- Even the dogs were better to Lazarus than was the rich man, who realizes too late his mistake. We are "the five brothers." Do we listen to Moses and the prophets, or the One who rose from the dead? As Jeremiah said, "More tortuous than all else is the human heart, beyond remedy; who can understand it?"

Masses with Children

- Jeremiah gives a great description of the person "whose hope is in the LORD." He or she bears fruit, even in the hard times.

- How many people like Lazarus are lying at our doors? What happened to the rich man, who didn't even give Lazarus the scraps from his table?

Missal Options

- Use the prayers for Thursday of the Second Week of Lent.
- Since music ministers may not be available for daily Mass, it might be better to pray form I or II of the PA on weekdays.
- Any Lenten Collect (except for today's) may be used to conclude the UP.
- Any Lenten Preface may be used.
- Consider using EP-III.
- Consider concluding the Lenten weekday Masses with a PP.

Song of the Day

"Have Mercy, Lord, on Us/*Attende Domine*" (various publishers)

Optional Memorial

Although born a prince of Poland, St. Casimir rejected political scheming, high office, personal indulgence, and warfare to live a life of chastity, simplicity, and good works until his early death in his mid-twenties. His single experience of combat, at age fifteen, left him concerned for the lot of the common people most affected by conflict and gave him an enduring love for the poor.

- The readings are from the SW.
- Use the Collect from the PS; the other prayers are from the PT.
- Use any of the Lenten Prefaces.
- Consider EP-II.
- Any Lenten Collect may be used to conclude the UP.
- Continue to use the same form of the PA.

LM #234 / LMC #176–184 / violet

Lenten Weekday

Scripture Insights

It is remarkable that the people of Israel kept alive stories like this one about Joseph and his brothers: let's not kill him, let's sell him instead! "After all, he is our brother, our own flesh." Such treachery among us humans is played out in Jesus' parable: "This is the heir. Come, let us kill him and acquire his inheritance." Jesus, always a son of Israel, remained ruthless in his critique of its leaders.

Preaching Points

Parish Masses

- Joseph's brothers say of him, "here comes that master dreamer," as they prepare the plot to kill their own flesh. Was it the dreams they were trying to kill? How often are we like Ruben, who speaks up but only half-heartedly?
- Jesus' story is the story of salvation history, the dark side. God sent the prophets, and they beat them. God sent his son, and they killed him. Yet to come is the Kingdom of God being "given to a people that will produce its fruit."

Masses with Children

- We often hear about "the God of Abraham, Isaac, and Jacob." This is the story of Joseph (as in the coat of many colors) and his brothers, all sons of Jacob. The meanness among us, even us followers of God, started early.
- Jesus' story about the vineyard is the story of how God tried to save us in different ways. God sent his prophets, then God's Son. We beat them and killed them. But Jesus, the one that the builders rejected, has become the cornerstone.

Missal Options

- Use the prayers for Friday of the Second Week of Lent.
- Since music ministers may not be available for daily Mass, it might be better to pray form I or II of the PA on weekdays.
- Any Lenten Collect (except for today's) may be used to conclude the UP.
- Any Lenten Preface may be used.
- Consider using EP-II.
- Consider concluding the Lenten weekday Masses with a PP.

Song of the Day

"Lord, Teach Us to Pray Aright" Henry Bryan Hays, OSB (Liturgical Press)

S A T 6 LM #235 / LMC #176–184 / violet
Lenten Weekday

Scripture Insights

Micah's words are beautiful, describing how God "delights in clemency." The parable of the Prodigal Son—really the story of the merciful father—wonderfully illustrates this. The details are key: the father sees the son "while he was still a long way off," which could happen only if he'd been watching for him. He ran to meet him (an earthly patriarch doesn't leave his land, and people come to him) and interrupted the penitential speech of his son with commands for the celebration to begin.

Preaching Points

Parish Masses

- The younger son's word are harsh: he is essentially telling his father to hasten the end result of his own death. Give me my inheritance now, not later, and we shall be rid of each other. Even at this, the father rejoiced at his return, with no words of repayment or restitution.
- The father also leaves the party to go out to the older son. Most of us are in his shoes, filled with resentment. The older son clearly had ideations of leaving; it was he who brought up the situation, but the father is merciful even to him, and calls him to celebrate.

Masses with Children

- This story is told by Jesus to show God's mercy and forgiveness. He means to contrast it to the earthly fathers of his day and to the religious leaders, who are more concerned about the rules than the people who broke them.
- One son took his father's money and wasted it (that's what prodigal means). The other son stayed home but was pouty and resentful. Neither fully appreciates the goodness of their father.

Missal Options

- Use the prayers for Saturday of the Second Week of Lent.
- Since music ministers may not be available for daily Mass, it might be better to pray form I or II of the PA on weekdays.
- Any Lenten Collect (except for today's) may be used to conclude the UP.
- Any Lenten Preface may be used.
- Consider using EP-II.
- Consider concluding the Lenten weekday Masses with a PP.

Song of the Day

"The Prodigal Father" by Bryan Flynn (WLP)

Something to Consider...

◈ Provide the parish ways to reflect on their role in the catechumenal process, such as the short booklet, *Disciples Making Disciples* by Victoria M. Tufano (LTP).

◈ Preparing to renew one's Baptism should be the center of our Lenten practices. Provide the assembly with copies of *Baptized for Discipleship* by Mary A. Ehle (LTP).

S U N 7 LM #29B or 28A / LMC #25B or 24A / violet

Third Sunday of Lent

Editorial Note

If your parish is celebrating the First Scrutiny today, you will need to use the Year A readings. The Scripture Insights for Year A along with Missal options are provided below.

Scripture Insights (Year B)

We commonly learn, read, and follow the Ten Commandments out of context. Whether in a religious education session or on a courtroom wall, they often stand alone like a timeless, universal statement of perfect morality. But the Bible places them firmly in their context within the story of Israel. In Exodus 3, God tells Moses that he is coming to deliver Israel from their oppressors. Exodus 4—11 narrates the struggle between Moses and the pharaoh before the deliverance. The first Passover celebration comes in chapters 12—13. The spectacular rescue from the Egyptians and its aftermath appear in Exodus 14—15, and the events of the journey to Mount Sinai, including the first manna and the water from the rock, happen in chapters 16—18. Finally in Exodus 19, the people reach Sinai, where God tells them through Moses, "You have see . . . how I bore you up on eagle wings and brought you here to myself. Therefore, if you hearken to my voice and keep my covenant, you shall be my special possession, dearer to me than all other people, though all the earth is mine. You shall be to me a kingdom of priests, a holy nation" (19:4–6). Then follows in chapter 20 the text we read today.

The proper setting for understanding the Decalogue is the mighty act of salvation and the covenant that God established as its result. Its Ten Commandments presuppose that one is already participating in the covenant. People obey out of love, faithfulness, and gratitude. The very first commandment emphasizes the context of salvation: "I, the Lord, am your God, *who brought you out of the land of Egypt* . . . you shall not have other gods besides me" (Exodus 20:2).

Moses sealed the people's participation in the covenant by sprinkling them with the "blood of the covenant" (Exodus 24:8). Jesus renewed that as "my blood of the covenant which will be shed for many" (Mark 14:24). For Christians, the context for understanding and obeying is the Paschal Mystery of our Lord, who through the Eucharist gives us the wisdom and power to obey.

Preaching Points

Parish Masses

- Love and faithfulness ought to outline all of our behavior in the face of God and one another. All of God's people are called to a life that is moral, upright, holy, and caring of others.
- The Ten Commandments are part of the story of God's people; they are God's expectations of a just society.
- "Love, faithfulness, and gratitude" toward God ought to be our motivation to obey the Ten Commandments.
- Jesus knows the hearts of his people and uniquely understands each of us. His words and actions in the Temple remind us that we too can rid ourselves of such vices.

Children's Liturgy of the Word

- The Ten Commandments explain to us the expectations God has of those who live in covenant with him.
- Instead of approaching the Ten Commandments like a checklist, we should strive to follow them in "love, faithfulness, and gratitude" toward God.

Scripture Insights (Year A)

Today's readings pose two questions that bring our Lenten journey into focus: "Is the Lord in our midst or not?" and "What are you looking for?"

The First Reading comes from Exodus 17, the early stages of Israel's forty-year journey in the desert. The Israelites had begun quarreling among themselves and grumbling against Moses, complaining about a lack of food and water. They even tested God, asking whether he was even in their midst. Moses pleads to God for intervention, and God responds by empowering Moses to draw water from the rock for the people to drink. Even though the Lord was indeed in the midst of the community during the desert journey, the Israelites' fears, intensified by their grumbling and complaining, blinded them to the Lord's presence.

In today's Gospel reading from John, Jesus meets a Samaritan woman at a well. With the simple request for her to give him a drink, Jesus initiates a dialogue that intrigues and transforms her. Just as she has come to believe in Jesus, the disciples return from their errand to a nearby town. John tells us in an aside that on seeing the woman, they fail to ask her what she is looking for—the very question Jesus had asked the first disciples, the question that initiated their conversion (see John 1:38). In the Gospel according to John, true discipleship involves first and foremost bringing others to Christ. The distracted disciples fail to evangelize—in contrast to the Samaritan woman, who, once she believes that Jesus is the Christ, hurries to her town to bring others to him.

As we continue through our Lenten journey, we are challenged to overcome fears and distractions, to find the Lord in our midst, and to bring others to him.

Preaching Points

Parish Masses

- Jesus violates a number of social norms to bring the Good News of God's forgiveness and restoration to the Samaritan woman. Explore the "risks for love" that disciples of Jesus must make to bring the Good News to those who are struggling with faith and faithfulness to pursue and fulfill their God-given potential.
- The readings and prayers for today pose some questions, and the liturgy points to some answers. Are we thirsting for the water of life? In what parts of our lives do we hunger and thirst for God's righteousness? The Preface sings about Jesus' thirst to receive our faith; the psalm emphasizes God's thirst for our response. Do we believe that God cares

and wants our response and the response of every person on earth? Our response must be to love him with our whole hearts and love our neighbor as ourselves.

- We thirst and yearn for the Lord. On this day, the elect participate in the first scrutiny. Unpack this rite theologically for the congregation. Emphasize that in this rite, we pray that God will open the elects' hearts and minds so they may give themselves over entirely into God's hands. But we also pray for ourselves, and for all the baptized, that we too may belong entirely to the Lord, for only the Lord can quench our thirst.

Children's Liturgy of the Word

- Jesus reaches out to the Samaritan woman, who would have been seen as "other," even the enemy. By telling her about her life, even though this is the first time they had met, she realizes that Jesus doesn't view her as an enemy but as worthy of God's love. Because of Jesus' kindness, she is able to change. When we are kind to others, chances are they will be kind to others as well.
- During this season of Lent, we are called to reach out to those in need. This is an opportunity for each of us, our parish, and our school to actively think of ways we can be of service, perhaps in collecting food or sending cards to people in prison.

Missal Options

- PA form III is a wonderful option for Lent. Use whatever form is chosen on every Sunday of Lent.
- The Gloria is not sung (or said).
- The Creed is recited or sung. Because of its baptismal significance, consider using the Apostles' Creed throughout Lent and Easter.
- Any Lenten Collect (except for today's) may be used or adapted to conclude the UP.
- If the Scrutinies are not taking place, use P-I or P-II of Lent; otherwise, the preface is found among the pages for the Third Sunday of Lent ("The Samaritan Woman").
- Consider the EPR-II.
- Lenten Sunday Masses conclude with a PP.
- If the Scrutiny occurs, the proper prayers should be used; these Mass formularies are found in the "Ritual Masses" section of the RM, under section I—For the Conferral of the Sacraments of Christian Initiation, #2: For the Celebration of the Scrutinies, A: For the First Scrutiny. For the actual ritual of the Scrutiny itself, consult RCIA, 150–56. The Scrutiny takes place after the homily.

Music Preparation

- We are reminded to keep Sunday sacred, but for those who work for the Church that is not easy. If you must work on Sunday you need to take time off on another day. Consider just doing the minimal hours on Sunday rather than a working a full-length day (if possible!) so that at least you can keep some elements of the Sabbath. Perhaps this means scheduling fewer events in your parish on a Sunday too!

Music Suggestions

- Gathering: "Forty Days and Forty Nights" (various publishers)
- Preparation of the Gifts: "Mercy, O God" by Francis Patrick O'Brian (GIA)
- Sending Forth: "Lord, Let Me Walk" by Jack Miffleton (WLP)

Mass Texts

Introduction to Mass

We are gathered here in our Father's house to seek a remedy for sin, to sing joyfully to the Lord, and to receive the Body and Blood of his Son, our Lord Jesus Christ. Let us continue our Lenten journey, preparing ourselves to celebrate this mystery of the Eucharist and the mystery of the Lord's Resurrection at Easter. *My brothers and sisters, let us acknowledge our sins, and so prepare ourselves to celebrate the sacred mysteries.*

Tropes for Penitential Act, Form III

While we were still sinners, you died for us: Lord, have mercy.

You rescue us from the snares of death: Christ, have mercy.

You are truly the savior of the world: Lord, have mercy.

Dismissal for Children's Liturgy of the Word

Dear children, you always have a home with God here in his house, which is your house since you are his sons and daughters. Here he gives you life-giving water and feeds you with his Word. Go now and listen to that Word and let it tell you how much God loves you.

Dismissal of Catechumens/Elect

My friends, we pray for you as you continue these days leading to your Baptism. May you grow in faith, hope, and love. We are eagerly awaiting the day when you will be one with us in the celebration of the Lord's Supper. Go in peace.

Dismissal of Extraordinary Ministers of Holy Communion

Friends, ministers of the Lord, we send you to the sick and homebound of our community with the words and Bread of everlasting life. Cheer the hearts of these brothers and sisters of ours, that they may rejoice with us in the love and mercy of our God. Go in peace.

Universal Prayer

The house of the Lord stands firm forever. As his living stones, we pray for the needs of our world.

1. That the Church may show that all creation is sacred and worthy of our respect, we pray:
2. That the buildings that house the Church may always be seen as places of hospitality, healing, and welcome for all, we pray:
3. That the sick and the suffering, especially those who are unable to gather with the Church, may know their participation in Christ's Body, we pray:
4. That the elect may reject what is false and continue to grow in relationship with the Lord this season, we pray:
5. That the dead, washed clean of their sins, may enter the heavenly city, the new and eternal Jerusalem, we pray:

Eternal God,
throughout human history,
you have chosen to be present wherever your people are.
In the fullness of time,
you sent Jesus to be the temple of God among us.
Help us to be living stones always joined to the cornerstone,
Jesus Christ.
Who lives and reigns with you in the unity of the
Holy Spirit,
one God, for ever and ever.
Amen

Other Rites and Customs

- Alert your readers, musicians, and clergy about which readings to prepare for this Sunday and the following two Sundays given the preference for using the readings of Year A when the Scrutinies are celebrated with the elect at Mass.
- During the third week of Lent, the community is going to "give" the Apostles' or Nicene Creed to the elect at a daily Mass (RCIA, 147–149; 157–163). Because this is an important step in their formation process, form a small schola, or at least include a well-prepared cantor to assist with this Mass.

Liturgy and Life

Today's readings are all about signs. Israel's fidelity to the commandments was the sign that they lived as God's people and that God was with them. Paul proclaims a paradox: the clearest sign of God-with-us is Jesus crucified. But, how could this be? How foolish to worship a weak God! Yet that precise absurdity is what we see in the cross. In today's Gospel, Jesus is told to produce some sign of his authority to cleanse the temple. His enigmatic answer baffles the people. But for us who believe, his words point to that moment when the "temple" of his body was raised up to glory after an ignominious death. Now we are to manifest the presence of the crucified and Risen Lord to the world. What sign do we give in our homes, our places of work, our neighborhoods, and our Church communities that we follow a Lord whose power lies in humility and sacrifice?

Taking Place This Week . . .

Consider what can be done liturgically, catechetically, and ministerially to respond to these important needs.

- Today is Girl Scout Sunday.
- International Women's Day and Commonwealth Day in Canada (3/8)
- National Catholic Sisters Week begins tomorrow (3/8).
- Isra and Mi'raj and World Kidney Day (3/11)

Optional Memorial of St. John of God, Religious / violet

Scripture Insights

Naaman goes to Israel to be healed (extraordinary) by dipping himself in a (ordinary) river. Jesus' preaching was extraordinary enough to incite the crowd to kill him, yet he escaped, "passed through the midst of them," probably due to his ordinary appearance.

Preaching Points

Parish Masses

- No prophet is accepted in his or her hometown. No ordinary healing seems sufficient. We want spectacular holy people and flashy miracles. We miss the wondrous gifts of ordinary time.

Masses with Children

- Christ said, "No prophet is accepted in his own native place." This means we often choose not to see the wonders in the "common" people and places around us.

Missal Options

- Use the prayers for Monday of the Third Week of Lent.
- Since music ministers may not be available for daily Mass, it might be better to pray form I or II of the PA on weekdays.
- Any Lenten Collect (except for today's) may be used to conclude the UP.
- The readings from LM #236 may be used any day this week.
- Any Lenten Preface may be used.
- Consider using EP-II.
- Consider concluding the Lenten weekday Masses with a PP.

Song of the Day

"Psalm 42: As the Deer Longs" by Danna Harkin (Word Music Group, LLC)

Optional Memorial

St. John of God was a Portuguese friar who became a leading religious figure. After a period in the army in Spain, he began to distribute religious books, using the new Gutenberg printing press. He cared for those with mental illness and founded what is now known as the Brothers Hospitallers of St. John of God.

- The readings are from the SW.
- Use the Collect from the PS; the other prayers are from the PT.
- Use any of the Lenten Prefaces.
- Consider EP-II.
- Any Lenten Collect may be used to conclude the UP.
- Continue to use the same form of the PA.

Optional Memorial of St. Frances of Rome, Religious / violet

Scripture Insights

Azariah speaks from the fiery furnace where the king had tossed him. Himself almost a burnt offering, he asks that hebe received "with contrite heart and humble spirit." Jesus' parable goes to great lengths to illustrate the debt for which we've been forgiven and how we too need to be forgiving to each other.

Preaching Points

Parish Masses

The parable of the king settling debts perhaps sounds harsh to us, with servants and selling people and their families to settle debts. Christ is trying to overemphasize how crucial it is that we forgive each other "from our hearts."

Masses with Children

The man asking Jesus how many times he should forgive thought he was being generous by suggesting seven times. Jesus multiplies that by seventy, by which he means "endlessly."

Missal Options

- Use the prayers for Tuesday of the Third Week of Lent.
- Any Lenten Collect (except for today's) may be used to conclude the UP.
- The readings from LM #236 may be used any day this week.
- Any Lenten Preface may be used.
- Consider using EP-III.
- Consider concluding the Lenten weekday Masses with a PP.

Song of the Day

"Forgive Our Sins" by Rosamond E. Herklots (Oxford University Press)

Optional Memorial

Although St. Frances' arranged marriage initially prevented her from pursuing a call to religious life, St. Frances' zeal for good works attracted a community of like-minded women, who became the Oblates of Mary, and the desire of her heart was finally fulfilled when her husband's death freed her to become religious superior.

- The readings are from the SW.
- Use the Collect from the PS; the other prayers are from the PT.
- Use any of the Lenten prefaces.
- Consider EP-II.
- Any Lenten Collect may be used to conclude the UP.
- Continue to use the same form of the PA.

WED 10 LM #239 / LMC #176–184 / violet
Lenten Weekday

Scripture Insights

Moses delivered to us God's law, and when we follow it others will say of us, "This great nation is truly a wise and intelligent people." And Jesus is greater still, not abolishing the slightest letter of the law but fulfilling it all.

Preaching Points

Parish Masses

- Moses reminds us that among the rewards of one covenant with God is God's closeness to us, "whenever we call upon him."

Masses with Children

- Moses helped the people receive and follow God's law, and he led them to the promised land. All of this is so that we may live and be intelligent and wise.

Missal Options

- Use the prayers for Wednesday of the Third Week of Lent.
- Any Lenten Collect (except for today's) may be used to conclude the UP.
- The readings from LM #236 may be used any day this week.
- Any Lenten Preface may be used.
- Consider using EP-II.
- Consider concluding the Lenten weekday Masses with a PP.

Song of the Day

"Draw Near" by Steven R. Janco (WLP)

THU 11 LM #240 / LMC #176–184 / violet
Lenten Weekday

Scripture Insights

Jeremiah is forever being crushed between God and God's people. God elaborates on how the people have rejected God, and God sends Jeremiah to scold them for their rejection. They will not listen once again, says God. The people observe Jesus casting out a demon and try to trap him. Jesus spins it back on them. God's house is not divided. The strong man has been found. You follow Jesus or you oppose him.

Preaching Points

Parish Masses

- The passage from Jeremiah is ultimately about God's relentlessness. I took you in as my people and you rejected me. I sent prophets to bring you back; you rejected them too. I am sending another, and I will keep on doing so.
- "Whoever is not with me is against me." Jesus is all about communion—all of us all with him. If Satan is divided against himself, how will his kingdom stand? Satan is about dividing, never uniting. His kingdom is forever falling.

Masses with Children

- To be a prophet is to speak for God. God makes it rough on them, or, rather, we make it rough on them, as we never listen. God sends them anyway.
- Jesus' call is stark. We are either for him or against him. Yet he is stronger than the enemy; he has bound him and keeps coming for us.

Missal Options

- Use the prayers for Thursday of the Third Week of Lent.
- Any Lenten Collect (except for today's) may be used to conclude the UP.
- The readings from LM #236 may be used any day this week.
- Any Lenten Preface may be used.
- Consider using EP-II.
- Consider concluding the Lenten weekday Masses with a PP.

Song of the Day

"Psalm 95: If Today You Hear God's Voice" by David Haas (GIA)

FRI 12 LM #241 / LMC #176–184 / violet
Lenten Weekday

Scripture Insights

The Book of Hosea, among the oldest of the prophetic writings, shows that God is relentless in pursuing us and forgiving us. Jesus, often harsh toward the scribes, this time gives all credit to the one asking the question about the greatest of the Commandments. The Commandments are repeated a second time, with slight variations, illustrating their importance.

Preaching Points

Parish Masses

- "'I will heal their defection,' says the LORD. 'I will love them freely; for my wrath is turned away.'" God is, from the first, relentless in forgiveness and love.

Masses with Children

- The greatest Commandments? You shall love God and you shall love his people.

Missal Options

- Use the prayers for Friday of the Third Week of Lent.
- Any Lenten Collect (except for today's) may be used to conclude the UP.
- The readings from LM #236 may be used any day this week.
- Any Lenten Preface may be used.
- Consider using EP-II.
- Consider concluding the Lenten weekday Masses with a PP.

Song of the Day

"Christians, Let Us Love One Another" by Claudia Foltz, SNJM, and Armand Nigro, SJ (OCP)

SAT 13 LM #242 / LMC #176–184 / violet
Lenten Weekday

Scripture Insights

Both of today's readings sum themselves up with wonderful final sentences ("it is love that I desire" and "everyone who exalts himself"), but the build-ups for both are also great. Both emphasize the need for inner devotion to God, not merely external observances.

Preaching Points

Parish Masses

- Micah always beckons the people back to God, yet he's brutally honest along the way. As God, through Micah, says: "I smote them through the prophets."
- The first line of the Gospel should give us pause. Jesus directed the parable to those who thought themselves righteous but "despised everyone else. "Let us stay as humble as the tax collector.

Masses with Children

- The Old Testament helped us worship God by way of sacrifices; often as little as a dove or as large as an ox, and those weren't burned and offered to God. Micah reminds us that love and knowledge of God are far more important.
- The Pharisee is a classic example of what we call "self-righteous." He is proud and thinks he did it all himself. The tax collector is humble, because he's been humbled by life, and feels the need for God.

Missal Options

- Use the prayers for Saturday of the Third Week of Lent.
- Since music ministers may not be available for daily Mass, it might be better to pray form I or II of the PA on weekdays.
- Any Lenten Collect (except for today's) may be used to conclude the UP.
- The readings from LM #236 may be used any day this week.
- Any Lenten Preface may be used.
- Consider using EPR-II.
- Consider concluding the Lenten weekday Masses with a PP.

Song of the Day

"Come, Return to the Lord" by Carey Landry (OCP)

SUN 14 LM #32B or 31A / LMC #28B or 27A / violet or rose
Fourth Sunday of Lent

Laetare Sunday

Editorial Note

If your parish is celebrating the Second Scrutiny today, you will need to use the Year A readings. The Scripture Insights for Year A along with Missal options are provided below.

About Laetare Sunday

We rejoice in the salvation the Lord is giving us as we continue entering into the discipline of Lent. The Entrance Antiphon sings: "Rejoice, Jerusalem!" If your parish is celebrating the Second Scrutiny today, you will need to use the Year A readings. The Scripture Insights for Year A along with Missal options are provided below.

Scripture Insights (Year B)

Today's Chronicles reading tersely ends the sorrowful story of Judah's disobedience toward God. For this writer, the exile to Babylon was a natural outcome of grievous sin. He was heir to the viewpoint: "If you obey God's commandments, you will prosper. If not, you will perish" (see Deuteronomy 4:25–27; 8:19; 11:13–17; 13:22–28.) In this way the writers explained Israel and Judah's respective defeats by foreign powers as acts of divine justice that had been foretold. In today's text, we can hear the priests' concern that the rituals associated with the code of holiness could no longer be performed. This is reflected in the report of the fiery destruction of the Temple and its vessels and the interpretation of the seventy years of exile as a Sabbath rest for the land. But suddenly the divine sun shines through the storm clouds of the exile when Cyrus proclaims the release of the captives; the people are freed to return to their land, to rebuild their temple, and to restore their spiritual fortunes. For the haggard exiles, the decree was an unimaginable grace, lavish and unexpected, an unparalleled act of Divine Mercy.

Imagining the beneficence of a new king and the state of the returning exiles gives us a perspective on the cornucopia of theological language of Ephesians. The Good News is the proclamation of favor issued by a powerful ruler and generous patron, "rich in mercy" (2:4), with "immeasurable riches of grace" (2:7) that are continually dispensed to the subjects. This generosity is beyond all measure, "far more than we can ask or imagine" (3:20), even when we were like the exiles, victims of our own disobedience, "dead through our trespasses and sins" (2:1, 5). This "kindness" is massively out of proportion to what we might have expected. Clearly, this situation is none of our doing but the result of God's unlimited favor. In Christian language, it is "grace," which excludes all boasting and spiritual preening.

Preaching Points

Parish Masses

- We are called to be the children of Christ's light; we are redeemed in him and through him—through his grace and not by our own accord.
- Just as the ancient Jews were kept from their holy land, we are kept from heaven by our sin. Like King Cyrus announcing the freedom of the people to return to the holy land, we are freed and given eternal life through Christ.
- Jesus' generosity is boundless, and the forgiveness of the Father is without end. He doesn't tire of forgiving his children.
- Our forgiveness comes through Jesus Christ, and it is not something we create or earn.

Children's Liturgy of the Word

- We are captive to our sin because sin is like a prison. Sin keeps us from the lives that God desires for us to have. Through Jesus we are freed from sin.
- We sometimes tire of forgiving people in our lives, but God never tires of forgiving his children.
- We do not earn God's forgiveness. Our good works have tremendous value in that they are a response to the grace of God.

Scripture Insights (Year A)

We learn in today's readings for the Fourth Sunday of Lent that divine vision penetrates beyond the superficial and sees into our deepest selves.

The First Reading, from 1 Samuel, recounts the anointing of the young shepherd boy, David, as king of Israel. In the story, God directs Samuel to Jesse of Bethlehem, who had eight sons. From Jesse's sons would come the next king of Israel. Jesse's eldest son, Eliab, was by all outward signs the logical choice among Jesse's sons. But to the surprise of all, God chooses Jesse's youngest son, David. It was what God saw in David's heart that made him different from his brothers. Israel was learning to rely on divine vision to guide its history and its destiny.

The divine vision of Jesus drives today's Gospel reading from John, the healing of the man born blind. The blind man's healing begins with a simple and logical question from the disciples: Was the man born blind because he or his parents had sinned? In fact, throughout this healing story, a total of sixteen questions are asked by various people. All of these questions express some form of limited human vision. It is Jesus alone who sees that the man was born blind not because of sin; rather, the man was born blind "so that the works of God might be made visible through him."

In his Letter to the Ephesians, Paul encourages the Ephesians to "live as children of light" (Ephesians 5:8), producing "goodness and righteousness and truth" (Ephesians 5:9). During this season of Lent, we are called to challenge our own limited human vision, to look beyond mere appearances, and to seek what is good and true and righteous. In this way, we will learn to see as God sees.

Preaching Points

Parish Masses

- Blindness manifests itself in many different ways: self-righteousness, closed-mindedness, lack of belief, fear, an air of superiority, and so on. Explore the life circumstances of people that we—as individuals, as family members, and maybe we as a faith community—are blind to, and how our faith in Jesus can expand our vision and our response to the needs of others.
- Lent is a time of enlightenment, when we ask to see how living in Christ is changing our worldview. In the Eucharist, we celebrate the great truth of God's self-giving love. If we let it, this celebration will teach us how to live in Christ.
- Many people in powerful positions, as well as those the powerful manipulate through fear and false promises, are blind to the hardships and injustices that pervade our world. Explore how as disciples of Jesus we are called to be "in the world" but not "of the world." As disciples, we must allow God to open our eyes, hearts, and voices in order to bring the Light of Christ to those who walk in darkness.
- Break open the second scrutiny, which draws on the Gospel message of Christ as the light of the world. Confident in the Father's love, we turn to Christ the healer, asking for awareness of our need for healing and for light to see the way that God sees, to love with God's heart.

Children's Liturgy of the Word

- Each of us has "blind spots"—that is, things we are not able to see or understand because of our prejudices or biases. Sometimes we have blind spots when we can't see the good in another person. Lent is a time to look at how we sometimes judge others too quickly and fail to see who they really are.
- Jesus uses the dirt from the earth to heal the blind man. In sacraments, we often use simple ordinary things to help us experience the holy in our lives—for example, in the Eucharist bread that becomes Christ's Body.
- Jesus came to earth to show us how much God loves us. When we act with love, we show God how much we love him.

Missal Options

- PA form III is a wonderful option for Lent. Use whatever form is chosen on every Sunday of Lent.
- The Gloria is not sung (or said).
- The Creed is recited or sung. Because of its baptismal significance, consider using the Apostles' Creed throughout Lent and Easter.
- Any Lenten Collect (except for today's) may be used or adapted to conclude the UP.
- If the Scrutinies are not taking place, use P-I or P-II of Lent; otherwise, the Preface is found among the pages for the Third Sunday of Lent ("The Man Born Blind").
- Consider the EPR-II.
- Lenten Sunday Masses conclude with a PP.
- If the Scrutiny occurs, the proper prayers should be used; these Mass formularies are found in the "Ritual Masses" section of the Missal, under section I—For the Conferral of the Sacraments of Christian Initiation, #2: For the Celebration of the Scrutinies, B: For the Second Scrutiny. For the actual ritual of the Scrutiny itself, consult RCIA, 150–56. The Scrutiny takes place after the homily.

Music Preparation

- Right about this point in Lent we run out of steam and are overwhelmed by the tasks of the coming Triduum. Take time in silence to glory in the cross. Let it strengthen you.
- Because there is no way to rehearse with the congregation during Holy Week, be strategic. "Crux Fidelis" (suggested below) is a beautiful piece to use during the Preparation of the Gifts on Palm Sunday and during the Adoration of the Cross on Good Friday. Continuing to use during the liturgy in this way will strengthen the congregation's ability to participate well.

Music Suggestions

- Gathering: "What Words Can Sing the Story" by J. Michael Joncas (OCP)
- Sending Forth: "Lift High the Cross" (various publishers)
- Preparation or Communion: "Crux Fidelis" by Steven J. Warner (WLP)

Mass Texts

Introduction to Mass

If anyone is wearied by their Lenten observance or disheartened by their sins, let them rejoice in the knowledge that Easter is on the way and in the faith that Christ has taken upon himself all our burdens and reconciled us to God. By grace we are saved, and so let us find joy in this Eucharist, which is the pledge of our salvation. *My brothers and sisters, let us acknowledge our sins, and so prepare ourselves to celebrate the sacred mysteries.*

Tropes for Penitential Act, Form III

We come to you, Lord, poor sinners in need of salvation: Lord, have mercy.

You are rich in compassion and abounding in steadfast love: Christ, have mercy.

You died for our sins and were lifted up that we might have eternal life: Lord, have mercy.

Dismissal for Children's Liturgy of the Word

Dear children, it is time for you to have your own celebration of the Liturgy of the Word. Listen to Jesus speaking tenderly to you in today's readings and know that he loves you more than you can possibly imagine. When you return to us you will increase our joy as we continue the Eucharist with gratitude.

Dismissal of Catechumens/Elect

My dear friends, we send you forth once again to reflect on the mystery of our redemption and of Christ at work in your lives. As we pray for you, our anticipation grows for your Baptism and for the day when you will join us in the celebration of the Eucharist. Go in peace.

Dismissal of Extraordinary Ministers of Holy Communion

My friends, speak a word of joy to our brothers and sisters who are prevented from joining us due to illness or injury or infirmity. Through partaking in Christ's Body, may they know their unity with us and grow in longing for the coming of God's Kingdom. Go in peace.

Universal Prayer

God so loved the world that he gave us his only Son. We show our love to God by serving him and loving others. And so, we turn to him in prayer for the needs of our world.

1. That the Church will be an instrument of reconciliation, we pray:
2. That civic leaders will be architects of peace and justice, we pray:
3. That we keep in mind the needs of the most vulnerable, we pray:
4. That our hearts will be open to reconcile with others, we pray:
5. That the elect throughout the world will continue to open themselves to God's love, we pray:
6. That all who mourn the loss of loved ones will be comforted by hope in the resurrection, we pray:

Loving Father,
your Son was lifted high upon the cross
so that the world might know the way to salvation.
May we be filled with joy this day
as we participate in the self-offering of Christ,
whose name is our hope and whose light is our truth.
Through Christ our Lord.
Amen.

Other Rites and Customs

- Rejoice—It's Laetare Sunday!
- If you've kept the organ and other instruments quiet throughout Lent, let them loose a little bit today.
- Decorate the sanctuary with some simple flowers in violet and rose.
- Have a Lenten soup supper and invite a guest speaker from the local food pantry or from Catholic Charities.

Liturgy and Life

"God writes straight with crooked lines." We often say this to encourage ourselves in the darkness of personal, social, or national disaster. Is it true? Witness unfaithful Israel. The people ignored the covenant and were humbled through exile; but, more important, this national disaster showed them that their God was really God of all the earth, a profound theological shift. In the Gospel, Jesus instructs Nicodemus in the mystery of the cross, the ultimate crooked line: "so must the Son of Man be lifted up, so that everyone who believes in him may have eternal life." This week, prepare for the Sacrament of Penance. Examine your own crooked life-line. Mark your turning points, your important encounters, the choices that have made all the difference. Tell your confessor what you learn. Then give thanks to God, who, as Paul says in his Letter to the Ephesians, is "rich in mercy."

Taking Place This Week . . .

Consider what can be done liturgically, catechetically, and ministerially to respond to these important needs.

- Today the special collection is for Catholic Relief Service.
- Daylight Saving Time starts (3/14).
- St. Patrick's Day (3/17)
- Solemnity of St. Joseph (3/19)
- March/Spring Equinox and International Day of Happiness (3/20)

MON 15 Lenten Weekday

LM #244 / LMC #176–184 / violet

Scripture Insights

Laetare Sunday spills over into Monday, as we get rejoicing and exultation from the prophet and a healing from Jesus. The long lives promised by Isaiah are revealed in Jesus' healing of the royal official's son. This is the second "sign" of Jesus. John's account of the Gospel speaks of signs, not miracles. Miracles are out of the ordinary occurrences. Signs are those acts that reveal Christ's creative power.

Preaching Points

Parish Masses

- God is always about new beginnings and new life, and that is what the prophet promises. No longer stuck in the things of the past, we are promised an end to weeping, and rejoicing that lasts into old age.
- Jesus often cures by touching. This time, as "in the beginning," the healing is done by command. Jesus never even sees the child.

Masses with Children

- God creates—it is what God does. In the First Reading God promises newness in both heaven and earth. No more crying, only rejoicing.
- Jesus sounds like he is scolding the crowd when he says, "Unless you people see signs and wonders, you will not believe." Yet he goes on to perform a sign. Perhaps it is just our nature.

Missal Options

- Use the prayers for Monday of the Fourth Week of Lent.
- Since music ministers may not be available for daily Mass, it might be better to pray form I or II of the PA on weekdays.
- The readings from LM #243 may be used any day this week (except for the Solemnity of St. Joseph).
- Any Lenten Collect may be used to conclude the UP.
- Any Lenten Preface may be used.
- Consider using the EPVN-IV
- Consider concluding the Lenten weekday Masses with a PP.

Song of the Day

"Trust in the Lord" by Roc O'Conner, SJ (OCP)

TUE 16 Lenten Weekday

LM #245 / LMC #176–184 / violet

Scripture Insights

Ezekiel's vision of water flowing from the Temple is all about life flourishing. Remember, these writings come from a desert environment. The sick and the lame waited by pools because they were sources of life and healing. Jesus' question is provocative, "Do you want to be well?" Jesus did heal the man on the Sabbath. The Jews scolded the man for carrying the mat and Jesus for healing on the Sabbath.

Preaching Points

Parish Masses

- Water is life. It begins as a trickle at the Temple and grows with leaps and bounds, and soon it is turn teeming with life.
- Jesus healed a man who had been sick for thirty-eight years. Rather than rejoicing over the man's healing, the religious leaders were angry that this was done on a Sabbath, a day of rest.

Masses with Children

- We know that water brings life—our bodies need it, we need it for cleansing ourselves, and all living creatures depend on it as well. Ezekiel's vision builds on all this.
- Jesus healed a man who had been sick for thirty-eight years. Rather than rejoicing over the man's healing, the religious leaders were angry that this was done on a Sabbath, a day of rest.

Missal Options

- Use the prayers for Tuesday of the Fourth Week of Lent.
- Since music ministers may not be available for daily Mass, it might be better to pray form I or II of the PA on weekdays.
- The readings from LM #243 may be used any day this week (except for the Solemnity of St. Joseph).
- Any Lenten Collect may be used to conclude the UP.
- Any Lenten Preface may be used.
- Consider using the EP-III.
- Consider concluding the Lenten weekday Masses with a PP.

Song of the Day

"Healer of Our Every Ill" by Marty Haugen (GIA)

W E D 17 LM #246 / LMC #176–184 / violet
Lenten Weekday

Optional Memorial of St. Patrick, Bishop / violet

Scripture Insights

Jesus takes the compassion expressed by the prophet, "Can a mother forget her infant?" and raises it to an even higher level. "The LORD comforts his people," says Isaiah. "So also does the Son give life to whomever he wishes." To go even further, Jesus tells us that even "all who are in the tombs will hear his voice and will come out."

Preaching Points

Parish Masses

- Our God is the God of life and compassion. God restores the land, releases the prisoners, and leads people to springs of water. All the while being even more tender than is a mother to her child.
- Jesus elaborates on the inseparable bond between the Father and him. The Father works on the Sabbath, so does he. The Father raises the dead, so does Jesus. As the Father "has life in himself," so does the Son.

Masses with Children

- Scripture often uses images from our lives so we may understand and raises them to an even higher level. Thus we get the image of a mother's love for her child. God loves us even more than that.
- The religious leaders of the day continuously challenge Jesus for doing things only God could do or should do, like curing on the Sabbath. Jesus here elaborates on the intimate, elaborate relationship he has with the Father, as a justification and explanation for doing that which God does.

Missal Options

- Use the prayers for Wednesday of the Fourth Week of Lent.
- Since music ministers may not be available for daily Mass, it might be better to pray form I or II of the PA on weekdays.
- The readings from LM #243 may be used any day this week (except for the Solemnity of St. Joseph).
- Any Lenten Collect may be used to conclude the UP.
- Any Lenten Preface may be used.
- Consider using the EPR-I.
- Consider concluding the Lenten weekday Masses with a PP.

Song of the Day

"Christ Be Beside Me" James Quinn, SJ (OCP)

Optional Memorial

After escaping slavery in Ireland, St. Patrick spent twenty-two years acquiring education and practical skills so that he could return to Ireland as a missionary witness to the God who had sustained him during captivity. In the end, he was wildly successful in his mission, peacefully converting thousands and building churches and monasteries across Ireland.

- The readings are from the SW.
- Use the Collect from the PS; the other prayers are from the PT.
- Use any of the Lenten Prefaces.
- Consider EP-II.
- Any Lenten Collect may be used to conclude the UP.
- Continue to use the same form of the PA.

T H U 18 LM #247 / LMC #176–184 / violet
Lenten Weekday

Optional Memorial of St. Cyril of Jerusalem, Bishop and Doctor of the Church / violet

Scripture Insights

As different as these two readings may seem, both are about the need for a relationship with God, which acknowledges how precarious that can feel. The Jews were nervous with Moses being gone for so long while talking to God on the mountain, so they made the golden calf. Christ calls the people to come to the Father through him, while pointing out all the ways the people try to replace him (clinging to the Scriptures, other teachers, the praise of people).

Preaching Points

Parish Masses

- Moses pleaded with God by reminding God of all his goodness to the people and by recounting all the promises made (land, descendants), and God relented.
- Christ is relentless and exhaustive: John foretold me, the Father sent me, the Scriptures testify to me, Moses wrote about me. I am the One "but you do not want to come to me to have life."

Masses with Children

- God was angry at the people for creating and worshiping the golden calf. Moses pleaded with God, reminding God of all God's kindness, and God relented.
- Christ wants us to be in relationship with him, and through him we get to the Father.

Missal Options

- Use the prayers for Thursday of the Fourth Week of Lent.
- Since music ministers may not be available for daily Mass, it might be better to pray form I or II of the PA on weekdays.
- The readings from LM #243 may be used any day this week (except for the Solemnity of St. Joseph).
- Any Lenten Collect may be used to conclude the UP.
- Any Lenten Preface may be used.
- Consider using the EP-II.
- Consider concluding the Lenten weekday Masses with a PP.

Song of the Day

"Make of Our Hands a Throne" by Cyril of Jerusalem, Steven C. Warner (WLP)

Optional Memorial

St. Cyril was frequently embroiled in the conflicts over Arianism and was exiled three times for his defenses of orthodoxy; however, his great work was not a work of polemics but a set of twenty-three lectures for catechumens. His love for Christ made him a natural preacher and teacher.

- The readings are from the SW.
- Use the Collect from the PS; the other prayers are from the PT.
- Use any of the Lenten Prefaces.
- Consider EP-II.
- Any Lenten Collect may be used to conclude the UP.
- Continue to use the same form of the PA.

FRI 19 Solemnity of St. Joseph, Spouse of the Blessed Virgin Mary

See page 130.

SAT 20 Lenten Weekday

LM #249 / LMC #176–184 / violet

Scripture Insights

The plots are in motion, to destroy Jeremiah, to arrest Jesus. Indeed Jesus is, as Jeremiah foretold, like a lamb being led to slaughter. Oddly, Jesus is nowhere to be found in this passage—only the plots and murmurings and the upheaval he has caused. Who is the only one to speak the truth about him? The guards: "Never before has anyone spoken like this man."

Preaching Points

Parish Masses

- Jeremiah, like many of the prophets before and after, incited the wrath of the powerful for speaking the Word of God.
- The Gospel starts with the truth and ends in rancor. Some in the crowd rightly see Jesus as the prophet and the Christ. Division and bickering ensue, over points of law and about Jesus' hometown. Only the guards really hear Jesus and let themselves be moved.

Masses with Children

- Jeremiah spoke God's Word, and it made some people angry. He was "like a trusting lamb led to slaughter," much like Jesus was.
- Jesus stirred up the crowds. Some knew he was the Christ and loved him for it. Others just knew of his power and wanted to destroy him since they didn't agree with him.

Missal Options

- Use the prayers for Saturday of the Fourth Week of Lent.
- Since music ministers may not be available for daily Mass, it might be better to pray form I or II of the PA on weekdays.
- The readings from LM #243 may be used any day this week (except for the Solemnity of St. Joseph).
- Any Lenten Collect may be used to conclude the UP.
- Any Lenten Preface may be used.
- Consider using the EP-II.
- Consider concluding the Lenten weekday Masses with a PP.

Song of the Day

"Broken for the Broken" by Chris DeSilva (GIA)

FRI **19** LM #543 / LMC #272 / white

Solemnity of St. Joseph, Spouse of the Blessed Virgin Mary

Today's Saint

Joseph was a just man. This is another way of saying that he was a fervent Jew who observed and revered the law. This fact underlines his great faith and docility to the Holy Spirit. Tempering his devotion to the law was his compassion. When he found out Mary was pregnant, his plan was to divorce her secretly. Scripture does not tell us how this would have been done. Like Joseph, the son of Jacob, this Joseph had the gift to interpret his dream accurately: "For it is through the Holy Spirit that this child has been conceived." We can only imagine the courage Joseph had in the milieu of his time.

Scripture Insights

God promised Abraham that he would be the father of all nations. Abraham believed God despite evidence to the contrary.

Abraham did nothing to earn God's favor. He accepted it as a gift, thereby making him the father of everyone—both Jew and Gentile—who accepts God's love and salvation knowing that such gifts cannot be earned, only received. King David had planned to build a temple in Jerusalem, but God sets that plan aside and declares that he will ensure that David's descendants always rule Israel. God's promise was fulfilled in a way that went well beyond the king's expectations.

By taking Jesus as his adopted son, Joseph, a descendant of David, fulfills God's promise. Jesus, however, will reign, not only over Israel, but over all of heaven and earth. In both options for this solemnity's Gospel passage St. Joseph is portrayed as a righteous man. Although he did his best to observe Jewish law, Joseph also proved that he was like Abraham in his righteousness, for when he was instructed to take the pregnant Mary into his home, he obeyed without question. Joseph modeled both trust and fidelity to the law for his new son.

In the passage from Luke, Joseph has taken his family to Jerusalem, a difficult journey that again shows Joseph's obedience to the law. We can imagine Joseph's terror at losing track of his adopted son, yet he lost Jesus while doing what he was supposed to do: raising the child well. By taking Jesus to Jerusalem, Joseph doubtlessly helped Jesus understand himself and his mission. Although Joseph may have been startled by the gift of Jesus, he modeled how we are to receive him. We accept salvation in faith even as we strive to be worthy of it.

Preaching Points

Parish Masses

- Joseph responded to God in faith, grace, and love. Certainly, he did not expect a family created in such a unique fashion, but he embraced God's request, loving and caring for his family. We too are called to respond to God's Word in love and compassion. To have faith in God and his Word is a noble and righteous quality.
- The house built from David's offspring is alive today. It is not a genetic line, but we are the family of God through adoption in Christ.
- Joseph showed goodness, gentleness, kindness, compassion, and bravery. The spouse of Mary and Jesus' earthly father was a man of God's grace and mercy.

Children's Liturgy of the Word

- Throughout the Bible, God promises descendants to his followers. They had faith in God and in God's Word that these descendants would come into being.
- David's descendants are living today—not only those who are related by blood, but through those of us who are adopted into God's family through Jesus.
- When we read the Gospel accounts, we find the expectations God has of his people. He expects kindness, mercy, and compassion from his people. We see St. Joseph embody all of those Gospel qualities.

Missal Options

- The prayers are found in the PS for March 19.
- Continue to use the same form of the PA that you use on the Lenten Sundays.
- The Gloria and the Creed are sung (or recited) because today is a solemnity.
- Any Lenten Collect may be used or adapted to conclude the UP.
- The Preface is proper and found in the RM on the pages for St. Joseph.
- Unlike the other days of Lent, a PP is not included in the texts for St. Joseph. To unify today's celebration with the Lenten season, consider the PP, #6, found after the SB at the end of the Order of Mass section in the RM.
- Even though it is Lent, you can pull out the stops (moderately) for today's solemnity. Use festive music (possibly inviting the choir to sing), incense, and a longer, more formal Gospel procession.
- If the parish has an image of St. Joseph, or of the Holy Family, see how it can be decorated this week with some flowers and candles. The image can be reverenced with incense at the beginning of Mass.
- Consider using EP-III.

Music Preparation

- While it is a festive day, the tone of the Gloria can be simple, like a chant setting or a through-composed setting.
- Secure a cantor or small schola to assist with today's Mass so the psalm and other parts of the ordinary can be sung.
- Consider chanting the Apostles' Creed on this solemnity and other solemn celebrations throughout the year.

Music Suggestions

- Gathering: "St. Joseph, Mary's Faithful Spouse" by D. Dufner, OSB (GIA) or "Come Now and Praise the Humble Saint" by G. W. Williams (Hope Publishing Company) or "O Joseph, Mighty Patron" by M. Keane (WLP)
- Preparation of the Gifts: "The Hands That First Held Mary's Child" by Thomas H. Troeger (GIA)

Mass Texts

Introduction to Mass

The Lord provides for us by sending us models, guardians, and intercessors, from Abraham, our father in faith, to Joseph, whom he chose to watch over his Son and his Church. Let us turn to the husband of Mary and seek his help, as we give thanks to God in the celebration of this Eucharist. *My brothers and sisters, let us acknowledge our sins, and so prepare ourselves to celebrate the sacred mysteries.*

Tropes for Penitential Act, Form III

You do not leave us alone in our sins:
Lord, have mercy.

You are faithful to the covenant you made
with your people: Christ, have mercy.

Your kingdom and your throne will endure
for all ages: Lord, have mercy.

Dismissal of Catechumens/Elect

My friends, St. Joseph was asked to have faith in the face of unbelievable circumstances, and he trusted in the Lord. We encourage you to find strength in his example and to place all your trust in the faithfulness of God who is leading you on this journey toward Baptism and union with his Son. We look forward, for your sake, to that union and to your union with us at the Lord's table. Go in peace.

Dismissal of Extraordinary Ministers of Holy Communion

Dear friends, as God provided for his Son through the love and protection of St. Joseph, so now he provides for his children who are sick and weak in body by giving us the Body of his Son. Take to them the Bread of Life, that they may be restored in faith and joy. Go in peace.

Universal Prayer

Obedient in faith in the Lord's desire that we should be conscious of the needs of others, we offer to him our prayers and petitions.

1. For our bishops and priests, that they may be inspired by the strength and gentleness of St. Joseph, we pray:
2. For people of every nation, instill in them the determination to work for peace and justice, we pray:
3. For our parish leaders, that they may model the prudence of St. Joseph, we pray:
4. For parents, that they seek the wisdom of Joseph, we pray:
5. For spouses, that they may live with trust in each other as did Mary and Joseph, we pray:
6. For the sick and the dying, that they will be comforted by the love of God, we pray:

God of wonders,
you chose Joseph to be the husband of Mary and
guardian of Jesus.
As he was attentive to your voice through the message
of an angel,
may we also discern your will for us.
As he provided a safe haven for Mary and her son,
may we prepare a loving welcome for Christ,
who comes to us in those who are
frightened or weary, poor or forgotten.
Through Christ our Lord.
Amen.

Other Rites and Customs

- Bless bread, pastries, and other foods using the Blessing of St. Joseph's Table from the *Book of Blessings*, 1679–1700. Usually the blessing takes place outside of Mass in the venue where the food is made available. A priest, deacon, or lay minister may lead the order of blessing. A shorter rite is offered (see BB, 1697). The introduction to the order of blessing explains that "we rejoice at this table, which is a sign of God's generous blessings and of our call to serve the poor and hungry" (BB, 1685).
- Share information about St. Joseph on the parish social media page. Consider including the Litany of St. Joseph, which is found in the BB, 1691.

Liturgy and Life

Sometimes God makes his plan known in dreams, as we see in today's reading. The Gospel accounts never quote Joseph, but his actions speak volumes. He does not allow fear to guide his life but recognizes that God saves. Rather than questioning, he commits and follows God's commands. Oh, that we might become as trusting as Joseph and open ourselves more fully to doing the work of God in the world.

S U N **21** LM #35B or 34A / LMC #31B or 30A / violet
Fifth Sunday of Lent

Editorial Note

If your parish is celebrating the Third Scrutiny today, you will need to use the Year A readings. The Scripture Insights for Year A along with Missal options are provided below.

Scripture Insights (Year B)

The short passage from the Letter to the Hebrews casts unusual light on Jesus. The Gospel accounts tell us that Jesus prayed (Matthew 14:23; Mark 1:35; Luke 6:12) and what he prayed about (Mark 14:36; Luke 22:22), but here we read that Jesus prayed "with loud cries and tears." John's account tells us that Jesus was confident that God heard his prayers (John 11:41–42), perhaps because he was God's Son; here we read that Jesus "was heard because of his reverence." The Gospel accounts tell us that Jesus remained in constant communion with the will of God (Matthew 26:39; John 8:29); here we read that "he learned obedience from what he suffered." The Gospel accounts tell us that at Jesus' baptism he was already "my Son, the beloved" in whom God was "well pleased" (Luke 3:22), but here we read that Jesus was "made perfect."

The letter's frank statement that Jesus progressed toward perfection stands alongside a Christology equal in majesty to any in the New Testament: This same human Jesus is the "heir of all things and through whom [God] created the universe," "the refulgence of [God's] glory, the very imprint of [God's] being," the one who "sustains all things by his mighty word" (Hebrews 1:2–4).

This writer grasped what many views of Jesus lack: a clear understanding of Jesus' humanity. Human beings develop over time, feel doubt and pain, do not know their fate, aspire to achieve. Hebrews makes explicit what the Gospel accounts imply: Jesus progressed toward God by suffering.

The Jeremiah passage speaks of the new covenant where rule-keeping cannot pass for true devotion and God will write God's law "on their hearts." Jesus' moment-by-moment practice of obedience fulfilled that prophecy by engraving God's covenant into the human heart forever. He wrote this inner law on our hearts with the stylus of his passion.

Preaching Points

Parish Masses

- We are called to be followers of Christ, obedient to him, and to act upon his Word. When we serve Christ, we serve the Father. God the Son was obedient to the Father; he was submissive to Father and was a true servant.
- Servanthood is not slavery; we serve Jesus voluntarily and joyfully.
- Jesus' entire life was spent within the will of God; Jesus is fully human and grew up oriented toward God and his will.
- Checking boxes and not breaking rules isn't the point of a Catholic life; we are called to submit our hearts and minds to the Father, in imitation of Jesus.

Children's Liturgy of the Word

- We are all called to serve God and one another with joy. Being a servant is a choice we make every day of our lives.
- Jesus was fully human and fully divine. Like all humans, he grew from a child into an adult. He was and is oriented toward God's will.
- The rules and laws of the Church are meant to help us on our journeys toward God, but rules are not the sum of Catholic life. We are called to submit ourselves to God, like Jesus.

Scripture Insights (Year A)

The First Reading describes a vision of the prophet Ezekiel during Israel's captivity and exile in Babylon, 587–538 BC. The Babylonian Empire had destroyed Jerusalem and carried Israel into exile. The Israelites felt dead and buried; Babylon had become their grave. But Ezekiel prophesied that God would one day open their graves and that together they would rise from the dead. Ezekiel's vision of the dry bones is grounded in a firm belief in the restoration of Israel. Historically, the Israelites did rise from the dead in their release from Babylon in 538 BC. Six hundred years later, Christians would look back at Ezekiel's prophecy and see its ultimate fulfillment in Jesus' Resurrection from the dead.

In the Gospel story, the sisters Mary and Martha are profoundly grieved by their brother's death, but each reacts differently. When Jesus arrives, Mary remains at home, mourning. Martha goes out to greet him. Jesus tells Martha, "I am the resurrection and the life" and then asks, "Do you believe this?" Martha responds, "Yes, Lord. I have come to believe that you are the Christ, the Son of God, the one who is coming into the world" (John 11:25). This confession of faith by Martha in John's account parallels Peter's confession of faith in the Synoptics (that is, Matthew 16:15–16; Mark 8:29; Luke 9:20).

It would take time for Martha and Peter to understand the implications of their confessions. Like them and the prophet Ezekiel, we are called to believe in God's power of life over death. And like Lazarus, we who believe in Jesus will rise from our graves at the sound of his voice.

Preaching Points

Parish Masses

- Jesus, lover and friend, is the one whom God sends to free us and give us life. Do we have any idea where our lack of life imprisons us? Where do we need to be raised? Can we ask the Lord to heal particular parts of our lives? Do we want to be freed from our responsibility to give of our surplus to feed the hungry, clothe the naked, and welcome the stranger?
- Explore the third scrutiny theologically with the congregation. In this rite, we ask the Lord to show the elect where they still need to be freed, where death is hiding in their spiritual lives, where they need to realize that in every part of our lives we may be reborn, raised by God to new life in Christ.

Children's Liturgy of the Word

- Do you ever think that God is sad, even suffers, when he sees his children suffering? God is our father and wants what is good for each of us.
- As Catholics we believe that death is not the end of life. In the Creed we say we believe in the resurrection of the body.
- Because Mary and Martha had faith in Jesus, Jesus raised their brother Lazarus from the tomb. Prayer and faith can bring about new and important changes for us and for others.

Missal Options

- PA form III is a wonderful option for Lent. Use whatever form is chosen on every Sunday of Lent.
- The Gloria is not sung (or said).
- The Creed is recited or sung. Because of its baptismal significance, consider using the Apostles' Creed throughout Lent and Easter.
- Any Lenten Collect (except for today's) may be used or adapted to conclude the UP.
- If the Scrutinies are not taking place, use P-I or P-II of Lent; otherwise, the Preface is found among the pages for the Third Sunday of Lent ("Lazarus").
- Consider the EPR-I.
- Lenten Sunday Masses conclude with a PP.
- If the Scrutiny occurs, the proper prayers should be used; these Mass formularies are found in the "Ritual Masses" section of the Missal, under section I—For the Conferral of the Sacraments of Christian Initiation, #2: For the Celebration of the Scrutinies, C: For the Third Scrutiny. For the actual ritual of the scrutiny itself, consult RCIA, 150–56. The Scrutiny takes place after the homily.

Music Preparation

- Prepare familiar music for Masses this week so you will not have to spend as much time practicing and will have more time for Triduum preparation in your final rehearsals with the choir.
- Sit down and make a to-do list of all your responsibilities and all the ministries and supplies necessary for the Triduum. Begin to accomplish tasks steadily so it is not overwhelming.

Music Suggestions

- Gathering: "We Remember" by Marty Haugen (GIA)
- Preparation of the Gifts: "Unless a Grain of Wheat" by Bob Hurd (OCP)
- Communion: "Unless a Grain of Wheat" by Bernadette Farrell (OCP) or "Now We Remain" by David Haas (GIA)

Mass Texts

Introduction to Mass

Jesus Christ handed himself over to death so that our death might be transformed and lead to eternal life. He is the source of our salvation and the source of our joy. Let us free ourselves of the burden of our sins and run after him with enlightened hearts, even as he draws us all to himself in the Eucharist we now celebrate. *My brothers and sisters, let us acknowledge our sins, and so prepare ourselves to celebrate the sacred mysteries.*

Tropes for Penitential Act, Form III

Lord Jesus, you forgive our wrongdoing and remember our sin no more: Lord, have mercy.

Lord Jesus, you give life to our mortal bodies: Christ, have mercy.

Lord Jesus, you are our food for eternal life: Lord, have mercy.

Dismissal for Children's Liturgy of the Word

My children, everything Jesus said and did was out of love for God and love for the human race. He lived so that he could be with us as one of us. He died so that death would not have the final word for us. He rose from the dead so that we could be with him forever. He is still present and active in the world today, and he will speak to you in the readings you are about to hear. Listen to him with faith in his great love.

Dismissal of Catechumens/Elect

My dear friends, we pray all the more eagerly that this grace will be yours and we look forward to having you join us around the table of our savior and Lord. Go in peace.

Dismissal of Extraordinary Ministers of Holy Communion

Dear ministers, the Lord desires to be with us in our weakness and frailty, and so we give you his Body to take to our sisters and brothers who have been weakened by illness, injury, or age. May he strengthen their spirits and fill them with peace and joy. Go in his love.

Universal Prayer

As baptized members of the Church, we are called to die to self so that we may be transformed into Christ. Let us be conscious of the needs of our world as we lift these needs to the Lord.

1. That the Eucharist may always be the source and summit of the Church's life and ministry, we pray:
2. That those who desperately cling to self and refuse to let go of established ways of being may fall to the ground and die to self, we pray:
3. That those responsible for harvesting the land may receive a bountiful crop from their next planting, we pray:
4. That those who manufacture the food we eat may receive a just reward for their labor, we pray:
5. That we may continue to follow our Lord this Lent with our eyes focused on the wood of the cross, we pray:

Benevolent God,
the suffering, death, and Resurrection of your Son
reveal the mystery of our life,
that to experience real transformation
we must be obedient to your will and die to self.
Like the grain of wheat that falls to the ground,
help us to let go of evil and selfish ways
and find our true life in you.
Through Christ our Lord.
Amen.

Other Rites and Customs

- Utilize the ancient practice of draping the statues and crosses in the church in violet cloth until the Easter Vigil.
- Gather the liturgical ministers this week to offer catechesis on the Sacred Paschal Triduum and encourage their full participation in these sacred days.
- This Sunday marks the transition to the last part of the Lenten season so be sure to include music that alludes to or references Christ's passion.
- Encourage families to watch some of the films that capture these moments, such as Jesus of Nazareth.

Liturgy and Life

Jesus tells us that he, like a grain of wheat, must fall to the ground and die in order to bear fruit for God's Kingdom. Lenten observances of prayer, fasting, and almsgiving (charity) similarly help us die to ourselves and our selfishness and draw us closer to him. In prayer, ask God to show you when and where during your life you have been charitable to others. What stands out? Is God calling you to be charitable in a specific way today? Is there a relationship in your life in need of healing? What steps can you take, in charity and with God's grace, to mend what is broken? Consider seeking counsel or support as you work toward reconciliation.

Taking Place This Week . . .

Consider what can be done liturgically, catechetically, and ministerially to respond to these important needs.

- World Day to Eliminate Racial Discrimination, World Poetry Day, World Down Syndrome Day, and International Day of Forests (3/21)
- World Water Day (3/22)
- World Meteorological Day (3/22)
- World Tuberculosis Day and World Day for Truth concerning Human Rights Violations (3/24)
- World Solidarity Day for Detained and Mission Workers and Day to Remember Slavery Victims and Transatlantic Slave Trade (3/25)
- Earth Hour (3/27)

MON 22 LM #251 / LMC #176–184 / violet Lenten Weekday

Scripture Insights

Both readings involve a woman allegedly caught in adultery. In both cases, the man of God treated her with dignity and respect. Daniel saw through the cruel deception of the men involved and saved the woman, who had acted with integrity. Jesus overrode the law and ignored the crowd, which had justification to stone her. None of us can condemn her. In Christ, mercy surpasses the law.

Preaching Points

Parish Masses

- Susannah herself had acted with integrity in a seemingly no-win situation. Daniel was an answer to Susannah's prayer. Though just a young man, the Spirit led him to speak up for her.
- This is one of the most well-known passages about Jesus, and justly so. No one quite knows what Jesus wrote in the sand. Everyone knows what he told the woman.

Masses with Children

- Daniel, though just a young boy, stood up to the elders and spoke up for Susannah. His courage and wisdom saved an innocent, honorable woman.
- "Let he who is without sin cast the first stone." Jesus reminds us that we all have sinned and have no right to condemn. He could have condemned her but instead treated her with mercy. He does the same to us.

Missal Options

- Use the prayers for Monday of the Fifth Week of Lent.
- Since music ministers may not be available for daily Mass, it might be better to pray form I or II of the PA on weekdays.
- The readings from LM #250 may be used any day this week (except for on the Solemnity of the Annunciation of the Lord).
- Any Lenten Collect (except for today's) may be used to conclude the UP.
- Use P-I of the Passion of the Lord.
- Consider using EP-II and concluding the Lenten weekday Masses with a PP.

Song of the Day

"Tree of Life" by Marty Haugen (GIA)

TUE 23 LM #252 / LMC #176–184 / violet Advent Weekday

Optional Memorial of St. Turibius of Mogrovejo, Bishop / violet

Scripture Insights

The story from Moses sounds odd to our ears—God punishing the complaints of the people by sending snakes, and Moses curing them by creating a bronze serpent in the form of a cross. The early followers of Christ, who were steeped in Jewish scripture, found new meaning in these old stories. The Jews in the Gospel should have recognized one key name: "I AM." It was the name God gave via the burning bush. They continually failed to recognize God in Christ.

Preaching Points

Parish Masses

- Moses was leading the people from slavery in Egypt to freedom in their own land, but the journey is hard. So Christ is leading us to new life in him, lest we die in the slavery of our sin.
- None of what Jesus says makes sense to the people until the crucifixion. "When you lift up the Son of Man, then you will realize that I AM." It is paradoxically in the crucifixion that we will realize Jesus' relation to the Father.

Masses with Children

- Moses was leading the people out of slavery, yet still they complained. God punished them yet also sent the healing.
- Jesus is speaking to those who were opposing him and said, "You belong to this world, but I do not belong to this world." Jesus' ways are very different from the ways of the world, and he invites us to live in him and thus live differently.

Missal Options

- Use the prayers for Tuesday of the Fifth Week of Lent.
- Since music ministers may not be available for daily Mass, it might be better to pray form I or II of the PA on weekdays.
- The readings from LM #250 may be used any day this week.
- Any Lenten Collect (except for today's) may be used to conclude the UP.
- Use P-I of the Passion of the Lord.
- Consider using EP-III and concluding the Lenten weekday Masses with a PP.

Song of the Day

"O Lord, Hear My Prayer" by Jacques Berthier (Taizé/GIA)

Optional Memorial

St. Turibius was a Spanish noble who became the missionary archbishop of Lima entrusted with the responsibility of evangelization of the people of Peru. His love for his adopted people led him to act as their advocate and defender against their mistreatment at the hands of their Spanish conquerors.

- The readings are from the SW.
- Use the Collect from the PS; the other prayers are from the PT.
- Use any of the Lenten Prefaces.
- Consider EP-II.
- Any Lenten Collect may be used to conclude the UP.
- Continue to use the same form of the PA.

WED 24 LM #253 / LMC #176–184 / violet

Lenten Weekday

Scripture Insights

We have today one of the great stories of resistance in the Bible, especially the wonderful ending with "the fourth looks like a son of God." God promises repeatedly to be with us during any persecution, and this vividly shows us that. Jesus promises the disciples that "the truth will set you free." Again we get life and freedom in Christ, and death and slavery everywhere else.

Preaching Points

Parish Masses

- The early Christians would have found great inspiration in the story, with Rome wanting obeisance and the pinch of incense and all. Among the great details is their attitude: maybe God will save us, but even if he doesn't "we will not serve your god."
- Jesus is insistent in his call to an intimate connection to the Father through him: "If God were your Father, you would love me, for I came from God."

Masses with Children

- The King was trying to get these prophets to renounce God and worship his false god. They refuse, and God saves them, and someone who looks like a son of God is there with them.
- In Christ there is truth, and the truth will set us free. We can be children of God or we can be slaves to sin.

Missal Options

- Use the prayers for Wednesday of the Fifth Week of Lent.
- Since music ministers may not be available for daily Mass, it might be better to pray form I or II of the PA on weekdays.
- The readings from LM #250 may be used any day this week.
- Any Lenten Collect (except for today's) may be used to conclude the UP.
- Use P-I of the Passion of the Lord.
- Consider using EPR-I and concluding the Lenten weekday Masses with a PP.

Song of the Day

"Unless a Grain of Wheat" by Bernadette Farrell (OCP)

THU 25 **Solemnity of the Annunciation of the Lord**

See page 138.

FRI 26 LM #255 / LMC #176–184 / violet

Lenten Weekday

Scripture Insights

Jesus and his foes are playing word games. They are trying to trap him, and he is trying to explain the complexities of his relationship with the Father. Calling himself God will get him stoned. Look at my works then, says Jesus, and believe what they say about me and the One who sent me.

Preaching Points

Parish Masses

- Jeremiah, like Jesus, was persecuted for speaking the Word of God. Note the difference though: Jeremiah wanted to witness the vengeance God inflicted on his foes. Jesus longs to draw them in.
- Jesus and the Father are distinct people but one in action, one in spirit. Jesus, with his works and with his being, shows us who the Father is. If he calls himself God he violates the first commandment. So he does the works of God and calls us to follow him.

Masses with Children

- Jeremiah was harassed and hated for speaking for God. Still he sang praises to God for rescuing him from his abusers.

- Jesus comes to show us who the Father is. How do we know who the Father is? Through Jesus' works.

Missal Options

- Use the prayers for Friday of the Fifth Week of Lent.
- Since music ministers may not be available for daily Mass, it might be better to pray form I or II of the PA on weekdays.
- The readings from LM #250 may be used.
- Any Lenten Collect (except for today's) may be used to conclude the UP.
- Use P-I of the Passion of the Lord.
- Consider using EP-II and concluding the Lenten weekday Masses with a PP.

Song of the Day

"I Love You, Lord/*Te Amo, Señor*" by Tim Smith and Julie Smith (OCP)

LM #256 / LMC #176–184 / violet
Lenten Weekday

Scripture Insights

Ezekiel offers a comprehensive vision of God's promise, then sums it up: "My dwelling shall be with them; I will be their God, and they shall be my people." Caiaphas speaks a deeper truth without knowing it: "It is better for you that one man should die instead of the people." The Jews had an uneasy peace with the Romans. They were afraid Jesus would upset it. He did.

Preaching Points

Parish Masses

- Ezekiel hits all the promises: cleansing from idolatry, a king, the land, the covenant. The culmination is this: "my sanctuary shall be set up among them forever," which took flesh in Jesus.
- Caiaphas was being practical; it is better that one man die than Rome destroy us all. His death did "gather into one that dispersed children of God."

Masses with Children

- Ezekiel tells about many promises God made and delivered to the people. The high priest, though, is God dwelling among us, which came true in Jesus.
- Jesus was gathering together many of the Jewish people. The religious leaders were getting nervous, since they were in control, or were supposed to be. They decided that Jesus' death would bring the people together. It did, but not in the way they expected.

Missal Options

- Use the prayers for Saturday of the Fifth Week of Lent.
- Since music ministers may not be available for daily Mass, it might be better to pray form I or II of the PA on weekdays.
- The readings from LM #250 may be used.
- Any Lenten Collect (except for today's) may be used to conclude the UP.
- Use P-I of the Passion of the Lord.
- Consider using EPR-I and concluding the Lenten weekday Masses with a PP.

Song of the Day

"Change Our Hearts" by Rory Cooney (OCP)

THU 25 LM #545 / LMC #274 / white
Solemnity of the Annunciation of the Lord

About Today's Solemnity

Today's solemnity highlights the very human role in Jesus' birth and upbringing and calls us to embrace life in the slowly growing springtime. We are reminded to keep looking for ways God is at work in our lives.

Scripture Insights *(From PS)*

King Ahaz of Judah refuses to ask for a sign that God is with him. He prefers to trust his own military and political skills in order to defend his people from an imminent attack. In response, Isaiah announces that Ahaz will lose his throne and that a child far more obedient to God will one day reign in his place. The story reminds us that we can't thwart God's will by refusing to hear it.

Mary understands the power of God's will. Although she is unsettled by the angel's announcement, she listens, and then she bows to what she hears. She receives the sign spoken by Isaiah, and the promised child is conceived within her. What God announced through Isaiah becomes in Mary real, alive, and incarnate.

Mary's son made announcements of his own. He announced that God's reign was coming about. He announced that this reign would be just, peaceful, and eternal. And as he announced God's Word, the Son of God made God's Kingdom real for those who believed and followed him. He fulfilled all that God had announced in different ways in ages past.

In the passage from Hebrews, we hear that Jesus took sin upon himself because no other act of sacrifice could permanently take away the world's sin. The sacrifices and offerings of his people pointed to what he would offer: himself. He would become the one, eternal sacrifice for sin in order to fulfill God's will that all people be cleansed, made whole, and brought together.

What God announces, God makes happen. When we listen to God's Word and let it overshadow us, we enter more fully into God's Kingdom. We also become better able to announce God's Word ourselves. As that happens, we become part of God's ongoing transformation of the world.

Preaching Points

Parish Masses

- God promised that he would be with his people. At the annunciation, he made his will known through the angel Gabriel's words. The Virgin Mary's assent to become the Mother of God is our beautiful example of cooperating with grace. God's people waited for the Messiah; this long-promised man would be "Emmanuel," God with us. How the world aches for union with God!
- Historically, the Jewish people made offerings of animals to God. The early Christians understood Jesus' sacrifice to be the only sacrifice needed for forgiveness.
- Jesus, the Son of God and fulfillment of God's promises, was made incarnate in the womb of a humble young woman. Emmanuel, "God with us," had become flesh.
- We are called to be like Mary who fully embraced her mission and cooperated with God and his grace.

Children's Liturgy of the Word

- All people crave union with God. For generations, God's people waited for Emmanuel, God with us.
- Jesus was born of a humble young mother; it was through her and her assent that God became a human person.
- We are called to be like Mary who fully embraced her mission and cooperated with God and his grace.

Missal Options

- The prayer texts, including the Preface, are proper and are found in the PS for March 25.
- Continue to use the same form of the PA prayed on the Sundays of Lent.
- Since today is a solemnity, the Gloria is sung (or recited).
- The Creed is also prayed. Today, like at Christmas, all genuflect at the words "and was incarnate."
- Any Lenten Collect may be used to conclude the UP.
- Consider using EP-II.
- Although it is not indicated by the rubrics, it is acceptable to conclude Mass with the SB for the Blessed Virgin Mary.
- Even though it is Lent, you can pull out the stops (moderately) for today's solemnity. Use festive music (possibly inviting the choir to sing), incense, and a longer, more formal Gospel procession.
- If the parish has a Marian image, especially of the annunciation, see how it can be decorated this week with some flowers and candles. The image can be reverenced with incense at the beginning of Mass.

Music Preparation

- Try to avoid Marian hymns that may be familiar but targeted for a certain observance, such as, "Immaculate Mary."
- Remember the Gloria today. Because this is a solemnity in the midst of Lent, celebrate it to its fullest degree.
- You will likely have a good crowd at Mass. Perhaps you can get a volunteer brigade if you need help preparing anything for Holy Week.

Music Suggestions

- Responsorial Psalm: "Here Am I, Lord" by Timothy Valentine (GIA)
- Presentation: "Luke: 1:46–55; Holy Is Your Name" by David Haas (GIA)
- Communion: "Magnificat" by Jacques Berthier (GIA)
- Sending Forth: "O Mary of Promise" by Steven C. Warner (WLP)

Mass Texts

Introduction to Mass

The divide between God and humans could only be bridged by one who was both divine and human—our Lord Jesus Christ. He became one of us that we might share in the life of God. Today, in the annunciation of the angel Gabriel to the Virgin Mary, we celebrate the moment when God's Word became flesh and entered into our world. May this Eucharist be our thanksgiving for the wondrous love and mercy of our God. *My brothers and sisters, let us acknowledge our sins, and so prepare ourselves to celebrate the sacred mysteries.*

Tropes for Penitential Act, Form III

Lord, we were lost in sin and you came to bring us back to the Father: Lord, have mercy.

Jesus Christ, you are Son of God and son of Mary: Christ, have mercy.

Word of God, you became flesh for our salvation: Lord, have mercy.

Dismissal of Catechumens/Elect

My dear friends, God chose the Virgin Mary to be the mother of his Son. He has now chosen you to follow in Jesus' footsteps. Through Mary's intercession, and by the help of our humble prayer, may you grow closer to him as you continue your formation. Go in peace.

Dismissal of Extraordinary Ministers of Holy Communion

My friends, may those who are experiencing the fragility of the human body through infirmity, find comfort and strength in the true Body of Christ we now entrust to you. Take him to them and assure them of our prayers for physical healing and spiritual consolation. Go in peace.

Universal Prayer

Behold, a virgin conceived and gave birth to a son, and he was called Emmanuel. May we, like Mary, be a handmaid of the Lord and bring our prayers before our God.

1. For the Church as she, like the Virgin Mary, seeks to say yes to all that God asks, we pray:
2. For the world as the message of Gabriel continues to be one of peace and joy for all generations, we pray:
3. For all who are filled with a spirit of humility, that they may one day receive the reward of God's glory, we pray:
4. For all mothers as they seek what is best for their children, we pray:
5. For the unborn, that we may protect life at all stages and seek to provide means for women to continue with their pregnancy, and that we may welcome and reconcile those who have had abortions, we pray:
6. For all the dead, that they may be raised to the fullness of life, we pray:

Lord God,
your Son, our Savior Jesus Christ,
emptied himself and was obedient unto his death.
In him, we see the perfection of our human nature at one with your divinity.
May we be his likeness in our world this day.
Who live and reign with God the Father in the unity of the Holy Spirit,
one God, for ever and ever.
Amen.

Other Rites and Customs

- Explain why we genuflect during the recitation of the Creed today. A short explanation could be added to the worship aid with directions helping parishioners to make this gesture. A longer explanation can be added to the parish bulletin and shared on social media.
- Gather parishioners to pray the Angelus in common after Mass.

Liturgy and Life

On the Solemnity of the Annunciation, the lives of young parents, especially mothers facing unanticipated pregnancies come to mind. Think about the story of angel Gabriel announcing to Mary that she was pregnant. What did the Virgin Mary endure when she had to explain her pregnancy to her wondering family and friends? What struggles did she face when she was so young and poor when having her first child? What challenges did she face living in an occupied land in a violent time? What kind of ministries does your community offer for young parents? Is there a place young women or couples can go if experiencing an unexpected pregnancy? Are there charities who help young parents provide clothing and diapers for their babies? Find out what resources your area has for struggling families, and learn what their needs are. See if you, and possibly your youth ministry group, can work to help one of the resource centers in your community. Purchase diapers or perhaps spend a weekend afternoon helping the center organize baby clothes. Your service can make a difference for families!

S U N **28** LM #37B and #38ABC / LMC #34B / red

Palm Sunday of the Passion of the Lord

About Palm Sunday

No other Sunday in the liturgical year reflects such dramatic contrast as today. What begins with songs of triumph quickly shifts into remembrance of the Lord's passion. His royal entrance into the holy city of Jerusalem was also an entrance into the mystery of his suffering, death, and Resurrection. As we enter this holiest of weeks with Christ, may our participation in each solemn liturgy draw us into deeper union with him and with one another.

Scripture Insights

Despite his apparently dispassionate reporting style, Mark gives an intensely theological portrayal of Jesus, inspired by the figure of the suffering servant, who "did not come to be served but to serve and to give his life as a ransom for many" (Mark 10:45). The focus of Mark's passion story is the crowning of the King. Because Jesus' coronation takes place through suffering, the story is unrelentingly ironic. Jesus' subjects flee (14:50); his court repudiates him (14:64); the state condemns him (15:15); soldiers pay mock homage with crown and cloak (15:16–20); his royal title sits atop the instrument of execution (15:26); his enthronement as Son of God occurs only at the moment of his death (15:39).

Paul's letter to the Philippians contains an early Christian hymn, already widely used in Paul's time, only thirty years after Jesus' crucifixion. Its theology of the passion unfolds in a sequence: (1) Christ begins in glory, equal with God, referring either to his divinity or perhaps to his perfect humanity in God's image; (2) he descends to a humiliating slave's death on the cross; (3) then, because he "humbled himself," God lifts him up again to unimaginable glory.

The prophet's ancient words poetically convey the inner experience of the suffering servant, personifying the narrative of Mark and the theological structure of Paul. The anonymous writer composed four "servant songs" (Isaiah 42:1–4; 49:1–6; 50:4–7; 52:13—53:12), perhaps based on the life of Jeremiah; this is a portion of the third song. The servant speaks in the first person, reflecting on the certainty of his mission and the strength he receives from the Lord. Jesus quoted and alluded to many Old Testament themes and figures to interpret his mission. But he especially adopted and fulfilled the persona of the suffering servant as a key to his passion. In this mysterious figure, we come close to Jesus' inner life and the meaning that he gave to his work.

Preaching Points

Parish Masses

- How do we begin to take it all in? On this Palm Sunday of the Passion of the Lord, we begin Holy Week. We are with Jesus as he is mocked, scourged, and crucified. We hear the centurion who declares, "Truly, this man was the Son of God" (Mark 15:39), and we are with Mary Magdalene and Mary the mother of Joses who watched where the crucified body of our Lord was laid. On this day, we confess that Jesus Christ is Lord, to the glory of God the Father.
- The King of Heaven and Earth gathered with friends, gave himself to his friends, and was betrayed by a friend. The readings work together seamlessly, illustrating a suffering servant who would serve his people, even to the point of death. Our Lord sought his people and served his people by giving himself.
- The understanding of royalty was turned on its head; our Lord and king did not seek servants, but friends; he did not seek to be served like a king, but to serve those he loved.
- Jesus' suffering was harsh: betrayal, arrest, scourging, and agonizing death. He took on the suffering for us in service to us. He serves us out of tremendous love for us. Like Christ, we are called to humble ourselves in service to one another.
- Christ's acceptance of his passion and crucifixion is a witness to the extent of God's love for humanity.

Children's Liturgy of the Word

- In Jesus' time and indeed in our own time, it was assumed that royalty should be served. Unlike other royals, Jesus sought to serve others.
- Jesus voluntarily took on suffering for his beloved people. He did this out of tremendous love for each of us.
- Like Jesus, we are called to be humble and to serve one another.

Pastoral Notes

- Palm Sunday ushers in Holy Week. Obtain plenty of palm plants and fronds to decorate the worship space and also the place where the first Gospel will be read and the procession begin. Attach large fronds with red ribbon onto a lectern. Add red ribbon and proportionate fronds to the processional cross. Outside, add more palm fronds and red ribbon to welcome the assembly. If you know someone skilled in weaving palm branches, have a large ornamental palm prepared for the presider to carry in procession. Add several large palm plants behind or on either side of the altar. You may choose to leave violet fabric in place, remove it altogether, or replace it with simple red runners or banners.
- Here is a unique idea to tie the Wood of the Cross to the Wood of the Stable: Save extra palms throughout the year. Use what you need for Ash Wednesday, but save the rest for next year's Christmas nativity. The palms can be used instead of straw for decorating the manger.
- A careful reading of the Missal by all those involved in the preparation of today's liturgy will help ensure a smooth flow to the ritual.

Missal Options

- Texts are found in the Holy Week section of the RM that follows the Saturday of the Fifth Week of Lent. A careful reading of the RM by all those involved in the preparation of today's liturgy will help ensure a smooth flow to the ritual.
- Gather for the main procession at a place apart from the main worship space, ideally, outside.
- The priest and the deacon wear red vestments; the priest may wear a chasuble, or he may wear a cope and then change into a chasuble when the procession is over.
- All Masses include one of the three forms of the procession: The Procession, the Solemn Entrance, or the Simple Entrance. The main procession and the solemn includes the proclamation of Jesus' entry into Jerusalem.
- The first form of the procession is more elaborate and should be done at the principal Mass. The Solemn Entrance is used if the main procession cannot take place outside. The Simple Procession is used at all other Masses.
- All sing a setting of "Hosanna" while the processions convene. Another hymn, such as "All Glory, Laud, and Honor" or "Jerusalem, My Destiny" may accompany the procession to the altar.
- The RM includes special instructions for the proclamation of the Lord's passion: It is to be read without incense, and there is to be no greeting.
- The processional cross may be decorated with palm branches. You might choose to add a few red flowers.
- Once the procession with palms reaches the altar, the Collect begins. The Kyrie may or may not be omitted before the Collect.
- Use any Collect from the Fifth Week of Lent to conclude the UP.
- Although the LMC includes the proclamation of the Gospel for the blessing of the palms, it would be very unlikely this will take place separately with children. Instead, children may remain with their parents for the blessing of palms and then depart for their own Liturgy of the Word after the Collect as usual.
- It is customary in many places to have several people participate in the reading of the passion, not just the priest and deacon. The part of Christ should, however, if possible, be read by the priest. Only a deacon asks for the blessing of the priest before reading the passion, as he does before reading the Gospel.
- There should be a brief homily after the Gospel.
- There is no PA.
- The Creed and the UP take place as usual (options are provided below).
- The Preface is proper and is found among the pages for Palm Sunday.
- Consider EPR-I.

Music Preparation

- If the congregation is processing with palms, it is good to have an order of worship with opening hymn so they may sing along.
- Study *The Roman Missal* and provide a script for priest, deacon, and musicians with opening procession and the passion with the ritual texts and Gospel readings.
- Make sure that musical breaks and/or speaking parts are clearly delineated.

Music Suggestions

- Prelude: "Ride on, King Jesus" (traditional; various publishers)
- Procession: "All Glory, Laud, and Honor" (various publishers)
- Responsorial Psalm: "Psalm 22: My God, My God" by Marty Haugen (GIA)
- Preparation of the Gifts: "From the Depths of Sin and Sadness" by Williard F. Jabusch (WLP)
- Passion Acclamation: "Passion Acclamation" by Christopher Walker (OCP)

Mass Texts

Introduction to Mass

[Use the proper text that is found in the Missal.]

Dismissal for Children's Liturgy of the Word

Dear children, the palm branches we hold today are symbols of victory, and they can remind us that Jesus won for us the greatest victory of all, one that makes it possible for us to be with God forever. In order to win this victory, though, he was willing to suffer and to die because he loves us so much. Keep this love of his in mind as you listen to today's Scriptures.

Dismissal of Catechumens/Elect

My friends, we stand at the beginning of Holy Week, this week in which we will solemnly walk with Jesus through his passion and death and at the end of which we will celebrate his Resurrection and your own initiation into these saving mysteries. Be attentive in these final days of your preparation. For our part, we will intensify our prayer for you that you may become beacons of light for the world. Go in peace.

Dismissal of Extraordinary Ministers of Holy Communion

Dear friends, we give you the Body of Christ for the nourishment of our sick and homebound brothers and sisters. May it invigorate them for their journey through Holy Week and strengthen their faith that they are one with us in the love of him who died for our sake. Go in peace.

Universal Prayer

The Son of God was obedient to his Father, even to the point of death. In humble obedience to our baptismal call, we pray for the needs of our world.

1. For the suffering Body of Christ throughout the world, afflicted by torture, betrayal, and abandonment, we pray:
2. For an end to capital punishment and for the freedom of innocent men and women who are unjustly imprisoned, we pray:
3. For the world's starving and the oppressed, we pray:
4. For those attracted to false gods in our society, we pray:
5. For the grace of a devout and holy observance of Holy Week and the Sacred Paschal Triduum, we pray:
6. For a genuine spiritual longing to renew our Baptism at Easter, we pray:
7. For the elect, who are in their final moments preparing for the Sacrament of Baptism, we pray:
8. For those who have died, and for those who mourn their loss, we pray:

King of kings and Lord of lords,
today we commemorate your solemn entrance
into Jerusalem.
It was there that you were betrayed, rejected, scourged,
and put to death.
May we see in your carrying of the cross our road
to salvation,
that in choosing to offer ourselves for others,
we grow more deeply in your likeness.
Who live and reign with God the Father in the
unity of the Holy Spirit,
one God, for ever and ever.
Amen.

Other Rites and Customs

- With Palm Sunday of the Lord's Passion, Holy Week begins. Keep activities to a minimum in order to set the week apart from all others. Plan ahead to participate in the liturgies of Holy Thursday, Good Friday, and the Easter Vigil or Easter Sunday.
- Utilize the Solemn Procession at the principal Mass this weekend.
- Decorate the processional cross with palm and ribbons.
- Make sure there is enough time in between Masses today as the Masses will run longer than usual.
- End Mass without a hymn, inviting everyone to reflect on the solemnity of these days.
- Give a special invitation to parishioners to attend the liturgies of the Sacred Paschal Triduum.
- Celebrate a solemn form of Evening Prayer II this Sunday evening.
- Publicize the opportunities for the Sacrament of Reconciliation during these final days of Lent.
- Passover begins on Saturday Evening so be sure to include prayers for our Jewish brothers and sisters (see below to see what else is taking place this week).
- When preparing for Palm Sunday, be conscious of the many environmental issues surrounding the harvesting of palm fronds, especially the Chamaedorea or Bella Palm. Ask questions. Be responsible and good stewards of natural resources. Look for fair trade, sustainable, wild-life, and eco-friendly distributers. Catholic Relief Services (www.crs.org/) has partnered with the Lutheran World Relief (lwr.org/) and the Presbyterian Church USA (www.pcusa.org/) to sell eco-friendly palms.

Liturgy and Life

It is hard to stay awake to the sin and suffering in this world. Even Jesus' disciples failed to keep watch with him in his deep sorrow. But the Gospel urges us to keep trying. It asks us to go with Christ to the heart of sorrow and to stand awake and in solidarity with the poor and suffering, who are Jesus in disguise. Our culture offers us many escapes, many ways to "sleep," but it is by encountering those who suffer, and by bringing God's love to them, that we come to know Christ and his cross and can look with hope to Resurrection.

Taking Place This Week . . .

Consider what can be done liturgically, catechetically, and ministerially to respond to these important needs.

- Holy Week begins today.
- The first day of Passover begins the evening of 3/27.
- National Vietnam Veterans Day (3/29)
- The Sacred Paschal Triduum begins on the evening of Holy Thursday on 4/1.
- The First Friday and First Saturday of the month is this week; however, these days do occur during the Triduum. Be aware of the sacramental limitations on these days.

MON 29 LM #257 / LMC #176–184 / violet
Monday of Holy Week

Scripture Insights

The servant song offers a different view of God's Messiah—one of justice and healing, not military deliverance. Jesus' gentle intimacy provides a further depth to the Messianic reality. Mary's generous act is moving and wonderfully human, though the anointing is a foreshadowing of his death.

Preaching Points

Parish Masses

- The servant of the Lord is gentle yet powerful. He is "the victory of justice" and "a light to the nations."
- "You always have the poor with you" is not a prophecy of inequality but a reminder that what we do to the poor we do to Christ himself.

Masses with Children

- There are four servants songs in Isaiah. They foretell Jesus' coming by describing how the Messiah will be a gentle force of justice and a healing, liberating servant to all the people.
- Mary anointed Jesus' feet with expensive oil. We are called to this sort of generous intimacy with each other, and when we are similarly generous to the poor, it is though we are treating Jesus this way.

Missal Options

- Use the prayers for Monday of Holy Week.
- Since music ministers may not be available for daily Mass, it might be better to pray form I or II of the PA on weekdays.
- Use any Collect from the Fifth Week of Lent to conclude the UP.
- Use P-II of the Passion of the Lord.
- Consider using EP-II.
- Consider concluding the Lenten weekday Masses with a PP.

Song of the Day

"The Servant Song" by Richard Gillard (various publishers)

TUE 30 LM #258 / LMC #176–184 / violet
Tuesday of Holy Week

Scripture Insights

The second servant song reveals more of God's plan: justice and healing begin in the people of Israel, so that God's salvation might reach "the ends of the Earth." Jesus, on his last night, has broken bread with a man who will betray him and his friend who will deny him. It is with the betrayal that Jesus' glorification begins.

Preaching Points

Parish Masses

- The people of Israel were by no means a powerful faction or well-organized country, yet God chose them and used them like a hidden weapon to be a "light to the nations" and the beginning of the salvation of the world.
- Jesus was betrayed by one of his own and denied by one of his best friends. It was by his death that his glory was revealed. The Kingdom of God proceeds in ways the world would never expect.

Masses with Children

- The nation of Israel (the Jewish people) was full of imperfections. God's servant will begin by healing and uniting them so they might emerge as "a light to the nations."
- The people closest to Christ betrayed him and denied him, and his death revealed his glory. God's salvation begins in the midst of our cruelty and imperfections.

Missal Options

- Use the prayers for Tuesday of Holy Week.
- Since music ministers may not be available for daily Mass, it might be better to pray form I or II of the PA on weekdays.
- Use any Collect from the Fifth Week of Lent to conclude the UP.
- Use P-II of the Passion of the Lord.
- Consider using EP-I.
- Consider concluding the Lenten weekday Masses with a PP.

Song of the Day

"Save Your People" by Jim Farrell (OCP)

W E D 31 LM #259 / LMC #176–184 / violet
Wednesday of Holy Week

Scripture Insights

There is a marked contrast between the Servant of YHWH, who is willing to suffer since he knows God is his help, and Judas, who sets in motion the betrayal of his friend and his Lord. Judas even lies to his face about it, after breaking bread with him. In years past, this was known as Spy Wednesday, and the sign of peace would be skipped, to acknowledge the possibility of betrayers among us.

Preaching Points

Parish Masses

- The Servant is given the ability "to speak to the weary a word that will rouse them." May all our preaching seek to do the same.
- The disciples were "deeply distressed," but Jesus carried on. Knowing Judas would betray him, he went on with his Last Supper.

Masses with Children

- Isaiah tells us of the "Suffering Servant" who willingly endures abuse and meanness for the sake of following God.
- Judas was one of Jesus' closest followers, yet still betrayed him. Jesus carried on with the meal, though his heart must have been sick and sad.

Missal Options

- Use the prayers for Wednesday of Holy Week.
- Since music ministers may not be available for daily Mass, it might be better to pray form I or II of the PA on weekdays.
- Use any Collect from the Fifth Week of Lent to conclude the UP.
- Use P-II of the Passion of the Lord.
- Consider using EP-II.
- Consider concluding the Lenten weekday Masses with a PP.

Song of the Day

"In These Days of Lenten Journey" by Ricky Manolo (OCP)

T H U 1 violet
Thursday of Holy Week (Holy Thursday)

Pastoral Notes

- Today is the last day of Lent. Lent concludes with the celebration of the Lord's Supper this evening.
- Masses without people present are forbidden.
- Usually, no Mass is celebrated before the Mass of the Lord's Supper except for the diocesan celebration of the Chrism Mass (which may be celebrated prior to today); however, the diocesan bishop may allow another celebration of the Mass of the Lord's Supper earlier in the day "where pastoral considerations require it . . . for those faithful who cannot otherwise participate in the evening Mass."
- Holy Communion may be given to the sick and homebound today.
- Ritual Masses are prohibited today. Find out when the Chrism Mass is celebrated in your dioceses. Make arrangements for who will transport the oils and organize transportation for parishioners who might wish to attend (be sure to find out if tickets are required).
- Revive the Rite for the Reception of Holy Oils, which takes place before the Evening Mass of the Lord's Supper. It is found on page 404 in this *Sourcebook*. You will want to explore music settings available from Catholic publishers, especially those with acclamations so that you involve the assembly in the ritual action. Be sure to publish an explanation about this ritual in the Triduum worship aid.

The prayer of the faithful responds not only to the needs of the particular Christian community but also to those of all humanity; and the church, coming together for the eucharistic celebration, shows to the world that she makes her own "the joys and hopes, the sorrows and anxieties of people today, especially of the poor and all those who suffer.

—*Dies Domini,* 38

The Sacred Paschal Triduum

If we keep the memorial of the Lord's paschal solemnity in this way, listening to his word and celebrating his mysteries, then we shall have the sure hope of sharing his triumph over death and living with him in God.

— Introductory words of the Easter Vigil, Lucernarium

The Meaning of the Season

In her overview of *Paschale solemnitatis*, the 1988 circular letter that enumerates liturgical guidelines celebrating the Triduum, Corinna Laughlin speaks of the importance of fullness in the letter. She notes that the letter speaks of fullness in reference to everything from the cycle of feasts to the participation of the people. She describes fullness as "the opposite of liturgical minimalism . . . what is special about each feast and celebration, its uniqueness, is allowed to shine forth in the way the liturgy is celebrated" (*The Liturgy Documents*, vol. 2, p. 457).

For those of us responsible for preparing and ministering during these liturgies, it is important to meditate on the meaning of this fullness. The First Reading for Good Friday, the "Suffering Servant" reading from Isaiah (52:13—53:12) speaks of one who was "crushed for our sins" yet "opened not his mouth; like a lamb led to the slaughter or a sheep before the shearers." This imagery echoes the passage from Philippians that we hear each Palm Sunday, when we are told that Jesus "emptied himself, taking the form of a slave" (2:6–11). This kenosis—this full, complete self-emptying—that Christ demonstrated through his passion and death is the very model of fullness. Christ loved us entirely and completely; he gave us his Body and Blood; he suffered immensely; he was crucified and buried that he might rise again and triumph over death in order to free us from sin and death. As we prepare to celebrate these most momentous events in salvation history, we must do all that we can to ensure that the liturgies reflect the fullness of this Paschal Mystery.

The Triduum liturgies are indeed "the summit of the whole liturgical year" (PSol, 2). Even though the liturgical rites of the Triduum underwent significant revision in the years prior to the Second Vatican Council, the now-familiar symbols and rituals themselves date back centuries. These symbols—and the liturgies as a whole—are emotionally evocative in large part because they are sensory. As liturgical theologian Martin Connell notes, "The fullness of the rites is realized when the senses of the members of the community are engaged, all five senses: sight, sound, smell, taste, and touch" (*Eternity Today*, vol. 2, pg. 154). *Paschale solemnitatis* and *The Roman Missal* offer detailed guidance about the proper time of the liturgies, their constitutive elements, and the various symbols and rituals—all with the goal of ensuring that the Triduum is celebrated fully and reverently in a way that does indeed engage the senses of all who gather.

During the Mass of the Lord's Supper on Holy Thursday, our senses are most attuned to the addition of sensory ritual and symbolic elements: the procession with the glistening oils, the joyous ringing of bells during the Gloria, the splashes of water during the washing of the feet, the incense, the candles, and the monstrance as the Blessed Sacrament is carried to the place of repose. In contrast, on Good Friday, the primary sensory experience is one of emptiness and subdued starkness. The liturgy begins with a silent procession and prostration of the priest and deacon. The Solemn Intercessions include periods of prolonged silent prayer. There is no incense, and candles are used only alongside the cross and the Eucharist. The Easter Vigil, the "greatest and most noble of all solemnities" (RM, The Easter Vigil in the Holy Night, 2), is a veritable feast for the senses. The fire and candles of the Lucernarium speak especially powerfully of the triumph of Christ our Light in the midst of darkness—as long as the Vigil itself, as prescribed, truly "begins after nightfall" (RM, The Easter Vigil in the Holy Night, 3). Finally, Easter Sunday is a day of resounding joy, one in which everything seems heightened: the music is boisterous and triumphant, the lights are bright, the flowers are blooming, and—hopefully—the church is full of Christians who have come to celebrate that Jesus has "conquered death and unlocked for us the path to eternity" (Collect, Easter Sunday).

While all Catholics are obligated to attend Mass on Easter Sunday (the obligation is fulfilled by attending the Easter Vigil), the other days of the Triduum—Holy Thursday, Good Friday—have not been holydays of obligation since Pope Urban VIII removed the obligation in 1642. Although they are not holydays of obligation, their sanctity has been recognized for centuries—even by those who do not generally attend the liturgies. Consequently, a host of devotional traditions have arisen. In the United States, many of these traditions are rooted in the traditions of European and Hispanic immigrants. Some of these practices are devotional (passion plays, living Stations of the Cross); some are liturgical outside of the primary liturgies (the blessing of Easter foods); some are domestic (the baking of traditional foods or the coloring of eggs). Some take place in church; some take place in the streets; some take place in the home. The importance of these practices in contributing to the sacredness of the Triduum cannot be understated. *Paschale solemnitatis* acknowledges the importance of these popular devotions throughout the letter, specifically noting that such practices on Good Friday "are not, for pastoral reasons, to be neglected" (72).

At the same time, though, *Paschale solemnitatis* is unambiguous that the liturgies of the Triduum are primary. It laments when "certain devotions and pious exercises are held at more convenient times, and so the faithful participate in them rather than in the liturgical celebrations" (3), and it urges the renewal of communally celebrated Tenebrae (a service for the Office of Readings and Morning Prayer) on Good Friday and Holy Saturday (40). It also admonishes that celebrations of Easter should not begin early; they should "be reserved for Easter night and the day that follows" (76). Drawing from CSL (13), the letter urges that the timing of devotions, as well as the texts and songs used, should reflect the "spirit of the liturgy" for the day, thus making it "quite clear that the liturgical celebration by its very nature far surpasses them in importance" (72).

All of these rubrical injunctions are designed to emphasize the primacy of the Triduum liturgies. During the Triduum, everything else should cease for Christians. The Triduum liturgies truly are sacred time, for we are not simply reenacting or remembering past events that have already happened. We are celebrating the Paschal Mystery, together as one Church, rejoicing in "the resurrection with uplifted and responsive minds" (CSL, 110). As Christians have for two millennia and as the choirs of heaven do unceasingly, we rejoice in the day that the Lord has made. He is risen! He is truly risen!

The Sounds of the Season

Triduum is a Latin word, formed from the Latin prefix *tri* (meaning "three") and the Latin word *dies* ("days"). The Paschal Triduum, although three days in length, is celebrated as one liturgy. If you have different ensembles serving the community, try to gather everyone together to form one ensemble. Don't have different groups from different cultures or languages "take a turn" within a single liturgy. Rather than portraying cohesion or unity, it suggests that the liturgy is divided up. The same principle applies if your parish is twinned or clustered with a neighboring parish community: invite all the music ministers to form one ensemble over these holiest of holy days. *Sing to the Lord* (110–14) stresses the importance of observing the principle of "progressive solemnity," and it doesn't get any more solemn ("solemn" is not synonymous with gloomy, sullen, or dreary but, rather, marked with sanctity and gravity) than the Triduum.

Holy Thursday (Evening Mass of the Lord's Supper): Consider using a setting of the Entrance Antiphon for Holy Thursday: "We should glory in the cross of our Lord, Jesus Christ." Many settings exist of this text that sums up the meaning of the Triduum in just a few words. If your parish sang the Penitential Act during Lent, sing it tonight followed by the Gloria. Save your festive setting for the Gloria for the Easter Vigil and utilize a simpler setting this evening. Immediately after the singing of the Gloria, the use of instruments should be scaled back to support the singing of the assembly. Try to focus energy on a cappella material. To add to the solemnity, consider having the readers chant the introduction ("A reading from . . .") and conclusion ("The word of the Lord") to the readings. The cantor can assist if the reader is not able to do this. For formulas, refer to appendix I in *The Roman Missal* ("Tones for the Readings"). The chanting of the Gospel is also very appropriate this evening. Look at *Sung Gospels for Major Solemnities in Multiple Voices* by Anthony Ruff, OSB (Liturgical Press) or *Book of Sung Gospels* by Gary Penkala (www.canticanova.com). Whatever you do along these lines tonight, strongly consider repeating it throughout the Triduum to maintain cohesion. This would also be true of the Responsorial Psalms. Luke Mayernik's collection titled "Responsorial Psalms for Holy Week" (Morning Star) is a good resource to consider.

Albeit optional, a beautiful ritual often overlooked due to the Mandatum and the Transfer of the Most Blessed Sacrament is the Rite of Reception of the Holy Oils. Effective when celebrated, this rite has the power to beautifully connect, and highlight, the important and vital presence of the blessed oils (which took place at the Chrism Mass) and the unique role of the bishop as shepherd of the church in each parish community. The ritual text is found at the USCCB website: http://www.usccb.org/prayer-and-worship/sacraments-and-sacramentals/sacramentals-blessings/blessing-of-oils-and-consecration-of-chrism.cfm. Recommended ritual music is Schiavone's "Rite for Receiving the Holy Oils" (OCP, 9120), Inwood's "Rite for Reception of the Blessed Oils" (OCP), or Paul French's "The Reception of the Holy Oils" (WLP).

The *Mandatum*, or washing of the feet, is one of the major rituals taking place this evening. For ritual music, choose any of the countless settings of the proposed antiphons based on John 13. Composer Peter Latona contributed greatly to this specific body of repertoire with his hauntingly beautiful, yet very accessible, *Mandatum* (GIA). Depending on how your parish approaches the rite and its duration, this might be a good time for a mixture of choral music with responsorial assembly singing. *The Roman Missal* suggests using the "Ubi Caritas" to accompany the Preparation of the Gifts. The choir may choose to sing the chant (either in Latin or a combination of English verses with Latin refrain) or choral settings by either Maurice Duruflé or by Ola Gjeilo (Walton Music/GIA). The iconic hymn "Where Charity and Love Prevail" would also be appropriate.

The other major ritual taking place this evening is the Transfer of the Most Blessed Sacrament. This is a unique and beautiful moment that has the power to leave a lasting imprint on the hearts and minds of the assembly. Admittedly, it can be challenging due to the unavoidable dimensions of singing and walking in the dark. If the transfer is taking place within two different locations, it might be best to split your choral ensemble up into three: have some at the beginning, middle, and end of the procession in order to maintain and support the assembly song. While many options are available, ranging from litanies to Taizé-style ostinato refrains to strophic hymns, traditionally the ancient *Pange lingua* is sung at this point in time. It could be sung in Latin or English or a combination. The last two verses (*Tantum ergo*) are not sung until the procession reaches the altar of repose and the presider, kneeling, incenses the Blessed Sacrament. After a time of silent adoration, many parishes end the day with compline.

Good Friday: Like a seamless garment, the Triduum is but one celebration so today's celebration begins where yesterday ended. Today's liturgy begins in silence while the priest and concelebrants process and prostrate themselves at the foot of the altar. The Collect follows without the customary greeting. The music today must be simple and, wherever possible, completely a cappella. In a situation where this is not possible, softly accompany the assembly with the choir or cantor singing verses a cappella. The use of a cappella music will deepen and heighten the liturgical and ritual action unlike anything that is accompanied. Music during the Adoration of the Holy Cross should be a good balance between assembly song and choral music. Some gems from the Taizé repertoire are quite appropriate.

Easter Vigil: Similar to the liturgy on Good Friday, the Great Vigil of Easter begins with a silent procession to where the fire pit is prepared for the blessing of the fire and the preparation of the Paschal candle. Following the solemn entrance (deacons may chant either "The Light of Christ" or "Lumen Christi"), the Exsultet ("Easter Proclamation") is chanted. Many consider the Exsultet to be the most beautiful prayer in the life of the Church as well as the most challenging. The Exsultet deserves proper respect and is not a chant to be looked at a week prior. Many individuals begin practicing it before Lent even begins. While there may be numerous settings—from choral to accompanied arrangements—many consider the chant in *The Roman Missal* to be the best option.

Concerning the Responsorial Psalms, it is noteworthy to utilize psalms having the same tone, or character, as the earlier Triduum celebrations. This helps to attain the feeling of "one liturgy." If the music at Good Friday was a cappella, try singing the psalms in the same manner. Bring out instruments in full splendor with the singing of the Gloria. After forty days of abstention, the Alleluia returns with solemnity. Tonight, the only time in the course of the year, it is sung with three versicles taken from Psalm 118. Traditionally, the Alleluia itself is sung three times, each time with the repeat a step higher. Needless to say, one needs to plan ahead carefully!

When the rites of initiation are celebrated, it is important to incorporate the various acclamations and responses. When celebrated fully, we have the Litany of the Saints, the acclamation during the blessing of the water, acclamation during the Rite of Sprinkling, and even an Alleluia following each Baptism. Use of these acclamations involves the entire assembly, not just the catechumens.

Customarily, the Easter Vigil and Easter Sunday ends with the chanted dismissal: "Go forth, the Mass is ended, alleluia, alleluia" or "Go in peace, alleluia, alleluia." This is followed by the people's response: "Thanks be to God, alleluia, alleluia." While much of the Vigil's assembly comprise those who are more deeply involved in the liturgical life of the parish, Sunday morning is more likely to have a higher percentage of visitors or those who might not have these chants memorized. Take the steps to rehearse this important dialogue with the choir well in advance. In order to have everyone participate, it may be beneficial to have the cantor "conduct" the flow of the words and melody for the assembly.

Easter Sunday: The music for Easter Sunday should be nothing short of splendid and glorious, thus mirroring the great solemnity itself. Draw out all the stops: engage full, combined choral ensembles (continuation of the combined vision is preferable over the "assignment" approach), utilize the beautiful blended sonorities of brass and timpani, and plan for full instrumental ensembles. This IS the day the Lord has made! It should be full of joy and grandeur!

The liturgy is at the center of the New Evangelization, and Easter Sunday often brings more visitors to church than does Christmas, so it is a wonderfully important opportunity for each community to be as hospitable, charitable, and welcoming as possible while simultaneously celebrating this solemnity in all its fullness. Utilize familiar hymns such as "Jesus Christ Is Risen Today," "Christ, the Lord Is Risen Today," and various Easter texts combined with the tune LASST UNS ERFREUEN. These are hymns that people know well and love to sing. Plan ahead by making sure there are sufficient hymnals or printed worship aids (be sure to secure necessary copyright permissions and licenses).

The great sequence *Victimae paschali laudes* is sung (preferably) today after the Second Reading. There are numerous settings of this and the beautiful Gregorian melody is found in both Latin and English in many worship resources.

For the Renewal of Baptismal Promises, utilize whatever settings were used at the great Easter Vigil and continue to use these settings for the Rite of Sprinkling throughout the fifty days of Easter. We are called to preserve and promote the great treasury of sacred music. Plenty of Easter gems exist from the Mozart, Thompson, or Boyce "Alleluia" to Handel's "Hallelujah Chorus" (or "Hallelujah, Amen" to Byrd's "Haec Dies" to Angotti's "He Is Risen" or Mahler's "We Arise." Choose choral repertoire wisely and always maintain an accessible level for your singers.

The Look of the Season

Immersion Baptism is the Church's preference. A parish that worships in a liturgical space that was built without an immersion font is left considering how to provide a suitable and worthy font for the celebration of adult Baptism by immersion.

The pastoral desire is to respect the liturgical vision found in the applicable documents without designing and constructing a large immersion font, a task that can be difficult and expensive. A number of solutions have been tried, not all of them suitable, with some appearing more like garden installations than worthy places for a sacramental ritual. One of the positive results of these attempts at providing a temporary font has been the pastoral decision to design and construct a better font "for next year" in order to provide a more worthy and hospitable arrangement for welcoming new members into the Church at the Easter Vigil. If the practical issues of cost, which include providing plumbing to the new font, connecting to a power supply for a circulating pump, and finding a suitable location that will allow for the ritual actions, preclude the construction of a permanent immersion font in an existing space, a temporary font may be the best solution.

There are two types of temporary immersion fonts. One type is designed and constructed for use only at the Easter Vigil when parishes typically baptize adults. At the end of Easter Time, this font is dismantled and stored until the following Easter. A second temporary immersion font is one that is designed and constructed with the intention of use for a longer period of time, possibly several months or even two to three years until the parish can afford to install a permanent immersion font as part of a renovation project.

In both cases, design and safety issues need to be considered in addition to ensuring that the font is worthy for the Sacrament of Baptism. Using an existing pedestal font that is fixed in place (fonts should not be movable), a vessel can be designed that is large enough to contain a generous amount of water and that would allow an adult to either stand or kneel in the water. The water can be taken from the upper or lower level and poured over the person being baptized. If the lower container is large enough and deep enough, the person could bend forward from a kneeling position to immerse a portion of their body in the water. This temporary vessel could be designed in such a way that it fits snugly around the base of the pedestal so that it appears to be a single font.

Many parishes have used this arrangement to incorporate an existing pedestal into the structure of a permanent immersion font. In this way a beautiful font that has served well the baptismal practice of the parish remains as part of its liturgical heritage.

One of the design features to be avoided is giving the impression that the temporary vessel is a wading pool that could be in a family's backyard. There are two reasons for this caution. First, wading pools do not have the rigidity of design for the ritual actions of adult Baptism. Second, their decorative features clearly speak of being a plaything and thus detract from the liturgical action of Baptism. Finding a suitable container for this lower vessel, however, can be a challenge.

One of the better solutions is to use a large (at least five feet in diameter) heavy, plastic membrane that is often used for ground water ponds. These items are constructed of a sturdy molded plastic, are usually black in color, and come in irregular shapes and various depths. But these "ponds" are not strong enough to stand on their own. They need an outer structure before they can be used safely. A carpenter can design and build a wooden frame to completely surround the membrane and hold it in place for as long as it is needed. This frame can be designed so that it can be taken apart with relative ease and stored until it is needed again. Place a bathtub mat on the floor of this membrane to avoid any slipping by the person being baptized and the deacon or priest who chooses to stand in the font.

Another material that can be used for this temporary font is metal, with sheet copper as likely the best solution. As with the plastic membrane, it would need a supporting outer structure for which a wood frame would work well. The photo shows a very handsome vessel that fits at the base of an existing pedestal font.

If this type of temporary font is left in place for the weeks of Easter Time, it is advisable to change out the water from time to time. If this lower vessel is going to act as a temporary font for an even longer period of time, for example, until a permanent font is constructed, it is important to investigate the use of a recycling pump that can keep the water from becoming stagnant.

If the font is located in a particularly large space, there may be some evaporation of water over time; fresh water can be added as needed. The height of the frame needs to provide safety for younger children and at the same time allow them to touch the water as they enter and leave the liturgical space. The placing of decorative elements around the font, such as plants or flower arrangements, should be done carefully and in moderation. Avoid placing any items in the font or under the water.

The principal liturgical elements that are well designed don't need to be decorated; they should stand alone as a work of art. The modest expense of designing and constructing this second vessel should not deter parishes from having one; the liturgical appointments and furnishings that we provide should be the best we can afford.

Though this solution may not have the presence and permanence of a newly designed immersion font, it should be a worthy and suitable vessel. For those situations where other options might be cost prohibitive or appear to be so makeshift as to be unworthy of the liturgical act, it is an appropriate response to an important liturgical and pastoral need. The provision of any worthy and well-designed liturgical furnishing or appointment in the liturgical environment is always a vehicle for catechesis.

An immersion font that is located in the liturgical space for the liturgies of Easter and the Easter season affords numerous opportunities for mystagogy as the newly baptized and the whole community continue to reflect on the new life of Christ into which they have been baptized. The references and images in the Scriptures of the Easter season that recall our dying and rising in Christ provide a rich resource for homilies. Being able to point to the place, the font, where that newness of life has been celebrated, is a visual reminder of the Church's tradition and its rich theology of Baptism.

Evangelizing the Parish through the Season

The Triduum is unparalleled as an opportunity for evangelization in the liturgy. But it is not an aspect of Christian practice that is likely to bring in people who are not already in the know. The combination of unusual times for prayer and often lengthy services make them unlikely to welcome in newcomers on their own. In some parishes, this can lead to a feeling that the Triduum liturgies from Holy Thursday through the Easter Vigil are time for the community to gather, and the Easter Sunday Mass is the public-facing offering. But this is unfortunate. The Triduum liturgies speak richly in the languages of Scripture, action, sacrament, and symbol. They are an underutilized opportunity for preaching the Gospel to others.

They are also an aspect of the liturgy that we share with a few other churches, especially the Orthodox, Episcopalians, and some Lutherans. So they can be an excellent time to invite in other Christians who would not ordinarily be available to visit during Sunday Worship. Now, to be clear, it is not being suggested that the liturgy be used to try and woo people away from their faith communities. But inviting other Christians to Catholic Triduum liturgies can be a way to help other Christians see why Catholics are as tied to the liturgy as they are. We can share our real riches with our friends, and help them to understand what it is that the Catholic liturgy is all about.

Such inter-Christian sharing is an aid to evangelism, although not directly in terms of increasing the numbers in your parish. In the Gospel according to John, when Jesus is praying for his disciples before he goes to be crucified, he prays that they might be one so that the world might believe (see John 17:21). The divisions and misunderstandings between Christians do not help the cause of the Gospel. The world sees a Church divided and often uninterested in healing those divisions. In the last fifty years, the Holy Spirit has done much to begin to salve these wounds, but there remains much to do. In this spirit, why not invite non-Catholics to come witness a Church that is dedicated to the reading of Scripture, a common meditation on the actions of Christ, and carries that faith out into the world.

Worship Committee Agenda for Triduum

Meeting Time

Members of the committee should begin to meet in early January to prepare the parish liturgies for the Sacred Paschal Triduum.

Opening Prayer

- Anticipating the season, ask each worship committee member to read aloud one of the prayers for the Triduum, using *The Roman Missal*. Allow ninety seconds for silent reflection after each one is shared. Finish together, praying the Glory Be three times.
- Using the Proper of Holy Thursday, invite a prayer leader to pray the Entrance Antiphon. Select and sing a well-known hymn used for Triduum; borrow a handbell or tone chime to provide the opening note.
- Intercessory prayer (think: asking God for what we need) is especially important during Triduum. Begin with an Our Father, then invite the group into three minutes of quiet reflection. Ask them to write, during the quiet time, one or two "petitions" that directly involve persons or groups in the parish.
- Add an introductory thought aloud, pray the Prayer of the Faithful for that meeting, and conclude as the priest does at Mass. (See sample Formularies in appendix V of *The Roman Missal.*)

Seasonal Questions and Initiatives

- Time to prepare for the Triduum: be present to the art and environment team and plan to share the Scripture and this *Sourcebook* for each movement (day) of the Three Days. Encourage them to divide into teams; if support is lacking, help them locate helping hands and divvy up the work. Make sure that an Easter Time team is in place, too, with the goal of celebrating *visually* the Great Fifty Days in the worship space especially.
- There are many different guides available for celebrating the Way of the Cross, for example, *Mary's Stations of the Cross*, *Scriptural Stations* (Little Sisters of the Poor), *Praying the Psalms on the Way of the Cross* (LTP). Review and enact a new format this year during Holy Week and on Good Friday.
- Seek to preserve the peace that Holy Saturday can bring: check with the RCIA team and invite them to use another room in the parish besides the worship space for a simple, prayerful retreat morning. Make this day a NRD (No Rehearsal Day), concentrating on supporting the liturgy team as they set up the liturgical items and flowers. Leave the space quiet and empty until the choir begins to arrive in the evening. Walk the Elect through the Vigil's ritual sometime during Holy Week, with the goal of making them comfortable with ritual movement.
- Locate archived articles and bulletin inserts at https://pastoralliturgy.org/archive and select one for committee discussion. Robert Valle's "A Prayerful Evaluation of the Parish Triduum Celebration" is a good starting point. "The Easter Vigil Readings: Our Story of Salvation" by Stephen Wilbricht opens hearts and minds to be able to truly appreciate "the night of all nights" and celebrate the "mother of all Vigils" as the epitome of the liturgical year.

Liturgical Catechesis for the Worship Committee

Every member should consult *Sourcebook* 2021 about the Triduum: assign sections for R & R (review and report) when this meeting is announced. This provides each member with time for intentional review. The reporting should be more of a pastoral conversation than an academic exercise, i.e., this is what I discovered in what I reviewed.

Liturgical Catechesis for the Assembly

Now is the time to use bulletin inserts, website posts, and even a liturgical homily or two to catechize the congregation regarding who the Easter Vigil is intended for (the unbaptized, for full initiation) and who those people are who will be welcomed into Full Communion at the Mass of their choosing during the season of Easter.

Closing Prayer

- Move to the parish church and gather around the baptismal font. Renew your baptismal promises with a prayer leader, in a spirit of gentle prayer. If a priest or deacon is present, ask them to bless you. If only laypersons are present, then dip your hand at the same time into the font and say the Sign of the Cross aloud as you bless yourself.
- Locate a recording or a parish musician who can accompany "Were You There," a well-known African American spiritual. Most hymnals can supply the text, and the musical accompaniment will add to prayerful singing. Alternate groups singing each stanza: All/Men/Women to add richness as you reflect on the text.
- In *The Roman Missal*, read from *Universal Norms of the Liturgical Year and the Calendar*, noting paragraphs 1 and 2, and 17–21. Then pray together the "Opening Prayer from Vatican Council II," which is easily found on the internet.

THU 1 LM #39ABC / white
Thursday of Holy Week (Holy Thursday)
Evening Mass of the Lord's Supper

About the Mass of the Lord's Supper

This liturgy celebrates the institution of the Eucharist and of the ordained priesthood, which are the means by which God continues to bring people of faith more deeply into the dynamic of the Father's gift of the incarnate Word and the Spirit-filled response of Jesus' opening himself in love of God and his neighbor.

Scripture Insights

When Jews celebrate Passover, they thank and praise God for freeing their ancestors from Egypt, making a covenant with them, and leading them to a land of their own. The meal is, however, more than a look back. Jews recognize that ritual brings them into the story of salvation. By ritually remembering the past, each new generation enters into that past, thereby becoming part of God's promises for the future.

Catholics follow Jews in our understanding of ritual remembrance. For us, however, the story we remember is the story of Christ. As he spoke the prayers over the bread and then the cup during his last ritual meal, Jesus instructed his followers to celebrate the meal because of what he had done and was about to do. No longer were they to remember events in Israel's past. Instead, every time they gathered for sacred meals, they were to thank and praise God for Jesus and all he had done for them.

The Christians in Corinth needed Paul to remind them that participating in the ritual meal was also a participation in selfless love. Some of them had grown self-satisfied and indifferent to the needs of others. They needed to remember Christ's death as well as his Resurrection.

In John's account Jesus explains what selfless love is. He removes all but his loin cloth, the only garment some slaves were permitted to wear, and then stoops to do the job only slaves did. Jesus, whose status makes him worthy of the highest honors, assumes the role of the least among us. Those who wish to follow him into glory must emulate his humility and sacrifice. We who gather to remember what he did, to become part of the story of salvation, must also treat others with selfless, even degrading, love.

Preaching Points

- Our Lenten observance is complete. We now prepare to enter into the three most sacred days of the liturgical year, the Sacred Paschal Triduum. The celebration of the evening Mass of the Lord's Supper commences the Triduum liturgy, through which we enter deeply into the heart of all we believe about Jesus Christ and to reflect on who we are called to be as disciples of the Lord Jesus.
- The brief, yet powerful passage from 1 Corinthians expresses what we know and believe about the Eucharist. St. Paul shared what he was told, that on the night before he died, Jesus took bread, blessed and broke it, and said, "This is my body that is for you. Do this in remembrance of me" (1 Corinthians 11:24). After supper, Jesus took the cup, saying, "This cup is the new covenant in my blood. Do this, as often as you drink it, in remembrance of me" (1 Corinthians 11:25).
- In the First Reading, we hear God give Moses and Aaron instructions for the Passover meal. While the Israelites are in exile in Egypt, Pharaoh is convinced to free the Israelites from their captivity through a series of plagues. The Passover takes place before the final plague, in which the firstborn children of the Egyptians will be killed. The angel of the Lord will pass over the children of the Israelites who have placed the blood of the lamb on their doorposts.

Missal Options

General Notes

- Holy Communion may be brought to the sick at any time this day.
- Enough trained lay ministers should be available to serve as liturgical ministers. Triduum rehearsals should be scheduled.
- Because of the solemnity of these holy days, the singing of the texts should be given priority. The Missal notes that the organ and other instruments are used only to support the singing of the assembly.
- The assembly should be properly catechized in various ways and methods before these days begin. Use social media to your advantage.
- Noble simplicity and progressive solemnity should be the guiding principles for preparation.
- Use the best vestments, linens, and vessels. Make sure they are laundered, pressed, and polished in advance. If new ones are used, this Mass is not the appropriate liturgy for blessing them.
- Although another Mass may be celebrated with permission of the bishop, the Mass of the Lord's Supper should ideally take place only once for a given community and in the evening.
- If it is not your practice to distribute both species to the assembly, please consider doing so today. Also, be aware of anyone in your assembly who is gluten intolerant.
- Ritual Masses are prohibited today.
- The sanctuary may be decorated, and only enough hosts for the sick should remain in the tabernacle. Enough hosts should be consecrated at tonight's Mass for the sick, for adoration, and for those attending Good Friday services.
- The texts for Mass are proper and are found in the Proper of Time.

Before Mass/Introductory Rites

- The oils may be received before Mass begins. The rite for receiving the oils is not found in the Missal. Instead, the US bishops have provided it on their website: http://www.usccb.org/prayer-and-worship/liturgical-year/triduum/reception-of-holy-oils.cfm. Find volunteers in the parish who are involved in the ministries the oils represent: Baptism preparation, Confirmation preparation, and ministers to the sick and homebound. It is also found on page 404 in this *Sourcebook*.

- Music directors should do their best to select a gathering hymn that is based on the very important words of the Entrance Antiphon. This antiphon sets the theological tone for the entire Triduum.
- The Gloria is sung, during which bells (including organ bells and the carillon) are rung.
- There is no dismissal for children's Liturgy of the Word.

Liturgy of the Word

See above under "Scripture Insights" and "Preaching Points."

Mandatum

- It may be surprising to some that the Mandatum, or Washing of Feet, is optional.
- Note that the Missal uses the term "feet" not "foot." Both feet should be washed.
- Those who prepare the liturgy should note the number of those having their feet washed is not mentioned in the ritual text. Tradition usually dictates twelve, but to do so could perpetuate the misconception that the Mandatum is a "reenactment." Men and women, adults and children, may have their feet washed. The USCCB provides a helpful clarification on this change to the rubric: www.usccb.org/prayer-and-worship/liturgical-year/triduum/holy-thursday-mandatum.cfm.
- When considering how many people to invite to have their feet washed, you will want to be sure that the rite does not become so long and emotionally engaging that it overpowers the Liturgy of the Eucharist. The Mandatum gives meaning and social context to the Eucharist, and it is the institution of the Eucharist that we celebrate this evening. Preparation should be focused and compelling.
- The Mandatum may be done only by a priest. He may remove his chasuble for the washing. Helpers should be on hand to change the water and provide clean towels if several people are having their feet washed.
- Use chairs that are appropriate for the liturgy; avoid metal fold-up chairs.
- Enough music should be prepared to unify and cover the ritual action and invite the assembly's participation. The Missal provides several options.
- If catechumens and elect are to be dismissed, do so after the Mandatum to reflect mystagogically on the rite during the dismissal. At this point in their formation, a catechumen may volunteer to lead the discussion so that the baptized dismissal leader does not miss the remaining part of Mass.
- After the Mandatum (or dismissal) the UP is prayed. Options are provided below under "Mass Texts." Consider a sung response or even chanted petitions.

Liturgy of the Eucharist

- On this night, the Missal directs that a special collection be taken for the poor and that these gifts are to be presented with the bread and wine.
- The Missal directs that "Ubi Caritas" be sung at this time. Although it is optional, the traditional texts are profoundly and poignantly connected with the meaning of today's liturgy: "Where true charity is dwelling, God is present there"—what is on the altar is at the altar.
- The Liturgy of the Eucharist proceeds as usual. Note that EP-I is called for and is reprinted among the pages for the Mass. The proper form of the Communicantes should be used.
- If there is more than one priest at the parish, these other ministers are encouraged to concelebrate. Concelebration notes are provided in the Missal texts.
- The Missal notes, "At an appropriate moment during Communion, the Priest entrusts the Eucharist from the table of the altar to Deacons or acolytes or other extraordinary ministers, so that afterwards it may be brought to the sick who are to receive Holy Communion at home."
- After all have received Communion, the remaining hosts are placed in a covered ciborium and left on the altar. The Prayer after Communion is then prayed.

Transfer of the Most Blessed Sacrament

- Unlike other Masses, the usual concluding rites are omitted and replaced by the transferal of the Eucharist.
- The rubrics for this ritual are quite detailed. Those who prepare the liturgy should review rubrics 37–44.
- The altar of repose should, if possible, be at a different location than the usual tabernacle.
- The assembly should be invited to join the procession to the altar of repose while singing "Pange, Lingua."
- Directions for the procession should be clearly noted in a worship aid; now is not the time for distracting announcements.
- At some point after Mass, the altar is stripped and crosses are removed if possible. If crosses remain in the church, they should be veiled.

Music Preparation

- Refer also to pages 149–150.
- PSol states: "Since the purpose of sung texts is . . . to facilitate the participation of the faithful, they should not be lightly omitted" (42C). This guiding principle should influence your preparation for the Triduum.
- If possible, limit the use of musical instruments after the Gloria, and use them only when essential to support the assembly (see PSol, 50).

- It is important to remember that for much of tonight's liturgy, the music serves the rite. You may have extra pieces prepared for footwashing that you do not need. That is just called being ready.
- During the procession with the Blessed Sacrament to the place of repose, use a flute or oboe to keep the pitch.
- As people leave the church, you might consider singing a Taizé chant to help people leave quietly (such as, "Stay Here and Keep Watch").
- Consider celebrating a sung, but simple, Night Prayer at the conclusion of the evening night watch.

Music Suggestions

- Reception of the Holy Oils: "Rite for Receiving the Holy Oils" by John Schiavone (OCP)
- Gathering: "We Should Glory in the Cross" by Tony Alonso (WLP)
- Responsorial Psalm 16: "Our Blessing Cup" by Scott Soper (OCP)
- Washing of the Feet: "Song of the Lord's Command" by David Haas (GIA), "Mandatum" by P. Latona (GIA) or "Jesu, Jesu" adapted by Tom Colvin (Hope Publishing Company)
- Preparation of the Gifts: "Where Charity and Love Prevail" by Paul Benoit, OSB (WLP)
- Communion: "In Remembrance of You" by Paul Tate (WLP)
- Transfer of the Holy Eucharist: "Hail Our Savior's Glorious Body/*Pange Lingua*" (various publishers)

Mass Texts

Introduction to Mass

My friends, on this night we call to mind Jesus' example of perfect love as we commemorate the institution of the Eucharist. Through the bread and the cup he gives us, his sacrifice on the cross, once and for all eternity, is present to us, and through it we are saved. Let us glory in the cross of Christ.

Tropes for Penitential Act, Form III

Lord Jesus, you are the sacrificial Lamb of God:
Lord, have mercy.

Lord Jesus, you give us a new commandment to love one another: Christ, have mercy.

Lord Jesus, we proclaim your death until you come again:
Lord, have mercy.

Dismissal of the Catechumens / Elect

Friends, very soon you will join us in sharing the Eucharist, and for that we rejoice. In the meantime, hold the love of God in your hearts and let it reveal to you greater depths of the Paschal Mystery. Go in the peace of Christ.

Dismissal of Extraordinary Ministers of Holy Communion

Ministers of the Lord, the Eucharist is our life and our salvation. We give it to you, along with the divine Word, to take to our sick brothers and sisters, that they may be one with us in the celebration of the Lord's Passover. Go in peace.

Universal Prayer

On the night before he was to suffer and die, the Lord Jesus washed the feet of his disciples and commanded them to do the same. Remembering the Lord's selfless love for us, we serve him with our prayers.

1. For the Church around the world as we enter into the Sacred Paschal Triduum, that all Christians may be drawn into deeper contemplation of the suffering, death, and Resurrection of Christ, we pray:
2. For all called to serve the Church, that the pope, all bishops, priests, and deacons may model for us the Lord's humble service, we pray:
3. For those preparing to receive the Body and Blood of our Lord for the first time this Easter, that they may learn to "proclaim the death of the Lord until he comes," we pray:
4. For those in our community who have washed our feet and have demonstrated for us the way of sacrifice, that they may know of our gratitude, we pray:
5. For those soon to be nourished with the Lord's Body on their journey to eternal life, that the dying may offer their lives to God as a "sacrifice of thanksgiving," we pray:

Lord God,
your son, Jesus Christ,
demonstrates for us the way of perfect humility.
Give us the strength to be like him in all that we do,
washing the feet of both friend and foe.
May these sacred days draw us into the mystery
of his suffering, death, and Resurrection.
Through Christ our Lord.
Amen.

Other Rites and Customs

- If Morning Prayer is prayed on Holy Thursday, Good Friday, or Holy Saturday, offer lay parishioners opportunities to preach.
- Throughout the Triduum, sing the various appointed antiphons given in *The Roman Missal* as they unpack the deep theology of these sacred days.
- Use one worship aid for the entire Triduum to reinforce the unity of these days.
- Invite parishioners to process with food for the poor during the Preparation of the Gifts.
- Involve children throughout the Triduum liturgies.
- Be careful of not historicizing the liturgies of the Triduum as they are not reenactments of past events but rather opportunities for immersion into the fullness of Christ's Paschal Mystery.

- Using the suggestion of PSol, 56, set aside some of the time of adoration to include the reading of some parts of the Gospel according to John (chapters 13—17) and sing some appropriate music.

Liturgy and Life

The actions of eating and drinking Christ's Body and Blood "proclaim the death of the Lord until he comes." We must be accountable for these sacramental actions, meaning that we must make the sacrificial death of our Lord real in our lives. We must be willing to allow our lives to be broken and poured out for others. On this day, when the Church washes feet and celebrates the Lord's Supper of humble service, we are invited to make of ourselves a living sacrifice. Take some time to reflect on how you might proclaim the Lord's death by offering yourself in service.

FRI **2** LM #40ABC / red

Friday of the Passion of the Lord (Good Friday)

About the Passion of the Lord

On Good Friday, we journey with the Lord, the innocent servant of God, who has taken our sins upon himself as he walks the path to Calvary. Through this liturgy, we share in Jesus' faith and love and participate in his self-opening to the Father's love.

Scripture Insights

Each reading invites us into deep self-examination. The mysterious servant of our First Reading lacks distinction and status and would, but for his remarkable action, be forgettable. Despite his innocence, the servant assumes responsibility for the wrongdoing of his people. We see in the servant not only the crucified Jesus but everyone who suffers for the sake of the Gospel. How readily do we stand with them? Do we leave it to others to pray and pursue justice and peace?

Jesus submitted to his Father by becoming fully human and enduring misunderstanding, hostility, rejection, and brutal violence. By remaining steadfast in his mission, Jesus proved his perfect obedience to God's will. We might pray for God's will to be done in our lives, but sometimes God's will doesn't match our own. In such moments do we act with the perfect obedience of Jesus?

The scenes between Jesus and Pilate are a culmination of the trial motif in John's Gospel. Just as others gave testimony for or against Jesus, so now Pilate must render his own verdict. The Gentile ruler first tries to sidestep the issue, then tries to avoid a negative verdict, and then finally, concerned only about political ramifications, sends Jesus to his death. As Jesus stood before Pilate, so Jesus stands before us. What verdict will we render? If we confess that Jesus is God's Son, do we really mean it? What do the choices we make reveal about whose side we're really on—are we choosing Jesus or the forces of evil?

These readings lead us to the Veneration of the Cross. As we come forward, we remember Jesus' courageous and life-giving act of love, and we commit ourselves to acting in the same way, no matter the cost.

Preaching Points

- Today we celebrate Good Friday of the Passion of the Lord. We call this Friday "good" in that, while we enter into Christ's passion and death, we know that through this ultimate act of sacrifice, humanity is offered salvation and eternal life. For this one day of the year, we thoroughly immerse ourselves in the reality of Jesus' passion and death. Yet throughout the liturgy of this day, we know that death does not have the final word.
- We take to heart the reality of Christ's passion and death on the cross. In today's First Reading, we hear a passage from Isaiah that is known as the Fourth Song of the Suffering Servant. When it was written, at the time nearing the end of Israel's Babylonian exile, the song may have referred to a particular person or the people of Israel. We hear the verses and see in them a profound prophecy of the passion of Jesus Christ.
- Through today's Responsorial Psalm, we sing the psalm that Jesus had on his lips and in his heart during his crucifixion. We sing his final words on the cross as the psalm refrain, "Father, into your hands I commend my spirit." With Jesus' words in our hearts and minds, we hear the Second Reading, from the letter to the Hebrews, which helps us reflect on Christ as the great high priest, who willingly accepted his suffering and sacrifice and became the source of eternal salvation.
- Jesus obediently accepted suffering and death, and in doing so he broke the bonds of sin and death. God has power and authority over all that is not loving, merciful, and forgiving in our lives and in the world. Christians throughout the world hold the passion and death of Christ in their hearts, taking to heart God's love for humanity.

Missal Options

Pastoral Notes

- Only the Sacraments of the Anointing of the Sick and Reconciliation take place today. Communion may be brought to the sick and homebound.
- In parish catechesis, it is important to assert that this liturgy is not a Mass.
- The worship space should be bare; remaining crosses are covered or removed; there are no cloths, candles, or any other accouterments.
- Although the vestments for today should be red, the cross is veiled in violet.
- It is preferred that the Good Friday liturgy take place at 3:00 PM, but it can also take place later for pastoral reasons.
- Ritual Masses are prohibited today.

Introductory Rites

- There is no procession. No gathering song. No spoken words of greeting. Instead, the liturgy begins starkly.
- The ministers enter in silence and prostrate themselves before the altar while the assembly kneels. Allow time for silent prayer.
- After an appropriate time for prayer, the ministers take their usual places and the priest offers a prayer, omitting the invitation "Let us pray." There are two options. The second reflects the assembly in a more direct way.
- There is no dismissal for children's Liturgy of the Word.

Liturgy of the Word

- Refer to the "Scripture Insights" and the "Preaching Points" above.
- There are special instructions for the proclamation of the Lord's passion: it is to be read without candles and without incense, and there is to be no greeting before the proclamation and no signing of the book. It is customary in many places to have several people participate in the reading of the passion, not just the priest and deacon. The part of Christ should, however, if possible, be read by the priest. Only a deacon asks for the blessing of the priest before reading the passion, as he does before reading the Gospel. Your community may wish to consider chanting the Gospel; this is a wonderful way of highlighting the solemnity of the day.
- Children's Liturgy of the Word should not take place today.

Solemn Intercessions

- If the elect are to be dismissed, do so after the homily and before the Solemn Intercessions.
- The Solemn Intercessions are ancient texts and are meant to be proclaimed. A deacon or lay minister may offer the invitation to prayer.
- "Let us kneel" is an invitation for the people of God to pray for a specific need. Allow the assembly time to do just that. If we take our time praying these intercessions, we come into contact with the breadth of the Church's intercession. We pray for everybody!
- If there is a "grave public need," the bishop might provide an additional intention for parishes to include.

Adoration of the Cross

- Those who prepare the liturgy should carefully review the rubrics for the Adoration of the Cross.
- Only one cross should be used; it may be bare or with the corpus.
- Use a cross that is substantially large and appropriate for adoration.
- There are two forms for the showing of the cross.
- In the first form of the showing, the deacon, accompanied by one or more ministers, goes to the sacristy and then returns in procession, accompanied by two ministers carrying lighted candles, carrying the cross (which is covered with a violet veil) through the church to the middle of the sanctuary. At three different points, more of the cross is unveiled while the priest chants, "Behold the wood of the Cross." The last time, the cross is put in place.
- In the second form of showing, the priest or the deacon, accompanied by one or more ministers, goes to the door of the church and takes up the unveiled cross as the ministers take up lighted candles. Then, in procession, they move through the church to the sanctuary, stopping in three locations at each of which the priest or deacon elevates the cross and sings, "Behold the wood of the Cross . . ." with all responding, "Come, let us adore."
- For adoration, members of the assembly approach the cross and make an act of adoration in a manner comfortable to them—for example, by genuflecting or bowing, or by kissing the cross.
- The procession to adore the cross should not be rushed; allow people to make this a moment of prayer, offering and uniting themselves to Christ's sacrifice for the world.
- Music should include congregational pieces.

Communion Rite

- After the Adoration of the Cross, the altar is prepared with the corporal and the Missal.
- The deacon (or priest), wearing a humeral veil, goes to the place of repose to retrieve the Blessed Sacrament. The assembly stands in silence. The deacon, with two candle-bearers, comes to the altar with the Blessed Sacrament by a shorter route.
- The Communion Rite includes the Our Father, Lamb of God, invitation to Holy Communion, and the reception of Holy Communion.
- The Missal recommends that Psalm 22 be sung during the reception of Holy Communion.
- If consecrated hosts remain, the deacon (or another minister) returns them to a place of repose, preferably outside of the church rather than the tabernacle. After this, the priest offers the Prayer after Communion.

Concluding Rite

There is no concluding rite per se; however, the priest does offer a Prayer over the People. The text is found on the pages for Good Friday.

Music Preparation

- Refer also to pages 149–150.
- The liturgy today begins and ends in profound silence.

- Because the music for this liturgy is so important, it is important to rehearse the priest-celebrant, the deacon, and cantors. At this rehearsal, determine if the priest will need a pitch for the "Behold the Wood" dialogue during the Adoration of the Cross.
- The music for today should be simple and should complement the solemn tone of the celebration and be accessible to the assembly. Plan to use "Jesus, Remember Me" as the last piece of music for the Adoration of the Cross. This will enable the choir to adore the cross and continue to support the singing of the assembly because they will know this piece by heart.
- Music should be familiar today. Many parisshes include more choir pieces during today's liturgy; do not neglect the assembly's singing. The assembly should be the musical focus.

Music Suggestions

- Responsorial Psalm 31: "Father, into Your Hands" by the Collegeville Composers Group (Liturgical Press) or "Abba, Father" by David Haas (GIA)
- Adoration of the Cross: "You Walked through Crowded Streets" by H. Stuempfle Jr. (GIA) and/or "Faithful Cross, O Tree of Beauty" by Delores Dufner, OSB (GIA), "Beneath the Cross the Mother Kept" by Genevieve Glen (OCP), "O Sacred Head Surrounded" (various publishers), or "Christ Has No Body Now But Yours" by Steven C. Warner (WLP)
- Communion: "O Wheat Whose Crushing Was for Bread" by D. Dufner, OSB (GIA)

Liturgical Texts

Dismissal of the Catechumens/Elect

My dear catechumens/elect, we send you forth for the final time before you are baptized into Christ's death. We pray that your hearts will ever be open to receive his mercy and forgiveness and that in the new life of the Spirit you will finally be one with us and with Jesus Christ our Lord. Go in peace.

Other Rites and Customs

- After the liturgy of Good Friday, the church should remain empty and stark.
- Stations of the Cross may take place during the day. Consider a living stations recognizing those who have suffered from oppression and acts of violence in your community. Make sure, however, that devotions and pious practices don't overshadow the Liturgy of the Hours and the principal liturgy of the day.
- Consider singing all music today without accompaniment.
- Encourage the faithful to continue the Paschal fast into Holy Saturday.
- Keep the cross used for adoration in the church throughout the day and evening for the purpose of individual prayer. Two or four candles may be placed around the cross (see RM, 33).
- Evening Prayer is celebrated by only those who did not participate in this Good Friday liturgy of the Passion of the Lord.
- It is a powerful symbol to invite the entire assembly to adore the cross barefoot or in stocking feet.
- Invite parishioners to leave the Good Friday liturgy in silence and keep this silence as part of the Paschal fast. Music ministers might offer a Taizé ostinato as a way to conclude the liturgy and create a more solemn tone, reducing the chances for idle chit-chat and conversation.
- Today the USCCB collection is for the Holy Land.

Liturgy and Life

Ecce homo! "Behold, the man." Once again we encounter the irony of the evangelist John. The mocked, scourged, thorn-crowned Jesus is presented by Pilate to the crowd, perhaps to win their pity for this wretched, powerless messiah. But those who have heard the Lord's teaching, witnessed his compassion, and been welcomed to his company do not pity Jesus. "Behold, the man." In Greek, "Look at the human being." Jesus is God's ideal of a human being: God-directed, loving, forgiving, steadfast. We must contemplate this human being every day.

SAT **3** violet
Holy Saturday Morning

About Holy Saturday Morning

Christ was in the tomb; he lay in darkness in the womb of the whole world. Holy Saturday commemorates that day and has a character all its own. It is a quiet day of meditation, reflection, and anticipation, especially for the elect preparing for Baptism.

Pastoral Notes

- Use the Proper Psalter for the Liturgy of the Hours.
- The Office of Readings provides the ancient homily about Christ's descent into hell.
- There are no Masses this morning, and Holy Communion should be received only as Viaticum.
- The Sacraments of Reconciliation and Anointing of the Sick may be celebrated, and ministers of care should make every effort to visit the sick on these days.
- RCIA, 185, envisions that Holy Saturday should be a day of prayer and reflection and be free from work. The RCIA also hopes that the elect will be gathered the morning of Holy Saturday to proclaim the Lord's Prayer, recite the Creed (193–196), celebrate the ephphetha rite (197–199), and choose a baptismal name (200–202).
- The liturgical environment team will be busy readying the church for the celebration of the Lord's Resurrection.
- Encourage parishioners to take part in the Paschal fast.

- In the midst of the many preparatory details for the Easter Vigil, be sure to take some time in silence to reflect on the significance of this day of waiting.
- Take time to read the ancient homily from the Office of Readings.
- Involve the Scouts in the lighting of the Easter fire.
- If your parish doesn't proclaim all seven Old Testament readings and psalms, consider adding one or two more—don't rush through the holiest night of the year!
- Enlist lots of help for decorating the church for Easter.
- Make sure an experienced photographer is on hand to take pictures and videos of the Vigil.

SAT **3** #41ABC / white

Vigil of the Resurrection of the Lord

About the Easter Vigil

The Paschal Mystery, already celebrated in various ways since the Evening Mass of the Lord's Supper, is clearly and joyfully announced from the very beginning of the Vigil liturgy. It is in the light of the Paschal candle that the liturgy continues to unfold. The Easter Vigil is the most beautiful of all liturgies. Ranking highest among the celebrations of the liturgical year, it should rank highest in the spiritual life of the parish community, not a small task in places where Christmas is considered the high point.

Scripture Insights

During the Easter Vigil we celebrate all that God has done for us. We gather in darkness because we are afraid of it no longer—God has vanquished darkness and all that belongs to darkness. We celebrate a new and eternal day, and so our readings begin with a proclamation of the gift of life, the gift of the world and all that fills it. We live in an era that recognizes the fragility of life and the harm that we inflict on our environment and other species. This story not only celebrates the magnitude of God's gift but also reminds us that salvation extends beyond us to include all of God's creative work.

Our next readings touch on parts of salvation history. We hear the agonizing story of Abraham preparing to sacrifice his son, the one through whom he thought he would become the father of many nations. In preparing to offer Isaac, Abraham acknowledges that his son and God's promise are gifts. He can receive them, but he can never claim them. God's gift of his Son is likewise a gift we receive without ever having earned it.

During the Exodus, God again displays his undeserved favor by privileging the weak over the strong. God frees the enslaved Israelites from the mighty Egyptians, leading them across the dry ground of the Red Sea. The story recalls the power God exercised over the primordial waters when he brought the world into being. The story also points ahead to Baptism, by which we are freed from our enslavement to sin and death.

The two passages from Isaiah were written after the Babylonian exile, the most traumatic event Israel had experienced up to that moment in its history. The people lost everything: king, land, temple. Enraged by their failure to uphold the covenant, God seemed to have cast his chosen people aside. Writing several centuries later, the prophet announces that a new era has dawned: God has forgiven his people. In deeply intimate language God assures his people that he is still with them. According to the terms of the covenant God did not have to take his people back, but out of love for them, he does. God promises that they will never again be so utterly devastated. The prophet calls the people to celebrate, to return home, to rebuild the Temple, and to throw a feast. God will glorify his people, but they must abandon their wrongdoing and embrace the covenant once again.

Both Isaiah and Baruch celebrate God's gift of wisdom, a gift we don't readily associate with Easter. Isaiah alludes to the banquet whereby "Lady Wisdom" nourishes those who seek her. Such wisdom ultimately comes from above, from the realm of the divine. Like all of God's gifts, wisdom can only be received, though we must seek wisdom diligently. God's wisdom became synonymous with Torah, God's law. Those who sought wisdom prospered and found peace. The wisdom we celebrate at Easter is the wisdom that became incarnate in God's Son. It is the hidden wisdom of the cross and Resurrection, the paradoxical wisdom that lights our way out of the darkness.

Ezekiel, who prophesied during the Babylonian exile, tells how once again God will take the initiative. Although God acted justly in allowing the Babylonian attack, the exile provoked other nations to declare that God was not so powerful after all. God, it seemed, had not been able to protect his people. In response, God vows to restore his people and elevate them so that all the world will see his glory. God will act despite the people's sins. In order to ensure that his people will remain faithful to him, God promises to give them his own spirit. Without this cleansing of our hearts and without God's spirit to guide and empower us, we would fall back into sin.

Baptism is a cleansing, a bestowal of God's Spirit and our inclusion into a new community. St. Paul presents another meaning of Baptism in his Letter to the Romans. At our Baptism we go down into a watery grave. Our ritual death becomes joined to the death of Christ. Because Christ died in an act of obedience and not as the result of sin, he has broken the link between sin and death. Just as the dead no longer have obligations in this world, so the baptized are no longer beholden to the forces of evil. We must, however, exemplify our freedom in all that we think, say, and do.

Despite all attempts by the darkness to overshadow the light, God will not let evil prevail. Jesus' tomb is open and empty. "He has been raised; he is not here." The women who come to the tomb are amazed, baffled. Crucifixion has ended in Resurrection. Nothing like this has ever happened before.

Preaching Points

Since there is no children's Liturgy of the Word this evening, the following preaching points are for the parish Mass.

- The readings from the Old Testament can be heard and interpreted anew in light of the mystery of Christ as proclaimed by Paul. In Christ there is a new creation, new freedom from enslavement, new release from exile. The transformation proclaimed by Israel's prophets is even greater than they could have hoped for, for the transformation entails a "newness of life" in Christ. Ezekiel's prophecy of a new heart and a new spirit, and the promise "You will be my people and I will be your God," find extraordinary, unimaginable fulfillment through the profound intimacy of life with Christ.
- Isaiah's promise of life-giving waters, bread that is freely given, and a rich banquet is particularly appropriate at the Easter Vigil. The waters of Baptism, the bountiful proclamation of God's Word, and the Eucharistic feast provide a banquet far richer than any envisioned by Isaiah. This night everyone is invited: come, eat, listen, and delight in the Lord's rich fare.
- In this Easter Vigil Gospel, we see the empty tomb but not the appearance of the Risen Christ. On Easter Sunday, the first day of the new creation, we will encounter him, far from the empty tomb, alive among us.

Missal Options

General Notes

- The Vigil takes the place of the Office of Readings.
- Vigil candles should be prepared ahead of time and distributed as people gather outside for the great fire. The only ones who do not light their candles during the service of light are those yet to be baptized. The church should be in darkness as people arrive.
- The Vigil must take place during the night. Consult this website to determine when nightfall will occur in your area: http://aa.usno.navy.mil/data/docs/RS_OneDay.php.

Lucernarium

- The "blazing fire" should be prepared before the Vigil begins.
- There is no procession; priest and ministers simply arrive at the fire, Paschal candle in hand. A processional cross and additional candles are not used in the procession.
- After the fire is blessed, the priest cuts a cross, the Greek letters for Alpha and Omega, and the date on the candle while reciting the beautiful text indicating that all time belongs to Christ. After this, five grains of incense representing Christ's wounds are placed into the candle, the candle is lit from the newly blessed fire, and the procession into the church begins. If there is a deacon, he carries the candle into the church, stopping three times while raising the candle and proclaiming "The Light of Christ," to which the assembly responds, "Thanks be to God." A thurifer leads the procession.
- After the second elevation of the candle, the candle flame is distributed to the assembly.
- Once the deacon (or priest, in his absence) reaches the sanctuary, the candle is placed in its proper place by the ambo. The lights in the church are lit.
- If the deacon sings the Exsultet, the priest will first bless him at the presider's chair.
- For the proclamation of the Exsultet, there is no shame in using the ancient and beautiful chant found in the RM. A ritual edition of this chant is published by LTP: *Proclamations for Christmas, Epiphany, and Easter.*
- If a cantor sings the Exsultet, the blessing is omitted as well as the dialogue (similar to the Preface dialogue) that is included in the text.

Liturgy of the Word

- See page 160 under "Scripture Insights" for pastoral commentary on the readings.
- After the Exsultet, the assembly's candles are extinguished and all are seated for the Liturgy of the Word.
- There are seven Old Testament readings—each followed by a psalm and Collect prayer—plus the sung Gloria, extended Gospel acclamation, and the Gospel proclamation. The Missal strongly encourages that all readings be proclaimed (especially given the solemnity and importance of this holy night!). Use great pastoral caution when choosing to eliminate the readings. If you find that it is best to omit readings, keep in mind that at least three readings must be proclaimed. Also, the reading from Exodus 14 and the Canticle of Miriam should never be omitted.
- Use your best proclaimers of the Word and psalmists.
- Parish teams should review the rubrics that are included in the LM. Some psalms are proclaimed specifically because Baptism will or will not take place this evening.
- Each Collect prayer is preceded by "Let us pray." Give the assembly time to do just that . . . pray.
- The Gloria is sung before the Epistle, complete with the ringing of bells. You might invite a group of children to help with the ringing!
- The Gospel Acclamation is combined with Psalm 118 (117). The priest (or cantor) intones the Alleluia acclamation three times, each successive time raising the beginning note by a step. If a deacon is present, he should proclaim the Gospel in the usual way. It is best, however, to do a more elaborate procession through the church with the Book of the Gospels (the book should have been placed on the altar before the liturgy begins since it is not included in the procession with the Paschal candle). There are no candle-bearers in the procession, only the thurifer.

- The homily may be brief but it should never be omitted. See above under "Preaching Points" for ideas.

Liturgy of Baptism

- The texts for the Baptism of adults was updated with the third edition of *The Roman Missal*. For pastoral consistency, it is best to use the language of the RM rather than of the RCIA.
- Infants as well as adults may be baptized this evening.
- The assembly should be able to see the baptismal font. If the font is in a large baptistery, invite the assembly to gather around the font. Only if the font is not visible should a temporary font be constructed and placed in the sanctuary. The presence of the community is essential; avoid doing Baptism apart from the community (or even filming it and broadcasting it in the church).
- The godparents, elect, and ministers process to the font while the Litany of Saints is sung. If there is to be no Baptism, the Litany of Saints is omitted. Note that the procession does not occur if the Baptism takes place in the sanctuary. If this is the case, the priest immediately addresses the assembly, and the Litany follows. If the Baptism occurs in a place apart from the sanctuary, the Litany begins the rite.
- The elect may be wearing dark-colored robes before they are baptized. This will highlight the clothing with the white garment that takes place later in the rite.
- The RM recommends that two cantors sing the Litany. The assembly stands at this time (because of the glorious nature of Easter).
- The Christian names of those to be baptized may be included in the Litany as well as the titular or patron saints of the parish.
- The blessing of water follows the Litany (or, if no Baptisms are taking place, the address to the people). Note that the Missal provides two options for the blessing of the water—the choice depends on whether or not Baptism will take place.
- The blessing of water may be chanted or spoken. Given the solemnity of this holy night, music ministers should make every effort to rehearse with pastors so they will be comfortable chanting this prayer.
- Following the formula of blessing, all sing the acclamation "Springs of water, bless the Lord; / praise and exalt him above all for ever." Do not omit this text.
- The priest then asks those to be baptized to renounce sin as found in the RCIA (or *Order of Baptism of Children*).
- If adults have not been anointed beforehand with the Oil of Catechumens, the anointing takes place at this time.
- Immersion is the preferred way to baptize infants and adults.
- After each person is baptized, sing an Alleluia acclamation.
- If infants are baptized, they are immediately anointed with the Sacred Chrism.
- Adults and children are then clothed with the white garment (use parish albs) and given their baptismal candles lighted from the newly blessed Easter fire (shared from the Paschal candle).
- After the candles have been given to the neophytes, and if the Baptisms have taken place apart from the sanctuary, the neophytes process to the sanctuary while the Vidi aquam (or another chant) is sung. Confirmation follows according to the newly translated *Order of Confirmation*.
- The Renewal of Baptismal Promises follows Confirmation. Invite the neophytes to go out into the assembly to relight the candles of the newly baptized. The "Vidi aquam" may also accompany the sprinkling rite or another acclamation baptismal in nature.
- After the Renewal of Baptismal Promises (which replaces the Creed), the UP takes place. This is the first time the now neophytes are exercising their priestly ministry flowing from Baptism! Sample texts are provided below under "Mass Texts." Consider chanting the text or at least the response. You might vary the response with "Risen Lord, hear our prayer." Use this throughout Easter Time.

Liturgy of the Eucharist

- The Liturgy of the Eucharist takes place in the usual way.
- The prayers are proper and are found among the texts for the Vigil.
- Invite the newly baptized and their godparents to bring forth the gifts.
- Use P-I of Easter.
- EP-I, EP-II, and EP-III include a special commemoration for the baptized and their godparents. EP-IV may not be used this evening.
- Enough hosts should be consecrated for the entire assembly. There is never the option to go to the tabernacle (unless absolutely necessary), and on this night, when the neophytes receive for the first time, they should be receiving the same hosts consecrated at Mass in which they presented their very selves to be united with the offering of Christ.
- The RM (#64) and the RCIA (#243) provide priests with the option to "briefly address the newly baptized about receiving" the Eucharist. RCIA #242 provides more clarification about what the priest may say: he "may remind the neophytes of the preeminence of the eucharist, which is the climax of their initiation and the center of the whole Christian life."
- Both the RM and the RCIA emphasize the reception of both species this night.
- Music accompanying the Communion procession should begin as the priest receives and should continue until all have received. The song selections should invite assembly participation.

Concluding Rites

- The Solemn Blessing must be done. The Missal provides the text, or this text may be replaced with the formula of final blessing from the Rite of Baptism of Adults or of Children.
- The priest or deacon chants the double Alleluia dismissal.
- Although a concluding song is not part of the rite, sing a rousing, jubilant hymn celebrating Christ's Resurrection!

Music Preparation

- Play an instrumental piece for Preparation of the Gifts. Given all the acclamations and assemnly singing that preceded this part of the Vigil, an instrumental will signify a contrast at the beginning of the Liturgy of the Eucharist; doing so will help place the focus on the altar for the climax of the liturical celebration.
- For the sprinkling with water, use the arrangement the parish sang on the Feast of the Baptism of the Lord.
- Tonight is not the night to introduce a new Mass Ordinary. Choose something festive, but familiar, so that all guests may fully participate.

Music Suggestions

- See also pages 149–150.
- Exsultet: traditional chant (*The Roman Missal*) or "This Is the Night" by Tony Alonso (GIA)
- Gospel Acclamation: "Festival Alleluia" by J. Chepponis (MorningStar)
- Communion: "Holy Banquet, Feast of Love" by D. Dufner, OSB (GIA)
- Acclamation for Baptism: "Rejoice, Rejoice" by "L. Stafford (WLP)

Mass Texts

Dismissal of Catechumens

My friends, on this night when we celebrate Christ's passage from death to life and rejoice in our own hope for resurrection, we long for you to share our joy and to join us at this table he has prepared for us. Until that day comes, go in peace to reflect on the Paschal Mystery.

Universal Prayer

In the fullness of Easter joy, let us bring our needs and hopes to the God of Life.

1. For the Church, that we may be renewed in grace on this most blessed of days, we pray:
2. That the Good News of a world redeemed might flour in every heart, we pray:
3. For the newly baptized, that God will bless them with his own wisdom and peace, on this day and every day of their lives, we pray:
4. For all who live under the shadow of death and war, that they may experience light, peace, and freedom, we pray:
5. For the sick, the suffering, the lonely, and the forgotten, that they may feel the joy of this holy night through our prayers and our loving support, we pray:
6. For all who have died, especially **N.**, that they may also share in his Resurrection, we pray:
7. For all of us gathered in this holy place, that the surpassing joy of this night may overflow in acts of loving kindness toward all we encounter in our daily life, we pray:

Loving and compassionate God,
by your Son's cross and Resurrection you have set us free.
Easter's light now shines upon us
to guide the path of your Church.
Keep us faithful to our baptismal calling
as we reveal by the witness of our lives
that nothing has the power to destroy what your love seeks to redeem.
May our hearts be filled with Easter joy.
Through Christ our Risen Lord.
Amen.

Other Rites and Customs

The great Vigil breaks the Paschal fast. Parishes will often schedule a reception for the newly initiated immediately following the Vigil service. Invite parishioners to bring a dish to pass and their Easter baskets. Begin the festivities with the blessing of the first meal of Easter, found in ch. 54 of the BB.

Liturgy and Life

The TV show *CSI: Crime Scene Investigation* would find little evidence in John's account of the Resurrection: a stone rolled away, an empty tomb, burial cloths, and a head covering in a separate place. Yet, such is the evidence that made Mary of Magdala, Simon Peter, and the disciple whom Jesus loved believe that Jesus was raised from the dead. Our witness stories can seem just as sparse: hope in the face of despair, acceptance of a terminal illness, unexpected forgiveness, or . . . fill in the blank. How has God raised you when death and darkness seemed stronger?

S U N **4** LM #42, 41, or 46 / LMC #36ABC / white

Easter Sunday of the Resurrection of the Lord

About Easter Sunday

Easter Sunday crowns the Triduum celebration and begins a new period of time within the liturgical year. Easter Sunday is the pattern and purpose for all other Sunday celebrations of the year and begins a time of reflecting on how the followers of Jesus came to receive and understand his Resurrection from the dead.

Scripture Insights

The Resurrection was too much for the disciples to take in. They were disoriented by terror, by wonder, and by joy. What could be the same if even death itself is unreliable? Mary thinks Jesus is the gardener, but when he speaks her name she melts. "the sheep follow him, because they recognize his voice" (John 10:4). Like the lover of the Song of Songs, her joy soon shivers into uncertainty when she moves to embrace him and he is changed. "Do not hold on to me," he says. What? Jesus asks Mary to adopt new ways of seeing and touching him, to know him in a new way, in spirit. But we learn the ways of spirit clumsily; like learning to write with the opposite hand, it means unlearning the old way. This bizarre experience of knowing but not knowing emerges in an odd line from the later story of the lakeshore breakfast: "None of the disciples dared to ask him, 'Who are you?' because they realized it was the Lord" (21:12).

Resurrection is more than a new phase of the old life. Jesus invites followers to rise with him into a strange, upside-down world where apparent irreversibles are reversed: life defeats death, love trumps evil, weakness means power, humility wins out, last come first, and "nothing will be impossible for God" (Luke 1:37).

Keeping this in focus demands an attitude of prayerful concentration like contemplation. The Letter to the Colossians urges believers to "think of what is above." This means not just having an idea but practicing habitual patterns of thinking. The marvelous news of Resurrection announces itself only to those who return repeatedly to question, ponder, and insist on understanding such statements as "you have died," "your life is hidden with Christ in God," and "you also will be revealed with him in glory." Members of the Christian community who listen intently and often to this message of Jesus' life gradually learn to live the resurrection as a fact of life.

Colossians 3:1–4 also is meant as a guide for community life. Each "you" is plural. Reread 3:1–4 from the plural perspective. What might "what is above" and "what is on earth" mean for life in a community of faith?

Preaching Points

Parish Masses

- The Son of God has been raised from the dead; death is defeated. Christ's promise is that in him we too shall be raised. The Apostles begin to spread the Good News and preach the Risen Lord.
- Because of Christ, we are a changed people. We have the freedom to look to Christ, and we are called to seek him rather than seek less worthy aspects of earthly life.
- Mary Magdalene went to Jesus' tomb and was the first to find it empty. She brought the disciples this marvelous news and was the first to share the news of the empty tomb.

Children's Liturgy of the Word

- The Apostles witnessed Jesus' teaching, healing, and preaching, and they shared that news with others. They preached the empty tomb and Jesus' victory over death.
- According to the Gospel according to John, Mary Magdalene was the first to witness the empty tomb. As she hurried back to the disciples, she held in her heart the great news of humanity's salvation.

Missal Options

- The Renewal of Baptismal Promises may take place in place of the Creed. The text is found among those for the Easter Vigil.
- The Gloria is sung or said.
- The Creed is sung or said only if the Renewal of Baptismal Promises does not take place.
- Offer P-I of Easter.
- If EP-I is prayed, use the proper form of the Communicantes.
- The SB from the Vigil may be used, and the double Alleluia is included in the dismissal.
- Ritual Masses are prohibited today.

Music Preparation

- Today, the parish will see many visitors, so choose music that is festive but familiar. Use as much traditional music as you can. For the Communion procession, prepare music the assembly can sing by memory.
- Use the same version of Psalm 118 at Vigil, Masses during the day, and throughout the Octave.
- There will be many visitors at today's liturgy. Be sure to make these liturgies just as festive as the Vigil. Muisc has the potential to evangelize the community and reach out to lapsed Catholics, hopefully enticing them to become more active in your parish. Make sure to include familiar pieces—but do them well!

Music Suggestions

- Gathering: "Christ the Lord Is Risen Today" arranged by Kevin Keil (OCP)
- Sprinkling Rite: "You Are Baptized, You Are Anointed" by Roger Stratton (WLP)
- Responsorial Psalm: "Psalm 118: Let Us Rejoice" by Marty Haugen (GIA) or "Psalm 118: This Is the Day" by Michael Joncas (OCP)
- Easter Sequence: "Christians to the Paschal Victim" (various publishers)
- Gospel Acclamation: "Festival Alleluia" by J. Chepponis (MorningStar)
- Communion: "Holy Banquet, Feast of Love" by D. Dufner, OSB (GIA)

Mass Texts

Introduction to Mass

This day God has made us through the Resurrection of his Son who died to bring us back to him. Indeed, we have been made one with Christ through baptism. He is our life, our way to the Father, our glory. Having been washed clean in his blood and clothed in the bright promise of salvation, let us celebrate this feast with thanksgiving and joy. *My brothers and sisters, let us acknowledge our sins, and so prepare ourselves to celebrate the sacred mysteries.*

Tropes for Penitential Act, Form III

Lord Jesus, you died for our sake and brought an end to death: Lord, have mercy.

Christ Jesus, you reconcile sinners to the Father: Christ, have mercy.

Lord Jesus, you are the Prince of life who died and reigns immortal: Lord, have mercy.

Dismissal for Children's Liturgy of the Word

Dear children, imagine the disciples' surprise and joy when Jesus, who had died and been buried, rose from the dead and again spent time with them! He still lives and will never die again. He is with us here, today, and he will be with you as you gather separately to listen to him. Go now in his love.

Dismissal of Catechumens

My friends, this day is the summit of the Church's liturgical life. The Lord's Resurrection is the source of all our hope and joy, which we long to share with you. As you take your leave from us to reflect on Christ risen from the tomb, know that we pray that his light will shine in your own hearts. Go in peace.

Dismissal of Extraordinary Ministers of Holy Communion

My dear ministers, we send you to those of our community who are experiencing in particular ways the weakness of the body. Share with them the Body of our Risen Lord Jesus and remind them of the bright promise of immortality. Go in the peace and joy of the Resurrection.

Universal Prayer

This is the day that the Lord has made! Let us rejoice and be glad! With faith in the Lord's Resurrection, we offer our prayers for the needs of the world.

1. That the pope, bishops, priests, deacons, and all who minister in the Church might reveal the power of the Resurrection by the hope they bear, we pray:
2. That the Good News of a world redeemed might flourish in every land and in every heart, we pray:
3. That life may be victorious over sin and death in the hearts of all who peer into the empty tomb, we pray:
4. That our parish community may be a sign of unity as we follow the Light of Christ, we pray:
5. That all the dead may be raised to new life, and that all who mourn may be comforted, we pray:

Risen and victorious Lord,
by your cross and Resurrection you have set us free.
Easter's light continues to guide the path of your Church.
Keep us faithful to our baptismal calling as we reveal in our lives
that nothing has power to destroy what the Father's love seeks to redeem.
May our hearts be filled with Easter joy.
Who live and reign with God the Father in the unity of the Holy Spirit,
one God, for ever and ever.
Amen.

Other Rites and Customs

- Provide a special bulletin for Easter that highlights the various ministries and activities of the parish. This serves as a great orientation to the parish for those who are visiting.
- Sing the Sequence at Mass—it's not optional today!
- Celebrate Easter Sunday Vespers to conclude the Triduum or at least provide parishioners with some form of adapted Evening Prayer for use before Easter dinner.
- Be sure the outside of the church is decorated for fifty days to let the world know that these days are very sacred.

Liturgy and Life

Being recognized and being named touches us deeply and can lead to mutual affirmation, respect, and healing. We often want to hold on to the moment, but life goes on. This is revealed in the memorial we celebrate in the Eucharist. Reflect on the power of your words. Relish the memory of people you have loved who have died. Allow the experience to one day free you to bring healing, new life, and good news to others.

Taking Place this Week

Consider what can be done liturgically, catechetically, and ministerially to respond to these important needs.

- The last day of Passover is 4/4.
- Mine Awareness Day (4/4)
- The Octave of Easter takes place throughout this week, ending next Sunday. Each day is treated as a solemnity.
- Yom HaShoah, United Nations World Health Day, and Day to Remember Rwanda Genocide Victims (4/7)
- April is Financial Literacy, Mathematics Awareness, National Child Abuse Prevention, National Volunteer, Prevention of the Cruelty to Animals, Black Women's History, and Sexual Assault Awareness Month.
- April is set aside by Catholics as the Month of the Holy Eucharist.

Easter Time

O God, who gladden us year by year with the solemnity of the Lord's Resurrection, graciously grant that, by celebrating these present festivities, we may merit through them to reach eternal joys.

— Collect, Wednesday within the Octave of Easter

The Meaning of the Season

ALLELUIA! It is impossible for us to sing alleluia too much as we celebrate this season of Easter. In fact, "these above all others are the days for the singing of the *Alleluia*" (UNLY, 22). No other word encapsulates the superabundance of joy, the triumph of Christ and his victory over the grave, and our identity as an Easter people living in the light of Christ with the promise of eternal life.

The Roman Missal includes five Prefaces for Easter—and all five begin "It is truly right and just, our duty and our salvation at all times to acclaim you, O Lord, but in this time [or, in Preface I, 'on this night'/'on this day'] above all to laud you yet more gloriously, when Christ our Passover has been sacrificed." All five conclusions are identical as well: "Therefore, overcome with paschal joy, / every land, every people exults in your praise / and even the heavenly Powers, with the angelic hosts, / sing together the unending hymn of your glory, / as they acclaim." These shared introductions and conclusions make clear that all fifty days are to be celebrated with exuberance. Indeed, citing St. Athanasius, UNLY decrees that the fifty days of this season "are celebrated in joyful exultation as one feast day, or better as one 'great Sunday'" (22).

Patrick Regan, OSB, offers a reflection on the history of these fifty days that can help us to understand and liturgically celebrate the season. Drawing on Tertullian, Augustine, and other Church Fathers, he explains that early Christians did not conceive of these days as "time-after" (after Easter Sunday) or "time between" (between Easter and Pentecost) but rather as a lengthy celebration of "rejoicing in the resurrection, ascension, bestowal of the Spirit, and founding of the church, understood not as separate episodes succeeding each other in time, but as different facets of one and the same mystery of Jesus' exaltation as Lord" ("The Fifty Days and the Fiftieth Day" in *Between Memory and Hope*, ed. Johnson, pp. 223–24).

This unified understanding of the fifty days as one celebration emphasizes the need to maintain our Easter joy throughout the entirety of the season. Fortunately, in most of the Northern Hemisphere, the season is happily concurrent with the arrival of spring, the gradual warming of temperatures, and the blooming of flowers. Also, unlike the overwhelming secular buildup to Christmas, there is less advance celebrating prior to Easter. Granted, stores do prominently advertise and sell plenty of candy and facilitate pictures with the Easter Bunny. But few radio stations or streaming channels play Easter hymns, and most homes are not decorated with Easter lights. As a result, we are not quite so exhausted by Easter prior to its arrival.

The prescribed liturgical texts and rubrics also do their part to help us sustain the joy. Bursting forth from the solemn celebrations of the Triduum and return of the Alleluia during the Easter Vigil, the Entrance and Communion Antiphons for the entire season end with Alleluia. The first eight days—the Octave of Easter—are celebrated as solemnities (see UNLY, 24). The Gospel readings for the first three Sundays and during the Octave of Easter "are accounts of the Lord's appearances" (LMI, 100–101). The lit Paschal candle remains by the ambo in the sanctuary. The vestments are white. Easter flowers adorn the church until they begin to wilt—at which time, hopefully, they can be replaced by others to last for the duration of the season. As previously mentioned, the shared Preface texts are unifying. All of these symbols continually proclaim the message that our Easter joy should not abate.

Easter Time is also the season of mystagogy. Yes, it is a time for catechizing those who were initiated into the Church at the Easter Vigil. Moreover, though, it is a time for these "neophytes" and the *entire community* "*together* to grow in deepening their grasp of the paschal mystery and in making it part of their lives through meditation on the Gospel, sharing in the Eucharist, and doing the works of charity" (RCIA, 244, see also 246; emphasis added). This deepening can happen in many ways, but the primary moment is "the Sunday Masses of the Easter season" (RCIA, 247). Celebrating the Rite of Sprinkling of Holy Water throughout the season is one way to symbolically emphasize the baptismal unity of the neophytes with the entire community.

In addition, the season of Easter is a preferred time for other celebrations of the sacraments of initiation. Many dioceses schedule Confirmations during Easter Time. For those parishes whose Confirmation celebrations occur close to or on Pentecost, the link between Baptism and Confirmation—between the Paschal Mystery and the descent of the Holy Spirit—is all the more apparent. Baptism itself has a "paschal character" (OBC, 9), and celebrating the Baptism of children on Sundays of Easter emphasizes the initiatory character of the season, especially for those who were not present for the Baptisms at the Easter Vigil (and doing so especially during the Eucharistic liturgy). First Communion practices vary widely from parish to parish and diocese to diocese, but one common thread is that they are often celebrated during Easter Time. Even other sacramental celebrations, such as ordinations and weddings, frequently occur during the Easter season. All of these celebrations are invariably joyful, and celebrating them maintains the joy of Easter throughout the entire season.

Finally, Easter Time continues well into the month of May, traditionally associated with Mary. From the May Crowning devotion to the recitation of the Rosary—particularly the first three Glorious Mysteries (the Resurrection, Ascension, and Descent of the Holy Spirit)—we rejoice with Mary in the Resurrection of her Son. The traditional "Regina Caeli," the traditional Marian antiphon for Easter Time, is a fine prayer for singing or reciting throughout the season.

We do indeed rejoice with Mary, the communion of saints, the angelic choirs, and the Church universal throughout this season. As Pope Francis said in his 2018 Easter *Urbi et Orbi* message, "We Christians believe and know that Christ's resurrection is the true hope of the world, the hope that does not disappoint." During the fifty days of Easter, that hope inspires us to live the message of Psalm 118: this is indeed the day that the Lord has made. Let us rejoice and be glad in it! Alleluia!

The Sounds of the Season

Pastoral musicians should take delight in the seven weeks of Easter because, in all actuality, each week is but one celebration. It is laudable that the sprinkling rite be utilized each week at each liturgy and that the same settings of the Gloria, Alleluia, and Eucharistic Prayer acclamations be retained. Utilize the rich hymn texts of Easter and employ the use of "Alleluia" throughout the entire season. Bear in mind that throughout Easter Time any Responsorial Psalm may take "Alleluia" as its antiphon. It is important that we do everything we can to convey our Easter joy!

Easter Time officially ends fifty days from Easter Sunday with the Solemnity of Pentecost. Because Easter Time concludes on Pentecost, it is appropriate to use the same ritual music. Similar to Easter Sunday, Pentecost Sunday calls for the beautiful and powerful "Golden Sequence" or "Veni, Sancte Spiritus," to be sung at the completion of the Second Reading. In addition to the chant, other settings are available and range from strophic settings to choral settings to contemporary settings. It is interesting to note that the solemn dismissal with double Alleluia is used today, just like on Easter Sunday and throughout the Octave of Easter (it is not, however, used on the Sundays between Easter and Pentecost).

The Look of the Season

First Communion and Confirmation often happen during the season of Easter, and so it is a good time to explore both of these sacraments.

The celebration of first Communion is usually scheduled in the spring on a date that often occurs during the weeks of Easter Time. The festive arrangements already in place would certainly be suitable for the celebration of first Communion. The art and environment team might want to examine the arrangements to determine if those around the altar need to be culled. Some parishes place so many plants and flowers around the altar that it is difficult to see the altar.

On this occasion when the emphasis is on the Sacrament of Eucharist, the altar, the table of the Lord, should be given prominence and not be overshadowed with extraneous decor. The altar vesture can be a festive fabric, but this should not take the form of a banner or a collage of names or symbols.

The altar is the symbol of Christ in the midst of his Body, the Church; it does not need any adornment. This principle applies to the ambo as well. It should not become a prop for banners or the backdrop for any sort of decorative display. Some parishes create large hangings or banners with the names of the first communicants placed on them. These can be quite beautiful and can honor the children at this important moment in their lives. These works of art can be suspended from the ceiling or attached to columns, making sure that they do not obstruct a view of the sanctuary or detract from the liturgical action. They can be left in place for a few days, but they are temporary additions to the environment and should be removed shortly after the celebration. These name banners could also be on a smaller scale and used in procession, even if more than one is necessary. Instead of placing them in the sanctuary, however, put them in floor stands around the inside perimeter of the church as a way to indicate that the first communicants are now part of the assembly that gathers at the table of the Lord.

The Roman Missal recommends that, in addition to the bread and wine offered at the Presentation and Preparation of Gifts, that "gifts for the Church and the poor" can be "gathered and brought to the altar" (Order of Mass, 22). Such gifts are usually monetary offerings, but certainly food items are appropriate. It is a worthy gesture, and a teaching moment for the children, to have each of them present at least one food item at this time. A large container, such as a wicker basket, could be placed adjacent to the sanctuary to receive these offerings.

If the group is large, most of the items could be placed prior to the liturgy and a few representatives of the group can carry items forward in the procession with the gifts of bread and wine. The Presentation of Gifts should not include any other items, such as catechetical books, Bibles, baptismal candles, etc.; nor should clusters of plastic grapes or strands of artificial grain be in this procession. The use of fake materials should not be considered in the liturgical environment. Some of the recommendations noted earlier, for example, the use of name banners, can be employed for the celebration of the sacrament.

Since the celebration of Confirmation often depends on the schedule of the bishop, it might be celebrated at any time of the year and thus in the midst of any of the liturgical seasons. Since the liturgy for Confirmation is a one-time event, it is not necessary to remove the existing and seasonal liturgical environment. On the other hand, any additional arrangements for the celebration of Confirmation should not overshadow the seasonal decor.

The usual liturgical color for Confirmation is red. Accents such as fabric hangings could be included; modest fresh flower arrangements with red blooms might be added to existing arrangements. Since the décor for the celebration of Confirmation is temporary, it isn't good stewardship to spend a lot of money on lavish displays.

A festive touch is the use of processional stands in an outdoor setting. These could be adorned with colorful fabric banners and used to mark the processional route if the candidates gather in another site and process into the church. Since Confirmation is one of the Sacraments of Initiation, is be appropriate to use some decor to draw attention to the baptismal font for this liturgy.

If this liturgy is outside the Easter season, the Paschal candle is located near the font and would, of course, be lighted.

The candidates are anointed with Sacred Chrism. The vessel for Chrism should be a beautiful one; it is removed from the ambry and presented to the bishop in a visible and reverent gesture.

Evangelizing through the Season

Easter Time is the season of mystagogy. It is the season in which the Church returns again and again to the central experience of the Paschal Mystery that has been celebrated again in the Triduum. Our attention is so closely focused on this story that it sometimes seems that we are hearing the same readings over and over at Mass. How is this an opportunity for evangelism? While it is certainly true that many in our culture have not heard the Gospel, it is also true that many who have heard the Gospel or grown up in the Church have become disillusioned with the Church and have stopped listening for God's Word there.

Easter Time can be a time of real growth for the Church, as she breaks open her own experience of the sacraments, of the stories, and of the Holy Spirit's work in the life of neophytes. And this work is an opportunity to invite those who might have become disillusioned back into the contemplation of what it is that the Church celebrates.

Mystagogical preaching is one place to begin in this task. How can homilies invite people to reflect more deeply on their experience of God? What common experiences from the liturgy might people reflect on together? This pattern can be expanded beyond the liturgy but will always return to the experience of being church together around the table. Common experiences of *lectio divina*, or *visio divina*, can open up the Scriptures read at the Mass. They can also be opportunities for inviting people to come and reflect together about the Bible. It's not uncommon to hear from those raised in the Catholic Church that they think that they cannot read or interpret Scripture themselves, and *lectio* can provide a place to start and permission to reengage. It can also be an experience to be shared with other Christians, by which the Gospel can be fostered together. Alternately, people might be invited to reflect on their memories of the rites, either from when they themselves were baptized or confirmed or from when they observed those close to them be received into Christ's Body. Learning to listen for God's action in our lives opens the ears of our hearts, allowing us to see more clearly the actions of grace throughout our lives. Learning to do this together can be an important first step toward healing the rifts that have come between people and the Church.

Worship Committee Agenda for Easter Time

Meeting Time

Members of the Worship Committee should gather during the Third Week of Easter Time, so that the memory of the Triduum's rite and rituals is still fresh. Group evaluation of Lent and the Triduum, along with some shared rejoicing among the committee members, are the reasons to meet. Easter seasonal preparation should, however, take place in late January.

Goal for the Meeting

- Evaluate the liturgies of Lent: use the form of "commendations" and "recommendations" to guide the committee's work.
- Evaluate the liturgy of the Triduum: again, use commendations and recommendations to move through each "day" that liturgy was celebrated. Be thoughtful, uncritical, and consider "what worked" and "what may not have worked" for each of the liturgies.
- Consider the RCIA process and the newly initiated: are the neophytes still rejoicing and coming to their reserved family pews at Mass? Does the congregation recognize who received the Easter sacraments (even if they didn't attend the Easter Vigil)? Is the parish welcoming persons who seek Full Communion, during the weekend Masses at Easter Time?
- Add any Marian celebrations such as a May Crowning of the Blessed Virgin Mary to the parish calendar, and encourage a multigenerational celebration.
- Recognize and make sure that the Vigil of Pentecost and Pentecost Sunday are celebrated boldly, continuing to catechize the assembly.
- Celebrate the season: a shared supper, special food at the meeting, gift books or small baskets of goodies to take home, individual thank-you notes from the priest and parish staff?

Liturgical Catechesis for the Worship Committee

- Consult *Sourcebook* 2021 as a group, regarding "The Look of the Season." It contains helpful and practical information and ideas for "keeping" the Easter season. Spend ten minutes in conversation with the art and environment leader, and determine if they have the support, creativity, and energy to continue the seasonal environment: ask if they have coordinated and shared responsibility for the special liturgies that happen each spring, such as first Communion, Confirmation for youth, graduation?
- Each member should familiarize themselves with the Universal Prayer suggestion provided for each Sunday, solemnity, and feast of the Lord in *Sourcebook*. Read the sample at the meeting, and consider using the sample "plus 2 others" on the Sundays of Easter until Pentecost.
- What does the Catholic Church say about the environment? Solicit three volunteers who are willing to read Pope Francis' *Laudato si'*, with encouragement to prepare a twenty-minute summary for the next meeting (which will be in summer, when it's "easier" to notice and appreciate the environment that we live in).

Liturgical Catechesis for the Assembly

- Review the content of the parish bulletin, asking, "Does our bulletin catechize or does it euthanize?" Invite the congregation to find and share, over a period of a month, any church bulletins that they think are helpful, informative, and catechetical. Set up a "bulletin basket" in the church narthex, or wherever people enter. The intended result would be learning what the assembly considers important and helpful, renewing what the assembly seeks in a communication tool, and how the assembly receives basic catechetical information.
- The concluding Sundays of Easter Time are great opportunities to bless those who minister as readers, sometime during each weekend Mass. Present the readers, in advance of Pentecost, with a copy of *Guide for Lectors and Readers, Second Edition* (LTP, The Liturgical Ministry Series) in celebration of their ministry.

Closing Prayer

Light a large candle in the center of the meeting space. Provide the text of the longer version of the Easter Proclamation for the worship committee (format it beautifully, so members can take it home and frame it). Divide into "sections" and begin with the Sign of the Cross. Pray the Exultet, with each group taking a part, prayerfully. A prayer leader could conclude by leading four minutes of lectio divina, if the committee chooses to reflect further.

M O N 5 LM #261 / LMC #185–192 / white
Monday within the Octave of Easter

Scripture Insights

Peter, speaking to Jews, drew on Jewish tradition. David foretold Christ, yet David is still in his tomb, while Christ has risen from his. We hear of the women's joy over seeing the Risen Christ, contrasted with the machinations of the chief priests to concoct a lie to cover up what the soldiers at the tomb saw.

Preaching Points

Parish Masses

- Peter's sermon was perhaps typical of the preaching done by the Apostles after the Resurrection. He builds on the best of Jewish tradition and shows how Christ fulfills and surpasses it.
- Mary and Mary were both afraid and joyful at seeing Christ, risen from the dead. The chief priests, in contrast, despite the firsthand witness of the guards, created a lie rather than rejoicing at what God had done.

Masses with Children

- The Apostles were emboldened at Christ's victory over death, and preached sermons like this to win the people over to Christ.
- The women were overjoyed at seeing Christ. The chief priests were concerned only about retaining power and created a lie about the disciples stealing the body.

Missal Options

- The prayers are proper and are found in the PT; use those for Monday within the Octave.
- Instead of the PA, offer the sprinkling rite.
- Sing or recite the Gloria.
- The sequence may be sung each day during the Octave.
- Although today is technically a solemnity, the Creed is not said or sung.
- Use any Easter Collect (expect for today's) to conclude the UP.
- Use P-I of Easter.
- If EP-I is used, the proper form of the Communicantes is said. Consider EP-II.
- The double Alleluia is used in the final dismissal.
- Although it's not called for in the Missal among the prayers of the day, you might consider concluding Masses this week with the SB for Easter Time.

Song of the Day

"Be Joyful Mary" (various publishers)

T U E 6 LM #262 / LMC #185–192 / white
Tuesday within the Octave of Easter

Scripture Insights

The Apostles still considered themselves to be Jewish, so they were aggressive in preaching to their own: God made Jesus both Lord and Christ, and you killed him. But many took the offer to repent and be baptized. Mary Magdalene quickly goes from grief to proclaiming the Resurrection. Four times the text mentions her weeping, but the story ends with her shouting the Good News.

Preaching Points

Parish Masses

- Such was Magdalene's devotion and love that she stayed with the Body of Jesus and was ready to pursue and protect Jesus' body when she thought it had been taken. All the greater was her joy at seeing the Risen Lord.
- Peter did confront the people for killing their Lord but offered a Baptism of forgiveness and reminded the people of God's continuing promise to the people and their children and others.

Masses with Children

- Peter pointed out that the people had done wrong by killing their Lord and the Christ but offered forgiveness and the Holy Spirit, despite their grave mistake.
- Mary Magdalene loved Jesus so much that she stayed with him even after his death. Imagine her joy as she finally recognized the Risen Lord.

Missal Options

- The prayers are proper and are found in the PT; use those for Tuesday within the Octave.
- Instead of the PA, offer the sprinkling rite.
- Sing or recite the Gloria.
- The sequence may be sung each day during the Octave.
- Although today is technically a solemnity, the Creed is not said or sung.
- Use any Easter Collect (expect for today's) to conclude the UP.
- Use P-I of Easter.
- If EP-I is used, the proper form of the Communicantes is said.
- The double Alleluia is used in the final dismissal.

- Although it's not called for in the Missal among the prayers of the day, you might consider concluding Masses this week with the SB for Easter Time.

Song of the Day

"Mary, Don't You Weep" arranged by Rory Cooney (GIA)

WED 7 LM #263 / LMC #185–192 / white
Wednesday within the Octave of Easter

Scripture Insights

Peter and John show early on that Christ will continue to heal through them, and thus we should be open to Christ's healing flowing through us. The Emmaus story has the disciples telling the Jesus story to the Risen Christ, who returned the favor by describing how the Scriptures had foretold his life and death. It is perhaps their hospitality to a stranger that allowed them to see Christ in that person.

Preaching Points

Parish Masses

- Acts of the Apostles is actually a continuation of the Gospel according Luke, and in it the Apostles go on to do what Jesus did in his public ministry, like healing the lame.
- The disciples' hearts were burning with joy as Jesus opened the Scriptures for them. So should our hearts burn as the Risen Christ continues to open the Scriptures for us.

Masses with Children

- The beggar was asking only for alms. Peter and John restore the beggar to the wholeness of life and leave him leaping and praising God.
- Jesus walks among us unrecognized all the time. When we are kind, when we listen to a stranger, when we invite people in and share a meal with them, then Christ makes himself known in the breaking of the bread, as he does in the Eucharist.

Missal Options

- The prayers are proper and are found in the PT; use those for Wednesday within the Octave.
- Instead of the PA, offer the sprinkling rite.
- Sing or recite the Gloria.
- Although today is technically a solemnity, the Creed is not said or sung.
- The sequence may be sung each day during the Octave.
- Use any Easter Collect (expect for today's) to conclude the UP and P-I of Easter.
- If EP-I is used, the proper form of the Communicantes is said. Consider EP-II.
- The double Alleluia is used in the final dismissal.
- Although it's not called for in the Missal among the prayers of the day, you might consider concluding Masses this week with the SB for Easter Time.

Song of the Day

"Are Not Our Hearts" by Carey Landry (OCP)

THU 8 LM #264 / LMC #185-192 / white
Thursday within the Octave of Easter

Scripture Insights

Again Peter preaches to his fellow Jews from their shared tradition, alluding to the covenant with Abraham and quoting Moses. Yet Peter pulls no punches when it comes to Jesus' execution. The Risen Lord is suddenly present as the disciples discuss what happened on the road to Emmaus, yet he is no ghost or apparition. He shows them his wounds, and he shares a meal. And once again he explains how the Scriptures foretold him all along.

Preaching Points

Parish Masses

- Peter scolds the people for being unaware yet offers repentance and more, so "that the Lord may grant you times of refreshment."
- Twice the Gospel mentions Jesus' hands and feet, which is to say that Risen Christ rose with the wounds still there. Yet he greets the disciples with peace.

Masses with Children

- Peter and John had just cured a man who was crippled from birth, yet they made clear that it was God who had cured the man, the same God of Abraham and Isaac and Jacob who spoke of Jesus through the prophets.
- The Risen Christ was no ghost. He showed his friends his wounds and ate a meal with them. He rose in bodily form.

Missal Options

- The prayers are proper and found in the PT; use those for Thursday within the Octave.
- Instead of the PA, offer the sprinkling rite.
- Sing or recite the Gloria.
- Although today is technically a solemnity, the Creed is not said or sung.
- The sequence may be sung each day during the Octave.

- Use any Easter Collect (expect for today's) to conclude the UP and P-I of Easter.
- If EP-I is used, the proper form of the Communicantes is said. Consider EP-II.
- The double Alleluia is used in the final dismissal.
- Although it's not called for in the Missal among the prayers of the day, you might consider concluding Masses this week with the SB for Easter Time.

Song of the Day

"That Easter Day with Joy Was Bright" (various publishers)

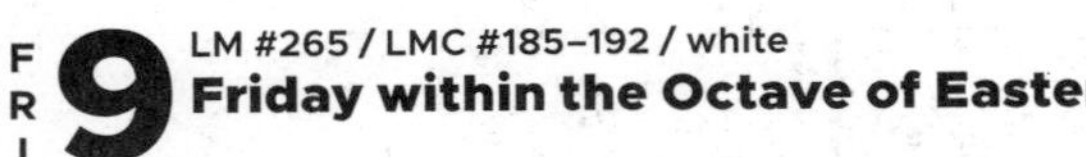

FRI 9 LM #265 / LMC #185–192 / white

Friday within the Octave of Easter

Scripture Insights

In chronological time, the events of the Gospel precede those of the story from Acts. In the Gospel, the Apostles were trying to go back to their old lives as fishermen, yet the Risen Christ has other plans, beginning with a meal of bread and fish. The power of the Risen Christ changes these men and flows through them.

Preaching Points

Parish Masses

- The same power struggles with the Jewish leaders continue after the Resurrection. They were troubled by Jesus in his earthly life, so they killed him. What can they do now that he is risen?
- In many of the Resurrection stories, Jesus is slow to be recognized, even by those who were closest to him. Once again, though, the shared meal reveals him.

Masses with Children

- "By what power or by what name have you done this?" the Jewish leaders ask John and Peter. They are delighted to be asked. Only by Christ. "There is no salvation through anyone else."
- This story of the Risen Christ hearkens back to two stories from his early life: the calling of the Apostles when they were still fishermen and the feeding of the multitudes. The Risen Christ continues to call us, continues to feed us.

Missal Options

- The prayers are proper and are found in the PT; use those for Thursday within the Octave.
- Instead of the PA, offer the sprinkling rite.
- Sing or recite the Gloria.
- Although today is technically a solemnity, the Creed is not said or sung.
- The sequence may be sung each day during the Octave.
- Use any Easter Collect (expect for today's) to conclude the UP.
- Use P-I of Easter, and if EP-I is used, the proper form of the Communicantes is said.
- The double Alleluia is used in the final dismissal.
- Although it's not called for in the Missal among the prayers of the day, you might consider concluding Masses this week with the SB for Easter Time.

Song of the Day

"Lord, When You Came/*Pescador de Hombres*"
by Cesáreo Gabaráin (OCP)

SAT 10 LM #266 / LMC #185–192 / white

Saturday within the Octave of Easter

Scripture Insights

The Jewish leaders were confounded: how did these "uneducated, ordinary men" cure the man? And how do we stop them, for the crowds are pursuing them? Will the Apostles keep quiet, as ordered by the leaders? Will the Eleven go "proclaim the Gospel to every creature," as commanded by the Risen Christ?

Preaching Points

Parish Masses

- The Jewish leaders were shocked by the "boldness" of these ordinary, uneducated men, and the crowds were "praising God for what had happened." The leaders tried to contest the situation, rather than rejoicing in the power of the Risen Christ.
- Jesus appeared to the Eleven while they were eating. The Risen Christ often appeared, or made himself known, at shared meals, as in the Eucharist.

Masses with Children

- The Jewish leaders tried to control the Apostles with threats and warnings of punishments. Who did the Apostles obey? The leaders or God?
- Christ rebuked the Eleven for not believing Mary Magdalene and the other disciples to whom he'd appeared. They were being as hard-hearted as the Jewish leaders, who also wouldn't believe what they heard.

Missal Options

- The prayers are proper and are found in the PT; use those for Saturday within the Octave.
- Instead of the PA, offer the sprinkling rite.
- Sing or recite the Gloria.
- Although today is technically a solemnity, the Creed is not said or sung.
- The sequence may be sung each day during the Octave.
- Use any Easter Collect (expect for today's) to conclude the UP and P-I of Easter.
- If EP-I is used, the proper form of the Communicantes is said. Consider EP-III.
- The double Alleluia is used in the final dismissal.
- Although it's not called for in the Missal among the prayers of the day, you might consider concluding Masses this week with the SB for Easter Time.

Song of the Day

"Go Make of All Disciples" by Leon M. Adkins (Abingdon Press)

Something to Consider...

◈ "Pastors must therefore realize that when the liturgy is celebrated something more is required than the mere observance of the laws governing valid and lawful celebration; it is also their duty to ensure that the faithful take part fully aware of what they are doing, actively engaged in the rite, and enriched by its effects" (*Sacrosanctum concilium*, 11).

S U N **11** LM #44B / LMC #38B / white

Second Sunday of Easter / Sunday of Divine Mercy

Octave Day of Easter

Scripture Insights

John 20:31 says the Gospel was written to nurture the act of committing oneself to the Son of God. For this act, John constantly uses the verb "believe" (*pisteuo*, ninety-eight times). It takes time and prayer to learn the spiritually powerful meaning of the word "believe" in John's account of the Gospel. Believing does not mean merely acting as if something is real. Believing means developing the spiritual faculty to perceive the invisible reality at the heart of all things, analogous to the ability to see and hear the physical world. Two levels of seeing operate in John. Physical seeing leads to an embryonic form of faith (see 6:30, "What sign can you do, that we may see and believe in you?"), which remains tied to earthly forms of existence (3:6). But true believing enables one to see beyond physical sight (6:40; 9:35–39).

For the early Christian communities, Apostles were those who had had the honor of being an eyewitness to the Risen Christ (Acts 1:22; 10:40–41; 1 Corinthians 15:3–8). The community of the Beloved Disciple that produced John's account accepted that tradition. "What we have seen with our eyes . . . and touched with our hands . . . we proclaim now to you" (1 John 1:1–4). But in a crucial sense, the Gospel subordinates apostleship to the task of ordinary Christians to *believe*. For John, believing in Jesus is the important step. Apostles might see Jesus risen, but they too must learn to believe. Thomas moves in one instant from earthly to spiritual believing. Jesus teaches that anyone who knows him through believing is equal to the Apostles, who know him by sight.

The power of believing in Jesus to transform human existence is evident in Luke's vignettes of the early Jerusalem community. "Those who believed" throbbed with Paschal life, conquered deeply rooted human habits, and became "one heart and soul."

Preaching Points

Parish Masses

- Jesus invites Thomas to touch his wounds, and when Thomas experiences Jesus in this manner, he proclaims the highest Christological pronouncement: "My Lord and my God." From this man's doubt, we see our Lord's identity gladly proclaimed.
- Like Thomas, we are called to believe in our Lord Jesus. Belief in Christ is a transformative reality in the life of Christians.
- How do the faithful people in the Church help one another to grow in faith and belief in the Lord?
- People grow in their faith from childhood to adulthood.

Children's Liturgy of the Word

- Thomas didn't yet understand that Jesus had risen from the dead, and he doubted what the other Apostles told him about seeing Jesus. When he witnessed the resurrected Jesus, Thomas believed. Like Thomas, we are called to belief in Jesus Christ.
- God's people are called to help each other grow in the faith that Jesus gave to us.
- Every year of your life you can grow closer to God. How has your faith changed as you grow older?

Missal Options

- Although today is Sunday of Divine Mercy, the prayer texts are those for the Second Sunday of Easter. These texts must not be replaced.
- Continue to offer the sprinkling rite instead of the three forms of the PA.
- The Gloria and the Creed are sung or said. Because of its baptismal significance, consider using the Apostles' Creed throughout Easter.
- Since it is the last day in the Octave of Easter, the Sequence may continue to be sung.
- Use any Easter Collect (expect for today's) to conclude the UP.
- Use P-I of Easter.
- Consider using EPVN-III.
- The SB for Easter Time may be prayed.
- Use the double Alleluia in the final dismissal.

Music Preparation

- Although they are written in different keys, use either accompaniment for "O Sons and Daughters" and the "Easter Alleluia" to put together a full Communion procession today. Stylize as traditional chant or the more driving beat in the Haugen arrangement.
- Explore some of the more contemporary Easter offerings as a contrast to the simplicity of Lent.

Music Suggestions

- Gathering: "Now the Green Blade Rises" (various publishers)
- Communion: "O Sons and Daughters" (various publishers) or "Easter Alleluia" adapted by Marty Haugen (GIA)
- Sending Forth: "I Know That My Redeemer Lives" (various publishers) or "Christ the Lord Is Risen Today (various publishers)

Mass Texts

Introduction to Mass

Like the Apostles in today's First Reading, we are called to witness to the Resurrection of the Lord Jesus. We are not, however, left to our own devices in this task, for the Second Reading reminds us that it is the Spirit that testifies. This same Spirit, the Spirit of Jesus, has been given to us through our Baptism, to inspire our testimony. Furthermore, we are strengthened for this mission by Christ's Body and Blood that we will receive from this altar. So let us approach with gratitude and joy. *My brothers and sisters, let us acknowledge our sins, and so prepare ourselves to celebrate the sacred mysteries.*

Tropes for Penitential Act, Form III

Lord Jesus, you redeemed us in your Blood:
Lord, have mercy.

Lord Jesus, we are reborn in your Spirit:
Christ, have mercy.

Lord Jesus, we have life in your name: Lord, have mercy.

Dismissal for Children's Liturgy of the Word

My dear children, the Apostle Thomas needed to see the Risen Christ before he believed in him. Sometimes it's hard not to be like Thomas, but the Risen Lord tells him and us that those who believe without seeing are blessed. And that is all of us. By listening to Christ in the Scriptures we pray that you will grow in faith in him who loves you very much. Go in peace.

Dismissal of Catechumens

My friends, we strive to be like the community of believers in the First Reading, of one heart and one mind, and we look forward to the day when you will join us in that spiritual communion, sharing in our faith, hope, and love and in the Body and Blood of our Lord Jesus. Go now in peace.

Dismissal of Extraordinary Ministers of Holy Communion

Dear friends, with care and concern for our sick and homebound brothers and sisters in Christ, we give you his Body to share with them. Share with them, too, the assurance that they are one with us in heart and mind and in the everlasting love and mercy of the Risen Lord. Go in peace.

Universal Prayer

This is the day that the Lord has made! Let us rejoice and be glad! With faith in the Lord's Resurrection and confident in his loving mercy, we offer our prayers for the needs of the world.

1. That our Christian assemblies may support and nurture the faith of the Body of Christ, we pray:
2. That all who assemble in fear, especially those who face political persecution, may know peace, we pray:
3. That divine mercy may wash away the doubt of all who reject the Lord and his resurrected life, we pray:
4. That all those who are excluded from our community, may receive welcome, we pray:
5. That we may be a people who open locked doors to those who are different from ourselves, we pray:

Risen Lord,
your mercy extends to all the earth
and calls us to gather together in faith.
May you walk into our midst this day and guide us to new life.
In moments of doubt and despair,
may we never forget that you are always near.
Who live and reign with God the Father in the unity of the Holy Spirit,
one God, for ever and ever.
Amen.

Other Rites and Customs

- Utilize the option in *The Roman Missal* of reciting the Apostles' Creed throughout Easter Time.
- Use incense throughout Easter Time to highlight the preeminence of the season.
- Include the Divine Mercy devotions but be sure they don't overshadow the celebration of the eighth and final day of the Octave of Easter.
- Keep good notes of what worked and what didn't during the past Triduum.
- Share the wonderful writings of the mystagogues from the Office of Readings throughout Easter Time in the bulletin and whatever social media platforms the parish uses.
- Encourage families to keep their homes decorated for the fifty days of Easter.

Liturgy and Life

Divine Mercy, which we celebrate today, takes many forms. For instance, our polluted air and land and water surely need some form of mercy. The United States Conference of Catholic Bishops has an Environmental Justice Program, which you can read about at http://www.usccb.org/sdwp/ejp/. Named "Caring for God's Creation," the program calls Catholics to greater reverence for creation, providing educational resources for parishes and dioceses.

Taking Place This Week . . .

Consider what can be done liturgically, catechetically, and ministerially to respond to these important needs.

- International Day of Human Space Flight (4/12)
- First day of Ramadan (4/13)
- Yom Ha'atzmaut and US Tax Day (4/15)

MON 12 LM #267 / LMC #185–192 / white
Easter Weekday

Scripture Insights

After the death and Resurrection of Jesus, the disciples interpreted everything in light of Easter, and so should we. Twice the reading mentions how the disciples would "speak the word of God with boldness," and so should we. Jesus spoke to Nicodemus about Baptism, which, like the Resurrection, changes how we see everything.

Preaching Points

Parish Masses

- Peter and John had been ordered to keep silent about the Risen Lord. How could they? When they returned to the disciples, the disciples together proclaimed this hymn of praise that is recorded in Acts.
- Nicodemus came at night. He was one of the rulers of the Jews but hid his attraction to Jesus. Jesus told him to start over, to be "born from above," to die and rise in Baptism. There is no indication that Nicodemus understood what Jesus told him.

Masses with Children

- The religious leaders of the day told the Apostles to keep quiet about the Risen Christ. Instead, they sang his praises with boldness.
- Nicodemus was one of the religious leaders. He came at night to see Jesus, who spoke to him about baptism—about being "born of water and Spirit." And the Spirit will set you free.

Missal Options

- Presiders may choose to offer any of the three forms of the PA or continue to sprinkle the gathered faithful. It might be best to reserve the sprinkling rite for Sundays and solemnities.
- Use any Easter Collect (expect for today's) to conclude the UP.
- The prayers for today are from Monday of the Second Week of Easter in the PT.
- Any of the five Prefaces of Easter may be used.
- Consider EP-II.

Song of the Day

"Easter Alleluia" by Marty Haugen (GIA) or "O God, You Search Me" by Bernadette Farrell (OCP)

TUE 13 LM #268 / LMC #185–192 / white
Easter Weekday

Optional Memorial of St. Martin I, Pope and Martyr / red

Scripture Insights

Nicodemus is a "teacher of Israel" but doesn't realize he is speaking to the fulfillment of God's promises. Christ speaks of being born of the Spirit, of heavenly things revealed by earthly things, of being "lifted up," which leads to eternal life. The end result is the sort of communion described in Acts, but one must be transformed to be able to love and share like that.

Preaching Points

Parish Masses

- Christ came to unite us all in his love, and the disciples were living it out.
- Perhaps Nicodemus expected mere knowledge and wisdom. Christ instead offered rebirth, life in the Spirit, even eternal life.

Masses with Children

- The community of believers were so in love with each other and with the power of the Resurrection that they shared everything.
- Jesus was trying to explain life in the Spirit and that his earthly way of living was meant to show a little bit of what heavenly life is like.

Missal Options

- It might be best to reserve the sprinkling rite for Sundays and solemnities. Presiders may choose from among the three options for the PA.
- Use any Easter Collect (expect for today's) to conclude the UP.
- The prayers for today are from Tuesday of the Second Week of Easter in the PT.
- Any of the five Prefaces of Easter may be used.
- Consider EP-III.

Song of the Day

"Lift High the Cross" by George Kitchen, Michael R. Newbolt, and Sydney H. Nicholson (Hope Publishing Company)

Optional Memorial

St. Martin I was a Roman of noble birth and had a reputation for intelligence, learning, and charity. He fought against the Monothelite heresy, which claimed that Jesus had two natures—human and divine—but only one will. At that time, the government was deeply involved in theological controversies. If the Church was torn by doctrinal conflicts, the emperors felt it threatened public order. They sought peace at all costs, even sacrificing orthodoxy. Martin was tried by Emperor Constans II in Constantinople and was imprisoned and exiled. He died from mistreatment at the hands of fellow Christians in 655.

- The readings may be taken from the SW, #551, CM or CP (For a Pope), or LMC #280.
- The Collect is from the PS; other texts are from the CP (For a Pope).
- Use P-I or P-II of Saints, or the Preface of Holy Pastors.
- Consider using EP-II.

WED 14 LM #269 / LMC #185–192 / white
Easter Weekday

Scripture Insights

John 3:16 is set alongside the Apostles being imprisoned and set free by the angel of the Lord. Indeed, the angel commands them to the public square to "tell the people everything about their life," which is the fullness of life described in John's account of the Gospel. The leaders are stuck in the darkness and choose not to see the Light of the World.

Preaching Points

Parish Masses

- As the tomb could not hold Christ, neither could a jail hold the Apostles. The Word of God breaks free.
- Christ did not come to condemn the world but that the world might be saved through him. Those who prefer darkness have condemned themselves.

Masses with Children

- The leaders feared the Apostles and their preaching, so they imprisoned them. The angel of the Lord set them free in the middle of the night, and they returned to preaching.
- God loves the world. This world matters. God loves us enough to send his only Son, not to condemn us, but to save us.

Missal Options

- It might be best to reserve the sprinkling rite for Sundays and solemnities. Presiders may choose from among the three options for the PA.
- Use any Easter Collect (expect for today's) to conclude the UP.
- Any of the five Prefaces of Easter may be used.
- The prayers for today are from Wednesday of the Second Week of Easter in the PT.
- Consider EPR-I.

Song of the Day

"We Are the Light of the World" Jean A. Greif (Vernacular Hymns Publishing Company)

THU 15 LM #270 / LMC #185–192 / white
Easter Weekday

Scripture Insights

Why were the Jewish leaders so enraged by the Apostles and their proclamation of the Risen Christ? Is it that the leaders were "of the earth" and thus stuck on earthly things? Thus they failed to see and hear, and then believe in, "the one who comes from heaven." Peter accentuates this point by saying "the God of our ancestors raised Jesus." The God who called Abraham also called Jesus out of the tomb.

Preaching Points

Parish Masses

- "We must obey God rather than men," says Peter to the men he disobeyed. He then asserts that the God of their shared ancestors is the one who raised Jesus from the dead.
- Christ shows us who God is. God sent him, and "he does not ration his gift of the Spirit."

Masses with Children

- Peter and the Apostles were in a tough spot: their religious leaders had forbidden them to speak of the Risen Christ. But how could they possibly keep quiet? "We must obey God rather than men."
- "Whoever believes in the Son has eternal life" because the Father sent the Son. Knowing Christ gives us a glimpse into the heavenly life of God.

Missal Options

- It might be best to reserve the sprinkling rite for Sundays and solemnities. Presiders may choose from among the three options for the PA.
- Use any Easter Collect (expect for today's) to conclude the UP.
- The prayers for today are from Thursday of the Second Week of Easter in the PT.
- Any of the five Prefaces of Easter may be used.
- Consider EP-II.

Song of the Day

"Jerusalem, My Happy Home" (various publishers)

FRI 16 LM #271 / LMC #185–192 / white
Easter Weekday

Scripture Insights

Why would we read John's account of the multiplication of the loaves during Easter? Because this was a foretaste of the heavenly banquet and a glimpse into God's generosity.

Preaching Points

Parish Masses

- Before Christ, the longing for a "messiah" was primarily about political liberation. Christ and his Apostles put a whole new spin on things.
- The boy had five barley loaves and two fish, "but what good are these for so many?" God's generosity will not be outdone. Our meager offerings are always enough when multiplied by God.

Masses with Children

- The leaders were furious at the Apostles, but Gamaliel's wisdom calmed them: if this movement is of human origin, it will fall apart on its own, he said, but if it's of God you will not be able to stop it.
- Jesus took five loaves and two fish from a boy and fed thousands. What will he do with your generosity?

Missal Options

- It might be best to reserve the sprinkling rite for Sundays and solemnities. Presiders may choose from among the three options for the PA.
- Use any Easter Collect (expect for today's) to conclude the UP.
- The prayers for today are from Friday of the Second Week of Easter in the PT.
- Any of the five Prefaces of Easter may be used.
- Consider EPR-I.

Song of the Day

"Eucharistic Litany" by Paul Hillebrand (WLP)

SAT 17 LM #272 / LMC #185–192 / white
Easter Weekday

Scripture Insights

The Apostles see the need for deacons. The word *deacon* means "ones who serve." Deacons are to care for the widows and needy. Stephen, the first martyr, was also the first deacon. The Gospel reading sounds like an appearance of the Risen Christ; the message is simple and profound: "It is I (literally: I AM), do not be afraid."

Preaching Points

Parish Masses

- We get insight into the early community life. The Greeks (Hellenists) complained that the Jews (Hebrews) were neglecting their widows. This was important enough of a duty that the Twelve laid hands (ordained) seven men to the task.
- We are always a boat at sea, buffeted by the waves and the wind. Jesus always comes to us and comforts our fears.

Masses with Children

- Deacons were created in the early church to ensure that widows and other vulnerable people got what they needed. These deacons were "filled with the Spirit and wisdom."
- Whenever you feel scared, like a little boat on a raging sea, just imagine Jesus coming to you, walking on the water, saying, "It is I. Do not be afraid."

Missal Options

- It might be best to reserve the sprinkling rite for Sundays and solemnities. Presiders may choose from among the three options for the PA.
- Use any Easter Collect (expect for today's) to conclude the UP.
- The prayers for today are from Saturday of the Second Week of Easter in the PT.
- Any of the five Prefaces of Easter may be used.
- Consider EPR-II.

Song of the Day

"Be Not Afraid" by Robert J. Dufford, SJ (OCP)

Love for others, and in the first place love for the poor, in whom the Church sees Christ himself, is made concrete in the promotion of justice.

—*Centesimus annus*, 58

S U N 18 LM #47B / LMC #41B / white
Third Sunday of Easter

Scripture Insights

Knowing something of the Holocaust, we are troubled by the way Peter accuses the Jews of crucifying Jesus: "Jesus, whom *you* handed over" (3:13–15). Are these and similar words in Acts 2:23, 36; 4:10–11; 5:30; 7:52 not unjust and implicitly anti-Jewish? The important search for the sense intended by Luke (who composed Peter's speech as a way of summarizing his essential message) should take into account these things:

1. Peter carefully restricts his accusation to those Jews who were actually involved in the Lord's death. Later Christian preachers in Acts do not accuse Jews of other times and places.
2. Significantly, Peter implicitly groups himself with those he accuses. He says the Jews had "handed over" and "rejected" Jesus. These are exactly the same Greek words that Luke's account uses not only to describe Judas's betrayal (22:48) but also Peter's own denial (22:57). Peter for this reason considers himself no different than the people he is accusing.
3. Peter immediately attaches an offer of forgiveness (Acts 2:38; 3:19; 5:31). Undeniably, the crucifixion was a malicious act, but God has reversed that evil in the Resurrection and so shows the cross to be the very means of salvation.
4. Peter readily offers pardon because "I know . . . that you acted in ignorance" (Acts 3:17). Is this why the Lord forgave him? It certainly evokes Jesus' prayer of forgiveness for his crucifiers, "for they know not what they do" (Luke 23:34). The deep irony of Christian anti-Judaism through the centuries is that Christ explicitly forbade it even as he suffered on the cross.

Far from stirring up Christian hatred for Jews, Peter maps a path to mercy. Jesus forgave both Peter and his crucifiers. Against this backdrop, the assurance of 1 John 2:1 is dramatic and solid: "If anyone does sin, we have an advocate with the Father, Jesus Christ the righteous one."

Preaching Points

Parish Masses

- When the Lord rose from the dead, he physically returned to life in his glorified body. Jesus Christ accompanied his Apostles, spoke with them, and ate with them. He helped them to understand Scripture and the forgiveness of sin for all people.
- Jesus preached forgiveness in his life, crucifixion, and Resurrection. His incarnation, ministry, death, and Resurrection were the pursuit of humanity's reconciliation with the Father.
- Historically, St. Peter's words regarding the Jews who turned over Christ were misused to persecute the Jewish people. It is important to remember that St. Peter considered himself among those who unjustly turned Christ over to the authorities. His message in this reading is one of forgiveness, not condemnation.
- All people act in ignorance at times and need forgiveness. We are called to help one another walk in the faith.

Children's Liturgy of the Word

- Forgiveness was a central message of Jesus' teaching, and his Incarnation, ministry, death, and Resurrection were lived so that we might have reconciliation with God.
- Christian people used to blame all Jewish people for Jesus' death. Jesus and St. Paul both told the faithful people that God forgives his people and that we should not spend time blaming one another.
- Everybody does things that are naughty or wrong sometimes. We are all in need of forgiveness at different times in our lives.

Missal Options

- If you have been sprinkling the faithful instead of praying the PA, continue to do so today.
- Sing or recite the Gloria and the Creed. Because of its baptismal significance, consider using the Apostles' Creed throughout Easter.
- Use any Easter Collect (expect for today's) to conclude the UP.
- Any of the five Prefaces of Easter may be used.
- Consider using EP-III.
- The SB of Easter Time may be prayed.
- There is no double Alleluia in the final dismissal.

Music Preparation

- We are still in the midst of Easter Time, but the rest of the world is long beyond it. So keep the Alleluias and Easter songs coming!
- By this point you are probably noticing a decline in attendance at choir practices and other events as people get busy with spring activities. Schedule familiar music that will work with whatever ensemble you have in your parish.

Music Suggestions

- Responsorial Psalm: "Lord, Let Your Face Shine upon Us" by Tom Booth (OCP)
- Communion: "In the Breaking of the Bread" by Bob Hurd (OCP) or "Bread of the World" by Paul A Tate (WLP)
- Sending Forth: "Singers, Sing" by Michael Gannon (WLP)

Mass Texts

Introduction to Mass

We gather here in confident hope for the joy of our own Resurrection. The Risen Lord has called us to touch him in this Eucharist so that we may go into the world and enable the people we encounter to touch him and to be touched by him through our loving service. May we all be one on the day of

Resurrection. *My brothers and sisters, let us acknowledge our sins, and so prepare ourselves to celebrate the sacred mysteries.*

Tropes for Penitential Act, Form III

You, the author of the life, were put to death for our sins: Lord, have mercy.

God raised you from the dead, that we may live with you forever: Christ, have mercy.

Let your face shine on us, that we may be saved: Lord, have mercy.

Dismissal for Children's Liturgy of the Word

Dear children, beloved by God, the disciples were afraid when the Risen Christ appeared to them, and they thought they were seeing a ghost. But he assured them that there was nothing to fear, that he was truly alive, the same Christ they knew and loved. He will now speak to you in today's readings, reminding you that there is nothing to fear and that he loves you very much.

Dismissal of Catechumens

My friends, we give you this time now to consider the Word that God is speaking to you. Ask Christ to open your mind to understand the Scriptures, that you may come to know him, in union with us, in the breaking of bread. Go in peace.

Dismissal of Extraordinary Ministers of Holy Communion

Dear ministers of the Lord, in his tenderness the Risen Christ provides for us in his Eucharistic Body and he asks us to share his Body with those who cannot join us due to physical injury or infirmity. Go now to them that the Lord may feed them with the Bread of Life.

Universal Prayer

This is the day that the Lord has made! Let us rejoice and be glad! We are at peace for we know the Lord is in our midst. Let us now pray for his peace to embrace our world.

1. That the Church may persist in the of manifesting the Lord's peaceful presence to all the world, we pray:
2. That leaders of every nation will discover ways to bring peace with justice into our world, we pray:
3. That the Lord's gift of real and lasting peace may overturn powers that threaten warfare and violence, we pray:
4. That those who dwell in fear and resist facing the truth of their lives may know conversion, we pray:
5. That those who suffer from chronic illness or terminal disease may persevere in their faith, we pray:
6. That the dead may be washed clean in the Blood of the Lamb and welcomed into the Kingdom of Heaven, we pray:

Lord God,
you never cease to gather us together to praise your holy name.
May your Son appear to us this day and extend the gift of his peace—
a peace that overwhelms our every fear.
Let the glory of Easter shine in our hearts and in our actions.
Through Christ our Lord.
Amen.

Other Rites and Customs

- Keep the Alleluias going!
- Schedule an ecumenical concert of Easter music for your local community.
- Host an Easter party for the neophytes and create a slideshow with pictures and videos from the Triduum, especially the Easter Vigil.
- Consider receiving baptized candidates into the Catholic Church today or one of the other Sundays of Easter, or whenever they are ready, leaving the Vigil for those to be baptized.
- Review your parish practices for first Communion and consider giving the option of having children receive their first Communion at Sunday Mass.

Liturgy and Life

Open your mind and heart to a deeper understanding of the Easter Scriptures. Read the Acts of the Apostles from start to finish. Imagine your way into the experience of the first Christians. Where do you encounter the Risen Christ during your day? Take your own Emmaus walk. Head outside one day this spring, paying close attention to everyone you encounter along the way. Be open to meeting Christ in the person of a stranger along the way.

Taking Place This Week . . .

Consider what can be done liturgically, catechetically, and ministerially to respond to these important needs.

- Administrative Professionals Day (4/21)
- Earth Day and Take Our Daughters and Sons to Work Day (4/22)
- World Book and Copyright Day (4/23)

MON 19 LM #273 / LMC #185–192 / white
Easter Weekday

Scripture Insights

Recall that Acts is actually the second part of the Gospel of Luke, and the Apostles endure what Jesus did, thus Stephen is being persecuted by the Jewish leaders just as Jesus was. Jesus admonishes the crowd for trying to fill their bellies rather than seeking the Bread of Eternal Life.

Preaching Points

Parish Masses

- Stephen was drawing attention for his wonders and signs as well as for his preaching and debating. His enemies could only concoct lies in their efforts to thwart him. Despite the antagonism, "his face was like the face of an angel."
- The crowds are pursuing Jesus for all the wrong reasons. They want full bellies; he wants their hearts.

Masses with Children

- Stephen was so full of the Spirit that he performed signs and preached just as Christ did. Like Christ, he provoked the jealousy and suspicions of the religious leaders. Despite it all, his face was like that of an angel.
- Christ had just fed the five thousand, and many were pressuring him. Was it because they saw him as the Son of God and the way to eternal life, or were they just hungry again?

Missal Options

- It might be best to reserve the sprinkling rite for Sundays and solemnities. Presiders may choose from among the three options for the PA.
- Use any Easter Collect (expect for today's) to conclude the UP.
- The prayers for today are from Monday of the Third Week of Easter in the PT.
- Any of the five Prefaces of Easter may be used.
- Consider EPVN-I.

Song of the Day

"Praise the Risen Lord" by Grayson Warren Brown (WLP)

TUE 20 LM #274 / LMC #185–192 / white
Easter Weekday

Scripture Insights

Both Jesus and Stephen are having trouble with crowds. The crowd pursuing Jesus wants more bread, like the manna their ancestors got. Jesus tries to get them to seek higher things, like the Bread of Life, who is right in front of them. Stephen's words and actions brought him harassment and death, just as what happened with Jesus. Like Jesus, he offered up his spirit, and prayed forgiveness on his persecutors.

Preaching Points

Parish Masses

- Stephen, filled with the Spirit, is the first martyr for Christ. In the crowd, orchestrating the murder, was Saul, who became Paul, who spread Christ's word far and wide. We never know who the Spirit will touch.
- The crowd, who were part of the feeding of the five thousand, asks Jesus for a sign. You want a sign from God? You're looking at it. You want the bread that comes from heaven? I am the Bread of Life.

Masses with Children

- Stephen was filled with the Spirit and performed signs and preached wonderfully. He paid the price and, like Christ, forgave the ones who did it to him.
- The crowd that is pursuing Christ has just been part of the feeding of the five thousand, and still they want more. Jesus tells them that he is more—he is the Bread of Eternal Life.

Missal Options

- It might be best to reserve the sprinkling rite for Sundays and solemnities. Presiders may choose from among the three options for the PA.
- Use any Easter Collect (expect for today's) to conclude the UP.
- The prayers for today are from Tuesday of the Third Week of Easter in the PT.
- Any of the five Prefaces of Easter may be used.
- Consider EP-II.

Song of the Day

"Eat This Bread" by Jacques Berthier (GIA)

WED 21 LM #275 / LMC #185–192 / white
Easter Weekday

Optional Memorial of St Anselm, Bishop and Doctor of the Church / white

Scripture Insights

The reading from Acts starts with persecution and ends with joy. Saul is getting more aggressive as Philip has Christ's power flowing through him. Christ reiterates that the Father wills all of us to come to him.

Preaching Points

Parish Masses

- Christ promises to raise us with him on the last day. Even the sort of persecution described in Acts will lead to our sharing in the Resurrection.
- The eternal life promised by Christ is available to all. As the Bread of Life, Christ feeds us and nourishes us.

Masses with Children

- In John's account of the Gospel, Jesus has seven great "I am" statements. Today, "I am the Bread of Life." This statement leads us to the Eucharist, where Christ feeds us.
- The Apostles went through all that Jesus went through. Today, they are persecuted, yet they go on preaching and end with joy.

Missal Options

- It might be best to reserve the sprinkling rite for Sundays and solemnities. Presiders may choose from among the three options for the PA.
- Use any Easter Collect (expect for today's) to conclude the UP.
- The prayers for today are from Wednesday of the Third Week of Easter in the PT.
- Any of the five Prefaces of Easter may be used.
- Consider EP-III.

Song of the Day

"I Am the Bread of Life" by Suzanne Toolan (GIA)

Optional Memorial

St. Anselm wrote devotional and spiritual treatises as an abbot, defended the Church against secular incursions as bishop of Westminster, and is known as the Father of Scholasticism for his theological works, particularly the *Proslogion*, a rational proof for God's existence. Anselm was stubborn in his defense of truth and the spiritual authority of the Church, even when it put him in conflict with worldly authorities.

- The readings may be taken from the SW, #552, CP or CDC, or LMC #281.
- The Collect is from the PS; other texts are from the CP (For a Bishop) or CDC.
- Use P-I or P-II of Saints, or the Preface of Holy Pastors.
- Consider using EP-I.

THU 22 LM #276 / LMC #185–192 / white
Easter Weekday

Scripture Insights

Christ elaborates on the Bread of Life: like manna, yet wondrously greater, in that Christ brings eternal life. The Ethiopian had already been touched by the Word of God (Isaiah's Suffering Servant, no less). Philip knew the One who fulfilled the prophecy and baptized the Ethiopian official into new life in Christ.

Preaching Points

Parish Masses

- Christ often takes stories from Jewish history—like the manna from heaven—but takes them to a new level. Like manna, he comes from heaven. Unlike manna, those who eat the Bread of Life will live forever.
- The Ethiopian had been to Jerusalem to worship. Philip introduced him to the One foretold by the Scriptures and baptized him into that life.

Masses with Children

- Jesus came to show us who God is. He often did so by using things we know of, like Bread and Light, and using them to describe himself. Bread feeds our bodies; Jesus as the Bread of Life feeds our souls and leads us to eternal life.
- The Ethiopian already knew of God. Philip drew him closer and immersed him into the life of Christ by baptizing him.

Missal Options

- It might be best to reserve the sprinkling rite for Sundays and solemnities. Presiders may choose from among the three options for the PA.
- Use any Easter Collect (expect for today's) to conclude the UP.
- The prayers for today are from Thursday of the Third Week of Easter in the PT.
- Any of the five Prefaces of Easter may be used.
- Consider EP-II.

Song of the Day

"I Am the Bread of Life" by John Michael Talbot (OCP/Universal Music)

FRI 23 LM #277 / LMC #185–192 / white
Easter Weekday

Optional Memorials of St. George, Martyr / red; St. Adalbert, Bishop and Martyr / red

Scripture Insights

Christ's words in the synagogue must have shocked his listeners: unless you consume my flesh and blood you do not have life within you. Almost as shocking for the community was how a man like Saul would meet Christ and be transformed. A man "breathing murderous threats" becomes a great Apostle. Christ's body, broken and poured out, gives us life.

Preaching Points

Parish Masses

- In this Resurrection appearance, the Risen Lord confronts Saul. The Risen Christ lives in his people and calls his persecutors to repentance and discipleship.
- Jesus' words about eating his flesh and drinking his blood must have made sense only after the Last Supper and the death and Resurrection. The Eucharist recalls all of these.

Masses with Children

- Christ tells the disciples they must eat his flesh and drink his blood. Flesh that is broken, blood that is poured, both of which happened in his death, which leads us to life.
- Saul had been there as Christians were killed and imprisoned. He was looking to do more of this when Christ knocked him down and led him to new life. Christ never gives up on any of us.

Missal Options

- It might be best to reserve the sprinkling rite for Sundays and solemnities. Presiders may choose from among the three options for the PA.
- Use any Easter Collect (expect for today's) to conclude the UP.
- The prayers for today are from Friday of the Third Week of Easter in the PT.
- Any of the five Prefaces of Easter may be used.
- Consider EPR-II.

Song of the Day

"Bread of Life" by Michael John Poirier (WLP)

Optional Memorials

St. George

St. George of Lydda was a soldier under Diocletian, likely a military tribune, who resigned his commission rather than follow orders to participate in worship of Roman gods and was subsequently martyred. George demonstrated great faith and courage when he defied Diocletian at the cost of his life.

- The readings may be taken from the SW, #553, CM, or LMC #282.
- The Collect is from the PS; other texts are from the CM (For One Martyr during Easter Time).
- Use P-I or P-II of Saints, or P-I or P-II of Holy Martyrs.
- Consider using EP-I.

St. Adalbert

St. Adalbert served as a missionary at the pope's request, evangelizing pagan populations in Prague and in Prussia until his martyrdom. Twice Adalbert tried to trade episcopal life for the quiet of a monastery, but he was obedient to his call to the mission field and died as an example of heroic faith.

- The readings may be taken from the SW, #553A, CM, or CP. There are no separate readings in the LMC; use the SW or those from the CM or CP.
- The Collect is from the PS; other texts are from the CM (For One Martyr during Easter Time) or from the CP (For a Bishop).
- Use P-I or P-II of Saints, P-I or P-II of Holy Martyrs, or the Preface of Holy Pastors.
- Consider using EP-I.

S A T 24 LM #278 / LMC #185–192 / white
Easter Weekday

Optional Memorial of St. Fidelis of Sigmaringen, Priest and Martyr / red

Scripture Insights

Jesus had just told the people that they must consume his flesh and blood or they would have no life in them. Many left. Peter's great line sums up the steadfastness of the Twelve: "Master, to whom shall we go? You have the words of eternal life." In Acts, the Twelve continue to do as Jesus did, even raising the dead.

Preaching Points

Parish Masses

- The reading says, "As a result of this, many of his disciples returned to their former way of life and no longer walked with him." Yet many did continue to "walk with him." His words were those of eternal life.
- The widows, often the objects of pity and almsgiving, have become powerful in the early Church. Tabitha had made many tunics and cloaks, probably to give to the needy. So important was she that Christ, through Peter, raised her from the dead.

Masses with Children

- Many left Jesus after he told them they must eat his flesh and drink his blood. The Apostles remained, knowing that Jesus was for real when he said that doing this would lead to eternal life.
- The Apostles continued the work of Jesus, even raising a widow from the dead. Tabitha was her name. She and other widows had been doing good deeds for many in their town.

Missal Options

- It might be best to reserve the sprinkling rite for Sundays and solemnities. Presiders may choose from among the three options for the PA.
- Use any Easter Collect (expect for today's) to conclude the UP.
- The prayers for today are from Saturday of the Third Week of Easter in the PT.
- Any of the five Prefaces of Easter may be used.
- Consider EP-I.

Song of the Day

"Look Beyond" by Gary Daigle and Darryl Ducote (GIA)

Optional Memorial

St. Fidelis was a Capuchin friar known for his learning, charity, and devotion, whether serving as prior in Germany or preaching to former Catholics in the north of France, where he was martyred by Calvinists. His combined wisdom and humility allowed Fidelis to convert many by his example.

- The readings may be taken from the SW, #554, CM, CP, or LMC #283.
- Use the Collect from the PS; the other prayers may be taken from the CM (For One Martyr during Easter Time) or from the CP (For One Pastor).
- Consider P-I or P-II of Saints, P-I or P-II of Holy Martyrs, or the Preface of Holy Pastors.
- You might use EP-I.

S U N **25** LM #50B / LMC #44B / white
Fourth Sunday of Easter

Scripture Insights

Today's readings crackle with the Apostles' excitement over the new understandings they were experiencing after the Resurrection and with their work of creating a new way of life, a community of the resurrected Christ — living and life-giving. In the light of Resurrection, Jesus' words in the Gospel, spoken before the Passion, take on new meaning.

The First Reading is part of a lengthy story that began with Peter healing a crippled man near the Jerusalem Temple and then addressing the people who stood around him, amazed at what he had done. As the crowds continued to grow, Peter and John were arrested, and his accusers demanded to know by whose authority they did such a thing. Peter is answering that question in today's First Reading. His sense of urgency and conviction ring out as he testifies that "there is no salvation through anyone else." He is, after all, "filled with the Holy Spirit."

Likewise, in the Second Reading we can hear a deep sense of community identity. Thanks to the loving gift of the Father, which is his Son, we have become "children of God" both now and in the future, when God (or Christ) is fully revealed and we become like him.

In today's Gospel, John uses the image of the Good Shepherd to explain what it means to be a faith community. It is about our shared trust in Christ who put his life on the line to take care of his flock and keep them secure. It is about a flock that can be open and welcoming to others without fear for its safety, because the one who laid down his life for them has taken it up again as the Father commanded.

Preaching Points

Parish Masses

- Love, devotion, and gentleness: these words describe our savior, the Good Shepherd, as he cares for us, his sheep. Jesus cares for us tenderly, not like a hired hand who might save himself rather than fight a wolf, but as the devoted shepherd who guides his flock. Jesus' love for us and his humanity shine brightly in this Gospel. Through use of agrarian terminology, we realize the great love that Jesus has for his people.
- Jesus is the source, cause, and reason of our salvation. It is in him that we may see heaven and be reconciled with the Father.
- We are called to shepherd those in our care; as teachers, parents, grandparents, and godparents we care for those in our care as Jesus would care for them.

Children's Liturgy of the Word

- People in Jesus' time understood stories about farmers and shepherds, so Jesus used those sorts of jobs to help explain his love for his people.
- Jesus cares for his people like a loving shepherd cares for his sheep. He's not like a hired man; he is more like the flock's owner. He ensures our care and safety.
- Jesus is the one person who gives us salvation. Our salvation is through him only. Because of Jesus, human beings can be reconciled to the Father.

Missal Options

- If you have been sprinkling the faithful instead of offering the PA, continue to do so today.
- Sing or recite the Gloria and the Creed. Because of its baptismal significance, consider using the Apostles' Creed throughout Easter.
- Use any Easter collect (expect for today's) to conclude the UP.
- The SB for Easter Time may be used.
- Consider EPVN-I.
- Any of the Prefaces for Easter may be used.
- There is no double Alleluia in the final dismissal.

Music Preparation

- The Fourth Sunday of Easter is traditionally called "Good Shepherd Sunday" but don't just schedule every sheep song you know and love in the liturgy. There are many other rich elements for today that shouldn't be missed!
- Around this time of year, many communities will have a "day of reflection" for parish liturgical ministers. Does your parish community have such a day? Does it include pastoral musicians? Bringing all of the liturgical ministers together for a joint day of reflection builds community and underscores the importance of their role in the liturgy.

Music Suggestions

- Gathering: "Christ in Me Arise" by Trevor Thompson (OCP)
- Responsorial Psalm: "*El Senor es Mi Pastor*/The Lord Is My Shepherd" by Michelle Abeyta (WLP)
- Preparation of the Gifts: "Christ, Our Cornerstone" by Martin Willet and Kevin Keil (WLP)
- Communion: "Like a Shepherd" by Robert J. Dufford, SJ (OCP)

Mass Texts

Introduction to Mass

We have come here in response to the voice of the Lord who has called us as a shepherd calls his sheep. We are his flock and Christ is our shepherd who gave his life so that we might live abundantly. In this Eucharist he offers us life, his own divine life. Let us put aside all fear of being fully alive and approach this table with confidence and hope. *My brothers and sisters, let us acknowledge our sins, and so prepare ourselves to celebrate the sacred mysteries.*

Tropes for Penitential Act, Form III

Put to death on the cross, you were raised to new life by the Father: Lord, have mercy.

Your merciful love fills the whole world: Christ, have mercy.

You are the Good Shepherd, leading us to eternal life: Lord, have mercy.

Dismissal for Children's Liturgy of the Word

Dear children, with you we are all children, God's beloved children, and he is the Father of us all. As deep and wide and high as your parents' love for you is, it is held within the love of God, who will never fail. He speaks his Word of love to you now. Go and listen to him who will always listen to you.

Dismissal of Catechumens

My friends, God has called each of you by name so that you may be one with him through the sacrament of his Church. As you leave us now to explore what this promise means in your own lives, know that we pray for your continued growth in Christ, who calls you as a gentle, loving shepherd. Go in peace.

Dismissal of Extraordinary Ministers of Holy Communion

Dear friends, the Good Shepherd knows his sheep; he knows the suffering and hardship of those who are prevented from joining us due to sickness or injury. Take this Eucharist to them and remind them that he hears their prayer and that he lay down his life for them, who are one with us as God's children. Go in peace.

Universal Prayer

The Lord is our Good Shepherd. He lays down his life for his flock. Following his example, may we heed his voice and offer our prayers for the needs of the world.

1. For all Christians who seek to follow the Good Shepherd, that they may be one, we pray:
2. For vocations to the priesthood and religious life, that many young people may choose a life of service in the Lord's name, we pray:
3. For those who seek to do violence to the Christian community by causing division, that they may be converted, we pray:
4. For those who tend sheep and for all farmers who make their living by the fruit of the earth, for a productive season ahead, we pray:
5. For all who close their ears to the voice of the Shepherd, that they may be humbled, we pray:

Lord Jesus,
you are the Good Shepherd who never leaves
the flock unattended
and who always watches over us with care.
May all who believe in you come together as one family,
united in your love.
Raise up in your Church effective leaders
who are willing to give their lives for the sheep.
Who live and reign with God the Father in the unity of
the Holy Spirit,
one God, for ever and ever.
Amen.

Other Rites and Customs

- On this Good Shepherd Sunday and World Day of Prayer for Vocations, be sure to include a petition in the Universal Prayer for those discerning a call to the priesthood, diaconate, or consecrated life.
- Replace the spent Easter lilies and other plants with fresh flowering shrubs or other plants that will continue to bloom until Pentecost.
- Celebrate Taizé Prayer around the Cross this week.

Liturgy and Life

On the Fourth Sunday of Easter we always celebrate Jesus, our Good Shepherd, who protects his flock, provides for our needs, and goes in search of any sheep that are lost. The Good Shepherd lays down his life for the sheep and seeks to restore all sheep into his sheepfold. As Christians, we are called to extend the hospitality of the Good Shepherd to members of the flock who have wandered or become disconnected from the Church.

Taking Place This Week . . .

Consider what can be done liturgically, catechetically, and ministerially to respond to these important needs.

- Today the special collection is for the Catholic Home Missions Appeal.
- Orthodox Palm Sunday (4/25), Orthodox Good Friday (4/30), and Orthodox Holy Saturday (5/1)
- World Malaria Day (4/25)
- World Intellectual Property Day and International Chernobyl Disaster Remembrance Day (4/26)
- Anzac Day (Australia/New Zealand; 4/26)
- World Day for Safety and Health at Work (4/28)
- Day to Remember Chemical Warfare Victims (4/29)
- Lag BaOmer (4/30)
- National Explosive Ordinance Disposal Day (5/1)
- First Saturday (5/1)

MON 26 LM #279 / LMC #185–192 / white
Easter Weekday

Scripture Insights

Jesus expands on the imagery of the Good Shepherd, describing the mutual knowledge that shepherd and sheep have of each other. The first disciples were Jewish, and as the movement spread they began to deal with questions like: Do we still keep kosher? Must a Gentile first become a Jew to become a Christian? Ultimately, we learn that Baptism was the key.

Preaching Points

Parish Masses

- This reading from John gives one of the great summations of why Jesus took flesh—so that we might have life.
- The Jews always humbly knew that they had been chosen by God. Here, the expansion of God's invitation to all people is made clear: "God has then granted life-giving repentance to the Gentiles too."

Masses with Children

- Shepherds know each one of their sheep, each little lamb. And each sheep knows the sounds of their shepherd's voice. In the same way, Christ knows each of us, and his voice speaks to our souls.
- Christianity started among the Jewish people. Many non-Jews were attracted to the movement, and the early Church had to decide which Jewish rules to keep and which not. In the end, Baptism was seen as the key to belonging.

Missal Options

- It might be best to reserve the sprinkling rite for Sundays and solemnities. Presiders may choose from among the three options for the PA.
- Use any Easter Collect (expect for today's) to conclude the UP.
- Any of the five Prefaces of Easter may be used.
- The prayers for today are from Monday of the Fourth Week of Easter in the PT.
- Consider EPVN-III.

Song of the Day

"Psalm 100: We Are God's People" by David Haas (GIA)

TUE 27 LM #280 / LMC #185–192 / white
Easter Weekday

Scripture Insights

Often Jesus did speak plainly and openly, and it was the crowds who did not or could not hear and understand. So it is in today's reading: The Father and I are one, my sheep know my voice and have eternal life. In Acts, the disciples scattered due to persecution but then took the opportunity to preach in their new cities. Thus the Good News spread, even in hard times.

Preaching Points

Parish Masses

- Jesus had in fact told the people plainly, in many different ways, that he was the Christ. Those who belonged to him recognized his voice and followed him.
- The Gospel had spread to some Greeks (non-Jews). Barnabas came to meet them, saw the grace of God active among them, and rejoiced in it. Then he went and met Paul, with whom he would have many journeys.

Masses with Children

- Some people just couldn't see Jesus' work and hear his words. Those who did, however, became his own and received eternal life.
- The disciples scattered during persecutions but kept preaching the Word even in their new locals. This was one of the ways that Christianity spread throughout the region and beyond the Jewish community.

Missal Options

- It might be best to reserve the sprinkling rite for Sundays and solemnities. Presiders may choose from among the three options for the PA.
- Use any Easter Collect (expect for today's) to conclude the UP.
- The prayers for today are from Tuesday of the Fourth Week of Easter in the PT.
- Any of the five Prefaces of Easter may be used.
- Consider EP-II.

Song of the Day

"Oh, Bless the Lord, My Soul" by Isaac Watts (various publishers)

WED 28 LM #281 / LMC #185–192 / white
Easter Weekday

Optional Memorials of St. Peter Chanel, Priest and Martyr / red; St. Louis Grignion de Montfort, Priest / white

Scripture Insights

Christ forces us to choose or, rather, our reaction to him and his words will be the judge of us. Christ did not come to condemn us, but if we reject his words we condemn ourselves.

Preaching Points

Parish Masses

- "I came into the world as light," says Christ. Light ends darkness and reveals wickedness.
- The Apostles were spreading the Word rapidly. They discerned the Spirit together, then laid hands on their companions and sent them off on new missions.

Masses with Children

- Jesus was sent by God to reveal to us who God is. If we reject Jesus and his Word, we condemn ourselves.
- The Apostles were energized by the Resurrection. They prayed together to decide where and how to spread the Word. They laid hands on the ones being sent forth.

Missal Options

- It might be best to reserve the sprinkling rite for Sundays and solemnities. Presiders may choose from among the three options for the PA.
- Use any Easter Collect (expect for today's) to conclude the UP.
- The prayers for today are from Wednesday of the Fourth Week of Easter in the PT.
- Any of the five Prefaces of Easter may be used.
- Consider EPR-II.

Song of the Day

"I Am the Light of the World" by Greg Hayakawa (OCP)

Optional Memorials

St. Peter Chanel

As superior of a group of Marist missionaries, St. Peter Chanel brought the Gospel to the South Pacific, including the Canary Islands and Tahiti, before being martyred in Futuna at the hands of a local king. St. Peter's zeal for Christ took him halfway around the globe to France, where he had begun as a shepherd boy.

- The readings may be taken from the SW, #556, CM, CP (For Missionaries), or LMC #285.
- Use the Collect from the PS; the other prayers may be taken from the CM (For One Martyr during Easter Time) or from the CP (For Missionaries).
- Consider P-I or P-II of Saints, P-I or P-II of Holy Martyrs, or the Preface of Holy Pastors.
- You might use EP-II.

St. Louis Grignion de Montfort

St. Louis' emotional language and flair for the dramatic attracted many to the practice of the faith and Marian devotion.

- The readings may be taken from the SW, #556A, or CP (For Missionaries). There are no texts in the LMC, but you can use those from the CS.
- Use the Collect from the PS (two options are provided); the other prayers may be taken from the CP (For One Pastor).
- Consider P-I or P-II of Saints, or the Preface of Holy Pastors.
- You might use EP-II.

THU 29 LM #282 or #557 / LMC #185–192 or #286 / white
Memorial of St. Catherine of Siena, Virgin and Doctor of the Church

Today's Saint

Catherine of Siena (1347–1380) was a lay Dominican who devoted her life to her beloved Jesus. After a time of solitude in contemplative prayer, Jesus sent her into the world on two feet to love those he loved. She was named a Doctor of the Church and has been known for her dialogues, letters, and prayers. She cared for the sick and dying and had a ministry of reconciliation between political states and Church leaders. We can look to Catherine as an example of a person who dialogued with Jesus in prayer, loved those he loved, and built bridges of reconciliation and trust.

Scripture Insights

The foot washing looks slightly different after the Resurrection. Judas had his feet washed, along with the rest, and still betrayed Jesus. Yet even betrayal and death did not stop Christ, and we once again are reminded to wash each other's feet. In Acts, the Apostles are using "the law and the prophets" to show Jews how Jesus had been foretold all along.

Preaching Points

Parish Masses

- Christ washed the feet of all the disciples, even though he seemed to know that one would betray him and one would deny him. We are called to wash the feet of all people, just as our master did.
- Paul gives the worshipers at the synagogue a lesson in the history of salvation, all of it leading to Jesus.

Masses with Children

- Jesus knew his disciples would betray him and deny him. He washed their feet anyway and commanded them, and us, to do the same.
- Paul goes to a synagogue and reminds the people how God chose them, and from the Jewish people rose Jesus, the savior of the world.

Scripture Insights (PS)

We are all sinners in need of forgiveness. The mystery of humility can never be understood by the proud and the arrogant.

Preaching Points

Parish Masses

- The Blood of Christ, poured out for us, is the source of forgiveness. We refuse that forgiveness in many ways, especially when we tell ourselves we don't need it because we haven't sinned. We need the humility to acknowledge that we are sinners.
- St. Catherine was illiterate but advised popes and prelates. Wisdom comes from surprising places. Jesus reveals the greatest mysteries to those who are childlike. Are we open to learning, especially from unexpected sources?

Masses with Children

- Christ comes to us in the Eucharist. When we receive Christ in the Eucharist, we are forgiven from sin. There are times when we refuse his forgiveness. We must be humble and come to Christ and admit that we do sin.
- St. Catherine of Siena did not know how to read. But she was still able to advise the popes and other important priests in the Church. She was a very wise woman. Wisdom comes to us in many places and from many people, especially those who come to Jesus like a child. We should be open to learning throughout our life, just like you are open to learning right now in school. You never know where you will find great wisdom.

Missal Options

- The readings may also be taken from the CV and CS or CDC in the LMC.
- The prayers are proper and are found in the PS.
- Consider P-I or P-II of Saints, or the Preface of Holy Virgins and Religious.
- You might use EP-II.
- It might be best to reserve the sprinkling rite for Sundays and solemnities. Presiders may choose from among the three options for the PA.
- Use an Easter Collect to conclude the UP.

Song of the Day

"For All the Faithful Women"
by Herman G. Stuempfle Jr. (GIA)

FRI **30** LM #283 / LMC #185–192 / white
Easter Weekday

Optional Memorial of St. Pius V, Pope / white

Scripture Insights

Jesus promises he is going to prepare a place for each of us. Paul, having just given the listeners at the synagogue a history lesson, explains who this history led to: the "word of salvation," Jesus. Talking to Jews, he reminds them that this is "what God promised our fathers."

Preaching Points

Parish Masses

- Jesus paints a beautiful portrait of his Father's house. There is room for all, Jesus is preparing a place, and he will come get us "so that were I am you also may be."
- Paul is illustrating to his fellow Jews how all their history and Scriptures led to Christ himself—"this word of salvation."

Masses with Children

- Christ reportedly has said he came from the Father and he will return to him. What is the way to God? "I am the way and the truth and the life," Jesus tells us.
- Paul was a Jew, like those who he is speaking to in Antioch. He tells the people that all their scriptures and history led to Jesus. The leaders in Jerusalem didn't recognize him, but God raised him from the dead so all may know.

Missal Options

- It might be best to reserve the sprinkling rite for Sundays and solemnities. Presiders may choose from among the three options for the PA.
- Use any Easter Collect (expect for today's) to conclude the UP.
- The prayers for today are from Friday of the Fourth Week of Easter in the PT.
- Any of the five Prefaces of Easter may be used.
- Consider EP-II.

Song of the Day

"Come, My Way, My Truth, My Life" (various publishers)

Optional Memorial

Pope St. Pius V (1504–1572) grew up as a shepherd boy. A founder of seminaries, he brought financial accountability to the Church and reformed education for the clergy and young people. Like Paul, he lived through the decisions of an important council, the Council of Trent (1545–1563). He sought to help the Church live the Gospel more faithfully so that people would come to know Jesus Christ.

- The readings may be taken from the SW, #558, CP (For a Pope), or LMC #287.
- Use the Collect from the PS; the other prayers may be taken from the CP (For a Pope).
- Consider P-I or P-II of Saints, or the Preface of Holy Pastors.
- You might use EP-I.

SAT **1** LM #284 / LMC #185–192 / white

Easter Weekday

Optional Memorial of St. Joseph the Worker / white

Scripture Insights

The Gospel according to John repeatedly tells us that Christ and the Father are one, yet still Philip demands, "Master, show us the Father." Christ chides him yet offers a powerful summation: "The Father who dwells in me is doing his works." The Apostles began by spreading the Word among their fellow Jews. Here we have the ultimate rejection by the Jews, so they turn to the Gentiles.

Preaching Points

Parish Masses

- We read this with new eyes after the Resurrection, as Jesus promises us we will do the works he does, "and will do greater ones than these, because I am going to the Father."
- Paul and Barnabas preached the Word, were rejected by the Jews, had persecution incited against them, but ended with being "filled with joy and the Holy Spirit."

Masses with Children

- Jesus came to show us who God is, and he says this again and again, yet still Philip asked Jesus to show them the Father. See me, see the Father, says Jesus. What I do the Father does through me.
- The Apostles went to the Jewish people first but were rejected and even persecuted by them. So they went to the Gentiles (which means non-Jews), where they found greater reception.

Missal Options

- It might be best to reserve the sprinkling rite for Sundays and solemnities. Presiders may choose from among the three options for the PA.
- Use any Easter Collect (expect for today's) to conclude the UP.
- The prayers for today are from Saturday of the Fourth Week of Easter in the PT.
- Any of the five Prefaces of Easter may be used.
- Consider EPVN-III.

Song of the Day

"Seek Ye First" by Karen Lafferty (various publishers)

Optional Memorial

St. Joseph, foster father to Jesus and a carpenter, is silent in the Gospel accounts, but his actions speak for the kind of man he was. His compassion in sparing Mary public humiliation, his obedience and faith in response to the angel's instructions, and his faithful protection and care for Mary and Jesus through exile and danger reveal Joseph as a model of integrity, industriousness, and gentle righteousness.

- The readings may be taken from the SW, #559, or LMC #288. The Gospel from the PS is proper.
- The prayer texts are proper and are found in the PS, including the Preface.
- Consider EP-I.

SUN 2 LM #53B / LMC #47B / white
Fifth Sunday of Easter

Scripture Insights

When he brought Saul to the Apostles, Barnabas told the story of how in Damascus Saul "had spoken out boldly in the name of Jesus." The phrase "spoken out boldly" uses a form of the Greek *parrhesia,* often translated in the New Testament as "boldness." It combines the words for "everything" *(pan)* and "speaking" *(rhesis).* Words spoken with *parrhesia* say everything there is to be said. *Parrhesia* suggests the act of communicating ideas directly, bluntly, without elaborate logic and vague metaphors—plain speaking.

Parrhesia suggests not so much a talent for speaking as a habit of speaking candidly, born of honesty and simplicity. The word also came to be used for the inner attitude of confidence that lay behind this practice of plain speaking. Intimate friends and family normally speak with *parrhesia* because they can speak without shame or fear of embarrassment or recrimination.

Preaching the Gospel with *parrhesia* was prized in the early Church as strong evidence that the Holy Spirit had certified one's authenticity as a disciple. This is what Barnabas saw in Paul. It is also something Luke himself saw and admired in the apostle, as we can see in his stories of Paul's courageous speaking in the latter half of Acts. Paul himself once described the effect of this gift of boldness. When he found himself poised to receive a Roman sentence of death, he wrote confidently: ""with all boldness [*parrhesia*], now as always, Christ will be magnified in my body, whether by life or by death" (Philippians 1:20).

These uses of *parrhesia* help illumine the theme of confidence in prayer in today's other texts. John's letter says that Christians who act in love receive new assurance of God's love that swallows up self-condemnation. Freedom from self-condemnation in turn nurtures courageous boldness—John uses the word *parrhesia*—in prayer to God. This creates the confidence that we have received whatever we ask for from God. The passage from John's account of the Gospel grounds this confident prayer in the indwelling life of Jesus (John 15:7).

Preaching Points

Parish Masses

- Barnabas saw that Saul/Paul was speaking honestly, clearly, and plainly as the latter preached the Gospel of Jesus Christ. This new man was suspect until the Apostles realized that, through Christ, the persecuting Saul had become a follower and lover of Christ.
- Sharing the Gospel with others doesn't require fancy words, special knowledge, or memorization of Scripture. Indeed, when we speak plainly and show the Gospel in our lives, we are sharing Jesus with others.
- Love is more than a feeling of warmth toward another person; love is something to be lived in truth and action. Love is a choice we make each moment of our days.
- When we abide in the Word of God, namely, believing in Jesus Christ and loving one another, we are abiding in God, and it is promised that God then abides in us.

Children's Liturgy of the Word

- We are all called to share the Gospel with others. Like St. Paul, we can speak plainly and without fancy words. We don't need to be adults to let others know about Jesus.
- Love is something we should commit to showing all the time. While we will never be perfect in our love of one another, we must always strive to choose love over selfishness or meanness.

Missal Options

- If you have been sprinkling the faithful instead of offering the PA, continue to do so today.
- Sing or recite the Gloria and the Creed. Because of its baptismal significance, consider using the Apostles' Creed throughout Easter.
- Use any Easter Collect (expect for today's) to conclude the UP.
- Any of the Easter Prefaces may be used.
- Consider EPVN-II.
- The SB for Easter Time may be used.
- There is no double Alleluia in the final dismissal.

Music Preparation

- The Gospel proclaims "whoever remains in me . . . will bear much fruit." Sometimes in ministry we are weary and question if we are doing this. Perhaps it is time to do what the vine-growers do. Pare down the branches. Select the best options and remove the extras.
- For some this may mean decluttering, delegating, or letting go of a program that is not growing.

Music Suggestions

- Gathering: "I Am the Vine" by Bob Hurd (OCP)
- Preparation of the Gifts: "Alleluia No. 1" by Donald Fischel (International Liturgy Publications)
- Communion: "*Surrexit Christus*" by Jacques Berthier/Taizé (GIA)
- Sending Forth: "All the Earth" by Lucien Deiss (WLP)

Mass Texts

Introduction to Mass

As disciples of the Lord Jesus, we have his life in us. Gathered together in his name, we have faith that he is in our midst, here and now. Let us remain in his love, as his love is the life of us, and, receiving his Body and Blood, let us then be life and love for all the world. *My brothers and sisters, let us acknowledge our sins, and so prepare ourselves to celebrate the sacred mysteries.*

Tropes for Penitential Act, Form III

You are greater than our sins and strengthen us to love: Lord, have mercy.

You cause us to grow, as branches on the vine, through the waters of Baptism: Christ, have mercy.

You will send down the consoling dew of the Holy Spirit: Lord, have mercy.

Dismissal for Children's Liturgy of the Word

My children, Christ tells us today that he is the vine and we are the branches on the vine. Though we might not see it or feel it, we are connected to him at all times, and because of that we are full of his life and love. So what kind of fruit might you bear? Go now to think about that and to listen to what else Christ has to say to you, and then we will welcome you back with joy.

Dismissal of Catechumens

Dear friends, this community now sends you forth to consider the Lord's invitation to life with him and his commandment to love one another. We pray that his Word will bear fruit in you as you continue your journey of discernment, until that day when you may join us around the table of the Eucharist. Go in peace.

Dismissal of Extraordinary Ministers of Holy Communion

My friends, though separated from us in body due to physical weakness, our sick and homebound brothers and sisters are still one with us in Christ. Go, therefore, to them and share with them the Bread of Life, that they may thrive with us in him.

Universal Prayer

Our Lord Jesus is the true vine, and his Father is the vine grower. Remain in Jesus and bear fruit in prayer for the needs of the world.

1. That all grafted onto Christ through the Sacrament of Baptism may be responsible in their Christian faith, we pray:
2. That those places in our world that have gone astray from the Gospel message of peace may be pruned by the Word, we pray:
3. That all who refuse to let go of a past injury or who resist reconciliation may hear Christ calling them to die to self, we pray:
4. That all gardeners and landscapers who work with the beauty of nature may have a season of abundant fruit, we pray:
5. That we may always give thanks for the mysterious ways in which we are pruned by the Word, we pray:

Lord Jesus,
you are the living vine, and we are the branches.
Help us to remain in you always,
just as you remain forever in your Church.
Prune from our hearts those things that prevent us from following you in freedom.
Who live and reign with God the Father in the unity of the Holy Spirit,
one God, for ever and ever.
Amen.

Other Rites and Customs

- Keep singing Easter music while being mindful that the celebration of Christ's Resurrection continues past the empty tomb into the joys and struggles of the early Church and Christ's call that all might be one in his love.
- Invite the neophytes to give witness talks so they can share the experience of their journey in the RCIA. These witness talks may be done at Mass but only after the Prayer after Communion.

Liturgy and Life

Spend time in your yard or take a walk to notice the plant life emerging from the ground and budding on vines. Give thanks for the wondrous glory of God's creation.

Taking Place This Week . . .

Consider what can be done liturgically, catechetically, and ministerially to respond to these important needs.

- Today is Orthodox Easter Sunday.
- Orthodox Easter Monday (5/3)
- World Press Freedom Day (5/3)
- National Nurses Day and the National Day of Prayer (5/6)
- Military Spouse Appreciation Day (5/7)
- First Friday (5/7)
- Lailat al-Qadr, Time to Remember Lost Lives from World War II, World Migratory Bird Day, and World Ovarian Cancer Day (5/8)
- Today is Bereaved Mother's Day.
- May is ALS Awareness, Asian Pacific American Heritage, Celiac Awareness, Haitian Heritage, Jewish American Heritage, Mental Health Awareness, National Foster Care, National Guide Dog, and National Stroke Awareness Month.
- During the month of May, Catholics around the world honor the Blessed Virgin Mary.

MON 3 LM #561 / LMC #185–192 or #290 / red
Feast of Sts. Philip and James, Apostles

Today's Saints

As Apostles, Philip and James were part of Jesus' inner circle. Philip had invited Nathanael to "come and see" Jesus. Now Philip asks Jesus to "show us the Father." Jesus answers that to see him is to see the Father. Like Philip, we invite people to see Jesus by the way we live. First Corinthians 15:1–8 notes that Jesus appeared to James after the Resurrection. Philip and James were martyrs. Jesus still appears to others through us. We can stand firm on Philip and James by announcing the Gospel with our lives so that people see Jesus in us.

Scripture Insights

With the reminder of Christ's victory over death in the First Reading, it is good for us to sing praise to God, declaring with all on earth and in heaven God's glory. The message of Christ's Resurrection must be proclaimed throughout the earth, to which Philip and James attest.

Preaching Points

Parish Masses

- At Baptism, we were anointed as priest, prophet, and king. As such, we share in the ministry of Christ.
- Baptism endows us with the responsibility to give witness to Christ in the world.

Masses with Children

- Tell the children about Sts. Philip and James.
- You can use the same preaching points for adults with children. Stress how Baptism changes us and, through the Holy Spirit, gives us the strength to be like Christ in the world.

Missal Options

- The prayers are proper and found in the PS.
- If the sprinkling rite is used on Sundays, it is good to do so today since it is a feast of the Apostles.
- The Gloria is sung or said.
- Use P-I or P-II of Apostles and consider EP-I.
- You may use the SB for Apostles today.

Song of the Day

"Ye Watchers and Ye Holy Ones" (various publishers)

Other Rites and Customs

Hours: Use the Proper Psalter from the PS.

TUE 4 LM #286 / LMC #185–192 / white
Easter Weekday

Scripture Insights

Christ gives his peace to the disciples, but he gives it as he is going to the Father. He gives peace "not as the world gives" peace. In the same way, he calls us to "rejoice" because he is "going to the Father." This makes sense after Easter but must have been jarring. At this point in Acts, the disciples have broken away from the Jewish community. They are setting up churches with presbyters (priests) to guide them.

Preaching Points

Parish Masses

- The way of Christ is nothing like the way of the world.
- The Apostles learn the way of suffering: "It is necessary for us to undergo many hardships to enter the Kingdom of God."

Masses with Children

- Jesus was "going away" ("dying") but he leaves his peace and promises he will be back (the Resurrection).
- The Apostles suffered greatly in preaching the Word. They stoned Paul so badly that some thought he was dead. They realized they must undergo many hardships to enter the Kingdom of God.

Missal Options

- It might be best to reserve the sprinkling rite for Sundays and solemnities. Presiders may choose from among the three options for the PA.
- Use any Easter Collect (expect for today's) to conclude the UP.
- The prayers for today are from Tuesday of the Fifth Week of Easter in the PT.
- Any of the five Prefaces of Easter may be used.
- Consider EPVN-I.

Song of the Day

"Peace" by Gregory Norbet, OSB (OCP)

WED 5 — LM #287 / LMC #185–192 / white
Easter Weekday

Scripture Insights

Jesus expands on the connectivity, the mutuality, of life and our dependence on him as the source. In Acts, we hear the beginnings of the first council of the Church as they gather to discuss whether one must obey the Mosaic Law in order to be a follower of Christ.

Preaching Points

Parish Masses

- The extremes are stark: with Christ we "bear much fruit," and without him we "can do nothing." Yet the glory of God is in our bearing fruit and becoming Christ's disciples.
- The Apostles and presbyters illustrate this living relationship with Christ as they gather from all over to share the joy of spreading the Word but also to discuss serious issues facing the Church.

Masses with Children

- Christ is the vine, and we are the branches. If we separate ourselves from him, we wither, just as a branch cut from a tree. Yet with Jesus as our source of life we are strong and bear much fruit.
- The Apostles spread the Church rapidly, yet serious questions also arose. They gathered to share their joy and solve these problems.

Missal Options

- It might be best to reserve the sprinkling rite for Sundays and solemnities. Presiders may choose from among the three options for the PA.
- Use any Easter Collect (expect for today's) to conclude the UP.
- The prayers for today are from Wednesday of the Fifth Week of Easter in the PT.
- Any of the five Prefaces of Easter may be used.
- Consider EP-II.

Song of the Day

"Remain in Me, I Am the Vine" by Curtis Stephan and Steve Angrisano (OCP)

THU 6 — LM #288 / LMC #185–192 / white
Easter Weekday

Scripture Insights

The Church gathered to address questions raised by their expansion to include the Gentiles. Peter pointed out that the Spirit was active among the Gentiles. He also proclaimed that the law has always been a burdensome yoke, whereas we are saved through the grace of Christ. Therefore the Gentiles were freed from the burden of the law, save a few prohibitions as mentioned.

Preaching Points

Parish Masses

- What a great gift from Christ—"Remain in my love . . . and your joy might be complete."
- The Apostles started by spreading the Word among the Jewish people but soon spread the good news to non-Jews as well, with great success. Peter declared that adherence to the law doesn't save us—only the grace of Jesus does that.

Masses with Children

- When we follow Christ's commands and remain in his love, then his joy is within us as well.
- God began his salvation through the Jewish people. The Apostles spread the Word of Christ to them first and then to the rest of the world.

Missal Options

- It might be best to reserve the sprinkling rite for Sundays and solemnities. Presiders may choose from among the three options for the PA.
- Use any Easter Collect (expect for today's) to conclude the UP.
- The prayers for today are from Thursday of the Fifth Week of Easter in the PT.
- Any of the five Prefaces of Easter may be used.
- Consider EP-III.

Song of the Day

"I Have Loved You" by Michael Joncas (OCP)

FRI 7 LM #289 / LMC #185–192 / white
Easter Weekday

Scripture Insights

Jesus commands us to love one another, even to the point of laying down our lives as he did. He calls us friends, but reminds us that he chooses us, not the other way around. The Apostles send delegates and a letter to clarify some imperfect teaching.

Preaching Points

Parish Masses

- Christ gives one big command: Love one another, even if it costs everything. He pulls us in close and calls us friends and appoints us "to go and bear fruit that will remain."
- The Church is growing before us as we read through Acts, and there are growing pains. Delegates and a letter were sent to correct some misguided teaching.

Masses with Children

- Christ's commandment is that we love one another, and "no one has greater love than this, to lay down one's life for one's friends."
- Who are Christ's friends? We are. And what did he do for us? Laid down his life.

Missal Options

- It might be best to reserve the sprinkling rite for Sundays and solemnities. Presiders may choose from among the three options for the PA.
- Use any Easter Collect (expect for today's) to conclude the UP.
- The prayers for today are from Friday of the Fifth Week of Easter in the PT.
- Any of the five Prefaces of Easter may be used.
- Consider EP-I.

Song of the Day

"May Love Be Ours" by Timothy Dudley Smith (Hope Publishing Company)

SAT 8 LM #290 / LMC #185–192 / white
Easter Weekday

Scripture Insights

Christ's words get even more bold: "If the world hates you, realize that it hated me first." We are reading this after the Resurrection, yes, but also after the crucifixion. The difference between us and the world has become more stark.

Preaching Points

Parish Masses

- Christ has chosen us, but because he has chosen us, the world hates us. In the end it is because, as Jesus says, "they do not know the one who sent me."
- We get some insight into how Paul and the other Apostles made decisions and were guided by the Spirit.

Masses with Children

- Jesus' words can shock us a little: "If you belonged to the world, the world would love its own." But we don't, and the world hates us.
- "No slave is greater than his master," says Jesus. If they mistreat him, our master, we can expect the same, yet we are set free by believing in the Resurrection.

Missal Options

- It might be best to reserve the sprinkling rite for Sundays and solemnities. Presiders may choose from among the three options for the PA.
- Use any Easter Collect (expect for today's) to conclude the UP.
- The prayers for today are from Saturday of the Fifth Week of Easter in the PT.
- Any of the five Prefaces of Easter may be used.
- Consider EP-II.

Song of the Day

"All the Earth" by Lucien Deiss (WLP)

When we read the Gospel we find a clear indication: not so much our friends and wealthy neighbors, but above all the poor and the sick, those who are usually despised and overlooked, "those who cannot repay you" (Luke 14:14) . . . We have to state, without mincing words, that there is an inseparable bond between our faith and the poor. May we never abandon them.

—*Evangelii gaudium*, 48

SUN 9 LM #56B / LMC #50B / white
Sixth Sunday of Easter

Scripture Insights

The Lectionary's snippets often drop us into the middle of a story, like latecomers to a movie. Today, we are in the midst of the Acts of the Apostles. From a human point of view, this haphazard, surprising sequence of events in Acts leaves two impressions about the infant Church: its vulnerability and its energetic joy. The larger spiritual view sees the steady hand of providence as God gradually unveils a master plan of salvation.

These surprises culminate in the greatest shock of all, as Luke explains in today's passage: the dramatic shift to include the Gentiles among the People of God. Since the second century, the Church has been almost exclusively made up of Gentiles—non-Jews—a situation that none of the Apostles or New Testament writers could have imagined. In turn, it is hard for us to imagine how wrenching this change was for them. Israel had always expected the Gentile nations to come to their God (see Isaiah 2:1–4) but thought they would do so by way of Judaism.

Peter's remark in verse 28 supplies context: "God has shown me that I should not call any person profane." It dawned on him and the young Church that God was going to save the Gentiles not as Jews but as Gentiles. Note their astonishment in 10:34. The Greek phrase calls to mind something like an overpowering idea suddenly taking hold. Gentiles were no longer dogs under the Jewish table begging for the children's bread (see Matthew 15:27) but full partners and joint heirs with the ancient people of the covenant.

This shift signals a major new theme in Acts. Jesus says in our Gospel today, "I no longer call you slaves . . . [but] friends." The reason for this is the unconditional and total love with which the Father loves the Son: "As the Father loves me, so I also love you" (15:9). This in turn requires the same surrender to each other: Now "love one another as I have loved you" (15:12).

Preaching Points

Parish Masses

- The first Christians were Jewish people who joined Christianity as a sect of Judaism. Today's reading from Acts of the Apostles outlines the introduction of Gentiles directly into Christianity.
- The Jewish people knew that the savior was promised to the world, but they assumed that Gentiles would become Jewish in order to know God through Christ. Instead, Gentiles came to know God through Jesus, becoming Christians from their Gentile state, instead of becoming Jewish first.
- St. Peter did not withhold Baptism from believers because they were not what he expected. Instead, he met the new believers in the waters of Baptism without hesitation.
- God does not desire for us to be like servants; we are not blindly following orders he gave to us. Instead, Jesus calls us his friends and expects us to love one another in the same fashion.

Children's Liturgy of the Word

- Jesus and all of his disciples were Jewish. The first Christians were also Jewish people; they knew about the promised Messiah from the Jewish teachings they had learned since childhood.
- In the Acts of the Apostles we hear about the first believers who were not Jewish; at this time, Gentiles became Christians but without being Jewish first.
- Jesus calls us friends and not servants because we are meant not to follow mindless orders but to respond to his teaching out of love for God and neighbor.

Missal Options

- If you have been sprinkling the faithful instead of offering the PA, continue to do so today.
- Sing or recite the Gloria and the Creed. Because of its baptismal significance, consider using the Apostles' Creed throughout Easter.
- Use any Easter Collect (expect for today's) to conclude the UP.
- In those dioceses that celebrate the Ascension of the Lord on Sunday, the Second Reading and the Gospel from the Seventh Sunday may be read today instead of those for the Sixth Sunday.
- Any of the Easter Prefaces may be used.
- Consider EP-III.
- The SB for Easter Time may be used.
- There is no double Alleluia in the final dismissal.

Music Preparation

- In our profession we deal with many people. Sometimes it can be hard to like, let alone love, someone. When dealing with difficult parishioners it can be helpful to remember that if they bug you there is usually some characteristic you share in common with them. Try to find common ground (especially when hearing complaints about the music you have selected!).
- Today is also Mother's Day. You may wish to include special music or a blessing for this celebration. Consider "Hail Mary, Gentle Woman," or "On This Day, O Beautiful Mother."

Music Suggestions

- Gathering: "Love Divine, All Love's Excelling" (various publishers)
- Preparation of the Gifts: "Give Us Your Peace" by Jesse Manibusan (OCP)
- Communion: "Christians, Let Us Love One Another" by Claudia Foltz, SNJM, and Armand Nigro, SJ (OCP)
- Sending Forth: "Love Has Come" by Matt Maher (OCP)

Mass Texts

Introduction to Mass

Continuing these days of Easter joy and awaiting the outpouring of the Holy Spirit, let us remember that out of love for us God sent his Son as expiation for our sins. Through the risen Lord's sacrifice we now celebrate and receive, we are strengthened to go and do likewise: to give our lives in love for all our brothers and sisters. *My brothers and sisters, let us acknowledge our sins, and so prepare ourselves to celebrate the sacred mysteries.*

Tropes for Penitential Act, Form III

You have revealed to the nations the saving power of God: Lord, have mercy.

You are God's love, sent into the world that we might have life: Christ, have mercy.

You no longer call us slaves, but friends: Lord, have mercy.

Dismissal for Children's Liturgy of the Word

My dear children, today's readings are full of God's love, for his love is everything. It's how we know him and it is the reason why Christ came to us and why he is here with us today. You will hear him speaking to you now, encouraging you to share with others the love he gives you. Go in peace.

Dismissal of Catechumens

Dear friends, Christ reveals the Good News of salvation to all the world and now you are recipients of that revelation. We dismiss you now to reflect together on the power of God's salvation in your own lives, and we look forward to the day when you will join us in celebrating this feast of thanksgiving. Go in peace.

Dismissal of Extraordinary Ministers of Holy Communion

My dear ministers, take the Word and Body of the Lord to our friends who are suffering illness or injury, that by his nourishment they may continue to bear fruit and may know that they remain one with us in God's love. Go in peace.

Universal Prayer

Jesus commands us to love one another as he loves us. In doing so, we pray for the needs of our world.

1. That the pope, all bishops, priests, deacons, and lay ministers may model discipleship by laying down their lives for the good of God's people, we pray:
2. That political leaders may be selfless in the way of serving those who have elected them into office, we pray:
3. That all friendships may be blessed with a true desire to sacrifice oneself for the good of the other, we pray:
4. That all married couples may know what it means to live as friends with the Lord at the center of their marriage, we pray:
5. That all mothers will foster the love and protection of their children, we pray:

Lord Jesus,
you call your disciples friends not slaves,
as you show them the meaning of selfless love.
May we participate fully in in your life this day
by forsaking our will and following your commands.
Reveal to us this day
the way of loving without counting the cost.
Who live and reign with God the Father in the unity of the Holy Spirit,
one God, for ever and ever.
Amen.

Other Rites and Customs

- Use the Order for the Blessing of Mothers on Mother's Day from the *Book of Blessings* (chapter 55).
- Be sensitive to those for whom Mother's Day is not a happy day because of death, divorce, separation, or other tragic circumstances.

Liturgy and Life

In turbulent times, it can be challenging to truly love those who are different from us, who look different, come from a different country or culture, or hold different political or religious views. Our media culture fuels this divisiveness, turning the "other" into the enemy. Yet Jesus commands us: "love one another." Often we love only when it is easy; Jesus asks us to love when it's hard, just as he did. If we are commanded by Christ to love one another, then contempt or hatred for another is a sin. Is there an individual or group that you find difficult to love? In prayer, ask for God's heart of love and forgiveness. Pray this way each day until you can hold them in God's love. Make an effort to get to know the "other" in your world.

Taking Place This Week . . .

Consider what can be done liturgically, catechetically, and ministerially to respond to these important needs.

- Today is Mother's Day.
- International Nurses Day (5/12)
- Ascension will either be this coming Thursday (5/13) or Sunday (5/16). Check with your diocese if you are unsure.
- Eid al-Fitr (5/13)
- International Day of Families, Peace Officers Memorial Day, Armed Forces Day (5/15)

MON 10 LM #291 / LMC #185–192 / white Easter Weekday

Optional Memorial of St. Damien de Veuster, Priest / white

Scripture Insights

Christ warns of hard times to come but promises the Advocate will be there for us. Lydia teaches us about hospitality—she accepts Baptism for her family and right away invites the Apostles into her home.

Preaching Points

Parish Masses

- The Spirit of Truth testifies to Christ, but so do the disciples, and so do we, because we know Christ, and by him we know the Father.
- Lydia's family already believed in God. God opened their hearts, and they took it to a deeper level, accepting Baptism and then insisting the Apostles stay with them.

Masses with Children

- Christ wants us to know that we will face hard times, but he promises to send his Spirit to help us through them.
- A woman named Lydia was baptized by the Apostles. She was so enthusiastic about her new life that she insisted the disciples stay with her family.

Missal Options

- It might be best to reserve the sprinkling rite for Sundays and solemnities. Presiders may choose from among the three options for the PA.
- Use any Easter Collect (expect for today's) to conclude the UP.
- The prayers for today are from Monday of the Sixth Week of Easter in the PT.
- Any of the five Prefaces of Easter may be used.
- Consider EP-II.

Song of the Day

"The Spirit Sends Us Forth" by Delores Dufner, OSB (OCP)

Optional memorial

St. Damien was a Hawaiian missionary and worked closely with the lepers on the island of Moloka'i. Outraged by the deplorable conditions of the island, he sought to restore a sense of dignity. Within a short period of time, the sick were living in clean houses instead of caves, and upon death they were given a proper burial rather than being dumped into mass graves. Even though leprosy was highly contagious, he chose to remain in close contact with the people. Damien eventually contracted the disease and died from it.

- The readings may be taken from the SW, #561A (LS), CP, or CHMW (including Masses with children).
- The Collect is found in the PS; the other prayers may be from the CP (For Missionaries). You might use P-I or P-II of the Saints, or the Preface of Holy Pastors.
- Consider EP-I.

TUE 11 LM #292 / LMC #185–192 / white Easter Weekday

Scripture Insights

Christ foretells his death but also promises the Advocate, who will "convict the world." Paul and Silas not only rejoice in prison but also take the opportunity to baptize the jailer and his family.

Preaching Points

Parish Masses

- The Advocate reveals the truth: the world has sinned by not believing, Jesus has returned to the Father, and the ruler of the world is condemned.
- The Apostles show us the freedom of the Resurrection. The beatings and imprisonment cannot stop their joy. Even when nature breaks the chains and opens the doors, they remain with the jailer, to bring him to Christ.

Masses with Children

- Christ and the Spirit reveal the Father to us. We lose Jesus but gain the Advocate, who reveals the Truth to us.
- Paul and Silas are put in the deepest, darkest part of prison. It's like the tomb. The earth quakes, and they're free, but they don't leave. Instead, they bring their jailer and his family to Christ!

Missal Options

- It might be best to reserve the sprinkling rite for Sundays and solemnities. Presiders may choose from among the three options for the PA.
- Use any Easter Collect (expect for today's) to conclude the UP.
- The prayers for today are from Tuesday of the Sixth Week of Easter in the PT.
- Any of the five Prefaces of Easter may be used.
- Consider EP-III.

Song of the Day

"How Can I Keep from Singing?" (various publishers)

WED 12 LM #293 / LMC #185–192 / white
Easter Weekday

Optional Memorials of Sts. Nereus and Achilleus, Martyrs / red; St. Pancras, Martyr / red

Scripture Insights

The Spirit of Truth will come and complete the revelation of Christ and the Father. Paul shows creativity in evangelization—seizing on a statue built "To an Unknown God" and building on some Greek poetry to tell the Athenian about the Lord of Heaven and Earth.

Preaching Points

Parish Masses

- The Spirit of truth guides us to all truth by continuing to reveal Christ and the Father.
- Paul's evangelization of "the Unknown God" is beautiful. "It is he who gives to everyone life and breath and everything" yet "he will judge the world with justice."

Masses with Children

- The Spirit, like Christ, will come to lead us to the Father. The Spirit of truth will lead us to all truth.
- Think of the great Greek statues that still survive. Paul found one and used it to tell the story of our God, from creation to Christ.

Missal Options

- It might be best to reserve the sprinkling rite for Sundays and solemnities. Presiders may choose from among the three options for the PA.
- Use any Easter Collect (expect for today's) to conclude the UP.
- The prayers for today are from Wednesday of the Sixth Week of Easter in the PT.
- Any of the five Prefaces of Easter may be used.
- Consider EP-II.

Song of the Day

"You Are Near" by Dan Schutte (OCP)

Optional Memorials

Sts. Nereus and Achilleus

Nereus and Achilleus were soldiers who converted to Christianity and were subsequently martyred. Although nothing else is known of their lives, we know of their martyrdom and can guess something of their inspirational influence from the Church their fellow Roman Christians erected over their grave in the fourth century.

- The readings may be taken from the SW, #562, CM, or LMC #291.
- Use the Collect from the PS; the other prayers may be taken from the CM (For Several Martyrs during Easter Time).
- Consider P-I or P-II of Saints, or P-I or P-II of Holy Martyrs.
- You might use EP-I.

St. Pancras

St. Pancras was only fourteen when he was martyred in the Diocletian persecutions. Although he was offered power and money, St. Pancras refused to sacrifice to the Roman gods and was subsequently decapitated.

- The readings may be taken from the SW, #563, CM, or LMC #292.
- Use the Collect from the PS; the other prayers may be taken from the CM (For One Martyr during Easter Time).
- Consider P-I or P-II of Saints, or P-I or P-II of Holy Martyrs.
- You might use EP-I.

THU 13 LM #294 / LMC #185–192 / violet
Easter Weekday

Optional Memorial of Our Lady of Fatima / white

Editorial Note

Some dioceses celebrate Ascension today. Information is provided on page 206.

Scripture Insights

Christ and the Father exist together in unity. Christ had to explain to the disciples that his home was heaven too and that he would soon leave the disciples to return home. The Father, Son, and Holy Spirit desire for us to share their heavenly home with us.

Preaching Points

Parish Masses

- Jesus prepared the disciples for his Ascension by explaining that they would soon no longer see him. They would miss him but would soon rejoice.
- We continue to carry this same rejoicing today: death has been conquered, and Christ resurrected and ascended into heaven. We too hope to participate in that Resurrection.

Masses with Children

- When we have to be apart from the people we love, it is difficult, and we have to prepare for it. Christ prepared the disciples for the time when he would no longer be with them in his physical body. The Holy Spirit would be sent to them, and, in that way, God would still be with the Church.
- We can take great joy in Christ's Resurrection and ascension and remember that we have faith that we will someday join him in the resurrection of the body.

Missal Options

- It might be best to reserve the sprinkling rite for Sundays and solemnities. Presiders may choose from among the three options for the PA.
- Use any Easter Collect (expect for today's) to conclude the UP.
- The prayers for today are from Thursday of the Sixth Week of Easter in the PT.
- Any of the five Prefaces of Easter may be used.
- Consider EPVN-I.

Song of the Day

"O Bless the Lord, My Soul" (various publishers)

Optional Memorial

Our Lady of Fatima is a title given to Mary based on her appearance to three children in Portugal in 1917. The Virgin requested that the world consecrate themselves to her Immaculate Heart in order to bring forth peace.

- The readings may be taken from the SW, #563A (LS), CBVM, or CMML.
- Use the Collect from the PS; the other prayers may be taken from the CBVM or CMMM.
- Use either P-I or P-II of the BVM.
- You might use EP-I.

FRI 14

LM #564 / LMC #293 / red

Feast of St. Matthias, Apostle

Today's Saint

Matthias was chosen by lots following prayer, which asked God to show the early community which candidate God had chosen. John's Gospel account reminds us that Christ chooses us to go and bear fruit by loving one another. We sometimes sing, "God has chosen me." Do you believe these words? We are to love in ways that tell the world God's Kingdom is here. God has chosen you. Consider saying a prayer of gratitude voicing your appreciation of that choice.

Scripture Insights

Our joy is complete when we love one another. It is the joy of Christ, the love of Christ, "no greater love than this." The Eleven needed to replace Judas, so they chose Matthias, "a witness to his resurrection."

Preaching Points

Parish Masses

- Tradition tells us that most of the Apostles died for their faith, as their master did. "It was not you who chose me, but I who chose you."
- Christ calls us "friends," which implies a great intimacy with him and thus with the Father. "As the Father loves me, so I also love you."

Masses with Children

- Jesus invites us to love one another, as he loved us. When we live like this, his joy lives in us.
- "No one has greater love than this, to lay down' one's life for one's friends." The Apostles chose Matthias to replace Judas. Matthias likely died a martyr's death.

Missal Options

- If using the readings from the LMC, the First Reading is proper. The other readings may be from the CA.
- The prayers are proper and are found in the PS.
- Since today is a feast of an Apostle, it is appropriate to offer the sprinkling rite.
- The Gloria is sung or recited; the Creed is omitted.
- Use either of the Prefaces for Apostles.
- You might use EP-I.
- The SB for the Apostles may be used.

Song of the Day

"We Have Been Told" by David Haas and Marty Haugen (GIA)

Other Rites and Customs

Hours: Use the Proper Psalter from the PS.

S A T **15** LM #296 / LMC #185–192 / white
Easter Weekday

Optional Memorial of St. Isidore / white

Scripture Insights

Christ tells us before the crucifixion and Resurrection of how much deeper our relationship will be with the Father after these events. His return to the Father will draw us even closer to the Father. In Acts, the community continues to expand and grow as different paths to Christ are shared.

Preaching Points

Parish Masses

- Christ can tell us that "whatever you ask the Father in my name he will give you" because Christ's time in the world has united us with the Father. Because we love Christ, the Father loves us.
- Apollos believed in Christ based on Scripture and John's Baptism. Priscilla and Aquila took him deeper into "the Way of God." The believers taught and strengthened each other as they spread the Word.

Masses with Children

- Christ draws us closer to the Father by way of love. As we love Jesus, so the Father loves us, and this guides our prayer.
- The Word of Christ was spread by people who believed and shared the Word with others, teaching each other as well.

Missal Options

- It might be best to reserve the sprinkling rite for Sundays and solemnities. Presiders may choose from among the three options for the PA.
- There are two options for the Collect depending on when Ascension is celebrated.
- Use any Easter Collect (expect for today's) to conclude the UP.
- The prayers for today are from Saturday of the Sixth Week of Easter in the PT.
- Any of the Prefaces for Easter or the Ascension may be used.
- Consider EPVN-II.

Song of the Day

"Seek Ye First" by Karen Lafferty (various publishers)

Optional Memorial

St. Isidore and his wife Maria stand as an example of sanctity in the midst of an everyday life, one balanced between work and prayer. There is a story that angels helped Isidore complete his work in the fields when he was lost in prayer, rewarding his rightly ordered devotion.

- The readings may be taken from the SW, #564A, CHMW, LMC #294, or CS (LMC).
- Use the Collect from the PS; the other prayers may be taken from the CHMW (For One Saint).
- Consider P-I or P-II of Saints.
- You might use EP-II.

Something to Consider...

◈ Continue to celebrate the season as a parish staff: a shared supper, special food at the meeting, gift books or small baskets of goodies to take home.

T H U **13** LM #58B / LMC #53B / white

Solemnity of the Ascension of the Lord

Holyday of Obligation

About Today's Solemnity

Jesus Christ is Lord of heaven and earth. While no longer physically here on earth, Christ is with us through the power and presence of the Holy Spirit. The Risen Christ taught the disciples how his life, death, and Resurrection fulfilled what had been written in Scripture. As he prepared to ascend, he instructed them to wait together for the descent of the Holy Spirit upon them. Through the Spirit's presence, they will understand what they must do and will be given the power to share the Good News through word and deed. On this Solemnity of the Ascension of the Lord, we will consider the call of every Christian to continue Jesus' ministry of love.

Scripture Insights

Luke constructs a bridge between the Gospel and Acts when Jesus and the two mysterious men of the Resurrection story in Luke 24 reprise their roles at the Ascension in Acts 1. Curiously, Jesus ascends on the evening of Easter Day in Luke 24, while in Acts 1 he ascends after forty days. This is a reminder that we can't read Bible narratives as though they were news reports. The Scripture texts deal with real events that were well known in the Christian community of their day, but Luke and the other evangelists reserved the freedom to shape the stories to bring out their deepest meanings. We need to let go of our modern expectations for literal facts and to learn the Biblical writers' symbolic approach. Take Luke's use of the forty days between Easter and the Ascension. The number deliberately evokes related events in the Bible.

The disciples themselves at first tended to see matters in the literal terms of the old life. When Jesus promises the outpouring of the Spirit, they rightly remember that as a signal that the final days are coming. A little too eagerly, they ask about finally getting their share in Israel's enthronement. (This recalls the remarkable inattention of Christian literalists in every age who plot the date of the Lord's return.) But, Jesus says, basically, "None of your business." He tells the disciples to take their faith to another level as his witnesses to the ends of the earth. Verse 8 in fact outlines Acts' progression from Jerusalem in chapter 1 to Rome in chapter 28.

Jesus then vanishes from sight, literally "taken from their eyes." His ascending body takes their worldly hopes and self-interested ideas away. In the same vein, the writer to the Ephesians calls everyone to "the work of ministry . . . until we all attai . . . to the extent of the full stature of Christ." This cultivation of unity and spiritual maturity is both the theme of Acts and the never-ending task of the Christian disciple.

Mark 16:19 alludes to Jesus at God's "right hand," a phrase found in our Creed. Check Psalm 110:1; Acts 2:33; Romans 8:34; Hebrews 1:3; 1 Peter 3:22. What does it seem to mean?

Preaching Points

Parish Masses

- Our Lord ascended to heaven and now lives with the Father in God's home. Though he lives in heaven, he is with his brothers and sisters too, as we live our lives on earth. Jesus will be with his people until the end of time.
- Throughout history people have claimed special knowledge about the end of time. Only the Father in heaven knows the timing of his will.
- Jesus ascended into heaven; his body was not left on earth because his resurrected person went to heaven.

Children's Liturgy of the Word

- Jesus went to heaven at the ascension. When this event happened his resurrected body and soul went to heaven so he could remain there with the Father. He wants to share his heavenly home with us someday.
- Jesus commanded his disciples to carry on his mission and to help others to know him. How do we help others to know about Jesus through our words and actions?

Missal Options

- There are two sets of formularies: one for the Vigil and the other for the Mass during the Day.
- The Vigil Mass may occur before or after Evening Prayer.
- There are two forms of the Collect for the Mass during the Day. Use the one not used to conclude the UP at all Masses.
- The Gloria and the Creed are sung or recited at both Masses. Because of its baptismal significance, consider using the Apostles' Creed throughout Easter.
- Use P-I or P-II of the Ascension.
- If EP-I is used, the proper form of the Communicantes is said.
- Use the SB for the Ascension.
- The double Alleluia is not sung during the dismissal.

Music Preparation

- There are great traditional hymns for today's solemnity. It crosses the distance between Easter and Pentecost. So, we are still singing "Alleluias" but looking forward to the coming of the Holy Spirit. You have many choices.
- Give people the opportunity to embrace their discipleship this week, as they leave singing or whistling something from the liturgy.
- The solemnity should be marked with the fullness of Easter joy replete with Alleluias.

Music Suggestions

- Gathering: "Hail the Day That Sees Him Rise" (various publishers)
- Responsorial Psalm: "Psalm 47: God Mounts His Throne" by Paul Inwood (OCP)
- Preparation of the Gifts: "Behold We Are Witnesses" by Alan J. Homerding (WLP)
- Sending Forth: "Go Ye Out" by Tom Booth (OCP)

Mass Texts

Introduction to Mass

Today's celebration is one in which our hope comes to the fore. Jesus Christ, who died and rose again to bring us back to the Father, has ascended above the highest heavens. Fixing all our hopes on him, we live in longing for his return and for the coming of God's Kingdom. In the meantime, we also wait for the outpouring of the Holy Spirit, by whose power Christ is still present to us in the Eucharist. Therefore, let us rejoice and give God thanks. *My brothers and sisters, let us acknowledge our sins, and so prepare ourselves to celebrate the sacred mysteries.*

Tropes for Penitential Act, Form III

You have risen from the dead and have ascended to God in glory: Lord, have mercy.

You will come again to take us to our heavenly homeland: Christ, have mercy.

You, our Lord, are the great king over all the earth: Lord, have mercy.

Dismissal for Children's Liturgy of the Word

My dear children, Christ, though he is no longer present to us in the exact same way he was present to his disciples before his death, promised that he would be with us always, even to the end of the world. He might not be apparent to our senses, but we believe he is still here among us and within us, teaching us, helping us, and listening to us. Go now and listen to the Scriptures with faith in his ever-present love.

Dismissal of Catechumens

My friends, we speak of Christ as our head and of the Church as his Body. We wait with eager anticipation for the day when you will join us as members of Christ's Body, that you will know the joy and hope that come from his call. Go now in peace and ponder the wonder of his promise.

Dismissal of Extraordinary Ministers of Holy Communion

Dear friends, we charge you with carrying Christ, in his Eucharistic Body, to the ill and infirm members of our community, that he may strengthen them in faith and hope and in the unity of the Holy Spirit who binds us all together in love. Go in peace.

Universal Prayer

Jesus commands us to proclaim the Gospel to all nations and to all creatures. That all peoples will know we are Christians by our actions, let us pray for the needs of our world.

1. That the Church may truly reflect the radiance of the ascended Lord, we pray:
2. That every aspect of the world created by God's love may be redeemed at the end of time, we pray:
3. That all of our works of justice may be patterned after our expectations of God's heavenly Kingdom, we pray:
4. That the light of Christ may shine brightly on all those who suffer in darkness, especially those who are poor or homeless, we pray:
5. That the grace of the Lord's Ascension may give comfort to all those who mourn, we pray

Lord God of heaven and earth,
you crown Jesus' earthly mission
by giving him a place at your right hand.
As his earthly body,
may we remain in him always
and look forward with hope to our future glory.
Who live and reign with God the Father in the unity of the Holy Spirit,
one God, for ever and ever.
Amen.

Other Rites and Customs

- Keep the Paschal candle lit.
- Begin the Novena to the Holy Spirit, one of the Church's most ancient novenas.

Liturgy and Life

As the Apostles watch Jesus ascend into heaven, two angelic figures ask: "Why are you standing there looking at the sky?" Their message seems twofold: "Don't worry, he'll be back," and "Get on with it!" Indeed, the rest of the Acts of the Apostles is about how Jesus works through his people, by the power of the Holy Spirit, to bring about God's purposes. How might the Holy Spirit be moving you toward action in the world? In what ways are you called to action?

SUN **16** LM #60B / LMC #56B / white

Seventh Sunday of Easter

Editorial Note

If your diocese celebrates the Ascension today, refer to the commentary on pages 206–207.

Scripture Insights

In this Acts passage, Luke is shifting the focus from Jesus to the disciples. Followers in other traditions simply carry out the vision of their teacher, but here the disciples are important in their own right. We know their ideas and writings, even their weaknesses, failures, and arguments.

More remarkable still, Luke places the story of the Church in Acts on the same level of importance as the story of Jesus in the Gospel. Note the strong sense of destiny that flows through our passage: Peter twice uses the strong phrase "it had to be" (*dei:* 16, 21), the same word Jesus used in speaking about his coming suffering (see Mark 8:31). Events that were not of their own making or choosing were happening all around them. A sense of the Lord's hidden, guiding hand pervades the atmosphere of Acts 1.

More was at work than a sense of destiny; the Apostles fulfilled unique roles in the salvation story. Their symbolic number, "Twelve," recalls the twelve tribes of Israel. Despite the emphasis on choosing a replacement for Judas, Matthias disappears from Scripture after his election; so when the Apostle James was killed (Acts 12:2), no one replaced him. The Twelve performed a symbolic role that was unrepeatable.

Jesus' prayer in John shows how he continues to pray for the Church even now. Here the symbolic number is "one": "that they may be one just as we are one." Jesus prays that the community may not be subverted by treachery like that of Judas or by the hatred of the world. The oneness of the disciples is the basis of their mission in the world. Laying the passages from Acts and John side-by-side on a spiritual plane, one surmises that although the disciples draw straws, it is really Jesus' prayer for the Church's protection and unity that guides its destiny.

Preaching Points

Parish Masses

- Today we are presented with a model for Christian discernment and decision making, we bless and thank God for his everlasting kindness, and we reflect on the gift of union with God in Christ through the Holy Spirit. Living in love is a lifetime expression of the truth of Christ through which we are consecrated at Baptism.
- When the Risen Christ was in the world, he initiated the Apostles into the care and keeping of the Church. The Church was established as one holy, catholic, and apostolic Church. In this reading, we clearly see the four marks of the Church.
- The Apostles needed to replace Judas, and together they selected Matthias, who then became one of the first Apostles. In a similar manner, the Church still replaces bishops who retire or die.
- When we abide in God's love, then God is with us and in us; we are given God's Spirit. Through Christ, God is with humanity.
- The Church is a gift Jesus gave to his people out of love for them. When he returned to heaven, he desired for his ministry to be continued by all people and that the faithful would be guided by the bishops and priests.

Children's Liturgy of the Word

- Modern bishops are the descendants of the Apostles through ordination and the laying on of hands.
- When we follow God's instructions to love one another, we are abiding in God. We are called to act in God's love at home, at school, and with our friends.
- Jesus did not want his followers to be left guessing what they should do after his ascension into heaven. He gave his people the gift of the Church, and the Church still guides us today.

Missal Options

- Continue to offer the sprinkling rite if you have been doing so throughout Easter.
- The Gloria and the Creed are sung or said. Because of its baptismal significance, consider using the Apostles' Creed throughout Easter.
- Use the Collect for the Ascension to conclude the UP if today is celebrated as the Seventh Sunday or vice versa.
- Any of the Prefaces of Easter or the Ascension may be used.
- Consider EP-III.
- The SB for Easter Time may be prayed.
- There is no double Alleluia in the dismissal.

Music Preparation

- Be aware in advance whether your parish is celebrating Ascension or the Seventh Sunday of Easter. Check your Ordo or any information from the diocese.
- Songs of Easter and the Ascension are both appropriate today.
- Consider celebrating the extended Pentecost vigil. It is a beautiful liturgy. Be sure to have the extra readings and psalms prepared.

Music Suggestions

- Gathering: "Christ Is Risen!, Shout Hosanna!" text by Brian Wren (various publishers)
- Preparation of the Gifts: "Earth, Earth, Awake!" text by Herman G. Stuempfle Jr. and tune by Sally Ann Morris (GIA)
- Communion: "Taste and See" by James Moore (GIA)
- Sending Forth: "Go to the World!" by Sylvia Dunstan (GIA)

Mass Texts

Introduction to Mass

In his great mercy, God has cast our sins far from us, so that nothing might stand between him and us. Let us, therefore, not cling to sin but open ourselves to the coming of the Holy Spirit, who is our unity and who is poured out upon us through the death and Resurrection of our Lord Jesus Christ. *My brothers and sisters, let us acknowledge our sins, and so prepare ourselves to celebrate the sacred mysteries.*

Tropes for Penitential Act, Form III

Lord, you deliver us from the power of evil:
Lord, have mercy.

Christ, we belong not to the world but to you:
Christ, have mercy.

Lord, you are the fulfillment of our joy: Lord,
have mercy.

Dismissal for Children's Liturgy of the Word

Dear children, in today's Gospel, we hear Christ praying for us to the Father. We can be sure that he continues to pray for us, so that we will be safe from evil, that we will know joy, and that we will be one with him. Go now and listen to him, and when you return to us we will continue to give God thanks and praise.

Dismissal of Catechumens

Dear friends, the Church's joy is unity in the Holy Spirit, and we long for you to join us in that unity, that you may know our joy. Reflect well on the word of truth spoken to you by God, whose only Son, Jesus Christ, is risen from the dead. Go in peace.

Dismissal of Extraordinary Ministers of Holy Communion

My friends, our sick and homebound brothers and sisters do not belong to the world, but they belong to us and we belong to Christ. So, we give you his Body to take to them, that we all may be one in him and in the joy of the coming Holy Spirit. Go in peace.

Universal Prayer

We are sent into the world to be bearers of Christ's truth. May we lift up those who suffer in these prayers we offer to the Father.

1. That the Church may embrace the world in love but resist ever being settled in it, we pray:
2. That leaders of nations may work for fuller and more visible unity among their peoples, we pray:
3. That all those responsible for scientific and technological developments may remember to give thanks and praise to God, we pray:
4. That all those who find themselves caught in a web of lies may seek to tell the truth, we pray:
5. That all the poor and those who live on the fringe of society may be welcomed into the fullness of communal life, we pray:
6. That all who reject God at the moment of death may be granted mercy, we pray:

Lord God of power and might,
your Son Jesus consecrates us in truth
and teaches us to resist the entrapments of our world.
Help us to live simple lives, fully devoted to you.
May we cast aside the material things
of our world
that prevent us from truly appreciating
the great gift that is your love.
Through Christ our Lord.
Amen.

Other Rites and Customs

- Choose music that mentions the coming of the Holy Spirit.
- Encourage parishioners to wear red to Mass next weekend.

Liturgy and Life

In the days after Christ's death and Resurrection, the Apostles moved to make their community whole. They knew that to effectively witness to Christ's rising, unity was required. Help create wholeness in your parish, bit by bit. After Mass today, reach out to someone on the margins and invite him or her to sit with you for coffee and a doughnut.

Taking Place This Week . . .

Consider what can be done liturgically, catechetically, and ministerially to respond to these important needs.

- Today the special collection is for the Catholic Communication Campaign.
- Shavuot and World Information Society Day (5/17)
- Emergency Medical Services for Children Day (5/19)
- World Autoimmune/Autoinflammatory Arthritis Day (5/20)
- World Day for Cultural Diversity (5/21)
- World Biological Diversity Day (5/22)
- The full Pentecost Vigil may be celebrated the evening of 5/23.
- Today is World Communication Day.

MON 17 LM #297 / LMC #185–192 / white

Easter Weekday

Scripture Insights

The disciples think they understand, but they will be shattered by the crucifixion. We read this post-Resurrection, so when Jesus says, "I have conquered the world," we believe him. Paul expands on what Baptism is and invites the Spirit to descend on a community of believers.

Preaching Points

Parish Masses

- Christ was abandoned by his followers but not by the Father. In one sentence, he promises us peace, troubles, and courage. The Resurrection proves he has indeed conquered the world.
- John's Baptism was one of repentance, and that was good. The Apostles bring a baptism in the Spirit, which is far greater.

Masses with Children

- Christ wants to give us his peace. "In the world you will have trouble," he tells us, but we have courage, since he conquered the world.
- Paul baptized in the name of Jesus and "laid his hands on them," and they received the Spirit, as we continue to do in the Sacrament of Confirmation.

Missal Options

- It might be best to reserve the sprinkling rite for Sundays and solemnities. Presiders may choose from among the three options for the PA.
- Use any Easter Collect (expect for today's) to conclude the UP.
- The prayers for today are from Monday of the Seventh Week of Easter in the PT.
- Use any of the Prefaces for Easter or the Ascension.
- Consider EP-II.

Song of the Day

"If You Believe and I Believe" by John L. Bell (GIA)

TUE 18 LM #298 / LMC #185–192 / white

Easter Weekday

Optional Memorial of St. John I, Pope and Martyr / red

Scripture Insights

Jesus, knowing the end is near for him, emphasizes once again that eternal life is knowing God through Christ. Further, when Jesus speaks of being glorified, he is speaking of the cross. Paul knows of great hardships to come but continues on with his call to bear witness to God's grace.

Preaching Points

Parish Masses

- Christ's glorification comes by way of the cross. In this way he returns to the Father, and the Father's goodness and power is shown.
- The sufferings continue with Paul and the Apostles as the Word is spread, just as their Master suffered. Yet the power and the promise of the Resurrection pushes them onward.

Masses with Children

- Christ knew the cross was coming, yet he spoke of it as the time when the Father and he would glorify each other. He faced it with love, knowing the Father's power.
- Paul had been treated harshly for spreading God's Word and knew there was more suffering to come, yet he kept going.

Missal Options

- It might be best to reserve the sprinkling rite for Sundays and solemnities. Presiders may choose from among the three options for the PA.
- Use any Easter Collect (expect for today's) to conclude the UP.
- The prayers for today are from Tuesday of the Seventh Week of Easter in the PT.
- Use any of the Prefaces for Easter or the Ascension.
- Consider EP-II.

Song of the Day

"Lord of All Nations, Grant Me Grace" by Olive W. Spannaus (Concordia Publishing House)

Optional Memorial

St. John I, a defender of the divinity of Christ, is not only revered as "a victim for Christ" but also remembered for introducing the Alexandrian system of calculating the date of Easter.

- The readings may be taken from the SW, #565, CM or CP (For a Pope), or LMC #295.
- Use the Collect from the PS; the other prayers may be taken from the CM (For One Martyr during Easter Time) or the CP (For a Pope).
- Consider P-I or P-II of Saints, P-I or P-II of Holy Martyrs, or the Preface of Holy Pastors.
- You might use EP-I.

WED 19 LM #299 / LMC #185–192 / white **Easter Weekday**

Scripture Insights

The cross is near, and the divisions are stark. Christ has called us out of the world, and so the world hates us as it hated him. Yet Christ sends us out into the world, "consecrated in truth." Paul also prepares to move on from a community he's invested much time in. He warns of men who will come after him "perverting the truth."

Preaching Points

Parish Masses

- Jesus is praying to the Father, for us. He gives us the Father's Word, and for this the world hates us. Yet he sends us back into the world and prays for our protection.
- Paul recounts how he has poured himself out for his community, citing Christ's works: "It is more blessed to give than to receive."

Masses with Children

- Christ prays for his disciples. He prays that we may be one, just as he and the Father are one. Praying that the Father protects us from the Evil One, he sends us back into the world.
- Paul warns the Church of God to keep watch, for "savage wolves" are coming to twist around the message he left with them.

Missal Options

- It might be best to reserve the sprinkling rite for Sundays and solemnities. Presiders may choose from among the three options for the PA.
- Use any Easter Collect (expect for today's) to conclude the UP.
- The prayers for today are from Wednesday of the Seventh Week of Easter in the PT.
- Use any of the Prefaces for Easter or the Ascension.
- Consider EP-I.

Song of the Day

"Be My Hands and Feet" by Mary Louise Bringle and Tony Alonso (GIA)

THU 20 LM #300 / LMC #185–192 / white **Easter Weekday**

Optional Memorial of St. Bernardine of Siena, Priest / white

Scripture Insights

Jesus prays that we all may be one, as he and the Father are one. Paul creates trouble in Jerusalem among the Jewish leaders, proclaiming his hope in the resurrection of the dead.

Preaching Points

Parish Masses

- Jesus' final prayer to the Father is "that the love with which you loved me may be in them and I in them."
- Christ prays not only for his disciples who are present with him "but also for those who will believe in them through their word." That's us, two thousand years later.

Masses with Children

- The Father sent Christ so we would be one as they are one, so we would love each other as much as they love each other.
- God sent Paul to Jerusalem, the center of the Jewish world, to proclaim the Resurrection. "Take courage," says God to Paul, as God sends him to Rome, the capital of the civilized world.

Missal Options

- It might be best to reserve the sprinkling rite for Sundays and solemnities. Presiders may choose from among the three options for the PA.
- Use any Easter Collect (expect for today's) to conclude the UP.
- The prayers for today are from Thursday of the Seventh Week of Easter in the PT.
- Use any of the Prefaces for Easter or the Ascension.
- Consider EP-II.

Song of the Day

"Psalm 16: Keep Me Safe, O God" by Owen Alstott (OCP)

Optional Memorial

St. Bernardine was an Italian Franciscan and preacher who attracted thousands to his preaching with his accessible language and eloquence. Although he upheld strict discipline as general of his order, his exhortations to laypeople were marked by encouragement and understanding of human weakness.

- The readings may be taken from the SW, #566, CP (For Missionaries), or LMC #296.
- Use the Collect from the PS; the other prayers may be taken from the CP (For Missionaries) or CHMW (For Religious).
- Consider P-I or P-II of Saints, or the Preface of Holy Pastors.
- You might use EP-I.

FRI 21 LM #301 / LMC #185–192 / white
Easter Weekday

Optional Memorial of St. Christopher Magallanes, Priest, and Companions, Martyrs / red

Scripture Insights

A troubling Resurrection appearance. Three times Jesus asks Peter if he loves him, just like the three denials, followed by the foretelling of Peter's death, by which "he would glorify God." Paul, like Jesus, was accused by the Jewish leaders and then handed to the Romans to await punishment.

Preaching Points

Parish Masses

- "Do you love me?" Christ asks three times. Yes, we say. "Feed my lambs." Yes, we say. "Tend my sheep." Yes, we say. "Feed my sheep," he replies.
- After Jesus' interrogation and description of Peter's upcoming death, Jesus ends as he started, saying to him, and us, "Follow me."

Masses with Children

- Peter had denied Jesus three times, so three times Jesus asks Peter if he loves him. Three times Peter affirms his love.
- Jesus tells Peter about how he will stretch out his hands and die as Jesus did. "Feed my sheep," says Jesus. "Follow me," says Jesus.

Missal Options

- It might be best to reserve the sprinkling rite for Sundays and solemnities. Presiders may choose to offer the sprinkling rite or any form of the PA.
- Use any Easter Collect (expect for today's) to conclude the UP.
- The prayers for today are from Friday of the Seventh Week of Easter in the PT.
- Use any of the Prefaces for Easter or the Ascension.
- Consider EP-I.

Song of the Day

"Do You Really Love Me" by Carey Landry (OCP)

Optional Memorial

St. Christopher Magallanes was one of twenty-two priests martyred in Mexico during a period of extreme anticlericalism in the early twentieth century. His prayers for his executioners and for the Mexican people in the moments before his martyrdom revealed both courage and love.

- The readings may be taken from the SW, #566A (LS), or CM (including Masses with children).
- Use the Collect from the PS; the other prayers may be taken from the CM (For Several Martyrs during Easter Time).
- You might use EP-I.
- Consider P-I or P-II of Saints, P-I or P-II of Holy Martyrs, or the Preface of Holy Pastors.

SAT 22 LM #302 / LMC #185–192 / white
Easter Weekday

Optional Memorial of St. Rita of Cascia, Religious / white

Scripture Insights

John's account of the Gospel refers many times to "the disciple whom Jesus loved," and here the writer reveals himself to be that disciple. Further, the early Church thought Christ's return to be imminent and that "John" might live long enough to see it. In the end, "What concern is it of yours?" says Jesus. "You follow me." And Paul, even as a prisoner/guest of the Romans, "proclaimed the Kingdom of God."

Preaching Points

Parish Masses

- Think of the many other things that Jesus did. What wonders, what miracles, what wisdom went on that is lost to history? And yet Christ and the Spirit are still active in the world, with wisdom and wonders and miracles.
- Paul never gave up on his Jewish people. "It is on account of the hope of Israel that I wear these chains."

Masses with Children

- Jesus has promised us he will return, and the early Church thought it would be very soon. Jesus tells us not to worry about when or where. "You follow me," he says.
- Paul was chained up as a prisoner in Rome for two years, yet he kept preaching the Kingdom of God to all who came to him.

Missal Options

- It might be best to reserve the sprinkling rite for Sundays and solemnities. Presiders may choose from among the three options for the PA.
- Use any Easter Collect (expect for today's) to conclude the UP.
- The prayers for today are from Saturday of the Seventh Week of Easter in the PT.
- Use any of the Prefaces for Easter or the Ascension.
- Consider EP-II.

Song of the Day

"May God Remain with Us" by James V. Marchionda, OP (WLP)

Optional Memorial

St. Rita was married against her wishes to an abusive and unfaithful man and grieved over her two sons, who followed their father's poor example and, like him, came to a violent end. Rita united her suffering to the wounds of Christ, and eventually her persistence, devotion, and endurance were rewarded when she was accepted into an order of Augustinian nuns.

- The readings may be taken from the SW, #566B (LS), or CHMW (For Religious) (including for Masses with children).
- Use the Collect from the PS; the other prayers may be taken from the CHMW/CS (For Religious).
- Consider P-I or P-II of Saints, P-I or P-II of Holy Martyrs, or the Preface of Holy Virgins and Religious.
- You might use EP-I.

Something to Consider...

◈ Recognize and make sure that the Vigil of Pentecost and Pentecost Sunday are celebrated boldly.

S U N **23** LM #62ABC and 63B / LMC #58ABC / red
Solemnity of Pentecost

About Today's Solemnity

Today we celebrate the gift of the Holy Spirit and the ways in which the Spirit inspires, guides, and strengthens us to live as Christian disciples. Especially in the later weeks of Easter Time, we have anticipated the advent of the Holy Spirit in the lives of the disciples and in the Church. Now we hear the account of the first Pentecost, when, through the presence and power of the Holy Spirit, the Good News of Christ was shared with people from throughout the world. Those who heard the disciples speaking were amazed and astonished at the power of God.

Scripture Insights: Vigil

The following insights concern all the readings for the extended Vigil.

During Easter Time, we hear about the brave, faith-filled activity of the Apostles as they continue the ministry of Jesus. We conclude Easter Time with an appeal for God's Spirit to fill us too. Although we cannot live without the breath of God, and we know that God calls us to live within his Kingdom, we do not always welcome God's presence.

The passage from Genesis is the culmination of a series of dispiriting stories that tell how sin spread throughout the world. When people attempt to construct a city with an awe-inspiring tower, we recognize that human beings have so utterly turned away from God they no longer acknowledge him as their creator. They prefer to "make a name for themselves" rather than call on the name of the Lord. God intervenes: he scatters the self-aggrandizing people before they construct a society that will harden in sin.

In the centuries that follow, God makes his own nation. He gathers an oppressed people, leads them into the Sinai desert, and invites them into a covenant. The reading from Exodus elevates these chosen people while noting that the whole world still belongs to God. God intends to free his creation from sin by first revealing himself to this one group.

He will build the people up into a nation that will call on his name and reveal his presence to others. The people accept the terms of the covenant. They come together at the base of a mountain on which God reveals his glory in cloud and storm and fire. The Spirit of God that quietly sustains all creation here manifests itself in ways so palpable and awe-inspiring that the people tremble.

After God allowed his wayward people to be defeated by foreign armies, Ezekiel, filled with God's Spirit, prophesied that the Lord would breathe life into his people once again. God would re-create them as a nation and restore them to the land he had once given them. Ezekiel's imagery of enlivened bones and open graves becomes a double promise: God will not only gather the descendants of his holy people but also breathe new life into those who have died.

Joel prophesied that the Spirit that sustains creation and empowers particular individuals will fill all of God's people so that even the least among them will exhibit the presence of God in dramatic ways. God's Spirit keeps people faithful, enabling them to profess God's holiness when he reveals himself on that "great and terrible day." Joel describes the Lord's day using imagery that recalls the events surrounding the Exodus but that also reminds us of Jesus' crucifixion.

In John's account of the Gospel we hear how blood and water flowed from the pierced side of Jesus as he hung on the cross. In the passage we have for this evening, Jesus foretells that this water is God's Spirit poured forth upon all creation.

The Spirit flows into the world and into us, a renewed gift of life and union for which we thirst. Just as God provided water in the desert, so Christ gives us eternal life by the waters of Baptism. The Spirit that pervades creation now becomes present within us as the holy and eternal presence of God. This divine indwelling empowers us to follow God's Spirit-filled Son and to become part of God's holy nation, his special possession, his re-created people.

We "have the firstfruits of the Spirit," yet we await the final transformation of the world, which continues to endure suffering and death. We celebrate all that God's Spirit is doing—sustaining, enlivening, guiding, empowering, consoling, and liberating—even as we call on this Spirit to complete the work of salvation. Because God's creation is not finished, we strive to participate in the Spirit's life-giving work, but sometimes we tremble. God's presence can be overwhelming.

The Spirit reaches depths in us that we cannot reach ourselves and that we might not have known were there. We need the Spirit. We need the awe-inspiring, challenging, and fearsome indwelling of the divine, for we cannot re-create ourselves. We cannot make a name for ourselves. We cannot unify ourselves, live justly, ensure peace, resist sin, or defeat death by ourselves. Only God's Spirit can do that. As we gather at the end of our Easter season, we pray for the Spirit to do all that we can't, and we pray for the Spirit to do all that it can in us.

Scripture Insights: Day

The texts invite us to consider the Spirit's vast activity in both an outer, geographical sense and an inner, spiritual sense. Jesus apparently lived his life within a tiny territory, but the outpouring of his Spirit at Pentecost sent his disciples to the ends of the earth. The same Spirit pressed them deep within themselves to explore the truth about Jesus.

Outwardly, Luke's list is a roll call, not of people who literally heard Peter's Pentecost sermon, but of people who had heard the Gospel by Luke's time in the late first century. The places named can be found on a good Bible map. They form a circle around Jerusalem, always the spiritual starting point for Luke. In Luke's Gospel, the devil showed Jesus "all the kingdoms of the world" because they were his to give (Luke 4:5–6); Acts shows us the kingdoms that became Christ's by the power of the Holy Spirit.

The list symbolizes the scope of God's grace and the Spirit's power. It also previews the rest of Acts. The Apostles would experience many successes and much rejoicing but also many conflicts and reversals. "It is necessary for us to undergo many hardships to enter the kingdom of God" (Acts 14:22). The Spirit's relentless energy constantly stirred and pushed the disciples beyond themselves. Their story became part of the story of "the mighty acts of God" (2:11).

Inwardly, the Spirit comes from Jesus to guide the disciples to all the truth about him. In the context of John's Gospel, this means penetrating to the awesome mystery of Jesus' divine being, the Word made flesh who in the beginning was with God and is himself God (John 1:1, 14).

Galatians says that by grace the Spirit instructs Christians about life by uniting them with Jesus' crucifixion. For those who understand, Christ's death powerfully centers the inner life of individuals and communities in the fruit of the Spirit.

Preaching Points

Parish Masses

- At Pentecost, the Church received the gift of the Holy Spirit. The third person of the Blessed Trinity guides the Church as Christ promised—God shares himself with Christ, who shares God with us through the Holy Spirit.
- When we abide in God, the fruits of his goodness show in our lives. Love shines clearly and brightly through love, joy, peace, patience, kindness, generosity, faithfulness, gentleness, and self-control. These attributes help us to form a holy, healthy, and joy-filled community.
- Through Pentecost, humanity begins to enter into the life of our triune God.
- The Holy Spirit is active in the life of the Church both in the guidance of the hierarchy and in the lives of the baptized.

Children's Liturgy of the Word

- God's great love for us helps us to love one another. When we live in God's love, others see evidence of that love in our actions.
- God desires all people to be close to him, and he wants to share his life with those created in his image. At Pentecost, the faithful people began to join in the life of the Father, Son, and Holy Spirit.
- The Holy Spirit guides the Church and lives with each person; each of us can ask the Holy Spirit for wisdom and guidance.

Missal Options

- There are two sets of Mass formularies: Vigil and Day.
- The Vigil Mass may precede or follow Evening Prayer I. There are two forms of the Vigil: extended and simple.
- Evening Prayer I may be combined with the extended Vigil. If so, the celebration may either begin with the introductory verse and the hymn from the Office or with the singing of the Entrance Antiphon. If the celebration is combined, the PA is omitted. After the psalmody, the Collect of the day is prayed. The PA is not omitted if Mass begins in the usual way.
- The Vigil includes a special introduction.
- If the extended Vigil is done, the Collect of the day is not said. Instead, various Collects are prayed after each psalm. The Gloria follows. The readings for the full Vigil with psalms are found in the LS.
- The simple form follows the regular form of Mass. The Gloria is sung or said.
- The Creed is said at the Vigil and the Mass during the Day.
- The Preface of Pentecost is used at both Masses. The texts are found in the Mass for the Day.
- If EP-I is prayed, the special form of the Communicantes is said.
- A solemn blessing may be used, and the double Alleluia is added to the final blessing.
- There are no readings for the Vigil in the children's Lectionary.

Music Preparation

- The Pentecost sequence is not an option and should be sung after the Second Reading. Settings abound!
- If you use a song like "One Spirit, One Church" by Kevin Keil and Maryanne Quinlivan, OSU (OCP), you are merging a new text with a traditional chant. The refrain was composed in 1990 and the verses are from a nineteenth-century hymn.

Music Suggestions

- Sequence: "Come, O Holy Spirit" by Owen Alstott (OCP)
- Sequence or Communion: "Come, Holy Spirit, On Us Shine" translated by Jerome Siweck (WLP)
- Preparation of the Gifts: "Holy Spirit, Come Now" by Jesse Manibusan (OCP)

Mass Texts

Introduction to Mass

Today we celebrate the outpouring of the Holy Spirit—the Spirit of love, truth, and unity—upon the Church. We are brought together as God's children and drawn up into the life and love of the Trinity by this same Spirit, who also transforms our humble offering of bread and wine, our offering of our very selves, into the Body and Blood of Christ. For this, let us give thanks and sing praise to our God. *My brothers and sisters, let us acknowledge our sins, and so prepare ourselves to celebrate the sacred mysteries.*

Tropes for Penitential Act, Form III

Through your Spirit, renew us who have grown old in sin:
Lord, have mercy.

Replace our hearts of stone with hearts of flesh:
Christ, have mercy.

Write the law of your love upon our hearts:
Lord, have mercy.

Dismissal for Children's Liturgy of the Word

My dear children, before he ascended into heaven, Christ promised to send his Spirit to us as our helper and constant companion. Today we celebrate the fulfillment of his promise. The Holy Spirit is within you, helping you to understand the Scriptures, and when you return to us we will continue our celebration together in the joy of the Holy Spirit. Go in peace.

Dismissal of Catechumens

My friends, it is our sincere prayer that as you take your leave from us to reflect on God's Word, the Holy Spirit will lead you into greater understanding and will mold your hearts into vessels of God's love. We look forward to the day when you will stand in unity with us around the table of the Lord's Supper. Go in peace.

Dismissal of Extraordinary Ministers of Holy Communion

Dear ministers of the Lord, take Christ to our sick and suffering friends, that he may pour his Spirit into their hearts, filling them with joy and uniting them with us in giving glory to God. Go in peace.

Universal Prayer

As we bring our prayers before the Lord, may he send out his Spirit and renew the face of the earth.

1. For all who are to receive the Sacrament of Confirmation, that they may use the Spirit's gifts wisely, we pray:
2. For those who have never heard of the Holy Spirit, that they may come to know the triune God of perfect relationship, we pray:
3. For nations that are at war, that a spirit of peace may reign in the hearts of all responsible for the violence and discord, we pray:
4. For ourselves, that we may find new and creative ways of expressing our love of the Lord by embracing the gifts of the Spirit, we pray:
5. For all who have died, especially for those who have experienced great suffering in their final days, that they may know God, we pray:

Creator God,
you offer us new life through our Baptism in Christ
and our communion in the Holy Spirit.
May we always renew our commitment to this invitation
so as to respond to you with great joy.
Help us to use wisely the gifts bestowed on us by the Spirit.
Through Christ our Lord.
Amen.

Other Rites and Customs

- Celebrate the Vigil of Pentecost, with its full complement of readings and psalms and with great solemnity.
- Host a ministry fair to emphasize the gifts of the Holy Spirit descending on the Church.
- At the conclusion of Mass or Evening Prayer, process the Paschal candle from its place of prominence in the sanctuary or near the ambo to the baptistery where it will remain until next year's Easter Vigil.
- Use lots of (hypoallergenic) incense!

Liturgy and Life

Take some time today and be mindful of your breathing. Close your eyes, quiet your mind, and take deep breaths. With each breath, recognize you are in the presence of God. Rest in this quiet of God's peace and love and acknowledge the presence of the Holy Spirit. After some time, bring to mind different images of the Holy Spirit you have encountered, such as fire, wind, or water. Think about how each of these images, like the image of breath, draw you deeper into the reality of God.

Taking Place This Week . . .

Consider what can be done liturgically, catechetically, and ministerially to respond to these important needs.

- Ordinary Time begins after Evening Prayer II this evening.
- Tomorrow is Whit Monday (5/24).
- Canada celebrates Victoria Day tomorrow (5/24).

Ordinary Time during Summer and Fall

All human life and therefore all human time, must become praise of the Creator and thanksgiving to him.

—*Dies Domini*, 15

The Meaning of the Season

THIS lengthy stretch of Ordinary Time is indeed a time of praise and thanksgiving when the Church lives its apostolic mission. During this season, we are nourished by the "carousel of sayings and stories, songs and prayers . . . in which the mysterious ways of God are not merely presented but experienced, not merely perused but lived through" (Mark Searle, "Sunday: The Heart of the Liturgical Year" in *Between Memory and Hope*, ed. Johnson, p. 59).

For many people, there is a rhythm to this portion of the year. It begins with summer and its long days, time for vacations and time to be outdoors (if the heat and humidity are not unbearable). It continues through the early fall, when the many aspects of modern life structured by the academic calendar begin anew. It progresses through fall and ends with the shortening of days as November winds its way to Thanksgiving.

So too is there a rhythm to the life of the Church during this season of Ordinary Time. Many musical groups and religious education programs go on hiatus during June, July, and August. As people travel, Mass schedules may be adjusted in locations that are popular tourist destinations. Pastoral assignments often begin and end, and parishes transition as they welcome new priests, deacons, and lay ministers and bid farewell to those who have served.

What anchors our faith during this season is Sunday—the Lord's Day. *Dies Domini* offers a beautiful extended meditation on the rich theological importance of Sunday for Christians. It emphasizes that from the early days of the Church, "Christians celebrated the weekly day of the risen Lord primarily as a day of joy" (55). As Ordinary Time progresses, our celebration of the Mass anchors the changing seasons, for as the *Catechism of the Catholic Church* reminds us, "The Sunday celebration of the Lord's Day and his Eucharist is at the heart of the Church's life" (2177).

These Sundays of Ordinary Time begin with two "idea feasts": the Most Holy Trinity and the Most Holy Body and Blood of Christ (Corpus Christi). Trinity Sunday has been celebrated on the first Sunday after Pentecost since the fourteenth century, when Pope John XXII universalized a practice that had already been growing for centuries. Corpus Christi and its traditional procession developed amid the devotional Eucharistic spirituality of the Middle Ages. The calendar reform of 1969 combined the Feast of Corpus Christi with the Feast of the Precious Blood. In doing so, it recognized the presence of Christ in both species. Some countries celebrate it as a holyday of obligation on the Thursday after Trinity Sunday, but in the United States, it is always transferred to a Sunday "so that the faithful are not denied the chance to meditate upon the mystery" (DD, 79). These celebrations of the Trinity and the Body and Blood of Christ are not simply moments for considering abstract theological ideas. They celebrate the Trinitarian God, who is always with us, and the Eucharist, which nourishes us. Thus, they are "a celebration of the living presence of the Risen Lord in the midst of his own people" (DD, 31).

We continue to celebrate the Risen Lord as we move through the ordinal Sundays of Ordinary Time. This year, July 4 coincides with the Fourteenth Sunday of Ordinary Time. The degree to which national holidays should be acknowledged at Mass with patriotic hymns, intercessions, or other elements can be a source of contention. *The Roman Missal* for use in the United States includes a Mass formulary for Independence Day that may be used with readings from the Masses "For the Country or a City" (882–86) or "For Peace and Justice" (887–91). These are to be used when Independence Day falls on a weekday. The Mass for Independence Day is to be treated as if an "optional memorial." It is optional—it is not required. GIRM, 374, however, permits "an appropriate Mass" to be celebrated on Sundays of Ordinary Time "If any case of a graver need or of pastoral advantage should arise, at the direction of the Diocesan Bishop or with his permission." Consult your local diocesan office of worship before preparing Mass for this Sunday.

The cycle of ordinal Sundays is interrupted this year by the Solemnity of the Assumption of the Lord on August 15. The Assumption is usually a holyday of obligation, and with it falling on a Sunday this year, it is indeed a fine day for us to recall that "she who is *Mater Domini* and *Mater Ecclesiae*" is always present "on the day which is both *dies Domini* and *dies Ecclesiae*" (DD, 86).

As we proceed through late August, September, and October, we have a long stretch of ordinal Sundays from which Ordinary Time takes its name. In this part of the Lectionary, with its readings primarily from the Gospel according to Mark, a dominant theme is what we must do as followers of Christ. We are to deny ourselves and take up our crosses (Twenty-Fourth Sunday; 8:27–35); make ourselves the last (Twenty-Fifth Sunday; 9:30–37); cut off all that causes us to sin (Twenty-Sixth Sunday; 9:38–43, 45, 47–48); accept the Kingdom of God like a child (Twenty-Seventh Sunday; 10:2–16); sell what we have and give up everything to follow Christ (Twenty-Eighth Sunday; 10:17–30); and be the slave of all (Twenty-Ninth Sunday; 10:35–45). These Gospel accounts remind us of what is perhaps the largest challenge of Ordinary Time: in our everyday lives, in all that we do, "to animate the world with the spirit of Christianity" and "to be witnesses to Christ in all circumstances" (GS, 43).

The Sundays of November, then, offer us meaning amid the shortening days. As the skies darken earlier and earlier, we are reminded that the skies will also darken at the Second Coming of Christ (Thirty-Third Sunday; 13:24–32), which is highlighted by Christ, King of the Universe, a solemnity whose eschatological readings remind us that the Kingdom of the Son of Man is not of this world.

Of course, Ordinary Time extends through weekdays too because "the weeks unfold under the influence of the Sundays that begin them" (P. Jounel, "The Year" in *The Liturgy and Time, ed. Martimort*, vol. 4, p. 27). In addition to the ferial days, there are other weekday moments that invite us to reflect on God's presence in the events of our lives. Personal and parish patron feast days, the remembrance of our beloved dead and departed at All Saints and All Souls' Day, and giving thanks to God on Thanksgiving Day are all moments by which we sanctify the year, especially when we gather together as one Church to receive the Eucharist.

When we celebrate these days throughout the week and keep the Lord's Day holy, we avoid the "dichotomy between the faith which many profess and the practice of their daily lives" (GS, 43). Our lives then become lives of prayer and praise without ceasing throughout this longest season of the liturgical year.

The Sounds of the Season

Following the Solemnity of Pentecost, we celebrate the Solemnities of the Most Holy Trinity and the Most Holy Body and Blood of Christ. Although in many of our communities the early weeks of June mark a shift into a lighter summer mode, be sure to give these celebrations their musical due because they are very important moments.

On the solemnity of the Most Holy Body and Blood of Christ, be aware that there is an option to sing the sequence, Lauda Sion. An excellent setting is available from World Library Publications: Richard Proulx's arrangement of "Praise, O Zion" utilizing Alan Hommerding's translation paired with the familiar tune TANTUM ERGO (WLP 8739).

Due to varied and legitimate reasons, many choral ensembles go on summer hiatus after the Solemnity of the Body and Blood of Christ. While this may be necessary in some locations, the music should never come to a complete halt. We cannot authentically catechize those in music ministry and model for our colleagues on the parish staff the importance of music's contribution to the liturgy if we ourselves are so willing to shut off the organ, or close the piano lid, from mid-June through September. What does doing otherwise suggest? At the very least, a combination of an organist (or other instrumentalist) and cantor should be present to lead, support, and encourage the assembly in their sung prayer. Perhaps, instead of having the entire choral ensemble take off for the summer, you may experiment with having a quartet, men's schola, women's schola, or some other varied combination drawn from the regular ensemble(s) to be present throughout the summer months. This may take some effort in terms of imagination and scheduling, but doing so will speak volumes as to the degree and importance of music's unique service to the liturgy. We are not just church musicians September through June but rather pastoral musicians 365 days of the year. We are called to serve our parish communities throughout the course of the year! Establishing smaller choral ensembles and thinking outside the box will serve your communities well and even serve your musicians well by affording them the opportunity to continue music study and further develop their talents and craft.

This time of year also provides a good opportunity to introduce new hymns and ritual music. If introducing a new hymn to the core repertoire, consider using the tune as a prelude or postlude for a few weeks before introducing it to the assembly. Once you do introduce it, try to use it for a few weeks so that the assembly gets the chance to truly know and own the piece. This way, they can sing it with full enthusiasm and transform it into prayer. The same rule of thumb applies to any new ritual music: use whatever it is throughout the summer and into the fall.

Be sure to get some well-deserved rest in order to recharge yourself for the busy fall months. Try to get as much preparation done over the slower summer months as you can. This may seem like a lot of work, but tackling it during a quieter time of year will reduce the stress you will face if trying to prepare in the fall when everything starts up fully.

The fall months also bring about the annual push for new recruits. Ask your current choristers to invite someone they may know or hear singing in the pews at Mass to come to choir. Consider having an open rehearsal in order to provide prospective choristers a glimpse into the workings of the choir. Develop well-worded and interesting press releases for your bulletin and local newspaper. Use social media sites to help get the word out to the community that you are looking for additional singers. Use your parish's website as well. Contact your local AGO and NPM chapter. Does your parish community have a parochial school or local community music school? Communication with the music teacher may yield additional singers for various choral ensembles. Advertise in all these varied media a few weeks before the start of your choral season.

The Look of the Season

In addition to the liturgical space that is common to every faith community, there are one or more auxiliary spaces that provide for the various ministries associated with that community.

The parish office is primarily a workplace, and the level of busyness doesn't usually need much by way of environment apart from the requisite furnishings and equipment. Some artistic items can, however, enhance the ambiance and contribute a measure of hospitality and joy.

It is fairly common for the main parish office, the one where people come to do parish business, to display a framed photo of the pope and one of the local bishop. A framed photo of the current pastor is less common, though some parishes like to honor former pastors with their portraits or photos.

A simple crucifix in a prominent place is always appropriate. Some image of the patron saint of the parish—for example, a painting, mosaic, or sculpture—can be placed in a waiting area.

Typically, Catholic school classrooms display a wall-mounted crucifix. These are readily available from religious goods suppliers; usually every room has the same one. There are creative options, though. The teachers could research local artists, perhaps among the students or parents, and commission them to design and fabricate a crucifix for each classroom.

An image of the patron of the school or parish can be given a place of honor in the classroom. On the feast day, if the patron is a saint, that image could be placed in a prayer corner and used as the focal point for prayer on that day.

Parish meeting rooms can be good spaces to display works of art. If the parish is part of a merged arrangement with other parishes, the meeting rooms can be excellent places to display artifacts from the closed parish facilities. These items should be clearly identified as to their source and the connection that they have had with a previous site or community. Every meeting room should include a cross, with or without a corpus affixed; it could be wall mounted or free standing. Framed religious themed art prints, or originals if resources allow, is suitable. If the meeting room is used for a particular purpose on a regular basis, for example, for Christian initiation gatherings, a simple prayer corner can be set up as a permanent arrangement. This is a good place to make use of last year's Paschal candle.

Simple seasonal items can be included. For example, a fabric swag over the doorways during Advent and Lent and Christmas decorations for the Christmas season. If round-table gatherings occur from time to time, consider a simple centerpiece of spring flowers during the Easter season. Of course, making these arrangements happen requires that someone be both willing and responsible; it is a good ministry for the person who doesn't want to be on a committee but would like to offer her or his talents to bring delight to others.

Some parishes designate the meeting rooms using the names of popular saints (a good exercise for a few folks to decide who this includes). Some image, a painting or sculpture of that saint, can be displayed on the wall or on a pedestal in the room. One trend today is to commission a series of icons depicting those saints; the icons can be attached on the door of each room.

Perhaps the primary difference between the vestibule of the church and that in the ministry center is that the first is a liturgical space and the latter is more functional. There is a marked difference in the size of the vestibule in older and newer churches. Most older churches had a simple vestibule that was primarily intended to be a weather-break, providing a transition space between the outdoors and the main body of the church. The space was not intended for gathering and had very little, if any, room for furnishings or art pieces. In more recently constructed and renovated churches, there are gathering spaces, some quite large, that offer more possibilities for specific types of environment.

As a liturgical space, the vestibule is a place of hospitality: the place where greeters can be stationed and where various activities can be held to enhance the bonds of community. As a ritual space, this is where wedding parties gather before the ceremony, where catechumens wait to be called to the baptismal font, where funeral processionals are formed and where mourners bid farewell, and where the entrance rites of Palm Sunday can take place.

These various uses need to be considered so that the environment is both suitable and welcoming. Seasonal drapery can be placed over the portal to the main body of the church for Advent, Lent, and Easter. A large cross, possibly the same one used for the Adoration of the Cross can be in this area during the seasons of Lent and Easter. In other liturgical seasons, live plants and fresh flower arrangements are always appropriate.

A large and well-crafted sculpture of the patron of the parish, if one is not present in the main body of the church, can find an honored place in the gathering area. Some parishes place a well-designed lectern in this space. This can display the Book of the Gospels before it is carried in procession at Sunday liturgies. On other days it might hold a large Bible. It could also hold the Book of the Names of the Dead during November. In each of these scenarios, a simple seasonal arrangement as well as a candle stand can be placed adjacent to the lectern.

Other items that could find a home in the gathering space might include a bulletin board for announcements of parish events—or a large TV monitor for this purpose—or a photo collage of first Communion candidates, Confirmation candidates, catechumens, wedding couples, etc. It is important to remember that the gathering area is primarily a place that allows members and visitors to mingle and interact with each other. Furnishings and other items should be kept to a minimum to avoid unnecessary clutter and to provide a hospitable environment for everyone. The vestibule of the ministry center will vary in size from one parish to another. The amount of space available will determine what environment can be arranged.

Some of the items mentioned for the gathering area of the church could be replicated in this space. For example, items that reflect the liturgical season, bulletin board displays of parish events, or, if the resources allow, a large-screen monitor that offers all manner of information about the life of the parish. If the ministry center comprises of many rooms, make sure that there is helpful signage for everyone, including the necessary information on accessibility.

In all of these spaces, the most important part of the environment is the people who minister in them: the parish receptionist, the liturgical greeters, teachers and catechists, meeting facilitators, the custodian and the security personnel. A friendly smile, a cheerful greeting, a respectful attitude, all make the experience of those who occupy these spaces even more pleasant than a vase of flowers or a box of chocolates.

Evangelizing the Parish through the Season

The bulk of the Church's liturgy falls into the long season of Ordinary Time. We count away the weeks, following along in the Lectionary as God interacts with his chosen people, sends prophets and calls them to justice. We listen in as Jesus proclaims the Gospel in Word and in deed, making God's reign visible wherever he goes. And we listen to the early Christian leaders work out what Jesus' teaching, his life and his death and Resurrection mean for how communities that follow him should live.

All of this is part of the long process by which God evangelizes the world. God has reached out to people in particular times and places throughout human history, and they have had to struggle to consider what that Word called them to do. This year, we will again work our way through this season, counting down the weeks as we go. As we do this, we should remember just how strange this all is and try to see it with new eyes—the eyes of the neophyte.

The liturgy brings words, structure, action, and even time together to speak this Word of God anew. As we approach the liturgy with new eyes, we may notice the strangeness of it all, but how do we help the newcomer to enter into the strangeness? Some Christian communities have chosen to change the liturgy to make it simpler. But this is not really an option for Catholics. So what to do? Like learning a foreign language, the best way to be able to hear the liturgy is to build experience of it in the company of generous hosts and in a variety of settings.

Your parish may already have people who keep an eye out for newcomers and sit with them, helping them to find things in the worship resource or hymnal. You probably have sheets with the people's words, perhaps left over from the 2011 Missal retranslation (keep in mind these are still useful as we welcome new Christians, new Catholics, returning Catholics, and visitors). These are excellent starting points. And certainly, the personal aspect of someone noticing new people and providing whatever help they need is particularly important. Maybe your parish has someone who leads tours of the space after the Mass—this can provide an opportunity for a kind of mystagogy as people reflect on what they experienced there. Maybe your priest regularly preaches not just on the lessons or on the seasons but breaks open the liturgical actions. Maybe you gather for the Liturgy of the Hours during the week, offering a different window into the liturgical actions of the Church, and giving people space for quiet and for prayer with the psalms.

Whatever your parish does to open doors into the liturgy for people, these are truly works of evangelization that serve newcomers, those who have been distant from the Church, and those who are there daily. The liturgy calls all of us to listen for God's Word, to receive it in the sacraments, and to be changed by the patterns of engaging with time, feasting and fasting, listening, repentance, and joy.

Worship Committee Agenda for Ordinary Time during Summer

Meeting Time

Members of the committee should begin to meet in the early spring to prepare the parish liturgies for Ordinary Time during Summer.

Goals for Meeting

- Determine how the Solemnity of the Holy Trinity, occurring when Ordinary Time "picks up" again, and the Solemnity of the Body and Blood of Christ will be emphasized and celebrated.
- What public devotions—perhaps to Mary, the saints, or Solemn Exposition of the Blessed Sacrament—take place for the parish or school? Who is responsible for planning and implementing these devotions?
- How will the parish music ministry plan to continue, even with smaller groups of volunteer singers, while the choir is on summer hiatus? Can the assembly learn a new hymn or two this summer, to add freshness and joy to their repertoire?
- How does the worship committee plan to support the volunteers who will do the music ministry at Vacation Bible School? Could the "official" music ministry offer music and some simple guidelines, so that "VBS" truly evangelizes through music?

Seasonal Questions and Initiatives (Meeting #1)

- The little things provide richness to the worship space: could families volunteer to contribute to the worship environment, with basic instruction and minimal oversight? Can volunteers bring out a nuanced Ordinary Time environment, using the *Guide for Ministers of the Liturgical Environment* (LTP, The Liturgical Ministry Series)?
- Regarding the celebration of the Body and Blood of Christ (Corpus Christi), is there a special litany or prayer to publish for the assembly? What about a procession (and is the bishop's permission needed)? Ask: how would a procession evangelize the local neighborhood community? Is there parish interest in joining a diocesan procession? Who will take photos to share online?
- Churches often welcome visitors and guests in summer. Can the announcements be eliminated at the end of Mass (people might read the bulletin more intentionally), and visitors in the congregation be recognized and blessed? "Pioneer" this idea at the most crowded Mass and determine in the fall if the assembly felt a longing for the return of the announcements.

Liturgical Catechesis for the Worship Committee

Provide electronic copies for all members and encourage a thoughtful rereading of the *Constitution on the Sacred Liturgy* (CSL). Its wisdom and clarity continue to instruct, and possibly even surprise, considering that the document was promulgated in 1963.

Liturgical Catechesis for the Assembly

- Is it time to create some short "infomercials" for the parish website? Consider one or two persons, provide them with a short script, and begin filming. Even an unseasoned "performer" can accomplish this with a good script. Topics such as (what is . . .) Liturgy of the Word with Holy Communion, the Sacrament of Confirmation for Youth, A Seasonal Shrine (use Peter Mazar's *To Crown the Year*, 2nd ed.), and The Role of an Extraordinary Minister of Holy Communion will interest the assembly. Think of other topics that people often ask questions about. LTP offers many resources for review, crafting a script using this information.
- Every month of the year, not only May and October, offers a significant celebration of the Blessed Mother. Learn, name, and publish these special days of Mary.

Closing Prayer

- Proclaim Ephesians 1:3–14, found on the Fifteenth Sunday in Ordinary Time, or from the Mass for Giving Thanks to God for the Gift of Human Life. Ask each member to share a gift of life that is evident to them. Conclude with any part of the Universal Prayer Attributed to Pope Clement XI, located in appendix VI of *The Roman Missal*.

Worship Committee Agenda for Ordinary Time during Fall

Meeting Time

Members of the committee should begin to meet in the late spring or early summer to prepare the parish liturgies for Ordinary Time during fall.

Goal for the Meeting

- Reenergize the worship committee, welcome new members, send a special thank-you gift (such as a *Year of Grace* calendar from LTP) to those members who are retiring from the worship committee.
- Make certain that the parish catechists are honored with a blessing on Catechetical Sunday in September.
- Thanksgiving (US) is Thursday, November 26. Plan now for a blessing of the Thanksgiving food, and connect a food drive with the Preparation of the Gifts at Mass (and the collection today goes to the local food pantry).
- Anticipate Advent—now or at another meeting? Schedule with sensitivity!

Opening Prayer

- The prayers for Thanksgiving are found in the Proper of Saints in *The Roman Missal*: pray the Collect as the opening prayer for the meeting.
- Provide copies of the Apostles' Creed and recite together. Light a candle in front of each committee member and read Romans 8:28–39 (as used in the RCIA) to remind members that we are created as images of Christ.

Seasonal Questions and Initiatives

- Retrieve notes, photos, and electronic catechetical materials and review activity of the worship committee from the previous year.
- Looking toward the Solemnity of All Saints on Monday, November 1, who will create the catechesis for understanding this day and also publicize the Mass schedule well in advance? Since this solemnity falls on Monday, would a simple supper "for all of the saints in the parish" build community after the evening Mass?
- How will the worship space reflect the increasing darkness of the days of late fall and the deepening colors of green in Ordinary Time?
- How will those who died and were buried from the parish this year be celebrated and lifted up for prayer?
- Decide what can be done to emphasize the end of the liturgical year, without pushing too quickly for the season of Advent.

Liturgical Catechesis for the Worship Committee

- Spend a half hour in dialogue, regarding summer's "homework": what surprised you or what did you discover as "new" in the *Constitution on the Sacred Liturgy* (CSL)? Use a similar criteria to share new learnings from the Scripture reading of Luke's Infancy Narratives.
- What did the worship committee learn from celebrating Ordinary Time last year that could be of assistance in preparing the end of Ordinary Time this year? Use notes and photos, if available, from the previous year's archived data.

Liturgical Catechesis for the Assembly

- Make available two copies per family of His Mercy Endures Forever: Encountering God's Mercy in the Mass (LTP, in English). Encourage "supper and sharing" on Sunday evenings for a month, using this as a resource. Discover how many families take advantage of this opportunity to gather as faithful witnesses to the mercy of God.
- Schedule and host a Fall Update for all liturgical ministers, "Liturgy and Lunch," and scout the diocese for a guest speaker to renew and energize the ministries represented. Make sure that there is a supply of books for all liturgical ministers, as gift, from The Liturgical Ministry Series, published in English and in Spanish by LTP.

Closing Prayer

- Invite a priest, deacon, or layperson to preside over the closing prayer and offer order of blessing for those who exercise pastoral service (it's found in the Book of Blessings). After the final blessing, offer each person on the worship committee a copy of *Sourcebook* 2022, to support their work and ministry to the parish.

MON 24 LM #572A / LMC #193–232 / white
Memorial of the Blessed Virgin Mary, Mother of the Church

About Today's Memorial

Today's memorial is the newest observance on the calendar. It is obligatory and was established on February 11, 2018. It occurs each year the Monday after Pentecost and recognizes Mary as the Mother of the Church.

Scripture Insights

Mary is the mother of the living, the new Eve. The early followers of Jesus were one with her in prayer.

Preaching Points

Parish Masses

- Mary is an image and model for the Church.
- Mary points to the redemption of the entire Church.
- Mary is worthy of honor and devotion.

Masses with Children

Reflect with the children about how they feel about their own mother or a mother figure; note examples about what their mother does for them. Compare this to how Mary cared for Jesus throughout his life. Jesus gave the Church—us—Mary to pray for us and guide us. We can look to Mary as a role model—our mother—and ask her to relay our prayers to God.

Missal Options

- The readings for the memorial: Although they are designated as LM #572A, the readings are not found in the current LM. Because of this, the USCCB has prepared PDFs in both English and Spanish that may be used. Be sure to place the printouts in a ritual binder. You may refer to this website for the readings: http://www.usccb.org/about/divine-worship/liturgical-calendar/mother-of-the-church.cfm).
- Use the votive Mass #10/B: Blessed Virgin Mary, Our Lady, Mother of the Church. The Preface is found on the pages for this Mass.
- Since today is not only about Mary but about our redemption as well, consider offering the sprinkling rite.

Song of the Day

"*Salve Regina*" in English or Latin (available in most Catholic hymnals)

TUE 25 LM #348 / LMC #193–232 / green
Weekday

Optional Memorials of St. Bede the Venerable, Priest and Doctor of the Church / white; St. Gregory VII, Pope / white; St. Mary Magdalene de'Pazzi, Virgin / white

Scripture Insights

God does not play favorites with his beloved children, and believing in God does not guarantee a happy or complication-free life. Indeed, those who follow God will experience persecution. In many places in the world, there still exists terrible persecution.

Preaching Points

Parish Masses

- God is wonderful and good, and in his goodness he guides us to worship. God is generous and expects generosity in return.
- Sometimes we need to give up important things or even give up relationships to serve God.

Masses with Children

- God is loving and generous, and he wants us to be loving and generous too. Being loving and generous is one way we say "thank you" to God.
- Sometimes we need to give up important things in order to serve God. God repays us for our generosity!

Missal Options

- Consider using the prayers from the Fourth Sunday in OT.
- Use any of the three forms of the PA.
- Any of the eight Prefaces for OT or the six Common Prefaces may be used.
- You might use EP-II.
- Any OT Collect may be used or adapted to conclude the UP. You might even look at the Collects in the Masses for Various Needs and Occasions for possible concluding prayers.

Song of the Day

"If You Belong to Me" by Bob Hurd (OCP)

Optional Memorials

St. Bede

The Venerable Bede is known as the author of the Ecclesiastical History of the English People, which became an invaluable resource for later historians, and of many works of biblical commentary. Although St. Bede spent his entire adult life a cloistered monk, the light of this "candle of the Church," as St. Boniface called him, shed light on Scripture for men and women across England and Germany.

- The readings may be taken from the SW, #567, CP, CDC, or LMC #297.
- Use the Collect from the PS; the other prayers may be taken from the CDC or the CHMW (For a Monk).
- Consider P-I or P-II of Saints, Preface of Holy Virgins and Religious, or the Preface of Holy Pastors.
- You might use EP-I or EP-II.

St. Gregory VII

Pope Gregory VII clashed with Holy Roman Emperor Henry IV and often with his own bishops in his relentless drive for reform in the Church, and in the end he died in exile. He accepted the division and exile he suffered as the present price of the unity and purity he desired for his beloved Church.

- The readings may be taken from the SW, #568, CP (For a Pope), or LMC #298.
- Use the Collect from the PS; the other prayers may be taken from the CP (For a Pope).
- Consider P-I or P-II of Saints or the Preface of Holy Pastors.
- You might use EP-I or EP-II.

St. Mary Magdalene de'Pazzi

St. Mary Magdalene de'Pazzi was born into wealth in Florence, but her love of Christ and desire to atone for sinners led her to devote her life to contemplation and penance as a Carmelite nun. She learned to mystically unite her own mental and physical sufferings with Christ's passion and taught the novitiates in her care to seek Christ in all circumstances.

- The readings may be taken from the SW, #569, CV, CHMW (For Religious), or LMC #299 or CS (For Religious/LMC).
- Use the Collect from the PS; the other prayers may be taken from the CV (For One Virgin) or from the CHMW (For Religious).
- Consider P-I or P-II of Saints or the Preface of Holy Virgins and Religious.
- You might use EP-II.

WED 26

LM #349 or #570 / LMC #193–232 or #300 / white

Memorial of St. Philip Neri, Priest

Today's Saint

St. Philip Neri (1515–1595) could "read" people's hearts. A confessor and spiritual director, he tried to free others from fear so they could live as God's chosen ones. Through study, prayer, sharing, and music, he invited others to union with Christ and one another through love.

Scripture Insights

A holy people should have a just and caring society. We are called to live lives of service to God and one another. As he stated in the reading, Jesus himself didn't come to rule but to serve his people. We are called to be like him.

Preaching Points

Parish Masses

- A key component of the Wisdom literature is that a wise society is one that meets the needs of the people, especially the most helpless of society. Such a people are rewarded by God and blessed by his favor.
- The King of the Universe is not a king like other kings, nor are the seats next to his like those of other kings. People who follow Jesus must be prepared to walk similar walks to his walk.

Masses with Children

- The Wisdom books of the Bible speak to a just society in which its members care for widows and orphans. Such societies are obedient to God, and God blesses such societies.
- Jesus does not want us to be concerned with seats of honor. Jesus himself is king, yet he came to serve. We too are called to lives of service.

Scripture Insights *(PS)*

Jesus wants us to share in the love of the Father and the Son and to be with him forever. We have nothing to fear.

Preaching Points

Parish Masses

- St. Paul urges the Philippians to focus on what is good, true, and just, because this is where God dwells. What experiences or people in your own life come to mind as you hear St. Paul's litany?
- God loves us even as he loves Christ. Why is it so hard to believe in this love? Is it because, in the words of the old hymn, "love so amazing, so divine / Demands my life, my soul, my all"? (lyric from the hymn, "When I Survey the Wondrous Cross"). Today's large-hearted saint, Philip Neri, knew and shared this amazing love.

Masses with Children

- God is found in all goodness. Today, St. Paul tells us to focus on goodness because that is where you will find God.
- Tell the children about St. Philip Neri. Emphasize that he also tried to invite others to be one with Christ through love. Tie this into the readings of the day.

Missal Options

- The readings may also be taken from the CP or CHMW/CS (For Religious).
- The prayers are proper and found in the PS.
- Presiders may choose from among the three options for the PA.
- You might use EP-II.
- Consider P-I or P-II of Saints, or the Preface of Holy Pastors.

Song of the Day

"Jerusalem, My Happy Home" (various publishers)

THU 27 LM #350 / LMC #193–232 / green Weekday

Optional Memorial of St. Augustine of Canterbury, Bishop / white

Scripture Insights

The Jewish people believed and experienced the wonders of the Lord. They waited for God's promised one, knowing God's goodness. In the person of Jesus Christ, the wonder of the Lord was shown and known fully.

Preaching Points

Parish Masses

- God is filled with greatness and goodness, and he knows his human creation better than they know themselves. He is able to act in our lives and bring us into life.
- Jesus is an image of justice and care of the helpless. The blind man, Bartimaeus, reminds us of the poorest in society—those who cannot provide for themselves. Jesus is moved to help the man, and Bartimaeus is healed.

Masses with Children

- When Jesus heals blindness, we are reminded of our own spiritual blindness. Ask Jesus to help and guide you in the difficult situations of your life.

Missal Options

- Consider using the prayers from the Thirty-Second Sunday in OT.
- Use any of the three forms of the PA.
- Any of the eight Prefaces for OT or the six Common Prefaces may be used.
- You might use EPVN-IV.
- Any OT Collect may be used or adapted to conclude the UP. You might even look at the Collects in the Masses for Various Needs and Occasions for possible concluding prayers.

Song of the Day

"Open My Eyes, Lord" by Jesse Manibussan (OCP)

Optional Memorial

St. Augustine was the first bishop of Canterbury and the founder of the Church in England, following a commission from Pope St. Gregory the Great. Augustine sought permission from King Ethelbert to evangelize in the south of England and sought to draw people to the light of Christ through the message of salvation for all, while affirming all that was good in their own traditions.

- The readings are from the SW, #571, CP (For Missionaries), or LMC #301.
- Use the Collect from the PS; the other prayers may be taken from the CP (For Missionaries or For a Bishop).
- You might use EP-I.
- Consider P-I or P-II of Saints, or the Preface of Holy Pastors.

FRI 28 LM #351 / LMC #193–232 / green Weekday

Scripture Insights

God is merciful, and we see his mercy in Jesus. While today's Gospel reading is not a peaceful one, it is a reminder that we put our faith in God who is merciful and filled with justice.

Preaching Points

Parish Masses

- The ancient Jewish people didn't believe in an afterlife but did believe that God's blessings were passed down from generation to generation. Through Scripture and tradition the Church understands God's promise of heaven.
- When Jesus saw injustice, he corrected the matter. We too are called to fearlessly seek justice.

Masses with Children

- The ancient Jewish people did not understand heaven in the same sense that we understand heaven. They did believe blessings could pass down generations.
- Do you ever see people treated unjustly? Deep down we can tell when something or someone is being treated badly. It is our job to stand up for what is just, right, and good.

Missal Options

- Consider using the prayers from the MPVN-1/D.
- Use any of the three forms of the PA.
- Any of the eight Prefaces for OT or the six Common Prefaces may be used.
- You might use EP-II.
- Any OT Collect may be used or adapted to conclude the UP. You might even look at the Collects in the Masses for Various Needs and Occasions for possible concluding prayers.

Song of the Day

"Faith of Our Fathers" (various publishers)

Optional Memorials of St. Paul VI, Pope / white; Blessed Virgin Mary / white

Scripture Insights

Jesus taught by God's authority, and the wise submit themselves to his authority. How do we submit ourselves to Christ's authority? How does it affect our lives and our decisions? How does it change or impact the world around us?

Preaching Points

Parish Masses

- Wisdom is frequently portrayed as a woman in the Wisdom literature. The reading reminds us that we are called to seek God's wisdom and delight in it.
- Jesus taught by God's authority. Jesus and the Father are one, and he carries out the will of the Father. The chief priests, elders, and scribes frequently tried to trick Jesus with questions, hoping he would blaspheme in reply.

Masses with Children

- Wisdom is sometimes portrayed as a woman in the Bible. What does it mean to understand God's wisdom and delight in it?
- Jesus and the Father are both God; they are united in all they are and in all they do. Some people tried to trick Jesus into blasphemy so they could find him guilty.

Missal Options

- Consider using the prayers from the Thirtieth Sunday in Ordinary Time.
- Use any of the three forms of the PA.
- Any of the eight Prefaces for OT or the six Common Prefaces may be used.
- You might use EP-III.
- Any OT Collect may be used or adapted to conclude the UP. You might even look at the Collects in the Masses for Various Needs and Occasions for possible concluding prayers.

Song of the Day

"Wisdom Has Built a House" by Lucien Deiss (WLP)

Optional Memorials

St. Paul VI

Italian-born Pope Paul VI succeeded Pope John XXIII, who died in the midst of the Second Vatican Council. Closing the Second Vatican Council, Paul VI was instrumental in implementing and launching the changes called for by the Council Fathers, such as the revision of the liturgical books. It was he who officially named Mary as the Mother of the Church, emphasized the preferential option for the poor, and defined that the Church's primary function is to evangelize. Paul VI was canonized by Pope Francis on October 14, 2018.

- In the January–February 2019 BCDW Newsletter, it was announced that Pope Francis requested that Pope St. Paul VI was to be added to the General Roman Calendar on May 29 as an optional memorial.
- As of now, proper texts in English and Spanish have yet to be prepared.
- In the meantime, if the optional memorial is celebrated, use the Common of Pastors: For a Pope.
- The readings may be from the SW, LMC, or CP (For a Pope). The Holy See recommends #571A from the Common of Pastors.
- Additional information is found on the USCCB website: www.USCCB.org/paulvi.

Blessed Virgin Mary

Refer to page 66 under "Optional Memorial" for liturgical suggestions.

S U N **30** LM #165B / LMC #159B / white

Solemnity of the Most Holy Trinity

About Today's Solemnity

The essential component of being in relationship with our Trinitarian God is to allow that relationship to impact all that we say and do. To be disciples of the Lord is to live according to Jesus' values and lifestyle and to model for others what relationship with God entails. Our mission is to do for others what Jesus had done for us, in both his words and his deeds, but most especially in his loving outreach to all. Blessed are we for having been chosen to be apostolic witnesses to all.

Scripture Insights

Scripture contains no philosophically mature doctrine of the Trinity; the word itself never appears. The reality of the Trinity lies deeply embedded in the New Testament and emerged over time. Painstakingly, the Church discerned and taught from Scripture the only doctrine adequate to the witness of both Testaments: that the one God of biblical Israel at the heart of creation and redemption is a reality of three persons. It is the mind of the Church interpreting Scripture, and not Scripture alone, that leads us to the truth of salvation.

Still, the best way to begin to learn about the Trinity is to go to Scripture. Who God *is* in heaven above (the deep mystery of God's being) can always be seen in what God *does* on earth below (God's relentless divine activity in the world for the sake of salvation).

In this week's Romans passage, Paul seems to presume three separate, self-aware divine persons in the Holy: Father-God, Christ-Son, and Spirit of God. Those who are led by God's Spirit are God's children, having lost servile fear of God when the Spirit bestows the consciousness of being God's beloved child. This "spirit of adoption" puts our relationship with God on an intimate basis; the Spirit inscribes its reality in our hearts. Paul also suggests that the Spirit's work infuses in us Jesus' own beloved-child relationship to God.

Preaching Points

Parish Masses

- The word *Trinity* does not appear in the Scripture readings, yet we see evidence of our Triune God throughout the Bible. It is through God the Son and the Holy Spirit that we can call on the Father, crying, "Abba!" to our Creator.
- We are made in the image and likeness of God. Our Triune God exists in relationship, and we too are made for relationship. We are not meant to be solitary creatures without community.
- When we share the faith through Baptism, we are following our Lord's instruction. How do we share the faith with others?

Children's Liturgy of the Word

- God is made of three divine persons: the Father, the Son, and the Holy Spirit. The three exist in perfect relationship. Since we are made in God's image and likeness, we are also called to live in community.
- God wants all of us to participate in the life of the Trinity. How do we share our faith with others so that they too can participate in the life of the Trinity?

Missal Options

- The Mass texts, including the Preface, are found at the end of the PT in the section for solemnities and feasts of the Lord.
- You might consider offering the sprinkling rite instead of the PA.
- Sing or recite the Gloria and the Creed.
- Consider using EP-III.

Music Preparation

- For solemnities like today, bring out some traditional favorites. You might consider revamping the style into a more upbeat way.
- Be mindful of the newer hymns and arrangements like John Angotti's "I Send You Out" (WLP). Contemporary songs may become parish favorites.

Music Suggestions

- Gathering: "Holy, Holy, Holy! Lord God Almighty!" (various publishers)
- Preparation of the Gifts: "Holy, Holy, Holy Cry" by Rick Modlin and Genevieve Glen, OSB (OCP)
- Communion: "Doxology" by Ken Canedo (OCP)
- Sending Forth: "All Praise and Glad Thanksgiving" (various publishers)

Mass Texts

Introduction to Mass

We were made that we might know and love God, the source of all things. Jesus Christ, the knowledge of God, unites us to himself in the love of the Holy Spirit, and offers us, with himself, to the Father. This is our joy, our hope, and our salvation, to be children of the living, Triune God. This Eucharist is our prayer of thanksgiving. *My brothers and sisters, let us acknowledge our sins, and so prepare ourselves to celebrate the sacred mysteries.*

Tropes for Penitential Act, Form III

You have made known to us the mystery of salvation:
Lord, have mercy.

Your Spirit cries out from our hearts, for we do not know
how to pray as we ought: Christ, have mercy.

You make us a pleasing sacrifice to the Father:
Lord, have mercy.

Dismissal for Children's Liturgy of the Word

My dear ones, the Holy Spirit lives within you, opening your hearts to receive the Word that Christ speaks to you. Both of them lead you to our Father who loves you as his very own children. Go and listen to them, and afterward we will celebrate together the love of our God.

Dismissal of Catechumens

Dear friends, we know of the Trinity only because God has revealed himself to us, and he has revealed himself because he wants to be in relationship with us. He is now calling you to that same relationship. Open your hearts to his call, and we will pray for the day when you will join us as brothers and sisters in receiving the sacrifice of his Son. Go in peace.

Dismissal of Extraordinary Ministers of Holy Communion

My friends, united in the Spirit to the ailing members of Christ's Body, we send you to them with the Eucharist, their spiritual food. May it strengthen them to rejoice in the Father's love. Go in peace.

Universal Prayer

Our God of love is Father, Son, and Holy Spirit. Doing as he commanded us, we lift up our prayers for the needs of the world.

1. For the Church, that she may be a sign of God's love for the world, embracing diversity and building community, we pray:
2. For leaders of nations who lack love for their people, that they might realize their oneness with those they serve, we pray:
3. For those who are preparing for Baptism and for those who catechize parents in the way of faith, we pray:
4. For families, especially for families who experience brokenness and division, that reconciliation may take place, we pray:
5. For all who mourn the death of a loved one, that they may be consoled by the merciful love of God, we pray:

Loving Father,
you sent your Son into the world
to save us and your Holy Spirit to sanctify us.
You are revealed to us
as a God of perfect relationship: love that knows no end.
May our relationships bear witness
to your presence and dominion in our world.
Through Christ our Lord.
Amen.

Other Rites and Customs

- If you are singing hymns about the Trinity at Mass, be sure to sing the entire hymn, not just the first few verses.
- Celebrate Baptism at Sunday Mass.
- Tomorrow is Memorial Day. Resist the urge to sing patriotic music at Mass. Instead, include prayers for those who have died serving our country in the Universal Prayer.

Liturgy and Life

For a reason we cannot know, God chooses to run the world through human beings. Our Trinitarian God, modeling community for us, continually frees us but also asks us to serve in the Kingdom, healing human community. Still God's Chosen People, our Jewish brothers and sisters are open to service projects done in conjunction with Christians. Join or suggest a joint Jewish-Catholic project in your city.

Taking Place This Week . . .

Consider what can be done liturgically, catechetically, and ministerially to respond to these important needs.

- World No Tobacco Day (5/31)
- Tomorrow is Memorial Day.
- Global Day of Parents (6/1)
- In some countries, Corpus Christi is celebrated on Thursday, June 3.
- World Day for Child Victims of Aggression (6/4)
- World Environment Day (6/5)
- First Friday (6/4) and First Saturday (6/5)
- June is African American Music Appreciation and National Safety Month.
- June is traditionally celebrated as the Month of the Most Sacred Heart.

MON **31** LM #572 / LMC #302 / white

Feast of the Visitation of the Blessed Virgin Mary

About Today's Feast

Luke places a canticle on Mary's lips as she visits her cousin Elizabeth. Mere prose would miss the mark for such a momentous occasion. Mary expresses in song her great joy in God. She was not able to respond to the angel Gabriel with the same amount of exuberance. Possibly it was Elizabeth's beautiful greeting that elicited such a poetic response. On this day, we join ourselves to Mary in proclaiming the greatness of the Lord. Like Mary, our spirits rejoice in God our Savior.

Scripture Insights *(PS)*

The greatness of God's great work was known to God, the angels, and the two women who embraced joyfully at Elizabeth and Zechariah's Judah home. We, the hearers of the Word, are held in sheer joy at their greeting and their recognition of the miracles taking place in their bodies.

Preaching Points

Parish Masses

- Elizabeth, pregnant with John the Baptist, and the Virgin Mary, pregnant with Jesus, visit together as the angel instructed Mary. The tiny babies growing in their wombs were together for the first time, and their lives began intertwining and preparing for their roles in God's plan for salvation.
- In today's Gospel reading, we find fulfillment of Zephaniah's words.

Masses with Children

- John the Baptist was a baby growing in Elizabeth's womb, and Jesus was the baby growing in Mary's womb. John the Baptist leapt for joy in his mother's womb when Mary spoke her greeting. John the Baptist already loved Jesus.
- The Hail Mary prayer from the Rosary is based on the Gospel reading. We repeat Elizabeth's words when we pray the Hail Mary.
- Long before Jesus was born, prophets told the people about Jesus and his earthly life. Zephaniah's words come to fruition in today's Gospel reading.

Missal Options

- The readings and prayers are proper and found in the PS.
- The Gloria is sung; however, the Creed is omitted.
- Any Collect from OT may be used to conclude the UP.
- Use P-II of the BVM and consider EP-III.
- The SB for the Virgin Mary may be used (#10).

Song of the Day

"Magnificat" by Alan J. Hommerding (WLP)

Other Rites and Customs

Hours: Use the Proper Psalter from the PS.

TUE **1** LM #354 or #574 / LMC #193–232 or #304 / red

Memorial of St. Justin, Martyr

Today's Saint

St. Justin, also called Justin Martyr (c. 100–165), was born in Judea and raised pagan by parents who were probably Greek or Roman. He studied philosophy, converted to Christianity, and spent his life teaching and writing. Justin's life ended in Rome, where he was martyred under Marcus Aurelius. He is one of the first Christian apologists and one of the first to employ philosophy as a tool toward greater understanding of revelation.

Scripture Insights

We are God's people, and we know well what he expects of us. We are called to echo his love in our own lives, living out his love through service and justice for those who are poor and suffering in our society.

Preaching Points

Parish Masses

- The psalm calls us to contribute to the justice for the poor and to strive to comprehend wisdom through fear of the Lord. Wisdom and justice are inexorably linked.
- Trying to trick Jesus, the Pharisees and Herodians questioned Jesus about taxes. Jesus' reply reminds us of what we need to render unto God, namely, love, service, kindness, and justice.

Masses with Children

- A wise society cares for the poor, and those who are wise seek justice for the poor and suffering. When we say we fear God, it isn't a definition of fear that means frightened but one that means respect.
- Jesus was never tricked by those who tried to make him blaspheme. In today's reading we are reminded that Caesar's picture is on the coins but that we render to God everything he requires of us: love, service, kindness, and justice.

Scripture Insights *(PS)*

We are not to hide away from the world, even though the sign of our faith, the cross, is incomprehensible without faith.

Preaching Points

Parish Masses

- Christians are not meant to live in enclaves with other Christians but to live in the midst of a diverse world. To the extent that we reflect the Christ whom we follow, we will be lights in darkness, the flavor of salt in insipid food.
- The cross is contradiction. It makes no sense by human standards. And yet, for those who believe, the cross is not weakness but strength, not foolishness but divine wisdom. We need to stay close to Christ's contradictory cross.

Masses with Children

- Tell the children about St. Justin.
- Christians are not meant to live with only like-minded people, that is, just among other Christians. We are to live in the world and tell other people about Jesus. We help others to understand what it means to be Christian and follow Jesus by the way we live our lives.
- The cross can be difficult to take upon ourselves. But, it gives us strength. We should always stay close to Jesus' cross. Make the connection about bearing the cross to St. Justin's martyrdom.

Missal Options

- The prayers are proper and found in the PS.
- You may also use the readings from the CM.
- Consider P-I or P-II of Saints, or P-I or P-II of Holy Martyrs.
- You might use EP-I.
- Any OT Collect may be used or adapted to conclude the UP.

Song of the Day

"Quietly Peacefully" by Lori True (GIA)

WED 2 Weekday

LM #355 / LMC #193–232 / green

Optional Memorial of Sts. Marcellinus and Peter, Martyrs / red

Scripture Insights

God is a God of mercy and goodness, and he brings us to wellness in virtue. He calls us to goodness and holiness and assists us in that call in our lives. We live in the Lord and through him.

Preaching Points

Parish Masses

- Again resisting the trickery of those who wished to harm him, Jesus answers the questions of the Sadducees, explaining that the question of whose wife a widow may be isn't the most important question about God and that in death people aren't married. The resurrection is real, and God's children live in peace at the resurrection.
- God hears our prayers and answers them. Even when we do not feel his presence, he is with each of his children.

Masses with Children

- The Sadducees tried to trick Jesus with their questions, but Jesus helped them understand more about God and God's ways. He taught the Sadducees that they didn't need to be concerned about marriage in the resurrection.
- God is with each of his children. He hears our prayers and answers them. Sometimes we might feel very close to God, and other times we might feel like he is far away. He is with us always.

Missal Options

- Consider using the prayers from the MPVN-6/1.
- Use any of the three forms of the PA.
- Any of the eight Prefaces for OT or the six Common Prefaces may be used.
- You might use EP-II.
- Any OT Collect may be used or adapted to conclude the UP. You might even look at the Collects in the Masses for Various Needs and Occasions for possible concluding prayers.

Song of the Day

"We Gather Together" (various publishers)

Optional Memorial

Sts. Marcellinus and Peter were martyred under Diocletian and memorialized by Pope Damasus. Marcellinus, a priest, and Peter, an exorcist, are reputed to have faced death with so much courage that their jailor and his family were all converted by their witness.

- The readings may be taken from the SW, #575, CM, or LMC #305.
- The Collect is from the PS; other prayers are from the CM (For Several Martyrs). Use the seasonal Collect to conclude the UP.
- Use any of the OT Collects to conclude the UP.
- Select from P-I or P-II of Saints, or P-I or P-II of Holy Martyrs.

THU **3** LM #356 or #576 / LMC #193–232 or #306 / red

Memorial of St. Charles Lwanga and Companions, Martyrs

Today's Saint

St. Charles Lwanga was martyred alongside twenty-one other Christian pages in the court of Ugandan King Mwanga II for resisting the king's immoral lifestyle, enraging Mwanga, and undermining his absolute authority over his subjects. Lwanga, a catechist, baptized his catechumens in preparation for execution, and together they were burned alive, steadfast in faith to the end.

Scripture Insights

We ask God for his love and mercy and prayerfully petition for his help in our lives. We are called to give the love and mercy that echoes that of God.

Preaching Points

Parish Masses

Loving God and loving our neighbors are Jesus' commandments and the essence of his teaching during his earthly ministry. When we prioritize love of God and neighbor, communities and societies are healthier places; they echo God's justice.

Masses with Children

The two greatest commands are to love God and love our neighbors. When we live in this way, we are living out Jesus' commands.

Scripture Insights *(PS)*

God's holy ones suffer for the sake of their faith because they believe in the resurrection.

Preaching Points

Parish Masses

- The seven brothers and their mother—like so many other martyrs before and since—are willing to die rather than betray their religious practice. Few of us are asked to give witness to the point of death, but all of us can give witness in other ways. Are we willing to suffer—even a little—for our faith?
- For the saints, heaven isn't just a distant goal—the hope of heaven motivates their actions. How often do we contemplate the Kingdom of God? How can the hope of bringing the Kingdom of God to fruition inspire our daily life?

Masses with Children

- Tell the children about St. Charles Lwanga.
- Dying for Christ isn't common. Few of us are asked to do this. But we can suffer, just a little, to be true to our faith.

Missal Options

- The readings may also be from the CM.
- The prayers are proper and are found in the PS.
- You might use EP-II.
- Use any of the three forms of the PA.
- Consider using any of the OT Collects to conclude the UP.
- Select from P-I or P-II of Saints, or P-I or P-II of Holy Martyrs.

Song of the Day

"I Am the Bread of Life" by Suzanne Toolan, RSM (GIA)

FRI **4** LM #357 / LMC #193–232 / green

Weekday

Scripture Insights

Sometimes people deliberately misunderstand a question or instruction. Tobit continuously looked to understand God and his ways, and scribes frequently looked to misunderstand Jesus. We should look to understand God and his ways.

Preaching Points

Parish Masses

In the First Reading, we hear that Tobit had cataracts peeled from his eyes and regained eyesight. How can we seek clearer vision of God and his ways? How can we more deeply understand and live out the Gospel?

Masses with Children

- Cataracts are body tissue that can grow on a person's eyes and cause blindness. In the Book of Tobit we hear how the cataracts are peeled from Tobit's eyes. How are we blinded to the world around us? How can we more clearly see the Gospel so we can live out Jesus' teachings?
- In the Bible there are many lists of descendants; Jesus' many-times-great-grandfather was King David. We say he is "from the line of David."

Missal Options

- Consider using the prayers from the Twelfth Sunday in Ordinary Time.
- Use any of the three forms of the PA.
- Any of the eight Prefaces for OT or the six Common Prefaces may be used.
- You might use EP-II.
- Any OT Collect may be used or adapted to conclude the UP. You might even look at the Collects in the Masses for Various Needs and Occasions for possible concluding prayers.

Song of the Day

- "Amazing Grace" (various publishers)
- When singing "Amazing Grace" be sure to change the line "saved a wretch like me" to "saved and set us free." This change reflects Catholic theology more accurately.

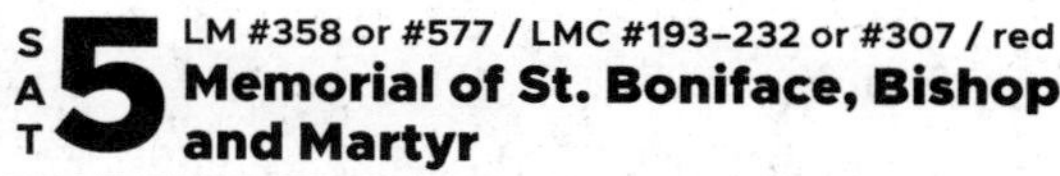

LM #358 or #577 / LMC #193–232 or #307 / red

Memorial of St. Boniface, Bishop and Martyr

Today's Saint

St. Boniface was an Anglo-Saxon monk and bishop who evangelized in Germany with such success that he was able to reform the Frankish Church with his monks, and he died while ministering to lapsed Christians in Friesland. His often-dramatic efforts succeeded in uniting Christians across the area in a common church and spread monasteries as centers of education across Germany and France.

Scripture Insights

At all times we are under God's ever-loving and watchful eye. What we choose to do in his name doesn't go unnoticed. Tobit and Sarah's deeds and the donation from the poor widow are known to our Lord; our deeds too are known.

Preaching Points

Parish Masses

- According to Catholic teaching, we are called give based on what others need, not according to what is comfortable to ourselves.

Masses with Children

- When we do good things for God, as Sarah and Tobit did, we should do them not to show off our faith but to live out Jesus' teaching.

Scripture Insights *(PS)*

This is what Christian leadership looks like: the shepherd who speaks truth to power and lays down his life for his sheep.

Preaching Points

Parish Masses

Before King Agrippa, Paul goes to the core of the Gospel: the Messiah has come, he has died and been raised so that Jews and Gentiles alike may have life in his name. Does the Paschal Mystery—the life, death, and Resurrection of Jesus—change our day-to-day lives?

Masses with Children

Tell the children about what shepherds do. Teach them how our leaders of the faith, parents, teachers, pastors, give their lives for us. This is what sacrifice is and what Jesus did for us.

Missal Options

- The readings may also be taken from the CM or the CP (For Missionaries).
- Use any of the three forms of the PA.
- The Collect is from the PS. The other prayers may be taken from the CM (For One Martyr) or the CP (For Missionaries).
- Select from P-I or P-II of Saints, P-I or P-II of Holy Martyrs, or the Preface of Holy Pastors.
- Consider EP-II.
- Use the seasonal Collect to conclude the UP.

Song of the Day

"Wisdom, My Road" by Leslie Palmer Barnart and arranged by Steven C. Warner (WLP)

S U N **6** LM #168B / LMC #162B / white

Solemnity of the Most Holy Body and Blood of Christ (Corpus Christi)

About Today's Solemnity

As Christians, we are called to share in Christ's life and sacrifice. On this Solemnity of the Most Holy Body and Blood of Christ, traditionally known as Corpus Christi, we delve into Christ's willingness to sacrifice himself for others. God becoming human in Christ was the beginning of a life devoted to others.

Scripture Insights

Blood is life. The people of ancient Israel knew that. They enacted laws against the spilling of blood (see Deuteronomy 19; 21; Leviticus 17) and used blood in rituals to sanctify altars, consecrate priests (see Exodus 29), and seal covenants between God and the people. It is fitting, then, that Jesus talks about his blood as the blood of the covenant. To drink his blood is to sprinkle it on one's heart, just as Moses dashed blood on the people as a sign of their relationship with God.

The Letter to the Hebrews contrasts the Blood of Christ with the blood of the sacrifice for atonement in Leviticus 16. Aaron was forbidden to enter the Holy Place until he had sacrificed a bull to atone for his sins and a goat to atone for the sins of the people. Jesus comes before God by way of his own blood. The blood of the old covenant, says the Letter to the Hebrews, sanctified the body; the blood of the new covenant sanctifies the mind and heart forever.

In the story of the Exodus, Moses sprinkled the blood of a lamb on the doorposts of the Israelites so that the angel of death who came to destroy the firstborn children of Egypt would pass over their houses. In his First Letter to the Corinthians, Paul states: "For our paschal lamb, Christ, has been sacrificed" (1 Corinthians 5:7). In Paul's theology, Christ becomes the means by which we escape the death caused by sin. It is the living sign of Christ's Blood that transforms our lives with grace.

We remember the Last Supper at every liturgy during the Eucharistic Prayer. We tell the full story of the Last Supper during the reading of the Passion on Palm Sunday and in Paul's letter to the Corinthians on Holy Thursday. In the readings for the Solemnity of the Body and Blood of Christ, we ponder the power and depth of Jesus' sacrifice for us. His Blood ratifies and sanctifies our relationship with God, atones for our sin, and protects us from "soul death." When we remember the Last Supper, Jesus' selfless act of love becomes present to us once again so that we can be transformed.

Preaching Points

Parish Masses

- The blood that pulses through our veins is a sign of our living state; without that blood, we die. Christ's Blood is that of the Lamb of God, and it is the blood of the final sacrifice, the only sacrifice needed for our salvation.
- Throughout Scripture, blood has tremendous significance. At the time of the Passover, the blood of the lambs served to protect God's people from the Angel of Death; likewise, Jesus' Blood served to save us from death.

Children's Liturgy of the Word

- Jesus' words in Scripture and the words at the Liturgy of the Eucharist are ancient Jewish prayers. When we participate in the liturgy we remember Jesus' sacrifice for his people and how that sacrifice is connected to the past.
- Christ wants us to receive him in the Eucharist. When we receive the Eucharist we receive the Body, Blood, soul, and divinity of our Lord, who saved us.

Missal Options

- The Mass texts, including the Preface, are found in the PT in the section for solemnities and feasts of the Lord.
- You might consider offering the sprinkling rite instead of the PA.
- Sing or recite the Gloria and the Creed.
- Consider using EP-I.
- You might consider singing the optional sequence, *Lauda sion*, before the Gospel.
- If the procession follows Mass, the normal Concluding Rites are omitted, which means there is no recessional hymn. Before the Prayer after Communion, consider singing a simple Song of Praise.

Music Preparation

- If you are not accustomed to doing the sequence, consider adding it. This is one of three that remain in our liturgies. Use a simple three-line psalm tone or traditional chant and do the short or long version.
- It will be valuable to incorporate music into the procession. Ensure that cantors or a choir are available and rehearsed to lead the music. Short simple refrains or psalms are ideal. Music selection from the Taizé tradition is also easy for an assembly to sing, especially during a procession.

Music Suggestions

- Gathering: "At the Lamb's High Feast" (various publishers)
- Communion: "Called to the Supper of the Lamb" by Alan J. Hommerding and Tony Alonso (WLP), "We Are One Body" by Dana Scallon (Heartbeat Music), or "In Remembrance of You" by Paul Tate (WLP)

Mass Texts

Introduction to Mass

So often do we celebrate the Eucharist that we may forget the wonder and mystery contained in this sacrament. The bread and wine we offer on this altar—the gift of God and the work of human hands—will become for us the true Flesh and Blood of our Lord Jesus Christ, who gave up his life that we might live forever. With renewed awareness and consciences washed clean, let us heed and do all that the Lord has commanded, and so give glory to God. *My brothers and sisters, let us acknowledge our sins, and so prepare ourselves to celebrate the sacred mysteries.*

Tropes for Penitential Act, Form III

You are our great high priest, offering yourself for our sins: Lord, have mercy.

You feed us with finest wheat and honey from the rock: Christ, have mercy.

Your sacrifice obtains for us eternal redemption:
Lord, have mercy.

Dismissal for Children's Liturgy of the Word

Dear children, Christ did not withhold anything in giving himself for us. He did not think of himself, but only of his love for us and our great need for him. As you listen to today's readings, give thanks to Christ and ask him to help you give yourself in love for others. Go in peace.

Dismissal of Catechumens

My friends, Christ is the mediator of a new covenant between us and God. May God's fidelity and the promise of eternal life through the Body and Blood of his Son give you confidence to grow more deeply into this great mystery, until the day when you will join us in receiving this sacrament of salvation. Go in peace.

Dismissal of Extraordinary Ministers of Holy Communion

Dear friends, go to our sick and homebound brothers and sisters and share with them this Living Bread come down from heaven, that with us they will live forever in Jesus Christ our Lord. Go in peace.

Universal Prayer

In preparation for the Bread of Life and Cup of Salvation let us call on the name of the Lord in prayer for the needs of our world.

1. For those in our Church entrusted with the ministry of presiding at the Eucharist, that they may always be willing to die to self, we pray:
2. For nations that do not have enough bread to feed their people and do not have the luxury of sharing wine, we pray:
3. For families who do not eat together regularly, that they may see the grace of sharing food and drink around a common table, we pray:
4. For those who have only recently begun to share in the Eucharistic feast, that they may continue to be drawn into the love of Christ, we pray:
5. For those preparing for their last Communion, that food for the journey may accompany them to heaven, we pray:

Lord Jesus Christ,
you feed us with your Body and Blood
to guide us on our pilgrim way
and to strengthen us in holiness.
May we return to the Father
all that he has given us through you.
Let our lives be broken in humble service
and poured out in love.
May we always be grateful
for the gift of the Eucharist in our lives.
Who live and reign with God the Father in
the unity of the Holy Spirit,
one God, for ever and ever.
Amen.

Other Rites and Customs

- Offer liturgical catechesis on the Holy Eucharist, what it means for the life of the Church, how we receive the Eucharist, and how we become what we receive. Here is a video you can share with the members of your assembly on social media: https://vimeo.com/247171726/419bd6e490.
- Bring Christ to the streets by having a Eucharistic procession.
- Invite back all the children who have received their first Holy Communion to one of the principal Masses followed by a breakfast of reception. Don't extend the invitation for them to rewear their Holy Communion outfits.

Liturgy and Life

Mark's account emphasizes that communion with Jesus includes sharing in his cup of self-sacrifice. As we rejoice in his love, we are called to let it flow through us. Extend Christ's love further afield through Catholic Relief Services. Visit http://crs.org/, and learn about the issues being confronted and the resources being shared by this organization. Make a contribution to their work.

Taking Place This Week . . .

Consider what can be done liturgically, catechetically, and ministerially to respond to these important needs.

- World Oceans Day (6/8)
- World Day Against Child Labor (6/12)

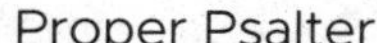

MON 7 LM #359 / LMC #193–232 / green
Weekday

Scripture Insights

Human suffering is not without merit. Grace can come to us in our suffering, and God can help us in the midst of our suffering. What's more, we can act and be of assistance to one another in suffering. Console the grieving, show mercy to others, and forgive debt.

Preaching Points

Parish Masses

- Christ knows our suffering, and in that suffering he can console each of us. Through grace, our suffering can bear fruit in our lives and in the lives of others. We, as a community, share in one another's suffering, and we share in relieving that suffering. Christianity is a communal faith as well as a personally held faith.
- Great things will come for God's people. Such things may not happen in this lifetime, but God's promises may be meant for heaven.
- God rewards his people and has special care for the poor that we too should prioritize.

Masses with Children

- Human suffering is a part of all human life. We are meant not to wallow in suffering but to look to God for consolation. Our friends and family will help us in suffering too. We are called to help one another.
- Along the same lines as "the first shall be last," we learn that those who suffer will be relieved. God rewards his people and has special care for the poor that we too should prioritize.

Missal Options

- Consider using the prayers from the MPVN-30/A/1.
- Use any of the three forms of the PA.
- Any of the eight Prefaces for OT or the six Common Prefaces may be used.
- You might use EPVN-I.
- Any OT Collect may be used or adapted to conclude the UP. You might even look at the Collects in the Masses for Various Needs and Occasions for possible concluding prayers.

Song of the Day

"Lead Me, Lord" by John Becker (OCP)

TUE 8 LM #360 / LMC #193–232 / green
Weekday

Scripture Insights

In Jesus' time, salt was a valuable resource because it was used to preserve and flavor food, and it was needed for the function of human bodies. By calling his people to be salt, Jesus was telling them to live out God's teachings and to be the ones who make changes in our society. We should stand firm in our words, like Jesus himself did when he lived on earth.

Preaching Points

Parish Masses

- God desires for his people to be an inspiration to all people. Our lives are meant to be an example of Jesus' teachings. What would people learn about Christianity from observing each of us? What do you need to change to better model Christ's teachings?
- We must be truthful and stand in our words, as God is truthful and deliberate in his promises.

Masses with Children

- If someone knew nothing of Christianity, they should be able to learn about it by witnessing the actions of Christ's people. What do people learn about Christianity from observing you and your actions?
- How do we effect change in the wider society? How can we be the love of Christ in our families, among our friends, in school, and in our activities?

Missal Options

- Consider using the prayers from the MPVN-10.
- Use any of the three forms of the PA.
- Any of the eight Prefaces for OT or the six Common Prefaces may be used.
- You might use EP-II.
- Any OT Collect may be used or adapted to conclude the UP. You might even look at the Collects in the Masses for Various Needs and Occasions for possible concluding prayers.

Song of the Day

"Christ, Be Our Light" by Bernadette Farrell (OCP)

WED 9 LM #361 / LMC #193–232 / green
Weekday

Optional Memorial of St. Ephrem, Deacon and Doctor of the Church / white

Scripture Insights

In many cases, the letter of the law and the spirit of the law are two different entities. We are called to obey not the letter of God's law but the spirit of it. Following the letter of the law can often stamp out the spirit of the law. We are not free from the law, and we find freedom in the spirit of the law.

Preaching Points

Parish Masses

- God's people are all called to ministry—not only the priests and religious, but all of the baptized. We are called to ministry of the spirit, not of the letter of the law. This reference is to how we obey and follow God; we are meant to live in the spirit of the law and not batter ourselves and others with the letter of the law.
- Jesus did not come in order to cancel out all of the Jewish faith, and he faithfully followed the Jewish law. He did come in order to fulfill the teachings of the faith.

Masses with Children

- By virtue of our Baptism, we are called to ministry in Christ's name. Ministry is for all of God's people, not only the priests and religious. We are meant to minister in the spirit of the law and not in the letter of the law.
- Jesus grew up as a faithful Jewish person. He and his family were subject to Jewish law and followed it. He didn't come to rid us of the Jewish tradition but to fulfill the Jewish tradition.

Missal Options

- Consider using the prayers from the MPVN-10.
- Use any of the three forms of the PA.
- Any of the eight Prefaces for OT or the six Common Prefaces may be used.
- You might use EP-II.
- Any OT Collect may be used or adapted to conclude the UP. You might even look at the Collects in the Masses for Various Needs and Occasions for possible concluding prayers.

Song of the Day

"Praise to the Lord" (various publishers)

Optional Memorial

St. Ephrem was a fourth-century Syrian deacon recognized as a Doctor of the Church for his prolific works of theology, scriptural commentary, and apologetics. For all his scholarship, St. Ephrem's greatest impact was probably via the over four hundred catechetical and devotional hymns he wrote to console, encourage, and teach his fellow Christians.

- The readings may be taken from the SW, #579, CDC, or LMC #309.
- The Collect is taken from the PS. The other prayers may be taken from the CDC.
- Use any of the OT Collects to conclude the UP.
- Select from P-I or P-II of Saints.
- Consider EP-I or EP-II.

THU 10 LM #362 / LMC #193–232 / green
Weekday

Scripture Insights

Because we are transformed in Christ, we should be careful of our own hearts and minds. How does anger influence us? How does anger take over our words or relationships? Do we healthfully manage anger, or does anger manage our relationships?

Preaching Points

Parish Masses

- Anger is something that naturally occurs in the range of human emotions. How we manage our anger matters absolutely, and reconciliation with our brothers and sisters is part of Christian life.
- Through Jesus we more clearly understand God and the Mosaic law. For Christians, the Ten Commandments are understood through Jesus' teachings.

Masses with Children

- People often become angry, and we need to understand our anger through our faithful lens. We must reconcile with those with whom we are angry. Reconciliation and apology are part of Christian living.
- Jesus helps us understand the Ten Commandments; we read the Old Testament in light of Jesus' teachings.

Missal Options

- Consider using the prayers from the MPVN-15/2.
- Use any of the three forms of the PA.
- Any of the eight Prefaces for OT or the six Common Prefaces may be used.

- You might use EPR-I.
- Any OT Collect may be used or adapted to conclude the UP. You might even look at the Collects in the Masses for Various Needs and Occasions for possible concluding prayers.

Song of the Day

"Sing a New Song" by Daniel L. Schutte (OCP)

FRI 11 Solemnity of the Most Sacred Heart of Jesus

See page 240.

LM #364; Gospel, #573 / LMC #193–232; Gospel, #303 / white

SAT 12 Memorial of the Immaculate Heart of the Blessed Virgin Mary

Today's Memorial

St. Louis Grignion de Montfort (1673–1716) spread devotion to the Immaculate Heart of Mary. Devotion to Mary's heart, like devotion to Jesus' heart, reminds us that God's saving love is offered to all. Mary treasured in her Immaculate Heart the joys and sorrows that came with being the mother of the Word made flesh.

Scripture Insights

Today's Scripture Insights focus on the Gospel from #573, which is proper. These reflections apply if the presider chooses to use the other readings from the SW or PS. Additional readings may come from the CBVM or CMML.

The Virgin Mary's heart must have raced as she and St. Joseph searched Jerusalem for their son. The Gospel, however, focuses on Mary's heart holding the wonder of her young son understanding and participating in rabbinic conversation. Instead of hearing of her terror, we hear about Mary's heart pondering her son's reference to his "Father's house." What did these words and experiences mean to our blessed mother?

Preaching Points

Parish Masses

- Our Lord has given us the gift of salvation in Jesus, and we rejoice in him. Like Mary, we rejoice in hearing Jesus teach the people.
- A faithful and observant Jewish couple, Mary and Joseph would have followed religious custom regarding Passover, so they celebrated the holy day in the holy city.
- In today's Gospel reading, we hear that after Passover Jesus helped the educated men of the Temple understand God. Years later, on that same holy day, Jesus would be arrested and begin his passion and death.

Masses with Children

- Jesus' family traveled to Jerusalem because they were faithful and observant Jewish people; they observed Passover in the holy city. Passover is also the meal Jesus celebrated at the Last Supper.
- When they found Jesus, he was speaking with the educated men of the Temple and had tremendous understanding of God. Jesus helps us know the Father every day. Through Jesus, we are drawn into the life of God.

Missal Options

- The Gospel for the memorial is proper; however, the other readings may come from the SW, CBVM, or CMML.
- The Gospel in the LMC is also proper. The other readings may be taken from the CBVM or SW.
- The prayers are proper and found in the PS at the end of the section for May.
- There is no Gloria or Creed.
- P-I or P-II of the Blessed Virgin Mary may be used. Consider EP-III.
- Use any of the three forms of the PA.
- Use any of the OT Collects to conclude the UP.

Song of the Day

"Jesus My Lord, My God, My All" (various publishers)

- Other Rites and Customs
- Hours: Use the Proper Psalter of the day.

In teaching us charity, the Gospel instructs us in the preferential respect due to the poor and the special situation they have in society: the more fortunate should renounce some of their rights so as to place their goods more generously at the service of others.

—*Octogesima adveniens*, 23

FRI **11** LM #171B / LMC #165B / white

Solemnity of the Most Sacred Heart of Jesus

About Today's Solemnity

In honoring the Sacred Heart, we are honoring the compassion and love of Christ: his human heart, moved with pity for his flock, his divine heart, pierced for the sins of his people. From the heart of Christ, pierced by the soldier's lance, blood and water poured out, "the wellspring of the Church's Sacraments" (Preface for the Sacred Heart).

Scripture Insights

Paul explains that he was commissioned to unveil the mystery of God's love. In Christ "we have boldness of speech and confidence of access [to God] through faith in him," a confidence made possible by the "inscrutable riches of Christ" and the "wisdom" in God's creation and purpose for all humankind.

Christ reveals God's character, and through the trust that Christ inspires, or "through faith in him," humankind draws near to God. With devotion and submission, Paul prays to the Father, from whom every family and nation has its identity. The petition has two parts; the first is a prayer for the community's spiritual condition. Relying on the riches of God's glory, Paul asks that the Ephesians be strengthened in their interior life. That strengthening comes about by God's Spirit at work among humans, and so Paul prays for Christ to dwell in their hearts.

Preaching Points

Parish Masses

- Our relationship with God is that of a child. The Lord taught Israel (a metaphor for God's beloved) to walk; he fed him and cared for him deeply.
- The goal for the early Christian community—and the Church everywhere—is to embody God's presence and love as Christ did. In this way they will experience the mystery of God's love.
- We are strengthened in love through the Spirit and Christ's indwelling. This love comes from God and enables our love to be directed to God and our neighbor.
- Jesus' heart remains forever aligned with those who believe in him.

Children's Liturgy of the Word

- Today we celebrate the Sacred Heart of Jesus. Focusing on Jesus' heart is a reminder that, through Jesus, God's love for the world and for each of us is unending.
- We remember that each of us is a beloved child of God. Just as our parents show how much they love us, God also cares for us. Because of Jesus' great love for us, we are strengthened by that love to show our care and concern for others. How do we show that love—to God and to one another?

Missal Options

- The prayers are proper and found in the PT for the Solemnities and Feasts of the Lord.
- The Gloria and the Creed are sung or recited.
- The Preface is also proper and found among the texts for the Sacred Heart.
- Consider EPR-I.
- Use any of the three forms of the PA.
- Use any of the OT Collects to conclude the UP.

Music Preparation

- If you have a violist or flutist add instrumental solo verses during "O Sacred Head Surrounded" (see below); this will provide a hauntingly beautiful time for the assembly to reflect on Jesus' heart.

Music Suggestions

- Gathering: "Love Divine, All Love's Excelling" (various publishers)
- Canticle: "Isaiah 12: You Will Draw Water" from *Psalms for Solemnities in Ordinary Time: Volume* 1 by Chrysogynous Waddell (WLP)
- Preparation of the Gifts: "O Sacred Head Surrounded" (various publishers)
- Sending Forth: "Heart of Christ" by Bob Hurd (OCP)

Mass Texts

Introduction to Mass

My brothers and sisters, although we were lost in our sins, God did not abandon us to death. In his compassion, he sent us his only Son. Though we each had a hand on the lance that pierced him on the cross, he poured out blood and water to wash us clean. Let us rejoice in the graces we receive from the heart of our Lord Jesus Christ. *My brothers and sisters, let us acknowledge our sins, and so prepare ourselves to celebrate the sacred mysteries.*

Tropes for Penitential Act, Form III

Though we are sinners, your love for us is everlasting: Lord, have mercy.

Your Sacred Heart is the fountain of our salvation: Christ, have mercy.

Your love or us surpasses all knowledge: Lord, have mercy.

Dismissal of Catechumens

My dear friends, as we send you forth to reflect on the Word you have heard, we encourage you to come to Jesus, who is meek and humble of heart. He knows your weaknesses and your burdens, and he will give you rest. We pray for you and for the coming of that day when he will give you his Body and Blood. Go in peace.

Dismissal of Extraordinary Ministers of Holy Communion

Friends, in his great love Jesus has given us his Word and the Sacrament of life. Now we give these to you so that you may strengthen and encourage the sick and homebound with the assurance that the love of the Lord is everlasting. Go in peace.

Universal Prayer

We offer our prayers and petitions to Jesus, who pours out his love on the world.

1. That the cross is embraced as the only way to salvation, we pray:
2. That religious leaders receive support in taking on the poverty and humility of the cross, we pray:
3. That those who suffer oppression at the hands of others will find in the cross a promise of freedom, we pray:
4. That all will imitate Christ by picking up their daily crosses and following him, we pray:
5. That our beloved dead, especially those who bore witness to Christ in the midst of their sufferings, will be received into the heavenly Kingdom, we pray:

Jesus, our Good Shepherd,
you call us to seek you with a sincere heart.
Help us to show your face
to those who are searching for love and forgiveness.
You live and reign for ever and ever.
Amen.

Other Rites and Customs

- It can be difficult to get "all-hands-on-deck" for solemnities that fall during the week. If these Masses are typically scheduled during the day, approach the parish council about rescheduling solemnities and feasts of the Lord as evening Masses. Present the liturgical principles of ranking and emphasize that these days are just as important as Sunday.
- Reflect on your parish's practices of Eucharistic adoration and exposition. Does adoration and exposition lead people back to the celebration of the Eucharist? Or does it surpass the meaning and practice of Mass?
- Encourage families to pray the Litany of the Sacred Heart.

Liturgy and Life

On the pedestal of the statue of the Sacred Heart on the campus of Notre Dame, we read Venite ad me omnes ("Everyone come to me"). This truncated sentence taken from Matthew's Gospel account (11:28) is so inclusive—all are called. Today we read that an eyewitness has given testimony so that "you also may come to believe." We come to belief through Jesus Christ. Each of the baptized also has a responsibility to spread the Good News of Jesus Christ so that others "may come to believe."

SUN 13 LM #92B / LMC #87B / green

Eleventh Sunday in Ordinary Time

Scripture Insights

In today's Gospel reading, we hear Jesus using parables to teach his disciples and the crowds about the Kingdom of God. For Jesus, the reality of the Kingdom of God was best explained by drawing on images and experiences from the daily life of the Galilean villagers.

As we hear in the First Reading today from the prophet Ezekiel, Jewish tradition sometimes compared God's work in the world to the growth of plants and trees. Ezekiel, a prophet in the early stages of Israel's exile in Babylon, prophesied that one day God would restore the exiled Israelites to a mighty and powerful nation, as in the days of King David, when Israel stood as "a majestic cedar." It was a message of hope for a broken and disheartened people.

We find a similar message of hope, with accompanying images of palm and cedar trees, in today's Responsorial Psalm. The psalmist offers a prayer of thanksgiving for God for his fidelity to those who are just and have remained faithful.

With such rich images and traditions embedded in Israel's prophetic writings and psalm prayers, it is understandable that Jesus would draw on similar agricultural metaphors, such as seeds and mustard plants, to teach the crowds and his disciples about the Kingdom of God. In his public ministry, Jesus was planting the seeds for the Kingdom of God that promised fulfillment in the future.

As Paul assures the Corinthians, we can be "courageous" in our faith in Christ. And the Kingdom of God continues to grow in our day in ways beyond human understanding.

Preaching Points

Parish Masses

- Plant and tree imagery would have been familiar for the ancient Israelites and ancient Jewish people. When we use it today, we can still hear and envision the message in Scripture. The Kingdom of God may start like a mustard seed, but it grows and branches into the sky. God's Word brings hope and wholeness to a people aching for the Lord.
- Through Christ, we take courage in all things, and in all things we aspire to do what is right and good, knowing that Christ is with us.
- Jesus taught his people using parables so that they could understand complex topics in common terminology.

Children's Liturgy of the Word

- God and his Word help people to be well in times of trouble.
- We must always choose what is right and good, knowing that Jesus is always with us and will help us to make good choices when we ask for his assistance.
- Jesus taught his people using parables so that they could understand complex topics in common terminology.

Missal Options

- Offer any of the three forms of the PA.
- Sing or recite the Gloria and the Creed.
- Any of the seasonal OT Collects may be used or adapted to conclude the UP.
- Select from any of the eight Prefaces of OT.
- Consider EPVN-III.
- There are six SBs for OT from which to choose.

Music Preparation

- Giant cedars and mustard trees start from small seeds. Be patient and give them time to grow. The one who planted them may not see the fruits. Did someone else plant good seeds in your program allowing you to reap the benefits?
- Be mindful of the seeds you plant and music choices you make. They shape the future of your parish worship and music ministry.
- Ordinary Time during the summer months presents the perfect opportunity to introduce new liturgical music (Mass settings, Gospel acclamations, and so on) and hymns. For new hymns, a good approach is to use the new tune a few weeks in advance as part of the prelude or maybe as an instrumental during the preparation of the gifts. Once you are ready to have the assembly sing it, it is a good idea to use it a few weeks in a row so that they have the opportunity to really learn it and transform it into prayer. If you introduce a new Mass setting, you will probably use it for a while. Introduce it gradually so as not to overwhelm the assembly.

Music Suggestions

- Entrance Antiphon and Hymn: "Seek First the Kingdom of God" by Charles Thatcher (WLP)
- Gathering: "Seed, Scattered and Sown" by Dan Feiten (OCP)
- Preparation of the Gifts: "Take My Life" by Scott Underwood (Mercy/Vineyard Publishing)
- Sending Forth: "Give Glory" by Jacob Israel Villalobos, Mathew Leon, and Michal Paul Leon (WLP)

Mass Texts

Introduction to Mass

God is working great things in us. Though we may not see or feel the evidence, still the witness of Scripture and our faith tell us that, provided our hearts are open, grace will flow through us and bring the Kingdom of God to fruition. Let us therefore unburden ourselves of our sins and allow the Body and Blood of our Lord Jesus to transform us into instruments of God's love and mercy in the world. *My brothers and sisters, let us acknowledge our sins, and so prepare ourselves to celebrate the sacred mysteries.*

Tropes for Penitential Act, Form III

O Lord, you will not abandon or forsake your people: Lord, have mercy.

You plant the seed of your Word in our hearts: Christ, have mercy.

Your Word will spring up like a majestic tree for the good of all: Lord, have mercy.

Dismissal for Children's Liturgy of the Word

My dear children, in today's Gospel, our Lord Jesus will remind you that God can do wonderful things with the smallest of beginnings. Though you may feel small and insignificant, God has chosen each of you for a very specific purpose, to share his love with the world in a way no one else can. This beautiful truth awaits you in Jesus' words. Go and listen to him.

Dismissal of Catechumens

My friends, with prayers for the coming of the day when you will join us in the celebration of the Eucharist, this community sends you forth to consider how God's Word is growing within you and what abundant harvest of love he might be preparing in you. Go in peace.

Dismissal of Extraordinary Ministers of Holy Communion

Dear sisters and brothers, take Christ's Body to our friends who are sick or injured or elderly and infirm, and remind them that God will not abandon or forsake them and that we have not forgotten them. May the Lord strengthen their faith and renew their joy. Go in peace.

Universal Prayer

With seeds scattered and sown, we till the soil of God's Kingdom with our prayers for the needs of this world.

1. For all Christians, that they may work together to heal division and establish unity in Christ, we pray:
2. For all who seek to break down boundaries between nations in the hope of revealing God's Kingdom, we pray:
3. For all gardeners and those who patiently attend to dormant seeds, that they may look forward to the first signs of life, we pray:
4. For the birds of the air and all creatures of the earth who seek a place of refuge and shelter, we pray:
5. For all the dead, as they await the time when they will be gathered into the fullness of God's reign, we pray:

Lord of all creation,
your loving providence
provides for the growth of the Kingdom.
Tend to us in your kindness,
and water the seeds of life
with the truth of the Gospel.
Open our hearts to perceive the mysterious ways
in which your will is active and alive in our world.
Through Christ our Lord.
Amen.

Other Rites and Customs

- Remind your music ministers about the need for ongoing formation and take advantage of some of the great summer programs that are available, particularly the NPM Convention.
- Honor those who have recently graduated from high school, college, or graduate school at a parish graduation Mass. You might adapt the Order of Blessing to be Used in Various Circumstances (chapter 71, BB) or the Order of Blessing of Students and Teachers (chapter 5, BB).

Liturgy and Life

Jesus truly understood his audience! In order to help his avid listeners ponder the Kingdom of God, he used the most familiar images from their everyday environment as doorways into his deeper teachings. Everyone in the crowd in today's Gospel knew the mustard seed to be the smallest of all seeds and how it could grow into a very large bush. Everyone knew the stages of growth of a grain of wheat through to harvest. Jesus led the people from what they already knew about seeds to discover the continuous and wondrous growth of the Kingdom of God. These parables offer us the same proclamation today. Try to protect God's creation.

Taking Place This Week . . .

Consider what can be done liturgically, catechetically, and ministerially to respond to these important needs.

- Today is Bereaved Father's Day.
- World Blood Donor Day and US Flag Day (6/14)
- World Elder Abuse Awareness Day (6/15)
- International Day of Family Remittances (6/17)
- World Day to Combat Desertification (6/17)
- International Day for the Elimination of Sexual Violence in Conflict and Juneteenth (6/19)

MON **14** LM #365 / LMC #193–232 / green
Weekday

Scripture Insights

Our faith in Christ should affect every aspect of our communal interaction. From family relationships to community socialization to communicating with enemies, Jesus' teaching influences our relationships with others.

Preaching Points

Parish Masses

- All people are called to ministry, and because we are ministers of God we have more reason to be aware of our behavior. We ought to mind our behavior in all areas of our lives.
- How we behave toward enemies matters; we do not have the power to change another person.

Masses with Children

- In all of our interactions with others, we must remember that we are Christ's ministers here on earth. We must be mindful of how we speak, how we behave, and how we may be perceived by others.
- We all make choices each day, and those choices matter. How we behave toward enemies matters, and we must realize that we do not have the power to change others.

Missal Options

- Consider using the Collect from the MPVN-30/B/2 and the rest of the prayers from option A.
- Use any of the three forms of the PA.
- Any of the eight Prefaces for OT or the six Common Prefaces may be used.
- You might use EP-II.
- Any OT Collect may be used or adapted to conclude the UP. You might even look at the Collects in the Masses for Various Needs and Occasions for possible concluding prayers.

Song of the Day

"God Has Spoken by the Prophets" by George W. Briggs (Hope Publishing Company)

TUE **15** LM #366 / LMC #193–232 / green
Weekday

Scripture Insights

Jesus became poor and suffered human suffering; because he was willing to take on such human poverty and pain, he offered us the gift of his grace, borne through his suffering.

Preaching Points

Parish Masses

- Everything Christ did, he did for our sake. He did not have to become human—a poor human—but he did so that we might have the riches of heaven. Like Jesus, we must have a passion for helping others.
- Loving those who love us is easy, but loving enemies is a lifelong challenge. What does it look like when we love our enemies?

Masses with Children

- Jesus did not have to become a person who endured poverty and suffering, but he did just that for each one of us. Like Jesus, we should have hearts that prioritize others' needs.
- Loving those who love us is easy, but loving enemies is a challenge. What does it look like when we love our enemies? How is loving our enemies different from making ourselves doormats for bullies?

Missal Options

- Consider using the prayers from the MPVN-42.
- Use any of the three forms of the PA.
- Any of the eight Prefaces for OT or the six Common Prefaces may be used.
- You might use EPR-I.
- Any OT Collect may be used or adapted to conclude the UP. You might even look at the Collects in the Masses for Various Needs and Occasions for possible concluding prayers.

Song of the Day

"*Ubi Caritas*" by Bob Hurd (OCP)

WED 16 LM #367 / LMC #193–232 / green
Weekday

Scripture Insights

Being a "cheerful giver" means that we take joy in generosity, and generous habits have become virtue. A cheerful giver doesn't whine or complain about giving, nor do they try to gain attention or accolades for giving.

Preaching Points

Parish Masses

- "You reap what you sow." This old saying has its roots in Scripture. How do we sow love? Generosity? Kindness? If we sow none of these things, we reap none of these things.
- Seeking the attention and approval of others is not our goal in doing good works. When making donations, doing good works, or fasting or praying, we are not to show off our charity. Charity is meant to benefit others, not benefit our reputations.

Masses with Children

- Farmers harvest the fruits of whatever seeds they plant. When we plant goodness, love, generosity, and kindness, those things return to us. When we plant lies, meanness, and dishonesty, we harvest those things.
- Showing off is something we must avoid in the spiritual life. Giving a donation or doing a good deed just for attention is not the aim of the Christian life.

Missal Options

- Consider using the prayers from the Thirty-Third Sunday in OT.
- Use any of the three forms of the PA.
- Any of the eight Prefaces for OT or the six Common Prefaces may be used.
- You might use EP-II.
- Any OT Collect may be used or adapted to conclude the UP. You might even look at the Collects in the Masses for Various Needs and Occasions for possible concluding prayers.

Song of the Day

"Here at This Table" by Janèt Sullivan Whitaker (OCP)

THU 17 LM #368 / LMC #193–232 / green
Weekday

Scripture Insights

We are always free to speak to God; we do not need to be in any special place or wear special clothing. God can hear us wherever and whenever we speak to him. He is near to us, and we are dear to him.

Preaching Points

Parish Masses

- Like Jesus, St. Paul preached without charging anyone money. Like Jesus, he was willing to live a poor life to share the Good News.
- When we pray we speak to God. Jesus taught us to address God as we would address a loving father.

Masses with Children

- Jesus lived a life of poverty and traveled from town to town spreading God's Word in his ministry. Like Jesus, St. Paul lived a simple life, preaching and teaching without charging money.
- In the Lord's Prayer, Jesus taught us to address God as we would address a loving father. God wants to hear from his children and likes for us to pray to him.

Missal Options

- Consider using the prayers from the Sixth Sunday in OT.
- Use any of the three forms of the PA.
- Any of the eight Prefaces for OT or the six Common Prefaces may be used.
- You might use EPR-I.
- Any OT Collect may be used or adapted to conclude the UP. You might even look at the Collects in the Masses for Various Needs and Occasions for possible concluding prayers.

Song of the Day

"Lord's Prayer" by Steven C. Warner (WLP)

F R I 18 LM #369 / LMC #193–232 / green
Weekday

Scripture Insights

St. Paul's treasure is in Christ, and so he served Christ's Church. His heart was filled with the Holy Spirit, and he lived to continue Jesus' ministry. His treasures were most certainly stored in heaven.

Preaching Points

Parish Masses

- St. Paul chose a life of danger and difficulty in his ministry. His store on earth was one of hunger and cold, but his store in heaven was great.
- Our treasures are those activities that take up our time, our care, and our energy. Our hearts naturally follow our time and energy. Where do your treasures lie, and is that where you want your heart to be? Our treasures should be those things of heavenly importance.

Masses with Children

- St. Paul chose a life that held hunger and cold on earth but riches in heaven.
- Our treasures are the things that are most important to us; our hearts naturally follow where we spend our time and energy. What are your treasures, and is that where you want your heart to be?

Missal Options

- Consider using the prayers from the MPVN-39.
- Use any of the three forms of the PA.
- Any of the eight Prefaces for OT or the six Common Prefaces may be used.
- You might use EPR-II.
- Any OT Collect may be used or adapted to conclude the UP. You might even look at the Collects in the Masses for Various Needs and Occasions for possible concluding prayers.

Song of the Day

"In Silence My Soul Thirsts" by Sheldon W. Sorge and Tammy Wiens (WLP)

S A T 19 LM #370 / LMC #193–232 / green
Weekday

Optional Memorials of St. Romuald, Abbot / white; Blessed Virgin Mary / white

Scripture Insights

St. Paul desired for the thorn to leave him, but the Lord's answer was no and that his grace was sufficient for St. Paul. Like St. Paul, we are called to remember that we mean more to God than the birds and wildflowers. God knows our needs.

Preaching Points

Parish Masses

- God knows our needs, and he cares for all of his children. This doesn't mean that God's people won't suffer the effects of poverty; we are called to care for those who suffer, as we are Christ's hands and feet in this world.
- Historically speaking, political leaders have had tremendous power over others. St. Paul, a leader in the early Church, highlighted his weakness rather than his power. He could see that in his weakness he could find strength in Christ.

Masses with Children

- God cares for all of his children and loves each of them very much. God's people don't avoid poverty because of their identity as God's people. We are called to care for our brothers and sisters in their suffering; we must be Christ's hands and feet in our world.
- In Christianity, realizing one's weakness is a good thing. We must know that through our weakness we have strength in Jesus.

Missal Options

- Consider using the prayers from the MPVN-23.
- Use any of the three forms of the PA.
- Any of the eight Prefaces for OT or the six Common Prefaces may be used.
- You might use EP-II.
- Any OT Collect may be used or adapted to conclude the UP. You might even look at the Collects in the Masses for Various Needs and Occasions for possible concluding prayers.

Song of the Day

"Taste and See" by James Moore (GIA)

Optional Memorials

St. Romuald

St. Romuald (c. 950–1027) was born in Ravenna and led a self-indulgent life as a young man, but when he saw his father kill an opponent in a duel, he fled to a monastery. Romuald yearned for a stricter life than he found there, and so he withdrew to become a hermit. Eventually, he founded the Camaldolese branch of the Benedictine family, integrating community life with the solitary life. His monks live and work in individual hermitages but come together to celebrate Eucharist and the Liturgy of the Hours.

- The readings may be from the SW, #582, LMC #312, or CHMW/CS (For Religious).
- The Collect is from the PS; the other prayers may be from the CHMW (for an Abbot).
- Consider P-I or P-II of Saints, or the Preface of Holy Virgins and Religious and EP-I.

Blessed Virgin Mary

- The readings may be taken from the SW, CBVM, or CMML.
- The prayer texts may be taken from the CBVM or CMMM. Any votive Mass for the BVM may be used.
- Use any of the three forms of the PA.
- Select from P-I or P-II of the BVM.
- Any of the OT Collects may conclude the UP.

Something to Consider...

◈ "Sunday should also give the faithful an opportunity to devote themselves to works of mercy, charity and apostolate" (*Dies Domini*, 69).

◈ "The Sunday eucharist but the whole of Sunday becomes a great school of charity, justice and peace" (*Dies Domini*, 73).

SUN 20 LM #95B / LMC #90B / green
Twelfth Sunday in Ordinary Time

Scripture Insights

Today's Scriptures set us in the midst of a raging sea, a mighty force of nature that only the Word of God can restrain. Anyone who has witnessed the violent winds and lashing waves of a storm at sea understands the terror of the disciples and the fearful hearts of the sailors described in today's Responsorial Psalm.

In Biblical tradition, the sea—particularly its stormy side—symbolizes chaos, all that threatens peace and well-being. Such was the experience of both Job and the disciples. Job's whole life had become an uncontrollable storm, having suddenly lost both family and possessions (see chapters 1–2). And the disciples, while attracted enough to Jesus to leave all and follow him, were still perplexed by his power and perhaps troubled by the negative reactions he sometimes received (see Mark 3:21–22).

In today's Scriptures, God's power over the storm is revealed in the midst: "The Lord addressed Job out of the storm" (38:1). Jesus was in the boat with his disciples, during the storm. Like the sailors of Psalm 107, "they cried to the Lord in their distress; from their straits he rescued them." The Word of God hushes the storm and stills the sea. In the midst of the storm, Job, the sailors, and the disciples all receive at least a glimpse of who God is and experience God's "kindness and wondrous deeds."

What wisdom for us as we encounter the storms of our own lives! What seems to be chaos, to threaten our very lives, is but the setting in which the power of the Divine can be revealed. Let us not forget that the Teacher will not let us perish. The power of his Word can still our storms as well.

Preaching Points

Parish Masses

- Christ is changed in his resurrected self, and in him we are changed and have the hope of resurrection. In our Lord we find the peace and goodness of God's love; we are made new through relationship with him.
- In ancient time, weather wasn't a predictable force, and the sea represented something wild and untamed. Jesus taming the sea was a calming of chaotic fear and unpredictability.
- God cares for us in the storms of our own lives; through his grace we can be made new.

Children's Liturgy of the Word

- Chaos is a word that describes extreme disorder. In ancient time, the sea was a chaotic figure to the people because it was unpredictable. When Jesus tamed the sea, he made order out of chaos.
- Jesus not only calms storms but also helps us make order out of chaos in our own lives. In him, we are made new.

Missal Options

- Offer any of the three forms of the PA.
- Sing or recite the Gloria and the Creed.
- Any of the seasonal OT Collects may be used or adapted to conclude the UP.
- Select from any of the eight Prefaces of OT.
- Consider EP-III.
- There are six SBs for OT from which to choose.

Music Preparation

- In our work as music ministers, there are moments of turbulence, storm, and destruction—it may seem like Jesus is asleep in the boat. We must pray to turn these moments over to God and to have the grace to see God in them.
- Consider your own calling and the moments in your music ministry that may have been difficult but have made you stronger in the end.
- Do you know that major publishers—OCP, GIA, WLP, MorningStar, Paraclete, EC Schirmer Music Company, and others—have choral subscriptions available? You receive a packet of scores and an accompanying CD on a quarterly basis. Although you need to weed through the material, you can usually find good choral gems for a wide variety of voices (children's choir, unison choir, SATB choir, women's voices, contemporary ensemble, etc.) and new or reworked liturgical/ritual compositions that you can add to the assembly's repertoire. Don't be afraid to check out what different publishers have to offer.

Music Suggestions

- Preparation of the Gifts: "Holy Darkness" by Daniel L. Schutte (OCP)
- Communion: "*Pescador de Hombres*" by Cesareo Gabarain, translation by Rev. Willard F. Jabusch (OCP)
- Sending Forth: "The Summons" by John L. Bell (GIA)

Mass Texts

Introduction to Mass

The One who created all things, who commands the wind and the sea and they obey him, is doing a new thing in us. In Christ, we are becoming a new creation. Such power is rooted in love, the love that led Jesus, God's only Son, to give his life, that we might live forever. With wonder and awe, let us approach this altar and give thanks to God for his tender love. *My brothers and sisters, let us acknowledge our sins, and so prepare ourselves to celebrate the sacred mysteries.*

Tropes for Penitential Act, Form III

In you our sins are nailed to the cross: Lord, have mercy.

In you our old life has passed away: Christ, have mercy.

In you we will be raised to eternal life at the end of days: Lord, have mercy.

Dismissal for Children's Liturgy of the Word

My children, God, who made the planets and the stars, also made the ladybug and the gentle breeze that cools you on a warm summer day. He is the King of all creation and he loves you as his own very dear children. Jesus Christ, our brother, reminds us in today's Gospel that with him we have nothing to fear. Go now and listen to him.

Dismissal of Catechumens

Dear friends, what old things is God asking you to leave behind? What new things might he be doing in you as you continue this journey of formation and discernment? We pray that the Lord will enlighten your hearts and minds and for the coming of that day when you will be one with us in faith, hope, and love. Go in peace.

Dismissal of Extraordinary Ministers of Holy Communion

My friends, having received this sacrament of love and unity, we are mindful of our sick and homebound brothers and sisters. Go to them; share with them the Word of life and the Bread of salvation. Assure them of our prayers that they may be free of all anxiety and know the love of Christ. Go in peace.

Universal Prayer

The Lord calms our fears and anxieties. Trusting in him, we turn to him to calm the storms this world endures. Please respond: Remain with us always, O Lord.

1. Remain with your Church as she seeks to reconcile sinners and awaken hearts to your gift of mercy, we pray:
2. Remain with all who are in the path of violence and war, we pray:
3. Remain with those at sea, especially fishers who are away from home for long periods of time, we pray:
4. Remain with those whose faith is weak and those who reject you, we pray:
5. Remain with the sick and those who suffer great pain on a daily basis, we pray:
6. Remain with the dying and those who have already died, as their souls negotiate the way to life eternal, we pray:

God, ever present in our times of need,
increase in us the gift of faith in you.
As your Son navigated the boat through the stormy waters
by teaching his disciples the importance of faith,
may we never fail to trust in your mercy.
With your forgiveness at hand,
may we live always anew in the Spirit.
Through Christ our Lord.
Amen.

Other Rites and Customs

- Include the Order for the Blessing of Fathers on Father's Day from chapter 56 of the *Book of Blessings*.
- Don't forget to pray for dads who have died and also step-fathers, foster and adoptive fathers, godfathers, and all who play a fatherly role.
- Give your regular music ministers a break for a few weeks by forming an intergenerational choir and offer a special welcome to college students who are home for summer break.

Liturgy and Life

From the time of Job to the days when Jesus sailed on Lake Galilee to today, people have been well aware of the power of water and what it means to feel terror when facing a storm. Those affected by recent hurricanes and tsunamis attest to the unimaginable damage water can bring to homes, lives, and communities. When water disasters hit communities, Catholic Charities is prepared to help. Provide your parish with information about the faithful response of this agency at http://catholiccharitiesusa.org/our-solutions/programs/.

Taking Place This Week . . .

Consider what can be done liturgically, catechetically, and ministerially to respond to these important needs.

- Today is Father's Day and the June/Summer Solstice. It is also American Eagle Day.
- National Indigenous Peoples Day takes place in Canada on 6/21.
- Public Service Day and International Workers Day (6/23)
- Day of the Seafarer (6/25)
- World Day against Drug Abuse and Trafficking and World Day to Support Torture Victims (6/26)

MON 21 LM #371 or #583 / LMC #193–232 or #313 / white
Memorial of St. Aloysius Gonzaga, Religious

Today's Saint

St. Aloysius Gonzaga, SJ (1568–1591), died at age twenty-three while tending the sick who were dying from an epidemic in Rome. He is patron of young people and individuals living with HIV/AIDS. Destined for wealth, his closeness to God moved him to give his property rights to his younger brother and profess poverty as a Jesuit. He lived the Jesuit motto, to the greater glory of God, by living the "Golden Rule." He lived the Gospel with integrity and thus chose the narrow path. Whether we are rich or poor, sick or healthy, older or younger, we are destined for closeness to God that is expressed in service and praise.

Scripture Insights

Each of us is called to follow the Lord as part of a community and as individuals. Abram followed God's instructions when instructed to leave the land of his ancestors and go to the new land God promised him.

Preaching Points

Parish Masses

- Most people don't hear God's voice in the same way Abram did, but we can all still follow God's directions. We hear his Word through Scripture and in the tradition of the Church.
- One of Jesus' teachings that we are called to follow was heard in the Gospel reading today. Being judgmental is not something Jesus wants us to be; instead of pointing out another person's faults, we are to look at our own faults. Hypocrisy is to be avoided.

Masses with Children

- Abraham heard God's voice in a different way than we do today. We follow God's voice by knowing and following truths revealed in Scripture and in the tradition of the Church.
- When a person is hypocritical, she negatively judges a person for an act that she herself commits. Jesus calls us to self-examination rather than being judgmental of others.

Scripture Insights *(PS)*

Keep the commandments: love God and neighbor. The call is simple and yet so difficult.

Preaching Points

Parish Masses

- Faith in Jesus Christ summons us to a new way of life, governed by the commandments. Faith does not stay in a private realm of God-and-me. Faith touches on every aspect of our lives, because love of God and love of neighbor are inseparable.
- How do we show our love of God? We have the perfect way to express our love: the way we treat our neighbor. This is the love that conquers the world.

Masses with Children

- Faith in God can't be a private action. It is meant to be shared with others! And we express our faith with how we treat others. The only way to conquer the problems in our world is though love.

Missal Options

- The readings may be from the SW, PS, or CHMW/CS (For Religious).
- Any of the three forms of the PA may be used.
- The prayers are proper and found in the PS.
- Look to the Collects of OT to use as the concluding prayer for the UP.
- Use P-I or P-II of Saints, or the Preface of Holy Virgins and Religious.
- Consider EPVN-IV.

Song of the Day

"The Faithful One" by Daniel L. Schutte (OCP)

TUE 22 LM #372 / LMC #193–232 / green
Weekday

Optional Memorials of St. Paulinus of Nola, Bishop / white; St. John Fisher, Bishop, and St. Thomas More, Martyrs / red

Scripture Insights

Abram treated Lot as he himself would want to be treated. Giving Lot the choice of land, Abraham secured friendship in a move of kindness and generosity. God promised Abraham that his descendants would be many.

Preaching Points

Parish Masses

- In Abram's time, fertile and grazing land was security for oneself and one's family. Taking the land that Lot didn't want was an act of faith and generosity. The land had significant meaning to Abram because he left the land of his ancestors, and God promised him descendants to populate the land.

- Treating others the way we would want to be treated is a basic principle in loving one's neighbor. We are meant to follow this Golden Rule in our interactions with others.

Masses with Children

- Fertile land that was tillable and that had space and vegetation for grazing animals was a measure of security and livelihood in Abraham's time. He gave Lot the first choice of land.
- We too are called to treat others as we wish to be treated; the Golden Rule is a basic element of kindness we are meant to give to all people.

Missal Options

- Consider using the prayers from the Ninth Sunday in OT.
- Use any of the three forms of the PA.
- Any of the eight Prefaces for OT or the six Common Prefaces may be used.
- You might use EPVN-III.
- Any OT Collect may be used or adapted to conclude the UP. You might even look at the Collects in the Masses for Various Needs and Occasions for possible concluding prayers.

Song of the Day

"That I May Serve You" by Janét Sullivan Whitaker (WLP)

Optional Memorials

St. Paulinus

After the loss of their only child, Paulinus and his wife, Theresia, dedicated themselves to philanthropy, becoming so known for their piety and works of charity that Paulinus was ordained a priest and later appointed bishop of Nola. St. Paulinus and Theresia turned the tragedy of their child's death into the seeds of a great outpouring of life for all those they encountered.

- The readings may be taken from the SW, #584, CP, or LMC #314.
- The Collect is from the PS, and the other prayers may be taken from the CP (For a Bishop).
- Use any of the OT Collects to conclude the UP.
- Select from P-I or P-II of Saints, or the Preface of Holy Pastors.
- Consider EP-I or EP-II.

Sts. John Fisher and Thomas More

Sts. John Fisher and Thomas More were martyred by their former patron and friend, Henry VIII of England, after refusing to recognize his claim to spiritual authority over the English Church. Although they loved their king and their lives, St. John Fisher and St. Thomas More loved truth more.

- The readings may be taken from the SW, #585, CM, or LMC #315.
- The Collect is from the PS, and the other prayers may be taken from the CM (For Several Martyrs).
- Use any of the OT Collects to conclude the UP.
- Select from P-I or P-II of Saints, or P-I or P-II of Holy Martyrs.
- Consider EP-I or EP-II.

WED 23 — LM #373 / LMC #193–232 / green — Weekday

Scripture Insights

A covenant is a solemn promise, and in today's First Reading we hear about the covenant between Abram and God. Abraham trusted in God's Word despite having no children and no descendants to whom his land would pass upon his death.

Preaching Points

Parish Masses

- Abram trusted in God even when he didn't understand how God's promise would come to fruition.
- The fruits of a person are the good things we see coming from them. While some people may hide their rottenness from immediate view, their rotten fruits will identify them. We should always be aware of those who seek to harm others.

Masses with Children

- Sometimes we can't see how something will work out the way it was promised to work out. Abraham trusted that God would keep his promise even when he didn't understand how God could make it work.
- What matters most about a person is what they are like on the inside. We are warned that some people may try to make themselves appear good but are very bad on the inside. The reading tells us that we can understand more about a person by observing his fruits.

Missal Options

- Consider using the prayers from the MPVN-27/A.
- Use any of the three forms of the PA.
- Any of the eight Prefaces for OT or the six Common Prefaces may be used.
- You might use EP-II.

- Any OT Collect may be used or adapted to conclude the UP. You might even look at the Collects in the Masses for Various Needs and Occasions for possible concluding prayers.

Song of the Day

"I Am the Vine" by Jack Miffleton (WLP)

THU 24 Solemnity of the Nativity of St. John the Baptist

See page 254.

FRI 25 Weekday

LM #375 / LMC #193–232 / green

Scripture Insights

In the First Reading, Abram and Sarai are given new names as they begin life in the covenant with the Lord. In the Gospel reading Jesus comes down from a mountain, which symbolizes something very important occurring. Isaac, a long-anticipated child, is promised in a miraculous birth, and Jesus performs a miraculous healing for a man with leprosy. Our God is a God of miracles!

Preaching Points

Parish Masses

- Abraham greets the news about Sarah's coming pregnancy with Isaac with laughter and seeks to protect Ishmael's interests.
- Jesus heals the man with leprosy. This man absolutely believes that Jesus can make him clean and has fully put his faith in Jesus.

Masses with Children

- The name *Isaac* means "laughter," and Abraham laughed at the thought of himself and Sarah becoming parents in their old age.
- The man with leprosy has faith that Jesus can heal him, if it is the Lord's wish. He put his faith in Jesus absolutely, fully believing in Jesus.

Missal Options

- Consider using the prayers from the Twenty-Fourth Sunday in OT.
- Use any of the three forms of the PA.
- Any of the eight Prefaces for OT or the six Common Prefaces may be used.
- You might use EPVN-IV.

- Any OT Collect may be used or adapted to conclude the UP. You might even look at the Collects in the Masses for Various Needs and Occasions for possible concluding prayers.

Song of the Day

"Covenant Hymn" by Gary Daigle and Rory Cooney (GIA)

SAT 26 Weekday

LM #376 / LMC #193–232 / green

Optional Memorial of the Blessed Virgin Mary / white

Scripture Insights

"Lord, . . . only say the word and my servant will be healed." These words, which are from the Gospel reading, can also be applied to Abraham and Sarah. Saddled with infertility, the couple desired a child who finally arrived when God announced his coming in their old age. Upon his Word, the reading tells us that this couple was healed and would expect a child.

Preaching Points

Parish Masses

- Sarah laughed to herself when told about a coming pregnancy when she was past the age of childbearing. Nothing is "too marvelous" for the Lord, she soon learned.
- The Roman centurion believed that Jesus could heal his servant; specifically, he believed that Jesus could speak the words and the man would be healed. Jesus praised his faith.
- The words of the centurion are the words we recite at Mass when the priest invites us to receive Holy Communion.

Masses with Children

- God is so great that nothing is too difficult for him; Sarah and Abraham experienced God's goodness when they learned they would have a child in their old age.
- The words of the centurion are the words we say at Mass when the priest invites us to receive Holy Communion.

Missal Options

- Consider using the prayers from the MPVN-17/B.
- Use any of the three forms of the PA.
- Any of the eight Prefaces for OT or the six Common Prefaces may be used.
- You might use EP-II.

- Any OT Collect may be used or adapted to conclude the UP. You might even look at the Collects in the Masses for Various Needs and Occasions for possible concluding prayers.

Song of the Day

"Healer of Our Every Ill" by Marty Haugen (GIA)

Optional Memorial

- The readings may be taken from the SW, CBVM, or CMML.
- The prayer texts may be taken from the CBVM or CMMM. Any votive Mass for the BVM may be used.
- Use any of the three forms of the PA.
- Select from P-I or P-II of the BVM.
- Any of the OT Collects may conclude the UP.

Something to Consider...

◈ "With zeal and patience pastors must promote the liturgical instruction of the faithful and also their active participation in the liturgy both internally and externally, taking into account their age and condition, their way of life, and their stage of religious development" (*Sacrosanctum concilium*, 19).

T H U 24 LM #586 and #587 / LMC #316 / white
Solemnity of the Nativity of St. John the Baptist

Today's Solemnity

The celebration of the birth of John the Baptist is one of three birthdays (along with the Nativities of Jesus and of the Blessed Virgin Mary) commemorated in the liturgical year. John's birth is observed during the summer solstice, on the longest day of the year, but immediately afterward the days begin to grow shorter. Jesus' birthday is celebrated, however, during the winter solstice, the shortest day of the year. But gradually and almost imperceptibly the days grow longer. It is no accident that John's Gospel account speaks about light. John was not the light but came to testify to the light. No wonder John states that he must diminish as Christ, the Light of the World, must increase, just like the phenomena of the solstices.

Scripture Insights: Vigil

God's call of Jeremiah echoes the call stories of people like Moses and Isaiah. Those men also expressed their unworthiness and their wish that God send someone else. God insists that Jeremiah's youth and lack of education is an asset, for then Jeremiah will speak God's Word just as it comes to him. God will also strengthen Jeremiah to persist in the face of harsh opposition. In the roughly fifty years that Jeremiah served as God's prophet, he experienced loneliness, grief, ridicule, and physical punishment. He obeyed God faithfully but at great cost.

John the Baptist was also set apart for a special role, and the circumstances of his conception echo stories from the Jewish tradition like that of Abraham, who conceived a son late in life, and Hannah, who dedicated her son to the service of God. The conception of John, however, marks the beginning of a new era. John bears the likeness of Elijah, the prophet who would return to prepare people for God's arrival. Zechariah and "the whole assembly" have been praying for this new era, yet John's proclamation of it will come at great cost.

We hear in our Second Reading that Jeremiah and John were among those inspired by "the Spirit of Christ" to proclaim a salvation that came ultimately through Jesus. Those who lived during and after the time of Christ rejoiced at seeing the fulfillment of God's long plan of salvation. This joy, however, comes at a cost. Jesus is the risen, glorified Son, but his glorification came after his crucifixion and death.

We must also be willing to bear the cost that comes from answering God's call if we wish to know the joy of salvation. As we celebrate the birthday of John the Baptist, the readings focus on John's role of inspiring people to prepare for the coming of the Messiah.

Preaching Points

Parish Masses

- At Baptism, the new Christian is anointed as Christ was anointed: priest, prophet, and king. If a prophet is one rooted deeply in faith and willing to call people away from the false idols of today's world, do we fulfill this baptismal role?
- Like John the Baptist, we are all called to be heralds of the Lord's desired coming (or coming more deeply) into our lives. How might we attract people to allow God into their lives and to expand their hearts in active compassion and care for those on the fringes of our society?
- Every prophet had to endure a cost for their faithfulness to speak on God's behalf. In today's secular culture we too must endure a cost. What are the challenges, the costs, and the benefits of speaking love to hate, hope to despair, and truth to power?

Masses with Children

- A prophet is someone who listens to God's message and shares it with others. Can you think of any prophets today?
- John the Baptist prepared people to be ready to recognize Jesus as the Messiah. Help the children reflect on what or who helps us recognize Jesus as the Savior.
- Reflect on how sometimes our faith means that we don't participate in things that hurt others.

Scripture Insights: Day

For the people of Israel, a person's name expressed an aspect of their identity. The name, John, a common one among the people of Israel, was not found in his family's lineage. It means "the Lord has been gracious" because the elderly parents, Elizabeth and Zechariah, had lost all hope of conceiving a child in their old age. God had certainly favored them. This raised the question "What, then, will this child be? For surely the hand of the Lord was with him."

The Second Reading, from the Acts of the Apostles, answers this question. When Paul speaks in the synagogue of Antioch, he identifies John's role as preparing the way for the Messiah. This shows how well the early Church understood that the Baptist was the forerunner of Christ. Like John the Baptist, our task is to continue his work of enabling the light of Christ to shine out more fully in our world.

Preaching Points

Parish Masses

- A miracle occurred in the very existence of John the Baptist. His parents' unexpected joy in such a long wait for a child, the miracle of the angel's appearance, and the remarkable event of his naming are all events that help us understand the extraordinary and exceptional person who is John the Baptist.
- From the womb, God knows each of his human creations. We are precious to him. God called some of his servants from before their births.
- John was humble and ready to serve God. Salvation had arrived on the earth, and John would prepare the people. How do we help others ready their hearts for the Savior?
- John's existence was propelled by God's call; from before his birth God's role can be clearly seen.

Children's Liturgy of the Word

- God has a special love of children, including children who are not yet born. Sometimes God's call to prophets was known before their births.
- John was humble; this means he didn't assume his own greatness. He helped the people get ready to meet Jesus.
- Because of the circumstances around his birth, people knew that John was destined for extraordinary ministry.

Missal Options

- The Vigil Mass may take place before or after Evening Prayer I.
- The prayers are proper and are found in the PS. A set of texts are provided for both the Vigil and the Mass during the day.
- Since John the Baptist prepares the way for our own Baptism in Christ, do the sprinkling rite today. Sing a song familiar to the assembly to accompany the rite at both Masses.
- The Gloria and the Creed are sung or said at both Masses.
- The Preface is proper and is found among the texts for the Mass during the day.
- Consider using EP-III (Vigil) or EP-I (Day).
- A SB is not provided for John the Baptist, but you could use any of the blessings for OT.

Music Preparation

- Sing the Benedictus, the Canticle of Zechariah, at Mass, the fixed Gospel reading at every celebration of Morning Prayer.

Music Suggestions

- Gathering: "The Great Forerunner of the Morn" (various publishers)
- Preparation of the Gifts: "Prepare the Way of the Lord" by Taizé (GIA)
- Communion: "As We Gather at the Table" by Carl F. Daw (Hope Publishing Company) and arranged by Kelly Dobbs Mickus (GIA)
- Sending Forth: "On Jordan's Bank" (various publishers)

Mass Texts

Introduction to Mass

Among those born of women there is no one greater than John the Baptist, whose birth we celebrate today. Yet, he glories not in drawing us to himself but in directing us to our Lord Jesus Christ, who tells us that the least in the Kingdom of God is greater than John. *My brothers and sisters, let us acknowledge our sins, and so prepare ourselves to celebrate the sacred mysteries.*

Tropes for Penitential Act, Form III

You are the eternal light come into the world, testified to by John: Lord, have mercy.

You sent John before you to prepare us for your coming: Christ, have mercy.

Your salvation will reach to the ends of the earth: Lord, have mercy.

Dismissal of Catechumens

Friends, on this journey toward Christian initiation, John the Baptist prepares the way of the Lord to your own hearts. Through his intercession, we pray that you may receive Christ with faith and joy and that the day will come when you will join us in receiving his Body and Blood in the Eucharist. Go in peace.

Dismissal of Extraordinary Ministers of Holy Communion

Dear ministers of the Lord, go to our sick and suffering friends, speak a word of comfort to them, and give them the Bread of life. Remind them of their unity with us in the Spirit and of the power of God's salvation. Go in peace.

Universal Prayer

John heralded the Savior's coming by proclaiming a baptism of repentance. Because we have been baptized into Christ, we are responsible for praying for the needs of the world. Let us turn now to Christ.

1. As John the Baptist was called to prepare the way of the Lord, may all ministers of the Church herald the Lord's presence, we pray:
2. As John the Baptist led a life of simplicity and poverty, may all nations care for the needs of the most vulnerable, we pray:
3. As John the Baptist proclaimed a baptism of repentance, may all those baptized into Christ be agents of reconciliation in our world, we pray:
4. As John the Baptist rejoiced in the womb of St. Elizabeth, may all pregnant women rejoice in the presence of loving and supportive friends, family, and community, we pray:
5. As John the Baptist was martyred for his faith, may all who have suffered and died for Christ be brought to the fullness of the resurrection, we pray:

Lord our God,
you chose St. John the Baptist
as the forerunner of your Son,
to prepare his way
and to herald his presence when at last he came.
Pour forth your Spirit of love on your Church this day
and guide her in the way of salvation.
Through Christ our Lord.
Amen.

Other Rites and Customs

Follow the tradition of having a great bonfire on this night in celebration of the Light that John the Baptist points to and prepares us to receive.

Liturgy and Life

Pray for the intercession of St. John the Baptist—that he will help you with your own mission as a disciple of Jesus.

S U N **27** LM #98B / LMC #93B / green

Thirteenth Sunday in Ordinary Time

Scripture Insights

"God did not make death, nor does he rejoice in the destruction of the living" (Wisdom 1:13). How powerfully this divine purpose is illustrated in the two stories in today's Gospel. Illness, death—both result from the "envy of the devil." Both are rendered impotent by the touch of Jesus.

In the Gospel, Mark frames the story of the woman who was sick for twelve years with the story of Jairus' daughter, a twelve-year-old-child on the point of death. The woman had suffered as long as the child had lived. Who cannot resonate with the frustration and expense of consulting doctor after doctor to no avail? With the anguished helplessness of Jairus?

At the same time, whose faith can even begin to approach that of Jairus and the woman? "If I but touch his clothes, I shall be cured," the woman believed. She touched Jesus and "felt in her body that she was healed of her affliction." Jairus asks Jesus to lay his hands upon his daughter, "that she may get well and live." At the word and touch of Jesus, the girl "arose immediately and walked around." What a contrast to Jairus' faith and the incredulity of the mourners who "ridiculed" Jesus! What a contrast between the life-giving power inherent in Jesus and the destructive forces of sin and death!

Today's psalm no doubt captures the joy of those Jesus healed: "I will praise you, Lord, for you have rescued me . . . You changed my mourning into dancing; O LORD, my God, forever will I give you thanks." May we, this day, seek the power of Jesus' touch for whatever is in need of healing. Then we too will rejoice and give praise.

Preaching Points

Parish Masses

- Death is not something God created for us; death is something that entered creation through sin. In Christ, death is not a final blow to each person's existence, and, in Christ, we do not fear death.
- God created us in his image and likeness, and he created us for existence, not for obliteration. Death is not something God manipulates for his pleasure or anyone's harm. We were not made to die; we were made to live.
- In Christ, we find the life that God has restored to his people. Through our Lord we are rescued from death. We are reminded of God's power over death when we hear about Jairus' daughter and the woman with the hemorrhage. Our faith in Christ brings life.

Children's Liturgy of the Word

- Death is not something humans were made to suffer; God intended for his people to live and to exist with him. Sin entered the world, and death accompanied that sin. God doesn't punish people by taking away those they love, and he doesn't enjoy earthly mortality.
- Death is not the final page of our books; in Jesus, our human death is the beginning of eternal life with God. He has rescued us from death, and we see his saving action in the story of Jairus' daughter and the story of the woman with a hemorrhage. In Christ, death is transformed to new life.

Missal Options

- Offer any of the three forms of the PA.
- Sing or recite the Gloria and the Creed.
- Any of the seasonal OT Collects may be used or adapted to conclude the UP.
- Select from any of the eight Prefaces of OT.
- Consider EPVN-I.
- There are six SBs for OT from which to choose.

Music Preparation

- For most musicians, we think of summer as our catch up and vacation time, but it can be gone before we know it, and nothing is prepared for the fall. Start listening to new hymns and octavos this summer while you work or give your office a good cleaning.
- As summer is still just beginning, make sure to take needed breaks in order to recharge and refresh! It is important for us to take opportunities to renew our energy. Summer may provide the opportunity for continued education. Check out various institutes and organizations for workshops, colloquiums, or retreats. If this is not possible, treat yourself to some relaxing downtime!

Music Suggestions

- Gathering: "I Heard the Voice of Jesus" (various publishers)
- Preparation of the Gifts: "Come, My Way, My Truth, My Life" (various publishers)
- Communion: "You Are Mine" by David Haas (GIA)
- Sending Forth: "Let All Things Now Living" (various publishers)

Mass Texts

Introduction to Mass

Between us all there is a radical equality, alluded to in today's Second Reading. We are all subject to death, but Christ came to save us all, surrendering his own prerogatives as God's only Son and taking on our mortal flesh. He offers each one of us his life in the bread and wine of the Eucharist, that we might together live forever with him in the peace of God's Kingdom. With grateful hearts let us prepare ourselves for these holy mysteries. *My brothers and sisters, let us acknowledge our sins, and so prepare ourselves to celebrate the sacred mysteries.*

Tropes for Penitential Act, Form III

You did not make death, but you destroy it in your own Body: Lord, have mercy.

For our sake you became poor, that we might be rich in grace: Christ, have mercy.

You raise us up from the netherworld and turn our mourning into dancing: Lord, have mercy.

Dismissal for Children's Liturgy of the Word

Dear children, God does not want us to suffer or our lives to end. He made us to live forever with him in joy and peace. Jesus is our way to God and our promise of life everlasting. It is he who speaks to you now in today's readings and he who guards you with his love. Go and listen to him.

Dismissal of Catechumens

My friends, the suffering and hardship of this world are real and unavoidable, but they are not the end and they do not get the last word. Jesus Christ, who died and rose again for our sakes, is himself the last word, God's Word of love, mercy, and new life. Reflect well on what he has spoken to you in these readings and on what he is saying in your own lives to lead you to conversion and transformation in him. Go in peace.

Dismissal of Extraordinary Ministers of Holy Communion

Dear friends, God desires life for all his children. Take to our ailing, weak, and injured sisters and brothers the Body of God's Son, who is our spiritual food and our pledge of eternal life. May we all be one in the love of Jesus Christ. Go in peace.

Universal Prayer

We give thanks to the Lord for his merciful love and turn to him in prayer with the needs of our world.

1. For the domestic Church, that Christian families everywhere may grow together in faith and holiness, we pray:
2. For the family of nations, that governments may work together toward a real and lasting peace, we pray:
3. For new mothers and fathers, that the birth of a child may spark wonder and awe, we pray:
4. For the sick, especially those in a coma or a persistent vegetative state, that the value of their lives may be respected, we pray:
5. For those who have died, that they may be raised to life with God, we pray:

Merciful God,
your Son raised Jairus' daughter to life
and bestowed on his family the gift of faith.
We pray, be the center of our
Christian families.
Through the Spirit of life,
renew in us the desire to serve you,
proclaiming to all the world
that Christ is the way to new and unending life.
Who lives and reigns with you in the unity of the Holy Spirit,
one God, for ever and ever.
Amen.

Other Rites and Customs

- Consider celebrating the Sacrament of Anointing of the Sick at one of the Masses today.
- Offer a blessing to those involved in healing professions such as doctors, nurses, EMT workers, etc., adapting the blessing found in chapter 7 of the *Book of Blessings*, Order for the Blessing of Organizations Concerned with Public Need.

Liturgy and Life

Jesus became poor that we might be rich. In today's reading, St. Paul urges us to create a balance between our abundance and the needs of others. Without this balance, material wealth can readily become an obstacle to spiritual growth. If we want to grow in love, we need to give. There are 37 million people in America currently living below the "poverty line." There are 12.9 million children growing up in poverty. The Catholic Campaign for Human Development urges us to show our love for the poor by learning the facts about poverty. Find out how you can make a difference as an advocate for change and how to make the most of your giving. Go to http:/www.povertyusa.org and click on "Get Involved" or call 202-541-3210. Learn, act, and give of your time, talent, or resources. Consider it an investment in the well-being of others and in your own spiritual growth.

Taking Place This Week . . .

Consider what can be done liturgically, catechetically, and ministerially to respond to these important needs.

- Today, the special collection is for Peter's Pence.
- World Asteroid Day (6/30)
- Canada Day (7/1)
- First Friday (7/2) and First Saturday (7/3)
- July is traditionally the month of the Most Precious Blood.

MON 28 Memorial of St. Irenaeus, Bishop and Martyr

LM #377 or #589 / LMC #193–232 or #318 / red

Today's Saint

As bishop of Lyons, Irenaeus clearly distinguished false teachings from those consistent with Christ's words and deeds. He hoped that clear teaching would invite his opponents to turn away from falsehood. Since it was a time flooded with political persecution and false teachers, many were martyred, including Irenaeus.

Scripture Insights

We are called to follow Christ with all our hearts. When we follow Jesus it isn't something that is just done on Sundays; it is a lifelong mission to engage in the Gospel and live out the Gospel message.

Preaching Points

Parish Masses

- God is merciful, and, in the First Reading, we hear Abraham witnessed his merciful nature. He does not desire destruction.
- Following Jesus should be our first priority in life; discipleship influences our lives, lifestyles, and decisions.

Masses with Children

- God is merciful. Abraham hears about God's mercy in the First Reading and intercedes for people in the city.
- When we follow Jesus it shows in our lives. The way we interact with others and the way we make decisions are influenced by our faith in Jesus. Following Jesus is our priority.

Scripture Insights *(PS)*

Christ prays that we may be one, and St. Paul shows us the way—through gentleness, kindness, and honesty.

Preaching Points

Parish Masses

- What do we do when someone we care about is going astray? We might follow St. Paul's advice to a young bishop. Speak gently and kindly, without argument and debate, and trust in God.
- Christ wants us to be one, not for the sake of uniformity, but for witness. Unity is a sign of God's presence, a path to belief.

Masses with Children

Jesus wants us to be one with each other. When we are one, we are a sign of his presence in the world.

Missal Options

- The readings may be from the SW, LM #589, LMC #318, or CM or CDC.
- The prayers are proper and found in the PS.
- Consider using P-I or P-II of Saints, the Preface of Holy Pastors, or P-I or P-II of Holy Martyrs as well as EP-II.

Song of the Day

"Make Your Home in Me" by Ben Walther (OCP)

TUE 29 Solemnity of Sts. Peter and Paul, Apostles

See page 262.

WED 30 Weekday

LM #379 / LMC #193–232 / green

Optional Memorial of the First Martyrs of the Holy Roman Church / red

Scripture Insights

The reading from Genesis illustrates for us again the great mercy that God has for the poorest and most downtrodden of his people. Hagar and Ishmael, a single woman and child alone, see God's intervention in their lives.

Preaching Points

Parish Masses

- Sarah did not want Ishmael and her son Isaac to have a shared life or compete in any way for their father's affection and blessing. She had Hagar and Ishmael sent away.
- Jesus' visit to a Gentile town ends in the eradication of demons; we witness here Jesus assisting people outside Judaism; Jesus came for all humankind.

Masses with Children

- Hagar and her son posed a threat in Sarah's mind, so she had them sent away from Isaac.
- Jesus had power over the supernatural world, and he helped a Gentile town in the eradication of evil. Jesus helped both Gentile people and Jewish people.

Missal Options

- Consider using the prayers from the Fourteenth Sunday in OT.
- Use any of the three forms of the PA.
- Any of the eight Prefaces for OT or the six Common Prefaces may be used.

- You might use EPR-I.
- Any OT Collect may be used or adapted to conclude the UP. You might even look at the Collects in the Masses for Various Needs and Occasions for possible concluding prayers.

Song of the Day

"The Cry of the Poor" by John Foley (OCP)

Optional Memorial

When Nero made Christians the scapegoats for the Great Fire of Rome, it kicked off a persecution that saw Christians tortured and killed for the next four years. The Church commemorates these nameless martyrs, whose sacrifice and steadfastness have inspired believers for two millennia.

- The readings may be taken from the SW, #592, CM, or LMC #320.
- The Collect is from the PS. The other prayers may be taken from the CM (For Several Martyrs).
- Use the seasonal Collect to conclude the UP.
- Select from P-I or P-II of Saints, or P-I or P-II of Holy Martyrs.
- Consider EP-I.

THU 1 LM #380 / LMC #193–232 / green
Weekday

Optional Memorial of St. Junípero Serra, Priest / white

Scripture Insights

In the story of Abraham and Isaac on the mountain, we see a preview of the love that God has for his people. God sent his Son to us, knowing what would happen to him; he did not hold back his Son out of love for us, and out of that same love, his Son willingly suffered death here on earth.

Preaching Points

Parish Masses

- In the Old Testament we see the importance of animal sacrifice and the forbidding of human sacrifice. Such sacrifice is not a part of our faith because of Christ's sacrifice.
- Jesus had the authority to forgive the sins of those he encountered. The people were surprised because only God can forgive sins.

Masses with Children

- Sacrifice has a foundational role in the Jewish tradition in the Old Testament. Through Jesus, we no longer offer such sacrifice.
- People were surprised to hear Jesus forgive the sins of those he encountered. Only God can forgive sins, so we see Jesus' divine identity revealed here.

Missal Options

- Consider using the prayers from the MPNV-38/A/; use the second option for the Collect.
- Use any of the three forms of the PA.
- Any of the eight Prefaces for OT or the six Common Prefaces may be used.
- You might use EPR-II.
- Any OT Collect may be used or adapted to conclude the UP. You might even look at the Collects in the Masses for Various Needs and Occasions for possible concluding prayers.

Song of the Day

"Let All Creation" by Paul Tate (WLP)

Optional Memorial

St. Junípero Serra walked 24,000 miles and founded a string of twenty-one missions from San Diego to Sonoma, California. Junípero Serra saw people of every race and origin as first and foremost sons and daughters of God, a conviction that drove his missionary work "to the ends of the earth."

- The readings may be taken from the SW, #592A (LS), CP (For Missionaries), CHMW/CS (For Religious), or LMC #321.
- The Collect is from the PS. The other prayers may be taken from the CP (For Missionaries or For One Pastor).
- Use the seasonal Collect to conclude the UP.
- Select from P-I or P-II of Saints, or the Preface of Holy Pastors.
- Consider EP-I or EP-II.

FRI 2 LM #381 / LMC #193–232 / green
Weekday

Scripture Insights

In the Genesis reading, we witness the founding of Isaac's family in his marriage to Rebekah. Abraham's life passes away, and Jacob is yet to be born, but his existence is a glimmer in the eyes of Abraham and Isaac. Promised generations to follow him, Abraham trusts in God as his earthly life ends.

Preaching Points

Parish Masses

- Abraham does not wish for Isaac to return to his homeland, because he desired for God's promise of his descendants filling the land.
- Jesus chooses Matthew, a despised tax collector, as a disciple. In this selection, we see that Jesus seeks, not the perfect, but the broken. We should recognize our brokenness and follow Jesus.

Masses with Children

- Abraham insisted Isaac stay in the land God promised him; he wanted to know his descendants would fill that land.
- Perfect people do not actually exist, but many people put on a show of perfection. Jesus doesn't choose perfect people to follow him; instead he seeks people who know they are broken. We should recognize our brokenness and follow Jesus.

Missal Options

- Consider using the prayers from the MPVN-9.
- Use any of the three forms of the PA.
- Any of the eight Prefaces for OT or the six Common Prefaces may be used.
- You might use EPVN-IV.
- Any OT Collect may be used or adapted to conclude the UP. You might even look at the Collects in the Masses for Various Needs and Occasions for possible concluding prayers.

Song of the Day

"The Servant Song" by Richard Gillard (various publishers)

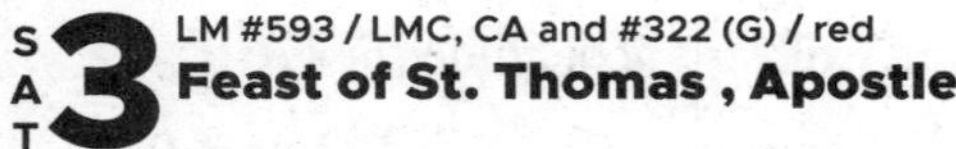

LM #593 / LMC, CA and #322 (G) / red

Feast of St. Thomas , Apostle

Today's Saint

Though labeled a doubter, Thomas asks for the same proof that the others had received. He only wants to see the Risen Lord and touch his wounds. But when he sees Christ, he moves from disbelief to belief suddenly and responds, "My Lord and my God!" This declaration of faith is unique. No other disciple in the Gospel accounts ever used such an advanced formula of faith. Thomas prepares the early Church for its Councils that ultimately define Jesus as Lord and God. It would take until the Council of Nicaea in AD 325 for such an advanced creed to be part of the profession in the Church.

Scripture Insights

A high Christological point in Scripture, the story of Thomas is often cited in terms of doubt: he is "doubting Thomas." Upon conversion of heart and mind to the truth of the Resurrection, Thomas identifies Jesus as "Lord and God." Understanding Jesus' divine identity is necessary to understand the Trinity, freedom from death and sin, and the Church in relationship with her Lord.

Preaching Points

Parish Masses

- Thomas needed to see Christ's wounds to believe he had truly risen from the dead, and he was able to witness the Risen Christ. We are called to believe in our Risen Lord without seeing or touching his wounds.
- Our identity as Church is found in our community of believers, which includes the ordained, vowed, and lay members of the faithful. As baptized people we are the dwelling place of the Lord; we are tabernacles.

Masses with Children

- Thomas wanted to see Jesus for himself before believing he had risen from the dead; we do not see Christ's risen body in our midst any longer, and we are called to believe in him without seeing his wounds.
- The Church is the community of baptized believers. Each of us is a tabernacle of the Lord. How does being a tabernacle change us and change our communities?

Missal Options

- The prayers are proper and are found in the PS.
- If you are using the LMC the Gospel is proper. The other readings may be from the CA.
- As a feast of an Apostle, you might do the sprinkling rite today. Sing or recite the Gloria.
- The Creed is not sung (or said).
- Use either of the Prefaces of the Apostles, and consider EP-I.
- Use any of the OT Collects to conclude the UP. You may end Mass with the SB for Apostles.

Song of the Day

"O Sons and Daughters" (various publishers)

- Other Rites and Customs
- Hours: Use the Proper Psalter of the day.

The Gospel requires that particular care be taken to welcome into the Church's assembly those often discarded by society—the socially and economically marginalized, the elderly, the sick, those with disabilities, and those with special needs.

—*Built of Living Stones*, 42

T U E **29** LM #590 and #591 / LMC #319 / red

Solemnity of Sts. Peter and Paul, Apostles

Today's Saints

In the Piazza San Pietro in Rome, statues of Sts. Peter and Paul flank the square, symbolizing the complementary nature of these saints' lives and mission. Paul symbolizes the person who comes to faith through a dramatic conversion, falling to the ground on his way to Damascus to persecute Christians. Peter is the person who comes to faith slowly and steadily, sometimes with two steps forward and one backward. He is the one who denies the Lord three times, then confesses his faith thrice. Regarding their complementary missions, Peter is the Apostle of the Jewish Christians, while Paul is the Apostle to the Gentile Christians. Today we celebrate their complementarity and pay homage to both saints.

Scripture Insights: Vigil

Paul confesses that he not only failed to follow Jesus but also vigorously attacked those who did. Only by God's intervention did Paul embrace the Gospel. To those in Galatia who were questioning the reliability of his words, Paul insists that God chose him from the womb for his mission and that human beings did not significantly shape him. What he preached came from God. Through Paul's devotion to his mission, the Gospel spread beyond Judaism.

Peter and Paul were vital to Christianity, but their success was due entirely to the grace of God. In the Gospel passage we hear the heart-wrenching story of Peter's rehabilitation. As the Risen Christ talks with Peter, he calls him "Simon," the name Peter had before Jesus called him to discipleship.

Three times Jesus asks if Peter loves him, just as three times Peter denied Jesus. Peter insists that he does love Jesus despite his past weakness. With the words "Follow me," Jesus commissions Peter again. This time Peter will not only lead the Church, as we heard in Acts, but also follow Jesus into martyrdom.

In giving their lives, both Peter and Paul followed Christ, the Good Shepherd, who perfectly modeled sacrificial love. We honor their courage and devotion. We also remember that God calls and empowers us, weak though we are, to follow his Son too.

Preaching Points: Vigil

Parish Masses

- "Keep your eye on the prize" is a motto that reminds us not to be distracted by what isn't in the bigger picture. In today's readings, we remember that our end goal is to be in right relationship with God and the world. Our actions here on earth are meant to help us grow in holiness and bring forth God's Kingdom.
- The Apostles carried on the ministry of Jesus after his death. Jesus shared his power and authority with the Apostles and they were able to perform miracles much like those of the Lord.
- St. Paul recalls his persecution of the Christians and his conversion. In his account, we see Paul become a man willing to die for the Lord. Paul learned about love—the deep, deep love that leads a person to truth and devotion.
- "Feed my lambs" and "Tend my sheep" are commands of leadership. Peter was charged with the leadership of the Church—God's flock—after Christ's ascension.

Children's Liturgy of the Word

- Jesus shared his authority with the Apostles and charged them with the task of continuing the Church.
- St. Paul was willing to die for his beliefs; we see Paul grow in his ability to love as a result of his transformation in Christ.
- St. Peter was changed with caring for us, who are God's sheep.

Scripture Insights: Day

Having heard what people are saying, Jesus now asks the disciples: "But who do you say that I am?" Here, Jesus refers only to himself. Peter brings in a different title: "You are the Christ, the Son of the living God." Peter's bold proclamation draws together identities expressed more evocatively in the Old Testament. There the title Messiah (Christ, anointed one) is associated with only two figures: the foreign King Cyrus, who freed the Jews from exile, and David, the anointed one of God, who is also referred to as God's son (Psalm 2:45). Matthew underscores the connection between Messiah and Son of God, giving the reader a fuller understanding of the nature of Jesus' mission and his close relationship with God. For this, Peter earns the blessing of Jesus, because he sees beyond what is merely expected to everything that can be hoped for.

Preaching Points: Day

Parish Masses

- Death will never own us, because we are claimed by Christ. Sts. Peter and Paul led the early Church, both facing death bravely, knowing their executions were pending. In this time, God was with them, and they were sustained by grace.
- In the darkest times of our lives, God's grace can help us persevere as we live our lives in the faith.
- St. Peter recognized Jesus as "the Christ, the Son of the living God" in this Gospel. The episcopacy commences in Jesus building the Church and rooting the future of the Church in the magisterium.
- Jesus promised that the gates of the netherworld would not win against the Church; indeed, the Church has not taught heresy.

Children's Liturgy of the Word

- All people have scary times in their lives, and God is always with us, even when we cannot feel his presence with us.
- Knowing who someone is helps you to understand the person. St. Peter identified Jesus as the "the Christ, the Son of the living God" in this Gospel. He helped the whole Church understand who Jesus is.
- God gives the Church authority to teach the truths of our faith, and the Church teaches truth.

Missal Options

- The texts are proper and are found in the PS.
- Use any of the three forms of the PA; however, you might consider offering the sprinkling rite.
- Use any of the OT Collects to conclude the UP.
- The Gloria and the Creed are sung or said.
- The Preface is proper and is found among the texts for the Mass during the day.
- Consider using EP-III for the Vigil and EP-I for the Mass during the Day.
- Conclude with the SB for Sts. Peter and Paul (#16).

Music Preparation

- Consider adding music on solemnities to send a message that your parish celebrates these days with great festivity.

Music Suggestions

- Gathering: "How Firm a Foundation" (various publishers)
- Preparation of the Gifts: "Balm in Gilead" (various publishers)
- Communion: "Bread of Life" by Bernadette Farrell (OCP)
- Sending Forth: "Those Who See Light" by Nancy Elze, Donald Osuna (OCP)

Mass Texts

Introduction to Mass

At the very beginnings of the Church stand these two giants, Sts. Peter and Paul, whose solemnity we celebrate today. Each in their own way, they testify to the Risen Christ, and by their prayers they strengthen our faith. Let us give thanks for them and with contrite hearts receive the sacrifice of the One they recognized as Son of God. *My brothers and sisters, let us acknowledge our sins, and so prepare ourselves to celebrate the sacred mysteries.*

Tropes for Penitential Act, Form III

You founded your Church on the rock of St. Peter:
Lord, have mercy.

Through St. Paul you taught the Good News to the Gentiles:
Christ, have mercy.

Their voices resound to the ends of the world:
Lord, have mercy.

Dismissal of Catechumens

My friends, Sts. Peter and Paul have given their lives for the sake of the Gospel, and they pray for us still, that we might one day join them in the joy of God's Kingdom. For your sake, we join our prayer to theirs and we look forward to the day when you will join us at the table of the Lord and in the communion of all the saints. Go now in Christ's peace.

Dismissal of Extraordinary Ministers of Holy Communion

Dear friends, the Lord Jesus still provides for his sheep. Take his Body to those of our community whose health prevents them from joining us in the flesh, that through you Christ may tend and feed all his lambs and unite us in his Spirit. Go in peace.

Universal Prayer

The message of Sts. Peter and Paul goes out to all the world! Seeking to win the race as did Peter and Paul, let us offer to God our petitions for those in need.

1. For the pope, the vicar of St. Peter, that he may ever increase in faith and wisdom, we pray:
2. For all missionaries who follow in the footsteps of St. Paul, proclaiming the Gospel in foreign lands, we pray:
3. For religious freedom in every land, that all governments will respect the right of people to worship God in their own way, we pray:
4. For all who find running the race of faith a challenge, especially for those burdened with illness and distress, we pray:
5. For those gathered here, that we may grow stronger in our faith, day by day, as we seek to emulate the Apostles and mature in Christ, we pray:

Almighty and ever-living God,
you raised up your servants St. Peter and St. Paul
as the sure foundation of the Church founded on the cornerstone that is Christ.
We give you thanks for the protection you have offered the Church throughout the ages.
Continue to pour on her the grace of the Holy Spirit
so that the Gospel may be heard in every corner of the world.
Through Christ our Lord.
Amen.

Other Rites and Customs

Given today's Gospel, celebrate the many people who serve your parish in a variety of ways. Include the Order of Blessing Those Who Exercise Pastoral Service (BB, ch. 60) at any of the Masses this weekend. Follow Mass with a thank-you party.

Liturgy and Life

Both Peter and Paul suffered martyrdom. Many may not know that the red hats worn by cardinals in the Church symbolize a willingness to undergo martyrdom for the faith. Today's solemnity invites us to consider how we might be called to sacrifice for our faith.

S U N **4** LM #101B / LMC #96B / green

Fourteenth Sunday in Ordinary Time

Scripture Insights

Ezekiel is the last of the major prophets, preaching in the period of the exile in Babylon (approximately 597 to 537 BC). In fact, he had already been taken captive to Babylon when he received his call. Ezekiel's prophesies stand out from those of the other prophets. The visions he reports are especially vivid and surreal: the wheel within the wheel (1:15) and the four living creatures with faces like an ox, a lion, an eagle, and a human being (1:10). (These would later be associated with the four evangelists, Mark, Matthew, John, and Luke, respectively.) Finally, Ezekiel speaks in the first person, as though he is relating his conversation with God as it happens, whereas most other prophets repeat what God has told them: "Thus says the Lord . . . "

We do not hear the subject of his preaching in this passage. In general, he prophesied the further destruction of Jerusalem by the Babylonians, an unpopular topic. When the Temple was destroyed in 587 BC, Ezekiel's prophecy was fulfilled. The subject of his preaching, however, is not as important as the outcome. The Lord tells Ezekiel to preach so that "they shall know that a prophet has been among them." Later in the prophecy, God tells Ezekiel: "They shall know that I, the LORD their God, am with them" (34:30). In the similarity of phrases, the reader can sense the close relationship between God and God's prophet.

In his hometown, Jesus faces similar issues. He must preach the good news whether people listen or not. Unlike Ezekiel, who expected a stubborn and rebellious people, Jesus is amazed and perplexed when people do not believe him. We readers, who have been following Mark's story as Jesus touches and heals every kind of separation that people experience, from sin to illness to death, are also surprised. And yet, in spite of firm disbelief, Jesus is able to effect some healing for those who sought it. It is enough. He continues teaching in every town that will have him.

Why does the crowd discuss Jesus' background and family? What does that have to do with their lack of belief?

Preaching Points

Parish Masses

- Matthew, Mark, Luke, and John are recognized in the Ezekiel reading's imagery. Like ancient Israel, we are called to love, embrace, and accept Jesus' way. We must seek the Lord and rely on his grace.
- We are a mission people, sent by our Lord to live as he taught us to live and to spread the good news of the Gospel.
- Through God's grace, we preach the Gospel. This grace is sufficient for each of us in our vocations.
- Jesus was rejected in his hometown; greeted with suspicion, he understood that most in Nazareth would reject him. Those who did seek him would receive his ministry.
- On this Sunday, we hear God call the prophet Ezekiel to proclaim the divine Word to a recalcitrant people. We, like the Israelites, sometimes close our hearts off to God. But one day amazement will fill our hardened hearts because we will know of God's abiding presence. Or, will amazement fill Jesus at the lack of faith he finds in us? Paul knows how sufficient the Lord's grace is for him. May amazement fill us on this Sunday as it did Paul—for God's sufficient grace is truly amazing grace! It is more than enough for us.

Children's Liturgy of the Word

- Each week at Mass we are sent forth into the world to carry on the Eucharistic life. We are a mission people.
- God's grace is sufficient for each of us, and we rely on that grace throughout our lives.
- Those in Jesus' hometown rejected him, seeing nothing special about Joseph and Mary's son. Despite that reception, Jesus still ministered to those who sought him.

Missal Options

- Offer any of the three forms of the PA.
- Sing or recite the Gloria and the Creed.
- Any of the seasonal OT Collects may be used or adapted to conclude the UP.
- Select from any of the eight Prefaces of OT.
- Consider EP-III.
- There are six SBs for OT from which to choose.

Music Preparation

The Fourteenth Sunday takes precedence over Independence Day. Resist the urge to sing patriotic songs at Mass. Instead, include petitions for the needs of our country (and of the entire world since God does not bless one country over another).

Music Suggestions

- Responsorial Psalm: "Our Eyes Are Fixed on the Lord" by Ephrem Feely (GIA)
- Preparation of the Gifts: "Make Us True Servants" by Susan G. Wente (WLP)
- Communion: "Spirit and Grace" by Ricky Manolo, CSP (OCP)
- Sending Forth: "This Is My Song" by George Harkness (various publishers)

Mass Texts

Introduction to Mass

God calls us day after day to walk humbly with his Son Jesus and to learn what it means to love. Let us not turn a hardened face to him or be stubborn in heart; rather, let us put aside all rebelliousness and plead for his merciful love. God's grace will be our help in weakness, and the Body and Blood of his Son that we receive here today will be our strength for the journey. *My brothers and sisters, let us acknowledge our sins, and so prepare ourselves to celebrate the sacred mysteries.*

Tropes for Penitential Act, Form III

Against you, O Lord, we have sinned and hardened our hearts: Lord, have mercy.

You come to us in the weakness of your cross: Christ, have mercy.

By the power of your Resurrection you have set us free from sin: Lord, have mercy.

Dismissal for Children's Liturgy of the Word

My dear children, in today's Gospel you will hear that Jesus' neighbors did not have faith in him and because of this he couldn't do any wonderful deeds among them. Faith, then, is very powerful. By our faith we invite Jesus into our lives to do wonderful things for us and for the world. Go and listen to him and welcome him into your hearts with faith.

Dismissal of Catechumens

Dear friends, in so many ways God speaks to your hearts, and today he has spoken to you through the Scriptures. How is he calling you to conversion and drawing you to greater love? We give you this time now to consider the Word you have heard—the challenge and promise contained therein. Open your hearts and continue on this path that will—we hope and pray— lead you to union with us in the Eucharist. Go in peace.

Dismissal of Extraordinary Ministers of Holy Communion

Dear friends, our sick and homebound brothers and sisters await your visit and the grace of this sacrament that is their spiritual food for eternal life. Take the Body of Christ to them along with our prayers for healing and our assurances that they are one with us in faith, hope, and love. Go in peace.

Universal Prayer

My brothers and sisters, have faith in Christ! Be a voice for the voiceless. Be a light in the darkness. Be a prophet against all that prevents God's creation from living to its fullness! Conscious of the brokenness in our world, let us raise up these needs to God.

1. For the Church, that she may always be a welcoming home, especially for the lost and forsaken, we pray:
2. For all nations at war, that they may cease their fighting and strive to live together in harmony, we pray:
3. That the United States may always stand as a beacon of hope in a darkened world, offering solace and refuge to those who seek a better life, we pray:
4. That we may seek the freedom of all those who are unjustly condemned, we pray:
5. That those who dedicate their lives to the protection of freedom throughout the world may be rewarded with honor and respect, we pray:
6. For the homeless and those who are struggling to keep a roof over their head, we pray:
7. For all missionaries and those engaged in extended service projects, that they may learn that no land on earth is their abiding home, we pray:
8. For the dead, that they may return home to God in peace, we pray:

Provident God,
we place all of our hope in you.
Through life's many storms,
we know that we may always turn to you in our time of need.
May Jesus, your Son, grasp us closer to himself
so that we may find a lasting family among his followers.
May the Gospel unfold in us
as we seek to make Christ known, loved, and served.
Who lives and reigns with you in the unity of the Holy Spirit,
one God, for ever and ever.
Amen.

Other Rites and Customs

Take advantage of the less busy summer months to review how your parish incorporates periods of silence into the liturgy, especially after the readings and the homily, after Communion, and after the invitation to pray during the Collect and Prayer after Communion (see GIRM, 43, 45, 51, 54, 55, 56, 66, 71, 78, 128, 130, 136, 147, 165, and 271).

Liturgy and Life

In the Jewish tradition, a prophet is one who is chosen by God, listens deeply to God, and is empowered to speak God's message for everyone. In the prophetic books of the Old Testament we read the sayings of the prophets and we also learn how they were called. God continues to call prophets as messengers to our modern world—people who give us hope. Be alert and discerning to recognize other modern-day prophets and take care not to reject their voices as the people of Nazareth dismissed Jesus. Listen carefully to the voice of God in your own life and allow God to speak words of wisdom, challenge, and guidance through you to those who seek your counsel.

Taking Place This Week . . .

Consider what can be done liturgically, catechetically, and ministerially to respond to these important needs.

- US Independence Day is 7/4 but observed on 7/5.
- July is National Park and Recreation month. Consider ways you as a parish can contribute to the protection of creation!

MON 5 LM #383 / LMC #193–232 / green
Weekday

Optional Memorials of St. Anthony Zaccaria, Priest / white; St. Elizabeth of Portugal / white

Scripture Insights

We are meant to dwell with God forever in heaven, and we know he has prepared a place for us in heaven. While we are on earth, we must also choose to dwell with God; doing so is a deliberate decision we make over hours, weeks, and years. Choosing God and his ways is a manner of living out our faith in our everyday lives.

Preaching Points

Parish Masses

- Abraham trusted God's promise to make his descendants as numerous as the stars, and in Jacob we see the third generation of Abraham's family interacting with the Lord and living in the covenant. God is always with his people.
- The woman who had a years-long hemorrhage put her faith in Jesus, knowing so clearly and absolutely that in him was a power to heal her. Because of her hemorrhage, she would have been ritually unclean, so her recovery was not just a return to physical health but also a return to a typical life.

Masses with Children

- God made a covenant with Abraham, and his grandson Jacob continued to live in that covenant. The Jewish people, including Jesus, descend from these faithful people.
- When Jesus healed a little girl who had died, we see that Jesus has power not only over nature but over death itself. The little girl coming back to the living is a reminder that the Lord too will die but will conquer death.

Missal Options

- Consider using the prayers from the MPVN-47.
- Use any of the three forms of the PA.
- Any of the eight Prefaces for OT or the six Common Prefaces may be used.
- You might use EPVN-IV.
- Any OT Collect may be used or adapted to conclude the UP. You might even look at the Collects in the Masses for Various Needs and Occasions for possible concluding prayers.

Song of the Day

"Strength for the Journey" by Michael John Poirier (WLP)

Optional Memorials

St. Anthony

St. Anthony was from Italy. He founded three religious orders: the Barnabites or Clerics Regular of St. Paul (the first order named for St. Paul), the Angelic Sisters of St. Paul for nuns, and a lay community.

- The readings may be from the SW, #595, LMC #325, or the CP or CS/CHMW (For Educators or For Religious).
- The Collect is from the PS; the other prayers may be from the CP (For One Pastor) or the CHMW (For Educators or For Religious).
- Consider P-I or P-II of Saints, the Preface of Holy Pastors, or the Preface of Holy Virgins and Religious. Consider also EP-I.

St. Elizabeth

Bearing the corruption and immorality of her husband's kingly court, St. Elizabeth joined the Third Order Franciscans following his death and lived a life of piety and prayer.

- The readings may be from the SW, #594 (LS), LMC #323, or CS/CHMW (For Those Who Work for the Underprivileged).
- The Collect is from the PS; the other prayers are from the CHMW (For Those Who Practiced Works of Mercy).
- Use either P-I or P-II of Saints, or the Preface of Holy Virgins and Religious.
- Consider also EP-I.

TUE 6 LM #384 / LMC #193–232 / green
Weekday

Optional Memorial of St. Maria Goretti, Virgin and Martyr / red

Scripture Insights

Through God's grace we are changed people. We encounter God's grace in many ways in our lives, primarily through the sacraments. In our lives we are called to look toward God and live in his ways; when we do that, we choose to be laborers for God.

Preaching Points

Parish Masses

- Like Abraham before him, Jacob is given a new name: Israel. The letters "el" at the end of an Old Testament name refer to God's name, "El." It is from Israel's name that the Israelites took their name and identity.

- Jesus wants us to look to him and join as laborers in God's harvest. Choosing Jesus and his ways is a way of living our lives.

Masses with Children

- Like Abraham before him, Jacob is given a new name: Israel. The letters "el" at the end of an Old Testament name refer to God's name, "El." It is from Israel's name that the Israelites took their name and identity.
- How do we choose to be laborers in God's harvest? What choices do we make every day that help us labor for God's harvest?

Missal Options

- Consider using the prayers from the MPVN-29.
- Use any of the three forms of the PA.
- Any of the eight Prefaces for OT or the six Common Prefaces may be used.
- You might use EP-II.
- Any OT Collect may be used or adapted to conclude the UP. You might even look at the Collects in the Masses for Various Needs and Occasions for possible concluding prayers.

Song of the Day

"Into the Fields" by Daniel J. Schutte (OCP)

Optional Memorial

St. Maria Goretti was killed while resisting her would-be rapist and has been held up as a model of chastity, but her resistance was also an act of charity and a desire to spare her attacker, Alessandro, from the stain of greater sin. The saint succeeded in redeeming Alessandro's soul after her death, appearing to him in a dream during his imprisonment, offering her forgiveness and urging him to turn to Christ's mercy.

- The readings may be taken from the SW, #596, CM, CV, LMC #326, or CS.
- The Collect is from the PS. The other prayers may be taken from the CM (For a Virgin Martyr) or CV (For One Virgin).
- Use any of the OT Collects to conclude the UP.
- Select from P-1 or P-II of Saints, P-I or P-II of Holy Martyrs, or the Preface of Holy Virgins and Religious.
- Consider EP-I.

WED 7 LM #385 / LMC #193–232 / green
Weekday

Scripture Insights

Joseph's brothers were like lost sheep; they had done wrong and were sorry for their sins against Joseph. They and their families were starving and were now depending on Joseph for survival.

Preaching Points

Parish Masses

- Joseph, who was given the very worst treatment by his brothers, found himself in a position of power over them. How would he use this power? Can reconciliation happen after such treatment?
- Who were the lost sheep of Israel, and what could a shepherd do for them? Jesus sent his disciples to preach to those who were God's people who desperately needed a shepherd.

Masses with Children

- The story of Joseph is one filled with lessons, but the primary question in this reading is one of power. How should power be used? How can power be used for good or bad purposes?
- The lost sheep of Israel were a primary concern in Jesus' ministry. Jesus had a deep love of God's people and desired to see them shepherded in the right direction.

Missal Options

- Consider using the prayers from the MPVN-3.
- Use any of the three forms of the PA.
- Any of the eight Prefaces for OT or the six Common Prefaces may be used.
- You might use EP-I.
- Any OT Collect may be used or adapted to conclude the UP. You might even look at the Collects in the Masses for Various Needs and Occasions for possible concluding prayers.

Song of the Day

"Go Out in the World" by Ed Bolduc (WLP)

THU 8 LM #386 / LMC #193–232 / green
Weekday

Scripture Insights

God's grace can be known to us when a terrible situation can be used for good. Joseph's brothers did something terrible when they sold him into slavery, but, by grace, the situation saved the lives of God's people.

Preaching Points

Parish Masses

- Joseph revealed his identity to his brothers and forgave them for their terrible act. Instead of reacting in retribution toward his brothers, in the reading he inquired about his father's wellness.
- The Word of God is meant to be free for all to hear, and the grace that comes from it is also free. Salvation itself, and all of its riches, is freely given.

Masses with Children

- Instead of taking revenge on his brothers, Joseph acts in love and forgiveness toward them.
- When Jesus sent his disciples out into ministry, he gave them the blessing to do his work. The people were to hear the words and receive the ministry without having to pay any money; God's goodness is free to all his beloved children.

Missal Options

- Consider using the prayers from the MPVN-18/B.
- Use any of the three forms of the PA.
- Any of the eight Prefaces for OT or the six Common Prefaces may be used.
- You might use EPR-I.
- Any OT Collect may be used or adapted to conclude the UP. You might even look at the Collects in the Masses for Various Needs and Occasions for possible concluding prayers.

Song of the Day

"God's Blessing Sends Us Forth"
by Omer Westendorf (WLP)

FRI 9 LM #387 / LMC #193–232 / green
Weekday

Optional Memorial of St. Augustine Zhao Rong, Priest, and Companions, Martyrs / red

Scripture Insights

When Israel saw Joseph, his heart must have burst with joy; his beloved son returned to his family was a joy like no other. Love of a parent for a child is a deep and abiding love; this love is one of the ways that we can begin to comprehend God's great love for us.

Preaching Points

Parish Masses

- Israel was the patriarch of the family, and the clan migrated to Egypt with God's blessing.
- In ministry, Jesus instructed the Apostles to be "as shrewd as serpents and simple as doves." Jesus understood that his message of love would not be easily received by the cold world.

Masses with Children

- The patriarch of a family is a "male leader." At this point in history, in this region and culture, families were known by their patriarchs. Israel was the oldest man in the family, and the reading shows us how, under his leadership and with God's blessing, the ancient Israelites arrived in Egypt.
- In ministry, Jesus instructed the Apostles to be "as shrewd as serpents and simple as doves." Jesus understood that his message of love would not be easily received by everyone in the world. Jesus promised that the Holy Spirit would help ministers who were persecuted.

Missal Options

- Consider using the prayers from the MPVN-19.
- Use any of the three forms of the PA.
- Any of the eight Prefaces for OT or the six Common Prefaces may be used.
- You might use EPVN-2.
- Any OT Collect may be used or adapted to conclude the UP. You might even look at the Collects in the Masses for Various Needs and Occasions for possible concluding prayers.

Song of the Day

"Take Up Your Cross" (various publishers)

Optional Memorial

St. Augustine Zhao Rong was a Chinese diocesan priest and one of one hundred Chinese Catholics and Western missionaries martyred in China between 1648 and 1930. These Chinese martyrs are examples of great faithfulness under persecution.

- The readings may be taken from the SW, #596A (LS), or CM.
- The Collect is from the PS. The other prayers may be taken from the CM (For Several Martyrs).
- Use any of the OT Collects to conclude the UP.
- Select from P-I or P-II of Saints, P-I or P-II of Holy Martyrs, and the Preface of Holy Pastors.
- Consider EP-I.

SAT **10** LM #388 / LMC #193–232 / green
Weekday

Optional Memorial of the Blessed Virgin Mary / white

Scripture Insights

As this chapter of Genesis closes, we hear that Joseph desires for his bones to be returned to the land of his birth. In our Catholic faith, we have a destination in common; we look to heaven as the place we seek upon our deaths.

Preaching Points

Parish Masses

- Despite living in Egypt, Jacob wished to be buried in the land of his forebears and to be buried near his forbears and his wife, Leah. Joseph instructed his family to take his bones to that same place when they returned to their homeland. Family, clan, and land united in God's blessing were of primary importance to Jacob and Joseph. They believed the Israelites would be returned to that land.
- The early Christians would face persecution. This Gospel reading reminds the believers that they do not need to fear the damage to their bodies; their souls will remain intact and can be with God in heaven. There is more to fear in that which can damage body and soul.

Masses with Children

- God, family, and land mattered greatly to Jacob and Joseph. Jacob wished to be buried with his wife, father, and grandfather in the land of his birth. Joseph requested that, when his descendants and surviving brothers returned to that land, they take his bones with them.
- The early Christians would face persecution. This Gospel reading reminds the believers that even if their bodies are hurt, their souls will remain intact, and they will be with God in heaven.

Missal Options

- Consider using the prayers from the Second Sunday in OT.
- Use any of the three forms of the PA.
- Any of the eight Prefaces for OT or the six Common Prefaces may be used.
- You might use EP-II.
- Any OT Collect may be used or adapted to conclude the UP. You might even look at the Collects in the Masses for Various Needs and Occasions for possible concluding prayers.

Song of the Day

"Daily, Daily Sing to Mary" (various publishers)

Optional Memorial

- The readings may be taken from the SW, CBVM, or CMML.
- The prayers may be taken from the CBVM or CMMM. You may also use the various Votive Masses for the BVM.
- Use any of the OT Collects to conclude the UP.
- Consider EP-III.

SUN 11 LM #104B / LMC #99B / green

Fifteenth Sunday in Ordinary Time

Scripture Insights

After Jesus' unfortunate experience in his hometown (Mark 6:1–6), he sends his disciples out to preach repentance, cast out demons, and anoint and heal the sick. Jesus' injunction to travel light appears to serve several purposes. The Apostles need to move easily and quickly from place to place. The directions to carry a staff and wear sandals are reminiscent of the instructions Moses gave for the Passover meal. "This is how you are to eat it: with your loins girt, sandals on your feet and your staff in hand, you shall eat like those who are in flight" (Exodus 12:11). Going out without food, baggage, or money forces the Apostles to depend on the hospitality of strangers and, ultimately, on God. It was a lesson the Jews learned in the wilderness, even though they carried personal belongings with them. The reader might also detect an urgency to reach as wide an area as possible, a mission certainly felt in the early Church. Baggage gets in the way. Finally, perhaps mindful of his own experience, Jesus urges the Apostles to leave any place that rejects them. Shaking off the dust is thought to be a Jewish custom that allows one to go on without dwelling on past troubles (see Acts 13:51).

Along with these specific instructions, Jesus commissions the Apostles to three particular tasks: they are to preach repentance, cast out demons, and anoint and cure the sick. Matthew and Luke record this story as well (Matthew 10; Luke 9), but Mark is the only one to associate anointing the sick with curing them. The Letter of James, written about the same time or slightly before Mark's account, also speaks of anointing with oil (5:14). It seems clear that this was a practice in at least some of the Christian communities. The contemporary Church has continued that practice in its Sacrament of Anointing. Through his disciples and in these three facets of the mission—healing, expelling demons, and preaching conversion—Jesus restores wholeness in mind, body, and soul to the whole world.

Preaching Points

Parish Masses

- Jesus instructed the Apostles not to be weighed down by baggage or by others' acceptance of their message as they began their mission. This mission was an instruction to continue Jesus' ministry of healing the "mind, body, and soul."
- God shares his plan for humankind with his beloved creation; we are meant to belong to God through Christ. We are sealed to God in the Holy Spirit, through Christ our Lord.
- The Apostles were commissioned by Christ to carry on his healing ministry.
- It does not matter where we are in our faith journey. Neither does our state in life or our chosen life's profession matter. Jesus sends us forth in mission from this unique point in time and our unique place in the world to preach repentance and bring life to others.

Children's Liturgy of the Word

- Our faith is not filled with secrets or special knowledge known by only a few people. God has made his plan for humankind clear for those who seek his wisdom.
- We belong to God, and uniquely belong to him in the Holy Spirit, through Jesus.
- Jesus wanted to be sure that his ministry would continue, so he helped his Apostles learn to minister in his name.

Missal Options

- Offer any of the three forms of the PA.
- Sing or recite the Gloria and the Creed.
- Any of the seasonal OT Collects may be used or adapted to conclude the UP.
- Select from any of the eight Prefaces of OT.
- Consider EPVN-II.
- There are six SBs for OT from which to choose.

Music Preparation

- As Jesus sends his disciples out to unknown territory, he tells them to trust and to live simply. He prepares them for new challenges. Perhaps there are tasks in your job as a music minister that you must turn over to God?
- One of the hardest things for many musicians to do is purge. Recycle single copies of octavos and old files. Go through your office and simplify things. Be considerate of the needs of creation and parishes that have less than you are fortunate to have. Do not throw away music—donate it to other parishes or recycle music that is too worn to give away. Copyright infringement is not only unethical but also illegal. Resolve to stop photocopying music if this has been your practice.
- One of the corporal works of mercy is to bury the dead. Many parish communities have a "Lazarus Ministry" or bereavement team in place to help assist the family in preparing the various funeral rites. The music ministry can assist by establishing a funeral choir to help support and encourage the assembly's sung prayer during these trying moments. Perhaps a cluster of parish communities (maybe even ecumenical in scope?) might be able to combine forces to provide a community-wide response to support those in need.

Music Suggestions

- Gathering: "God Has Spoken by the Prophets" by George W. Briggs (Hope Publishing Company)
- Preparation of the Gifts: "Lord, You Give the Great Commission" (various publishers)
- Communion: "The Hand of the Lord Feeds Us" by Steven R. Janco (WLP)

Mass Texts

Introduction to Mass

We have come here in answer to God's call to repentance and to faith in his Son Jesus who, through the Eucharist, provides us with the grace we need to go out into the world and extend that call to all people. Before we take up the tasks of Apostles and servants, let us look to our own hearts, to our own need for forgiveness, and thank God for his merciful love. *My brothers and sisters, let us acknowledge our sins, and so prepare ourselves to celebrate the sacred mysteries.*

Tropes for Penitential Act, Form III

We are like sheep who have gone astray: Lord, have mercy.

By your blood we have redemption, the forgiveness of sins: Christ, have mercy.

Show us, Lord, your kindness and grant us your salvation: Lord, have mercy.

Dismissal for Children's Liturgy of the Word

Dear children, family is a blessing, a gift from the God who loves us. St. Paul, in today's Second Reading, tells us that God blesses us even further by adopting us through his Son Jesus. We are daughters and sons of God himself, guaranteed the unconditional, never-failing love of our Father in heaven. Through Jesus, our brother, he now speaks to you in the Scriptures. Go and listen to him.

Dismissal of Catechumens

Dear friends, before the world began God knew you and loved you into being. The wisdom and love of your Creator have led you here today, to this specific place, this community, the particular words spoken to you in today's readings. Avail yourself of all the help God has put in your path and let it lead you to the further help of the sacrament of eternal life, Christ's Body and Blood. Go in peace.

Dismissal of Extraordinary Ministers of Holy Communion

My friends, God has entrusted to his Church the Bread of life, and now we send you to the sick members of Christ's Body with this spiritual nourishment, that it may renew in them the faith that, with us, they will behold God's face in the joy of his Kingdom. Go in peace.

Universal Prayer

Taking nothing on our journey but our trust in God, we turn to him now in prayer.

1. That the Church may always be hospitable, especially for the stranger and those in need, we pray:
2. That our Christian homes may be places where welcome is freely given and accepted, we pray:
3. That those who close doors to people of different views, colors, or nationalities may learn to be open, we pray:
4. That we may be filled with courage in our preaching of the Gospel in words we say and the actions we perform, we pray:
5. That those who have died may be raised to new life in the Spirit, we pray:

Compassionate and merciful God,
you are always open
to receiving our hearts when we turn to you in faith.
As followers of your beloved Son,
may we welcome not only our brother and sister,
but the stranger and the destitute.
Through Christ our Lord.
Amen.

Other Rites and Customs

- While the Memorial of St. Benedict is superseded by Sunday this year, offer catechesis on the Liturgy of the Hours in honor of the founder of Western monasticism.
- Invite a speaker from the missions to reflect on Jesus' commissioning of the Twelve to go out two by two.

Liturgy and Life

Jesus sent his disciples out to gain some experiential learning. He sent them two by two, without food or money, into communities to put into action all they had been taught. In a similar way, Jesus invites each of us to bring God's compassion and healing to others.

Taking Place This Week . . .

Consider what can be done liturgically, catechetically, and ministerially to respond to these important needs.

- World Population Day (7/11)
- The French celebrate Bastille Day (7/14).
- World Youth Skills Day (7/15)

MON 12 LM #389 / LMC #193–232 / green
Weekday

Scripture Insights

The killing of the Hebrew boys in Egypt reminds us of the killing of boys after Jesus' birth. Moses, a boy who would survive, would lead his people out of Egypt. Jesus, who would lead his people out of sin, would survive the infanticide when his parents fled to Egypt.

Preaching Points

Parish Masses

- The Egyptians forgot about Joseph and his wise management of the country. As the Hebrews prospered, the Egyptian officials enslaved them; the Hebrews became slaves.
- Jesus teaches us that he should be the priority above all else in our lives. When we prioritize Jesus and his teaching, the rest of our lives fall into place.

Masses with Children

- The Egyptians were threatened by the Hebrews who lived in Egypt. They were forced into slavery by the Egyptians, and their baby boys were killed.
- Jesus taught that people should always put him and his teaching first in their lives. When we live our lives the way he taught us to live, most of our lives fall into order.

Missal Options

- Consider using the prayers from the MPVN-31/2.
- Use any of the three forms of the PA.
- Any of the eight Prefaces for OT or the six Common Prefaces may be used.
- You might use EPVN-II.
- Any OT Collect may be used or adapted to conclude the UP. You might even look at the Collects in the Masses for Various Needs and Occasions for possible concluding prayers.

Song of the Day

"O Gracious Light, Lord Jesus Christ" translated by F. Bland Tucker (The Church Pension Fund)

TUE 13 LM #390 / LMC #193–232 / green
Weekday

Optional Memorial of St. Henry / white

Scripture Insights

Moses was saved from premature earthly death in order that he might save his people from slavery in Egypt. Jesus lived so that his people could escape the slavery of sin; we must open our hearts and minds to Jesus and his Word so that we may have life.

Preaching Points

Parish Masses

- The story of Moses is one that begins in a time of infanticide; his mother hid him to save him from those who sought to kill Hebrew boys. Despite his adoption by the Pharaoh's daughter, he maintained his allegiance to the Hebrews, and his heart was moved by their plight.
- How do we stand up for those who are helpless, like the Hebrews were helpless under Egyptian rule?
- Jesus taught that we must be open to him and to his teaching. How can we open ourselves to Jesus? How do we close ourselves to Jesus, and how do we change that behavior?

Masses with Children

- Moses' mother hid him from the Egyptians who tried to kill all the Hebrew boys. Little Moses was adopted by a daughter of the Pharaoh and survived the terrible infanticide. Despite being adopted into the Egyptian royal family, Moses didn't abandon his Hebrew origins. Knowing morally wrong treatment when he saw it, Moses objected to the Hebrews' slavery.
- We are called to stand for what is right. How do we stand for human rights?
- How do we open ourselves to Jesus and his Word? How do we close ourselves to him, and how can we change our behavior so that we may grow in Jesus?

Missal Options

- Consider using the prayers from the Twelfth Sunday in OT.
- Use any of the three forms of the PA.
- Any of the eight Prefaces for OT or the six Common Prefaces may be used.
- You might use EP-II.
- Any OT Collect may be used or adapted to conclude the UP. You might even look at the Collects in the Masses for Various Needs and Occasions for possible concluding prayers.

Song of the Day

"Praise to the Lord" (various publishers)

Optional Memorial

Although he did not choose his station or duties in life, King Henry II sought to glorify God and live a Christian life as king of Germany and made wise and prudent decisions for both Church and state during his reign.

- The readings may be taken from the SW, #598, CHMW/CS, or LMC #328.
- The Collect is from the PS. The other prayers may be taken from the CHMW (For One Saint).
- Use any of the OT Collects to conclude the UP.
- Use either P-I or P-II of Saints.
- Consider EP-I or EP-II.

WED 14 LM #391 or #599A / LMC #193–232 or #329 / white

Memorial of St. Kateri Tekakwitha, Virgin

Today's Saint

St. Kateri Tekakwitha (1657–1680) was the first Native American to be canonized. Hearing about Christ from Jesuit missionaries, she chose to be a Christian at seventeen. Since Christians also brought disease and destruction to some indigenous villages, her choice was opposed by her family. She gave birth to the Gospel by being faithful to prayer and caring for children and the sick. She promised to continue her care when she reached heaven. She died at age twenty-four.

Scripture Insights

What is it to be called by God? Most people do not experience God the way Abraham and Isaac experienced him, yet we all respond to God's call. Moses was called to lead his people out of slavery. We must discern our own calls in our lives.

Preaching Points

Parish Masses

- Moses left Egypt after he killed the Egyptian man, and he lived exiled in Midian with his wife and her family. His answer, "Here I am," is a reminder of how we should respond to God when we are called. Instead of responding in the negative, Moses responds in curiosity.
- God does not call people because of their looks, their wealth, or their sophistication. We do not have to be the most educated or richest people in order to know, love, and begin to understand God.

Masses with Children

- God calls people to different roles in life. Few people hear from God directly the way Moses and Abraham heard from him. How do we hear from God, and how do we respond to his call?
- Looks, wealth, and education do not limit God from revealing himself to people, and a person doesn't need to be the smartest or richest person to grow in understanding and love of God.

Missal Options

- The readings may also be taken from the #599A (LS), the CV. For Masses with children, the readings may also be from the CS.
- Use any of the three forms of the PA.
- Use any of the OT Collects to conclude the UP.
- Select from P-I or P-II of Saints, or the Preface of Holy Virgins and Religious.
- The Collect is from the PS. Notice that the Missal uses the term "Blessed." This should be updated to "Saint." The other prayers may be taken from the CV (For One Virgin).
- Consider EPVN-I.

Song of the Day

"Eat This Bread" by Jacques Berthier (GIA)

THU 15 LM #392 or #600 / LMC #193–232 or #330 / white

Memorial of St. Bonaventure, Bishop and Doctor of the Church

Today's Saint

A Franciscan bishop, Doctor of the Church, and teacher, Bonaventure served as Franciscan minister general at a time of great division. Because of his evident love for God, he is called the "Seraphic Doctor."

Scripture Insights

Called to lead his people out of slavery, Moses had to travel to Egypt and face the elders and explain that God had spoken to him. Despite having grown up in an Egyptian palace, despite having left in exile, Moses would have to face these hurdles as God requested him to do.

Preaching Points

Parish Masses

- Enslavement of any kind is wrong, and God desired for his people to be freed from slavery. What modern slavery exists, and how do God's people respond to such injustice?

- Juxtapose the slavery of the Hebrews with the yoke that Jesus offers to us; Jesus does not force his yoke on us but allows us to choose it.

Masses with Children

- The Egyptians held the Hebrews as slaves, and God desired for his people to be free from such injustice. Moses was the man God called to free his people.
- The Hebrews were enslaved to the Egyptians and it was not by choice. We willingly choose God's authority over us. Jesus tells us that his yoke is light.

Scripture Insights *(PS)*

Christ is our teacher and the foundation of all wisdom and understanding of God.

Preaching Points

Parish Masses

- Is Christ our teacher and our master? Are there other, noisier voices that drown out Christ's voice in our lives? Christ is always speaking to us through the Scriptures, in the Church, and in the quiet place within us where we pray.
- That place within us where we meet God needs to be expanded through prayer, so that Christ can dwell within us and reveal his mysteries to us.

Masses with Children

- Christ is always present and speaking to us. He finds us in the Church, in the quiet places within, in the Scriptures, in the Eucharist, and in other people.
- Pray often so that Christ can dwell within us and reveal what he wants from us in our life.

Missal Options

- The readings may also be taken from the CP or CDC.
- The Collect is from the PS. The other prayers are from the CP (For a Bishop) or CDC.
- Use any of the three forms of the PA.
- Use any of the OT Collects to conclude the UP.
- Select from P-I or P-II of Saints, the Preface of Holy Pastors, or the Preface of Holy Virgins and Religious.
- Consider EP-II.

Song of the Day

"Open My Eyes, Lord" by Jesse Manibussan (OCP)

FRI 16 LM #393 / LMC #193–232 / green

Weekday

Optional Memorial of Our Lady of Mount Carmel / white

Scripture Insights

The blood of the lamb would protect the inhabitants of each Hebrew household. The blood would signal the angel of death to pass over the homes of the Hebrews while God's angel of death made its way through Egypt. The meal, which was known as the Seder, was the last supper Jesus ate with his disciples. As the blood of the lambs slaughtered in Egypt preserved the enslaved Hebrews from death, the blood of the lamb of God would preserve his followers from death.

Preaching Points

Parish Masses

- When matters seem impossible, God makes a way for the impossible to become possible. God loves and protects his people.
- Jesus told the Pharisees that the disciples were not breaking God's law by picking and eating grain in the wheat field. God desires a merciful interpretation of the law, not a rigid interpretation.

Masses with Children

- Great things happen when God reaches his hand toward his people. With God, the Hebrews began their journey toward freedom.
- The Pharisees practiced a rigid interpretation of God's law and believed Jesus' disciples were violating that law. Jesus explained that his disciples were innocent and that God desires mercy and not rigid sacrifice.

Missal Options

- Consider using the prayers from the Twenty-Ninth Sunday in OT.
- Use any of the three forms of the PA.
- Any of the eight Prefaces for OT or the six Common Prefaces may be used.
- You might use EPR-II.
- Any OT Collect may be used or adapted to conclude the UP. You might even look at the Collects in the Masses for Various Needs and Occasions for possible concluding prayers.

Song of the Day

"Your Words Are Spirit and Life" by Bernadette Farrell (OCP)

Optional Memorial

Our Lady of Mount Carmel is a title given to Mary as patroness of the Carmelite Order. The Carmelites devote their lives to a relationship with Jesus, prayer, contemplation, and virtues, attributes they associate closely with the Blessed Virgin.

- The readings may be taken from the SW, #601, CBVM, CMML, or LMC #331.
- The Collect may be taken from the PS. The other prayers may be taken from the CBVM or CMMM.
- You may also use the various Votive Masses for the BVM.
- Consider EP-IIII.
- Use any of the OT Collects to conclude the UP.

SAT 17 LM #394 / LMC #193–232 / green

Weekday

Optional Memorial of the Blessed Virgin Mary / white

Scripture Insights

In the night of the Exodus, the Lord was clearly known to his people as he led them from slavery into the wild desert. In the Gospel reading, the people approached the Lord but were told not to make him known. We live in a time where we see these events through faithful and historic lenses; we see these events as days God reached out to his people to ease their pain and free them from what binds them.

Preaching Points

Parish Masses

- Before they left Egypt, families didn't have time to let their bread rise—they left in a terrible rush, without time to let the bread rise or make food. For this reason, flat bread is used at Seder meals and in the Eucharistic bread at Mass.
- There is a contrast between the Old Testament and Gospel readings, and it is one of life and death. The Hebrews begin to flee the prison of Egypt, and the Pharisees begin to close in on Jesus' life.

Masses with Children

- Bread rises with yeast, and the rising takes hours. Because the Hebrews left in a hurry, they didn't have time to allow their bread to rise, so the bread they ate was flat like a cracker. This is why the Hebrew people, and today the modern Jewish people, eat unleavened bread at Passover.
- Jesus' Last Supper was a Passover supper, a Seder meal. The bread he used was unleavened bread. This is why we use flat bread in the Eucharist.

Missal Options

- Consider using the prayers from the MPVN-1/B.
- Use any of the three forms of the PA.
- Any of the eight Prefaces for OT or the six Common Prefaces may be used.
- You might use EPVN-IV.
- Any OT Collect may be used or adapted to conclude the UP. You might even look at the Collects in the Masses for Various Needs and Occasions for possible concluding prayers.

Song of the Day

"At the Name of Jesus" by Christopher Walker (OCP)

Optional Memorial

- The readings may be taken from the SW, CBVM, or CMML.
- The prayer texts may be taken from the CBVM or CMMM. Any votive Mass for the BVM may be used.
- Use any of the three forms of the PA.
- Select from P-I or P-II of the BVM.
- Any of the OT Collects may conclude the UP.

S U N 18 LM #107B / LMC #102B / green

Sixteenth Sunday in Ordinary Time

Scripture Insights

Jeremiah's indictment of leaders who abandon the people is at once powerful and disturbing. The priests, rulers, and false prophets in the period just before the exile had predicted that God would never allow Jerusalem to fall. All the people had to do was wait a little longer for God's vindication. Jeremiah knew that something different was going to happen: Jerusalem would be destroyed by the Babylonians, and in 587 BC, it was. He saw that the false hopes and promises raised by the rulers had left the people of Jerusalem scattered like the sheep so many of them had pastured in the hills surrounding the city. And with no moral guidance, many Israelites had been led to sin. The leaders had driven them away from God.

God promises to gather the sheep and bring them back by raising up shepherds for them. The promise has much the same structure as the promise to raise up a prophet like Moses in Deuteronomy 18:15–20. There, the prophet will tell the people all God has said. In Jeremiah, the shepherd will shepherd (literally pasture) the people. Finally, God promises to raise up a righteous Branch. The Branch will reign as a wise king who will execute justice and righteousness. This description is important; in Jewish theology, the reign of God brings justice and righteousness. Here, a king from David's family tree will become God's shepherd on earth.

Another great vision of the Davidic shepherd is the restoration of the divided Israel (Ezekiel 37:23–36). Paul sees the restoration in his time as the coming together of Jews and Gentiles in Jesus Christ. For Paul, Jesus is the righteous Branch, bringing all people near to God.

In Mark, we hear again the image of shepherd. When Jesus sees the crowd hungry for guidance, he must reach out to them. But Mark gives us a different image for the shepherd of these sheep. This shepherd is not a king or a branch of David's tree; he is a teacher—yet another description that helps the reader grasp who Jesus is for the world.

Preaching Points

Parish Masses

- In the First Reading, we hear about God's people Israel being left without a shepherd; without anyone to guide them in God's ways, they struggle. In the Gospel, we see Jesus as the fulfillment of God's promise to give Israel a shepherd; Jesus is the Good Shepherd who guides the people in God's ways.
- Jesus was promised to the ancient Israelites, and they waited for him to emerge from David's line, knowing God keeps his promises.
- Though Jesus came from David's line, his Incarnation, crucifixion, and Resurrection were for all people—Jewish and Gentile.
- Jesus was deeply moved by the condition of the suffering people he encountered. Our Lord knows and understands our suffering.

Children's Liturgy of the Word

- Jesus was promised to the ancient Israelites. They knew he would be descended from King David, and they believed that God would keep his promise to his people.
- Jesus, Mary, and Joseph were all faithful Jewish people. Jesus came from the Jewish tradition, and he gathered Jewish people and Gentile people together.
- Jesus understands our suffering as one of us. Jesus is fully human and fully divine, so he lived suffering and witnessed it in others when he walked the earth.

Missal Options

- Offer any of the three forms of the PA.
- Sing or recite the Gloria and the Creed.
- Any of the seasonal OT Collects may be used or adapted to conclude the UP.
- Select from any of the eight Prefaces of OT.
- Consider EPR-I.
- There are six SBs for OT from which to choose.

Music Preparation

- People in ministry often work weekends and evenings with little down time. Jesus knew it was important for his people to get rest if they were going to serve others well.
- Even if you are not required to log your hours, do so. It may help you realize the time you spend working and give you permission to take off.
- Tap into social media to help recruit new members to the music ministry! Consider establishing a Facebook page, Instagram, or Twitter account specifically for the parish music ministry. Share with people your rehearsal and liturgical schedule as well as some of the music that you are doing. Getting this information out to the wider community may motivate and inspire new singers or instrumentalists to join or perhaps even to visit the parish for Mass. You need not take this on yourself! Chances are you may have someone in the parish community who might be able to assist and thus turn it into a unique ministry.

Music Suggestions

- Gathering: "Like a Shepherd" by Robert J. Dufford (OCP)
- Preparation of the Gifts: "O God of Love" (various publishers)
- Communion: "Blest Are We" by Vince Ambrosetti (International Liturgy Publications)
- Sending Forth: "I Heard the Voice of Jesus Say" (various publishers)

Mass Texts

Introduction to Mass

In the midst of our busy lives, Jesus invites us here to rest a while with him, to listen to his teaching, to sing his praises, and to receive his life-giving Body and Blood. So refreshed ourselves, we may then be able to serve in the world as the faithful shepherds he calls us to be. Let us enter into this celebration with willing hearts and give glory to our great God. *My brothers and sisters, let us acknowledge our sins, and so prepare ourselves to celebrate the sacred mysteries.*

Tropes for Penitential Act, Form III

We are your scattered sheep, O Lord;
bring us back to you: Lord, have mercy.

Your heart is moved with pity for us who
have no help but you: Christ: Christ,
have mercy.

You reconcile us to the Father through
your own flesh and blood: Lord,
have mercy.

Dismissal for Children's Liturgy of the Word

My children, we can receive help from many sources: friends, family, teachers, even total strangers. The greatest help we can possibly receive comes from God himself, the one who made us and everything that exists. He loves us with a never-ending love, through the heart of his son Jesus. He now speaks to you in today's readings, teaching you many things. Go and turn to him for help.

Dismissal of Catechumens

Friends, this community now sends you forth to reflect on the mystery of Christ who, as St. Paul says, makes us one in his Spirit and reconciles us to the Father. We pray that the power of Christ will work wonders in you and lead you to that day when you will stand with us in joy around the table of the Eucharist. Go in his peace.

Dismissal of Extraordinary Ministers of Holy Communion

Ministers of the Lord, Christ, our Good Shepherd, sends you to his ailing sheep who are in need of spiritual sustenance and a word of encouragement. May the Body of Christ fill them with joy and unite their prayer and praise to our own in the Holy Spirit. Go in peace.

Universal Prayer

The Lord is our shepherd. We turn to him in prayer so that he may guide our world with peace and harmony.

1. That ministers of the Church may never grow weary of the crowds that seek the Lord's kindness and compassion, we pray:
2. That we may never cease to take time each day to quietly attend to the Lord's voice in our lives, we pray:
3. That all who are making an annual retreat may be blessed with grace in their time of renewal, we pray:
4. That those fortunate to have a sabbatical year of rest from their labors may use this gift wisely, we pray:
5. That those who feel an absence of direction in their lives, like sheep without a shepherd, may soon find their way, we pray:

Good and glorious Father,
your Son drew great energy
from the time he spent with you in prayer,
and he showed his disciples the need to do the same.
May we never grow weary of quiet time spent
with you,
so that life around us may be kept in proper order.
Through Christ our Lord.
Amen.

Other Rites and Customs

- In observance of National Ice Cream Day today, celebrate Evening Prayer outdoors and conclude with an ice cream "sundae" social.
- Go through the closets in the sacristy and storage room, take inventory and get rid of things that aren't used. Be conscious of the environment and those parishes that have less. Do not throw items away but donate what you can.

Liturgy and Life

Last Sunday Jesus sent off his disciples two by two to evangelize and heal the suffering. In today's Gospel, they return to share their experiences. Jesus declares it is time for all of them to rest and regroup. So it is for us—it is midsummer and time for rest! Plan some time for yourself in a quiet place. Rest in the beauty of God's creation and allow the time of solitude and quiet to restore your soul.

Taking Place This Week . . .

Consider what can be done liturgically, catechetically, and ministerially to respond to these important needs.

- Tisha B'Av (7/18)
- Eid al-Adha (7/20)
- Natural Family Planning Week begins today.

MON 19 LM #395 / LMC #193–232 / green
Weekday

Scripture Insights

Sometimes when a parent has given a child something very good, the child might be ungrateful if the item isn't exactly what he wanted to receive. The Hebrews felt this way about Moses taking them out of Egypt when they realized the Egyptians were coming for them. God would fight for his children, but they did not yet know that. They didn't realize yet what God would do for them.

Preaching Points

Parish Masses

- Despite the plagues that struck Egypt, Pharaoh changed his mind about letting the Hebrews go and sent his chariots and charioteers after them.
- We aren't meant to demand signs from God or expect him to do what we say to prove his existence. Neither would Jesus play the role of a charlatan just to help the Pharisees understand his identity.

Masses with Children

- Despite the plagues that struck Egypt, Pharaoh changed his mind about letting the Hebrews go and sent his chariots and charioteers after the them.
- God isn't a vending machine from whom we can demand favors and signs. Jesus doesn't try to make signs to force the Pharisees and scribes to believe his words.

Missal Options

- Consider using the prayers from the Seventh Sunday in OT.
- Use any of the three forms of the PA.
- Any of the eight Prefaces for OT or the six Common Prefaces may be used.
- You might use EP-III.
- Any OT Collect may be used or adapted to conclude the UP. You might even look at the Collects in the Masses for Various Needs and Occasions for possible concluding prayers.

Song of the Day

"Give Glory" by Jacob Israel Villalobos, Matthew Leon, and Michael Paul Leon (WLP)

TUE 20 LM #396 / LMC #193–232 / green
Weekday

Optional Memorial of St. Apollinaris, Bishop and Martyr / red

Scripture Insights

The Hebrews doubted Moses' leadership and plan, thinking it was better to remain in Egypt in servitude than to die at the hands of the Egyptians in the desert. God parted the waters of the Red Sea, and the Hebrews walked through on dry land; the Egyptians were killed by the waters of the Red Sea when Moses, at God's direction, raised his hand to close the parting. The Hebrews quickly understood who they were and who God is.

Preaching Points

Parish Masses

- God did great things to protect his children, the Hebrews, from the Egyptians. His action in their lives was undeniable.
- When Jesus identified his mother and his brothers as those who do the will of his heavenly father, he identified those who follow him as his family. We must open our hearts to Jesus and his teachings, and we are his family. We are adopted into God's family through Jesus.

Masses with Children

- The Hebrews witnessed God's might when he parted the Red Sea and saved them from their captors. They are God's chosen people.
- Jesus says that those who do the will of God are his brothers and sisters. How do we do the will of God? How do we make that choice every day of our lives?

Missal Options

- Consider using the prayers from the Nineteenth Sunday in OT.
- Use any of the three forms of the PA.
- Any of the eight Prefaces for OT or the six Common Prefaces may be used.
- You might use EP-II.
- Any OT Collect may be used or adapted to conclude the UP. You might even look at the Collects in the Masses for Various Needs and Occasions for possible concluding prayers.

Song of the Day

"I Received the Living God" by Bernard Geoffroy and Brett Ballard (WLP)

Optional Memorial

St. Apollinaris was the first bishop of Ravenna, appointed during the Vespasian persecutions, a time when episcopal appointment meant extra risk rather than privilege. His people were sent into exile, but, as their bishop, Apollinaris was targeted with special treatment—he was tortured and beheaded.

- The readings may be taken from the SW, #601B (LS), or CM or CP.
- Use any of the OT Collects to conclude the UP.
- Use the Collect from the PS. The other prayers may be taken from the CM (For One Martyr) or from the CP (For a Bishop).
- Select from P-I or P-II of Saints, P-I or P-II of Holy Martyrs, or the Preface of Holy Pastors.
- Consider EP-I or EP-II.

WED 21 LM #397 / LMC #193–232 / green
Weekday

Optional Memorial of St. Lawrence of Brindisi, Priest and Doctor of the Church / white

Scripture Insights

Every morning, God provided the bread that his children would need to survive in the desert and each night he provided quail for their meat. Just as God provided bread for the spiritual sustenance of his children in the desert, Jesus provides the bread from heaven to provide for our spiritual sustenance.

Preaching Points

Parish Masses

- The people grumbled about not having enough food, and God sent them food. They had to trust in God's providence every day, because on all but the sixth day they could only gather as much as they needed for that day.
- Jesus asks us to make our hearts and minds fertile ground so that the grains he gives may sprout and flourish.

Masses with Children

- God sent the Israelites food when they were in the desert. Every day they could gather enough bread and quail to last them one day. On the sixth day they gathered extra for the Sabbath.
- How do we make our hearts and minds like fertile ground for Jesus and avoid becoming like rocky ground?

Missal Options

- Consider using the prayers from the MPVN-28/2.
- Use any of the three forms of the PA.
- Any of the eight Prefaces for OT or the six Common Prefaces may be used.
- You might use EPVN-I.
- Any OT Collect may be used or adapted to conclude the UP. You might even look at the Collects in the Masses for Various Needs and Occasions for possible concluding prayers.

Song of the Day

"Rain Down" by Jaime Cortez (OCP)

Optional Memorial

St. Lawrence is the patron saint of Brindisi for his defense of the city against the Turks, but his lasting legacy is as a theologian and linguist fluent in all of the languages of the Scriptures and many of those spoken around Europe.

- The readings may be taken from the SW, #602, CP, CDC, or LMC #332.
- Use any of the OT Collects to conclude the UP.
- Use the Collect from the PS. The other prayers may be taken from the CP (For One Pastor), CDC, or CHMW (For Religious).
- Select from P-I or P-II of Saints, or the Preface of Holy Pastors.
- Consider EP-I or EP-II.

THU 22 LS #603 / LMC, CS; Gospel, #333 / white
Feast of St. Mary Magdalene

Today's Saint

St. Mary Magdalene (first century) is Apostle to the Apostles and patron of the Order of Preachers (Dominicans) because she was the first to proclaim the Resurrection. Although women did not study with rabbis in Jesus' day, Mary was a disciple of the rabbi Jesus. Therefore, the seed of God's Word was firmly planted within her, so firmly that she stood at the foot of the cross with Jesus' mother and her sister, when the other disciples ran in fear. God's Word has been planted in each of us. By reading, studying, and praying with it, we are better able to proclaim the power of Jesus Christ to those we meet.

Scripture Insights

In these readings we hear about Mary Magdalene, the devoted follower of Jesus. She sought her beloved Lord and did not find him in his tomb. Instead, she was the first to learn that the Lord was alive, and she bore this Good News to the Apostles.

Preaching Points

Parish Masses

- Many people could have been the first to whom Jesus appeared, but in John's account of the Gospel we hear that Mary Magdalene was the first to witness our Lord's glorious Resurrection. She was the first to see that death had indeed been conquered.
- Each of us has a deep need and desire for God's presence in our lives. Mary Magdalene sought Jesus with all her heart.

Masses with Children

- Mary Magdalene was the first to witness the resurrected Christ. She carried this Good News to the Apostles; in this sense she was the first evangelist to preach the resurrected Lord.
- According to St. Augustine, each of us is born with a desire to be in relationship with God. Mary Magdalene sought Jesus with all her heart, and we are called to do the same.

Missal Options

- The Gospel in the LMC is proper. The other readings are from the CS.
- Use any of the three forms of the PA. Since today honors the Apostle to the Apostles, consider doing the sprinkling rite.
- Use any of the OT Collects to conclude the UP.
- The prayers are proper and are found in the PS. Presiders should be aware that the Holy See approved an English translation of a new Preface for this feast. It is available as a free PDF download on the USCCB website: http://www.usccb.org/about/divine-worship/liturgical-calendar/saint-mary-magdalene.cfm. A chant setting is also provided.
- Consider EPR-I.

Song of the Day

"For All The Faithful Women," vs. 6, by Herman G. Steumpfle Jr. (GIA)

FRI 23 LM #399 / LMC #193–232 / green Weekday

Optional Memorial of St. Bridget, Religious / white

Scripture Insights

The Ten Commandments were given by God to Moses. These commandments are the basic laws God expects for his people to follow in order to have a society that loves and honors God and one another.

Preaching Points

Parish Masses

- How do the Ten Commandments function in our lives today, and how do we understand them in light of Christ? How would the commandments change the lives of the Israelites?
- Rich soil produces an abundant crop. How do we cultivate our hearts into rich soil? How do we adapt any faults we have so that our soil might be richer for planting?

Masses with Children

- How did the Ten Commandments help the Israelites understand their relationships with God and one another? How do they help us to do the same?
- Consider what kind of ground you want to be for the grain seeds Jesus give us. Are you happy with your ground? If you need to change what kind of ground you are, how can you do that?

Missal Options

- Consider using the prayers from the MPVN-28/1.
- Use any of the three forms of the PA.
- Any of the eight Prefaces for OT or the six Common Prefaces may be used.
- You might use EPVN-II.
- Any OT Collect may be used or adapted to conclude the UP. You might even look at the Collects in the Masses for Various Needs and Occasions for possible concluding prayers.

Song of the Day

"Parable" by M. D. Ridge (OCP)

Optional Memorial

St. Bridget of Sweden was a mystic, a wife and mother, a queen's lady-in-waiting, and the founder of the Brigittines, a religious order of men and women united under the rule of an abbess. St. Bridget was indefatigable in her many works and spoke her prophetic words without fear to nobles, royals, and popes.

- The readings may be taken from the SW, #604, CHMW/CS (For Religious), or LMC #334.
- Use the Collect from the PS; the other prayers may be taken from the CHMW (For Holy Women or For Religious).
- Select from P-I or P-II of Saints, or the Preface of Holy Virgins and Religious.
- Consider EP-I or EP-II.

SAT 24 LM #400 / LMC #193–232 / green
Weekday

Optional Memorials of St. Sharbel Makhlūf, Priest / white; Blessed Virgin Mary / white

Scripture Insights

Through Moses and the Ten Commandments, a covenant, sprinkled in blood, was made between God and the Israelites. God had specific expectations of his people, and his people had seen God's might and power shown in their favor.

Preaching Points

Parish Masses

- God's commandments give us a basic understanding of how society ought to function. We are not meant to live focusing only on ourselves and our own wants, but instead we are called to consider God and one another in all that we do.
- Despite making his teachings clear, Jesus knew some people wouldn't follow his teachings. The weeds will sometimes be among the wheat plants.

Masses with Children

- The Ten Commandments help us understand the basic manner in which society is meant to function. We aren't meant to spend our lives doing whatever we want; instead, we are called to live our lives focused on God and one another.
- The Ten Commandments are divided into two groups: commandments about God and commandments about people interacting with each other. Discuss these divisions and what's in each group.

Missal Options

- Consider using the prayers from the MPVN-1/D.
- Use any of the three forms of the PA.
- Any of the eight Prefaces for OT or the six Common Prefaces may be used.
- You might use EPR-II.
- Any OT Collect may be used or adapted to conclude the UP. You might even look at the Collects in the Masses for Various Needs and Occasions for possible concluding prayers.

Song of the Day

"Blest Are They" by David Haas (GIA)

Optional Memorials

St. Sharbel Makhlūf

St. Sharbel Makhlūf was a Lebanese monk and hermit who was known for his wise counsel in life and for many miraculous healings after his death. Although Sharbel lived out his entire life near his home village and, near the end, left his hermitage only occasionally to perform the sacraments, his quiet example and powerful intercession reached far beyond the borders of Lebanon.

- You may use the readings from the SW, #604A (LS), CP, or CHMW/CS.
- Use the Collect from the PS; the other prayers may be taken from the CP (For One Pastor) or CHMW (for a Monk).
- Use any of the OT Collects to conclude the UP.
- Select from P-I or P-II of Saints, or the Preface of Holy Pastors.
- Consider EP-I or EP-II.

Blessed Virgin Mary

- The readings may be taken from the SW, CBVM, or CMML.
- The prayer texts may be taken from the CBVM or CMMM. Any votive Mass for the BVM may be used.
- Use any of the three forms of the PA.
- Select from P-I or P-II of the BVM.
- Any of the OT Collects may conclude the UP.

S U N 25 LM #110A / LMC #106B / green
Seventeenth Sunday in Ordinary Time

Scripture Insights

John's account of the Gospel often gives a different version of stories told in the Synoptic accounts, Matthew, Mark, and Luke. His account of the Last Supper, for example, is remarkably different. In the Synoptics, we hear the familiar story of breaking bread and blessing wine that is part of our liturgy. But John recalls how Jesus washed feet at the Last Supper (John 13:1–11). Eucharistic references are plentiful in John's account, however, especially in chapter 6. In the middle of Ordinary Time, the Church takes the time to read John 6 and savor the words and actions of Jesus as he talks about the bread of life and the hunger of humankind.

That chapter opens with the multiplication of five loaves and two fish. This is one of only two stories that all four Gospels relate. Jesus seems to be following in the footsteps of the great prophets like Elisha who multiplied loaves and grain, but two things set Jesus' action apart from the Old Testament prophets. First, he takes the bread and fish and gives thanks (in Greek, *eucharisteo,* from which our word *eucharist* comes) and then distributes them. Second, he has the disciples gather up what's left over. Twelve baskets of fragments are left, one for each of the disciples who doubted they could feed the multitude.

Some commentators refer to this passage as an institution of the Eucharist because of what Jesus does with the bread and the fish. There is no cup of wine, no table ceremony, no transforming words. Nevertheless, the ritual of giving thanks and giving to others to eat is highly symbolic. Later in the chapter, Jesus uses bread as a metaphor for himself.

The crowd follows Jesus because they see the signs he does. Believing only because of outward signs is the most tenuous form of faith. At the end of the passage, the crowd wants to make Jesus king because of what they have seen. They have misunderstood Jesus' person and message. He is forced into hiding because earthly kingship is not what Jesus came for (see John 18:36).

Preaching Points

Parish Masses

- The Greek word *eucharisteo* refers to "giving thanks." Our Lord gave thanks for the bread, as the people gave thanks for food and the presence of Christ. This breaking of bread is Eucharistic and miraculous.
- We are called to "bear . . . with one another through love," so that we may live in the love and peace that Christ has given his people.
- In Jesus, we do not need to be afraid, even in the darkest of storms that may occur in our lives.
- The feeding of the thousands is a Eucharistic story; thousands of people gave thanks and broke bread with our Lord.

Children's Liturgy of the Word

- Loving God and loving neighbors are the two greatest commandments, and in the Second Reading we are reminded that we are called to "bear . . . with one another through love."
- We all face troubling and scary times in our lives. Jesus is always with us during scary times, even though we cannot see or hear him.
- We give thanks for God, and we give thanks for his Son. We give thanks in the Eucharist each time we participate in Mass.

Missal Options

- Offer any of the three forms of the PA.
- Sing or recite the Gloria and the Creed.
- Any of the seasonal OT Collects may be used or adapted to conclude the UP.
- Select from any of the eight Prefaces of OT.
- Consider EPVN-IV.
- There are six SBs for OT from which to choose.

Music Preparation

- Have you begun preparing music for the fall? For those who may not be aware, CanticaNova Publications provides an excellent music preparation guide that lists propers (both Latin and English), choral anthems, hymns, readings, ordinaries, and other liturgical texts. It can be a great resource. Check them out at www.canticanova.com.

Music Suggestions

- Gathering: "As We Gather at Your Table" by Carl P. Daw (Hope Publishing Company)
- Preparation of the Gifts: "At the Table of the Lord" by Brian Wren and Carl Johengen (WLP)

Mass Texts

Introduction to Mass

We are here to offer ourselves in thanksgiving to God who has already given us the very stuff of our sacrifice. As Jesus did with the multiplication of the loaves and fish, and as the Father does now with the bread and wine we will place on this altar, God transforms what we offer and gives it back to us in abundance, as an overflowing source of life. With wonder and gratitude for this marvelous exchange, let us lift up our hearts in praise of our God. *My brothers and sisters, let us acknowledge our sins, and so prepare ourselves to celebrate the sacred mysteries.*

Tropes for Penitential Act, Form III

You are good and compassionate to all: Lord, have mercy.

You sacrificed yourself willingly for the salvation of all: Christ, have mercy.

You come to us in our need and feed us with the best of wheat: Lord, have mercy.

Dismissal for Children's Liturgy of the Word

My children, how can five loaves of bread and a couple of fish feed over five thousand people? I can't say that I know exactly, but I do know that it has something to do with the love of Jesus for his people. With love he will now lead you aside and speak to you, and when you come back to us we will continue together our celebration of his love that has no end.

Dismissal of Catechumens

You who are seeking the Lord on this journey of Christian initiation, Christ has fed you with his Word, and we now give you time to go and ruminate on its meaning for your own lives. Let his Word nourish you, inspire you, and challenge you to persevere on this path until you come to the day when Christ will feed you his Body and Blood. Until that time, go in peace.

Dismissal of Extraordinary Ministers of Holy Communion

Dear friends, some members of our community are unable to celebrate with us due to physical ailments, injuries, or weakness, yet because they are joined to us in the Spirit by the bond of love, we send you to them with this Eucharist. May the Body of Christ bring us all together to eternal life. Go in peace.

Universal Prayer

Jesus chooses the assistance from the powerless to humble the mighty and so we turn to him in prayer for the needs of our world.

1. That the celebration of the Eucharist may always have the effect of extending God's justice in the world, we pray:
2. That nations suffering from extreme poverty, unable to feed their people, may receive assistance from around the world, we pray:
3. That our tables may always be places where food and drink are shared readily with friend and stranger alike, we pray:
4. That little children may teach us many things about God's preferential option to choose the powerless, we pray:
5. That those who have died may be showered with God's loving mercy, we pray:

God of abundance,
your Son multiplied the loaves and the fish
and fed the hungry crowd.
May we too recline before your grace
and receive all the riches
you desire to pour out on us.
May the good we receive
be multiplied again and again
for the good of others.
Through Christ our Lord.
Amen.

Other Rites and Customs

- As we begin a brief respite from Mark's account of the Gospel and begin the Bread of Life Discourse from John's account of the Gospel, offer an adult faith formation session focused on the Eucharist.
- Try to work on the count of people at Mass so the proper number of hosts can be consecrated at Mass so that the faithful do not have to receive hosts from the tabernacle. Check out this video to help your sacristans keep proper count: https://vimeo.com/300328193.

Liturgy and Life

"There is a boy here who has five barley loaves and two fish; but what good are these for so many?" In today's Scripture readings, both the prophet Elisha and Jesus understand the essential human need to eat. Both feed large, hungry crowds. All were fed and no one was left hungry. We can strive to end hunger in our world today. The one thousand days from pregnancy through to a child's second birthday are the most crucial for a child's development. Without adequate nutrition during the first one thousand days of life, children suffer a lifetime of negative consequences. The "1,000 Days Movement" seeks to improve nutrition, eradicate hunger, improve maternal health, and reduce child mortality. Be a prophetic voice. Form a group and pledge to engage in one thousand conversations about maternal and child nutrition in one thousand days. For guidance, go to www.bread.org/hunger /maternal-child -nutrition/documents/1000-conversations.pdf

Taking Place This Week . . .

Consider what can be done liturgically, catechetically, and ministerially to respond to these important needs.

- Parents Day (7/25)
- National Korean War Veterans Awareness Day (7/27)
- World Hepatitis Day (7/28)
- World Friendship Day and World Day against Trafficking Persons (7/30)

M O N 26 LM #401 or #606 / LMC #193–232 or #336 / white
Memorial of Sts. Joachim and Anne, Parents of the Blessed Virgin Mary

Today's Saints

According to tradition, Mary spent her life at the Temple from the time she was a little girl. Her parents, Joachim and Anne, presented their young daughter to the Temple for service and study, in thanksgiving for the great gift God had given them through her. The memorial helps us think about the ways we prepare ourselves for Jesus Christ to be born into our lives.

Scripture Insights

While Moses was on the mountain, the people were unfaithful and made a false god out of gold. We are called to be faithful to God, and not put anything in God's place of honor in our lives. Each of us is called to live in God's Kingdom.

Preaching Points

Parish Masses

- Moses, in anger, threw the tablets; he was horrified at the unfaithfulness of the people. God's response was not one of anger toward Moses.
- The Kingdom of God is a living and growing reality. We are all called to participate in God's Kingdom.

Masses with Children

- The people were unfaithful to God while Moses was on the mountain. Moses wanted the people to be faithful whether or not he was present. God explained in the Ten Commandments that the people should not worship other gods.
- We are called to be a part of the Kingdom of God. It is a living and growing reality and a gift from Jesus!

Scripture Insights *(PS)*

We are doubly blessed—blessed in our ancestors, blessed in the mysteries that have been revealed to us because we have come to know Christ.

Preaching Points

Parish Masses

- Something in us instinctively wants to know where we came from and who our ancestors are. Today, let us give thanks for the people who have come before us and who have given us life and faith—in our human families and in our faith family, the Church.
- What do we see? Jesus Christ, living in each of us, living in the Church in his sacraments. What do we hear? Christ's saving Word in the Gospel. We are blessed indeed.

Masses with Children

Christ is present to us in many ways. Most especially, he is present in the Eucharist. But, he is also present when the Scriptures are read at Mass. How blessed we are to have him with us everywhere and always!

Missal Options

- The readings are from the SW, #606, or CS (LMC).
- The prayers are proper and found in the PS.
- Consider P-I or P-II of Saints and EP-II.
- Any OT Collect may be used or adapted to conclude the UP.

Song of the Day

"Seek Ye First" by Karen Lafferty (various publishers)

T U E 27 LM #402 / LMC #193–232 / green
Weekday

Scripture Insights

In the Exodus reading, we hear that Moses and God spoke as people might speak to one another. When the Son was made incarnate and came to the Earth, people were able to speak to him face to face. Our God is dedicated to his people and desires to draw us into the life of the Trinity. It is our hope that we too may go to heaven and live with God in the place he has prepared for us.

Preaching Points

Parish Masses

- In the desert, the Lord appeared as a column of cloud or as a column of fire. God was present with his people.
- Moses called his people "stiff-necked." We are called to be obedient to God's ways and to be the "good seed" sown by the Son of Man.

Masses with Children

- In the desert, the Lord appeared as a column of cloud or as a column of fire. God was present with his people.
- Because the Bible was written for an agrarian society, there are a lot of references to farming and herding. Today's reading tells us that we are to be the good seeds sown by Jesus and not grow to be the weeds.

Missal Options

- Consider using the prayers from the MPVN-46/2.
- Use any of the three forms of the PA.

- Any of the eight Prefaces for OT or the six Common Prefaces may be used.
- You might use EPR-II.
- Any OT Collect may be used or adapted to conclude the UP. You might even look at the Collects in the Masses for Various Needs and Occasions for possible concluding prayers.

Song of the Day

"Psalm 4: Lord Let Your Face Shine Upon Us" by Marty Haugen (GIA)

WED 28

LM #403 / LMC #193–232 / green
Weekday

Scripture Insights

A relationship with God changes a person ultimately and absolutely. In Exodus we hear that with Moses this change was a visible change; his face was radiant after speaking with God. Being in relationship with God calls us to conversion of heart and mind, and these realities are seen in our relationships with others.

Preaching Points

Parish Masses

- Moses transmitted God's Word to the people; it is through him that they came to know what God expected of him.
- The Kingdom of God is the most joy-filled and wonderful reality. The Gospel reading helps us understand it as something for which one would risk everything to partake in it.

Masses with Children

- While in the desert, Moses helped the people understand what God expected from them. He would speak to God, and God gave him the commandments for the people to follow. Those commandments are in Scripture.
- The Kingdom of God is such a wonderful reality that people go to great lengths to participate in it. God desires for his children to participate in the Kingdom.

Missal Options

- Consider using the prayers from the MPVN-14.
- Use any of the three forms of the PA.
- Any of the eight Prefaces for OT or the six Common Prefaces may be used.
- You might use EP-II.
- Any OT Collect may be used or adapted to conclude the UP. You might even look at the Collects in the Masses for Various Needs and Occasions for possible concluding prayers.

Song of the Day

"Come Now, Almighty King" (various publishers)

THU 29

LM #404, Gospel 607 / LMC, CS, Gospel #337 / white
Memorial of St. Martha

Today's Saint

St. Martha is remembered as the bustling woman chided by Christ for "burdened with much serving," while her more contemplative sister "has chosen the better part." But the Gospel accounts also record Martha's remarkable profession of faith in Jesus as "the Christ, the Son of God," placing her in the company of Peter as the only followers of Jesus to recognize his divinity before the Resurrection.

Scripture Insights *(PS)*

The Lectionary reflections below refer to the Gospel, which is proper and found in the PS, #607.

We think of Martha as "the busy one," but Martha is above all a woman of faith who loved Christ and knew him as the Son of God.

Preaching Points

Parish Masses

- Love is the key: God loves us, and so we must love one another. We have no way to express our love for God except by loving one another—loving God in one another.
- Martha and Mary: work and contemplation; service and love. If we learn from Mary the way of contemplation, we learn from Martha the way of faith and complete trust in the power of God.

Masses with Children

- Love is the key: God loves us, and so we must love one another. We have no way to express our love for God except by loving one another—loving God in one another.
- In today's Gospel, we hear about Martha and Mary hosting Jesus at their home. Martha went about her day, busily serving as host. Mary sat beside Jesus and listened. Today's story teaches us about different ways to be with God: active service or prayerful contemplation.

Missal Options

- The Gospel for the memorial is proper.
- You may use the other readings from the CHMW/CS.
- Use any of the three forms of the PA.
- Use any of the OT Collects to conclude the UP.
- The prayers are proper and found in the PS.
- Consider EP-II.
- Consider P-I or P-II of Saints.

Song of the Day

"Dwelling Place" by John Foley (OCP)

LM #405 / LMC #193–232 / green
Weekday

Optional Memorial of St. Peter Chrysologus, Bishop and Doctor of the Church/ white

Scripture Insights

Judaism is one of the world's oldest religions. In this reading from the Book of Leviticus, we hear about the holy days the ancient Jewish people observed. These holy days—known as Passover, Sabbath, Yom Kippur, and Succoth—are still observed by Jewish people today.

Preaching Points

Parish Masses

- The Book of Leviticus explains the necessary standards for holy days and other religious requirements. Numbers play a role in the book; for example, if a festival numbers seven days, the number seven represents perfection or fullness.
- In his hometown, Jesus was greeted by neighbors who were offended by his ministry. In a sense, they perceived that Jesus thought himself to be special instead of an ordinary Nazarene. He expected this reaction, and his ministry there was stunted by disbelief.

Masses with Children

- Leviticus is a book of the Bible that detailed instructions for the Israelites. In Leviticus they recorded the requirements for holy days and other religious obligations.
- In his hometown, Jesus was greeted by neighbors who couldn't believe their ears when they heard him speak. They considered him to be the boy next door and not a wise shepherd for God's people. Because of the people's lack of faith, he didn't perform miracles there like he did everywhere else.

Missal Options

- Consider using the prayers from the MPVN-15.
- Use any of the three forms of the PA.
- Any of the eight Prefaces for OT or the six Common Prefaces may be used.
- You might use EP-II.
- Any OT Collect may be used or adapted to conclude the UP. You might even look at the Collects in the Masses for Various Needs and Occasions for possible concluding prayers.
- Consider P-I or P-II of Saints.
- Given today's readings, include a petition for our Jewish brothers and sisters in today's UP.

Song of the Day

"Canticle of the Sun" by Marty Haugen (GIA)

Optional Memorial

St. Peter Chrysologus was a fourth-century bishop whose preaching earned him the sobriquet, "the golden-worded." His celebrated homilies explained doctrines like the Trinity eloquently, clearly, and concisely.

- The readings may be taken from the SW, #608, CP, CDC, or LMC #338.
- Use any of the OT Collects to conclude the UP.
- Use the Collect from the PS; the other prayers may be taken from the CP (For a Bishop) or CDC.
- Select from P-I or P-II of Saints, or the Common of Holy Pastors.
- Consider EP-I or EP-II.

SAT **31** LM #406 or #609 / LMC #193–232 or #339 / white
Memorial of St. Ignatius of Loyola, Priest

Today's Saint

St. Ignatius of Loyola changed the world as the founder of the Jesuits, and his *Spiritual Exercises* have become a model of Christian discernment and discipline. When his military career was cut abruptly short by injury, St. Ignatius found new purpose in following the example of Christ and the saints with the same vigor that would become characteristic of the order he founded.

Scripture Insights

The jubilee and sabbatical years were a form of caring for the poor in the ancient Israelite community. The poor were able to eat from the fields, and people were made free. God has a special love of those who are poor.

Preaching Points

Parish Masses

- Leviticus offers very specific instructions about the jubilee year and the right of the poor to consume food from the fields. People are called to be fair and just in interpersonal and business relationships with one another.
- John the Baptist was beheaded at the command of Herod; the death of Jesus' holy cousin was a terrible event. This man who spoke truth and readied people for the Messiah was killed for his effort.

Masses with Children

- Leviticus offers very specific instructions about the jubilee year and the right of the poor to consume food from the fields. God's people are meant to be honest and generous with one another and to take care of the poor.
- John the Baptist, Jesus' cousin who prepared the way for Jesus, was killed by Herod. He spoke goodness and truth during his life.

Scripture Insights *(PS)*

The work of the Gospel requires careful planning—and total dedication.

Preaching Points

Parish Masses

- The motto of the Jesuits is "*Ad Majorem Dei Gloriam*"— to the greater glory of God. Every action of our lives should be directed toward God's greater glory, so that the words of St. Paul may become a reality in us.
- Do we have what it takes to finish what we have begun? Are we willing to follow Christ all the way, or do we still cling to career or money or possessions for our sense of security?

Masses with Children

- Tell the children about St. Ignatius of Loyola. You will want to stress that he was the founder of the Jesuits, an order, or group, of priests. Their motto is "to the greater glory of God." This means that everything we do is in fact praising God and for him.

Missal Options

- The readings may also be taken from the CP or CHMW/CS (For Religious).
- Use any of the three forms of the PA.
- Use any of the OT Collects to conclude the UP.
- The prayers are proper and are found in the PS.
- Select from P-I or P-II of Saints, or the Preface of Holy Pastors.
- Consider EP-II.

Song of the Day

"Jubilee Song" by Bernadette Farrell (OCP)

Something to Consider...

◈ Hone your skills for writing the Prayer of the Faithful with *How to Write the Prayer of the Faithful* by Corinna Laughlin (LTP). Pass on to all those involved with this task.

S U N **1** LM #113B / LMC #108B / green

Eighteenth Sunday in Ordinary Time

Scripture Insights

Alongside John 6 and the discourse on the bread of life, the Church hears most of the fourth and fifth chapters of Paul's Letter to the Ephesians. Known as one of the captivity letters (Colossians, Philippians, and Philemon are the others) because it is apparently written from prison (Ephesians 4:1), the Letter to the Ephesians discusses the mystery of life in Christ. Paul's exhortation to "live in a manner worthy of the call you have received," which we heard last week, strikes at the heart of Christian discipleship. This week, Paul continues to call the Ephesians to a renewal in Christ—to "put away the old self of your former way of life . . . and be renewed in the spirit of your minds" (4:22–23). It was expected that Baptism into the death and Resurrection of Christ would bring radical life changes for early Christians. For some, this meant giving up jobs and wealth; for others, it meant hospitality or service. For everyone, life in Christ was life lived according to God and not according to the world. Christians were encouraged to embrace love rather than ambition, greed, or power and to focus on the treasure of heaven rather than on earthly wealth.

Consequently, this small section of the Letter to the Ephesians provides the perfect prelude to the discourse on the bread of life in John's account of the Gospel. Jesus warns the crowd that they are thinking wrongly—running to see him for perishable bread (6:26). In Paul's vocabulary, the crowd sees Jesus with old eyes, with their old selves. If they saw Jesus with spiritual eyes, they would know him as the Bread of Life. They would seek only the bread of life. They would hear Jesus' gentle correction to their assertion that Moses gave them manna from heaven. "My Father gives you the true bread from heaven" (6:32). Physical hunger and thirst made the Jews rely on God in the desert. Jesus shows the crowd that hunger has much deeper implications for the soul. If they believe Christ is food and drink, they will never be hungry or thirsty.

Preaching Points

Parish Masses

- Through Christ, we are able to put away that which is not of Christ. In him, we choose holy lives that are earmarked by kindness, love, and charity. In this life, we are fed and nourished by Christ himself, present in the Eucharist.
- In the desert, God provided the Israelites with manna that sustained their lives throughout their years in the desert following the exodus from Egypt.
- In the Gospel reading, Jesus references the manna and begins explaining the bread of life that has come from heaven.
- When we receive the Eucharist, we are consuming the bread that is Christ, and our spiritual hunger is filled.

Children's Liturgy of the Word

- Manna is the food that God sent the Israelites in the desert; this food kept the Israelites alive during their years in the desert.
- God sent the manna to the Israelites, and it filled their bellies. Christ is also bread from heaven, but he feeds our hungry souls.
- All people are made to crave God; each of us has a need for God's presence in our lives. Christ quenches our hunger for God in the Eucharist.

Missal Options

- Offer any of the three forms of the PA.
- Sing or recite the Gloria and the Creed.
- Any of the seasonal OT Collects may be used or adapted to conclude the UP.
- Select from any of the eight Prefaces of OT.
- Consider EP-III.
- There are six SBs for OT from which to choose.

Music Preparation

- During the next few weeks, you will probably try to use every "Bread of Life" song you know. Perhaps you may wish to use one piece for Communion for all five weeks or a seasonal psalm to help tie the discourse together.
- Instrumental pieces like "*Adoro Te*" and "*Panis Angelicus*" are fitting as preludes or for the Preparation of the Gifts.
- Make sure you are doing something to nourish your soul this summer.

Music Suggestions

- Gathering: "Alleluia! Sing to Jesus" (various publishers)
- Preparation of the Gifts: "Look Beyond" by Gary Daigle and Darryl Ducote (GIA)
- Communion: "I Am the Bread of Life" by Suzanne Toolan, RSM (GIA)
- Sending Forth: "Give Thanks to the Lord" by Daniel L. Schutte (OCP)

Mass Texts

Introduction to Mass

We come to the Lord with a host of needs, desires, and wishes. Let us not seek that which perishes, but let us set our hearts on that which endures for eternal life, the true bread from heaven, Jesus Christ, our Lord. Union with the Father in the Holy Spirit, through Christ's Body and Blood, is what we truly need and precisely what we are offered at this holy table. For this, we give thanks and praise. *My brothers and sisters, let us acknowledge our sins, and so prepare ourselves to celebrate the sacred mysteries.*

Tropes for Penitential Act, Form III

Lord Jesus, whoever comes to you will never hunger: Lord, have mercy.

Lord Jesus, whoever believes in you will never thirst: Christ, have mercy.

Lord Jesus, you satisfy the deepest desire of the human heart: Lord, have mercy.

Dismissal for Children's Liturgy of the Word

Dear children, the crowd that comes looking for Jesus in today's Gospel is thinking more about their stomachs than their hearts. Of course, God gives us good food to eat, but he also fills us with something more lasting and permanent, and that is his love. This is what we hunger and thirst for more than anything else. Believing in his love, go and listen to Jesus who is God's love in human form.

Dismissal of Catechumens

My friends, you have heard St. Paul exhort us to put aside the old self and to put on the new self. As you go forth from us to reflect on today's Scriptures, this community prays that you will open yourselves to this transformation being accomplished in you by God and that you will one day stand with us, fellow works in progress, to celebrate the Lord's Supper. Go in peace.

Dismissal of Extraordinary Ministers of Holy Communion

Dear friends, we send you to our sick and homebound brothers and sisters, that the Lord may give them the true bread from heaven that gives life to the world. May they be renewed in Spirit and remember that they are one with us in the peace and love of Jesus Christ, our Lord.

Universal Prayer

Our Lord Jesus Christ is the bread of life that truly satisfies. So that our world will hunger and thirst no more, let us turn to the Lord in prayer.

1. That the Church may seek to satisfy the deepest longings of Christians who hunger and thirst for Christ, we pray:
2. That world leaders may provide for the basic needs of their people and treat them with human dignity, we pray:
3. That all who are never satisfied with their material possessions may reject the false allure of wealth, we pray:
4. That those who guide the consumer market and sell their goods through advertising may not exploit consumers, we pray:
5. That those who have died may receive their eternal reward in heaven, we pray:

God of love,
you gave us your Son
as the true bread sent from heaven that satisfies our hunger
and makes us thirst for you.
May we always be grateful for this precious gift.
Send us out into a world
that tries to fill its longings with so many things but you.
May we be tangible signs of a love that never fails.
Through Christ our Lord.
Amen.

Other Rites and Customs

- Consider gathering the extraordinary ministers of Holy Communion for an afternoon of reflection.
- Explore the option of offering the Eucharist in the form of bread and wine at all Sunday Masses, if this is not done.

Liturgy and Life

Whether through manna in the desert or Christ, the Bread of Life, God feeds his people what they need. But, there is also an expectation that the People of God will live right. It's good for us to know that what sustains us comes from God. One good response is to develop habits toward food sustainability. You could eat food produced locally so that transportation does not create greenhouse gases that harm God's earth. Join a community-supported agriculture farm, which will sell you local produce. It's prime gardening season, with harvest at hand. Stand in your garden or yard, or over your vegetable drawer, and give thanks to God for the fruits of the earth, one of the oldest kinds of prayer known to humans.

Taking Place This Week . . .

Consider what can be done liturgically, catechetically, and ministerially to respond to these important needs.

- Feast of the Transfiguration (8/6)
- First Friday (8/6) and First Saturday (8/7)
- Purple Heart Day (8/7)
- August is National Water Quality Month, National Immunization Awareness Month, and National Back to School Month.
- August is traditionally celebrated as the Month of the Immaculate Heart.

MON **2** LM #407 / LMC #193–232 / green
Weekday

Optional Memorials of St. Eusebius of Vercelli, Bishop / white; St. Peter Julian Eymard, Priest / white

Scripture Insights

God provides us with many wonderful things, and we are called to be grateful for these gifts. Moses struggled with the complaints of his people and desired for them to be more agreeable. How are we grateful for that which God has given us? In what areas of our lives are we ungrateful?

Preaching Points

Parish Masses

- Moses wondered if God was displeased with him and so put him in the role of leadership of the Israelites.
- After the death of John the Baptist, Jesus performed the miracle of the loaves and the fishes. Jesus provided his people with food, and we are reminded of the Eucharistic supper yet to come.

Masses with Children

- Moses was so distraught at the complaints of his kin that he asked God if God was angry at him. He wondered if being the leader of his people was punishment.
- Jesus fed thousands of people with only five loaves and two fish. This miracle reminds us that Jesus would soon give the bread that feeds our souls—the Eucharist.

Missal Options

- Consider using the prayers from the MPVN-31/1.
- Use any of the three forms of the PA.
- Any of the eight Prefaces for OT or the six Common Prefaces may be used.
- You might use EP-II.
- Any OT Collect may be used or adapted to conclude the UP. You might even look at the Collects in the Masses for Various Needs and Occasions for possible concluding prayers.

Song of the Day

"You Satisfy the Hungry Heart" by Omer Westendorf and Robert E. Kreutz (various publishers)

Optional Memorials

St. Eusebius

St. Eusebius (+ 371) was born in Sardinia. He was made the first bishop of Vercelli, probably in the 340s, and formed his clergy into a monastic community.

- The readings may be from the SW, LMC #611, or CP.
- The Collect is proper; the other prayers may be from the CP (For a Bishop).
- Any Collect from OT may be used to conclude the UP.
- Use P-I or P-II of Saints, the Preface of Holy Pastors, or the Preface of Holy Virgins and Religious.
- Consider using EP-I.

St. Peter Julian Eymard

St. Peter Julian Eymard worked tirelessly to encourage frequent reception of Holy Communion and has been called the "apostle of the Eucharist." He was a friend of his contemporaries, St. Peter Chanel and St. John Vianney, and advised the sculptor Auguste Rodin not to give up art to become a lay brother in his Congregation.

- There are no alternate readings in the LMC. Use the SW or those from the CS (For Religious). The readings from the LM may be from the SW or #611A.
- The Collect is proper; the other prayers may be from the CHMW (For Religious) or CP (For One Pastor).
- Consider using P-I or P-II of Saints, the Preface of Holy Pastors, or the Preface of Holy Virgins and Religious.
- Any Collect from OT may be used to conclude the UP.
- Consider using EP-I.

TUE **3** LM #408 / LMC #193–232 / green
Weekday

Scripture Insights

Jealousy is a vice against which we must guard. Speak simply with friends and family members, not allowing jealousy to spoil relationships or make others' lives difficult. Strive for conscientious love instead of jealously.

Preaching Points

Parish Masses

- Moses had the gift of speaking with God and the blessing of being the leader of the Israelites in the desert. His sister Miriam was jealous of his position, importance, and relationship with God.
- Through Christ, we are able to do things and become people we could never do or become without him.

Masses with Children

- Miriam was jealous of the relationship her brother Moses had with God and spoke in complaint. God helped her understand his relationship with Moses and the difficult position Moses had in the community.
- Jesus helps each of us do things we couldn't do without him. What are some of the things that Jesus helps us do?

Missal Options

- Consider using the prayers from the MPVN-17/B.
- Use any of the three forms of the PA.
- Any of the eight Prefaces for OT or the six Common Prefaces may be used.
- You might use EPR-I.
- Any OT Collect may be used or adapted to conclude the UP. You might even look at the Collects in the Masses for Various Needs and Occasions for possible concluding prayers.

Song of the Day

"Here I Am" by Tom Booth (OCP)

LM #409 or #612 / LMC #193–232 or #342 / white

Memorial of St. John Vianney, Priest

Today's Saint

St. John Mary Vianney (1786–1859), patron of parish priests, was ordained because of his virtue. He was assigned to Ars, France, because the parish needed the love he could bring.

Scripture Insights

Sometimes having faith in God is a simple and easy task, and other times faith is difficult to maintain. We can take comfort in God and rely on him. He loves his people.

Preaching Points

Parish Masses

- Men from each of the twelve tribes of Israel investigated Canaan in preparation for taking over the land for their own. The people were hopeful that the years of desert living were coming to an end.
- The Canaanite woman would have been shunned by most Jewish people, but Jesus reached out to heal her child, as the woman requested. The woman had tremendous faith in Jesus.

Masses with Children

- The twelve tribes of Israel are the descendants of each of Jacob's twelve sons. One man from each of those tribes investigated Canaan as they prepared to enter and take over the land.
- In Jesus' time, the Jewish people shunned the Canaanites, but Jesus spoke with a Canaanite woman without fear. The woman had tremendous faith, and Jesus healed her daughter.

Scripture Insights

God's beloved people need shepherds to care for them and lead them in God's ways.

Preaching Points

Parish Masses

- It is not where we have been, but where we go that matters. It does not matter how virtuous a person has been in the past once they start down the path of sin. In the same way, God overlooks all past sins of a person who turns away from evil deeds and changes. St. John Vianney spent hours each day in the confessional because he knew this to be true. He knew that all are called to continuous conversion.
- Jesus looked at the crowd and was moved with pity. That hasn't changed: he still looks upon our world and is moved with pity. He still cares for his flock through the hands of those he calls to service. Let us pray for more laborers in the vineyard.

Masses with Children

- Tell the children about St. John Vianney.
- Make the connection that God forgives our sins to St. John's focus on confession.

Missal Options

- The readings may also be from the CP.
- Use the Collect from the PS; the other prayers may be taken from the CP (For One Pastor).
- Use any of the three forms of the PA.
- Use any of the OT Collects to conclude the UP.
- Select from P-I or P-II of Saints, or the Preface of Holy Pastors.
- Consider EPR-I.

Song of the Day

"Save Your People" by Jim Farrell (OCP)

THU 5 Weekday

LM #410 / LMC #193–232 / green

Optional Memorial of the Dedication of the Basilica of St. Mary Major / white

Scripture Insights

Our Lord is a God of abundance. He is filled with good things, and his action in the lives of his people bring an abundance of good things. The Israelites received an abundance of water, and, through Jesus, we receive an abundance of mercy.

Preaching Points

Parish Masses

- Moses and Aaron would not live to see the Israelites enter the promised land. Their posterity would live to see the promised land.
- "You are the Christ, the Son of the living God." These words identify Jesus; he is the Son of God, the Christ, the anointed one. Because of this identification, Jesus tells Peter that he will build his Church on this rock; after Jesus' death, Peter and the Apostles carry on the Church.

Masses with Children

- Moses and Aaron would not live to see the Israelites enter the promised land. Their children and children's children would live to see the promised land.
- Peter is the one who identifies Jesus as the Son of God and the Christ. Jesus builds his Church on this rock, a play on the name Peter. After Jesus' death, Peter and the Apostles would carry on Jesus' ministry.

Missal Options

- Consider using the prayers from the MPVN-2.
- Use any of the three forms of the PA.
- Any of the eight Prefaces for OT or the six Common Prefaces may be used.
- You might use EP-I.
- Any OT Collect may be used or adapted to conclude the UP. You might even look at the Collects in the Masses for Various Needs and Occasions for possible concluding prayers.

Song of the Day

"How Can I Keep from Singing" (various publishers)

Optional Memorial

The memorial commemorates Pope Sixtus III's dedication of a church to the Blessed Virgin Mary following the First Council of Ephesus, in which Mary was declared the *Theotokos*. It is the largest and oldest church dedicated to Mary found in Rome.

- The readings may be taken from the SW, #613, CBVM, CMML, or LMC #343.
- Use the Collect from the PS; the other prayers may be taken from the CBBM or CMMM. You may also use one of the various Votive Masses for the BVM, except for the Collect which is proper to the day.
- Consider EP-I or EP-II.
- Select from P-I or P-II of the Blessed Virgin Mary.
- Use any of the OT Collects to conclude the UP.

FRI 6 Feast of the Transfiguration of the Lord

See page 294.

SAT 7 Weekday

LM #412 / LMC #193–232 / green

Optional Memorials of St. Sixtus II, Pope, and Companions, Martyrs / red; St. Cajetan, Priest / white; Blessed Virgin Mary / white

Scripture Insights

The Shema is an ancient prayer and proclamation that the Israelites and the modern Jewish people recite and teach their children to recite. Mary and Joseph would have taught this prayer to Jesus, and indeed he also taught that we must love God with all of one's heart, mind, and soul.

Preaching Points

Parish Masses

- How do we love God with our hearts, minds, and souls? How do we keep God at the forefront of our lives, not forgetting about him?
- The Apostles served Jesus in their ministry. How do we serve God and God's people? How does this relate to loving God with our hearts, minds, and souls?

Masses with Children

- How do we love God with our hearts, minds, and souls? How do we concentrate on God and his love and not forget about him?
- The Apostles served Jesus by continuing his ministry and later becoming priests who offered the Eucharist to the people. How do you serve God and his people? How do we love God by serving others?

Missal Options

- Consider using the prayers from the Thirtieth Sunday in OT.
- Use any of the three forms of the PA.
- Any of the eight Prefaces for OT or the six Common Prefaces may be used.
- You might use EPVN-IV.
- Any OT Collect may be used or adapted to conclude the UP. You might even look at the Collects in the Masses for Various Needs and Occasions for possible concluding prayers.

Song of the Day

"I Love You, Lord/*Te Amo Senor*" by Tim Smith and Julie Smith (OCP)

Optional Memorials

St. Sixtus II

During his short tenure as pope, St. Sixtus II managed to restore the strained relationship between the Western and Eastern Churches. He was martyred by Emperor Valerian alongside several deacons.

- The readings may be taken from the SW, #615, CM, or LMC #345.
- Use any of the OT Collects to conclude the UP.
- Use the Collect from the PS; the other prayers may be taken from the CM (For Several Martyrs).
- Select from P-I or P-II of Saints, P-I or P-II of Holy Martyrs, or the Preface of Holy Pastors.
- Consider EP-I or EP-II.

St. Cajetan

St. Cajetan founded the Theatines, the Order of the Clerks Regular, to promote reception of the sacraments, do works of charity, and recall clergy to their vocations. St. Cajetan was an idealist who sought to demonstrate by example the power of virtue in a time when many in the Church were morally compromised.

- The readings may be taken from the SW, #616, CP, CHMW/CS (For Religious), or LMC #346.
- Use any of the OT Collects to conclude the UP.
- Use the Collect form the PS; the other prayers may be taken from the CP (For One Pastor) or from the CHMW (For Religious).
- Consider EP-I or EP-II.
- Select from P-I or P-II of Saints, the Preface of Holy Pastors, or the Preface of Holy Virgins and Religious.

Blessed Virgin Mary

- The readings may be taken from the SW, CBVM, or CMML.
- The prayer texts may be taken from the CBVM or CMMM. Any votive Mass for the BVM may be used.
- Use any of the three forms of the PA.
- Select from P-I or P-II of the BVM.
- Any of the OT Collects may conclude the UP.

F R I **6** LM #614 / LMC #344 / white

Feast of the Transfiguration of the Lord

About Today's Feast

The Transfiguration of the Lord refers to a mysterious event during which Jesus is transfigured, or changed, in the presence of three of his disciples, Peter, James, and John. Moses and Elijah, two Old Testament figures representing the Law and the Prophets, appear and converse with Jesus. The event highlights Jesus' divinity and glory that was hidden from the world but is now revealed to his closest disciples. Jesus is the fulfillment and completion of the Old Testament promises. This brief glimpse into Jesus' hidden power, divinity, and glory would be fully revealed in the Resurrection once the journey of suffering and death had been accomplished.

Scripture Insights

"And he was transfigured before the . . ." What awesome, mysterious words. It's an idea perhaps somewhat unfamiliar to us, but not so for the early Christians. In Jewish apocalyptic tradition, concerned with "revelations" about the end of time, the verb *metamorphoo* pointed to the miraculous change of form to be experienced by God's faithful in the age to come after a time of intense suffering. Although that verb isn't used in the vision of the prophet Daniel, the scene he pictures bears some similarities to the Gospel scene: One "like a Son of man" is given glory and kingship by God ("the Ancient One"). The phrase "Son of man"—in its most generic meaning, a human being—refers to an exalted figure who comes in triumph at the end of time. It is a title commonly used for Jesus in the Gospel accounts (see Mark 9:9).

In today's Gospel, the verb metamorphoo occurs in the passive voice. The transfiguration was something that happened to Jesus. All three Synoptic accounts (Matthew, Mark, and Luke) situate the event on a mountain. In Biblical tradition, human beings usually encounter God on mountains. Jesus is transformed into glory, or brilliant light, evoking the radiance of God (compare Daniel 7:9 and Mark 9:3).

The Transfiguration story in Mark's account comes midway in Jesus' journey to Jerusalem, the place of his suffering and death. In fact, the account follows his prediction of the passion and his teaching that disciples must be prepared to follow this same way. The transformation experienced at that moment was but a preview and perhaps a preparation for the glory that would be his when he rose from the dead. Mark suggests that, even on the way to Jerusalem, Jesus is mindful of a destiny beyond it. Let us listen to the voice of the Beloved Son, that we too may be transfigured in glory, both now and in the age to come.

Preaching Points

Parish Masses

- The glory of Christ had not yet occurred, but Peter, James, and John witnessed a foretaste of the victory Christ would have over death. We can look at the Transfiguration and realize that it is our future too. In Christ, we will be raised from the dead, our bodies renewed in his victory over death.
- What is it to "rise from the dead"? Peter, James, and John debated this very concept after the Transfiguration. What does it mean about death? What does it mean about life?
- The Transfiguration is a triumphal event for Jesus and one that helps the Apostles understand his identity as the Christ.
- What will it be like for us when we reach heaven and are living in God's radiance?
- The Lord is king over all creation. As king over our lives, God calls us to practice justice, modeling ourselves on Jesus, who promoted right relationship with all. As Jesus' disciples, we are called to make known to others God's power and glory visibly manifested by our words and actions.

Children's Liturgy of the Word

- Why is being raised from the dead important to the Gospel? What does it mean about death, and what does it mean about life?
- To *triumph* means "to have victory," and Jesus triumphed over death. The Apostles who witnessed the Transfiguration were able to contemplate Christ's coming triumph because they saw him transfigured.
- What will it be like for us when we reach heaven and are living in God's radiance?

Missal Options

- Offer any of the three forms of the PA.
- The prayers are proper and found in the PS. Sing or recite the Gloria. The Creed is omitted because today is not a Sunday.
- Any of the seasonal OT Collects may be used or adapted to conclude the UP.
- The Preface is proper and found among the texts for today's feast.
- Consider EP-II.

Music Preparation

- Parish communities considering music on this day should know the Gloria is prescribed and that the psalm and gospel versicle can be found in most psalm collections.

Music Suggestions

- Gathering: "'Tis Good, Lord, to Be Here" (various publishers)
- Responsorial Psalm: "Psalm 97: A Light Will Shine" by J. Robert Carroll (GIA)
- Preparation of the Gifts: "Transform Us" by Sylvia Dunstan (GIA); "Transfigure Us, O Lord" by Bob Hurd (OCP); or "Song of the Transfiguration" by David Haas (GIA)

Mass Texts

Introduction to Mass

It is good that we are here in God's house to listen to the voice of his Son. Jesus, transfigured in glory before his disciples, comes to us in the humble elements of bread and wine to make us more like himself. We see him in the Eucharist and in each other now with the eyes of faith, but the day is coming when we will see him face to face, as he is. Let us approach this altar with attentiveness and gratitude. *My brothers and sisters, let us acknowledge our sins, and so prepare ourselves to celebrate the sacred mysteries.*

Tropes for Penitential Act, Form III

You are the Son of the Ancient One,
worthy of all praise: Lord, have mercy.

Your dominion is an everlasting dominion
that shall not pass away: Christ,
have mercy.

All peoples on earth will adore you
forever: Lord, have mercy.

Dismissal for Catechumens

Friends, we accompany you on this journey of faith, but it is the Lord himself who is initiating you into the mystery of intimacy with him. Listen to him, follow where he leads you, and place all your trust in him. For our part, we will continue to pray that your hearts will be set on fire with love for Christ and that our joy will one day be yours in the celebration of the Eucharist.

Dismissal of Extraordinary Ministers of Holy Communion

My friends, the Lord of glory is hidden but truly present in this Eucharistic bread we give you. Take it—take Christ—to the sick and suffering members of our community, that they may be filled with his life and love and join their praise to ours. Go in peace.

Universal Prayer

Praise the Lord, for he is good! May our prayers ascend the mountain of the Lord.

1. That the ministry of the Church, especially with the celebration of the sacraments, may lead to the transfiguration of the Lord, we pray:
2. That world leaders may desire the transfiguration of all societies, we pray:
3. That those who are sick and suffer from disease may be healed and brought into new relationship with others, we pray:
4. That we may find beauty in places where others find only ugliness, we pray:
5. That the world may embrace the cross as true hope and perfect salvation, we pray:

Lord Jesus Christ,
on the holy mountain
your heavenly Father transfigured you in glory.
He called you his Beloved Son
for the world to see your life as a reflection of his love.
Your radiance continues to shine brightly in our world
wherever the hope of the cross leads to resurrected life.
Transfigure us with your glory
where you live and reign with the Father in the unity of the
Holy Spirit,
one God, for ever and ever.
Amen.

Other Rites and Customs

As August 6 and 8 mark the anniversaries of the dropping of the bombs on the Japanese cities of Hiroshima and Nagasaki, include a petition in the Universal Prayer for the people of Japan.

Liturgy and Life

When Jesus took Peter, James, and John up the mountain to witness his Transfiguration, he planted seeds of transformation in them. Taking inner-city children up a mountain or out into the country can provide a transformative experience for them also and can instill hope. A number of organizations across the country sponsor summer holidays, camps, or other outdoor experiences. For example, learn how the Fresh Air Fund places New York City children with rural or suburban host families for a summer visit: www.freshair.org. Or, explore wilderness opportunities for children in the Washington, DC, area: http://www.citykidsdc.org/. What similar services could you find in your own area that would offer a city child a change in the summer? How might you support it?

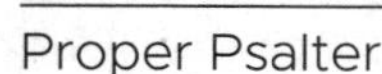

S U N 8 LM #116B / LMC #111B / green

Nineteenth Sunday in Ordinary Time

Scripture Insights

The Letter to the Ephesians seems to provide a marked contrast to the other two readings today. Paul continues his exhortation to live as new people, marked by the seal of the Holy Spirit (probably a reference to Baptism). Particular actions and attitudes, such as bitterness, anger, and slander, are unworthy of such people. On the other hand, kindness and forgiveness are to be encouraged, even expected. For the Ephesians, the best and only example of love and forgiveness was Jesus.

Two phrases from the other two readings might give clues as to how the Ephesians and the other members of the early Church were supposed to persevere in their spiritual transformation. In the First Reading, the Lord provides Ezekiel with food and drink in the wilderness. The first time, God simply commands Ezekiel to eat. The second time, God adds the single phrase, "else the journey will be too long for you." While the reference to Ezekiel's trip to Horeb is clear, the idea of a journey can apply also to the process of renewal—spiritual journey—apparent in Ephesians. The lesson seems clear. Eat the food that God provides and you will have strength for the journey.

John's account again identifies Jesus as the "living bread that came down from heaven." John adds, "Whoever eats this bread will live forever." Belief in Jesus yields eternal life. Belief is the fundamental, life-changing event. If the command of God in Ezekiel is to eat, the command of Jesus in John is to eat this bread from heaven and live forever. In Baptism, the Ephesians inherit both messages. Jesus is the food they must eat for the journey. In their love and forgiveness, they reflect the eternal life Jesus gave them through his own death on the cross. The Gospel according to John and the Letter to the Ephesians form interwoven pictures of a faith that leads to life and the discipleship that springs from that faith. Belief in Jesus Christ, as Paul is fond of saying, means the Christian is no longer a slave to sin but free to choose a different kind of life—one of kindness and love.

In what sense is faith in Jesus a gift of God? In what way do we have to work at it?

Preaching Points

Parish Masses

- God provides what each of us needs for our journeys in life. When God provides the food, we are called to respond to God's generosity and goodness; we must consume that which God has provided for us, because it is what our bodies and souls require.
- Through the Eucharist, we have the food that sustains us on our earthly journey. In Christ we also experience and behold the bread of salvation.
- In our lives we all experience anger, but we can control whether anger leads us to sin.
- Through Baptism and the Eucharist, we are called to holy lives and are sustained in living holy lives.
- We must eat and drink on the journey, for it is long and tiresome. The angel of the Lord reminds Elijah of this in the First Reading. We need strength. We need nourishment to carry out the mission on which God sends us. Without nourishment, we find it difficult to live virtuous lives. Malice and bitterness take over. Being imitators of God becomes impossible. But when we realize our nourishment comes from Christ, the One whom the Father sent, we shall live. Life forever is ours. Life for the world is Christ's gift.

Children's Liturgy of the Word

- The Eucharist helps us to live holy lives; Christ himself feeds us on our life journeys.
- Everybody is sometimes angry, but we are called to not act sinfully in our anger. We learn to control anger so others aren't hurt.
- The sacraments give us grace to live our lives, and, through Baptism and the Eucharist, we are called and supported to live holy lives.

Missal Options

- Offer any of the three forms of the PA.
- Sing or recite the Gloria and the Creed.
- Any of the seasonal OT Collects may be used or adapted to conclude the UP.
- Select from any of the eight Prefaces of OT.
- Consider EPVN-III.
- There are six SBs for OT from which to choose.

Music Preparation

Consider using technology for easier communications with people. There are programs to schedule ministries and cloud storage options for sharing music and schedules; it is also easy to make a recording of a piece with a simple app on your phone. (Note that you need the appropriate copyright license.) Calendar programs are also great for scheduling wedding preparation.

Music Suggestions

- Gathering: "I Am the Bread of Life" by Eugene Englert (WLP)
- Preparation of the Gifts: "Let Us Be Bread" by Thomas J. Porter (GIA)
- Communion: "God's Holy Mystery" by Paul Tate (WLP)
- Sending Forth: "Now Let Us from This Table Rise" (various publishers)

Mass Texts

Introduction to Mass

We are joined together as one body in the Holy Spirit who is our bond of love and peace. Let us lay aside all divisiveness, all murmuring and grumbling, and be willing to forgive others as God has forgiven us in Christ, who gives himself to us as the living bread for the life of the world. *My brothers and sisters, let us acknowledge our sins, and so prepare ourselves to celebrate the sacred mysteries.*

Tropes for Penitential Act, Form III

Lord, in your compassion, you do not forget your poor ones:
Lord, have mercy.

Christ, you loved us and handed yourself over for us:
Christ, have mercy.

Lord, whoever believes in you has eternal life:
Lord, have mercy.

Dismissal for Children's Liturgy of the Word

My children, in today's Gospel we hear of people complaining about Jesus and thinking they knew all there was to know about him. But Jesus is full of surprises, and his love is a never-ending and always-unfolding mystery of new and wonderful things. Go now and listen to his teaching, and on your return to us we will all rejoice together in the love of God.

Dismissal of Catechumens

Dear friends, God has given you life, and he now calls you to life in abundance and without end. As you go forth from us to reflect on this call and on the message of today's readings, we will pray for you, that Christ, who gave himself for the life of the world, will soon bring you to this banquet where he will feed you the bread of eternal life. Go in peace.

Dismissal of Extraordinary Ministers of Holy Communion

My friends, we give you this living bread, our Lord Jesus Christ, that you may share him with our sisters and brothers in hospitals, nursing homes, or sick at home. May they know healing and comfort and the joy of their fellowship with us. Go in Christ's peace.

Universal Prayer

The Lord Jesus is the bread that comes down from heaven. He fills our every need. Let us offer to him the needs of our world.

1. That the Church of God seek ever new ways to provide food to the hungry of the world, we pray:
2. That leaders of nations support every effort to distribute food justly and generously, we pray:
3. That every parish respond to the needs of those who go without food or shelter, we pray:
4. That each one of us is attentive to the needs of those who struggle for daily bread, we pray:
5. That those who hunger will not lose hope, we pray:

O God,
out of your goodness,
you fed the pilgrims in the desert.
Make us always mindful of those who continue
to need your gracious providence,
that we too might bring your unconditional love to all.
Through Christ our Lord.
Amen.

Other Rites and Customs

- Whenever school is back in your region, encourage students and teachers to bring their backpacks, schoolbags, and briefcases for a blessing, utilizing the Order for the Blessing of Students and Teachers found in chapter 5 of the *Book of Blessings*. This order of blessing acknowledges that God is the source of human knowledge and wisdom.
- In the Universal Prayer, in addition to praying for students and teachers, be sure to also pray for school personnel, administrators, maintenance workers, bus drivers, crossing guards, and everyone else who make it possible for schools to function.

Liturgy and Life

Family meals are sacred moments, even between couples. Meals in common signify unity but also are a time to thank God for blessings of food, both physical and spiritual. As with Elijah, meals strengthen us for mission—so does community life. Before praying over the food, light a candle as a concrete sign of the sacredness of the meal. The prayer leader can do the lighting, provided that would be safe.

Taking Place This Week . . .

Consider what can be done liturgically, catechetically, and ministerially to respond to these important needs.

- World Indigenous Peoples' Day (8/9)
- Muharram/Islamic New Year (8/10)
- International Youth Day (8/12)

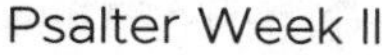

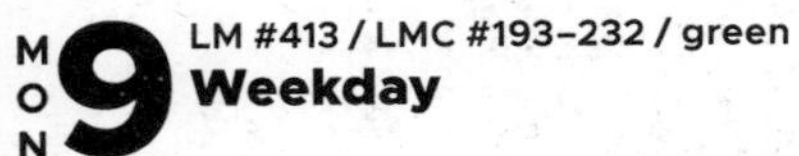

MON 9 LM #413 / LMC #193–232 / green
Weekday

Optional Memorial of St. Teresa Benedicta of the Cross, Virgin and Martyr / red

Scripture Insights

Justice is our God's mission. He cares for the widow and the orphan and cares for those foreign to the land. He enjoins us to have the same zeal for the helpless, the poor, and the lonely in our society.

Preaching Points

Parish Masses

- Childless Abram was promised that his descendants would number like the stars in the sky or grains of sand. We read today that God's Word had come to fruition.
- Jesus predicted his death, and the Apostles were dismayed. Jesus knew that his death would not be the end of his life but the beginning of Resurrection and the beginning of our freedom from death.

Masses with Children

- Abram had no children when God promised that he would have thousands of descendants. By the time the Israelites were ready to enter Canaan, it was clear that God's Word was true to Abram.
- Jesus predicted his death, much to the dismay of his Apostles. They did not yet know that Jesus' Resurrection was coming, which would mean that death would be defeated.

Missal Options

- Consider using the prayers from the MPVN-2.
- Use any of the three forms of the PA.
- Any of the eight Prefaces for OT or the six Common Prefaces may be used.
- You might use EP-II.
- Any OT Collect may be used or adapted to conclude the UP. You might even look at the Collects in the Masses for Various Needs and Occasions for possible concluding prayers.

Song of the Day

"Crux fidelis" by Steven C. Warner (WLP)

Optional Memorial

St. Teresa Benedicta of the Cross was born Edith Stein at Breslau in 1891 into an observant Jewish family, but by the time she reached her teens, she had become an atheist. She studied philosophy and received her doctorate at Freiburg under the philosopher Edmund Husserl but left her university career to teach at a girls' school when Husserl did not support her further studies. Influenced by her study of scholastic theology and spirituality, she became a Catholic in 1922. In 1932, she became a lecturer at Munster, but anti-Semitic laws passed by the Nazis forced her to resign, and she entered the Carmel at Cologne in 1933. In an attempt to protect her from the Nazis, she was transferred to a Carmel in the Netherlands, but when the Dutch bishops condemned Nazi racism, the Nazis retaliated by arresting Jewish converts. Edith, along with her sister Rosa, who had also become a Catholic, was deported to Auschwitz and died in the gas chamber on August 9, 1942.

- There are no readings in the LMC. Use those from the CS (For Religious).
- If using the regular Lectionary, the readings may be from the SW, LMS #617A (LS), or CM or CV.
- Consider using P-I or P-II of Saints, or the Preface of Holy Virgins and Religious.
- You might use EP-I.
- Any OT Collect may be used to conclude the UP.

TUE 10 LM #618 / LMC #348 / red
Feast of St. Lawrence, Deacon and Martyr

Today's Saint

St. Lawrence (+258) was a deacon. Arrested during a time of persecution, Lawrence sold the community's possessions to care for the poor and left nothing for his captors. Enraged, they roasted his body over an open fire, forcing the poor to watch. Legend holds that Lawrence cried out: "I'm done on this side. Turn me over."

Scripture Insights

We are called to know the difference between selfishness and selflessness and to choose the selfless path. When we live our lives in concern and care for others, we are following Jesus' path for us.

Preaching Points

Parish Masses

- God is generous with his children, and he calls us to be generous to one another. How can we show healthy generosity to one another?
- When we strive to be like Jesus in word, deed, and action, we are following our Lord. He promises us that we will be with him when we follow him.

Masses with Children

- God is generous in his love, goodness, and forgiveness. God is love, and he wants his children to love one another. How do we love each other with generosity?
- God wants his children to imitate Jesus with their words, good deeds, and actions. When we follow Jesus' example, we are following him. He promises to keep us near to him.

Missal Options

- In the LMC, the readings may also be from the CM.
- Use any of the three forms of the PA.
- Use any of the OT Collects to conclude the UP.
- The prayers are proper and are found in the PS.
- The Gloria is sung or said.
- Consider EP-I.
- Select from P-I or P-II of Saints, or P-I or P-II of Holy Martyrs. You might conclude Mass with the SB for Apostles.

Song of the Day

"Unless a Grain of Wheat" by Bernadette Farrell (OCP)

Other Rites and Customs

Hours: Use the Proper Psalter from the PS.

WED 11 Memorial of St. Clare, Virgin

LM #415 or #619 / LMC #193–232 or #349 / white

Today's Saint

St. Clare (1194–1253) was a friend and follower of St. Francis of Assisi. She was from a wealthy family and sold all she had to serve the poor Christ. Many women came to join Clare's Poor Ladies. Clare served her sisters, like Christ, the Servant King.

Scripture Insights

Christians are meant to be a communal people; the faith is not meant to be lived in solitary life without companions who are also on a faithful journey through life. Jesus helps us to understand how our communities ought to look and how we should expect to live within a social structure.

Preaching Points

Parish Masses

- Before he died, God allowed for Moses to see the land that God had promised his forebears. Joshua would be the new leader of the Israelites, and no other leader has ever been like Moses.
- We should be honest and forthright in our communication with others. Instead of gossiping or spreading tales, we ought to invite a person into conversation and settle matters that way. God is with us when we are gathered together in his name.

Masses with Children

- Moses was the leader of the Israelites from the time of Egypt and through the desert years. Joshua would be the new leader, because Moses would die before reaching the promised land.
- Jesus expects his people to have love and respect for one another; this love and respect dictates our choices, our relationships, and our communication with others.

Scripture Insights *(PS)*

The Christian life is always a pursuit of something we attain only in eternity: resurrection and life in Jesus.

Preaching Points

Parish Masses

- Jesus calls disciples to give up everything for the sake of the Gospel, to receive everything back, a hundredfold, in the Kingdom. Down through the ages, saints of every time and place show us what it looks like to give up everything for Christ.
- Ours is an "upward calling": in the life of faith there is no stopping place. We do not arrive, attain, or take hold in this life, but only in eternity. Are we resting on our laurels? Or, like St. Paul, are we "straining forward to what lies ahead"?

Masses with Children

- We are to give up everything to follow Christ.

Missal Options

- The readings may also be taken from the CV or the CHMW/CS (For Religious). Use any of the three forms of the PA.
- Use any of the OT Collects to conclude the UP.
- Use the Collect from the PS; the other prayers may be taken from the CV (For One Virgin) or from the CHMW (For a Nun).
- Consider EP-I or EP-II.
- Select from P-I or P-II of Saints, or the Preface of Holy Virgins and Religious.

Song of the Day

"Lord of All Hopefulness" by Jan Struter (Oxford University Press)

THU 12 LM #416 / LMC #193–232 / green **Weekday**

Optional Memorial of St. Jane Frances de Chantal, Religious / white

Scripture Insights

We are called to have God before us in all things we do in our lives. Jesus and his teachings ought to have an effect on the decisions we make and on the way we forgive others. How do we put Jesus at the forefront of our lives and relationships?

Preaching Points

Parish Masses

- In order for the Israelites to capture Canaan, we heard today that they carried the Ark of the Covenant at the front of the procession and depended on God's intervention to assist them to walk into the land.
- When we forgive others, we must forgive fully and forgive many times. This doesn't mean we allow people to hurt us again but that, when we are hurt, we can offer forgiveness.

Masses with Children

- We hear in the reading from Joshua that the Israelites depended on God's intervention to help them enter the land of Canaan. They carried the Ark of the Covenant ahead of them.
- We are called to be a forgiving people. We forgive others when they hurt us. This doesn't mean we encourage people to be bullies, just that we forgive others when they have hurt us in some way.

Missal Options

- Consider using the prayers from the Twenty-Sixth Sunday in OT.
- Use any of the three forms of the PA.
- Any of the eight Prefaces for OT or the six Common Prefaces may be used.
- You might use EPVN-IV.
- Any OT Collect may be used or adapted to conclude the UP. You might even look at the Collects in the Masses for Various Needs and Occasions for possible concluding prayers.

Song of the Day

"Forgive Our Sins" by Rosamond E. Kerkotlots (Oxford University Press)

Optional Memorial

St. Jane Frances de Chantal was still a young woman when her husband died in a hunting accident, leaving her with six young children and little comfort outside her devotion to Christ and the Church. Jane founded the Order of the Visitation as a religious community with a moderate rule accessible to widowed, old, and ill candidates.

- The readings may be taken from the SW, #623A (LS), CHMW/CS (For Religious), or LMC #354.
- Use any of the OT Collects to conclude the UP.
- Use the Collect from the PS; the other prayers may be taken from the CHMW (For Religious).
- Consider EP-I or EP-II.
- Select from P-I or P-II of Saints, or the Preface of Holy Virgins and Religious.

FRI 13 LM #417 / LMC #193–232 / green **Weekday**

Optional Memorial of Sts. Pontian, Pope, and Hippolytus, Priest, Martyrs / red

Scripture Insights

We give thanks to God because it is through him that all good things come to us. God loves his people and is active in our lives. We depend on him for life, goodness, and mercy.

Preaching Points

Parish Masses

- Joshua prepared the people to enter the promised land, reminding the Israelites of God's guidance through each step of the way; God led them out of Egypt, keeping them safe from the Pharaoh's men, and God was with them in the desert.
- Jesus looked to protect women by protecting marriage laws. Married people encounter God's grace in their sacramental marriages.

Masses with Children

- God loves his people and is always with his children. God was with the Israelites in a special way in the desert and as they entered Canaan.
- Jesus loves his people and wants married people to have holy marriages. He knows that children need parents to help them grow up. Marriage is a sacrament, and sacraments enable people to encounter God's grace.

Missal Options

- Consider using the prayers from the Second Sunday in OT.
- Use any of the three forms of the PA.
- Any of the eight Prefaces for OT or the six Common Prefaces may be used.
- You might use EPR-II.
- Any OT Collect may be used or adapted to conclude the UP. You might even look at the Collects in the Masses for Various Needs and Occasions for possible concluding prayers.

Song of the Day

"When Love Is Found" by Brian Wren (various publishers)

Optional Memorial

Sts. Pontian and Hippolytus were at odds during life but were reconciled at the end of life. St. Hippolytus was one of the most important theologians of the early Roman Church but allowed himself to be set up as antipope due to his impatience with what he saw as "laxness" in the Church. St. Pontian was the last of the three popes opposed by Hippolytus, but the two were both exiled by Emperor Maximinus and met martyrdom together, united in the end by their fidelity to Christ.

- The readings may be taken from the SW, #620, CM, CP, or LMC #350.
- Use any of the OT Collects to conclude the UP.
- Use the Collect from the PS; the other prayers may be taken from the CM (For Several Martyrs) or the CP (For Several Pastors).
- Consider EP-I or EP-II.
- Select from P-I or P-II of Saints, P-I or P-II of Holy Martyrs, or the Preface of Holy Pastors.

SAT 14

LM #418 or #602A / LMC #193–232 or #351 / red

Memorial of St. Maximilian Kolbe, Priest and Martyr

Today's Saint

St. Maximilian, a priest, preached the love of Christ during his life and demonstrated it in death, offering himself as substitute to save the life of a young father chosen at random for starvation by their Nazi captors.

Scripture Insights

We choose to love and serve God. Because we have chosen to love and serve God, we must not put anything before him in our lives. We ought to be aware of anything that prevents us from following God's laws or distracts us from carrying out his teachings.

Preaching Points

Parish Masses

- Before his death, Joshua reminded the people of God's expectations of them, and the consequences of not following what was set down in commandments.
- God shows us the way of life, and he guides us on our paths. Jesus wanted the little children to come to him and to bless them.

Masses with Children

- Before Joshua died, he reminded the people about the commandments and what God expected from them. He wanted to be sure that the people understood their role and God's role.
- God shows us the way of life, and he guides us on our paths. Jesus loves little children and wants to help them know his way.

Scripture Insights *(PS)*

We are not slaves of God but friends, and in the Body of Christ, we are not strangers, but brothers and sisters.

Preaching Points

Parish Masses

- We really have only one way to make our love for God concrete: how we treat other people. To lay down one's life for the life and growth of others is the greatest expression of love.
- St. John says it clearly: hatred cannot coexist with love of God. If we hate one another, our love for God is not real. If we withhold the help we could give to a needy person, our love for God is not real. Love of God has consequences in our daily lives and actions.

Masses with Children

- We show our love for God by how we love others.
- If we hate others, then our love for God is not real.

Missal Options

- The readings may also be taken from the CM or CP.
- Use any of the three forms of the PA.
- Use any of the OT Collects to conclude the UP.
- The prayers are proper and found in the PS.
- Consider EPR-IV.
- Select from P-I or P-II of Saints, P-I or P-II of Holy Martyrs, or the Preface of Holy Pastors.

Song of the Day

"I Want to Walk as a Child of the Light"
by Kathleen Thomerson (various publishers)

S U N **15** LM #621 and 622 / LMC #352 / white

Solemnity of the Assumption of the Blessed Virgin Mary

About Today's Solemnity

For her courageous discipleship, God blessed Mary during her difficult life, and at her death, God assumed her bodily into heaven, where she now enjoys full union with her Lord. Mary, as one of us, points to what awaits the Church and all disciples who wait in hope for full union with God. While not in Scripture, Mary's bodily assumption into heaven is an ancient Church belief. The solemnity not only celebrates Mary's assumption, but, as she is the primary symbol of the Church, Mary's assumption points to the fullness of salvation that will be given to the entire Church with the Lord's Second Coming.

Scripture Insights: Vigil

As the Israelites traveled through the desert, they carried the Ark of the Covenant, a large, ornately carved chest. Inside were the stone tablets of the Ten Commandments, a symbol of God's covenant with them. A chair rested on top of the ark as a representation of God's throne, a sign that God dwelled among his people. After King David made Jerusalem the capital of Israel, he brought the ark into the city to signify that God was with his people, blessing and protecting them.

Mary is the ark of the new covenant. As Elizabeth exclaims in Luke 1:42, Mary is blessed because she bears the living God. Tablets of stone are superseded by flesh and blood. The woman in today's Gospel passage declares that there is something special about Jesus that honors and elevates his mother.

She was probably startled by Jesus' invitation that she become blessed herself, not by bearing a son of importance, but by believing and living what Jesus taught. Mary did. Mary heard and submitted to God's Word when the angel announced it to her. After Jesus' death and Resurrection she continued to be obedient to God's Word. She gathered with the disciples, awaiting the gift of the Holy Spirit and devoting herself to prayer (Acts 1:14).

Our celebration of Mary's Assumption into heaven is a celebration of eternal life. Because she kept God's Word so faithfully, Christ "clothed" his mother "with immortality," thereby keeping her body from decay. There was probably a bigger, louder celebration when Mary entered heaven than there was when the ark of the first covenant entered Jerusalem. We pray that we will hear and observe God's Word so that we too will be joyously welcomed into eternal life.

Scripture Insights: Day

To picture Mary, still alive and with her son, our Lectionary turns to the Book of Revelation. In its Biblical context, this passage refers to the nation, Israel, and to the Church, who gave and still gives birth to Christ, the Savior of the world. We see, however, that the passage applies to Mary too. Mary, in a literal rather than in a metaphorical sense, gave birth to a son, a son who was "caught up to God and his throne" through his own Resurrection from the dead.

Today's psalm also presents a powerful image of Mary as a new queen leaving her (earthly) home and entering a (heavenly) palace. Reunion with God is pictured as a marriage.

The reading from Luke reminds us of why we honor Mary. She is the "mother" of our "Lord," Elizabeth says, and we also learn that Mary is the preeminent disciple when Elizabeth exclaims, "Blessed are you who believed that what was spoken to you by the Lord would be fulfilled."

Preaching Points

Parish Masses

- Mary heard God's Word, reflected on it, and allowed it to literally take flesh in her. Because of her willing cooperation, intimacy with God through Jesus is now a reality for all creation. Mary was the first to benefit from the intimacy by being bodily assumed into heaven. In Jesus, we are all called to the same intimacy, as we await the day when we will be united with God for all time.
- Mary fully rejoices in her Lord, who is faithful and keeps Old Testament promises. God is the mighty one who is always attuned to the needs of the poor, the oppressed, the outcast, and the stranger. The world's values are realigned to manifest God's ways. Like Mary, we disciples are called to rejoice in the Lord, who does wondrous things for us.

Children's Liturgy of the Word

- Mary became part of God's family by agreeing to be Jesus' mother. Because of this, God gave her a special place in heaven. We are also part of God's family because we have been baptized and share God's love with other people.
- God promised that he would take care of everyone who was hurting, sad, or sick. God loves everyone. Mary gave thanks to God for keeping his promises and we should also thank God for loving us and keeping his promises.

Missal Options

- Because today's solemnity is just as much about the Church as it is Mary, consider doing the sprinkling rite. The prayer texts are proper and are found in the PS. A set is provided for both the Vigil and the Mass during the Day.
- The Gloria and the Creed are sung or said.
- The Preface is proper and is used at both Masses but is found among the pages for the Mass during the Day.
- Consider EP-III.
- Use the SB for the BVM #15.
- If using the LMC, the Gospel is proper. The other readings are from the CBVM.

Music Preparation

Having the Assumption fall on a Sunday makes it a little bit easier for you than having extra Masses midweek. The Vigil readings are proper and should not be replaced with the texts from the Mass during the Day. Make sure your Saturday evening readers and cantors are aware of this.

Music Suggestions

- Gathering: "Virgin, Full of Grace" by Melvin L. Farrell (WLP)
- Responsorial Psalm: "Psalm 45: The Queen Stands" by Owen Alstott (OCP)
- Communion: "Arrayed in Gold" by Trevor Thompson (OCP) or "Sing 'Ave!'" by Alan J. Hommerding (WLP)

Mass Texts

Introduction to Mass

Today we celebrate the Assumption of the Blessed Virgin Mary. Her son, the Son of God, would not allow the sacred vessel of her body to undergo corruption and wanted her to be with him in the glory of heaven. Where she has gone, we poor sinners hope to follow. Until that day, we rejoice in the help of her prayers, and we unite ourselves to the sacrifice of Christ's Body and Blood, the pledge of our resurrection. *My brothers and sisters, let us acknowledge our sins, and so prepare ourselves to celebrate the sacred mysteries.*

Tropes for Penitential Act, Form III

By your death, O Lord, you have swallowed up death in victory: Lord, have mercy.

You remember the promises made to our ancestors: Christ, have mercy.

You scatter the proud and lift up the lowly: Lord, have mercy.

Dismissal for Children's Liturgy of the Word

Children, long, long ago, God protected Mary from all sin, and then, at the end of her earthly life, he took her to himself, both her body and her soul. One day we will be with God in the same way. But until then we can pray to Mary and ask her to help us follow her son and to teach us to be more like him. Go now and listen to the Word of God and observe it.

Dismissal of Catechumens

Friends, God has spoken his Word to you and we now give you time to go apart and reflect on this Word and its meaning in your own lives. Look to the Virgin Mary as a model of openness to God and, more, as a loving mother who can help you with her prayers. It is our prayer that the Word will lead you to newness of life and fellowship with us in the Church's sacraments. Go in peace.

Dismissal of Extraordinary Ministers of Holy Communion

My friends, we send you to those of our community who are ailing and in need of healing. Speak the Word of God to them and share with them Christ's Body that they may be strengthened in spirit and join their praises to ours. Go in peace.

Universal Prayer

The Lord fills the hungry with good things and sends the rich away empty. Trusting in his promise of mercy, we turn to him now in prayer.

1. That the Church, under the patronage of Mary, may always be a sign of humility, we pray:
2. That leaders of nations will act with humility and kindness, we pray:
3. That women of all nations may be respected and honored, we pray:
4. That single mothers receive the support and kindness they need to be good parents, we pray:
5. That Mary will guide all peoples to work together for peace in our world, we pray:
6. That society will come to respect all life from conception to natural death, we pray:
7. That those who have died may join the heavenly liturgy in singing the praises of God's goodness, we pray:

Good and gracious God,
you sent your Son to be born of a woman
and so enter our human condition as a sign of your love.
Grant that we may imitate Mary's humble service in all that we do
and be bearers of your love to the world.
Through Christ our Lord.
Amen.

Other Rites and Customs

If you live near a body of water, continue the ancient Catholic custom of blessing the sea and swimming in it to pray for healing. It is a custom in many coastal regions to have special blessings of the sea or ocean water on the Feast of the Assumption. The custom originated In Italy in the fifteenth century when the bishop of Venice, during a storm at sea on the Feast of the Assumption, prayed and threw his pastoral ring into the sea from the ship—and the waters were calmed.

Liturgy and Life

On this day, it is customary to bless fruit and herbs. Make your home and family meal heavenly with sweet-smelling herbs and flowers. Pray the Rosary as a family before bedtime.

Taking Place This Week . . .

Consider what can be done liturgically, catechetically, and ministerially to respond to these important needs.

- World Humanitarian Day (8/19)
- Senior Citizen Day (8/21)

MON 16 LM #419 / LMC #193–232 / green
Weekday

Optional Memorial of St. Stephen of Hungary / white

Scripture Insights

It is normal to have some attachment to things in our lives—a family needs a stove to cook food and a table for children to color pictures and do their homework. Jesus warns us that we shouldn't put our possessions above love of God and love of others, especially the poor.

Preaching Points

Parish Masses

- Called to listen to God and obey him, God's people are meant to live their lives under his wisdom, guidance, and rules. The ancient Israelites did not obey God and his commands; people would listen to the judges for a while and revert to their old ways.
- In the Gospel reading we recall the young man who obeyed all the commandments but was saddened by the idea of obeying Jesus' advice for him. He did not wish to part with the possessions he loved.

Masses with Children

- God desired for his chosen people to obey him and to live in harmony with his ways. They would sometimes listen to the judges (leaders) but would often revert to their old ways.
- In the Gospel reading, Jesus tells a man to sell what he owns and give to the poor; the man is sad because he doesn't want to part with his things. We can have possessions, but we mustn't let possessions stand in the way of our love for God and others.

Missal Options

- Consider using the prayers from the Thirty-Second Sunday in OT.
- Use any of the three forms of the PA.
- Any of the eight Prefaces for OT or the six Common Prefaces may be used.
- You might use EPVN-III.
- Any OT Collect may be used or adapted to conclude the UP. You might even look at the Collects in the Masses for Various Needs and Occasions for possible concluding prayers.

Song of the Day

"God Has Spoken By the Prophets" by George W. Briggs (Hope Publishing Company)

Optional Memorial

St. Stephen (+1038) is thought of as the founder of the kingdom of Hungary, was its first king, and established Christianity there.

- The readings may be from the SW, #623, LMC #353, or CS/CHMW.
- The Collect is proper and the other prayers are from the CHMW (For One Saint).
- Consider P-I or P-II of Saints and EP-I.

TUE 17 LM #420 / LMC #193–232 / green
Weekday

Scripture Insights

With God, all things are possible. This Scripture has been illustrated repeatedly through the Old and New Testaments and through the modern age. Gideon would press forward in his mission by the grace of God, and salvation itself comes through the very grace of our Lord.

Preaching Points

Parish Masses

- Gideon did not know that he was conversing with God's own angel; when we read that story we remember that we are always in the company of the angels and saints.
- We cannot attain salvation by our own merit; we depend on God for that gift.
- Jesus emphasizes again the heavenly reward for those who are made to suffer on the earth; his preference is always for the poor and suffering.

Masses with Children

- Each of us has a guardian angel with us, and we are surrounded by the communion of saints. Gideon did not know that he was conversing with an angel.
- Salvation isn't something we can do for ourselves; it is something we depend on Jesus to do for us.
- Jesus has a special love of the poor and suffering people of the world. Those who suffer on earth will have their reward in heaven.

Missal Options

- Consider using the prayers from the Third Sunday in OT.
- Use any of the three forms of the PA.
- Any of the eight Prefaces for OT or the six Common Prefaces may be used.
- You might use EP-II.

- Any OT Collect may be used or adapted to conclude the UP. You might even look at the Collects in the Masses for Various Needs and Occasions for possible concluding prayers.

Song of the Day

"Priestly People" by Lucien Deiss (WLP)

WED 18 LM #421 / LMC #193–232 / green Weekday

Scripture Insights

Generosity is a virtue highlighted in today's Gospel reading. God asks us to be kind and generous with one another, and the parable teaches us not to be jealous of others when they are the recipients of generosity. In terms of salvation, we remember that those who have always lived in Christ may be admitted to the same heaven as those who knew his Baptism in their final hours.

Preaching Points

Parish Masses

- How do we allow God to reign over us? How do we listen to his Word and live in his teaching?
- God's grace and mercy is endless, and it is his to give. We must have joy for all those who experience his abundant love, not jealousy because of our own self-importance.
- In the parable, the vineyard owner had the workers paid in order from the last to arrive to the first to arrive. We recall that in heaven the last shall be first as well; Jesus overturned the expectations of those in his time and in our own age.

Masses with Children

- Reign refers to "a king or queen ruling over a nation." Our desire is that God reigns in our lives and in our hearts. How do we allow God reign over our lives?
- God's grace is his own to give. How wonderful that he is generous with his abundant love. We can delight when we see his love showing in others' lives.

Missal Options

- Consider using the prayers from the MPVN-26/A.
- Use any of the three forms of the PA.
- Any of the eight Prefaces for OT or the six Common Prefaces may be used.
- You might use EP-III.
- Any OT Collect may be used or adapted to conclude the UP. You might even look at the Collects in the Masses for Various Needs and Occasions for possible concluding prayers.

Song of the Day

"For the Fruits of All Creation" by Fredd Pratt Green (Hope Publishing Company)

THU 19 LM #422 / LMC #193–232 / green Weekday

Optional Memorial of St. John Eudes, Priest / white

Scripture Insights

God is generous and invites all of humanity to partake in the Kingdom of Heaven. It us up to each of us to prepare ourselves for the banquet. We must do what we can to make ourselves worthy.

Preaching Points

Parish Masses

- Heaven is our life's mission, and we receive help from Jesus and the saints in our journey to grow in our faith.
- In our lives we strive for the Kingdom of God in the here and now and for heaven in our future. How do we prepare, and how do we help others on this journey?

Masses with Children

- Our goal in life is to go to heaven, and it is through Jesus that we can attain this goal. He gives help to all of God's children.
- In our lives we strive for the Kingdom of God here and in heaven. This means we must follow Jesus' teachings here on earth as we prepare for the Kingdom of God. How do we prepare, and how do we help others on this journey?

Missal Options

- Consider using the prayers from the MPVN-1/A.
- Use any of the three forms of the PA.
- Any of the eight Prefaces for OT or the six Common Prefaces may be used.
- You might use EP-II.
- Any OT Collect may be used or adapted to conclude the UP. You might even look at the Collects in the Masses for Various Needs and Occasions for possible concluding prayers.

Song of the Day

"Psalm 40: Here I am Lord" by Rory Cooney (GIA)

Optional Memorial

St. John Eudes left the Oratorians to found an order, the Congregation of Jesus and Mary, for the renewal of the diocesan priesthood dedicated to founding seminaries and educating seminarians and priests. In turbulent times, St. John always set his hand to whatever work needed to be done, whether it was nursing plague victims or educating and forming better priests and pastors.

- The readings may be taken from the SW, #624, CP, CHMW/CS, or LMC #355.
- Use the Collect from the PS; the other prayers may be taken from the CP (For One Pastor) or from the CHMW (For Religious).
- Select from P-I or P-II of Saints, or the Preface of Holy Pastors or of Holy Virgins and Religious.

FRI 20 LM #423 or #625 / LMC #193–232 or #356 / white

Memorial of St. Bernard, Abbot and Doctor of the Church

Today's Saint

St. Bernard was a nobleman who joined the abbey at Cîteaux, France. Many of his family members and friends joined him. Bernard wanted to follow and lead others to Christ, rather than to himself. He used his gifts for leadership, arbitration, writing, and creating harmony in the abbey to give glory to God.

Scripture Insights

Love and devotion come to us through others in this life. Naomi, a widow, enjoys the love and devotion of her daughter-in-law, Ruth, who does not leave her mother-in-law. She determines that the two shall make a life together. Like God, who never leaves his people, Ruth does not leave Naomi.

Preaching Points

Parish Masses

- Love God above all, and love your neighbor as yourself. These two greatest commands are the essence of Jesus' teaching.
- Ruth, who lived long before Jesus, personified Jesus' teaching. Her love of her mother-in-law is a beautiful example of human devotion.

Masses with Children

- The two greatest commands are loving God above everyone and everything, and loving our neighbors as ourselves. These two commandments are the sum of Jesus' teachings.
- Ruth, who lived a long time before Jesus, was a person who lived a vocation of love as she made her mother-in-law her family.

Scripture Insights *(PS)*

To learn God's ways and share what we learn with others is Christ's prayer for us. This is true wisdom.

Preaching Points

Parish Masses

- Christ prays that we may be one, not only with each other, but with Christ and the Father. Community matters: we need each other.
- The spirit of wisdom will come to those who seek her, and nurture them as a mother nurtures her child. Are we content to remain in infancy when it comes to our faith? Our faith and understanding should grow along with us as we age.

Masses with Children

- If we are one with each other, then we are one with God.
- God's wisdom will come to us when we seek him. And our own wisdom should grow along with us as we get older.

Missal Options

- The readings may also be taken from the CDC or CHMW/CS (For Religious).
- Use any of the three forms of the PA.
- Use any of the OT Collects to conclude the UP.
- The prayers are proper and are found in the PS.
- Select from P-I or P-II of Saints, the Preface of Holy Pastors, or the Preface of Holy Virgins and Religious.
- Consider EPR-II.

Song of the Day

"Covenant Hymn" by Rory Cooney and Gary Daigle (GIA)

SAT **21** LM #424 or #636 / LMC #193–232 or #357 / white

Memorial of St. Pius X, Pope

Today's Saint

As pope at the turn of the last century, St. Pius X reformed the liturgy and breviary, promoted Gregorian chant, opposed Modernism, and lowered the age of first Communion from twelve to seven. Although he rose to keep lofty company as pope, St. Pius had humble origins and never lost his love for simple, accessible liturgy and expressions of doctrine.

Scripture Insights

Those who pridefully show themselves as being the very best and holiest people are exalting themselves. They shall be last, and the humble and holy people shall find themselves exalted.

Preaching Points

Parish Masses

- Naomi was an unpresuming woman who found herself without husband or sons in her older age. This humble woman found herself exalted in the life she shared with her daughter-in-law, Ruth.
- The ancient Israelites believed that having progeny bore specific spiritual significance; despite having lost both of her sons, Naomi's family would live on through the children of the devoted Ruth.
- Jesus spoke against those who would weigh down others with heavy burdens of teaching and responsibility and not try to help bear that burden.

Masses with Children

- Naomi was a humble woman who was widowed and unexpectedly childless in her older age. In her humility she was exalted in the life she shared with her daughter-in-law Ruth.
- Jesus spoke against those who put heavy religious rules and expectations on others without trying to ease such a burden; we don't ask others to do what we ourselves won't help them do.

Scripture Insights *(PS)*

Paul is like a nursing mother; Jesus asks Peter to feed the flock and care for it. True leadership is gentle and compassionate.

Preaching Points

Parish Masses

- Three times Peter professes his love for Jesus and commits himself to the tending of the flock, the feeding of the sheep. We are fed in many ways, but first and foremost with the bread of heaven: the Eucharist. This is the food that nourishes us and makes us one.
- St. Paul is the ideal minister, proclaiming the Gospel with integrity and gentleness, asking nothing in return. When we proclaim the Gospel—whether as a priest, a catechist, a teacher, or a parent—we should do as St. Paul did, giving not only the message of the Gospel but something of ourselves as well.

Missal Options

- The readings may also be from the CP (For a Pope).
- Use any of the three forms of the PA.
- Use any of the OT Collects to conclude the UP.
- You may use the prayers from the PS or the CP (For a Pope).
- Select from P-I or P-II of Saints, or the Preface of Holy Pastors.
- Consider EPVN-I.

Song of the Day

"Wherever You Go" by Gregory Norbet, OSB (OCP)

S U N **22** LM #122B / LMC #117B / green

Twenty-First Sunday in Ordinary Time

Scripture Insights

In the reading from John's account of the Gospel the disciples are grappling with a difficult teaching from Jesus that they do not entirely understand, mainly because they cannot see beyond the literal interpretation of his words.

Paul's Letter to the Ephesians contains a text that is troubling for many today. The command for wives to be submissive to their husbands has been taken out of context and misused for centuries. In this section of Ephesians, Paul has been exhorting his listeners to give up all manner of vices, becoming people of love and forgiveness. He also envisions a different way for people to relate in marriage. Paul understands marriage as a metaphor for Christ's relationship with the Church and develops an image to express that relationship: the Church as a body with Christ as its head. Paul uses this image to frame his understanding of the marriage covenant.

Marriage was seen as a metaphor for God's relationship with Israel long before Paul used it to describe Christ and the Church. Paul adds the element of mutual reverence and love, using the image of the head and body to include interdependence in the hierarchical marriage relationship of that time. The body and the head work together in life. This is the obedience that Paul advocates for wife and husband—one that allows them to live as a united whole. Paul adds that the head must love the body, countering the notion of wives as property that was common in Paul's time. The husband must love his wife as Christ loves the Church. If such love is the foundation of the husband's part in the marriage, he cannot abuse or neglect, cannot be faithless, cruel, or cold. These are the vices that followers of Christ give up. Just as disciples become new people, husbands and wives become a new unity in the marriage covenant, practicing kindness and forgiveness. In the same way, Christ and his Church become a single entity in the new covenant.

How can mutual respect and self-sacrificing love be expressed in the marriage covenant today?

Preaching Points

Parish Masses

- Husbands and wives are called to live a life of love with one another and their families. Marriage is a sacrament, so it gives grace for husbands and wives to live out their mission of love and commitment.
- Even when Jesus' teaching was difficult to understand, Simon Peter trusted Jesus' words because he knew Jesus was the "Holy One of God."
- We are called to put God first in our lives and not put other things on a pedestal with him or above him.

Children's Liturgy of the Word

- We are called to put God first in our lives instead of being more concerned with popularity or recent fads.
- Sometimes Jesus' teachings are difficult to understand, but we can trust Jesus and ask him to help us grow in understanding.
- Husbands and wives live out the Sacrament of Marriage together, and they are called to love one another with a deep and abiding love.

Missal Options

- Offer any of the three forms of the PA.
- Sing or recite the Gloria and the Creed.
- Any of the seasonal OT Collects may be used or adapted to conclude the UP.
- Consider EP-IV with its proper Preface.
- There are six SBs for OT from which to choose.

Music Preparation

- Create a list of calendar events for you and your musicians of all their important dates for the coming year.
- Reserve all rehearsal spaces on your facilities calendar for the year.

Music Suggestions

- Gathering: "*Somos El Cuerpo De Cristo*/We Are the Body of Christ" by Jaime Cortez (OCP)
- Preparation of the Gifts: "Christians Let Us Love One Another" by Claudia Foltz, SNJM, and Armand Nigro, SJ (OCP)
- Communion: "Taste and See" by James Moore (GIA)
- Sending Forth: "We Will Serve the Lord" by Rory Cooney (GIA)

Mass Texts

Introduction to Mass

God has proven himself faithful to his people time and again, bringing the Israelites up out of captivity in Egypt, sending his only Son to walk among us in the flesh and to offer himself up for the sanctification of the Church. We have chosen to follow Christ, but today let us renew our commitment; let us once again choose to serve the Lord, who now gives himself to us in the Bread of Life and the Cup of Salvation. *My brothers and sisters, let us acknowledge our sins, and so prepare ourselves to celebrate the sacred mysteries.*

Tropes for Penitential Act, Form III

Your words, O Lord, are Spirit and life: Lord, have mercy.

You rescue us from all our distress: Christ, have mercy.

We believe that you are the Holy One of God:
Lord, have mercy.

Dismissal for Children's Liturgy of the Word

Dear children, Jesus is many things for us. He is our teacher, our companion, our friend, our savior. He is God. In today's Gospel you will hear that some of Jesus' disciples no longer believed in him and left. Peter, however, speaks for the rest of us when he says he has no one to turn to but Jesus. With Peter, turn to Jesus, listen to him, and trust him who is always with you and loves you very much.

Dismissal of Catechumens

Dear friends, like the Israelites in today's First Reading, or the disciples of Jesus in the Gospel, you have a choice about whom you will follow and serve and worship. This community is here to testify to you that God is true and Christ is faithful and to support you with our prayers. Open your mind to the Word you have heard and take it to heart, that you may taste and see for yourselves the goodness of God in the Eucharist. Go in peace.

Dismissal of Extraordinary Ministers of Holy Communion

Friends, we are mindful of our brothers and sisters who are separated from us by sickness or injury. Go to them and remind them that, in the Holy Spirit, they are united to us and that, through the Eucharist you will give them, they are one Body with us in Christ. Go in peace.

Universal Prayer

My sisters and brothers, we have been chosen for a special relationship with the Father through our participation in the life of the Son. We are "Spirit and life" for the world, because the Word animates our faith. Responding to this call, let us pray for the needs of our world.

1. For Christians everywhere to be united in their belief that they have been chosen to be in relationship with God and with each other, we pray:
2. For parts of our world that experience the pangs of civil strife and war, we pray:
3. For families that struggle with unity and forgiveness, we pray:
4. For all among us who feel estranged from family, may they soon find a welcome embrace, we pray:
5. For the sick, especially those who turn daily to the Lord in prayer for their healing, we pray:
6. For all who have abandoned the company of the Lord, we pray:
7. For those who have been victims of prejudice, may they not harbor revenge in their hearts, we pray:
8. For those who have died, may they give glory to God in the banquet of heaven, we pray:

God of love,
who have called us to be your own
and to praise you in all our works,
grant us, we pray, the courage to follow your Son in all things,
that we might be faithful disciples when we are tempted
and joyful disciples when we are anxious.
Through Christ our Lord.
Amen.

Other Rites and Customs

- Extend a special blessing to the many young adults who will be returning to college in the coming days. Use the Order for the Blessing of Students and Teachers (chapter 5, BB).

- Use the blessing of engaged couples found in appendix II of the *Order of Celebrating Matrimony*. Presiders and liturgists should take note that this blessing is not to take place during Mass.

Liturgy and Life

We cannot deny it; many young people step away from practicing their faith—at least temporarily. Like some of the disciples in today's Gospel, they find the ways of Jesus and the Church hard to accept. What is our response? Scripture makes it clear that Jesus and the Lord of Israel never forced adherence but instead invited, urged, and appealed. That is still how God works. Look up the Catholic campus ministry at the nearest college or university; volunteer, send a donation, or write a note of support. Pick one young person in your life, someone who has set aside faith life. Pray for that person and, if it feels appropriate, send a note that is encouraging but not condemning.

Taking Place This Week . . .

Consider what can be done liturgically, catechetically, and ministerially to respond to these important needs.

- World Day for Slave Trade Abolition (8/23)
- Women's Equality Day (8/26)

MON 23 LM #425 / LMC #193–232 / green Weekday

Optional Memorial of Rose of Lima, Virgin / white

Scripture Insights

God's people ought to draw others to the faith through examples of love and charity. The scribes and Pharisees would direct people to the faith, but spiritually bar them from the fullness of heaven; Jesus spoke against such atrocity.

Preaching Points

Parish Masses

- Some of the early Christians came into the faith from non-Jewish backgrounds; people were convinced by the Holy Spirit to depart from the religions in which they had grown up.
- Hypocritical behavior is a terrible behavior; Jesus spoke strongly against hypocrites and their lies.

Masses with Children

- Early Christians came to Christianity from Jewish and non-Jewish backgrounds. Many came from polytheistic religions and were convicted by the Holy Spirit to become Christians.
- Hypocrisy happens when people make a statement and claim it to be true but don't actually live out that belief. Jesus spoke strongly against those who live in such lies.

Missal Options

- Consider using the prayers from the MPVN-1/E.
- Use any of the three forms of the PA.
- Any of the eight Prefaces for OT or the six Common Prefaces may be used.
- You might use EP-II.
- Any OT Collect may be used or adapted to conclude the UP. You might even look at the Collects in the Masses for Various Needs and Occasions for possible concluding prayers.

Song of the Day

"How Firm a Foundation" (various publishers)

Optional Memorial

During St. Rose of Lima's (1586–1617) brief life, people noticed her physical beauty, but the beauty of her soul far surpassed her physical appearance. Rose longed to live solely for God by claiming Christ as her spouse. Basing her life on St. Catherine of Siena, she lived a penitential life, setting up an infirmary in the family home to care for impoverished children and the sick.

- The readings may be from the SW, #628, CV, CHMW (For Religious), LMC #359, or CS (For Religious).
- The Collect is from the PS; the other prayers may be from the CV: For One Virgin.
- Consider P-I or P-II of Saints, or the Preface of Holy Virgins and Religious and EP-I.
- Any OT Collect may be used to conclude the UP.

TUE 24 LM #629 / LMC #361 / red Feast of St. Bartholomew, Apostle

Today's Saint

St. Bartholomew was one of the Apostles, usually mentioned in the company of St. Philip. Little is known about Bartholomew, but legend holds that he brought the Gospel to India and was martyred in Armenia.

Scripture Insights *(PS)*

We are celebrating Bartholomew, but we read about Nathanael—it is the same Apostle, but a different name! The passage from John gives us a lively exchange. Nathanael is at first doubtful when Philip tells him that he has found the Messiah. But when he comes to meet Jesus, he finds that Jesus already knows him as a true and honest "child of Israel." Nathanael comes to believe because Jesus knows him—but Jesus assures him that he, Nathanael, will come to know more about Jesus as well. It is the same for us: Jesus knows us through and through and invites us on an adventure of discovery, to learn who Jesus really is.

Preaching Points

Parish Masses

- The Book of Revelation provides us with a glimpse of heaven, the new Jerusalem. The walls are marked with the names of the twelve tribes of Israel and the Twelve Apostles.
- Our faith is built on the witness and testimony of the other Apostles, and it is given to us in Baptism.

Masses with Children

- The children might be confused as to why Bartholomew is not mentioned in today's readings. Instead, focus on who Bartholomew is and how he is one of the Twelve Apostles.
- Instead of reflecting on the Gospel, talk about the Book of Revelation and how it presents us with a vision of heaven, or God's Kingdom. The Apostles' names are inscribed on the walls of heaven. The faith

that they had in Jesus is extended to us. Jesus extends God's Kingdom to us as well. We are given this faith at Baptism.

Missal Options

- Since today is a feast of an Apostle, consider doing the sprinkling rite.
- The Gloria is sung or said.
- Use any of the OT Collects to conclude the UP.
- The readings from the CA may be used with Masses with children.
- The prayer texts are proper and are found in the PS.
- Use either of the Prefaces of the Apostles.
- Consider EP-I.
- Conclude Mass with the SB for the Apostles (#17).

Song of the Day

"Beautiful City" (various publishers)

Other Rites and Customs

Hours: Use the Proper Psalter of the day.

WED 25 LM #427 / LMC #193–232 / green Weekday

Optional Memorials of St. Louis / white; St. Joseph Calasanz, Priest / white

Scripture Insights

We are called to be holy and pure on the inside and on the outside; we should engage in honesty and integrity and not hypocrisy. Jesus spoke strongly against the Pharisees who made themselves appear holy and good while not actually living what they taught.

Preaching Points

Parish Masses

- Righteousness is a good thing when a person is living a life of goodness and integrity.
- There is particular irony in the Pharisees claiming that they would not have shed the blood of the prophets had they lived in the time of those prophets.
- The work of the Gospel can be hard work, but the rewards are great. The early Christian leaders desired a positive and encouraging manner of learning the Gospel. They tried to be like loving fathers toward the communities.

Masses with Children

- Righteousness sometimes has a bad name, but it can be very good when a person is living a life of integrity.
- The early Christian leaders looked to encourage the believing communities in the faith. They worked to encourage and teach like good fathers teach their children.

Missal Options

- Consider using the prayers from the MPVN-30/A; use the second option for the Collect.
- Use any of the three forms of the PA.
- Any of the eight Prefaces for OT or the six Common Prefaces may be used.
- You might use EPR-II.
- Any OT Collect may be used or adapted to conclude the UP. You might even look at the Collects in the Masses for Various Needs and Occasions for possible concluding prayers.

Song of the Day

"O God, You Search Me" by Bernadette Farrell (OCP)

Optional Memorials

St. Louis

King Louis I of France dedicated his lengthy reign to the promotion of peace and justice in his domain, arbitrating cases between his subjects, feeding and housing the poor, and negotiating peace settlements with England.

- The readings may be taken from the SW, #630, CHMW/CS, or LMC #361.
- Use any of the OT Collects to conclude the UP.
- Use the Collect from the PS; the other prayers are taken from the CHMW (For One Saint).
- Select from P-I or P-II of Saints.
- Consider EP-I or EP-II.

St. Joseph Calasanz

St. Joseph Calasanz founded the Clerks Regular of the Pious School to educate the poor and improve their lives. With St. Camillus de Lellis, St. Joseph cared for plague victims, serving Christ in his "distressing disguise" wherever he saw need.

- The readings may be taken from the SW, #631, CP, CHMW (For Teachers), LMC #362, or CS (For Religious).
- Use any of the OT Collects to conclude the UP.

- Use the Collect form the PS; the other prayers may be taken from the CHMW (For Educators) or from the CP (For One Pastor).
- Select from P-I or P-II of Saints, or the Preface of Holy Pastors.
- Consider EP-I or EP-II.

THU 26

LM #428 / LMC #193–232 / green

Weekday

Scripture Insights

Love is central to the Christian life. This love stems from Christ, who first loved us, and it flows from each believer to another. When we love one another and live in that love, we are living out Christ's teaching on loving neighbors as ourselves.

Preaching Points

Parish Masses

- We shouldn't live planning to prepare for Jesus only at the last minute of our lives. This behavior is a sort of hypocrisy. Instead, our lives should be dedicated to living in Christ's love so that we are always ready to greet him in joy.
- How do we increase our love for family, friends, and community members? How do we love others in the midst of dislike?

Masses with Children

- We shouldn't live our lives planning to prepare for Jesus only at the last minute of our lives. Instead, our lives should be shining examples of Christ's love all the time.
- How do we increase our love for family, friends, classmates and those in our communities? How do we love others when they are unkind? How do we love others when dealing with feelings of dislike?

Missal Options

- Consider using the prayers from the Twenty-Seventh Sunday in OT.
- Use any of the three forms of the PA.
- Any of the eight Prefaces for OT or the six Common Prefaces may be used.
- You might use EP-II.
- Any OT Collect may be used or adapted to conclude the UP. You might even look at the Collects in the Masses for Various Needs and Occasions for possible concluding prayers.

Song of the Day

"Holy God, We Praise Thy Name" (various publishers)

FRI 27

LM #429 or #632 / LMC #193–232 or #363 / white

Memorial of St. Monica

Today's Saint

St. Monica was married to unfaithful and unbelieving Patricius. Monica's son, St. Augustine, was a handful. She tried to change him to no avail. Finally, she submitted to prayer after being advised it was her only help. Augustine was baptized at age twenty-eight, and the rest is history.

Scripture Insights

Marriage should be a life of love and concern for another person, not a decision based on power or ownership of another person. By their faith, Christians ought to engage in human respect, not human exploitation.

Preaching Points

Parish Masses

- We are called to lives that are moral and upright; our families should be formed in holiness, not in exploitation.
- We must be aware in our spiritual lives and be prepared. We wait for the coming of our Lord in joyful hope, as we say at Mass, and we joyfully prepare for his arrival.

Masses with Children

- When we behave with moral fortitude, we are treating people like human beings and not like things that can be owned or controlled. We are careful to respect others.
- Someday Jesus will return to us, as he promised. We wait for that day in joyful hope! Jesus wants us to always be ready to meet him. Out of love for him, we keep ourselves ready to greet him with joy.

Scripture Insights *(PS)*

To be a wife, to be a mother, is a great responsibility of immense value.

Preaching Points

Parish Masses

- When Jesus sees the funeral procession of the young man, he has pity on the childless widow. He gives her back her son and, in so doing, gives her back her own life and her place in society. God listens to the prayers of mothers.
- The lives of holy people—even when they are lived in a narrow compass—have a ripple effect. Each of us

has the power to change the lives of those around us, simply by the way we live our own lives.

Masses with Children

- Use the preaching points provided for Parish Masses with children, as well.

Missal Options

- The readings may also be taken from the CHMW/CS.
- Use the Collect from the PS; the other prayers may be taken from the CHMW (For Holy Women).
- Use any of the three forms of the PA.
- Use any of the OT Collects to conclude the UP, and P-I or P-II of Saints.
- Consider EP-II.

Song of the Day

"Keep Your Lamps" (various publishers)

SAT 28 LM #430 or #633 / LMC #193–232 or #364 / white

Memorial of St. Augustine, Bishop and Doctor of the Church

Today's Saint

St. Augustine had a formative influence on the early Church as bishop and was the author of works of apologetics and theology exploring the role of the Christian in the world and refuting popular errors. His Confessions gives an account of his attachment to sin, his restless spirit as a young man, and his path to the spiritual conversion that lit the fire of his love for God.

Scripture Insights

Human love and respect are a basic teaching of our faith. We should keep peace with each other and not spend time concerning ourselves with others' business. We must be faithful to God in our homes, among friends, and in our communities.

Preaching Points

Parish Masses

- Jesus wants us to be responsible, moral, and accountable in small and large matters. Like the servant in the parable, we will be rewarded for faithfulness.
- Love is a central Gospel message, and we are called to be faithful to this teaching. How are we loving in small matters? How are we loving in substantial matters?

Masses with Children

- Jesus wants us to be responsible, moral, and accountable in small and large matters. Like the servant in the parable, we will be rewarded for faithfulness. As you grow up, you will grow in your responsibility in your family, your classroom, and your community.
- Love is a central Gospel message, and we are called to be faithful to this teaching. How are we loving in small and large matters? How are we loving to others in our families and in our classrooms? What happens when we fail to love others as we ought?

Scripture Insights *(PS)*

We have but one teacher—Jesus Christ; and one law—love.

Preaching Points

Parish Masses

- God loves us first. Sometimes God calls the most unlikely of people, like St. Augustine, and when they respond to God's love, extraordinary things can happen. God never gives up on us. Who are the "hopeless" ones in our lives? Are there people we have given up on? Today is a day to pray for their conversion and response to God's love.
- St. Augustine restlessly sought the truth, and his search led him in many directions before it finally brought him to Christ. May our hearts be similarly restless until they rest securely in God.

Masses with Children

- Sometimes God calls unlikely people and extraordinary things happen. Tell the children about St. Augustine. He was an unlikely person, but he changed his ways and devoted himself to Christ.

Missal Options

- The readings may also be taken from the CP or CDC.
- Use any of the three forms of the PA.
- Use any of the OT Collects to conclude the UP.
- The prayers are proper and are found in the PS.
- Select from P-I or P-II of Saints, or the Preface of Holy Pastors.
- Consider EP-II.

Song of the Day

"Praise My Soul, the King of Heaven" (various publishers)

S U N **29** LM #125B / LMC #120B / green
Twenty-Second Sunday in Ordinary Time

Scripture Insights

Today all three readings are concerned with the disposition of the heart and its connection with outer actions. Moses begins the first of his exhortations to the Israelites before they cross the Jordan into Canaan. The law of God is just, more so than the laws of any other nation. Obedience to the law of God, says Moses, will show Israel's wisdom and discernment. But hearing the word and desiring it with the heart must come first. Conversion of the heart always has primary importance for Moses and the rest of the prophets. Moses spoke of circumcision of the heart as a sign of the interiorization of the covenant (Deuteronomy 10:16). Isaiah told the Israelites that God despised the festivals, sacrifices, and rituals because the Israelites were not caring for the orphan and the widow. They were going through the motions of obedience without care for God and God's justice. Their attitude was apparent in their lack of compassion.

James understands the implication of "hearing" the law for the Jews. To hear is to obey. According to James, a good Christian is in the same position. One cannot be a hearer of the Word without doing right as well, and following the law without a faithful heart has no place in the covenant relationship.

In Mark's account of the Gospel, Jesus speaks precisely to the last point. The Pharisees are concerned with outward appearances, not inner conversion. When Jesus quotes Isaiah, he reminds them that such scrupulous behavior without the necessary conversion of heart is not true worship of God. Jesus is not attacking the Jewish law here. His point is about the systematic judgment of the scribes and Pharisees that does not ask first what is the disposition of the heart but, rather, whether every letter of the law has been observed. Like Moses, Isaiah, and the other prophets before him, Jesus knows that lip service and outward obedience without inner transformation are not a sign of covenant relationship.

What examples do we see today in Church or society of outward obedience and inward rebellion?

Preaching Points

Parish Masses

- To truly hear the law is to listen with the ear of the heart and make its message part of one's automatic action. Outward appearances do not matter, but virtue and obedience do matter to the Lord. What is in our hearts can make us unclean more than the outward appearances of cleanliness.
- The ancient Israelites were subject to God's law as it was given to the people. They were not free to change God's laws and claim superiority over God's laws.
- We are charged with the responsibility of actively living out God's word in the care of the poor and helpless in our society.
- We are called not to just preach the Good News but to live out the Good News. We are not meant to direct others to do the good work of God's people in our stead.

Children's Liturgy of the Word

- God's law was given to the ancient Israelites and they were told not to change it.
- When we live out God's law in our society, we help the poor, helpless, and lonely people in our society.
- Nobody appreciates people who are bossy, especially when someone preaches a virtue but doesn't express or practice that virtue. We must live out God's law rather than just instruct others about it.

Missal Options

- Offer any of the three forms of the PA.
- Sing or recite the Gloria and the Creed.
- Any of the seasonal OT Collects may be used or adapted to conclude the UP.
- Select from any of the eight Prefaces of OT.
- Consider EP-III.
- There are six SBs for OT from which to choose.

Music Preparation

- This is a good time of year to start a new Mass setting that will take you through the end of Ordinary Time. When choosing a setting, ask: Is the voicing is right for my choir? How well will it work with a solo cantor? Does it work with piano, organ, or contemporary ensemble? Are there instrumental parts? Is it easy to learn and does it have the power to last?
- As many programs begin to get into gear, why not consider blessing your musicians? Check out the *Book of Blessings*, chapter 62: Order for the Blessing of Altar Servers, Sacristans, Musicians and Ushers. Having a formalized order of blessing should deepen the pastoral musician's sense of service to the liturgy and overall commitment. Perhaps each could receive a St. Cecilia medal.

Music Suggestions

- Preparation of the Gifts: "Psalm 51: Create in Me a Clean Heart" by Bob Hurd (OCP)
- Mass Setting: "Mass of St. Paul of the Cross" by Edward Eicker (WLP)
- Communion: "When You Fill Us with Your Word" by the Collegeville Composers Group (Liturgical Press)
- Sending Forth: "Christ's Church Shall Glory" by Christopher Idle (Hope Publishing Company)

Mass Texts

Introduction to Mass

What makes for the correct practice of our faith? Is it fulfilling our Sunday obligation or making our weekly offering to the parish coffers? Is it saying our prayers or adhering to the teachings of the Church? All of these are praiseworthy, but today's Second Reading informs us that an essential part of pure religion is to care for the needy and the oppressed. We must give our lives for the world as Christ gives himself in the bread and wine of the Eucharist. *My brothers and sisters, let us acknowledge our sins, and so prepare ourselves to celebrate the sacred mysteries.*

Tropes for Penitential Act, Form III

You call us to do justice and so to live in your presence: Lord, have mercy.

Your word is a light to our feet and a lamp to our path: Christ, have mercy.

We honor you not only with our lips but also with our hearts: Lord, have mercy.

Dismissal for Children's Liturgy of the Word

My children, we now give you your own time to go and hear God's Word and to think about how you might put it into practice. When you return to us we will rejoice and together give thanks for the great love God has given us in his Son, Jesus, who now calls to you.

Dismissal of Catechumens

My friends, the Word is being planted in you and we encourage you to receive it humbly. We send you forth to consider how God is calling you to embody it in your lives, and we pray that the Spirit will continue to enlighten you in this regard and that you may soon join us around the table of the Lord. Go in peace.

Dismissal of Extraordinary Ministers of Holy Communion

Dear ministers, the Lord is close to his people in their need, and so we give you his Body and the Word of life to take to the sick and suffering members of our community. Let them be consoled and strengthened in spirit, so that they may join their praise to ours and give thanks to our great God. Go in peace.

Universal Prayer

My brothers and sisters, we honor God with a heart that generates love. With love for all people, let us offer our prayers to God.

1. For Church leaders, for the pope, all bishops, priests, deacons, religious, and lay ministers, that they may witness to a way of following Christ that is honest and true, we pray:
2. For national leaders, that they may generate love with the policies they enact, we pray:
3. For all who defile our world through negative speech, that they may use words that build up, not tear down, we pray:
4. For all who seek the path of conversion, especially those who desire to celebrate the Sacrament of Reconciliation, that they may live anew, we pray:
5. For our faithful departed, especially those who honored God in this life with generous and loving hearts, we pray:

Merciful Father,
your Son teaches us to look deep within
to discover that which is the root of all sin.
Give us hearts that desire serious introspection,
so that we may know all that comes from within
might be fitting for your honor and glory.
Through Christ our Lord.
Amen.

Other Rites and Customs

- Make plans for a formational gathering for your liturgy or worship committee as a new season begins.
- These late summer days present a good opportunity to talk about the importance of Sunday Mass, especially as people return to their usual routines after summer vacation and with school and other activities starting up again. Consider providing parishioners with LTP's intergenerational series, *From Mass to Mission.*
- Members of the music ministry may want to take advantage of this time to recruit and form new music ministers.
- Reflect on Pope Francis' encyclical *Laudato si'* in preparation for the World Day of Prayer for the Care of Creation on September 1.

Liturgy and Life

There is a saying attributed to St. Francis of Assisi: Preach the Gospel always; when necessary use words."James challenges us to "be doers of the word and not hearers only," and the Gospel instructs us to honor God with both our hearts and our lips. The message seems clear: live our faith with integrity in such a way that what is true in our hearts shows through in all our words and action.

Taking Place This Week . . .

Consider what can be done liturgically, catechetically, and ministerially to respond to these important needs.

- International Day against Nuclear Tests (8/29)
- World Day of Victims of Enforced Disappearance (8/30)
- International Overdose Awareness Day (8/31)
- First Friday (9/3) and First Friday (9/4)
- September is traditionally celebrated as the Month of Our Lady of Sorrows.

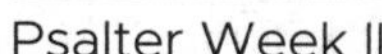

M O N 30 — LM #431 / LMC #193–232 / green
Weekday

Scripture Insights

Death is not the end of the Christian life; it is the beginning of eternal life. When our earthly lives are over, we trust in God's goodness and the hope of heaven. Jesus has promised to prepare a place for us.

Preaching Points

Parish Masses

- The early Christians were waiting for the immediate return of Jesus, and this epistle was meant to help them understand the faith in light of Jesus' promise and time continuing without his return.
- When the Nazarenes saw Scripture fulfilled before their eyes, they were not able to see Jesus for who he truly is and was. We must keep our eyes and ears ready for Jesus.

Masses with Children

- The early Christians assumed that Jesus would return very quickly. When he didn't return immediately, the leaders of the Church had to help the people understand death and Jesus' second coming in a new light.
- When the Nazarenes saw Scripture fulfilled before their eyes, they were not able to see Jesus for who he truly is and was. They could only see that Jesus, who they had known as a boy, was claiming something they believed impossible.

Missal Options

- Consider using the prayers from the MPVN-32.
- Use any of the three forms of the PA.
- Any of the eight Prefaces for OT or the six Common Prefaces may be used.
- You might use EP-II.
- Any OT Collect may be used or adapted to conclude the UP. You might even look at the Collects in the Masses for Various Needs and Occasions for possible concluding prayers.

Song of the Day

"You Have Anointed Me" by Mike Balhoff, Gary Daigle, and Darryl Ducote (GIA)

T U E 31 — LM #432 / LMC #193–232 / green
Weekday

Scripture Insights

The early Christians believed that Jesus' return was immanent; many were surprised when he did not immediately return and that the last day was something that didn't happen immediately. We do not know when that day will occur, but we wait for that day in joy, because Jesus has promised it. Instead of preparing when we think it may happen, we must always be prepared for Jesus.

Preaching Points

Parish Masses

- God desires for his children to be saved and join him in heaven one day. We should always be alert and ready for our Lord.
- Jesus spoke with authority over the supernatural world. This authority was unique and serves to illustrate Jesus' divinity.

Masses with Children

- God prepared a place for us in heaven, and he desires for all of his children to live there with him. We should always be ready to meet God.
- Jesus had authority over the supernatural world. That means the supernatural world had to obey him; this authority helps us understand that Jesus is God.

Missal Options

- Consider using the prayers from the MPVN-43.
- Use any of the three forms of the PA.
- Any of the eight Prefaces for OT or the six Common Prefaces may be used.
- You might use EPVN-IV.
- Any OT Collect may be used or adapted to conclude the UP. You might even look at the Collects in the Masses for Various Needs and Occasions for possible concluding prayers.

Song of the Day

"God of Day and God of Darkness"
by Marty Haugen (GIA)

WED 1 LM #433 / LMC #193–232 / green
Weekday

Scripture Insights

People who experience Jesus respond to him; Simon's mother-in-law was healed and began to serve. Jesus departed from there to preach throughout the region, because he knew the world needed his healing ministry.

Preaching Points

Parish Masses

- Jesus' mission was centered in the Holy Land, but through Scripture his preaching, teaching, and healing ministry have had long reach.
- Communities of Christians are meant to grow and bear fruit. How does your community bear fruit, and how is your community growing? How does your community reach out to the poor, the suffering, and the immigrants in your midst?

Masses with Children

- Christian communities are meant to bear fruit for one another and for strangers. How does your community care for one another? How do you care for others? How does your community reach out to those who need it most? How do you care for your family members or your friends at school?
- Jesus proclaimed the Good News throughout the Holy Land. Through Scripture we still hear his Good News proclaimed.

Missal Options

- Consider using the prayers from the MPVN-45/1.
- Use any of the three forms of the PA.
- Any of the eight Prefaces for OT or the six Common Prefaces may be used.
- You might use EPR-II.
- Any OT Collect may be used or adapted to conclude the UP. You might even look at the Collects in the Masses for Various Needs and Occasions for possible concluding prayers.

Song of the Day

"Song of Good News" by Williard F. Jabusch (WLP)

THU 2 LM #434 / LMC #193–232 / green
Weekday

Scripture Insights

Through Christ, we are delivered from darkness to light. In him we grow and produce fruit in his light. God has called us to this Christian life, and we walk with him on this journey.

Preaching Points

Parish Masses

- When Jesus called Simon, James, and John they left everything and followed him. While we are not typically called in the same way the Apostles were called, we still respond to Jesus' call in our lives each day; we are called to follow him.
- What must you leave behind in order to follow Jesus? Jealousy? Greed? What virtues do you possess that help you to follow Jesus?
- When we follow Jesus, we grow in the faith and our knowledge of God. How does our knowledge of God show in our lives? How does it transform us and our communities?

Masses with Children

- Simon, James, and John left everything and followed Jesus. Each of us are called to follow Jesus too, though not exactly in the same way the Apostles followed him.
- What must you leave behind to follow Jesus more nearly? Jealousy? Selfishness? What virtues do you possess that help you to follow Jesus?
- What does it mean to grow in the knowledge of God, and how does it change us?

Missal Options

- Consider using the prayers from the MPVN-38/A; use the first option for the Collect.
- Use any of the three forms of the PA.
- Any of the eight Prefaces for OT or the six Common Prefaces may be used.
- You might use EP-II.
- Any OT Collect may be used or adapted to conclude the UP. You might even look at the Collects in the Masses for Various Needs and Occasions for possible concluding prayers.

Song of the Day

"You Walk Along Our Shoreline" by Sylvia Dunstan (GIA)

FRI 3 LM #435 or #635 / LMC #193–232 or #366 / white

Memorial of St. Gregory the Great, Pope and Doctor of the Church

Today's Saint

St. Gregory the Great was responsible for promoting monasticism, patronizing the development of Gregorian chant, commissioning evangelists to Britain, and writing many theological and catechetical works. Pope Gregory led Rome and the Church through plagues, invasions, and political confusion, placing his talents for organization and leadership in the service of both political peace and the spread of Christianity.

Scripture Insights

In Christ and through Christ we find all things; we find ourselves created by God and saved from ourselves by Christ. In him we find our beginning and our eternal lives. Through him we live in our community, the Church, and are bound to him.

Preaching Points

Parish Masses

- In Christ we see God; through him we come to understand God and to know him. In Christ's love, charity, devotion, and love of justice, we understand God's expectation for his people. Jesus and the Father are one.
- When Jesus walked with his disciples on the earth, they were in a time of great joy. Emmanuel, God with us, was with his people. He is the bridegroom, and his people are the bride.

Masses with Children

- Jesus Christ helps us to understand God. Jesus does God's will always, so we can understand what God is like by understanding what Jesus was like. Jesus and the Father are one.
- Weddings are happy and exciting occasions—at these celebrations, people are ready to feast and not fast. When Jesus was on earth with his disciples, God was with us; it was a time of feasting and not fasting.

Scripture Insights *(PS)*

Jesus is among us as one who serves. It is because of his presence, not ours, that God's light shines forth in the work that we do.

Preaching Points

Parish Masses

- Jesus calls his disciples to turn the world upside down: the leader must be the servant. To lord it over others, to demand places and titles of honor, is typical of rulers; but that is not where Christ is to be found. To meet Christ, we must become servants to each other.
- Each of us is an "earthen vessel," a flawed and breakable container that is filled with something priceless and eternal: the Spirit of God. When we look at each other and interact with each other, too often we see only the earthen vessel, not the treasure within. What would happen if we all looked at each other as bearers of God's presence?

Masses with Children

- An "earthen vessel" is a flawed pot made from the clay of the earth, made by human hands. Likewise, we are "earth vessels," flawed and from the earth by made by God. Only God can fill us.
- We are to be servants of God. Only then will the world be a different place. We are to bring his Kingdom here on earth by the loving things we do.

Missal Options

- The readings may also be taken from the CP (For a Pope) or the CDC.
- Use any of the three forms of the PA.
- Use any of the OT Collects to conclude the UP.
- The prayers are proper and found in the PS.
- Select from P-I or P-II of Saints, the Preface of Holy Pastors, or the Preface of Virgins and Religious.
- Consider EP-II.

Song of the Day

"One Bread, One Body" by John Foley (OCP)

SAT 4 LM #436 / LMC #193–232 / green
Weekday

Optional Memorial of the Blessed Virgin Mary / white

Scripture Insights

We are transformed in Christ. None of us are without sin, perfect, or naturally irreproachable. Each of us has virtues, yes, but each of us has vices as well. In Jesus Christ we are a transformed people, as St. Paul says, made irreproachable through Jesus.

Preaching Points

Parish Masses

- The Pharisees questioned the legitimacy of Jesus' ministry and the behavior of the Jesus and the Apostles. When questioned about the Apostles consuming grain on the Sabbath, Jesus referred to himself as "lord of the sabbath." Jesus saw no sin in picking grain to eat on the Sabbath.
- We are called to stand solidly in the Good News of Christ. St. Paul calls us to persevere in this faith.

Masses with Children

- The Pharisees regularly questioned Jesus' ministry and behavior and that of his Apostles. When the Pharisees criticized the Apostles' picking and eating of grain on the Sabbath, Jesus corrected them by saying the men had not sinned.
- We are called to stand solidly in the Good News of Christ. St. Paul calls us to persevere in this faith. What does it mean to persevere in the faith? How do we stand firm in our faith and action?

Missal Options

- Consider using the prayers from the Twenty-Third Sunday in OT.
- Use any of the three forms of the PA.
- Any of the eight Prefaces for OT or the six Common Prefaces may be used.
- You might use EP-II.
- Any OT Collect may be used or adapted to conclude the UP. You might even look at the Collects in the Masses for Various Needs and Occasions for possible concluding prayers.

Song of the Day

"Sing of the Lord's Goodness"
by Ernest Sands and Paul Inwood (OCP)

Optional Memorial

- The readings may be taken from the SW, CBVM, or CMML.
- The prayer texts may be taken from the CBVM or CMMM. Any votive Mass for the BVM may be used.
- Use any of the three forms of the PA.
- Select from P-I or P-II of the BVM.
- Any of the OT Collects may conclude the UP.

SUN **5** LM #128B / LMC #123B / green

Twenty-Third Sunday in Ordinary Time

Scripture Insights

Isaiah's vision of the coming day of God reveals a world turned upside down. The blind see, the deaf hear, the mute speak and waters spring up in the desert. This is a world of the unexpected and surprising. It is a result that is as unsettling as it is joyful, for it is not what nature has intended. In the presence of the divine, anything needed is provided; anything broken is made whole. The laws of nature, created by God, are suspended when God comes in glory.

Mark's account of the Gospel describes the living fulfillment of Isaiah's prophecy when Jesus touches the deaf and mute man so that he hears and speaks. As in the other healing stories, Jesus demonstrates mastery over the limits of the human body. Already he has made the lame walk (see Mark 2) and the dead live (Mark 5). The next time he heals (see Mark 8:22–26), he will cure a blind man. Where Jesus walks, life in its wholeness abounds. The astonishment of the people suggests that they remember the prophecy of Isaiah and wonder if this might be the sign that God has come to save them.

In what way might these texts illuminate the epistle from James? James addresses a particular fault of a Christian community in the first century. The people show favoritism to the rich and well-dressed. James reminds them that God's preference is for the poor and disenfranchised. God did, after all, rescue poor Israel from wealthy Egypt. In that act, God displayed a fondness for turning things upside down. James reminds the Church that God's power is not limited to healing the sick or sending manna. God also has control over economic and social injustices. A society that allows these things will be surprised, unsettled, and ultimately changed at the coming day of the Lord. Just as God will heal our broken bodies, God will heal the broken relationships caused by unjust uses of wealth. That will be good news to some, but for those who define themselves by their wealth and the privilege it buys them, it will be a painful transformation.

How do we follow God in making a preferential option for the poor?

Preaching Points

Parish Masses

- Slipping into preferential treatment by social class is something that can happen anywhere. We must guard against nepotism and partiality for the wealthy and instead have deliberate care for the poor.
- In God's Kingdom the broken will find wellness, and God's people will be healed and made whole. If healed from fear, division, or any impediment, how would you choose to bring justice to the world?
- Our faith is alive in our works. We do not have fecund faith without works that accompany it.
- When Jesus healed people, he gave them a whole health that allowed them to fully participate in the lives of their community.

Children's Liturgy of the Word

- Isaiah is a prophetic book, and we see in Jesus all that was written about the coming Messiah. It is Jesus who brings his people from brokenness to wholeness.
- Our faith is not something that exists only in church on Sundays. Our faith is meant to be a living faith, something abundantly alive that helps transform the world into the Kingdom.
- Everywhere Christ visited, he brought healing and wholeness to the people.

Missal Options

- Offer any of the three forms of the PA.
- Sing or recite the Gloria and the Creed.
- Any of the seasonal OT Collects may be used or adapted to conclude the UP.
- Select from any of the eight Prefaces of OT.
- Consider EPVN-III.
- There are six SBs for OT from which to choose.

Music Preparation

- Sometimes we can get so caught up in our habits that we become blind, deaf, and closed to new ideas. Our ministers suffer these problems too. Consider bringing someone from outside in to evaluate one of your liturgies, or do a clinic day with your choir or cantors. Perhaps they can make suggestions and say things that you are not able to say.
- September can be a busy month with programs starting up after a bit of a summer break. Why not have an "open rehearsal" for the parish and wider community? Many community choruses do this, and the results appear to be very positive. Be sure to publicize the night well in advance and to multiple sources. Many dioceses have a free online calendar for parishes to post various events and activities. Does your diocese provide something like this? Contact your local chancery office and inquire.

Music Suggestions

- Gathering: "Ready the Way" by Bob Hurd (OCP)
- Preparation of the Gifts: "Open My Eyes, Lord" by Jessie Manibussan (OCP)
- Communion: "The Cloud's Veil" by Liam Lawton (GIA)
- Sending Forth: "O God, Our Help in Ages Past" (various publishers)

Mass Texts

Introduction to Mass

In his love for the world, God has chosen us as his instruments of mercy. Strengthened by the Eucharist we celebrate here today, by the life and love of Jesus Christ, we may speak a word of encouragement to the fearful, do justice for the oppressed, and feed the hungry, that all people may know the joy of God's goodness. *My brothers and sisters, let us acknowledge our sins, and so prepare ourselves to celebrate the sacred mysteries.*

Tropes for Penitential Act, Form III

You, O Lord, open the eyes of the blind and the ears of the deaf: Lord, have mercy.

You cause streams of life to burst forth in the desert: Christ, have mercy.

You promise the Kingdom to those who love you: Lord, have mercy.

Dismissal for Children's Liturgy of the Word

Dear children, God can do all things, but in his kindness he has allowed us to help care for the poor and unfortunate people in our midst. Jesus came to teach and to heal, and we are called to continue his work of love in the world. Go now and listen to him and ask him to help you help others.

Dismissal of Catechumens

Friends, God is faithful forever. To us he has promised eternal life and he now offers that same promise to you in his Church. May his Word find welcome in you and take root in your hearts, and may the day quickly come that will find you standing with us to receive his Body and Blood. Go now in peace.

Dismissal of Extraordinary Ministers of Holy Communion

Dear friends, Jesus Christ has done all things well. He has fed us the Bread of Heaven and now makes provision for our sick and homebound sisters and brothers, that they too may be nourished with this spiritual food. Go to them now, fulfilling Christ's commandment of love.

Universal Prayer

My brothers and sisters, the Lord opens our eyes, our minds, and our hearts to his grace so that we may be able to serve him and those in need. Let us look past our own desires and lift up to the Lord our prayers for the world.

1. That the Church may always proclaim the wonderful works of God, we pray:
2. That those who have been abandoned along this world's roadsides may be welcomed into our lives, we pray:
3. That all who use language to dishonor others may have their mouths cleansed, we pray:
4. That all who are deaf may be guided by others who have a good sense of hearing, we pray:
5. That the dead may be purified by the loving mercy of our God, we pray:

Lord Jesus Christ,
out of loving mercy you healed all the distressed,
and you opened the ears and loosened the tongue of the man who could neither hear nor speak.
Open our ears anew this day,
so that we might hear your Word,
and touch our tongue so that every sound we make
might give praise and glory to God
through your most holy name.
Amen.

Other Rites and Customs

- On this Labor Day weekend, be sure to include a petition in the Universal Prayer for those who labor as well as for those who are unemployed or underemployed.
- Publish excerpts of Pope Leo XII's encyclical, *Rerum novarum* in the bulletin.
- Consider having a Mass for those with special needs, particularly those who are deaf or blind.
- Consider how you will mark the twentieth anniversary of the September 11, 2001, attack on the United States this Saturday.

Liturgy and Life

The Letter of James continues to challenge us, perhaps even to the point of discomfort. He names a human tendency played out across time and cultures: we give preference and honor to the rich and easily dismiss the poor. Catholic social teaching instructs us to work against this instinct and give preferential option to the poor. This means creating conditions for marginalized voices to be heard, defending the vulnerable, and evaluating lifestyles, policies, and social constructs in terms of how they impact the poor in society.

Taking Place This Week . . .

Consider what can be done liturgically, catechetically, and ministerially to respond to these important needs.

- International Day of Charity (9/5)
- Labor Day (9/6 in the US and Canada)
- Rosh Hashana (9/7)
- International Literacy Day (9/8)
- World Suicide Prevention Day (9/10)
- National Day of Mourning and Remembrance/ Patriot Day (9/11)
- September is National Childhood Cancer Awareness, National Literacy, National Suicide Prevention, National Hispanic Heritage, and Pain Awareness Month.

MON **6** LM #437 / LMC #193–232 / green
Weekday

Scripture Insights

Human suffering is not useless. Certainly we relieve suffering when we can do so, yet suffering can serve to unite us with Jesus. Paul rejoiced in his persecution as he suffered to serve Christ. When Jesus healed the man with the withered hand, the suffering and subsequent healing served to unite him to Jesus.

Preaching Points

Parish Masses

- Life circumstances are never perfect, and total alleviation of all suffering isn't possible. In our suffering we can look to God and ask for his grace to help us grow in him during painful periods of our lives.
- Keeping the Sabbath wasn't meant to make or keep people sick. Jesus healed on the Sabbath to help people understand that relieving human suffering doesn't fall second to the Sabbath.

Masses with Children

- Suffering can help us understand Jesus and his mission to us all. When we suffer, we can ask for God's grace to help us know him. We should not seek suffering and should relieve suffering when we can do so.
- Jesus prioritized healing a person's hand over keeping the letter of the law on the Sabbath. The Pharisees decided that Jesus was troublesome and a threat to their power.

Missal Options

- Consider using the prayers from the MPVN-48/2.
- Use any of the three forms of the PA.
- Any of the eight Prefaces for OT or the six Common Prefaces may be used.
- You might use EP-II.
- Any OT Collect may be used or adapted to conclude the UP. You might even look at the Collects in the Masses for Various Needs and Occasions for possible concluding prayers.

Song of the Day

"For the Fruits of All Creation" by Fred Pratt Green (Hope Publishing Company)

TUE **7** LM #438 / LMC #193–232 / green
Weekday

Scripture Insights

In Christ and his Church we find the fullness of faith. We must adhere ourselves to these truths rather than fall for the false teachings of others. Other beliefs and belief systems may appear attractive, but they do not have the fullness of faith that Christ offers his Church.

Preaching Points

Parish Masses

- Jesus brings us to life from the depths of our human sinfulness, and our sin no longer has hold on our souls. Through him, we reach for a holier life and for heaven after death.
- Jesus had many followers and specifically selected the Twelve Apostles from among them. These twelve, minus Judas, would become the bishops of the early Church.

Masses with Children

- Through Jesus, our sin no longer has attachment to our souls. Jesus comes to each of us while we are still in human sin. Through him, we reach for a holier life and for heaven after death.
- Many people followed Jesus because his preaching and teaching and miracles were changing people's lives. They saw in him a person they wanted to follow. Jesus selected the Twelve Apostles from among his many followers.

Missal Options

- Consider using the prayers from the MPVN-29.
- Use any of the three forms of the PA.
- Any of the eight Prefaces for OT or the six Common Prefaces may be used.
- You might use EPVN-IV.
- Any OT Collect may be used or adapted to conclude the UP. You might even look at the Collects in the Masses for Various Needs and Occasions for possible concluding prayers.

Song of the Day

"I Bind unto Myself Today" by Jennifer Kerr Budziak (GIA)

W E D **8** LM #636 / LMC #367 / white

Feast of the Nativity of the Blessed Virgin Mary

About Today's Feast

Only the births of Christ, Mary, and John the Baptist are celebrated in our liturgical calendar. All three are integral to the mystery of the Incarnation. Most of what we know about the early life of Mary is found in the *Protoevangelium* of James, an apocryphal gospel from the second century, a source that does not bear the authority of canonical Scripture. Indeed, Mary's birth was the first of many holy events for this daughter of Israel through whom God chose to carry out the plan of salvation.

Scripture Insights

Throughout history, the Jewish people waited for the Messiah, the one who was promised by God to save his people. The line was established—it is the line of Abraham and of King David. Jesus was born into this line, as God's will for salvation and the history of God's people meet in the womb of Mary.

Preaching Points

Parish Masses

- The Blessed Virgin Mary was pregnant with the child of God, and an angel instructed Joseph to take her into his home despite her pregnancy. Mary's faith, seen in her assent to God, and Joseph's faith, seen in his obedience to God's angel, are beautiful examples of people cooperating with God's will.
- *Emmanuel* means "God-with-us," and in the person Jesus, God came to be with us, his people. It is through the Virgin Mary that Jesus came into the world, and it was she who was conceived without the stain of Original Sin in her own mother's womb.

Masses with Children

- Joseph had great faith in God and was obedient to God's angel. Most people do not hear and see angels, so we are called to be obedient to God through the teaching of Scripture and the tradition of the Church.
- God loves us so much that he became one of us, a human person, through the Incarnation of Jesus. This beautiful gift to us occurred through the Virgin Mary, who agreed to be Jesus' mother. St. Joseph, who is descended from Abraham and King David, agreed through faith to be Jesus' earthly father.

Missal Options

- Use any of the three forms of the PA.
- The readings for children's Masses may by from the CBVM.
- Use any of the OT Collects or those from the CBVM or CMMM to conclude the UP.
- The prayers are proper and found in the PS.
- The Gloria is sung or recited; the Creed is not said or sung.
- Use P-I or P-II of the BVM.
- Consider EP-II.
- The SB for the BVM (#15) may conclude the Mass.

Song of the Day

"Mary, First Among Believers" by Delores Dufner, OSB (GIA)

Other Rites and Customs

Hours: Use the Proper Psalter of the day.

T H U  LM #440 or #636A (LS) / LMC #193 - 232 or #368 / white

Memorial of St. Peter Claver, Priest

Today's Saint

Peter Claver (1580–1654), a Spanish Jesuit priest, spent his life tending to the needs of African slaves in Columbia, South America. While serving as a missionary, he ministered to the slaves by providing them with food and medicine, washing their wounds, preparing them for Baptism, and witnessing their marriages. He actively recruited lawyers to plead the cases of imprisoned slaves and prepared criminals for death. He not only cared for the slaves but also preached missions to plantation owners and sailors. The "saint of the slaves," as St. Peter is often called, died after contracting the plague.

Scripture Insights

Compassion, kindness, humility, gentleness, and patience; these attributes are the characteristics of those who follow Christ's teachings. We are called to engage with our families and communities in light of his teaching and in imitation of him.

Preaching Points

Parish Masses

- Love is the mark of a Christian person; we are called to do everything in Christ's name. Like Christ, and in obedience to him, we are called to love one another.
- We are called to love our enemies; Jesus explained that any person can be loving toward those who love them but that we ought to love those who are not our friends.

- When we love those who treat us badly, it doesn't mean that we let people abuse us. We can have reasonable boundaries with people who do not treat us well and still love them.

Masses with Children

- Love is the mark of a Christian person. We are called to follow Jesus' example and follow his rules for us. Both his example and his instruction tell us to love one another.
- We are called to love those who are enemies as well as those who treat us well. Jesus explains that it isn't difficult to love those who love us but that it is challenging to love those who are enemies.
- Loving our enemies doesn't mean that we let people continue to bully or hurt us. It is not loving to allow a person to continue to behave badly.

Scripture Insights *(PS)*

God asks us to love and serve each other. Whatever we do for one of the least, we do for God.

Preaching Points

Parish Masses

- If we want to serve Christ, to love Christ, to tend his wounds, and be with him in his loneliness, none of us needs to look far: in every community, people are suffering, sick, impoverished, alone, rejected. That is where we will find Christ.
- Fasting from food is a prayerful offering in many religious traditions, including ours. The kind of fast God asks of us is not about giving up but about going forth, advocating for justice, and sharing what we have with those most in need.

Masses with Children

- If we want to serve Christ, to love Christ, to tend his wounds, and be with him in his loneliness, none of us needs to look far: in every community, people are suffering, sick, impoverished, alone, rejected. That is where we will find Christ.

Missal Options

- The readings may also be taken from the #636A (LS) or the CP (For Missionaries). The readings for children may be taken from the CP or CS (For Those Who Work for the Underprivileged).
- Use any of the three forms of the PA.
- Use any of the OT Collects to conclude the UP.
- Use the Collect from the PS; the other prayers may be taken from the CP (For One Pastor) or CHMW (For Those Who Practiced Works of Mercy).
- Select from any of the eight Prefaces of OT or the six Common Prefaces.
- Consider EPVN-IV.

Song of the Day

"The Peace of God" by David Haas (GIA)

FRI 10 Weekday

LM #441 / LMC #193–232 / green

Scripture Insights

In Christ we can turn around our lives; we are not stagnant beings but rather have the ability to grow and change. We can look to Christ and ask him for transformation. In Christ, we can continue the mission to healing from our sin.

Preaching Points

Parish Masses

- St. Paul states that he was arrogant and was a persecutor of Christians, but because of Jesus' intervention in his life he experienced metanoia, a deep spiritual change.
- We must avoid hypocrisy in our lives. Before correcting others, we must be free of whatever fault we are finding.

Masses with Children

- Arrogance is the sin of pride, and Paul explains that, before Christ transformed him, he was arrogant and persecuted Christians. With his transformation in Christ, he was no longer arrogant or filled with hate.
- Hypocrisy is something we must avoid. When people are hypocritical, they find fault with others that they themselves still exhibit. Jesus warns us to be aware of not committing such sin.

Missal Options

- Consider using the prayers from the Tenth Sunday in OT.
- Use any of the three forms of the PA.
- Any of the eight Prefaces for OT or the six Common Prefaces may be used.
- You might use EPVN-III.
- Any OT Collect may be used or adapted to conclude the UP. You might even look at the Collects in the Masses for Various Needs and Occasions for possible concluding prayers.

Song of the Day

- "Amazing Grace" (various publishers)
- When singing "Amazing Grace" be sure to change the line "saved a wretch like me" to "saved and set us free." This change reflects Catholic theology more accurately.

SAT 11 LM #442 / LMC #193–232 / green
Weekday

Optional Memorial of the Blessed Virgin Mary / white

Scripture Insights

Grace transforms that which it touches. Sin that is touched by grace can become a testament to the power of God and the resurrected Lord. Each of us is called to be open to Jesus and his transforming love.

Preaching Points

Parish Masses

- St. Paul humbly recognizes his sin and states that because of his sin, he is able to share with others the beautiful attributes of Christ's love shining in his transformed life. His story helps others recognize the value and power of the faith.
- What sort of fruit do you bear in your life? Jesus' teaching is that we shall know others by their fruits. We choose the people we stay near and choose how we are ourselves will be.

Masses with Children

- St. Paul teaches that Jesus' intervention in his life caused love to shine through him. St. Paul went from a sinful life to a holy life.
- What sort of fruit do you bear in your life? Jesus' teaching is that we shall know others by their fruits. What kind of fruit do you want to bear? What sort of fruit-bearing people do you want to be near?

Missal Options

- Consider using the prayers from the Twenty-Fourth Sunday in OT.
- Use any of the three forms of the PA.
- Any of the eight Prefaces for OT or the six Common Prefaces may be used.
- You might use EP-II.
- Any OT Collect may be used or adapted to conclude the UP. You might even look at the Collects in the Masses for Various Needs and Occasions for possible concluding prayers.

Song of the Day

"Church of God" by Margaret Daly (OCP)

Optional Memorial

- The readings may be taken from the SW, CBVM, or CMML.
- The prayer texts may be taken from the CBVM or CMMM. Any votive Mass for the BVM may be used.
- Use any of the three forms of the PA.
- Select from P-I or P-II of the BVM.
- Any of the OT Collects may conclude the UP.

SUN **12** LM #131B / LMC #126B / green

Twenty-Fourth Sunday in Ordinary Time

Scripture Insights

"Who do people say that I am?" Jesus poses this question to his disciples on his journey through Caesarea Philippi. It elicits Peter's acknowledgment that Jesus is the Messiah. For centuries Israel had looked forward to God fulfilling his promise to King David by raising up another great leader to restore Israel's kingdom (see 2 Samuel 7). These hopes had become clouded in political and earthly expectations.

Peter's response, in unambiguous terms, "You are the Christ [or the Messiah]," gives Jesus the opportunity to offer a different understanding. Jesus says that he has come to establish not an earthly kingdom in power but rather a spiritual kingdom in weakness. God's Kingdom will be established through Jesus' death and Resurrection.

The First Reading, from the third of Isaiah's "Servant Songs," belongs to another tradition pointing to the Messiah's coming in humiliation and suffering. Jesus draws on this tradition in referring to his own ministry of suffering and death on behalf of God's people.

Peter fails to take this tradition into account when he tells Jesus not to talk about suffering and death. He is utterly perplexed and alarmed, for Peter believed that the Messiah would come in power and glory. When Jesus says to Peter, "Get behind me, Satan," he is referring to Satan in the Book of Job, where Satan, as the name actually means, is God's adversary. Jesus reinforces this by saying that Peter's thoughts reflect human ways of thinking, not God's way.

A further challenge emerges for Jesus' followers from his revelation that he is going to suffer and die. His followers' lives will embrace the same path of suffering, death, and resurrection. As true Christians, our lives too will share in Jesus' redemptive suffering.

Preaching Points

Parish Masses

- Jesus is a king unlike any other king in human history. Kings are typically greeted with fanfare and given grand palaces; instead, the King of the Universe traveled without an entourage arranging his comfort and looked to the end of his earthly life knowing he would be mercilessly persecuted and broken.
- Believing in God doesn't make our lives easy, flawless, or without struggle. God helps us in our struggles and gives us assistance in our difficulty.
- Lofty spirituality doesn't matter if we allow others to go hungry and cold. Our faith is meant to be seen and understood in the context of works.
- Jesus knew that he would have to suffer and taught his disciples that he would endure persecution. This reading foreshadows the persecution and suffering that the Apostles themselves would one day bear.
- When we follow Jesus, we will know life. When we take up the cross, we will know our salvation. We do not earn salvation by the works we do to follow Jesus, James tells us in the Second Reading. But the good works we do are our response to the gift of faith and grace and life we have in God through Jesus Christ. And what a gift that we can present to others by the good we do!

Children's Liturgy of the Word

- Everyone's lives have difficulties and struggles. We all have things we worry about and things that make us sad. God is always with us in our sadness and struggles.
- Having deep spirituality doesn't matter if we do not make sure that our neighbors have food and shelter. Our acts matter absolutely.
- Ancient kings were given every comfort and lived lavish lives. Jesus, the King of the Universe, led a simple life and bore suffering other earthly kings never bore.

Missal Options

- Offer any of the three forms of the PA.
- Sing or recite the Gloria and the Creed.
- Any of the seasonal OT Collects may be used or adapted to conclude the UP.
- Select from any of the eight Prefaces of OT.
- Consider using EP-II.
- There are six SBs for OT from which to choose.

Music Preparation

Our readings speak of Isaiah's suffering servant, faith and good works, and carrying our cross. Here are some positive things you can do to help balance your workload: (1) schedule a session with a spiritual director or confessor; (2) build practice time into your schedule; and (3) treat yourself to a manicure or a massage!

Music Suggestions

- Gathering: "Festival Canticle/This Is the Feast" John Arthur and Richard Hillert (various publishers)
- Responsorial Psalm: "Walk in the Land" by Joe Mattingly (WLP)
- Preparation of the Gifts: "O Cross of Christ, Immortal Tree" (Stanbrook Abbey Hymnal)
- Sending Forth: "Take Up Your Cross" (multiple tunes by various publishers)

Mass Texts

Introduction to Mass

We believe that Jesus Christ is the Son of God, but does our faith have any impact on how we live in the world, or is it merely a sort of security blanket to make us feel comfortable and safe? Our faith must be accompanied by works of courage, love, and compassion, or it is empty. We must take up our cross and follow in the footsteps of Christ, who is here in our midst to give us his Body and Blood as food for the journey. *My brothers and sisters, let us acknowledge our sins, and so prepare ourselves to celebrate the sacred mysteries.*

Tropes for Penitential Act, Form III

You surrendered yourself into the hands of sinners: Lord, have mercy.

You gave your life that all may have life in abundance: Christ, have mercy.

You call us to give our lives for your sake and the sake of the Gospel: Lord, have mercy.

Dismissal for Children's Liturgy of the Word

My children, today you will hear Jesus ask his disciples who they think he is. He asks you that same question. In order to know someone, we have to spend time with them, talk to them, ask them questions, listen to them, and, as the saying goes, walk a while in their shoes. You can get to know Jesus by praying, listening to the Scriptures, and living as he did: with love for others. We pray that this time together today will help you know Jesus a little more. Go in peace.

Dismissal of Catechumens

My dear friends, we send you forth with our prayers that Christ himself will teach you the true meaning of the Gospel and of life lived in service of one another. We look forward to sharing with you the one Bread and one Cup of eternal life. Go in peace.

Dismissal of Extraordinary Ministers of Holy Communion

My friends, we send you to our brothers and sisters who are carrying the heavy cross of illness or injury. May Christ, whose Body you will share with them, ease their burdens and refresh them with his love. Go in peace.

Universal Prayer

Conscious of the needs of others, we take up our cross and empty ourselves before the Lord so that he might save us.

1. That Christians may sit patiently with those who are negotiating whether to carry the cross, we pray:
2. That laws created by legislators may be just and might not place unnecessary burdens on people, especially the poor, we pray:
3. That doctors and nurses may listen carefully to their patients and not create rushed solutions to their problems, we pray:
4. That those who have shirked the cross may not be afraid to pick it up again, we pray:
5. That those who have died may be counted among the first in God's glory, we pray:

Almighty God,
you love the world with abundant care and mercy.
Your Son mandates that the cross is the way to life with you.
May we pick it up with great hope this day
and never seek shortcuts that would bypass
the transforming lessons of obedient and sacrificial love.
Through Christ our Lord.
Amen.

Other Rites and Customs

- Introduce the practice of the children's Liturgy of the Word to the parish—see LTP's resources *How to Lead Children's Liturgy of the Word* and *Children's Liturgy of the Word.*
- Today is National Grandparents' Day so be sure to include a petition for grandparents in the Universal Prayer. You might also adapt the Order of Blessing of Parents (chapter 1 in the BB) for this need and bless grandparents at the end of today's Masses.

Liturgy and Life

This week's reading from James's letter continues to challenge us to live our faith with integrity so that what is true in our hearts shows through in our actions. What "works" will express our faith? In the Catholic Tradition, the Corporal Works of Mercy include feeding the hungry, sheltering the homeless, clothing the naked, visiting the sick and imprisoned, burying the dead, giving alms to the poor, and caring for creation.

Taking Place This Week . . .

Consider what can be done liturgically, catechetically, and ministerially to respond to these important needs.

- National Grandparents Day (9/12)
- International Day of Democracy (9/15)
- World Ozone Layer Day and Yom Kippur (9/16)
- Constitution Day, Citizenship Day, and National POW/MIA Recognition Day (9/17)
- National CleanUp Day (9/18)

M O N 13 LM #443 or #637 / LMC #193–232 or #369 / white
Memorial of St. John Chrysostom, Bishop and Doctor of the Church

Today's Saint

After a short stint as a monk, St. John Chrysostom (c. 350–407), whose surname means "golden mouth," returned to Antioch, where he was ordained a priest and became a noted preacher. During his free time he wrote commentaries on the Pauline letters as well as the Gospels according to Matthew and John. Due to his reputation for preaching and writing, he was appointed bishop of Constantinople. As bishop, he initiated a program of reform that challenged clerical abuses and the extravagant lifestyle of the upper class. His reforms were not always received well, especially on the part of Empress Eudoxia; therefore, he was exiled from the city for a period of time.

Scripture Insights

None of us are worthy of the Lord entering under our roofs, as the Roman centurion stated about himself. God desires, however, for all of his human creation to be saved. He loves every one of us and desires for each of us to share in his life in heaven.

Preaching Points

Parish Masses

- The Roman centurion knew that Jesus could heal his slave but did not believe he was worthy for Jesus to enter his home. His faith in Jesus was tremendous, and it was praised by Jesus. We are reminded that Jesus came to the world for all people—the Jewish people and the Gentile people.
- God desires for his children to speak to him in prayer. St. Paul encourages us to pray for our leaders for two reasons: so that we may live in peace and so that they may come to know the truth of the faith.

Masses with Children

- The Roman centurion had tremendous faith in Jesus. The words he used, "I am not worthy to have you enter under my roof," are the words we recite at Mass before we receive Communion.
- God wants all of his children to speak to him in prayer. One of the ways St. Paul encourages us to pray is to pray for our leaders. We pray for them because we want peaceful lives for ourselves and others and so that the leaders may come to know the faith of the Church.

Scripture Insights *(PS)*

There are many ways to serve—not everyone is called in the same way. God's Word needs to be proclaimed everywhere, even though not all will receive it.

Preaching Points

Parish Masses

- The sower scatters the seed over the land, knowing that not every seed will grow and yield at harvest time. In the same way, in the work of faith, we need to keep at it patiently, carrying out our work knowing we will not necessarily see the results.
- What kind of words do we speak? Today's saint spoke of God so beautifully and eloquently that he earned the name Chrysostom, "golden-mouthed." Do we watch the way we speak, so that our words build up and give life rather than tear down?

Masses with Children

- When a farmer or a gardener scatters seeds on the ground, he or she knows that not every seed will grow. They also know that they need to be patient and tend to the seeds, pulling weeds and watering the seeds regularly so that they have a chance to grow. In the same way, our faith in God is like a seed. We need to tend to it and watch it grow.
- Tell the children about St. John Chrysostom. Point out that he spoke of God in a beautiful way. Draw the comparison to our life of faith—do we watch what we say or do we tear others down? Make references to how the children treat each other at school; bullying and teasing other children because they are different or not popular enough is not the way of God.

Missal Options

- The readings may be from the SW, #637, CP, or CDC.
- Consider using EP-II and P-I or P-II of Saints, or the Preface of Holy Pastors.
- The presidential prayers are proper and are found in the PS.
- Any Collect from OT may be used to conclude the UP.

Song of the Day

"Keep in Mind" by Lucien Deiss (WLP)

T U E 14 Feast of the Exaltation of the Holy Cross

See page 332.

WED 15

LM #445, Gospel #639 / LMC #371 (G) / white

Memorial of Our Lady of Sorrows

About Today's Memorial

The scene of a mother watching her only son dying is beyond imagination. All the accounts of the Gospel bear witness to Mary, the mother of Jesus, being present at his crucifixion. One can speculate that knowing his mother's presence intensified the suffering of Jesus. He would know that a widow would be vulnerable without a male to look over her. Beyond this practical concern, the Gospel according to John suggests the birth of a new spiritual family under the cross, represented by two exemplary disciples: Mary and the Beloved Disciple.

Scripture Insights

The household of God refers to a place like a parish church; St. Paul desired for Timothy and the others in Ephesus to know and understand the reverence due to a place where believers gathered to share in the Eucharistic celebration.

Preaching Points

Parish Masses

St. Paul wrote the letter to Timothy not knowing if he would be there to instruct in person; he desired for the people to understand the sacredness of Christian worship and Eucharistic sacrifice.

Masses with Children

St. Paul traveled to the different groups of believers in different cities in the region. He wrote letters to the different groups between visits, and those letters have become part of the canon of Scripture. Today's letter was one he wrote to Timothy in Ephesus, which is in Asia Minor/Turkey.

Scripture Insights *(PS)*

When Jesus was hanging on the cross, Mary was standing nearby. She shared in his suffering.

Preaching Points

Parish Masses

- Simeon not only recognized who Jesus was: he recognized Mary as someone who would suffer greatly and even be pierced with a sword. Simeon's prophecy would be fulfilled throughout Mary's life, at moments of intense fear, sadness, and separation, above all, as she stood at the foot of the cross, sharing in her Son's agony. Let us ask for a share in Mary's compassion, so that we also may "feel with" the pain of others.
- "He learned obedience from what he suffered." Has the suffering we have endured made us bitter? Or has it taught us obedience?

Masses with Children

In the first option for the Gospel we hear how Jesus' mother, Mary, was standing at the foot of the cross when he was crucified. He told his disciples to "Behold, your mother." Even though Mary is not our "biological" mother, she is our "spiritual" mother. Mary is often referred to as the Mother of the Church. The Church is made up of all of Jesus' followers. So, Mary is our mother too.

Missal Options

- The Gospel from the PS is proper to the day. There are two options for the Gospel (either John 19:25–27 or Luke 2:33–35).
- The Gospel from the LMC is proper. Other readings may be taken from the CBVM.
- Use any of the three forms of the PA.
- Use any of the OT Collects to conclude the UP.
- The prayer texts are proper and are found in the PS.
- Use P-I or P-II of the BVM.
- You might choose to sing the sequence—*Stabat mater*—after the psalm. It is found in the #639. Musicians might effectively incorporate the Gospel Acclamation to the end of the text.
- Consider EPVN-III.

Song of the Day

"Litany of Mary" by Tony Alonso (GIA)

Other Rites and Customs

Hours: Use the Proper Psalter of the day.

THU 16

LM #446 or #640 / LMC #193–232 or #XX / red

Memorial of Sts. Cornelius, Pope, and Cyprian, Bishop, Martyrs

Today's Saints

Pope Cornelius and Bishop Cyprian disagreed on how to treat Christians who had apostatized under persecution, with Cyprian favoring re-Baptism and the pope declaring that only a period of penance should be required. The two saints are, however, remembered together as martyrs who themselves accepted death rather than renounce their shared faith.

Scripture Insights

All people sin, and all people have need of Jesus' forgiveness. The woman who visited the Pharisee's house felt the weight of Jesus' forgiveness more heavily than others because she had such tremendous need of Jesus and his love. Each of us knows our need for God, and such need is written on each of our hearts.

Preaching Points

Parish Masses

- "Your faith has saved you; go in peace." Jesus' response to the woman who anointed his feet reminds us that each of us are forgiven for our sins too, when we approach the Lord in the Eucharist and the Sacrament of Reconciliation with repentant hearts.
- The early Church was growing and was being shepherded by its bishops and presbyters. In today's 1 Timothy reading we hear that Timothy should have confidence in priesthood.

Masses with Children

- "Your faith has saved you; go in peace." Jesus said these words to the woman who anointed his feet with ointment. We remember that when we approach Jesus in repentance, he forgives our sins too.
- Since the earliest days of the Church, we see that "presbyters" (priests) served the local congregations of believers. They helped the people learn about God and how Jesus fulfilled the Scriptures.

Scripture Insights *(PS)*

Jesus does not promise his disciples an easy life. But their sufferings, united with Christ's, will bear fruit in the Church.

Preaching Points

Parish Masses

- St. Paul is able to endure great suffering with tranquility because he knows that his suffering, united with Christ's, has value and meaning. When we are perplexed, persecuted, or struck down, we have something to offer to God on behalf of the Church.
- In his prayer to the Father, Jesus asks God not to take his followers out of the world but to protect them from evil. The world, with all its challenges, is where Christ's followers need to be. We are to be a leaven of the Gospel in our complicated world.

Masses with Children

It is not easy to follow Jesus. But if we persevere in faith, he will always stand by us and help us to do everything for his glory.

Missal Options

- The readings may also be taken from the CM or CP.
- Use any of the three forms of the PA.
- Use any of the OT Collects to conclude the UP.
- Although a full set of prayers is provided in the PS, you may also use those from the CM (For Several Martyrs) or CP (For a Bishop).
- Select from P-I or P-II of Saints, P-I or P-II of Holy Martyrs, or the Preface of Holy Pastors.
- Consider EP-I.

Song of the Day

"Great Is Thy Faithfulness" by William M. Runyan (Hope Publishing Company)

FRI **17** LM #447 / LMC #193–232 / green
Weekday

Optional Memorial of St. Robert Bellarmine, Bishop and Doctor of the Church / white

Scripture Insights

Useless argument and accusation do not make for a peaceful community or a peaceful home. Instead we strive for the contentment that our faith can give to us. Rather than strife and unpleasantness, we may exist in peace and harmony.

Preaching Points

Parish Masses

- Striving for wealth alone with singular desire is not a Christian's call. Our love must be pointed to Christ and his Church and living out our Christian lives. Like many things in life, an item, money in this case, is not the evil; the misplaced affection is outside of the order Jesus has given us. When we love money instead of people, our priorities are out of order.
- Some of Jesus' followers were women, and some of those women used their own money to fund Jesus' needs during his ministry. Later, in the early Church, widows also offered their money for others in the same way.

Masses with Children

- Money is used in most societies. The paper and metal elements of money are not evil, but when people love money more than they love other people, their priorities are outside the order Jesus has given us.
- Several women followed Jesus during his ministry, and many of them helped him by funding his needs during that time.

Missal Options

- Consider using the prayers from the MPVN-41.
- Use any of the three forms of the PA.
- Any of the eight Prefaces for OT or the six Common Prefaces may be used.
- You might use EP-II.
- Any OT Collect may be used or adapted to conclude the UP. You might even look at the Collects in the Masses for Various Needs and Occasions for possible concluding prayers.

Song of the Day

"For All the Faithful Women" by Herman G. Stuempfle, Jr. (GIA)

Optional Memorial

St. Robert Bellarmine was a Jesuit scholar and rigorous academic theologian who defended and clarified Church teaching during the Reformation as an adviser to two popes, and he was a prolific writer. Bellarmine's many gifts lifted him to reluctant prominence without making him prideful, and he continued to serve others through both his own works of charity and his generous sponsorship of other reformers.

- The readings may be taken from the SW, #641, CP, CDC, or LMC #373.
- Use the Collect from the PS; the other prayers may be taken from the CP (For a Bishop) or CDC.
- Select from P-I or P-II of Saints, or the Preface of Holy Pastors.
- Consider EP-II.

SAT 18 Weekday

LM #448 / LMC #193–232 / green

Optional Memorial of the Blessed Virgin Mary / white

Scripture Insights

Timothy, a presbyter, was called to keep the commandment until Jesus returned again to earth. At the time, the faithful believed that Jesus would return soon. We too, thousands of years later, can remember the importance of keeping Jesus' command until he comes again.

Preaching Points

Parish Masses

- We are called to keep Jesus' commands; in the Gospel reading we hear about seed falling on different types of ground. We must choose to be the fertile earth on which the seeds of Jesus' Word falls.
- How do we keep away the weeds and the thorns that threaten to choke out the desired harvest?

Masses with Children

- What kind of ground do you want to be for Jesus' Word? We are called to be the fertile earth so that God's Word can grow in us.
- What does a person's life look like when they have made themselves fertile ground for God's Word? How do they maintain such ground, and keep away the thorns and weeds?

Missal Options

- Consider using the prayers from the MPVN-18/A; use the second option for the Collect.
- Use any of the three forms of the PA.
- Any of the eight Prefaces for OT or the six Common Prefaces may be used.
- You might use EP-III.
- Any OT Collect may be used or adapted to conclude the UP. You might even look at the Collects in the Masses for Various Needs and Occasions for possible concluding prayers.

Song of the Day

"I Will Be the Vine" by Liam Lawton (GIA)

Optional Memorial

- The readings may be taken from the SW, CBVM, or CMML.
- The prayer texts may be taken from the CBVM or CMMM. Any votive Mass for the BVM may be used.
- Use any of the three forms of the PA.
- Select from P-I or P-II of the BVM.
- Any of the OT Collects may conclude the UP.

TUE 14 LM #638 / LMC #370 / red

Feast of the Exaltation of the Holy Cross

About Today's Feast

This feast commemorates the finding of the Cross of Jesus by St. Helena, mother of the first Christian emperor, Constantine. The cross is no longer a sign of torture but of triumph. It leads our processions and stands near the altar of Christ's sacrifice. A symbol of death overcame death because of the perfect obedience of Jesus, who freely accepted it. Jesus reigns from the cross. We should reflect frequently on what the cross represents, as expressed in today's reading from Philippians.

Scripture Insights

Consider the contrasts in Philippians and in John: between Jesus relinquishing himself and God exalting him, and between Jesus lifted up like the serpent and Jesus saving the world. These juxtapositions are as challenging as they are compelling. What savior would take the form of a slave? What power can there be in crucifixion and death? How can we believe that someone who dies brings eternal life?

Moses lifted up the serpent in the desert so that the people might look at what was killing them. In their prayer to God, they opened themselves to God's grace and so recovered. When they looked at the serpent, they lived. In John's account of the Gospel, Jesus is lifted up like the serpent. John's clear reference to the Numbers passage and his repetition (three times) of the "lifting up" of the Son of Man (see 8:28 and 12:32–34) are indicative of the way he contrasts the old and new covenants. Jesus, like the serpent, is a figure of horror. When the witnesses to the crucifixion gather below the cross, they confront the reasons for death—greed, hatred, envy, and fear. But, in the self-giving of Jesus on the cross, they receive more than human life. They receive the gift of God's never-ending love and grace, which makes life eternal. The Church lives forever in the presence of God.

John is the only evangelist to discuss why God sends Jesus to the world. Matthew, Mark, and Luke tie Jesus to the fulfillment of the prophecies of old, but John speaks about the love of God for the world. Moses told Israel that God chose them, not because they were the greatest nation in the world, but because God loved them (Deuteronomy 7:8). John places Jesus' birth into the world in that same context of love from God. Jesus is the center of God's new relationship with human beings. He was never meant to condemn the world, but to save it, and so, as the hymn from Philippians tells us, Jesus' self-sacrificing love was not a sign of weakness and slavery but a sign of his lordship over heaven and earth.

Preaching Points

Parish Masses

- God made the tremendous "self-gift" of Jesus to the world. It is in him that we clearly see the greatness of God's love for every person among his vast creation. God's love and grace have no end, and, through Christ, we are the recipients of that love and grace.
- Being God's people doesn't mean our lives are free from unpleasantness or distress, but we can know that God is with us in our distress.
- Jesus did not ever abuse the power he has as God; indeed, he never brandished his power as a weapon. Instead, Jesus was humble and taught his followers to grow in humility.
- God loves his human creation so much that he sent the Son to us. God the Son came to earth to save humanity, willingly living and dying for us.
- As Jesus' disciples, our baptismal call is to take on the mind and heart of Christ. We model ourselves on the total self-giving love of Christ, loving ourselves and others the way God loves us. We willingly love all so that others may live and experience the love with which we are loved.

Children's Liturgy of the Word

- God loves us very much, but this doesn't mean our lives are easy or free from suffering. Jesus is with us in our suffering.
- Our Lord is powerful and mighty, yet he never used his power as a weapon. Jesus was humble and taught his followers to be humble too.
- Parents love their children with all their hearts. God loves his son and his human creation. God the Son came to earth to save humanity, and God loves us so much that he sent his son to us.

Missal Options

- Use any of the three forms of the PA.
- Use any of the OT Collects to conclude the UP.
- The prayer texts, including the Preface, are proper and are found in the PS.
- The Gloria is sung or said; the Creed is not sung or said.
- Presiders should note that the Entrance Antiphon is the same as the one used on Holy Thursday. This might be a source text for today's homily.
- P-I of the Passion of the Lord is used.
- Consider EPR-II.

Music Preparation

Those preparing music for the liturgy should know that the use of the Gloria is prescribed and the psalm and Gospel versicles can be found in most psalm collections. A little choral gem is "*O Crux benedicta*" by Claudio Monteverdi (arranged by Bruce Smedley; GIA).

Music Suggestions

- Gathering: "Lift High the Cross" (various publishers)
- Responsorial Psalm: "Psalm 78: Do Not Forget" by Robert Batastini (GIA)
- Communion: "*Crux Fidelis*" by Steven Warner (WLP)
- Sending Forth: "Take Up Your Cross" by Jaime Cortez (OCP)

Mass Texts

Introduction to Mass

The Cross of our Lord Jesus Christ stands as, in a sense, the pole of the world, or the focal point, certainly of our lives as Christians. To it we come and through it we have access to the Lord's Resurrection and our own. This is a deep mystery and cause for rejoicing, that by means of something so horrible we receive so great a treasure: the Risen Lord who even now offers us his Body and Blood. *My brothers and sisters, let us acknowledge our sins, and so prepare ourselves to celebrate the sacred mysteries.*

Tropes for Penitential Act, Form III

It was our sins that led you to suffer and die on the cross: Lord, have mercy.

You did not deem equality with God something to be grasped: Christ, have mercy.

Yet God exalted you far above the heavens: Lord, have mercy.

Dismissal of Catechumens

My friends, it was God's love for the world that drove Jesus to the cross, where he stretched out his arms to embrace everyone who comes to him. You yourselves have come near. Stand fast in patience and hope, and reflect well on Christ's promises, that your faith may continue to grow until that day when you receive his life poured out in the Eucharist. Go now in peace.

Dismissal of Extraordinary Ministers of Holy Communion

Dear ministers of the Lord, we give you the Body of Christ, sacrificed and risen from the dead, to take to our infirm brothers and sisters. Encourage them to unite their sufferings to his and to find consolation in his cross. Go in peace.

Universal Prayer

My sisters and brothers, we adore the Lord because by his holy cross he has redeemed the world. In obedience to him let us offer our prayers for the needs of the world.

1. Through the Lord's holy cross, may all Christians be led into the mystery of redemptive suffering, we pray:
2. Through the Lord's holy cross, may the hearts of political leaders be softened and no longer tempted to persecute and oppress, we pray:
3. Through the Lord's holy cross, may courage and hope be granted to those who suffer great pain in their bodies, we pray:
4. Through the Lord's holy cross, may the weak be strengthened, the downtrodden be raised, and the dying be comforted, we pray:
5. Through the Lord's holy cross, may those who have died be given admittance to the joy of God's Kingdom, we pray:

Beloved Savior,
you chose to reign from a cross
instead of to sit on a throne.
Grant us the grace, we pray,
to carry our cross patiently,
without fear or dread.
You live and reign with God the Father in the unity of the Holy Spirit,
one God, for ever and ever.
Amen.

Other Rites and Customs

- Celebrate Taizé Prayer Around the Cross.
- Bless new altar servers using the Order for the Blessing of Altar Servers, Sacristans, Musicians and Ushers found in the *Book of Blessings*, chapter 62.

Liturgy and Life

Reflect on this text from *Gaudium et spes* (37): "Christians reply that all these human activities, which are daily endangered by pride and inordinate self love, must be purified and protected by the cross and resurrection of Christ. Redeemed by Christ and made a new creature by the holy Spirit, a person can, and indeed must love the things which God has created: it is from God that they have been received, and it is as coming from God's hand that they are seen and revered."

S U N **19** LM #134B / LMC #129B / green

Twenty-Fifth Sunday in Ordinary Time

Scripture Insights

Among biblical texts, the Letter of James is one of the most direct in its description of the causes of war and injustice. James does not blame the devil, unjust authority, or outside forces. "Where do the wars and where do the conflicts among you come from? Is it not from your passions that make war within your members?" (4:1). Envy, greed, and ambition are at the heart of much of the world's trouble. According to James, these are precisely the emotions that bind someone to the world rather than to God (see 4:4). Writing to Christians in the first century, James focuses on Christian conduct—utter devotion to the things of God.

James' identification of the sin in our lives provides a lens through which we might view all three readings. His manner of teaching resembles wisdom literature, from which the first reading comes. The picture of the wicked sketched in the verses we read today is fleshed out in the entire second chapter of Wisdom. There we are shown wild desire for the things of this world. When godless people realize that someone who is righteous indicts their ambition and greed, they want to torture the righteous one because he opposes them. They want free rein to do whatever they wish. The last verse of the chapter speaks directly to James' concern. "But by the envy of the devil, death entered the world, and they who are in his possession experience it" (Wisdom 2:24).

In Mark's account of the Gospel, the disciples argue about who is the greatest among them. This dispute, set between a prophecy about the crucifixion and a teaching about the presence of Christ in the most unimportant of people, underscores the disciples' ignorance of Jesus' mission. Envy demands a better position, greed desires wealth, and ambition seeks power. Jesus' life, death, and teaching contradict all three. The Apostles show they are still tied to the values of the world. To be true disciples of Christ, they must set aside envy and ambition and open themselves to the fruits of wisdom and the Spirit.

Preaching Points

Parish Masses

- The consequences of sin affect the daily lives of all people. We are called to live lives that are holy and abundant with the grace and peace that Jesus provides when we strive to serve one another. To serve one another we must have humility.
- We recognize God's grace and wisdom by the fruits produced; peace, gentleness, and mercy are abundant.
- That which is good and right may not always be convenient and easy to manage. Moral rightness doesn't change based on convenience. We cannot claim convenience as a mitigating factor in determining rightness or wrongness of an action.
- Jesus taught his disciples that they should be servants of one another rather than seeking recognition and power over one another.

Children's Liturgy of the Word

- Some of the most important deeds we accomplish may not be simple, easy, or convenient, but we must still choose what is right and good.
- We recognize God's grace and wisdom by the fruits produced; peace, gentleness, and mercy are abundant.
- Jesus' disciples argued about which of them was the greatest, but Jesus taught them they ought to work toward serving one another rather than striving toward ruling over one another.

Missal Options

- Offer any of the three forms of the PA.
- Sing or recite the Gloria and the Creed.
- Any of the seasonal OT Collects may be used or adapted to conclude the UP.
- Select from any of the eight Prefaces of OT.
- Consider EPR-I.
- There are six SBs for OT from which to choose.

Music Preparation

What are the important parts of the Mass to sing? Sing to the Lord is quite clear in this regard: "singing by the gathered assembly and ministers is important at all celebrations. Not every part that can be sung should necessarily be sung at every celebration; rather preference should be given to those parts that are of greater importance" (115). Dialogues and acclamations—"especially to those to be sung by the priest or the deacon or the lector, with the people responding, or by the priest and people together"—rank as the most important. Antiphons and psalms rank second, refrains and repeated responses are third, and hymns are fourth.

Music Suggestions

- Gathering Song: "Christ in Me Arise" by Trevor Thompson (OCP)
- Preparation of the Gifts: "O God Beyond All Praising" (various publishers)
- Communion: "From the Many, Make Us One" by Gabe Huck and Tony Alonso (GIA)

Mass Texts

Introduction to Mass

Fellow children of God, we are sometimes tempted to jealousy of the good we see in others, and we may harbor resentments or outright hatred toward them. But the gifts God has given some are for the good of all, and we are all one in his Spirit. Let us therefore rejoice in one another and in the generosity of Christ who gives himself to us in the Eucharist, that we may have peace. *My brothers and sisters, let us acknowledge our sins, and so prepare ourselves to celebrate the sacred mysteries.*

Tropes for Penitential Act, Form III

We are full of deceit, but you come to us with the innocence of a child: Lord, have mercy.

In receiving you, we receive the One who sent you: Christ, have mercy.

You have made yourself the servant of all: Lord, have mercy.

Dismissal for Children's Liturgy of the Word

Dear children, you are the future of the Church and from you we learn so much about what it means to be children of God. As you go to listen to Jesus, know how dear you are to him and that he dwells in your hearts, shining out as an example for all of us. Go now in his love.

Dismissal of Catechumens

Dear friends, greatness in Christ is not defined by worldly standards. Rather, the first shall be last and the servants of all. As you seek him, seek also the welfare of all your brothers and sisters, that you may truly be children of God and stand with us at the table of his Son who is in our midst as one who serves. Go in peace.

Dismissal of Extraordinary Ministers of Holy Communion

My friends, our sisters and brothers who are confined by physical weakness rely on your ministry to bring them Christ's Body. Through him, may God bless them with peace and may he bless you for your generosity. Go in God's love.

Universal Prayer

My sisters and brothers, in today's Gospel the Lord said that those who wish to be first must be servants of all. With humble service, we pray for the needs of the Church and for the world.

1. That the leaders of the Church may see themselves as servants, we pray:
2. That government leaders may serve their people without hoarding power, we pray:
3. That heads of households may count themselves among the last, we pray:
4. That we may all work together within our communities to promote harmony, we pray:
5. That all who are homeless may find a place to call their own, we pray:
6. That all who have died may be raised to new life in Christ, we pray:

Lord Jesus,
you foretold your passion and death
as you journeyed with your disciples along the way.
In the house, you reveal that true discipleship
is found in the desire to become the servant of all.
May we, the household of the Church,
be willing to shed our lives
for your sake and the sake of the Gospel,
so as to serve without counting the cost.
You live and reign for ever and ever.
Amen.

Other Rites and Customs

- In commemoration of Catechetical Sunday, offer a blessing of catechists during Mass, using the Order for the Blessing of Those Appointed as Catechists found in chapter 4 of the *Book of Blessings*.
- Be sure your parish's copyright licenses for music are up to date and accurate reporting of usage has been done. Resist the urge to photocopy music, for it is illegal and unethical.

Liturgy and Life

Jesus says that those who receive a child receive him. Today, the scourge of human trafficking continues to make the lives of some children a hellish slavery. They are laborers and often sex objects. Read paragraph 4 of Pope Francis' statement for World Day of Peace, 2015, "No Longer Slaves, but Brothers and Sisters." The United States Conference of Catholic Bishops operates an anti-trafficking program that includes the Amistad Movement, named after the Amistad slave ship, site of an 1839 revolt that eventually resulted in freedom for the Africans who had been seized. The movement offers awareness programs and training to immigrants to help them avoid becoming trafficking victims. To schedule training in your area, go to www.usccb.org/about/anti-trafficking-program/amistad.cfm.

Taking Place This Week . . .

Consider what can be done liturgically, catechetically, and ministerially to respond to these important needs.

- The first day of Sukkot is 9/21.
- International Day of Peace (9/21)
- September/Autumnal Equinox (9/22)
- World Maritime Day (9/23)

MON **20** LM #449 or #642A / LMC #193–232 or #375 / red

Memorial of Sts. Andrew Kim Tae-gŏn, Priest, Paul Chŏng Ha-sang, and Companions, Martyrs

Today's Saints

From age to age, various means helped to plant the Gospel. Interestingly, Christianity did not reach Korea through foreign missionaries. Rather, a Korean diplomat in China returned to Korea with books written by the Italian Jesuit missionary to China, Matteo Ricci. The seed was planted in this way among the laity. Later, St. Andrew Kim became the first Korean priest. He and countless others were executed for the faith, confirming Tertullian's adage that "the blood of the martyrs is the seed of the Church."

Scripture Insights

God's people are called to bring his Word to the world. Meant to be a bright light shining in the world for all to see, God's people should put themselves on lampstands and not hide their grace-filled lives.

Preaching Points

Parish Masses

- In the Book of Ezra, we enter the post-exile time period for God's people. We begin hearing about Cyrus and the rebuilding of Jerusalem; the temple had already been rebuilt at this time.
- We are a light for others when they can see how Jesus has transformed us in this life. What does a transformed life look like? How is Jesus transforming you, and how have you already been transformed?

Masses with Children

- The weekday readings have switched back to the Old Testament for the First Readings. In this particular reading, we go back to the time of King Cyrus, who allowed the Jewish people to return to Jerusalem after the Babylonian exile.
- We are a light for others when they can see how Jesus has transformed us in this life. What does a transformed life look like? How is Jesus transforming you? Do you admire anyone whose life you have seen transformed, either a saint or someone you know? Do they hide that transformation or let others see it?

Scripture Insights *(PS)*

We must lose our lives—spend them on behalf of others—in order to gain lasting life. Nothing can separate us from God's love; therefore, we have nothing to fear.

Preaching Points

Parish Masses

- What are we afraid of? St. Paul urges us to fear nothing in the cosmos, because nothing can separate us from God, and separation from God is the only thing we need to fear. What risks might we take if we really believed we had nothing to be afraid of?
- We cannot save ourselves: only God can save us. The more we lose on behalf of Christ, the more we gain. What do we stand to lose? Only our time, our possessions, our ego. What do we gain? Eternity.

Masses with Children

- We have nothing to fear in this world because nothing separates us from the love of God. To be separated from God is the only thing we should fear, which is why we should live a life rooted in love.

Missal Options

- The readings may be from the SW, #642A, CM, or CP.
- Consider EP-II and P-I or P-II of Saints, or the Preface of Holy Martyrs or Holy Pastors.
- The prayers are proper and found in the PS.
- Use any OT Collect to conclude the UP.

Song of the Day

"Christ, Be Our Light" by Bernadette Farrell (OCP)

TUE **21** LM #643 / LMC, CA, #376 (G)/ red

Feast of St. Matthew, Apostle and Evangelist

Today's Saint

St. Matthew was a tax collector when Christ called him to leave his former ways to follow him. The Gospel accounts tell us that Matthew invited Jesus to his home to dine with tax collectors and prostitutes, bringing Christ to others who on the margins of society.

Scripture Insights

Each of us are called into different roles, according to our talents and gifts. Whatever our roles are in the community, each of us are called to lives of goodness and mercy. No matter what our roles may be, we must be humble and willing to sacrifice for others.

Preaching Points

Parish Masses

- Matthew was a tax collector, and the people questioned Jesus for eating with a man of such a despised profession. Jesus was concerned, not with others' opinions, but instead with Matthew himself.

- In our lives we minister to others in many ways. In each of these varied roles we are called to build the Body of Christ in our community.

Masses with Children

- Later in life you may realize a call to a religious vocation, to the single life, or to marriage. These vocations are a response to God's call to love others and to help them go to heaven someday. People in all vocations are called to treat others as Jesus taught us to treat them.
- In Jesus' time, tax collectors were despised. Jesus didn't mind people's criticism of his choice to spend time with the shunned people in the community. We too must care more about what God wants of us than what people demand of us.

Missal Options

- The Gospel from the LMC is proper. The other readings are from the CA.
- Since today is a feast of an Apostle, consider doing the sprinkling rite.
- Use any of the OT Collects to conclude the UP.
- The prayer texts are proper and are found in the PS.
- The Gloria is sung or said; the Creed is not sung or said.
- Use P-I or P-II of the Apostles.
- The SB for Apostles may conclude the Mass (#17).
- Consider EP-I.

Song of the Day

"Lord, You Give the Great Commission" (Hope Publishing Company)

Other Rites and Customs

Hours: Use the Proper Psalter of the day.

WED 22

LM #451 / LMC #193–232 / green

Weekday

Scripture Insights

God loves his people and is always with them. In the Old Testament reading we hear about God caring for Israel despite exile and sin. Jesus sends out his disciples, and his authority is with them as they preach and cure the sick.

Preaching Points

Parish Masses

- All of God's people (except Jesus and Mary) live with sin. In the Ezra reading we hear about the writer being overwhelmed by sinful conviction, and we hear about God being faithful to his people despite that sin.
- The Apostles begin their ministry, which will someday continue Jesus' ministry after Jesus' ascension. Taking nothing with them would necessitate their confidence and trust in God.

Masses with Children

- God has mercy for his children; despite our shortcomings and sin, God loves us and has mercy for us.
- When the Apostles took nothing with them when they began their ministry, they had to learn to depend on God to help them meet their daily needs.

Missal Options

- Consider using the prayers from the MPNV-1/B.
- Use any of the three forms of the PA.
- Any of the eight Prefaces for OT or the six Common Prefaces may be used.
- You might use EP-RI.
- Any OT Collect may be used or adapted to conclude the UP. You might even look at the Collects in the Masses for Various Needs and Occasions for possible concluding prayers.

Song of the Day

"Journey of Faith" by Delores Dufner, OSB (WLP)

THU 23

LM #452 or #643A (LS) / LMC #193–232 / white

Memorial of St. Pius of Pietrelcina, Priest

Today's Saint

Padre Pio was a popular modern saint who bore the stigmata, visible replicas of the wounds of Christ on his body, which caused him much embarrassment and suffering throughout his life. Nonetheless, the saint spent hours every day hearing confessions for the many thousands who flocked to him to receive counsel and God's mercy.

Scripture Insights

Where do the peoples' values lie? Who or what is their priority? In the Book of Haggai the prophet warns the people that God and his house ought to be given priority in the social order.

Preaching Points

Parish Masses

- In Jerusalem the people began having beautiful homes that showed off the owners' wealth. The prophets warned that it is not reasonable for the temple to become run down while the people make their own homes rich with beauty.

- The first commandment is not to put any other gods before God. In our own lives, what do we put before God? How can we put him first?

Masses with Children

- In Jerusalem the wealthy people spent their money decorating their homes to show off their wealth instead of giving some of that money to the upkeep of the temple. The prophet warned the people that they should not let the temple, God's house, deteriorate.
- The first commandment is not to put any other gods before God. In our own lives, what do we put before God? How can we put him first?

Scripture Insights (PS)

The disciples of Jesus must follow Jesus—carrying his cross, even bearing his wounds.

Preaching Points

Parish Masses

- Did St. Paul have the stigmata? That is one way to read the First Reading today. This rare gift is a visible sign of something that is true for all Christians: we are sharers in the mystery of Christ, and the more fully we live our faith, the more conformed to Christ we will be. His life is not something quite separate from us. His life lives in us and is the model for our own lives.
- We who follow Jesus must also carry the cross, not once, Jesus says, but "daily." What are the daily crosses that you carry? A troubled relationship? A difficult job? A child you worry about? Financial uncertainty? Self-doubt? The crosses we carry are part of being a Christian. Today, let us ask Jesus to carry them with us.

Masses with Children

- Think about the troubles that children have—homework, getting in trouble at home, other children who might be picking on them. These troubles are our crosses in life. But Jesus helps us carry them. Encourage the children to bring their troubles to Jesus.

Missal Options

- The readings may also be taken from #643A (LS), the CP, or the CHMW/CS (For Religious)
- The Collect is from the PS; the other prayers may be from the CP (For One Pastor) or CHMW (For Religious).
- Use any of the three forms of the PA.
- Use any of the OT Collects to conclude the UP.
- Consider EP-III.

Song of the Day

"At the Table of the Lord" by Brian Wren and Carl Johengen (Hope Publishing Company/WLP)

FRI 24

LM #453 / LMC #193–232 / green

Weekday

Scripture Insights

In the Old Testament reading we are reminded that God was with his people, and that he upheld the covenant from the time of the exodus. In the New Testament reading we see fulfillment of God's promises made in the Old Testament; an anointed one would be sent, and we see that anointed one clearly in the person Jesus.

Preaching Points

Parish Masses

- God brings love and peace to his people. Through God the people know who they are; their identity as chosen people is in him.
- Jesus predicts his death and Resurrection; he predicts his terrible suffering.

Masses with Children

- God brings love and peace to his people. By being reminded of the exodus and Moses' covenant with God, the people are reminded of their identity as God's chosen people.
- Jesus predicts his death and Resurrection; he predicts his terrible suffering. Later, the disciples will remember his words when they wonder where his body has gone.

Missal Options

- Consider using the prayers from the MPVN-2.
- Use any of the three forms of the PA.
- Any of the eight Prefaces for OT or the six Common Prefaces may be used.
- You might use EPR-I.
- Any OT Collect may be used or adapted to conclude the UP. You might even look at the Collects in the Masses for Various Needs and Occasions for possible concluding prayers.

Song of the Day

"For You I Long" by Paul Nienaber, SJ, and J. Michael Joncas (WLP)

SAT 25 LM #454 / LMC #193–232 / green
Weekday

Optional Memorial of the Blessed Virgin Mary / white

Scripture Insights

God was in the holy of holies in the Temple, and before that time he was seen as the pillar of fire or cloud in the desert. God dwelt among his people in that sense. But he also dwells with us in the person of Jesus.

Preaching Points

Parish Masses

- In the antiphon for the psalm we hear that God "guards us as a shepherd guards his flock." This psalm reminds us that Jesus, the Good Shepherd, would someday come to his people on earth and guide them, having become one of them.
- The Good Shepherd would not have a life of peace, nor would kindness be shown to him by the leaders of his time. The disciples didn't understand when Jesus told them he would suffer.

Masses with Children

- In the biblical time, shepherds guarded their flocks carefully; the sheep were everything the shepherd families needed to survive. God guides us carefully and with love.
- Jesus told the disciples that he would suffer, but they didn't understand what he was saying.

Missal Options

- Consider using the prayers from the MPVN-43.
- Use any of the three forms of the PA.
- Any of the eight Prefaces for OT or the six Common Prefaces may be used.
- You might use EP-II.
- Any OT Collect may be used or adapted to conclude the UP. You might even look at the Collects in the Masses for Various Needs and Occasions for possible concluding prayers.

Song of the Day

"Receive in Your Heart" by Elinor J. DiFalco (WLP)

Optional Memorial

- The readings may be taken from the SW, CBVM, or CMML.
- The prayer texts may be taken from the CBVM or CMMM. Any votive Mass for the BVM may be used.
- Use any of the three forms of the PA.
- Select from P-I or P-II of the BVM.
- Any of the OT Collects may conclude the UP.

Something to Consider…

◈ "The food of truth demands that we denounce inhumane situations in which people starve to death because of injustice and exploitation, and it gives us renewed strength and courage to work tirelessly in the service of the civilization of love" (*Sacramentum caritatis*, 90).

S U N **26** LM #137B / LMC #132B / green
Twenty-Sixth Sunday in Ordinary Time

Scripture Insights

In his letter, James defines the actions of a believer and also defines the actions that lead one away from God. For James, wealth ties people to the world's values. He is particularly critical of the rich whose wealth was acquired through fraud and injustice. Verse 5:4 reminds us of two places in the Pentateuch: "The wages you withheld from the workers who harvested your fields are crying aloud" is an echo of Abel's blood that cries out from the earth in Genesis 4:10 after Cain murders him. The cries of the harvesters reach the ears of the Lord of Hosts just as the cries of the widows and orphans do in Exodus 22:22. Those who are oppressed and marginalized have the attention of God. James makes it clear that wealth gained through the suffering of the innocent condemns those who have it. They will weep in misery.

While James urges his readers to humility, gentleness, mercy, and righteousness (see last week's reading), Jesus warns his followers not to be a stumbling block to the "little ones" who believe in Jesus. He is warning listeners that their own actions are an example, good or bad. His second teaching echoes the language of the first: Remove whatever causes you to stumble. Hands, feet, and eyes are often the instruments of sin. Jesus' graphic illustration reminds the disciples that they must be ready to let go of everything, including their pride, in order to enter the Kingdom of God.

The hell that Jesus names in Mark's account of the Gospel is not the Hebrew *Sheol* but a place outside Jerusalem believed to have been a site of child sacrifice to pagan gods in its earlier history, later converted to a dump in which fire burned continuously. In the original text, it is called Gehenna. Later it became the model for the Christian concept of hell as a place of fire. Isaiah's description of the bodies of those who rebelled against God also influenced this text: "Their worm shall not die, nor their fire be extinguished . . ." (Isaiah 66:24). Discipleship leads to life; any other path means death.

Preaching Points

Parish Masses

- Since the dawn of civilization, some people have been mistreated by those who have power over them. As Catholics, we are called to stand for what is right and good, always resisting oppression of those who have less power.
- In the Old Testament, we hear about those who prophesied, and we hear about how God communicated with his people, Israel.
- Work is a foundational aspect of human existence. Fair wages, fair work, and care of workers has a prominent place in Catholic Social Teaching and has roots in Scripture, such as today's reading.

Children's Liturgy of the Word

- During the years of desert wandering, God was present in a pillar of smoke or of fire. He communicated with his people, Israel.
- All people have value in our society. The majority of people work in our society; work has value, and workers should be treated well.

Missal Options

- Offer any of the three forms of the PA.
- Sing or recite the Gloria and the Creed.
- Any of the seasonal OT Collects may be used or adapted to conclude the UP.
- Select from any of the eight Prefaces of OT.
- Consider EP-III.
- There are six SBs for OT from which to choose.

Music Preparation

As important as music is, silent reflection is also important. "Music arises out of silence and returns to silence. God is revealed both in the beauty of song and in the power of silence. The Sacred Liturgy has its rhythm of texts, actions, songs and silence. Silence in the Liturgy allows the community to reflect on what it has heard and experienced, and to open its heart to the mystery celebrated. Ministers and pastoral musicians should take care that the rites unfold with the proper ebb and flow of sound and silence. The importance of silence in the Liturgy cannot be overemphasized" (STL, 118).

Music Suggestions

- Gathering: "What Is This Place" by Huub Oosterhouse (OCP)
- Preparation of the Gifts: "Here I Am, Lord" by Daniel J. Schutte (OCP)
- Communion: "Life-Giving Bread, Saving Cup" by James J. Chepponis (GIA)
- Sending Forth: "The Church of Christ Cannot Be Bound" by Adam M. Tice (GIA)

Mass Texts

Introduction to Mass

Today we are presented with a mystery: that sometimes those who are not members of Christ's Church can further God's will in the world; that some of those who are outside the fold may, in some way, recognize the voice of the Good Shepherd. Let us not begrudge them the good that they do but instead give thanks to God and examine ourselves all the more to make certain that we are truly pleasing to God. *My brothers and sisters, let us acknowledge our sins, and so prepare ourselves to celebrate the sacred mysteries.*

Tropes for Penitential Act, Form III

We have sinned against you and not been faithful to your commandments: Lord, have mercy.

You deal with us not according to our sins, but according to your merciful love: Christ, have mercy.

You came not to condemn but to reconcile all people to the Father: Lord, have mercy.

Dismissal for Children's Liturgy of the Word

My dear children, we give you this time together to listen to God's Word and sing his praises. Place all your trust in him and do not be afraid to share with Jesus everything that is in your hearts. When you return to us you will increase our joy and help us to give glory to God for all his blessings. Go in peace.

Dismissal of Catechumens

Friends, today's Gospel reminds us of the importance of removing all obstacles to receiving Christ with joy. As you continue your journey of formation, we pray that your hearts will open ever more to him until they overflow with the graces he will give you in the Sacrament of his Body and Blood. Go now in peace.

Dismissal of Extraordinary Ministers of Holy Communion

Dear friends, speak God's Word to our sick and homebound brothers and sisters and share with them the Eucharist, that Christ may enlighten their hearts and may fill them with the Holy Spirit, who is our source of unity and joy. Go in peace.

Universal Prayer

My sisters and brothers, by Baptism we belong to Christ. May we always be conscious of the needs of others and may others always recognize Christ within us. Let us turn to him now in prayer.

1. For the Church as she makes the desire to "belong to Christ" an attractive option for those outside the Church, we pray:
2. For all peacemakers, including those who do not follow Christ, that they may unite hearts together in love, we pray:
3. For a willingness on the part of all religions to work together for the prosperity of our planet, we pray:
4. For those who do not believe in God, that all atheists may embody love and concern for others, we pray:
5. For those who have died, especially for Christians who died outside the Church, that they may be washed clean by God's loving mercy, we pray:

Lord Jesus,
you are leading all men and women to yourself,
though often by different paths.
Inspire us to recognize the good works of all people,
to encourage them, to be influenced by them,
and always to praise you.
You live and reign for ever and ever.
Amen.

Other Rites and Customs

Considering the upcoming Feast of the Archangels (September 29) and the Memorial of Holy Guardian Angels (October 2) provide the parish catechesis about the Catholic theology of angels.

Liturgy and Life

Today the Letter of James challenges our tendency toward accumulating wealth and our dependence on material items. Materialism is not just a personal sin; it is a social sin with enormous consequences in first-world cultures. Pope Paul VI called us to live simply so that others might simply live. We can do this!

Taking Place This Week . . .

Consider what can be done liturgically, catechetically, and ministerially to respond to these important needs.

- Today is the World Day of Migrants and Refugees and Priesthood Sunday.
- World Day to Eliminate Nuclear Weapons (9/26)
- Last Day of Sukkot/Hoshana Rahhab (9/27)
- World Tourism Day (9/27)
- Shmini Atzeret (9/28)
- World Rabies Day (9/28)
- Simchat Torah (9/29)
- World Heart Day (9/29)
- International Day of Older Persons and World Vegetarian Day (10/1)
- International Day of Non-Violence (10/2)
- First Friday (10/1) and First Saturday (10/2)
- October is Filipino American History, Italian-American Heritage and Culture, National Bullying Prevention, National Cyber Security Awareness, National Disability Employment Awareness, National Work and Family, and Polish American Heritage Month.
- October is traditionally celebrated as the Month of the Most Holy Rosary. It is also Respect Life Month.

MON 27 LM #455 or #645 / LMC #193–232 or #378 / white
Memorial of St. Vincent De Paul, Priest

Today's Saint

St. Vincent de Paul (1581–1660), a French priest, gradually became aware of the growing disparity between the rich and poor; therefore, he laid the framework for a confraternity of caring, called the Servants of the Poor, which provided for the physical needs of the poor. Recognizing the call to care for not only their physical needs but also their spiritual needs, he established a society of priests, the Congregation of the Mission (Vincentians), dedicated to preaching to peasants, catechesis of the marginalized, and other charitable works. In collaboration with St. Louise Montfort de Marillac, he founded the Daughters of Charity, a new community of sisters not bound by traditional vows or enclosure, devoted to the sick, orphaned, and imprisoned.

Scripture Insights

Jesus again overturns the world's perception of greatness. We mustn't trouble ourselves with comparison and ranking of our faithfulness to Jesus. It is folly to make such comparison, and it misses the point of Jesus' teaching.

Preaching Points

Parish Masses

- In Zechariah we hear that God desired to draw his children back to Jerusalem. Some of his people were not yet back in Jerusalem, but God desired their return to the city.
- Jesus said the little children must be loved and welcomed like himself. Those who are the least are the greatest in God's Kingdom.

Masses with Children

- Jerusalem was God's holy city; the Temple was there. In Zechariah we hear that God desired for those Israelites in other countries in exile return to Jerusalem.
- Jesus said the little children must be loved and welcomed like himself. Those who are the least are the greatest in God's Kingdom.

Scripture Insights *(PS)*

Does God have favorites? Both readings today would answer yes. God has a special compassion for the little ones of this world.

Preaching Points

Parish Masses

- God chooses the foolish, the weak, the lowly, and the despised; Christ has compassion on the sheep who are without a shepherd. This is what Catholic Social Teaching calls "the preferential option for the poor." What if we are not poor? St. Vincent de Paul gives us the answer: make friends with the poor. Serve Christ in them.
- When Jesus comes proclaiming the Gospel of the Kingdom, he comes not only teaching but also curing diseases and illnesses and reaching out to those who were abandoned. In our ministry, we must do the same: caring for the little ones is integral to the proclamation of the Gospel.

Masses with Children

- Tell the children about St. Vincent de Paul.
- Make the connection between St. Vincent's life and today's readings. God has compassion on the poor. So too are we to serve the poor, for God dwells within them.

Missal Options

- The readings may be from the SW, LM #645, CP (For Missionaries), or CMHW/CS (For Those Who Work for the Underprivileged).
- The prayers are found in the PS.
- Consider using the Preface of Holy Pastors, or P-I or P-II of Saints and EPVN-IV.

Song of the Day

"Jerusalem, My Happy Home" (various publishers)

TUE 28 LM #456 / LMC #193–232 / green
Weekday

Optional Memorials of St. Wenceslaus, Martyr / red; St. Lawrence Ruiz and Companions, Martyrs / red

Scripture Insights

Our Lord is the God of all people. People who live in many places would come to know God because we are made to know him and to crave relationship with him. God has made himself known to the world in relationship with the Jewish people, and the world knows him through the Jewish people and their tradition.

Preaching Points

Parish Masses

- In ancient time, cultures had varying beliefs, and they believed in deities that they adored, implored, and worshiped. The Lord our God is not bound by cultural beliefs but is sovereign and for all people.
- Jesus began his journey to Jerusalem; he knew what awaited him in the holy city. Jesus sought Jerusalem and God's will despite persecution, and it was done out of love for his people.

Masses with Children

- Most ancient cultures had belief systems that included gods, goddesses, and other deities that they believed controlled the world around them. The Lord our God is not bound by such cultural beliefs—and is for all people, not just the people of one land and culture.
- Jesus knew that his journey to Jerusalem would end in his final persecution, yet he steadfastly remained obedient to God.

Missal Options

- Consider using the prayers from the Ninth Sunday in OT.
- Use any of the three forms of the PA.
- Any of the eight Prefaces for OT or the six Common Prefaces may be used.
- You might use EPR-II.
- Any OT Collect may be used or adapted to conclude the UP. You might even look at the Collects in the Masses for Various Needs and Occasions for possible concluding prayers.

Song of the Day

"Jerusalem, My Destiny" by Rory Cooney (GIA)

Optional Memorials

St. Wenceslaus

St. Wenceslaus was a Christian king in Bohemia known for his opposition to capital punishment and his works of charity, until his brothers and other nobles conspired to kill him for his attempts to rule by Christian principles. Demonstrating the same mercy in death that he prized in life, Wenceslaus was heard to pray for God's forgiveness for his brother before he died.

- The readings may be taken from the SW, #646, CM, or LMC #379.
- Use the Collect from the PS; the other prayers may be taken from the CM (For One Martyr).
- Use any of the OT Collects to conclude the UP.
- Select from P-I or P-II of Saints, or P-I or P-II of Holy Martyrs.
- Consider EP-I or EP-II.

St. Lawrence Ruiz and Companions

St. Lawrence Ruiz's peaceful family life in Manila was shattered by a false accusation that drove him to flee with a Dominican mission to seek refuge in Japan. A new imperial edict against Christianity awaited them in Japan, and St. Lawrence Ruiz was martyred in Japan alongside fifteen others who refused to dishonor Christian images and disavow their faith.

- The readings may be taken from the SW, #645A (LS), CM, or LMC #380.
- Use the Collect from the PS; the other prayers may be taken from the CM (For Several Martyrs).
- Use any of the OT Collects to conclude the UP.
- Select from P-I or P-II of Saints, or P-I or P-II of Holy Martyrs.
- Consider EP-I or EP-II.

WED **29** LM #647 / LMC #381 / white

Feast of Sts. Michael, Gabriel, and Raphael, Archangels

Today's Feast

Jews and Christians have always recognized and revered angels, spiritual beings created by God who are neither human nor divine. Scripture depicts angels as messengers of God and manifestations of God's glory and power, but only three are named in the Scriptures. Michael, Gabriel, and Raphael have traditionally held special roles in salvation history as agents of God who minister to human beings.

Scripture Insights

Because of Jesus, our sin holds no power over us. Our Lord has conquered the trappings of sin and has released his people. He is the Lamb of God, and it is by his authority that we are no longer bound by our sin.

Preaching Points

Parish Masses

- St. Michael the Archangel is associated with battle; he fights against evil with the angels. They fight for God and his goodness. The authority and love of Christ overpowers all else.
- Nathanael was a holy man, and Jesus identified him as a "true child of Israel" because he had no duplicity. We too are called to be holy and truthful people who serve God and one another, not ourselves alone.

Masses with Children

- Many children learn the St. Michael prayer at home and know that he is associated with battles. In today's reading, St. Michael the Archangel defends what is holy and good from the threats of evil.
- Jesus found Nathanael to be a holy man who was truthful and free from self-serving untruthfulness. We too are called to serve God and one another without lies or other untruthfulness.

Missal Options

- Because of the eschatological nature of today's feast, consider doing the sprinkling rite.
- The Gloria is sung or said; the Creed is not sung or said.
- The prayer texts, including the Preface, are proper and are found in the PS.
- Use any of the OT Collects to conclude the UP.
- Consider EP-I or EP-III.

Song of the Day

"Holy, Holy, Holy! Lord God Almighty!" (various publishers)

Other Rites and Customs

Hours: Use the Proper Psalter of the day.

THU 30 LM #458 or #648 / LMC #193–232 or #382 / white Memorial of St. Jerome, Priest and Doctor of the Church

Today's Saint

St. Jerome was the author of the Vulgate translation of the Bible and of many biblical commentaries. St. Jerome spent his most productive years in seclusion, offering pastoral guidance to noble women, writing, and living an ascetic life.

Scripture Insights

When the people experienced the words of God and comprehended them, they had great joy and celebrated.

Preaching Points

Parish Masses

- Nehemiah contributed to the rebuilding of Jerusalem, and Ezra was instrumental in reestablishing the religious aspects of Jewish life.
- Jesus' disciples were called to a simple life of eating what they were offered and sleeping where they were welcomed. They were called to carry on Jesus' ministry.

Masses with Children

- After the Jewish people began returning to Jerusalem after the exile, Nehemiah helped the people reestablish the city, and Ezra helped them reestablish Jewish worship.
- Jesus' disciples were called to a simple life of eating what they were offered and sleeping where they were welcomed. This simple life wasn't at all grand, nor was it about anything but the Good News. The disciples were called to carry on Jesus' ministry.

Scripture Insights *(PS)*

The Scriptures are an inestimable treasure, the best of old and new, opening for us a window on the very mind of Christ.

Preaching Points

Parish Masses

- The Scriptures are not just for Sundays! The Scriptures can guide us in the circumstances of our day-to-day lives, not just the big moments. If we let them, the Scriptures will speak to us in a variety of circumstances—teaching, correcting, equipping us for the decisions we make and the work we do.
- St. Jerome is like that scribe, bringing forth both the new and the old. His translation of the Old and New Testaments into Latin made the Bible accessible to countless people.

Masses with Children

- The Scripture readings guide us in our daily life. It gives us advice and wisdom for living the way of God.
- St. Jerome saw the need for people to live by the Scriptures, and he made them accessible to the people of his day.

Missal Options

- The readings may also be from the CDC or CP.
- Use any of the three forms of the PA.
- Use any of the OT Collects to conclude the UP.
- The prayer texts are proper and found in the PS.
- Consider EP-II.
- Select from P-I or P-II of Saints, or the Preface of Holy Pastors.

Song of the Day

"Gather Us In" by Marty Haugen (GIA)

FRI 1 LM #459 or #648 / LMC #193–232 or #383 / white

Memorial of St. Thérèse of the Child Jesus, Virgin and Doctor of the Church

Today's Saint

Despite their youth, certain saints especially manifest God's grace. Early efforts to sentimentalize St. Thérèse's autobiography and spiritual doctrine have been ultimately overcome by critical texts of her writings and the awarding to her the title Doctor of the Church. Her "little way" is pure Gospel wisdom: Be childlike in trusting God and offer every action, even the simplest, to God's glory.

Scripture Insights

Jesus is the Son of God, and we are called to heed his word and authority. Heeding God's Word is something to which we dedicate our lives; we must work each day to produce the fruit of obedience to God in our lives

Preaching Points

Parish Masses

- During the Babylonian exile, God's people understood that they must be obedient to God. Obedience isn't always easy, but it is fruitful and good.
- Rejecting God and his ways can be done through small actions and through public actions. We are called to be obedient to God in all things.

Masses with Children

- Exile means that "the people were sent out and away from somewhere"; in today's reading we hear about a time in which the Jews were exiled from the holy land after the Babylonians conquered them. During this time the people realized that they had been disobedient to God, and they desired to return to obedience.
- We are all called to be obedient to God. Sometimes people are obedient only when others can see their faithfulness—we are called to be obedient in all things and at all times.

Scripture Insights *(PS)*

We must become like children in order to reach the heavenly Jerusalem, our mother.

Preaching Points

Parish Masses

- God is both father and mother to us: holding us close like an infant at the breast, carrying us, and comforting us.
- What does it mean to become little? It means to let go of our need to dominate, to be right, to understand, and to have. It means simply to trust God the way children depend on their parents for everything.

Masses with Children

- The preaching points for parish Masses also work well with children today.

Missal Options

- The readings may also be taken from the CV or CHMW/CS (For Religious).
- Use any of the three forms of the PA.
- Use any of the OT Collects to conclude the UP.
- The prayer texts are proper and are found in the PS.
- Select from P-I or P-II of Saints, or the Preface of Holy Virgins and Religious.
- Consider EP-II.

Song of the Day

"God Weeps with Us Who Weep and Mourn"
by Thomas Traeger (Oxford University Press)

SAT 2 LM #460; Gospel, #650 / LMC #384 / white

Memorial of the Holy Guardian Angels

Today's Memorial

According to both Scripture and Tradition, God assigns guardian angels to individuals, communities, countries, groups, and even planets. One's guardian angel presents personal prayers to God. Angels guide us on our way and protect us from troubles—even children have guardian angels, showing how precious children are in the sight of God. Angels, of course, are spirits, bodiless, pure intellect. Art and Christmas have sentimentalized angels. This is too bad, because they are strong advocates and necessary messengers to God on our behalf.

Scripture Insights

The following reflections refer to the LM #460 (FR and RP). We should not fear because our God is always with us, even when we stray or are heavily burdened. God loves the poor and hears their cries.

Preaching Points

Parish Masses

- The holy city, Jerusalem, speaks to the people, urging them to call on God, who will forgive their many sins, answer their prayer, and bring them home.
- God loves the lowly and the poor. Consider incorporating the Church's teaching on the preferential option for the poor today.

Masses with Children

- There is no reason to be afraid because God is always with us.
- God loves all people, especially the poor.
- Even when we do bad things, God is there, trying to comfort us and bring us back to him. God is all-loving and all-forgiving.

Scripture Insights *(PS)*

We do not walk alone in our lives. God is with each of us and, in his goodness, has given us guardian angels to watch over us. We do not see or hear our guardian angels, but they are present with us, out of God's love for us.

Preaching Points

Parish Masses

- In the Exodus, God promised protection from an angel; this protection was given in love and devotion to his people.
- God desires for us to be like little children in our faithfulness to him. Children are humble and not full of themselves; we too must live humble lives.

Masses with Children

- God sends us the protection of the angels. Everyone has a guardian angel. We may not be able to see them, but they help God to protect us.
- We are always to be childlike in our faith. God is our Father, and he is humble. We too must be humble, just like God.

Missal Options

- The Gospel from the LM and LMC is proper.
- Because of the eschatological focus of today's memorial, consider doing a sprinkling rite.
- Use any of the OT Collects to conclude the UP.
- The prayers, including the Preface, are proper and are found in the PS. Presiders should note that the chanted version of the Preface is found with the texts for the Feast of the Archangels on September 29.
- Consider EP-I or EP-III.

Song of the Day

"All Through the Night" (various publishers)

Other Rites and Customs

Hours: Use the Proper Psalter of the day.

From the liturgy, therefore, particularly the eucharist, grace is poured forth upon us as from a fountain; the liturgy is the source for achieving in the most effective way possible human sanctification and God's glorification, the end to which all the Church's other activities are directed.

—*Sacrosanctum concilium*, 10

S U N **3** LM #140B / LMC #135B / green
Twenty-Seventh Sunday in Ordinary Time

About Today

The Second Sunday of Easter also bears the title of Sunday of Divine Mercy. The Divine Mercy is not a new solemnity or feast, nor does it celebrate a new or separate mystery of redemption, but rather, it leads into the continuing celebration of God's mercy during Easter Time. As the Octave Day of Easter, the Lectionary readings and prayer texts highlight the mystery of divine compassion that underlies the Church's Easter faith.

Scripture Insights

When the Pharisees test Jesus, they question him on points of the law. Rabbinical discussion frequently included arguments about how the law was to be interpreted. Those promoting a particular viewpoint would use Scripture to persuade others. In the question of divorce, Jesus tests the Pharisees' knowledge of Mosaic law and then counters their answer with his own interpretation and biblical text. Quoting Genesis 1:27 and Genesis 2:24, Jesus points to the intimate relationship of men and women from the beginning of creation. Both are created in God's image, destined to live in relationship with one another. For Jesus, marriage is a blessed relationship and the proper arena in which to fulfill the original biblical commands to be fruitful and multiply.

Jewish law provided for a certificate of divorce (see Deuteronomy 24:1), but Jesus sees this as a compromise for human weakness. He does not specifically condemn divorce but lays out the ideal on which all marriages are based. The implication is that divorce is an aberration and a sign of the brokenness of the world. In later discussion with the disciples, Jesus defines remarriage as an occasion of adultery against a spouse.

Jesus protests the easy ending of a marriage in his society. His teaching protects women, who could be dismissed from a marriage with a piece of paper, and promotes the idea that adultery is a sin against a woman as much as against a man. Jesus also makes a woman's responsibility equal to a man's in marriage, forbidding wives to divorce their husbands or commit adultery by marrying another. The Mosaic law had not considered either possibility. Most important, Jesus focuses on the sanctity of marriage rather than on the lawfulness of divorce for any reason. He raises the understanding of marriage from a civil institution to a state of life blessed by God.

Preaching Points

Parish Masses

- Great care is required in relationships, particularly in marriage. When Jesus spoke about the legal allowances for divorce in Mosaic law, he identified the allowances as serving the "hardness of hearts" rather than serving the couple. Jesus' teaching brought protection for women; unjust divorce could ruin a woman's life, but Jesus taught that people shouldn't simply divorce for inconsequential reasons.
- The union of a couple in marriage has its roots in Genesis. The marriage relationship is holy and exists to help couples and their children grow in love and holiness.
- Because our Lord tasted death and conquered it, we no longer fear death.
- In the Sacrament of Marriage we find the sign of consent that is used with free will. When a couple consents to marriage, they are able to form a bond so strong that it cannot be broken at will.
- Divorce is reality of our modern society, and the divorced should be treated with the love and respect due to all people.

Children's Liturgy of the Word

- From the beginning of time, God made humans to live in relationship with each other. Marriage is a basic element of our society's structure.
- Jesus taught that marriage is something that lasts and cannot be cancelled for silly reasons.
- Because our Lord tasted death and conquered it, we no longer fear death.

Missal Options

- Offer any of the three forms of the PA.
- Sing or recite the Gloria and the Creed.
- Any of the seasonal OT Collects may be used or adapted to conclude the UP.
- Consider EP-IV with its proper Preface.
- There are six SBs for OT from which to choose.

Music Preparation

Pastors should ensure "'that the faithful may also be able to say or to sing together in Latin those parts of the Ordinary of the Mass which pertain to them.' They should be able to sing these parts of the Mass proper to them, at least according to simpler melodies" (STL, 61). "Each worshiping community in the United States, including all age groups and all ethnic groups, should, at a minimum, learn *Kyrie XVI, Sanctus XVIII* and *Agnus Dei XVIII*. . . . More difficult chants, such as *Gloria VIII* and settings of the *Credo* and *Pater Noster*, might be learned after the easier chants have been mastered" (STL, 75).

Music Suggestions

- Gathering: "When Hands Reach Out" by Carolyn Winfrey Gillette (available on composer's website: https://www.carolynshymns.com/when_hands_reach_out.html)
- Preparation of the Gifts: "All My Days" by Daniel J. Schutte (OCP)
- Communion: "*Ubi Caritas*" by Jacques Berthier /Taizé (GIA)
- Sending Forth: "Shall Tribulation or Distress" by Mary Louise Bringle and Sally Ann Morris (GIA)

Mass Texts

Introduction to Mass

Christ is not ashamed to call us his brothers and sisters. Though he is Lord of all and dwells in the highest heavens, he, for a time and of his own free will, was made lower than the angels and allowed himself to experience death in order to save us poor sinful creatures. His love has gathered us here and now overflows in the sacrament of our salvation, the bread and wine of the Eucharist, which will transform us into himself, that we might rise up to be where he is. *My brothers and sisters, let us acknowledge our sins, and so prepare ourselves to celebrate the sacred mysteries.*

Tropes for Penitential Act, Form III

All things in heaven and earth were made for you and through you: Lord, have mercy.

You lead us to salvation through your death and Resurrection: Christ, have mercy.

You remain in us through the love we share: Lord, have mercy.

Dismissal for Children's Liturgy of the Word

Children, our relationships are signs of God's love. Through the love of family and friends, God reminds us that we are made to be in relationship with each other and that he wants to be in relationship with us. Jesus is our way to friendship with God. He comes to you and now speaks to you in today's readings. Go and listen to him and let him into your hearts.

Dismissal of Catechumens

My dear catechumens, the fidelity of friends and companions, between husbands and wives, points us to the absolutely dependable fidelity of God. He is calling you and promising you eternal life, and he is trustworthy and true. May the testimony and prayers of this community give you confidence and help you arrive at the day when you will receive Christ in his Body and Blood. Go in peace.

Dismissal of Extraordinary Ministers of Holy Communion

Dear friends, take the Bread of Life to our ailing and infirm sisters and brothers. In his communion with them, may Christ heal the deepest wounds of their souls and bring them comfort in body and mind. Go in peace.

Universal Prayer

Let us come to Jesus as little children. May he embrace the needs we place before him.

1. For the children whom we are called to be through our Baptism into Christ, we pray:
2. For the children who experience war, shootings, abuse, bullying, and violence, we pray:
3. For the children who will not grow into adulthood due to abuse, violence, starvation, and incurable disease, we pray:
4. For the children who are orphaned and for all those willing to adopt or foster children, we pray:
5. For the children we have known who have taught us lessons of God's love and joy, we pray:
6. For the children who have died, that they may be embraced by the love of God in the heavenly Kingdom, we pray:

Lord Jesus,
you demanded that the little children have access to you,
as you announced that to know the Kingdom of God is to embrace it as a child.
Make us childlike in our service of you this day.
Help us to see that we discover God's love more easily when our hearts are not burdened with selfish pride.
Who live and reign with you in the unity of the Holy Spirit,
one God, for ever and ever.
Amen.

Other Rites and Customs

- Offer a blessing of animals in commemoration of tomorrow's Memorial of St. Francis. The *Book of Blessings* includes an order of service that can be adapted to the situation.
- In honor of the Month of the Holy Rosary, encourage participation in a communal recitation of the Rosary after one of the Masses.

Liturgy and Life

In the Genesis creation story, everything was called good until God said, "It is not good for the man to be alone." This section of Genesis teaches us that human beings are made for one another and that no other creature or thing can replace the human relationships that help us grow in holiness. God created a partner for Adam. Take time this week to make a list of the people with whom God has enriched your life. Thank God for them, and let them know you are grateful for their presence.

Taking Place This Week . . .

Consider what can be done liturgically, catechetically, and ministerially to respond to these important needs.

- Memorial of St. Francis/Pet Blessing (10/4)
- World Habitat Day and Child Health Day (10/4)
- World Teachers' Day (10/5)
- World Cerebral Palsy Day (10/6)
- Today is Respect Life Sunday.

MON 4 LM #461 or #651 / LMC #193–232 or #385 / white
Memorial of St. Francis of Assisi

Today's Saint

St. Francis tried to live the Gospel message of simplicity literally: Do not be weighed down by possessions. Do not tarry. Preach the Gospel. Spread peace. Do not engage anyone in conflict. Not all Christians can live with the heroism of St. Francis, but we must strive always for detachment from whatever leads us astray.

Scripture Insights

We are called to loving obedience to God; we ought to obey him in all things. We are called to love God with everything we have and to love our neighbors as ourselves. When we listen to God and obey him, we change our families and communities for the better.

Preaching Points

Parish Masses

- Jonah did not wish to listen to God's call and sailed to avoid him; in this story we hear that Jonah's actions did not ultimately avoid God or his request.
- Jesus explained the idea of who our neighbors are; they are the people we know and love, but they are also the strangers we do not know. Our neighbors are those of other races and creeds, those whom we perceive as different from us, yet are made in the image and likeness of the same God.

Masses with Children

- In the First Reading, Jonah didn't want to go to Nineveh as God requested of him. We heard that despite Jonah running away from God, he was not able to avoid the Lord.
- Who are our neighbors? Our neighbors are all people; family, friends, teachers, and others in our community. Each human person bears the image and likeness of God.

Scripture Insights *(PS)*

The childlike enter into great mysteries; in the saints, we glimpse the life of Christ.

Preaching Points

Parish Masses

- Francis was a worldly young man until Christ called him. But the more closely he followed Christ, the more childlike he became: living in total dependence on God as a Father, with simplicity, trust, and joy.
- Like St. Paul, Francis bore the marks of Jesus on his body—in prayer, he received the stigmata, the mysterious wounds of Christ. But he bore the marks of Jesus in other ways too. His radical poverty and the way he lived Jesus' Gospel have led to him being called "another Christ."

Masses with Children

- Tell the children about St. Francis. Share a story or two about St. Francis and animals that will resonate well with the children. Bring the stories around to Francis' life with the poor and his life of simplicity. Make the connection to how we are to live by Francis' example.

Missal Options

- The readings may be from the SW, #651, or CMHW/CS (For Religious).
- The prayers are proper and are found in the PS.
- Use P-I or P-II of Saints, or the Preface of Hoy Virgins and Religious.
- Consider using EP-II.
- Any OT Collect may be used to conclude the UP.

Song of the Day

"All Creatures of Our God and King" (various publishers) or "The Prayer of St. Francis" by Sebastian Temple (OCP)

TUE 5 LM #462 / LMC #193–232 / green
Weekday

Optional Memorial of Bl. Francis Xavier Seelos, Priest / white

Scripture Insights

God has mercy on his human creation, and in our sorrow, God finds mercy. Jesus shows mercy, love, and gentleness to the frustrated Martha; we too should choose Jesus and show love and mercy to others.

Preaching Points

Parish Masses

- We must choose to hear the Word of God, like Mary. We must act on it. How do we respond to God's Word?
- The people of Nineveh listened to Jonah and let the Lord see their sorrow; God did not punish the city because of his tremendous mercy for those who turn from sin.

Masses with Children

- Mary chose to listen to Jesus teach. Like Mary, we should listen to Jesus and learn from him. How do we respond to God's Word?
- The people of Nineveh listened to Jonah and were sorry for their sin. God did not punish them because they turned from sin. God has tremendous mercy!

Missal Options

- Consider using the prayers from the Seventh Sunday in OT.
- Use any of the three forms of the PA.
- Any of the eight Prefaces for OT or the six Common Prefaces may be used.
- You might use EP-II.
- Any OT Collect may be used or adapted to conclude the UP. You might even look at the Collects in the Masses for Various Needs and Occasions for possible concluding prayers.

Song of the Day

"All Who Hunger, Gather Gladly" by Sylvia Dunstan (GIA)

Optional Memorial

Francis Xavier Seelos was a Redemptorist priest whose missionary work in the United States for twenty-three years was marked by compassion and pastoral care. He died while tending to the ill in New Orleans during a yellow fever epidemic.

- The readings may be taken from the SW, PS #651A (LS), or CP (For Missionaries).
- Consider EP-I or EP-II.
- Select from P-I or P-II of Saints, or the Preface of Holy Pastors.

Optional Memorials of St. Bruno, Priest / white; Bl. Marie Rose Durocher, Virgin / white

---

Scripture Insights

Jonah was angry that Nineveh wasn't punished for their transgressions, and God desired for Jonah to find mercy in his heart. We are meant to be merciful people, ready to offer forgiveness, and not relish punishment of others.

Preaching Points

Parish Masses

- Are our hearts hardened and looking to find our own virtues while looking for others' faults? If so, we must seek God's grace in such matters.
- When Jesus taught the Our Father prayer to his disciples, he used the word *Abba*, which means "Father."

Masses with Children

- Jonah wanted to see Nineveh punished because he saw its faults so clearly. Do we ever look for others' faults while praising our own virtues?
- When Jesus taught the Our Father prayer to his disciples, he used the word *Abba*, which means "Father." What does Jesus tell us about God when he teaches us to call God by such a familiar name?

Missal Options

- Consider using the prayers from the Twenty-Second Sunday in OT.
- Use any of the three forms of the PA.
- Any of the eight Prefaces for OT or the six Common Prefaces may be used.
- You might use EP-III.
- Any OT Collect may be used or adapted to conclude the UP. You might even look at the Collects in the Masses for Various Needs and Occasions for possible concluding prayers.

Song of the Day

"Our Father" by Steven J. Warner (WLP)

Optional Memorials

St. Bruno

St. Bruno and six companions together founded the Carthusians, a strict order dedicated to prayer and work in eremitical seclusion. St Bruno's oratory in the French Alps, La Chartreuse, was physically austere and geographically remote so that this external seclusion might nourish an internal stillness and lead to deeper communion with God.

- The readings may be taken from the SW, PS #652, CP, CHMW/CS (For Religious), or LMC #386.
- Use the Collect from the PS; the other prayers may be taken from the CHMW (For a Monk) or CP (For One Pastor).
- Use any of the OT Collects to conclude the UP.
- Select from P-I or P-II of Saints, the Preface of Holy Pastors, or the Preface of Holy Virgins and Religious.
- Consider EP-I or EP-II.

Bl. Marie Rose Durocher

Bl. Marie Rose Durocher was born into a prosperous and devout Quebecois farming family, but her ill health prevented her from joining a religious order in her teen years, and it took years for her to find her vocation as the founder of the Congregation of the Sisters of the Most Holy Names of Jesus and Mary. While acting as a housekeeper for a brother who was a priest, Bl. Marie-Rose noticed that there was a shortage of schools for rural children in his parish, and she devoted the rest of her life to bringing education to children with the teaching order she founded.

- The readings may be taken from the SW, PS #652A, CV, CHMW/CS (For Religious), or LMC #387.
- Use the Collect from the PS; the other prayers may be taken from the CV (For One Virgin).
- Use any of the OT Collects to conclude the UP.
- Select from P-I or P-II of Saints, or the Preface of Holy Virgins and Religious.
- Consider EP-I or EP-II.

Today's Memorial

Our Lady appeared to St. Dominic and presented him with the Holy Rosary as a means to convert those who did not believe in the Christian faith. Although this vision is attributed to legend, the Dominicans are credited with developing this traditional prayer. Pope St. John Paul II added the Luminous Mysteries in 2002.

Scripture Insights

Persistence is a quality of not giving up. We are called to be persistent in our calling on God. God desires to hear from his children in prayer and wants us to approach him.

Preaching Points

Parish Masses

- After they returned from exile, the ancient Jewish people resumed religious activity at the rebuilt temple. Malachi preaches about those who are humble and respect God and about the justice they will someday receive.
- God loves his children, and he wants to help us with our needs. Jesus compares him to a father whose son requires necessities; that father will supply what he can for his child.

Masses with Children

- Malachi preached about having humility and not pride and about the importance of respecting God.
- God wants to hear us ask for what we need, and he likes to help us with those needs. Jesus compares God to a father helping a child.

Scripture Insights *(PS)*

When the Word became flesh, Mary was present. When the gift of the Spirit was poured out, Mary was there, witness to the mysteries of Christ.

Preaching Points

Parish Masses

- Through Mary's yes, God's marvelous plan was set in motion. The mysteries of the Rosary trace key moments along the journey, intense moments of joy, light, sorrow, and glory. When we pray the Rosary, we contemplate the mysteries of Christ in company with Mary.
- As the disciples await the gift of the Holy Spirit after the Resurrection of Jesus, Mary is with them, praying in the midst of the Apostles. Mary is always with the Church, praying for and with us.

Masses with Children

- Tell the children about this memorial by explaining what the Rosary is.
- Emphasize how Mary's yes is a model for how we are to live our Christian life. Mary's life reveals key moments in the life of Christ, and praying the Rosary with Mary helps us to understand his life and how that affects us from day to day.

Missal Options

- The readings may also be taken from the CBVM or CMML.
- Use any of the three forms of the PA.
- Use any of the OT Collects to conclude the UP.
- The prayers are proper and are found in the PS.
- Use P-I or P-II of the Blessed Virgin Mary.
- Consider EP-II.

Song of the Day

"My Shepherd, You Supply My Need" by John L. Bell (GIA)

Other Rites and Customs

Hours: Use the Proper Psalter of the day.

F R I 8 LM #465 / LMC #193–232 / green
Weekday

Scripture Insights

In the First Reading, God's people faced a terrible infestation of locusts; God assisted them in ridding the land of the pests. Jesus faced doubters who believed he drove out demons by the devil's authority. Jesus' authority came from God, however, and he rid the people of the evil present.

Preaching Points

Parish Masses

- Different parts of the Bible have different historical and spiritual significance to our faith. The Book of Joel was written during a time of an infestation of locusts, which were a threat to crops, livelihood, and survival itself.
- Jesus used logic to explain that his authority was from God and that, because he was driving the demons out by God's authority, God's Kingdom was before them all.

Masses with Children

- We read different parts of the Bible in different ways. When the Book of Joel was written, Israel was facing an infestation of locusts. Such bugs could eat crops and destroy industries.
- Jesus used logic to explain that his authority was from God and that, because he was driving the demons out by God's authority, God's Kingdom was before them all. God was very near to those questioning Jesus, but they couldn't see him for what he was.

Missal Options

- Consider using the prayers from the Twenty-Eighth Sunday in OT.
- Use any of the three forms of the PA.
- Any of the eight Prefaces for OT or the six Common Prefaces may be used.
- You might use EP-II.
- Any OT Collect may be used or adapted to conclude the UP. You might even look at the Collects in the Masses for Various Needs and Occasions for possible concluding prayers.

Song of the Day

"Mercy, O God" by Francis Patrick O'Brian (GIA)

S A T 9 LM #466 / LMC #193–232 / green
Weekday

Optional Memorials of St. Denis, Bishop, and Companions, Martyrs / red; St. John Leonardi, Priest / white; Blessed Virgin Mary / white

Scripture Insights

What does it mean to have a heart open to God and his Word? When we have open hearts we are ready for transformation in Christ and are transformed for the Kingdom of God. We will seek our Lord and to follow his Word.

Preaching Points

Parish Masses

- Our God stands firmly for justice, and he expects the same of his people. We can delight in his justice, because God loves the poor, the meek, and the suffering.
- Anyone can hear the Word of God being spoken, but we must open our hearts to actually internalize the message and be courageous to act on it. Jesus explained that those who listen and act on his Word are blessed.

Masses with Children

- What does it mean to stand for justice? God shows his love for the poor, suffering, and meek over and over in Scripture; how do we stand for those same groups?
- Most people can hear the Word of God proclaimed, but not everyone opens their hearts to truly understand God's message. Jesus explained that those who listen to his Word and act on it are blessed.

Missal Options

- Consider using the prayers from the MPVN-20/1.
- Use any of the three forms of the PA.
- Any of the eight Prefaces for OT or the six Common Prefaces may be used.
- You might use EP-III.
- Any OT Collect may be used or adapted to conclude the UP. You might even look at the Collects in the Masses for Various Needs and Occasions for possible concluding prayers.

Song of the Day

"Lord, Your Almighty Word" (various publishers)

Optional Memorials

St. Denis

St. Denis was a third-century bishop who was martyred on the highest hill in Paris during the persecutions under Decius, along with his companions, Sts. Eleutherius and Rusticus. Devotion to the three martyrs led St. Genevieve to begin the construction of a basilica in their honor on the hill where they died.

- The readings may be taken from the SW, PS #654, CM, or LMC #389.
- Use the Collect from the PS; the other prayers may be taken from the CM (For Several Martyrs).
- Use any of the OT Collects to conclude the UP.
- Select from P-I or P-II of Saints, or P-I or P-II of Holy Martyrs.
- Consider EP-I or EP-II.

St. John Leonardi

St. John Leonardi was the founder of the Clerks Regular of the Mother of God, a small order dedicated to the reform of the diocesan priesthood and renewal of the Church from the top down. St. John trained as a pharmacist in his youth but spent most of his life seeking remedies for the spiritual ills that plagued the Church of his time.

- The readings may be taken from the SW, PS #655, CP, CHMW/CS (For Those Who Work for the Underprivileged), or LMC #390.
- Use the Collect from the PS; the other prayers may be taken from the CP (For Missionaries) or CHMW (For Those Who Practiced Works of Mercy).
- Select from P-I or P-II of Saints, or the Preface of Holy Pastors.
- Consider EP-I or EP-II.

Blessed Virgin Mary

- The readings may be taken from the SW, CBVM, or CMML.
- Use any of the prayers from the CBVM or the CMMM.
- You may also use any of the Votive Masses of the BVM.
- Select from P-I or P-II of the BVM.
- Consider EP-I or EP-III.

From the liturgy, therefore, particularly the eucharist, grace is poured forth upon us as from a fountain; the liturgy is the source for achieving in the most effective way possible human sanctification and God's glorification, the end to which all the Church's other activities are directed.

—*Built of Living Stones*, 20

S U N 10 LM #143B / LMC #138B / green

Twenty-Eighth Sunday in Ordinary Time

Scripture Insights

Legend connects the book of Wisdom with Solomon, who succeeded his father, King David, on the throne of Israel. In the story of Solomon (see 1 Kings 3:4–9), the young king prays to God, not for riches or power, but for an understanding heart to govern the people. God grants his request and also rewards him with riches and glory beyond compare. In the passage from Wisdom, we hear the narrator (usually thought to be Solomon) tell how he prayed for wisdom, desiring her more than any earthly treasure. The author writes in the style of much of the wisdom literature (Proverbs, Job, and Ecclesiastes, for instance). Unlike the prophets who got their message from visions or the voice of God, the lessons in wisdom literature are drawn from life experience.

Wisdom (in Hebrew, *hokmah,* and in Greek, *Sophia*) was paired with understanding and discernment. Wisdom is feminine; she is depicted as the reflection of God and image of God's goodness (see Wisdom 7:26). She is also God's master crafter and the first of God's acts (see Proverbs 8:22). In Wisdom 10, she is cast as God in the retelling of stories from Genesis and Exodus. Some scholars have called her the feminine face of God. Whatever her identity, ancient writers saw great beauty and treasure in Wisdom. They considered her a pathway to God. Thus wisdom literature is full of prayers for wisdom.

The Wisdom reading provides a nice counterpoint to the Gospel, where Jesus discusses the price of discipleship. "Riches" in the Gospel means everything related to worldly wealth, possessions, and relationships. None of these can stand in the way of the service of God. When the disciples look at the implications of the word "rich" and realize there are many ways of being rich, they cry out in frustration: "Then who can be saved?" For Jesus, the answer is not in doubt. Rich or poor, God must be the center of life, but the rich must work especially hard to overcome attachments to their worldly goods. He might have recited Wisdom's prayer for them.

Preaching Points

Parish Masses

- Our attachment to worldly things has a warning from the Lord. Our material possessions should not take precedence over the Wisdom gifts, nor should they overtake the importance of care of the poor.
- The spirit of Wisdom is a tremendous gift. Wisdom is often personified as a woman in the wisdom literature.
- Jesus understands human life perfectly, being a fully human (and fully divine) person. Being omnipotent, God knows our inmost hearts and minds.
- Our riches are best gathered in the form of Wisdom rather than material wealth.

Children's Liturgy of the Word

- In Wisdom literature, Wisdom is often personified as a woman. Wisdom is a great gift.
- Jesus came to the earth as a fully human, fully divine person; he understands our lives perfectly, and God knows our inmost hearts and minds.
- Our material possessions don't matter; what matters is living out life the way Jesus instructed us to live.

Missal Options

- Offer any of the three forms of the PA.
- Sing or recite the Gloria and the Creed.
- Any of the seasonal OT Collects may be used or adapted to conclude the UP.
- Select from any of the eight Prefaces of OT.
- Consider EPVN-II.
- There are six SBs for OT from which to choose.

Music Preparation

An important role that pastoral musicians frequently find themselves in is that of a music educator. This comes into play particularly during rehearsals where we may find ourselves working with a variety of singers or instrumentalists who need a little bit of assistance in theory, score reading, technique, and music history. It is important to use standard musical terminology at all times, and it is ok to explain what it is that you are speaking about. Do not presume that the musicians know what a system is, what dynamic markings are, or even where the key or time signature is. Music is a language, and it is important that our musicians develop their understanding of their craft. Keep a little pocket music dictionary nearby to help answer any questions you may not know immediately.

Music Suggestions

- Preparation of the Gifts: "Your Words Are Spirit and Life" by Bernadette Farrell (OCP)
- Communion: "Broken for the Broken" by Chris de Silva (GIA)
- Sending Forth: "In Christ There Is No East or West" (various publishers)

Mass Texts

Introduction to Mass

Many supposed treasures compete for our attention: money, fame, property, the latest gadgets, and a host of other baubles that will all pass away. But the true treasures come from God and are everlasting: love, wisdom, union with him through Jesus Christ. Let us pray for the grace of discernment, that we may seek after and prefer the things from above, beginning here with the Bread of Heaven we will receive from this altar. *My brothers and sisters, let us acknowledge our sins, and so prepare ourselves to celebrate the sacred mysteries.*

Tropes for Penitential Act, Form III

Lord, you have compassion on us in our weakness:
Lord, have mercy.

O Christ, your love is better than life itself:
Christ, have mercy.

Lord, you grant wisdom to all who seek you:
Lord, have mercy.

Dismissal for Children's Liturgy of the Word

Dear children, gold is spectacular, but today's First Reading tells us that, compared to wisdom, it's no more remarkable than sand. The Church teaches us what we must value above all else: our faith, love for other people, following Jesus. Christ is God's living Word and he speaks to you now. May you always place him first in your hearts.

Dismissal of Catechumens

My friends, God calls you not to half measures but to give all you have, all you are for love of him. You have made seeking him through this process of initiation a priority in your lives, and we pray that you will continue to do so even after you come to full communion with us and begin to be nourished by his Body and Blood. Go in peace.

Dismissal of Extraordinary Ministers of Holy Communion

Friends in the Lord, we give you Christ, our treasure, in his Eucharistic Body to take to our members who are sick and suffering. May he fill them with his joy and peace, and may they know and rejoice in their unity with us. Go in his love.

Universal Prayer

My sisters and brothers, nothing is impossible for God! Let us all place our faith in his loving mercy and trust that he hears and will respond to our prayers for the world.

1. That Christian men and women may seek first the Kingdom of God before any material possessions, we pray:
2. That nations may not use their wealth as a weapon against underdeveloped nations, we pray:
3. That those who are entrusted with great wealth may strip from themselves the temptation to worship money and possessions and use their wealth for personal gain and privilege, we pray:
4. That the poor and those who labor under unjust conditions may turn their need into true love for God, we pray:
5. That those who died hoarding their wealth may receive the gift of God's mercy, we pray:

Loving Father,
your kingdom of mercy and redemption
is the greatest gift we can hope to receive.
Your Son promises that it belongs
to those who have renounced the allure of wealth
and see you as the source of their salvation.
With you all things are possible.
Open our eyes to this truth apparent in our world.
Through Christ our Lord.
Amen.

Other Rites and Customs

- With today's readings inviting the Church to reflect on how we treat the poor and the least among us, offer a blessing for those involved in parish social ministry or parish outreach. Use the Order for the Blessing of Those Who Exercise Pastoral Service (chapter 60, BB).
- Reflect on how your ushers, greeters, or ministers of hospitality offer a welcoming presence to guests.

Liturgy and Life

In today's Gospel, Jesus encounters a man who wants to belong to God, to inherit eternal life, but who is unable to let all of his security rest in God's promises. We are challenged to consider how much our faith lies in God and how much in our possessions. St. John Chrysostom (in *On Wealth and Poverty*, 55) taught that refusing to share wealth with the poor is the same as stealing from them. Discuss that statement with your faith community or a friend. What does it say about the righteousness of the man who spoke with Jesus? This week, give something you think you need to the poor.

Taking Place This Week . . .

Consider what can be done liturgically, catechetically, and ministerially to respond to these important needs.

- World Mental Health Day (10/10)
- Columbus Day or Indigenous Peoples' Day (US; 10/11)
- Canadian Thanksgiving Day (10/11)
- World Day for Natural Disaster Reduction Day (10/13)
- World Sight Day (10/14)
- International Day of Rural Women and Boss' Day (10/15)
- World Food Day (10/16)

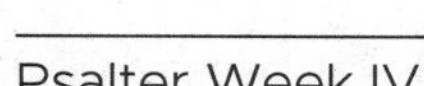

MON 11 — LM #467 / LMC #193–232 / green — Weekday

Optional Memorial of St. John XXIII, Pope / white

Scripture Insights

Our identity is found in Christ and through Christ. We are his disciples and we follow him. We are called to live in obedience to him; we are meant to live holy lives, dedicated to living out Jesus' teaching.

Preaching Points

Parish Masses

- What does it mean to be set apart? Are Christians not a part of the world? Do we hold ourselves to a particular standard of love, care, and charity? How do these attributes help us to grow in holiness?
- Jesus healed the sick and raised the dead, yet people still sought signs that he was the Messiah.

Masses with Children

- Why are Christians set apart? How does our love for others, our charity, and our care for the poor affect our faith and help us to grow in holiness?
- Jesus healed the sick and raised the dead, yet people still sought signs that he was the Messiah.

Missal Options

- Consider using the prayers from the Second Sunday in OT.
- Use any of the three forms of the PA.
- Any of the eight Prefaces for OT or the six Common Prefaces may be used.
- You might use EP-II.
- Any OT Collect may be used or adapted to conclude the UP. You might even look at the Collects in the Masses for Various Needs and Occasions for possible concluding prayers.

Song of the Day

"All the Ends of the Earth" by Bob Dufford (OCP)

Optional Memorial

Known for his modesty and pastoral concern, "Good Pope John" dedicated his ministry to placing the Church at the service of the needs of the world. As supreme pontiff, John XXIII refused to be a prisoner of the Vatican and instead modeled his papacy on the Good Shepherd, visiting the prisons of Rome, reaching out to the sick, and welcoming visitors of every faith and nation. He surprised the world by announcing the Second Vatican Council on January 25, 1959. His hope was that the Council would signal a new style for the Church and her authority.

- There are no readings in the LMC, but you could use those from the CP.
- The readings from the LM may be from the SW or LS #655A or CP (For a Pope).
- In 2019, an English translation of a proper Collect was approved by the Holy See. The Collect is available on the USCCB website: http://www.usccb.org/about/divine-worship/liturgical-calendar/saint-john-xxiii.cfm. The other prayers are from the CP: For a Pope.
- Consider EP-I.

TUE 12 — LM #468 / LMC #193–232 / green — Weekday

Scripture Insights

Humanity has needed a savior since Adam and Eve and the fall. The Gospel teaches us about Jesus and God's salvation through Jesus. We put our faith in him, fully relying on him for our salvation.

Preaching Points

Parish Masses

- St. Paul says he is "not ashamed of the Gospel." How are people ashamed and unashamed of the Gospel? Do parts of the Gospel exist that you haven't yet fully embraced?
- Hypocrites make themselves look good while engaging in unsavory practice or behavior. We are not to be hypocritical people but instead embrace goodness and honesty.

Masses with Children

- How can we embrace the Gospel more fully? How can we be unashamed like St. Paul?
- Jesus wants our souls to be clean inside and out; we shouldn't put on a good face in order to look good but then act as if we are rotten when we think nobody can see.

Missal Options

- Consider using the prayers from the Fifth Sunday in OT.
- Use any of the three forms of the PA.
- Any of the eight Prefaces for OT or the six Common Prefaces may be used.
- You might use EPVN-III.

- Any OT Collect may be used or adapted to conclude the UP. You might even look at the Collects in the Masses for Various Needs and Occasions for possible concluding prayers.

Song of the Day

"Canticle of the Sun" by Marty Haugen (GIA)

WED 13 LM #469 / LMC #193–232 / green Weekday

Scripture Insights

Our behavior in life matters absolutely. We know what God expects of us; we hear the expectations throughout the Old Testament, we hear them personified in the wisdom tradition, and we hear it in the Gospel. Each of us can expect to stand before God and reap the fruit of our actions in life.

Preaching Points

Parish Masses

- St. Paul again addresses dangerous hypocrisy—we ought not behave judgmentally toward others, especially when the same or similar sin is present in our own lives.
- Jesus criticized the scholars for burdening people with overly heavy expectations and then not assisting those they burdened. This sort of situation can happen in many types of power structures.

Masses with Children

- When we claim another person is sinning, we mustn't be judgmental about it, especially when we have our own sins.
- Jesus criticized the scholars for burdening people with too many rules and then not helping the people to follow them.

Missal Options

- Consider using the prayers from the MPVN-8.
- Use any of the three forms of the PA.
- Any of the eight Prefaces for OT or the six Common Prefaces may be used.
- You might use EPR-I.
- Any OT Collect may be used or adapted to conclude the UP. You might even look at the Collects in the Masses for Various Needs and Occasions for possible concluding prayers.

Song of the Day

"We Walk By Faith" by Marty Haugen (GIA)

THU 14 LM #470 / LMC #193–232 / green Weekday

Optional Memorial of St. Callistus I, Pope and Martyr / red

Scripture Insights

We are saved from the consequences of sin by our faith in Christ. Christians—whether they were Jewish people or Gentile people—are saved by Jesus.

Preaching Points

Parish Masses

- St. Paul doesn't believe that we ought to neglect good works but that we may not brag about them.
- Jesus criticized the scribes and Pharisees for leading the people astray. They began looking for ways to find fault with Jesus' teaching.

Masses with Children

- St. Paul says that we shouldn't brag about the good works we do for others.
- Jesus told the scribes and Pharisees that they shouldn't lead people astray. They didn't like what Jesus told them and looked for ways to trick him into saying something against the law. They tried to create trouble for Jesus.

Missal Options

- Consider using the prayers from the Eighth Sunday in OT.
- Use any of the three forms of the PA.
- Any of the eight Prefaces for OT or the six Common Prefaces may be used.
- You might use EP-I.
- Any OT Collect may be used or adapted to conclude the UP. You might even look at the Collects in the Masses for Various Needs and Occasions for possible concluding prayers.

Song of the Day

"Christ Before Us" by Janèt Sullivan Whitaker (OCP)

Optional Memorial

Pope Callistus I instituted the ember days of fast and abstinence as pope and is remembered as a martyr. In keeping with the redemptive nature of his ember days, the saint was known as an advocate for mercy toward apostates who desired to rejoin the Church.

- The readings may be taken from the SW, PS #656, CM, CP (For a Pope), or LMC #391.
- Use the Collect from the PS; the other prayers may be taken from the CM (For One Martyr) or from the CP (For a Pope).
- Use any of the OT Collects to conclude the UP.
- Select from P-I or P-II of Saints, P-I or P-II of Holy Martyrs, or the Preface of Holy Pastors.
- Consider EP-I or EP-II.

FRI 15 LM #471 or #657 / LMC #193–232 or #392 / white
Memorial of St. Teresa of Jesus, Virgin and Doctor of the Church

Today's Saint

In the midst of political and social upheaval as well as religious reform, St. Teresa of Avila lived as a Carmelite nun. She used her many gifts in service of her order and the Church and grew in holiness. The abundant fruits of her contemplation survive in writings such as *The Interior Castle* and continue to offer spiritual wisdom to many who desire a deeper union with God and neighbor.

Scripture Insights

We have received forgiveness as a gift from God. We have not earned it like a person earns an income at a job, but it is a gift given freely by our God.

Preaching Points

Parish Masses

- Through Jesus, our sins are forgotten by God. We can confess our sins and through Jesus we are forgiven.
- "Do not be afraid." These words are heard many times throughout Scripture. Any fear we have ought to be for that which can hurt our souls and not our bodies.

Masses with Children

- We confess our sins to God, and we are sorry for any sins we commit. Through Jesus, our sins are erased.
- "Do not be afraid." These words are heard many times throughout Scripture. Because of Jesus and his gift to us, we have no reason to be afraid.

Scripture Insights *(PS)*

Remaining is the key: when we remain in Christ, we bear much fruit; the Holy Spirit remains in us, praying in us.

Preaching Points

Parish Masses

- Remaining in Christ is not static but a process of growth. Like branches on the vine, we can bear fruit only as long as we remain joined to Christ. We also need pruning from time to time, the stripping away of destructive relationships or habits that block our growth. And that can be painful and difficult.
- Growth is always possible. St. Teresa had been a Carmelite for years when she heard a new call to a more radical response to the Gospel. Creation is still groaning in labor pains; something new is always coming to birth.

Masses with Children

- In order for plants to grow, they need to be pruned from time to time. This is like our faith. We need to cultivate and help our faith grow.

Missal Options

- The readings may also be taken from the CV or CHMW/CS (For Religious) or CDC.
- Use any of the three forms of the PA.
- Use any of the OT Collects to conclude the UP.
- The prayers are proper and are found in the PS.
- Select from P-I or P-II of Saints, or the Preface of Holy Virgins and Religious.
- Consider EP-II.

Song of the Day

"All That Is Hidden" by Bernadette Farrell (OCP)

SAT 16 LM #472 / LMC #193–232 / green
Weekday

Optional Memorials of St. Hedwig, Religious / white; St. Margaret Mary Alacoque, Virgin / white; Blessed Virgin Mary / white

Scripture Insights

The faith has been passed down from Abraham and his descendants, but Christ has come so that all may join God's family by proclaiming Christ's name, and the faith that he has given to God's human creation.

Preaching Points

Parish Masses

- We trust in God to guide our words in difficult situations. We do not need to fear persecution because God is with us, and his presence assists us.
- Our faith is descended through the line of Abraham, and we believe in Christ who fulfilled the teachings of the ancients.
- God is always with his people, never forgetting his beloved creation.

Masses with Children

- In the ancient Church many people were persecuted for their faith, and the Gospel writers assured the persecuted people that God would be with them in their struggles. When Christians were questioned, the Gospel according to John helps us understand that the Holy Spirit guides the answers people give to the persecutors.
- Our faith is rooted in a time long before Jesus' birth. Abraham helped people know and love God, and our faith is a fulfillment of the promises God made to his people.

Missal Options

- Consider using the prayers from the MPVN-19.
- Use any of the three forms of the PA.
- Any of the eight Prefaces for OT or the six Common Prefaces may be used.
- You might use EPR-I.
- Any OT Collect may be used or adapted to conclude the UP. You might even look at the Collects in the Masses for Various Needs and Occasions for possible concluding prayers.

Song of the Day

"Jesus Christ, by Faith Revealed" by Delores Dufner, OSB (WLP)

Optional Memorials

St. Hedwig

St. Hedwig was a Bavarian noble who, with her husband Henry of Silesia, dedicated her wealth and energy to charitable works and funded religious communities. Although Hedwig was married at a very young age, she must have had a strong personality, for her devout influence shaped her marriage and her husband's governance until Henry's death, after which Hedwig finished out her years in the convent she had endowed in Treibniz.

- The readings may be taken from the SW, PS #658, CHMW/CS (For Religious), or LMC #393.
- Use the Collect from the PS; the other prayers may be taken from the CHMW (For Religious or For Holy Women).
- Use any of the OT Collects to conclude the UP.
- Select from P-I or P-II of Saints, or the Preface of Holy Virgins and Religious.
- Consider EP-II.

St. Margaret Mary Alacoque

St. Margaret Mary Alacoque received visions of Christ that led her to promote devotion to the Sacred Heart. Although she was met with initial skepticism within her community, she persisted in sharing her visions until her confessor, St. Claude de Colombiere, declared them to be genuine and helped spread her message of union with Christ through devotion to his Sacred Heart.

- The readings may be taken from the SW, PS #659, CV, CHMW/CS (For Religious), or LMC #394.
- Use the Collect from the PS; the other prayers may be taken from the CV (For One Virgin).
- Use any of the OT Collects to conclude the UP.
- Select from P-I or P-II of Saints, or the Preface of Holy Virgins and Religious.
- Consider EP-II.

Blessed Virgin Mary

- The readings may be taken from the SW, CBVM, or CMML.
- Use any of the prayers from the CBVM or CMMM. You may also use any of the Votive Masses of the BVM.
- Select from P-I or P-II of the BVM.
- Consider EP-I or EP-III.

S U N **17** LM #146B / LMC #141B / green

Twenty-Ninth Sunday in Ordinary Time

Scripture Insights

The First Reading is probably familiar to us as the Good Friday reading about the suffering servant of God. From early times, the Christian Church has applied this image to Jesus. The prophecy of a servant who would redeem Israel through suffering is unique among prophetic books. To say that Isaiah predicted the coming of Jesus is not accurate, but Isaiah did see the world turned upside down by God's victory and the restoration of Israel. Mountains would be made low, what is crooked made straight, rivers run in the desert, and those who were humiliated and brought low would be raised up. In Isaiah's imagination and poetry, the suffering servant enhanced the "new creation" God was working out.

Those who witnessed the crucifixion and Resurrection of Jesus Christ were trying to describe something they had never experienced. Children who are learning to speak do much the same thing. Early Christian communities found the most apt descriptions for Jesus in the words and prophecies of the Old Testament. For them, Jesus was the fulfillment of those Scriptures because what they read there fit their experience of Jesus so closely. As Christians, we need the Old Testament to explain the identity of Jesus. The words of Isaiah help us understand the object of our belief; in turn, our belief provides some illumination on the words spoken so long before Jesus.

The New Testament quotes Isaiah more than any other Old Testament book except for the Psalms. It is Isaiah's strong poetry and imagination, as well as his insight into God's actions in history, that make his prophecy such a rich resource for understanding who Jesus is in the life of the world. Isaiah's description of the suffering one also paints a sobering picture for any disciple who would drink the cup Jesus drinks and follow in his footsteps for the sake of God and the world.

Preaching Points

Parish Masses

- The readings from Isaiah and Mark remind us that while following Christ is inherently dignity-filled, it is not meant to be an enterprise of power or luxury. Greatness is achieved through humility and servanthood.
- To the ancient Jewish people who became believers in Jesus, the latter's identity was clearly recognizable in the description from Isaiah. As modern Christians read the words from Isaiah, we see our Lord, persecuted and gravely injured, who bore the suffering for our sakes.
- In his life on earth, our Lord lived in the human condition. He understands the struggles of our lives, and we can approach him, knowing that Jesus understands human life.
- Christ's purpose and that of the Gospel isn't meant to grant greatness to believers; Christ's followers are called to servanthood.
- Jesus invites his disciples to share in his baptism and drink the cup of his Blood that he will pour out in his suffering and death. Suffering is not the end for Jesus or his disciples, but hope in God's kindness and grace is.

Children's Liturgy of the Word

- Isaiah, an Old Testament book, speaks of a "suffering servant" who early Christians recognized as Jesus.
- Jesus understands our human struggles because, while he is fully God, he is also fully human.
- Jesus does not show us his grace and love by giving us power or wealth; we engage ourselves in Jesus' love by being servants to others.

Missal Options

- Offer any of the three forms of the PA.
- Sing or recite the Gloria and the Creed.
- Any of the seasonal OT Collects may be used or adapted to conclude the UP.
- Select from any of the eight Prefaces of OT.
- Consider EP-I.
- There are six SBs for OT from which to choose.

Music Preparation

By now, you should have all your music in folders for Christmas. The next six weeks are going to be rushing by. Set a timeline and a list of goals for the music ministry and share it with your choirs and cantors. The more they know your gameplan, the more receptive they may be to your methods.

Music Suggestions

- Gathering: "Come, Christians, Join to Sing" (various publishers)
- Preparation of the Gifts: "O Bless the Lord, My Soul" (various publishers)
- Communion: "*Pan de Vida*" by Bob Hurd (OCP)
- Sending Forth: "May You Walk with Christ" by Stephen Dean (OCP)

Mass Texts

Introduction to Mass

Jesus is our great high priest who offers himself for our sins, to reconcile us to the Father. He took to himself our humanity and all our suffering and sorrow. Therefore, let us gladly offer ourselves to him, approach this altar with confidence in his love and mercy, and receive with gratitude the spiritual food that makes us whole. *My brothers and sisters, let us acknowledge our sins, and so prepare ourselves to celebrate the sacred mysteries.*

Tropes for Penitential Act, Form III

Upon yourself you bore the guilt and sin of us all: Lord, have mercy.

You came not to be served but to serve and to give us your life: Christ, have mercy.

The will of the Father is accomplished through you: Lord, have mercy.

Dismissal for Children's Liturgy of the Word

My children, there is no part of human experience that Jesus is unfamiliar with. He knows our joys and our sorrows. He knows what it is like to be a child, to grow and learn, to be excited and to be afraid. You can turn to him with whatever is in your heart and he will never stop loving you. Go now and listen to him speaking to you in today's readings.

Dismissal of Catechumens

Friends, we give you this time to reflect on the message of Christ, who knows your strengths and weaknesses and comes to meet you where you are. May you find confidence in his mercy and grow in faith, hope, and love, until the day when you join us as one family, one body, around the table of the Lord. Go in peace.

Dismissal of Extraordinary Ministers of Holy Communion

Dear ministers of the Lord, go to our brothers and sisters who are weak in health and body and share with them the Body of Christ, who knows and bears their sufferings. May he lift their spirits and enable them to join their praise with ours. Go in peace.

Universal Prayer

The Son of Man did not come to be served but to serve and give his life as a ransom for many. He calls us to do the same. And so we now pray for the needs of our world.

1. That those ordained for service in the Church may willingly carry the Cross of Christ so as to give their lives for others, we pray:
2. That elected officials may lead as servants, we pray:
3. That those who abuse power in any way, especially those who lord their authority over others, may be humbled, we pray:
4. That the powerless, especially those who suffer from poverty, imprisonment, or rejection, may turn to the Lord for a renewed sense of strength, we pray:
5. That those who have died may be counted among the chosen in the Kingdom of Heaven, we pray:

Lord God,
your Son Jesus Christ
teaches us that to serve and not to be served
is the way to live in your Kingdom.
Help us to be selfless
and to freely give up our place of honor and prestige
for the benefit of others.
Make our world a place of genuine equality
in which there are no rich and no poor.
Through Christ our Lord.
Amen.

Other Rites and Customs

- With the change in seasons, organize a coat or clothing drive.
- Advent will be upon us in a few short weeks—are you ready?

Liturgy and Life

We all want to be somebody. Today's readings contrast celebrity with service. We remember Isaiah's Suffering Servant because he was faithful in spite of the world's judgment. Jesus tries to teach the disciples that status-seeking leads to emptiness. Rather than buy into popularity, we're invited to anchor our hope in God as we pray, "Lord, let your mercy be on us, as we place our trust in you." And trust brings hope. This week, perform three acts of service that no one will see or know about.

Taking Place This Week . . .

Consider what can be done liturgically, catechetically, and ministerially to respond to these important needs.

- World Day for Poverty Eradication (10/17)
- Mawlid (9/19)

MON 18 LM #661 / LMC, CA, #396 (G) / red
Feast of St. Luke, Apostle and Evangelist

Today's Saint

St. Luke the Evangelist (first century) is traditionally known as the author of the Gospel that bears his name as well as of the Acts of the Apostles. He is also identified with the "beloved physician" referred to by St. Paul (Colossians 4:14). Luke was a Gentile from Antioch in Syria, and his roots show both in his writing style and in his sympathetic treatment of Gentiles in the Gospel that bears his name. According to Acts of the Apostles, he accompanied St. Paul on some of his evangelizing journeys, and he stays with Paul when he is imprisoned in Rome. Some sources claim he was martyred, but some sources indicate that he died an old man of natural causes.

Scripture Insights

To evangelize is to share the Good News of Jesus with others. Jesus sent his disciples out in pairs, warning them that they would not always be warmly received. We are called to be faithful to Christ in our earthly mission.

Preaching Points

Parish Masses

- Jesus did not call the wealthy and important to evangelize; he called faithful people to this work. We too are called to spread God's Word and to be faithful to Christ in this mission.
- When we are in times of fear (such as in the First Reading) God is with us, and he gives us his love and support.

Masses with Children

- God is always with his people, especially in times of trouble. You are never alone!
- What are the ways that we share the Good News of Jesus with others? How do we help others understand Jesus and his teachings?

Missal Options

- Since today is a feast of an evangelist, consider offering the sprinkling rite.
- The Gospel is proper in the LMC. The rest of the readings are from the CA.
- The prayers are proper and found in the PS.
- The Gloria is sung or said; the Creed is not prayed.
- Use P-II of Apostles and consider EPVN-II.
- You may conclude Mass with the SB for Apostles.
- Any OT Collect may be used to conclude the UP.

Song of the Day

"By All Your Saints Still Striving" (various publishers)

TUE 19 LM #474 or #662 / LMC #193–232 or #397 / red
Memorial of Sts. John de Brébeuf and Isaac Jogues, Priests, and Companions, Martyrs

Today's Saints

Sts. Jean de Brébeuf and Isaac Jogues were Jesuit missionaries who were martyred in North America with their fellow missionaries. For love of Christ, both Isaac Jogues and Jean de Brébeuf returned to the Huron missions voluntarily, despite knowing that hardship and likely martyrdom awaited them there.

Scripture Insights

The first sin changed the course of humankind, and sin grew in God's creation. One sin triggered humanity's fall, and one action—that of Jesus—brought about humanity's salvation.

Preaching Points

Parish Masses

- Each of us has sin and each of us bears that burden; through Christ that burden is relieved, and we are transformed in him. Grace grows in our lives.
- We must always be prepared for the Lord's coming. Even if we will not see the Lord's coming in our lifetimes, we must always be ready to act as his hands and feet in our families, our communities, and the world.

Masses with Children

- Sin is something each of us commits, and through Jesus our sins are forgiven. Grace grows abundantly, and it is rooted in Christ.
- The Gospel accounts speak of Jesus' second coming; this is an event we anticipate in joy. We must always be ready for our Lord's coming, and we must always be ready to greet him in the hungry.

Scripture Insights *(PS)*

Jesus gives us a mission, to make disciples of all nations, a task that is possible only because he remains with us.

Preaching Points

Parish Masses

- We have been given an awesome responsibility: to proclaim the Gospel to all nations. This is not a one-time task that can be completed; it is the ongoing mission of the Church, for the message of the Gospel must be preached anew to every generation. It is a task that will require all our energy and all our creativity and that is utterly impossible unless we rely on Christ.

- Death and life are never far apart. Through their sufferings and death, the martyrs—from St. Paul down to the martyrs of North America, who gave their lives bringing the Gospel to this land—give witness to the life of Jesus.

Masses with Children

- When we were baptized, we were given an awesome responsibility—to act like Jesus! We should tell his story to everyone we meet, not just with what we say but with how we act. It takes all of our energy to do this! So we must rely on Jesus to do his will.

Missal Options

- The readings may also be from the CM or CP (For Missionaries).
- Use the Collect from the PS; the other prayers may be taken from the CM (For Missionary Martyrs).
- Use any of the three forms of the PA.
- Use any of the OT Collects to conclude the UP.
- Select from P-I or P-II of Saints, P-I or P-II of Holy Martyrs, or the Preface of Holy Pastors.
- Consider EPVN-I.

Song of the Day

"Here Am I, Lord" by Curtis Stephan (OCP)

WED 20

LM #475 / LMC #193–232 / green

Weekday

Optional Memorial of St. Paul of the Cross, Priest / white

Scripture Insights

Free will is something each of us uses every day—do we use it for good things? We are not free to choose sin because we know we are under Christ's grace; we must use our free will to choose goodness and not sin.

Preaching Points

Parish Masses

- Our hearts must be converted from sin to righteousness. Our hearts and minds should be entertaining that which leads to goodness and righteousness, not that which leads to sin. We are to have freedom from sin!
- We should orient ourselves to God's will, as did the wise servant who considered his master's arrival at any time. When we are oriented to him, we are preparing for him.

Masses with Children

- God wants us to have freedom from sin through his Son, Jesus. We use our free will to choose that which is righteous and not sinful to help ourselves grow in goodness.
- God is like the master, and we are like the servants. All of us will meet him someday, and we are called to keep ourselves ready to meet him.

Missal Options

- Consider using the prayers from the MPVN-40.
- Use any of the three forms of the PA.
- Any of the eight Prefaces for OT or the six Common Prefaces may be used.
- You might use EP-II.
- Any OT Collect may be used or adapted to conclude the UP. You might even look at the Collects in the Masses for Various Needs and Occasions for possible concluding prayers.

Song of the Day

"Our Help Is from the Lord" by Dean Olawski (OCP)

Optional Memorial

St. Paul of the Cross founded the Passionists to spread devotion to the passion and cross of Jesus. Single-minded in his dedication, St. Paul found the topic of the passion to be an inexhaustible source of meditations and preaching.

- The readings may be taken from the SW, PS #663, CP, CHMW/CS (For Religious), or LMC #398.
- The prayers are proper and are found in the PS.
- Use any of the OT Collects to conclude the UP.
- Select from P-I or P-II of Saints, or the Preface of Holy Pastors.
- Consider EP-I or EP-II.

THU 21

LM #476 / LMC #193–232 / green

Weekday

Scripture Insights

We have life in our Lord Jesus Christ, and in that life we have the gift of grace. We are to embrace that grace, rise from sin, and embrace righteousness.

Preaching Points

Parish Masses

- We will never be perfect in the face of sin, but we can remember that sin does us no favors, while grace draws us nearer to God.

- People have a choice as to whether or not they accept Jesus and his teachings. We must be responsible for our own choices and do our best to set an admirable example of Christianity for others.

Masses with Children

- None of us will reach perfection in this life, but we can remember that sin isn't helping us or others in our lives. We can remember that God's grace draws us closer to our Lord.
- Each person has a choice as to whether they accept and embrace Jesus and his teachings. We make our own choices in this matter. We should always try to set a good example for others so they can understand our faith through our actions.

Missal Options

- Consider using the prayers from the MPVN-12.
- Use any of the three forms of the PA.
- Any of the eight Prefaces for OT or the six Common Prefaces may be used.
- You might use EPR-I.
- Any OT Collect may be used or adapted to conclude the UP. You might even look at the Collects in the Masses for Various Needs and Occasions for possible concluding prayers.

Song of the Day

"Send Down the Fire" by Marty Haugen (GIA)

FRI 22 Weekday

LM #477 / LMC #193–232 / green

Optional Memorial of St. John Paul II, Pope / white

Scripture Insights

We are called to delight in God's goodness and mercy and to embrace his teachings. Even when we sin, we can stop that sin and, with God's grace, work toward a more righteous life.

Preaching Points

Parish Masses

- Each of us falls to sin at times. When this happens we must confess our sins, make reparations as best we can, and work to not repeat that sin again.
- Jesus said that the people need to look around them and notice the situation to understand who he is and what spiritual reality is at hand. God stood before the people, and the people did not know he was in their midst.

Masses with Children

- Nobody in the world does not sin. When we sin, we can confess our sins and try not to repeat that sin again.
- Jesus knew that the people could understand the weather by observing the wind, and so he wanted them to understand who he was based on the signs around him. God was with his people, and the people didn't know it!

Missal Options

- Consider using the prayers from the Twenty-First Sunday in OT.
- Use any of the three forms of the PA.
- Any of the eight Prefaces for OT or the six Common Prefaces may be used.
- You might use EP-II.
- Any OT Collect may be used or adapted to conclude the UP. You might even look at the Collects in the Masses for Various Needs and Occasions for possible concluding prayers.

Song of the Day

"All People That on Earth Do Dwell" (various publishers)

Optional Memorial

The holiness of St. John Paul II was reflected through his humanity, that of a tireless, gifted, and charismatic pastoral leader.

- The readings may be taken from the SW, #663A (LS), or CP (For a Pope).
- In 2019, an English translation of a proper Collect was approved by the Holy See. The Collect is available on the USCCB website: http://www.usccb.org/about/divine-worship/liturgical-calendar/saint-john-paul-ii.cfm. The other prayers are from the CP: For a Pope.
- Consider EP-II.
- Select from P-I or P-II of Saints, or the Preface of Holy Pastors.

S A T 23 LM #478 / LMC #193–232 / green
Weekday

Optional Memorials of St. John of Capistrano, Priest / white; Blessed Virgin Mary / white

Scripture Insights

Christ resides in us, and that indwelling gives us the gift of eternal life. Because we are living humans, we worry about death, but in Christ, we have the promise of resurrection and life eternal with our Lord.

preaching Points

Parish Masses

- To say that we "are not in the flesh" reminds us that, while we are living people now, through Christ we are also in the spirit. We also understand that eternal life begins when earthly life ends.
- God has tremendous love, understanding, and patience for his children. Like the gardener who tends the soil for the tree to produce fruit, our Lord waits patiently for us to bloom.

Masses with Children

- We are living human beings right now, and we understand that after this life we begin eternal life in heaven with God.
- The gardener in the Gospel parable tends the soil as he patiently waits for the tree to bear fruit. God waits for each of us to grow and mature in the faith.

Missal Options

- Consider using the prayers from the MPVN-28.
- Use any of the three forms of the PA.
- Any of the eight Prefaces for OT or the six Common Prefaces may be used.
- You might use EPVN-III.
- Any OT Collect may be used or adapted to conclude the UP. You might even look at the Collects in the Masses for Various Needs and Occasions for possible concluding prayers.

Song of the Day

"I Received the Living God" (various publishers)

Optional Memorials

St. John of Capistrano

St. John of Capistrano was a Franciscan priest and reformer whose preaching called both laity and clergy to a renewed life of virtue through Christ.

- The readings may be taken from the SW, PS #664, LMC #399, or CP (For Missionaries).
- Use the Collect from the PS; the other prayers may be taken from the CP (For Missionaries) or CHMW (For Religious).
- Use any of the OT Collects to conclude the UP.
- Select from P-I or P-II of Saints, or the Preface of Holy Pastors.
- Consider EP-II.

Blessed Virgin Mary

- The readings may be taken from the SW, CBVM, or CMML.
- The prayer texts may be taken from the CBVM or CMMM. Any votive Mass for the BVM may be used.
- Use any of the three forms of the PA.
- Select from P-I or P-II of the BVM.
- Any of the OT Collects may conclude the UP.

SUN **24** LM #149B / LMC #144B / green
Thirtieth Sunday in Ordinary Time

Scripture Insights

Jesus' departure from Jericho signals the beginning of his final journey to Jerusalem and the passion that awaits him there. Mark takes a break from his terse writing style to describe the healing of the blind Bartimaeus in detail.

In both Old and New Testaments, blindness is often a symbol of ignorance, particularly the ignorance of unbelief and lack of insight (see Isaiah 6:9–10; Matthew 15:14; Romans 2:19). The servant of the Lord was to open the eyes of the blind (see Isaiah 42:7). Thus, healing blindness became a mark of the Messiah.

The story of *Bartimaeus* (the name in Hebrew or Aramaic means "son of Timaeus"; it is translated for the Greek-speaking audience) is the story of a simple healing by Jesus, another example of his election by God and his compassion for others. A deeper interpretation focuses on the beggar's shout to the "Son of David" and on his identification of Jesus as "my teacher" (*Rabboni,* the same word used by Mary Magdalene in John 20:16). This suggests that the one who is blind sees more clearly than those who are sighted. Still another emphasis can be placed on the closing line, "Immediately he received his sight and followed [Jesus] on the way." Coming just before the entry into Jerusalem and the passion, the story of Bartimaeus provides a sterling example of Christian discipleship, particularly after the difficult teachings on divorce, ambition, and riches. Finally, note the question Jesus asks: "What do you want me to do for you?" It is the same question he asked James and John when they wanted to be placed at his right and left hand. In both cases, the availability and vulnerability of Jesus as he awaits the answer gives some indication of the openness we must have toward others who call on us. The faith of Bartimaeus, his willingness to speak the deepest desire of his heart, and his immediate response of following Jesus remains a constant source of inspiration for the Church.

Preaching Points

Parish Masses

- Bartimaeus, blind since birth, was healed by Jesus. After Jesus healed him, he began to follow Jesus. Like Bartimaeus, we are called to respond to the healing Jesus offers us in our lives.
- When we read that Jesus healed the blind, we understand that he could control nature and change the biology of a person. Those who were healed could go forth and live a regular life in their communities.
- Some blindness references a spiritual blindness or being unaware of something. How can Jesus heal our blindness?
- The priesthood vocation is meant to be a life of ministry and sacrifice for Christ and for others.

Children's Liturgy of the Word

- All people are called to love and sacrifice in their vocation. The priests are called to a life of love and sacrifice in the Church's ministry.
- When Jesus healed the blind, we see that he had influence over nature and the physical world.
- Often, blindness refers to a "spiritual blindness" or an inability to see one's own faults. We must pray for Jesus to heal our blindness and that we begin to understand our own blindness.

Missal Options

- Offer any of the three forms of the PA.
- Sing or recite the Gloria and the Creed.
- Any of the seasonal OT Collects may be used or adapted to conclude the UP.
- Select from any of the eight Prefaces of OT.
- Consider EP-III.
- There are six SBs for OT from which to choose.

Music Preparation

- Our readings today are about rejoicing and giving thanks. Take time to pray in thanksgiving for the way God is present in your life.
- Consider doing some sort of thanksgiving gesture for all ministerial volunteers. It could be as simple as coffee and donuts after Mass or as elaborate as a banquet. Just hearing the words "thank you" will mean so much.

Music Suggestions

- Gathering: "I Rejoiced When I Heard Them Say" by Richard Proulx (GIA)
- Preparation of the Gifts: "God, Who Made the Earth and Heaven (various publishers)
- Communion: "This Is the Body of Christ" by John Bell (GIA)
- Sending Forth: "Immortal, Invisible, God Only Wise" (various publishers)

Mass Texts

Introduction to Mass

The goodness of God is evident in so many ways. He has given us the beauty of the created world, the blessings of life, family, and friends. The Scriptures tell us of the marvelous deeds he worked for Israel and of his promises for future deliverance and salvation. Greatest of all, he has given us his only Son, our Lord Jesus Christ, who is present with us here and now and offers us life through his Body and Blood. Mindful of such wonderful gifts, let us cry out to God with joy. *My brothers and sisters, let us acknowledge our sins, and so prepare ourselves to celebrate the sacred mysteries.*

Tropes for Penitential Act, Form III

You, O Lord, are the Son of God, begotten before the ages: Lord, have mercy.

You are our great high priest for ever and ever: Christ, have mercy.

Your gift of faith is the source of our salvation: Lord, have mercy.

Dismissal for Children's Liturgy of the Word

Dear children, today we hear of the healing of blind Bartimaeus. When he heard that Jesus was passing by, he cried out for Jesus to restore his sight. When people told him to keep quiet, he only cried out more boldly than before, for he believed that Jesus was both powerful and merciful. Listen to this story and always remember that Jesus is eager to hear your prayer and to grant you his help. Go now in his love.

Dismissal of Catechumens

My dear catechumens, you leave us now to reflect more deeply on the message of Christ. As he asked Bartimaeus, he now asks you, what do you want him to do for you? May your faith in Jesus' saving help grow day by day, until you may remain with us to celebrate these sacred mysteries. Go in peace.

Dismissal of Extraordinary Ministers of Holy Communion

My friends, our sick and homebound sisters and brothers await your visit. They await Christ, who will come to them by your ministry to nourish their souls. May his Word and Body fill them with joy and strengthen their bond with us in the Holy Spirit. Go in peace.

Universal Prayer

Let us come to the Lord with a faith that is seeking and crying out for mercy in our world.

1. For all called to discipleship, that their greatest gift to offer others may be their faith, we pray:
2. For the citizens of this country, that our love for justice and freedom may be matched by our desire for mercy and compassion, we pray:
3. For those who are blind and for those who work to prevent blindness, we pray:
4. For all who earn what little they have through begging by the side of the road, that they may find dignified employment and housing, we pray:
5. For all the deceased whose faith has been rewarded with God's merciful and loving embrace, we pray:

Compassionate Father,
your Son gives sight to the blind
and calls the lowly to a life of discipleship.
May we be among those whose faith is demonstrated
by a willingness to call out for healing and mercy.
Correct our vision, Lord,
so that we may see this world according to your loving design.
Through Christ our Lord.
Amen.

Other Rites and Customs

- If your parish uses the same option for the Penitential Act each week, consider introducing one of the less often used options.
- Since Pastoral Care Week begins today, offer the Anointing of the Sick at one of the Masses.

Liturgy and Life

At every time in our life, God is trying to bring us back from exile to guide us to wholeness. But as with the blind man Bartimaeus, a key to our healing is a faithful response to God's loving presence. For ideas about how you or someone you love might respond to God's personal offer of healing to you, go to www.vocationnetwork.org. There, take the Vocation Match survey, which is for those who are single, married, widowed, and divorced. The survey will suggest organizations you can contact for a possible life of service. This time of year, many parishes have people in the process of responding to God's call through the process of Christian initiation. They are discerning, praying, and being formed by the community to take their place in the Body of Christ through the Roman Catholic Church. Pray for those in this process and prayerfully let their search inspire your ongoing response to God.

Taking Place This Week . . .

Consider what can be done liturgically, catechetically, and ministerially to respond to these important needs.

- United Nations Day and World Development Information Day (10/24)
- World Stroke Day (10/29)
- Today is World Mission Sunday.
- Pastoral Care Week begins today.

MON 25 LM #479 / LMC #193–232 / green
Weekday

Scripture Insights

We are God's children through our adoption in Jesus. Being a child of God transforms each of us, and in that transformation we become new people in and through our Lord. Transformed people live transformed lives.

Preaching Points

Parish Masses

- *Abba* means "Father" in Hebrew. This familiar term is one that indicates a close and loving relationship between human beings and God.
- Jesus taught the people that humans who were suffering needed and should receive care on the Sabbath. Jesus relieved human suffering everywhere he went.

Masses with Children

- The word that is used in the Scripture today, *Abba*, is a Hebrew word. It means "Father." This word has a close and familiar sound to it and reminds us of a loving father. This is the term St. Paul used when describing our relationship with God.
- Jesus healed a woman on the Sabbath, which was against the law at the time. Jesus helped the people understand that if a person needed help on the Sabbath, she should be helped.

Missal Options

- Consider using the prayers from the MPVN-43.
- Use any of the three forms of the PA.
- Any of the eight Prefaces for OT or the six Common Prefaces may be used.
- You might use EPVN-II.
- Any OT Collect may be used or adapted to conclude the UP. You might even look at the Collects in the Masses for Various Needs and Occasions for possible concluding prayers.

Song of the Day

"Healer of Our Every Ill" by Marty Haugen (GIA)

TUE 26 LM #480 / LMC #193–232 / green
Weekday

Scripture Insights

Heaven is so magnificent that St. Paul doesn't mind his earthly suffering for the sake of Christ and his heaven. The Kingdom of God is something that grows, though it begins as something small; we are the small and suffering seeds that grow, enriched in the Holy Spirit.

Preaching Points

Parish Masses

- St. Paul says that we wait with endurance—his community waited for Christ in suffering and in joy, just as we wait for Jesus' return. At each Mass we hear how we wait for our "joyful hope," Christ.
- What is the Kingdom of God? How do we participate in it?

Masses with Children

- Our endurance is in the hope and patience that allows us to continue our earthly journey. St. Paul's communities waited out suffering, and at Mass each week we hear that we wait for Christ, our "joyful hope."
- What is the Kingdom of God? How do we participate in it?

Missal Options

- Consider using the prayers from the MPVN-43.
- Use any of the three forms of the PA.
- Any of the eight Prefaces for OT or the six Common Prefaces may be used.
- You might use EP-II.
- Any OT Collect may be used or adapted to conclude the UP. You might even look at the Collects in the Masses for Various Needs and Occasions for possible concluding prayers.

Song of the Day

"Seek Ye First" (various publishers)

W E D 27 LM #481 / LMC #193–232 / green
Weekday

Scripture Insights

The Gospel accounts, and indeed the Wisdom influence on Scripture, show God's special love for the poorest of his creation. God creates a way for the poorest to be exalted and for the exalted to learn what it is to be last.

Preaching Points

Parish Masses

- We must strive for God's narrow way; we do not look to culture or popular opinion for what is good and right. We look only to God's ways to know his way.
- Knowing that all things work for the good doesn't mean that our lives will be easy. Indeed, faithful people can face terrible events in their lives. Grace changes us, and grace can help us in trying times in our lives.

Masses with Children

- God's ways aren't found where people often seek opinions; TV, pop culture, and governments are not primary sources for seeking God's ways. We find God's ways in Scripture and in the tradition of the Church.
- Today's Scripture tells us instead that we may face terrible events in our lives but that God's grace can bring healing out of difficult times.

Missal Options

- Consider using the prayers from the MPV-17/A; use the second option for the Collect.
- Use any of the three forms of the PA.
- Any of the eight Prefaces for OT or the six Common Prefaces may be used.
- You might use EPVN-II.
- Any OT Collect may be used or adapted to conclude the UP. You might even look at the Collects in the Masses for Various Needs and Occasions for possible concluding prayers.

Song of the Day

"Blest Are They" by David Haas (GIA)

T H U 28 LM #666 / LMC #401 / red
Feast of Sts. Simon and Jude, Apostles

Today's Saints

St. Simon the Zealot and St. Jude Thaddeus were Apostles mentioned in the New Testament. After the Resurrection, Sts. Simon and Jude are believed to have evangelized and been martyred together in Persia.

Scripture Insights

The Latin word *discipulus* is the root of the word "disciple." *Discipulus* means "student." Each of us are called to be Jesus' students, and we join generations of Jesus' followers who craved knowledge and understanding of him.

Preaching Points

Parish Masses

- We are Jesus' family, and Jesus is the head of our family. How do families love and help one another? How do they care for one another?

Masses with Children

- Families are meant to love and support one another. We are all Christ's family, and we are called to help one another grow closer to him. How do we support one another as we grow in our Catholic faith?

Missal Options

- As a feast of the Apostles, consider doing the sprinkling rite today.
- The Gloria is sung or said; the Creed is not sung (or said).
- For Masses with children the readings may be from the CA.
- The prayers are proper and are found in the PS.
- Use either of the Prefaces of the Apostles.
- The SB for Apostles may conclude the Mass (#17).
- Consider EP-I.

Song of the Day

"A House of Prayer" by Tony Alonso (GIA)

Other Rites and Customs

Hours: Use the Proper Psalter of the day.

FRI 29 LM #483 / LMC #193–232 / green Weekday

Scripture Insights

The law of the Pharisees brings death; Jesus brings life and peace.

Preaching Points

Parish Masses

Jesus healed people on the Sabbath because he saw the need of the sick and had the ability to heal them. Though the Pharisees doubted his orthodoxy, they couldn't answer his rhetoric.

Masses with Children

Jesus helped people understand that focusing on the letter of the Law sometimes made them miss the spirit of the law. By using the story of the ox, Jesus was able to help people understand why he healed others on the Sabbath.

Missal Options

- Consider using the prayers from the MPVN-45/2.
- Use any of the three forms of the PA.
- Any of the eight Prefaces for OT or the six Common Prefaces may be used.
- You might use EP-II.
- Any OT Collect may be used or adapted to conclude the UP. You might even look at the Collects in the Masses for Various Needs and Occasions for possible concluding prayers.

Song of the Day

"We Choose Life" by David Haas (GIA)

SAT 30 LM #484 / LMC #193–232 / green Weekday

Optional Memorial of the Blessed Virgin Mary / white

Scripture Insights

Humility is a foundational mind-set in Christianity. We are called to reject pride and embrace humility. Humility is needed in our relationship with God and our relationships with one another.

Preaching Points

Parish Masses

- God has not rejected his people, Israel, and he does not turn away Gentiles. Through Christ, all have recourse to God the Father.
- Those who lack humility steep themselves in pride. Pride swells our self-assessment, while humility helps us to grow in our relationships with God and one another.

Masses with Children

- God was known to humanity through his people, Israel. Through Jesus he can be known to the world, and all of humanity, regardless of bloodlines, can approach the Lord.
- Pride is sin in which people hold themselves in such high esteem that they disregard God and his ways to uphold their own thoughts and their own ways. We are called to humility, which is a sense of knowing our own limitations, lowliness, and humanness before God and others.

Missal Options

- Consider using the prayers from the MPVN-1/E.
- Use any of the three forms of the PA.
- Any of the eight Prefaces for OT or the six Common Prefaces may be used.
- You might use EPVN-III.
- Any OT Collect may be used or adapted to conclude the UP. You might even look at the Collects in the Masses for Various Needs and Occasions for possible concluding prayers.

Song of the Day

"Let All Mortal Flesh Keep Silence" (various publishers)

Optional Memorial

- The readings may be taken from the SW, CBVM, or CMML.
- The prayer texts may be taken from the CBVM or CMMM. Any votive Mass for the BVM may be used.
- Use any of the three forms of the PA.
- Select from P-I or P-II of the BVM.
- Any of the OT Collects may conclude the UP.

The Son of God became man in order to restore all creation,
in one supreme act of praise, to the One who made it from nothing.

—*Ecclesia de eucharistia*, 8

S U N **31** LM #152B / LMC #147B / green

Thirty-First Sunday in Ordinary Time

Scripture Insights

"Love God and love your neighbor" captures the essence of Jesus' message. Today's First Reading contains a passage known as the Shema Israel ("Hear, O Israel," Deuteronomy 6:4), the central statement of belief of the Jewish people. A high point in the synagogue service still today is the recitation of these words. There is only one God, and God alone is Israel's God. This belief calls forth a total dedication to God with your heart, your soul, and your strength—God must be loved with our entire being.

A scribe (someone well trained in interpreting the Jewish Law) comes to Jesus in today's Gospel with a question: "Which is the first of all the commandments?"

This was a much discussed question in Israel at that time, with two main schools of thought: Rabbi Shammai was very strict, while Rabbi Hillel was more pastoral and taught that the whole law is summed up in the words "What you hate for yourself, do not do to your neighbor." Against this background the scribe wishes to see where Jesus stands. Jesus quotes the words of the Shema Israel, but goes even farther by adding a second part: "You shall love your neighbor as yourself" (from Leviticus 19:19). By bringing together these two commandments, Jesus makes an important point. While he upholds the Old Testament, he also offers a clear way of interpreting the numerous laws—through the lens of love: love God and love your neighbor as yourself. Jesus offers us today a path to follow in life: love of God and love of neighbor should direct every action. When faced with decisions in life, our first question must always be: How does the law of love of God and neighbor influence this situation?

Preaching Points

Parish Masses

- The Ten Commandments, at their core, boil down to love. When a person loves God, he will keep the Sabbath holy and will not take the Lord's name in vain. When a person loves her neighbors, she will not steal from them or lie to them. Each of the Ten Commandments falls under loving God and/or loving others.
- The Shema is a basic understanding of God that is explained in today's reading from Deuteronomy. The children of Israel passed down this teaching to each generation.
- Jesus is the one sacrifice whose salvific act is our saving. He is both priest and lamb.
- When the Sadducees tried to trick Jesus into blasphemy about the most important of the commandments, he gave an answer that is the sum of the commandments and one that we still call on today; both are a prioritization of love.

Children's Liturgy of the Word

- The Shema is a basic teaching of Judaism that observant Jewish people learn as children. Jesus would have learned to recite the Shema as a child.
- Jesus' sacrifice is our saving; he is part of the one God we hear about in the Shema.
- Instead of being tricked into blasphemy, Jesus helps the scribe understand how his teaching fits into God's laws for his people.

Missal Options

- Offer any of the three forms of the PA.
- Sing or recite the Gloria and the Creed.
- Any of the seasonal OT Collects may be used or adapted to conclude the UP.
- Select from any of the eight Prefaces of OT.
- Consider EPVN-III.
- There are six SBs for OT from which to choose.

Music Preparation

Working with couples preparing for Marriage may be a source of frustration for many liturgists and musicians. Put together a good set of explanations for upcoming weddings, listing fees, musical options, clothing restrictions, audio visual guidelines, and rules on alcohol. The clearer your information, the better.

Music Suggestions

- Gathering: "A New Commandment" by James Quinn and Steven R. Janco (WLP)
- Preparation of the Gifts: "Set Your Heart on the Higher Gifts" by Steven C. Warner (WLP)
- Communion: "We Are the Light of the World" by Jean Anthony Greif (OCP)
- Sending Forth: "Love Divine, All Love's Excelling" (various publishers)

Mass Texts

Introduction to Mass

God has loved us into being and has gathered us here as his children in Christ. All that we have and all that we are we owe to our heavenly Father. Let us therefore strive to love him with every fiber of our being—in our silence and our speech, in our thoughts and our actions—and to love our fellow children of God, for whom also he gave his only Son. *My brothers and sisters, let us acknowledge our sins, and so prepare ourselves to celebrate the sacred mysteries.*

Tropes for Penitential Act, Form III

In your great love, O Lord, remember not our sins:
Lord, have mercy.

You live forever to make intercession for us before the Father: Christ, have mercy.

You yourself are the fulfillment of God's promises:
Lord, have mercy.

Dismissal for Children's Liturgy of the Word

My dear children, each of you is enough in God's eyes. There is no need to compare yourself with someone you think loves God more than you or who is holier than you. You each have within you, by God's grace, all you need to love him perfectly: *your* heart, *your* soul, *your* strength. That is enough, and in you God rejoices. Go and listen to his Word and rejoice in his love.

Dismissal of Catechumens

Dear friends, the love of God has brought you here and is at work in your hearts and souls. As you go now to consider his Word and his commandment of love, know that we hold you in prayer and eagerly await the day when you will stand with us to receive the Body and Blood of his Son, Jesus. Go in peace.

Dismissal of Extraordinary Ministers of Holy Communion

My friends, take the Body of the Lord and go to his servants whose sickness or injuries prevent them from joining us. Let them know that, though absent in body, they are with us in the Spirit and love of God who desires to feed them the Bread of life. Go in peace.

Universal Prayer

The Lord God is our strength, our rock, our fortress, our deliverer. May we find the hope to bring our prayers before God.

1. For our Holy Father, that he may show us how to be holy and lead with laws of love, we pray:
2. For our nation's leaders and for all those running for office; that all elections may be peaceful and calm, and all may be led by the Spirit to vote their consciences, we pray:
3. For our Jewish and Muslim brothers and sisters, that interreligious dialogue among the Catholic, Jewish, and Muslim communities may continue and be strengthened, we pray:
4. For all those who struggle to love neighbor, family, or self, that they may be strengthened and formed in God's ways, we pray:
5. For the faith community gathered here today, that they may continue to call on God their strength in times of joy, in times of turmoil, and in times of sorrow, we pray:
6. For all our beloved dead, that they may come into God's Kingdom of light, love, and peace, we pray:
7. For God to hear the prayers we hold in the silence of our hearts [*reader should pause*], we pray:

Hear, O Israel!
The Lord our God is God alone!
Hear our prayers, O God,
and always draw us closer to you
through your gracious laws of love.
Through Christ our Lord.
Amen.

Other Rites and Customs

- Publish in the bulletin the names of all those who have died in the parish in the past year.
- Invite young children to dress up as saints and have a parade after one of the Masses.

Liturgy and Life

Jesus' command to love our neighbor as ourselves is one of his best-known sayings. Those who speak my language or look like me or share my religious practices are easier to love than those who seem different, yet hope for peace in today's world depends on embracing the "other."

Taking Place This Week . . .

Consider what can be done liturgically, catechetically, and ministerially to respond to these important needs.

- World Cities Day and Halloween (10/31)
- All Saints Day (11/1)
- World Vegan Day (11/1)
- All Souls' Day (11/2)
- First Friday (11/5) and First Saturday (11/6)
- World Day to Protect the Environment in War (11/6)
- November is Homeless Youth Awareness Month, National Adoption Awareness Month, Native American Heritage Month, World Vegan Month, National Veteran and Military Families Month, and National Career Development Month.
- The dead are honored throughout the month of November.

MON 1 LM #667 / LMC #402 / white
Solemnity of All Saints

Not a holyday of obligation this year

About Today's Solemnity

Today's Solemnity of All Saints celebrates those who have committed themselves to Christ and striven to be like him. It includes all who are living and all "who have gone before us with the sign of faith" (Eucharistic Prayer I). In a more restrictive sense, it refers to those whom the Church names as saints and all those unnamed who are with the Lord. We publicly commit ourselves to Christ at our Baptism and join a community that strives to follow Christ in all things. Therefore, today, as we celebrate all those who are with God already, our hope is that we too, by being faithful to our baptismal call, may one day join them in complete union with God.

Scripture Insights

The Solemnity of All Saints is a celebration rooted in both faith and hope: faith that through Jesus Christ all of humanity has been offered redemption and hope that someday we and our dearly departed ones will be together with Christ in heaven.

The First Reading, from the Book of Revelation, was intended to offer just this hope, based on faith in Jesus Christ, to early Christians whose relatives had been martyred during the reign of Emperor Domitian (81–96). The book was written in a code of elaborate symbols so that its intended audience (persecuted Christians) could safely read it without fear of punishment from their persecutors.

We recognize part of the code because it has entered our liturgy: The Lamb who offers salvation is Jesus Christ. Those marked with the seal of our God are the baptized. Those who have survived the persecution are martyrs who are alive in heaven, who have "washed their robes and made them white in the Blood of the Lamb."

Heaven is full of people. The number marked with the seal, 144,000, is a symbolic number (12 × 12 × 1000 = 12 tribes of Israel × 12 Apostles × magnitude or fullness). In addition to the 144,000, there is "a great multitude, which no one could count, from every nation, race, people, and tongue." There is room for everyone, and we hope that we shall one day join it. In 1 John we are assured that "we are God's children now; what we shall be has not yet been revealed. We do know that when it is revealed we shall be like him, for we shall see him as he is."

We are a people that long to see God's face. Let us live according to the Beatitudes Jesus gives us in today's Gospel so that we may rejoice and be glad in heaven.

Preaching Points

Parish Masses

- Heaven is filled with saints, and the gates are open to us in Jesus, because God desires for his children to abide with him in heaven. In this earthly life, heaven is our goal. Through Christ, we are transformed. Our souls are washed clean in him, and we become a new creation through his Incarnation, life, death, and Resurrection.
- The saints are those who have already reached heaven; they intercede for those of us still on earth. When they walked this earth, they embodied the Beatitudes.
- Which of the Beatitudes are easiest to embrace? Which are more difficult to embrace or understand?

Children's Liturgy of the Word

- Through Jesus, we are made into new people. God's grace changes us and helps us to grow more like Jesus.
- The saints are those who have already reached heaven; they intercede for those of us still on earth. When they walked this earth, they embodied the Beatitudes.
- Who do you see embracing the Beatitudes? How do you strive toward righteousness, mercy, and peacemaking?

Missal Options

- The prayer texts, including the Preface, from the Proper of Saints may be used. You may also use the votive Mass of All Saints. The Gloria and the Creed are sung or said.
- The SB for All Saints may be used (#18).
- Because of the eschatological nature of today's solemnity, consider doing the sprinkling rite.
- Use any of the OT Collects to conclude the UP.
- Consider EP-I or EP-III.

Music Preparation

The Beatitudes call us to think about those who are poor and are seeking justice or liberation from oppression. How can the music you prepare call your assembly members to think about the poor and the oppressed? The music you prepare isn't just to make the liturgy beautiful (although this is important too!)—music is another opportunity to preach the Gospel.

Music Suggestions

- Gathering: "We Sing of the Saints" by Alan J. Hommerding (WLP)
- Responsorial Psalm: "Psalm 24:We Long to See Your Face" by Kevin Keil (GIA)
- Preparation of the Gifts: "*Adoramus Te Domine*" by Jacques Brethier/Taizé (GIA)
- Sending Forth: "Sing with All the Saints in Glory" (various publishers)

Mass Texts

Introduction to Mass

God calls us to holiness, to a life lived in love and service of one another. As our models, he gives us the example of the saints, these holy women and men who have founded their lives on Christ. They help us not just by their example but by the power of their prayer, interceding for us before the throne of God until we too, united with them in heaven, are made perfect in Christ, who even now purifies us by his Blood. *My brothers and sisters, let us acknowledge our sins, and so prepare ourselves to celebrate the sacred mysteries.*

Tropes for Penitential Act, Form III

You desire to present us as a pleasing offering to your Father: Lord, have mercy.

Your Spirit of holiness is the inspiration of all the saints: Christ, have mercy.

You are the beloved Lamb of God who takes away all our sins: Lord, have mercy.

Dismissal of Catechumens

My friends, holiness is within reach of all of us. We are all called to be saints. You yourselves are even now responding to this call from God. We join our prayers to those of all the saints in heaven, that you may continue courageously on this journey, that Christ will one day soon feed you the Bread of angels, and that you will grow in faith in the power of God to fulfill what he has promised. Go now in peace.

Dismissal of Extraordinary Ministers of Holy Communion

Dear friends, the Lord forgets no one in their suffering, and so we send you to the ailing and infirm members of his Body, that he may nourish them with his Word and with Bread from heaven, with his very self. Remind them of his love and of their union with us and with all the holy men and women of God. Go in peace.

Universal Prayer

My sisters and brothers, rejoice and be glad! The Kingdom of God is ours! But we must share its Good News. And so we pray for the needs of our world.

1. That the Church may always lead others to holiness, we pray:
2. That the baptized may always follow the path of virtue and holiness and share the Good News by the witness of their life, we pray:
3. That peacemakers of the world will continue to call nations to justice, we pray:
4. That men and women in our families, workplaces, and other intentional communities will inspire us to be more like Christ, we pray:
5. That those gathered here will be aware of Christ's presence within all people, we pray:
6. That those who have died may now join the saints in heaven, we pray:

Father,
all-powerful and ever-living God,
we give you thanks
for the blessing of all the saints who have inspired us
by their holy way of life.
Like them, we are called to holiness.
Guide us on our way,
and may all that we do
serve as a blessing on this world.
Through Christ our Lord.
Amen.

Other Rites and Customs

- Sing the Litany of the Saints as the entrance hymn or at the Preparation of the Gifts.
- Encourage families to set up a devotional area in their home where they assemble pictures or statues of various saints.
- Remind parishioners of the civic duty to vote on Tuesday.

Liturgy and Life

The Beatitudes teach us that the "blessed" are those who are poor, meek, ridiculed, and grieving; those who yearn for justice and peace, who act with mercy, and whose hearts remain focused on God. But is this not what all of us are called to be and do? We often say self-deprecatingly, "I'm no saint." But can we allow ourselves to dare to think, "but I would like to be"?

T U E **2** LM #668 or #1011–1016 / LMC #403 / white, black, or violet
Commemoration of All the Faithful Departed (All Souls' Day)

About Today's Commemoration

Today we remember and pray for all those who have died. We do not know for certain what happens after death, but we live in hope of eternal union with our loving God, who initiates a relationship with us at our birth and continually invites us to respond. How we respond to God in our lifetime will determine if our life beyond death will be in union with God or separate from God. Thus, we believe that our love relationship with God endures for all eternity, with God always ready to welcome and embrace us. We also believe that death does not separate the living from those who have died. Just as we ask each other for prayers during our lifetime, we continue that practice even beyond death.

Scripture Insights

There are many options for today's readings. The author has chosen to reflect on Wisdom, Romans, and Matthew.

The Church chooses three readings to teach us about death in God. The Book of Wisdom opens with an exhortation to seek justice and an assurance that "the souls of the just are in the hand of God." The vision of reward after death suggests the beginnings of a belief in resurrection, which the Pharisees of the New Testament confessed. There is comfort in the understanding that the grace and mercy of God surround us, even in death.

The reading from Romans describes the source of eternal life even for those who are sinful. The death of Jesus justifies all people before God, including God's enemies. This not only proves God's love for the world but also opens us to an understanding of that love even for those we feel may not deserve it. God's compassion is not limited to those who are perfect in their obedience.

Jesus' Beatitudes single out various groups of people and assert that they are "blessed." The Greek word for "blessed" could just as easily be translated as "happy" or "fortunate." But why would the poor, hungry, mourning, or meek be fortunate? Jesus is certainly not teaching that poverty, hunger, grief, or lowliness are good things in which we should rejoice.

He is rather saying that all of those who are now experiencing these burdens are destined for a better future. The tense of the verbs is crucial to the Beatitudes. Those who are grieving or hungry now, will be comforted and satisfied then. The blessed future will be realized in the kingdom of God. The Beatitudes, therefore, assert that God is establishing a kingdom in which every evil will be destroyed. Those who are a part of God's people—however burdened they might be—are blessed, because God's Kingdom will be theirs. In that Kingdom, every evil will be replaced with good.

Preaching Points

Parish Masses

- So many souls have left earthly life, and we trust them to God's great mercy. Death, for Christians, is not merely the end of earthly life but the beginning of life in heaven with our Lord.
- Jesus did not die for us while believing us to be perfect; he died for us knowing our imperfection. He loves us despite our sin and made his sacrifice for our sin out of love for us.
- Those who have had difficult lives filled with poverty, hunger, and injustice can rest knowing that God has a deep and special love for those who suffer. We are called to ease the suffering of others.
- God has prepared a place for each of us in heaven, and he holds a special place in his heart for those who have been persecuted. Like God, we must take care to love and assist the persecuted.

Children's Liturgy of the Word

- Jesus knew and understood human beings when he died for us. He loves us despite our sin.
- God has a deep and abiding love for those who suffer, and he has instructed his people to cultivate this love too.
- Jesus has made a place for each of us in heaven. Always, but especially during November, we remember those who have died who are meeting Jesus.

Missal Options

- There are three formularies from which to choose for today's Mass in the PS.
- Use any of the three forms of the PA or even the Sprinkling Rite.
- The Gloria and the Creed are not said or sung.
- Any readings from the Masses for the Dead may be used (LM and LMC).
- Select from any of the five Prefaces for the Dead.
- Consider EP-III.
- The SB in Celebrations for the Dead may be used (#20).
- Use one of three options for the Collect not used at today's Mass to conclude the UP.

Music Preparation

Music can be extremely healing for people, not only in the hymns and songs that are chosen, but also in the way in which it is executed. Prepare music that proclaims the love and mercy of God and our hope in the resurrection. Be sure to invite all the parish choirs to take part in All Souls' Day liturgies. This will speak to those who are grieving that "the parish is here for you!"

Music Suggestions

- Responsorial Psalm: "How Lovely Is Your Dwelling Place" by Randall DeBruyn (OCP)
- Preparation of the Gifts: "We Will Rise Again" by David Haas (OCP) or "You Are Mine" by David Haas (OCP)

- Communion: "In the Arms of the Shepherd" by Marcy Weckler (WLP)
- Sending Forth: "I Know That My Redeemer Lives" by Scott Soper (OCP)

Mass Texts

Introduction to Mass

We gather here to honor the memory of all our deceased friends and loved ones, but more than that we pray for them, that Christ, over whom death has no more power, may hold them safely in his arms. We also encourage ourselves in the faith and hope that we will one day be reunited with them in the newness of resurrected life and the joy of the heavenly banquet, of which this Eucharist we now celebrate is a foretaste. *My brothers and sisters, let us acknowledge our sins, and so prepare ourselves to celebrate the sacred mysteries.*

Tropes for Penitential Act, Form III

We have died in Adam and are brought to life in you: Lord, have mercy.

You have destroyed death forever: Christ, have mercy.

You prepare a place for us and will take us to yourself: Lord, have mercy.

Dismissal of Catechumens

My dear catechumens, it is the message of the Church that death, this greatest mystery of human existence and source of fear and sorrow, has been transformed into a passageway to God, through the death and Resurrection of his Son. We hand this message on to you. Reflect deeply on it, learn to place your trust and hope in it, and allow it to change you and bring you to the banquet of Christ, who is our resurrection and our life. Go in peace.

Dismissal of Extraordinary Ministers of Holy Communion

Dear ministers of the Lord, as we pass through this vale of tears we have opportunities to lighten each other's load and to spread the light of Christ. We send you now to do just that for our sick and suffering brothers and sisters by sharing with them Christ's life-giving Body. May it bring them, with us, to everlasting life. Go in peace.

Universal Prayer

This is the day that the Lord has made! He has conquered death! Let us rejoice and turn to him in prayer.

1. That all who participate in the ministry of comforting the dying and consoling those who mourn might be blessed with grace, we pray:
2. That nations responsible for inflicting death on their populations and people of other nations may repent, we pray:
3. That all who approach death's door alone may be surrounded by God's peace, we pray:
4. That all who fear death may trust in the bright promise of immortality, we pray:
5. That all of our loved ones who have died may join the angels and saints in paradise, we pray:

Merciful Father,
you hold out before us
the promise of eternal life,
as we look forward to that day
when death will for ever be destroyed.
Wipe away the tears from the eyes
of all those who mourn this day.
May we be a source of blessing for
all who grieve,
and may the souls of the faithful departed,
through your mercy, rest in peace.
Through Christ our Lord.
Amen.

Other Rites and Customs

- Invite the parish to attend the Order for Visiting a Cemetery on All Souls' Day (November 2). The order of prayer is found in the *Book of Blessings* (chapter 57).
- Offer a special Mass in the evening for all families in the parish who have lost loved ones in the past year.

Liturgy and Life

Yesterday we celebrated God's own ingathering: the saints. Today we remember the faithful departed. Having in common the tender care of God, together we all form one magnificent community, the communion of saints. Mexican families celebrate this communion with zest, picnicking in cemeteries during *Días de los Muertos*, the Days of the Dead. In your home, you could display photos of your family's beloved dead this November. Near the photos, place a white candle on a white cloth, recalling Easter Resurrection. Burn your Easter candle while telling favorite stories about each remembered loved one.

WED **3** LM #487 / LMC #193–232 / green
Weekday

Optional Memorial of St. Martin de Porres, Religious / white

Scripture Insights

Loving one another is a central teaching in the Gospel. In the Ten Commandments we see this teaching laid out in specifics, but such specifics aren't necessary when we simply remember that, when we love our neighbors, we always do good for them. God's commandments fall in line under the command to love one another.

Preaching Points

Parish Masses

- Each of the Ten Commandments fall into two categories: love of God and love of neighbor. When we love one another, we won't be stealing others' belongings, their spouses, or their lives.
- We follow Jesus by carrying our own crosses in imitation of him. What is your cross, and how can Jesus assist you in carrying it?

Masses with Children

- When we love one another we do not act in cruelty, jealousy, or theft. When we love one another as we love our own selves, we treat people well and work to keep right relationships with one another.
- Jesus doesn't mean for us to actually hate our family members; this passage is a reference to the importance of putting Jesus first and foremost in our lives. When Jesus and his ways are first, the rest of our lives fall into better order.

Missal Options

- Consider using the prayers from the MPVN-1/C.
- Use any of the three forms of the PA.
- Any of the eight Prefaces for OT or the six Common Prefaces may be used.
- You might use EP-III.
- Any OT Collect may be used or adapted to conclude the UP. You might even look at the Collects in the Masses for Various Needs and Occasions for possible concluding prayers.

Song of the Day

"Take Up Your Cross" by Jaime Cortez (OCP)

Optional Memorial

St. Martin's holiness was grounded in a deep life of prayer and in the charity with which he carried out his daily work in the kitchen, laundry, and infirmary.

- The readings may be taken from the SW, PS #669, CHMW/CS (For Religious), or LMC #404.
- Use the Collect from the PS; the other prayers may be taken from the CHMW (For Religious).
- Use any of the three forms of the PA.
- Any of the OT Collects may conclude the UP.
- Select from P-I or P-II of Saints, or the Preface of Holy Virgins and Religious.
- Consider EP-II.

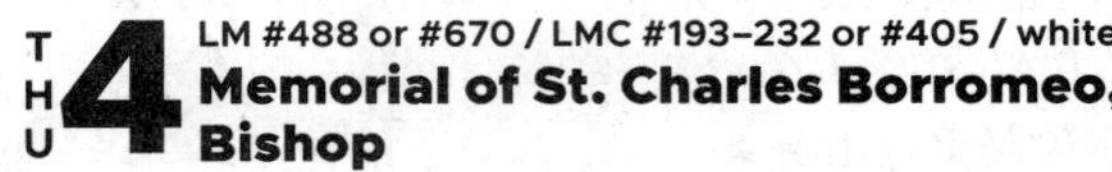

THU **4** LM #488 or #670 / LMC #193–232 or #405 / white
Memorial of St. Charles Borromeo, Bishop

Today's Saint

As cardinal, archbishop, and papal legate, St. Charles Borromeo played a role in the final session of the Council of Trent and supported clerical codes of conduct and seminary reform while setting an example of clerical simplicity and charity in his own life.

Scripture Insights

We are God's children and brothers and sisters to one another. We should love and help others rather than look down on them. Kindness wins over being judgmental; each of us faces God, not one another, for judgement.

Preaching Points

Parish Masses

- Jesus was criticized for dining with sinners; in the Gospel accounts, he does not seem to pay mind to the criticism or judgmental talking others make about his habits.
- Jesus and heaven delight in the repentance of one person who repents from sin. Repenting and seeking goodness are truly wonderful events.

Masses with Children

- Jesus never seemed to show concern for what others thought of him; he dined with people with whom others wouldn't speak.
- Jesus and all of heaven have great joy when a person who was sinning repents of his sin and commences good work.

Scripture Insights (PS)

Each of us has been given a gift to use in service of the whole community. This diversity is essential to the unity Jesus wants for the Church.

Preaching Points

Parish Masses

- A good leader recognizes people's gifts and finds ways for them to put them to good use. That takes discernment. Who are the people in our lives who have helped us recognize our gifts? Are we able to recognize the giftedness of others and foster it?
- Jesus is the Good Shepherd, who stays with the sheep in spite of danger and even lays down his life for them. St. Charles Borromeo strove to keep the flock together in the midst of challenging times and, in so doing, reminded the whole Church what a good shepherd looks like.

Masses with Children

Use the same preaching points as those for the parish Masses.

Missal Options

- The readings may also be taken from the CP.
- Use any of the three forms of the PA.
- Any of the OT Collects may conclude the UP.
- Although a full set of prayers is found in the PS, you may also use those from the CP (For a Bishop).
- Select from P-I or P-II of Saints, or the Preface of Holy Pastors.
- Consider EP-II.

Song of the Day

"We Belong to You" by Trevor Thompson (OCP)

FRI 5 LM #489 / LMC #193–232 / green
Weekday

Scripture Insights

Christians live and worship in communities and have done so since the earliest of Christian times. We are meant to help one another grow in our Christian faith and to bear one another on our life's journey toward heaven.

Preaching Points

Parish Masses

- The first Christians were considered to be a new sect of Judaism; the Greeks who became Christians entered the Church without first becoming Jewish. St. Paul ministered to these groups.
- When St. Paul preaches, he teaches the people that the good things he says is Christ working in him.

Masses with Children

- Greek believers did not become Christians by becoming Jewish first. St. Paul ministered to the Greek and Jewish peoples.
- When St. Paul preaches, he teaches the people that the good things he says are due to Christ working in him.

Missal Options

- Consider using the prayers from the Twenty-Seventh Sunday in OT.
- Use any of the three forms of the PA.
- Any of the eight Prefaces for OT or the six Common Prefaces may be used.
- You might use EP-II.
- Any OT Collect may be used or adapted to conclude the UP. You might even look at the Collects in the Masses for Various Needs and Occasions for possible concluding prayers.

Song of the Day

"Lord of All Hopefulness" by Jan Struther (Oxford University Press)

SAT 6 LM #490 / LMC #193–232 / green
Weekday

Optional Memorial of the Blessed Virgin Mary / white

Scripture Insights

In the early Church many women and men served the growing Body of Christ. St. Paul mentions several of these ministers by name in today's reading. We too are called to serve the Church in various ways.

Preaching Points

Parish Masses

- How do we balance our human need for sustenance, trade, and money? How do we live lives that are committed to trustworthy stewardship?
- Trustworthiness is something that must be built over years but may be broken in an instant. We must be trustworthy with others' matters and our own.

Masses with Children

- Stewardship is taking care of something or someone; for example, we are stewards of the earth God gave us. How do we develop good stewardship skills in our school years?
- Trustworthiness is something that must be built over time. We must be trustworthy with others' matters and our own.

Missal Options

- Consider using the prayers from the Seventeenth Sunday in OT.
- Use any of the three forms of the PA.
- Any of the eight Prefaces for OT or the six Common Prefaces may be used.
- You might use EPR-II.
- Any OT Collect may be used or adapted to conclude the UP. You might even look at the Collects in the Masses for Various Needs and Occasions for possible concluding prayers.

Song of the Day

"Simple Gifts" (various publishers)

Optional Memorial

- The readings may be taken from the SW, CBVM, or CMML.
- The prayer texts may be taken from the CBVM or CMMM. Any votive Mass for the BVM may be used.
- Use any of the three forms of the PA.
- Select from P-I or P-II of the BVM.
- Any of the OT Collects may conclude the UP.

If it is true that the sacraments are part of the Church's pilgrimage through history towards the full manifestation of the victory of the risen Christ, it is also true that, especially in the liturgy of the Eucharist, they give us a real foretaste of the eschatological fulfillment for which every human being and all creation are destined (cf. Romans 8:19ff).

—*Sacramentum caritatis*, 30

SUN 7 LM #155B / LMC #150B / green

Thirty-Second Sunday in Ordinary Time

Scripture Insights

"The widow's mite" would be a suitable headline for today's readings. True generosity is portrayed through the lives of two widows, the most vulnerable people in society. In the First Reading a widow, in the middle of a great famine, shares the last of her resources with the prophet Elijah. Elijah's trust and encouragement ("Do not be afraid.") strengthen her trust in God, and her generosity in sharing her last meal with Elijah is rewarded with a supply of food that lasts throughout the famine.

Today's Gospel reading opens with Jesus' remarks about the scribes, and these provide the context for what follows. He is criticizing the Jewish scribes, the legal experts, for being more interested in receiving honor from people than serving them.

Jesus singles out the way "they devour the houses of widows"—a devastating criticism! In contrast to their selfishness, Jesus observes a widow in the Temple who provides an authentic example of sacrificial giving. Jesus draws attention to her putting "two small coins worth a few cents" into one of the thirteen collection boxes. Sadly, this translation has lost the beauty of a long English tradition! Literally, the translation should read: "a poor widow came and threw in two mites that make up half a farthing!" The coin referred to here as "a mite" (from the Greek word, *lepton*) is the lowest denomination of a coin that has ever been struck by any nation in history! And yet she is giving to the treasury what in fact she could not afford.

Both readings illustrate the genuine self-sacrificing nature of giving. The widows gave to the extent of hurting! These acts of self-sacrifice by the poorest and most vulnerable offer a beautiful foreshadowing of the genuine self-sacrifice of Jesus, whereby he gave his very life for our salvation.

Preaching Points

Parish Masses

- A community that is living in the right ways of God is one that feeds the hungry and doesn't let anyone go without shelter. In such communities the widows and the orphans have great care taken for them. Those who are helpless have the watchful eye of others caring for their needs.
- Appearances are not what is important to God; the goodness and purity of our hearts are what matters to the Lord.
- The widow gave out of her daily bread and not merely out of her excess; her gift came at great cost to her.
- The mother to whom Elijah spoke fed him and trusted that her jar and jug would last her and her son. She too gave out of her daily bread rather than out of her excess.

Children's Liturgy of the Word

- Appearances can be deceiving. Something that looks good and pretty may not actually be either on closer examination—God doesn't care what it looks like we are doing; he cares what we are actually doing.
- The widow in Jesus' story didn't have much to give, but she shared her money anyway. Jesus teaches us that we should be generous with others.
- The mother to whom Elijah spoke trusted in Elijah and the Lord when she shared her grain and oil. She was rewarded for her trust and generosity.

Missal Options

- Offer any of the three forms of the PA.
- Sing or recite the Gloria and the Creed.
- Any of the seasonal OT Collects may be used or adapted to conclude the UP.
- Select from any of the eight Prefaces of OT.
- Consider EP-III.
- There are six SBs for OT from which to choose.

Music Preparation

- The readings are about giving and hospitality. Ask yourself, "How is our liturgy hospitable?" Provide clear worship aids and signing ministers and listening devices for the deaf. Never assume that people know the service music. Visitors from other churches may not know the settings that are chosen for your particular parish. Make sure these settings are accessible by all who are in attendance.

Music Suggestions

- Gathering: "Table of Plenty" by Daniel J. Schutte (OCP)
- Preparation of the Gifts: "Where Charity and Love Prevail" by Paul Benoit (WLP)
- Communion: "Here at This Table" by Janèt Sullivan Whitaker and Max Whitaker (OCP)
- Sending Forth: "Lead Me, Guide Me" by Doris M. Akers (OCP)

Mass Texts

Introduction to Mass

Let us not be afraid to come into God's presence and offer to him all we have, including our poverty and weakness. In exchange, he gives us all he has, all that he is, through the offering of Christ, once for all. We will place bread and wine on this altar, and God will give us the Body and Blood of his Son for the life of the whole world. Therefore let us praise him with joy and thanksgiving. *My brothers and sisters, let us acknowledge our sins, and so prepare ourselves to celebrate the sacred mysteries.*

Tropes for Penitential Act, Form III

You did not enter a sanctuary made by hands but heaven itself: Lord, have mercy.

You appear before God on our behalf, to reconcile us to the Father: Christ, have mercy.

You will come again to bring salvation to all who eagerly await you: Lord, have mercy.

Dismissal for Children's Liturgy of the Word

Children, today we hear of two widows who willingly gave what little they had because they believed in God who cares for the poor. Let them inspire you and help you trust in the God who loves you, not for what you have, but for who you are, his beloved children in Christ. Go now and listen to him.

Dismissal of Catechumens

Dear friends, God can do wonders with small things. He asks of you only an open heart in which to put his Spirit. Let the Word you have heard today soften the ground of your heart, that new life may spring up from within you and that you may soon rejoice with us to receive Christ, his Son, in the Eucharist. Go in peace.

Dismissal of Extraordinary Ministers of Holy Communion

My friends, we entrust to you our Lord Jesus Christ in his Word and Sacrament, that you may take him to our sick and homebound sisters and brothers. May he fill them with joy and encouragement and unite their prayers to ours in his Spirit. Go in peace.

Universal Prayer

My sisters and brothers, in today's Gospel the widow's gift of her money was a sign of her piety and her trust in God. May our prayers for those in need be a sign of our discipleship and dedication to sharing the Good News.

1. That all Christians may give, not from their surplus wealth, but from their trusting dependence in God, we pray:
2. That our spiritual leaders and all who minister in the Church may be men and women committed to a spirit of poverty, we pray:
3. That world leaders may establish programs and pass laws that benefit human welfare, we pray:
4. That the government may work to prevent corruption on the national and international level, we pray:
5. That the rich may be willing to share with the poor, we pray:
6. For those who have died, may they be received into God's heavenly Kingdom, we pray:

Lord God,
you ask us to come to you empty-handed,
discovering in your infinite mercy
and your unending compassion all that we need.
Help us to be like the widow,
who out of trusting dependence on you,
gave not from her wealth but from her poverty.
Through Christ our Lord.
Amen.

Other Rites and Customs

- Offer a blessing of veterans to mark Thursday's observance of Veterans' Day, adapting chapter 71 in the *Book of Blessings*.
- With Christmas coming up, publicize various bereavement groups in the parish or around the diocese.
- The stories of the generosity of the widows in the First Reading and the Gospel afford a good opportunity to introduce or reflect on the concept of stewardship as a spirituality of gratitude, rather than simply as a way of raising funds or increasing the number of volunteers.

Liturgy and Life

The widow who fed Elijah with the last food she had and the widow who contributed her whole livelihood to the Temple treasury inspire us: "If they can do that, I can at least do something!" Heroes have that effect on us because they are not centered on themselves. The Church has reemphasized stewardship as an approach to life, not just a matter of giving money. It is centered on living out of gratitude. When we receive gifts, we naturally want to respond. Take a look at your giving practices—in terms of money, time, and talent. Does what you are doing fit your values? Meditate on the gifts God has given you and consider a fitting response.

Taking Place This Week . . .

Consider what can be done liturgically, catechetically, and ministerially to respond to these important needs.

- Vocation Awareness Week begins today.
- Daylight Saving Time ends (11/7).
- World Science Day (11/10)
- Veterans Day (USA; 11/11)
- Canadian Remembrance Day (11/11)
- World Pneumonia Day (11/12)

MON 8 LM #491 / LMC #193–232 / green
Weekday

Scripture Insights

Jesus' teaching is that we must love God and love neighbors. Sin is what separates us from God and from our neighbors. We are called to live in right relationship with God and one another.

Preaching Points

Parish Masses

- Justice is a major biblical theme and one with which we interact each day. We are faced with justice issues in micro and macro forms: family, community, country, and world.
- We must never make ourselves the cause of a person's sin. Certainly others are responsible for their actions, but we mustn't encourage sin or participate in it.

Masses with Children

- Justice is something for which we strive. We start small, in our families and communities. How can your class help bring justice and comfort to the poor, to immigrants, or to the elderly in your community?
- We are called to forgive people repeatedly, and to be forgiving people. With regard to issues of bullying in school, forgiving is not an action of allowing ourselves to be hurt.

Missal Options

- Consider using the prayers from the Sixteenth Sunday in OT.
- Use any of the three forms of the PA.
- Any of the eight Prefaces for OT or the six Common Prefaces may be used.
- You might use EPVN-II.
- Any OT Collect may be used or adapted to conclude the UP. You might even look at the Collects in the Masses for Various Needs and Occasions for possible concluding prayers.

Song of the Day

"All Creatures of Our God and King" (various publishers)

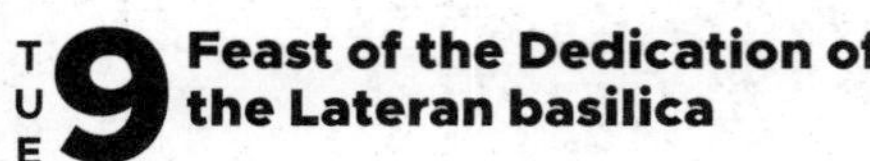

TUE 9 Feast of the Dedication of the Lateran basilica

See page 390.

WED 10 LM #493 or #672 / LMC #193–232 or #407 / white
Memorial of St. Leo the Great, Pope and Doctor of the Church

Today's Saint

Pope Leo acted to protect the physical welfare of the people of Rome, negotiating with Attila the Hun for the safety of Rome and organizing relief efforts after the Vandals attacked the city.

Scripture Insights

People are called to radical obedience to God despite having earthly powers and riches. Even the wisest among us are called to bow to his wisdom and not rely only on their own minds.

Preaching Points

Parish Masses

- Leaders are meant to set a good example for the people, because many look to them in admiration. Leaders must be aware of God and God's wisdom.
- In the Gospel reading we are reminded of the universality of Jesus' earthly mission; he came through the Jewish line of David and was promised though Jewish revelation, yet his coming was for all people.

Masses with Children

- Our leaders are held to a higher standard in terms of their leadership skills. They must seek God and his wisdom.
- When a foreign person returned to Jesus to thank him for his healing ministry, we are reminded that Jesus came for all people, and through him non-Jewish people came to know the one Lord.

Scripture Insights *(PS)*

Jesus gives authority to Peter, whose response of faith is prompted by the Holy Spirit.

Preaching Points

Parish Masses

- In Europe, the first universities grew up around the great cathedrals. Learning and study, the pursuit of wisdom, has always been part of the Church's mission, because study, with prayer, can open us up to understand the Scriptures, the wisdom of heaven.
- Peter is the rock on which Christ established the Church. All authority in the Church starts here. For all his doubts and flaws, Peter is also filled with flashes of profound insight, wisdom from the Holy Spirit.

Masses with Children

Use the same preaching points as those for parish Masses.

Missal Options

- The readings may also be taken from the CP (For a Pope) or CDC.
- The prayers are proper and are found in the PS.
- Use any of the three forms of the PA.
- Any of the OT Collects may conclude the UP.
- Select from P-I or P-II of Saints, or the Preface of Holy Pastors.
- Consider EP-II.

Song of the Day

"Healer of My Soul" by John Michael Talbot (GIA)

T H U **11** LM #494 or #673 / LMC #193–232 or #409 / white

Memorial of St. Martin of Tours, Bishop

Today's Saint

St. Martin of Tours was a Roman soldier who converted after he had a vision of Christ wearing the cloak Martin had given a freezing beggar. St. Martin may have been the first Christian conscientious objector; after his conversion, he rejected violence and left the army for the life of an eremitic monk, eventually being elected bishop of Tours.

Scripture Insights

Wisdom is filled with virtue; it is she who helps and inspires us to fulfill God's will. In Wisdom we find the quality of love focused toward God and neighbor. How is Wisdom's example to us inspirational, and how does she relate to the Kingdom of God?

Preaching Points

Parish Masses

- In Wisdom is "the image of [God's] goodness." How do we perceive wisdom, and how do we orient ourselves toward wisdom?
- The Kingdom of God is something in which we participate now and will continue to experience in fullness in heaven.

Masses with Children

- In the Wisdom books, Wisdom is personified as a woman. How do we understand wisdom, and how do we seek wisdom?
- What is the Kingdom of God? How do we participate in it now, and how do we participate in it after we die?

Scripture Insights *(PS)*

What we do for one of the least, we do for God.

Preaching Points

Parish Masses

- Martin, a Roman soldier, took pity on a beggar and gave him half his cloak. Only afterward was the beggar revealed to be Christ. Christ's presence is seldom obvious. We won't always know who it is we are helping—or neglecting.
- Christ's mission—to proclaim the Good News and bring freedom, healing, and comfort—has become our mission. It is a huge task, but it is not impossible, because Christ is with us. For us, as for St. Martin, it can all start with one encounter.

Masses with Children

Use the same preaching points as those for the parish Masses.

Missal Options

- The readings may also be taken from the CP or CHMW/CS (For Religious).
- The prayers are proper and are found in the PS.
- Use any of the three forms of the PA.
- Any of the OT Collects may conclude the UP.
- Select from P-I or P-II of Saints, or the Preface of Holy Pastors.
- Consider EP-II.

Song of the Day

"Wisdom Has Built a House" by Lucien Deiss (WLP)

F R I **12** LM #495 or #674 / LMC #193–232 or #409 / red

Memorial of St. Josaphat, Bishop and Martyr

Today's Saint

St. Josaphat worked relentlessly toward the goal of reconciliation between the Orthodox and Catholic communities of Kiev. Many of his flock came into the full communion of the Catholic Church, and St. Josaphat was murdered by a violent mob while preaching his ecumenical message, becoming a martyr for Christian unity.

Scripture Insights

In the Wisdom reading, we learn that ignorance of God and his ways makes people foolish. We must seek God and learn his ways to lose that ignorance and gain wisdom. How do we seek God in order to grow in wisdom? What is fear of the Lord?

Preaching Points

Parish Masses

- We can understand more about God in his creation. How do we learn to understand God in his created work?
- We do not know when Jesus will return to us, but we know that at the end of time, Jesus will return to the earth.

Masses with Children

- We can learn about the creator through his creation. How do we learn more about God through his creation?
- Jesus promised the people he would return to earth; we wait for Jesus' coming in joyful hope; we hear these words at each Mass.

Scripture Insights *(PS)*

Unity is Christ's will for us; unity is the call for each of us.

Preaching Points

Parish Masses

- Writing from prison, Paul has one wish for the community at Ephesus: unity. The work of unity is not just the work of one person. It will take all of us, working together—patiently bearing with each other—to build and preserve our unity. This holds true for our Church, our families, our nation, and our world.
- Unity is more challenging than division. It is easier to split off, to isolate ourselves, than it is to stay together. But unity is the attribute of God, and when we stay united, we give witness to God in a divided world.

Masses with Children

- In today's reading, St. Paul is writing from prison. He is writing to the community in Ephesus, and he has one wish for them: unity of faith. It is not just our individual responsibility to spread the Word of Christ. It takes all of us: our families, our friends, and everyone we meet.

Missal Options

- The readings may also be from the CM or CP.
- The prayers are proper and are found in the PS.
- Use any of the three forms of the PA.
- Any of the OT Collects may conclude the UP.
- Select from P-I or P-II of Saints, P-I or P-II of Holy Martyrs, or the Preface of Holy Pastors.
- Consider EP-II.

Song of the Day

"The Summons" by John L. Bell (GIA)

SAT 13

LM #496 or #674A / LMC #193–232 or #410 / white

Memorial of St. Frances Xavier Cabrini, Virgin

Today's Saint

Mother Cabrini founded the Missionary Sisters of the Sacred Heart after she was rejected by other religious orders, demonstrating the determination and firmness of purpose that allowed her to spread missions across North America and made her the first canonized United States citizen.

Scripture Insights

God protected his people, Israel, as they escaped Egypt and crossed the Red Sea. God keeps his promises to the people and loves his chosen ones.

Preaching Points

Parish Masses

- Persistence is a skill that we must use as we seek God and as we seek justice in our communities.
- God will protect and love his people on earth; we are part of God's family, adopted through Jesus.

Masses with Children

- Persistence means that we do not give up on that which we are trying to accomplish. We must be persistent as we seek God and as we seek justice in our communities and in the world.
- We are God's creation and are made in his image and likeness. He loves his chosen people and protects them. We are part of God's family by our adoption through Jesus.

Missal Options

- The readings may also be from PS #674A, the CV, or the CHMW/CS (For Religious).
- Use the Collect from the PS; the other prayers may be taken from the CV (For One Virgin) or CHMW (For Those Who Practiced Works of Mercy).
- Use any of the three forms of the PA.
- Any of the OT Collects may conclude the UP.
- Select from P-I or P-II of Saints, or the Preface of Holy Virgins and Religious.
- Consider EP-II.

Song of the Day

"Praise the One who Breaks the Darkness" by Rusty Edwards (Hope Publishing Company)

Commitment to justice, reconciliation, and peace finds its ultimate foundation and fulfillment in the love revealed to us in Christ.

—*Verbum Domini*, 103

T U E 9 LM #671 / LMC #406 / white

Feast of the Dedication of the Lateran Basilica

About Today's Feast

Today's feast celebrates the Mother Church of all churches in the city of Rome and the world. St. John Lateran is the cathedral church of the bishop of Rome, the pope, given to him by the Roman Emperor Constantine in AD 324. Its yearly celebration is focused not so much on the building but on the people who gather therein. What we celebrate today is the definition of Church retrieved by the Second Vatican Council, that of the Church as the pilgrim people of God (see *Lumen gentium*, chapter 7). We are the Church, the living temples of God's Spirit, called to make Christ's presence real in our lives and be living signs of that presence in the world. God's healing spirit flows through us to the world.

Scripture Insights

St. John Lateran is the cathedral of Rome and the site of several councils of the Church. Less familiar than, say, St. Peter's in Vatican City, St. John's is the church of the pope as the bishop of Rome. Churches remind us that God is present in the world. When we enter the church's space and time, we bring the world with us; when we go back into the world, we bring God with us.

The key word used in today's texts is *temple*, the gathering place for the faithful in Old Testament and very early Christian times. In the Gospel, the merchants were bringing the world's values into the sacred space of the Temple where God's values should reign. In this first part of the Gospel according to John, Jesus defends the Temple as a place of prayer. In the second part of the Gospel, Jesus uses the word *temple* as a metaphor for his own Body. His Body defines sacred space and time and calls attention to the presence of God in the world. This Temple might be killed, but will be raised up in three days. But those listening could not see beyond the literal understanding of the word.

Paul also uses the word *temple* metaphorically to speak of our bodies as temples of the Holy Spirit. As such, we are to behave as though the presence of God shines through us.

Finally, Ezekiel shows us a mystical vision of the Temple in the day of the Lord. Water from this Temple brings life to the whole earth. It is a symbol of wholeness and restored relationship between Israel and God. John would adapt this vision in the last chapters of Revelation.

The words *temple* and *church* continue to have multiple meanings today. We mean the building, the people, and the dwelling place of God in eternity. Church is the means of relationship with God and the people of God. A feast devoted to a church allows us to reflect on who and what church is for us.

Preaching Points

Parish Masses

- Justice is a buzzword on many platforms today, but in the Catholic tradition, justice is something that is based in the Gospel. Justice is what we see Jesus teaching his disciples to bring to the poor and the downtrodden. Each of us is a temple of the Holy Spirit; how do we bring justice to each poor and downtrodden temple we encounter in our lives?
- In every parish one can find a tabernacle—it is the place where the Body of Christ rests in the parish church. Each of us is also a tabernacle, because the Holy Spirit resides in us.
- If each person is a holy temple of God, how should we treat one another? How should we treat ourselves?
- In the Gospel reading, Jesus speaks about the destroying the temple and raising it in three days. He was referring to his own death and Resurrection.

Children's Liturgy of the Word

- Tabernacles have had a special place throughout history—in the Old Testament we read about the tabernacle in the temples and in the desert. We have tabernacles in parish churches too. Each person you encounter is a tabernacle of the Holy Spirit.
- Do we always treat each other like a temple of God? What should you do if you, a living tabernacle, are not being treated in a respectful manner?
- Jesus frequently spoke in stories and pictures, and he did this when he spoke about destroying the temple and raising it back up in three days. Jesus was referring to Good Friday and Easter.

Missal Options

- Offer any of the three forms of the PA.
- Sing or recite the Gloria.
- Any of the seasonal OT Collects may be used to conclude the UP.
- The Preface is found within the texts for the feast ("The Mystery of the Church, the Bride of Christ and the Temple of the Spirit).
- Consider EPVN-III.
- There are six SBs for OT from which to choose.
- The readings from the CDC may be used from the LMC.

Music Preparation

Today, take time to review paragraphs 110–114 in Sing to the Lord, where the principle of progressive solemnity is discussed. This will help as you continue to plan for major feasts.

Music Suggestions

- Gathering: "Christ Is Made the Sure Foundation" (various publishers)
- Preparation of the Gifts: "Dwelling Place" by John B. Foley (OCP)
- Communion: "Taste and See" by James Moore (GIA)
- Sending Forth: "Sing a New Church" by Dolores Dufner, OSB (OCP)

Mass Texts

Introduction to Mass

God cannot be confined to a building. Nevertheless, he chooses to meet us in this holy space where we gather to celebrate the sacraments, just as he dwells in the temple of our bodies, in the sanctuary of our souls. As we remember the dedication of the Lateran Basilica, the bishop of Rome's cathedral, let us cleanse our hearts of all unworthy thoughts, and so prepare ourselves to receive Christ in the Eucharist. *My brothers and sisters, let us acknowledge our sins, and so prepare ourselves to celebrate the sacred mysteries.*

Tropes for Penitential Act, Form III

You, Lord, are the foundation of our lives: Lord, have mercy.

You are God's dwelling with the human race:
Christ, have mercy.

Life-giving water flows out from you,
for our nourishment and healing:
Lord, have mercy.

Dismissal of Catechumens

Friends, we are bound together into the living structure of the Church by the Holy Spirit, with Jesus Christ as our cornerstone. You are called to make your home here in the Church, just as God is making his home within you. As you reflect on this mystery, may you continue to be built up in faith, hope, and love, until you join us around the Lord's table. Go in peace.

Dismissal of Extraordinary Ministers of Holy Communion

Dear friends, our brothers and sisters who are ailing and infirm cannot join us in this temple, so we send you to them bearing Christ's sacred Body, their spiritual food and medicine, to strengthen them in the belief that he dwells with them and that God has chosen them as his holy temple. Go in peace.

Universal Prayer

My sisters and brothers, we are living stones of the Church whose cornerstone is Christ, and so we have the strength to pray for those in need.

1. For the Church of Rome on the anniversary of the dedication of the mother church, St. John Lateran, we pray:
2. For the bishop of Rome, Pope N., that God may continue to bless and guide his ministry, we pray:
3. For all nations, that they may seek justice, renew efforts to support and sustain our planet, and seek to end poverty and hunger, we pray:
4. For all who provide financial resources for the care and maintenance of our church building, that may also care for the living temple of the Body of Christ, we pray:
5. For a desire to celebrate the sacraments, which provide for our renewal of the new and eternal covenant, we pray:
6. That the sick and homebound may be frequently reminded of their oneness with us around the table, we pray:
7. For communities that are preparing for or are in the process of building and dedicating a new church building, we pray;
8. For the faithful departed, that the Father's house may be open to all who have died, we pray:

God our Father,
we are the living stones
out of which you build a temple
to the praise and glory of your name.
Pour forth your Spirit so that we may continue
to realize the gifts that flow from your abundant love.
As we come before you in faith,
help us to build up a world fitting for your coming Kingdom.
Through Christ our Lord.
Amen.

Other Rites and Customs

Organize a pilgrimage to the cathedral of your diocese or a nearby basilica.

Liturgy and Life

The People of God who are the Church are the living temples where he chooses to dwell. St. Augustine reminds us that all who believe in Christ are truly built into the house of the Lord when they are fitted together through love.

SUN **14** LM #158B / LMC #153B / green

Thirty-Third Sunday in Ordinary Time

Scripture Insights

Apocalyptic literature arose in periods of strife and persecution. Two examples are the latter half of Daniel, written around 150 BC, and the Revelation of John, written during the Roman persecution of Christians at the end of the first century AD. Presented as God's revelations to the faithful who live in fear, they exhort people to remain true to God, who will not desert them. Usually a cataclysmic battle ensues between the forces of evil and God, who is the ultimate victor. A glorious ending is painted for those who remain true to God. Apocalyptic literature uses symbols easily recognizable to the audience but often strange to subsequent generations. Many of our images of heaven come from scenes at the end of Daniel and Revelation.

The reading from Daniel shows a shift in Jewish thinking about life after death. According to the Pentateuch and the prophets there was no afterlife. People lived on in the memories of their descendants, and punishment and reward were carried out in subsequent generations. This is why God talks about blessings being carried into the thousandth generation of those who love God, while curses last through the third or fourth generation. (Notice the disparity in duration.) With the advent of unceasing persecution, however, some Jews developed a theology that allowed for God's reward or punishment to take place after death, when "those who sleep in the dust of the earth shall awake." The idea of an afterlife would eventually call up images of fire, heavenly cities, deep pits, and the names of the faithful written in the book of life.

There is a flavor of the apocalyptic in Mark's account of the Gospel this week. Cosmic reversals will occur, the Son of Man will come in the clouds to gather the elect, and heaven and earth will pass away. But Jesus assures us that his words will not pass away and the Father will be in control.

Preaching Points

Parish Masses

- Belief in the afterlife developed over time in Jewish history. The ancients did not believe in an afterlife but did believe that actions would carry over to descendants. Jesus taught us about the Father, heaven, and God's plan for his beloved creation.
- We believe in the resurrection of the dead at the end of time. We will be like Jesus and will have resurrected bodies.
- How do the faithful encourage one another in love, goodness, and good deeds? This encouragement is what we must commit to do for one another.
- We must understand what is forever and what is temporary in our lives. That which is of God and life eternal is forever; so many small things in life are passing minutia.

Children's Liturgy of the Word

- We believe that death is not the end of our lives; because of Christ, our souls can go to heaven when we die. At the end of time, we can become like Jesus and have resurrected bodies.
- We are called to help each other in kindness, love, and in good deeds. We should encourage others when they show such Christ-like behavior.
- Some things in life are temporary, like fashion fads and popular video games. Other things in life are permanent and eternal, such as salvation and that which makes us Christian. We must be careful to understand the difference between these things.

Missal Options

- Offer any of the three forms of the PA.
- Sing or recite the Gloria and the Creed.
- Any of the seasonal OT Collects may be used or adapted to conclude the UP.
- Select from any of the eight Prefaces of OT.
- Consider EP-III.
- There are six SBs for OT from which to choose.

Music Preparation

Our readings speak of awakening and recognizing signs and symbols. It is a call to be prepared. So, it is not too early to be practicing music for Advent and Christmas Time. Consider working with a weekly checklist or a monthly/yearly tickler file (date labeled filing system) to help you be organized. Put due dates on your calendar a week or month ahead of time to stay on task.

Music Suggestions

- Gathering: "Awake, O Sleeper" by Ike Ndolo (OCP)
- Preparation of the Gifts: "Awake, My Soul, Awake" by Harry Hagain, OSB (OCP)
- Communion: "My Lord, What a Morning" (various publishers)
- Sending Forth: "Awake to the Day" by Ed Bolduc (WLP)

Mass Texts

Introduction to Mass

Although we are sinners, God gives us the means of reconciliation, our sacrifice for sin, his own Son, Jesus Christ, our Lord, who has offered himself once for all. Love drove God to do this for us. His love has brought us back, and his love now comes to us in the sacrament of eternal life that he pours out for us from this altar. In gratitude and joy, let us sing his praises. *My brothers and sisters, let us acknowledge our sins, and so prepare ourselves to celebrate the sacred mysteries.*

Tropes for Penitential Act, Form III

You have taken your seat at the right hand of God Most High: Lord, have mercy.

You will gather the elect from every corner of the earth: Christ, have mercy.

Heaven and earth will pass away, but your Word is eternal: Lord, have mercy.

Dismissal for Children's Liturgy of the Word

Dear children, though the sun and the moon and the stars will one day, far from now, fade away, Jesus' words are forever because he is forever and will never leave us. He calls to you now from today's Scriptures. Go and listen to him, and afterward, when you return to us, we will welcome you back with love and joy.

Dismissal of Catechumens

My friends, this community holds you up in prayer as you go forth from us to reflect on the presence and meaning of God's Word in your own lives. Let that Word be your help and guide, your constant companion, leading you deeper into wisdom and faith and bringing you into the fullness of communion with us in the celebration of the Eucharist. Go in Christ's peace.

Dismissal of Extraordinary Ministers of Holy Communion

Friends, those of our members who are absent in body due to physical or mental weakness have need of the Eucharist, as do we all. Take Christ's Body to them, and let them not think they are isolated from us but rather that they are with us in the bond of the Holy Spirit, who is love. Go in peace.

Universal Prayer

My sisters and brothers, we do not know the day or the hour when Christ will return. We must stay vigilant in prayer and in action. Let us bring to the Lord the needs of this world.

1. For the Church, that she may be vigilant in waiting for the Lord's coming and the dawning of God's Kingdom, we pray:
2. For kingdoms in this world that function according to tyranny, that their people may know and experience freedom, we pray:
3. For people who live in fear of the end of the world, that they may convert this fear into action that promotes peace and justice, we pray:
4. For those gathered here as we continue to be built up into the Body of Christ, we pray:
5. For Christians, who commit their lives to daily prayer and to charity, love, and justice, that they may persevere in hopeful expectation of the coming of the Son of Man, we pray:

Lord Jesus, Prince of Peace,
you foretell the dawning of God's Kingdom.
May we discover it
as clearly as we are able to discern the change of seasons.
Let us not fear your imminent return
but await it with hope and joy,
where you live with God in the unity
of the Holy Spirit,
one God, for ever and ever.
Amen.

Other Rites and Customs

- Since we will begin to hear from St. Luke's account of the Gospel in two weeks, offer a Scripture study class that focuses on this Gospel.
- Have copies of LTP's annual resource *At Home with the Word 2022* available for purchase or free distribution.
- Organize a day of recollection for those involved in the Ministry of Consolation, the parish's funeral ministry or bereavement ministry. Provide them with copies of LTP's *Do Not Let Your Hearts Be Troubled: The Catholic Understanding of Death and Eternal Life* by Victoria M. Tufano. It is available in both English and Spanish.

Liturgy and Life

If there were a tornado coming or a great sale, we'd let others know. So why would we keep silent about the greatest news the world has ever received? Today's Gospel tells us to expect the coming of the Son of Man. For Christians, this expectation is a source of hope, not dread, and certainly not indifference. The Second Vatican Council emphasized the missionary nature of the Church. Many of us are uncomfortable with this call to evangelize. We don't want to impose, be intolerant, or act superior. St. Thérèse of Lisieux spent her brief life in a Carmelite monastery, yet she is the patron saint of missionaries. Maybe we need to rethink our ideas about evangelization.

Taking Place This Week . . .

Consider what can be done liturgically, catechetically, and ministerially to respond to these important needs.

- World Diabetes Day (11/14)
- International Day for Tolerance (11/16)
- World Prematurity Day (11/17)
- World Philosophy Day (11/18)
- International Men's Day (11/19)
- Universal Children's Day (11/20)

MON 15 LM #497 / LMC #193–232 / green
Weekday

Optional Memorial of St. Albert the Great, Bishop and Doctor of the Church / white

Scripture Insights

To prefer death to breaking God's commands and laws is to truly prioritize love of God over all else in one's life. In the Maccabees reading, we hear about such people who loved God so deeply that they would rather face death than break God's Word. When are we asked to put our own faith on the line? How do we respond to such a challenge?

Preaching Points

Parish Masses

- Throughout salvation history, we see Israel struck with many difficult times, but there are stories of God's children persevering in the faith. How do we persevere in the faith?
- The blind man whose vision Jesus restored demonstrated perseverance as he sought healing from Jesus.

Masses with Children

- We are called to persevere in our faith. The ancient Israelites demonstrated tremendous courage and perseverance in their faith as they kept the Jewish law.
- The blind man persevered in seeking Jesus as he sought healing, and Jesus healed him because of his faith.

Missal Options

- Consider using the prayers from the Thirty-Second Sunday in OT.
- Use any of the three forms of the PA.
- Any of the eight Prefaces for OT or the six Common Prefaces may be used.
- You might use EPVN-IV.
- Any OT Collect may be used or adapted to conclude the UP. You might even look at the Collects in the Masses for Various Needs and Occasions for possible concluding prayers.

Song of the Day

"Remember Me" by Alan J. Hommerding (WLP)

Optional Memorial

To the great disappointment of his father, St. Albert the Great (1206–1280), known as "the universal doctor," entered the Dominican order, where he was recognized for his acumen. Ahead of his time, he believed that learning did not take place in a vacuum; one must be an interdisciplinary learner. As a prestigious teacher, he had the privilege of instructing and mentoring St. Thomas Aquinas, author of the *Summa theologiae.*

- The readings may be from the SW, #675, LMC #41, or CP or CDC.
- The Collect is proper and found in the PS; the other prayers may be from the CP (For a Bishop) or CDC.
- Consider using P-I or P-II of Saints, or the Preface of Holy Pastors.
- Also consider EP-I or EP-II.
- You may use any OT Collect to conclude the UP.

TUE 16 LM #498 / LMC #193–232 / green
Weekday

Optional Memorials of St. Margaret of Scotland / white; St. Gertrude, Virgin / white

Scripture Insights

Most of us will never face trials like those of Eleazar. We may, however, find ourselves in circumstances where we will need to stand in defense of our faith. How will you stand when challenged in your faith? What issues are you likely to face?

Preaching Points

Parish Masses

- Eleazar's faith was not shaken by his tormentors attempting to force him to break the law; indeed, he preferred death to eating that which God forbade. The virtue of such faith in God and God's ways was clearly illustrated in Eleazar.
- Jesus sought to save those who needed the most help. This is why he went to Zacchaeus' home. Zacchaeus was converted to Jesus' teaching that day.

Masses with Children

- The Jewish people were not allowed to eat pork—it was an ancient dietary law. When people attempted to force-feed Eleazar some pork, he stated that he would rather die. Eleazar demonstrated a tremendous virtue of faith.
- Jesus didn't seem to mind what people said about him or his friends. He went to Zacchaeus' house and the man developed a faith in Jesus and his Word.

Missal Options

- Consider using the prayers from the MPVN-18/2.
- Use any of the three forms of the PA.

- Any of the eight Prefaces for OT or the six Common Prefaces may be used.
- You might use EPR-I.
- Any OT Collect may be used or adapted to conclude the UP. You might even look at the Collects in the Masses for Various Needs and Occasions for possible concluding prayers.

Song of the Day

"All Things Bright and Beautiful" (various publishers)

Optional Memorials

St. Margaret of Scotland

St. Margaret was a Queen of Scotland who dedicated herself to prayer and good works, sheltering pilgrims, restoring monasteries, and promoting Church reform. Her marriage was a happy one, and Margaret and her husband, King Malcolm III, raised eight children together.

- The readings may be taken from the SW, PS #676, CHMW/CS (For Those Who Work for the Underprivileged), or LMC #412.
- Use the Collect from the PS; the other prayers may be taken from the CHMW (For Those Who Practiced Works of Mercy).
- Any of the OT Collects may conclude the UP.
- Select from P-I or P-II of Saints, or the Preface of Holy Virgins and Religious.
- Consider EP-II.

St. Gertrude

St. Gertrude the Great was a Benedictine nun and mystic whose ecstasies and visions are recorded in The Life and Revelations of St. Gertrude the Great. The saint had a great devotion to the Sacred Heart of Jesus, and her visions speak of the ardent love Christ has for each soul.

- The readings may be taken from the SW, PS #677, CV, CHMW/CS (For Religious), or LMC #413.
- Use the Collect from the PS; the other prayers may be taken from the CV (For One Virgin) or from the CHMW (For a Nun).
- Any of the OT Collects may conclude the UP.
- Select from P-I or P-II of Saints or the Preface of Holy Virgins and Religious.
- Consider EP-II.

WED 17 — LM #499 or #678 / LMC #193–232 or #414 / white

Memorial of St. Elizabeth of Hungary, Religious

Today's Saint

As queen of Hungary, St. Elizabeth demonstrated a special care for the poor and underprivileged, nursing the sick and feeding the hungry with her own hands. After her husband's death, the saint became a Third Order Franciscan and devoted herself to prayer, simplicity, and almsgiving.

Scripture Insights

When lives are lost in the name of God, the lives are not forever ended. Indeed, God has prepared a place for each of us in heaven, and our lives are made new for us in our heavenly home.

Preaching Points

Parish Masses

- The mother of the seven sons encouraged one of the men as he faced death. Who encourages you in your faith? How do you encourage others?
- What are the small matters in life in which we must be faithful? Are we always truthful? Stewardly? Helpful? Generous to the poor? Which matters in our own lives need to change?

Masses with Children

- The mother of the seven sons did her best to help her son be faithful as he faced death. Who helps you find faith in God in your life?
- How are we faithful or unfaithful in small matters? Are we always honest, even in small matters? Are we practicing truthfulness and charity toward others?

Scripture Insights *(PS)*

Radical and generous love of the other is the call of the Gospel, because this is the love most like God's love.

Preaching Points

Parish Masses

- St. John says it bluntly: we cannot love God if we neglect our neighbor. Such love is empty, merely "word or speech" rather than "deed and truth." We have just one chance to demonstrate our love for God—this life we have been given. And we have just one way to do it—through our generous love and care for those in need.
- St. Elizabeth cared so much for the poor that she gave up her own bed to a beggar. When her husband went to throw the beggar out, he discovered Christ himself.

Elizabeth is an example of the extraordinary, radical generosity Jesus describes in the Sermon on the Mount.

Masses with Children

- For reflecting on St. Elizabeth, refer to the preaching points for adults.
- We cannot love God unless we love others. We must extend God's generous love to all people.

Missal Options

- The readings may also be taken from the CHMW/ CS (For Those Who Work for the Underprivileged or For Religious).
- Use the Collect from the PS; the other prayers may be taken from the CHMW (For Those Who Practiced Works of Mercy).
- Use any of the three forms of the PA.
- Any of the OT Collects may conclude the UP.
- Select from P-I or P-II of Saints, or the Preface of Holy Virgins and Religious.
- Consider EP-II.

Song of the Day

"In This Place" by Trevor and Victoria Thomson (OCP)

THU 18 LM #500 / LMC #193–232 / green Weekday

Optional Memorials of the Dedication of the Basilicas of Sts. Peter and Paul, Apostles / white; St. Rose Philippine Duchesne, Virgin / white

Scripture Insights

We are not called to blindly follow culture or unjust laws, we are called to be the faithful people of God. We do not give up our faith for the platitudes of political parties.

Preaching Points

Parish Masses

- We do not offer ourselves in the service of other deities because we are the servants of God. We serve God and live our lives following his ways.
- Jesus wept for Jerusalem, knowing the destruction that would visit the holy city.

Masses with Children

- We are called to be God's servants, which means we follow God and his ways and not the ways of other religions. Nor do we worship as forced by civil authorities.
- Jerusalem, the Holy City, had fallen to invading forces in the past, and Jesus wept, knowing Jerusalem would again fall.

Missal Options

- Consider using the prayers from the Twenty-Ninth Sunday in OT.
- Use any of the three forms of the PA.
- Any of the eight Prefaces for OT or the six Common Prefaces may be used.
- You might use EPVN-II.
- Any OT Collect may be used or adapted to conclude the UP. You might even look at the Collects in the Masses for Various Needs and Occasions for possible concluding prayers.

Song of the Day

"God, We Praise You" by Christopher Idle (various publishers)

Optional Memorials

Dedication of the Basilicas of Sts. Peter and Paul

Today's memorial recognizes the dedication of churches constructed on the place of the martyrdom of Sts. Peter and Paul.

- The readings are proper and are from PS #679 and LMC #415.
- A full set of prayer texts is found in the PS.
- Use P-I or P-II of the Apostles.
- Use any of the three forms of the PA.
- Any of the OT Collects may conclude the UP.
- Consider EP-I or EP-II.

St. Rose Philippine Duchesne

St. Rose Philippine Duchesne came to Missouri with the Society of the Sacred Heart to educate and care for Native Americans and the poor of St. Louis. Her zeal and leadership led the sisters to establish schools and orphanages across the United States.

- The readings may be taken from the SW, PS #679A, CV, CHMW/CS (For Religious), or LMC #416.
- Use the Collect from the PS; the other prayers may be taken from the CV (For One Virgin).
- Any of the OT Collects may conclude the UP.
- Select from P-I or P-II of Saints, or the Preface of Holy Virgins and Religious.
- Consider EP-II.

FRI 19 Weekday

LM #501 / LMC #193–232 / green

Scripture Insights

In the Book of Maccabees, we hear about Gentiles having desecrated the holy Temple and the Temple's return to order. In the Gospel reading we hear that Jesus works to restore the Temple to its intended purpose. What does place have to do with God, and how does it affect our behavior and our worship?

Preaching Points

Parish Masses

- We see in the Maccabees reading the historic beginning of the Jewish holy days of Hanukkah, the festival of lights. The people rejoiced in the recovery of their Temple. They wanted to worship God and serve him as their faith directed.
- God's house isn't meant to be a circus-like marketplace or anything but a place of worship. Jesus set right the wrongs that had begun residing at the Temple.

Masses with Children

- The Jewish holiday Hanukkah originated in the Book of Maccabees. They rejoiced that their Temple was back in the order God intended.
- God's house is meant to be a place of prayer and worship. Jesus set right the wrongs that existed at the Temple during his time.

Missal Options

- Consider using the prayers from the MPVN-30/A; use the second option for the Collect.
- Use any of the three forms of the PA.
- Any of the eight Prefaces for OT or the six Common Prefaces may be used.
- You might use EP-II.
- Any OT Collect may be used or adapted to conclude the UP. You might even look at the Collects in the Masses for Various Needs and Occasions for possible concluding prayers.

Song of the Day

"We Acclaim the Cross of Jesus" by Jerome Siwek (WLP)

SAT 20 Weekday

LM #502 / LMC #193–232 / green

Optional Memorial of the Blessed Virgin Mary / white

Scripture Insights

God's laws are not meant to weigh heavily on us, nor are they meant to make us stumble. God doesn't give us laws for the sake of bearing heavy loads. God's laws are meant to give us a path or a light in the darkness. His ways are meant to bring us closer to him.

Preaching Points

Parish Masses

- In Maccabees we see a clear picture of good and evil reaping their harvest in the fight over the holy land. The people of Judah and their Temple should not have been disturbed.
- In God we are alive. Through Jesus we have the joy and promise of eternal life, and we look forward to heaven. This is what it means when we say that God is the God "of the living."

Masses with Children

- Bad decisions are punished, as we read in Maccabees. The Jewish people and their holy Temple should have been left alone.
- We say that God is God "of the living" because through him we have the promise of eternal life.

Missal Options

- Consider using the prayers from the MPVN-16; use the second option for the Collect.
- Use any of the three forms of the PA.
- Any of the eight Prefaces for OT or the six Common Prefaces may be used.
- You might use EP-IV with its proper Preface.
- Any OT Collect may be used or adapted to conclude the UP. You might even look at the Collects in the Masses for Various Needs and Occasions for possible concluding prayers.

Song of the Day

"Virgin, Full of Grace" by Melvin L. Farrell (WLP)

Optional Memorial

For guidance, please refer to page 66 under "Optional Memorial."

SUN 21 LM #161B / LMC #156B / white

Solemnity of Our Lord Jesus Christ, King of the Universe

About Today's Solemnity

On this day, we celebrate the universal kingship of Jesus Christ. He is the fulfillment of the vision of the Son of Man coming in the First Reading from Daniel. Dominion and glory are his as he reigns over all peoples and nations. He is the beginning and the end, as we hear in the Second Reading, from Revelation. His Kingdom does not belong to this world, he tells Pilate in the Gospel reading from John. Pilate names him a king, though Jesus did not identify himself as such. Truth is the basis of Jesus' Kingdom—a far different basis than that of earthly kings and rulers. As his followers, we belong to the truth. The truth of Jesus is the basis on which we can build to transform the world so it more closely mirrors God's Kingdom of love and justice here and now.

Scripture Insights

The Solemnity of Our Lord Jesus Christ, King of the Universe closes the liturgical year with a paradox. Two images of royalty and power confront us. Daniel's visions portray a powerful being who looks like a human being. The original Aramaic says "son of man," but this is not the semi-divine figure of the early first century. In the Old Testament, the phrase "son of man" refers to a human being. What appears to Daniel, however, is no ordinary human being. The power accorded him is greater than any king's power; his kingship is over the whole earth. The figure shares God's power in both the service of peoples and everlasting kingship.

Readers and writers of the New Testament found the Daniel passage and the title "Son of Man" to be profoundly significant in their discussion of Jesus. Much of the image of Jesus' glorious reign at the end of time has its roots in Daniel's vision.

The paradox arises in the passage from John's account of the Gospel. Jesus is brought before Pilate, scourged, insulted, spat upon. He endures interrogation about his kingship and kingdom that Pilate has no possibility of understanding because Pilate's definition of kingship belongs to the world. It is too narrow to contain the broken man who stands before him. If Pilate had looked at the Jewish understanding of kingship found in Deuteronomy 17, he would have understood better. The king of Israel was not to plan battles, attack nations, or make laws. He was not to protect the people. The sole duty of the king was to read the law of God and obey it. He was to provide the example of what it meant to follow God's commandment. In this context, Jesus was truly king in a way the world could not understand.

The Church chooses to portray the broken king on a cross as a symbol of faith, love, and obedience: Deuteronomy's definition. Yet Christians also revere the visions described in the books of Daniel and Revelation, of Christ sitting at the right hand of the Father and reigning gloriously at the end of time. This paradox is the legacy of the Incarnation.

Preaching Points

Parish Masses

- Jesus' glory reigns in our hearts. He directs us, guides us, and helps us to discern our vocation as his disciples. We can come away with him to rest when we need to rejuvenate ourselves for our mission or when we need to understand more clearly how it is he is calling us to reflect his glory. Our relationship with him is one where heart speaks to heart. This strengthens us as we enter another year in our faith journey.
- The Lord's glory is in us and all around us. We celebrate this truth today! As we go through the day and week, notice the many ways the Lord is present around you. Take time to breathe in the glory that surrounds you. Praise God for the glory and splendor of Jesus Christ, King of the Universe!

Children's Liturgy of the Word

- Jesus has many titles that tell us more about him. Titles mentioned today are "faithful witness, the firstborn of the dead and ruler of the kings of the earth."
- Jesus' Kingdom is God's entire creation, the universe and it endless space. Pilate couldn't understand "kingdom" as it pertained to Jesus. Pilate's small view of "kingdom" doesn't begin to encompass the vastness of Christ's Kingdom.

Missal Options

- Consider using the Rite for the Blessing and Sprinkling of Water as a reminder of the Kingdom to which we belong, a Kingdom into which we have been baptized.
- Consider form III of the PA with the tropes found on the next page.
- The Gloria and the Creed are sung or said.
- The Preface is proper and is found in the PT with the texts for Christ the King.
- Consider EP-III.

Music Preparation

- Make this day as bombastic as you can in honor of "Christ the King" and in sharp contrast to the simple Advent that is to come. It doesn't matter how powerful the Scripture readings are or how well the pastor preaches. Music trumps it. It is much more subliminal. Leave everyone with a strong hymn that will make them smile and hum through the coming week.

Music Suggestions

- Gathering: "Crown Him with Many Crowns" (various publishers)
- Preparation of the Gifts: "King of My Heart" by Greg Walton (OCP)
- Communion: "Jesus, the Lord" by Roc O'Connor (OCP)
- Sending Forth: "Soon and Very Soon" by Andre Crouch (various publishers)

Mass Texts

Introduction to Mass

The One who made the far-flung stars and galaxies comes to us as our King, but not as a fearsome tyrant. He is our gentle and merciful ruler. He came to us as a helpless child and as an innocent man sentenced to die for our sins. Love is the scepter of his throne and his own Body and Blood are the food and drink of this kingly banquet to which we are invited. Let us receive him with praise and thanksgiving. *My brothers and sisters, let us acknowledge our sins, and so prepare ourselves to celebrate the sacred mysteries.*

Tropes for Penitential Act, Form III

You are the Alpha and the Omega, the first and the last, the almighty: Lord, have mercy.

You are the firstborn from the dead, the ruler of the kings of the earth: Christ, have mercy.

You love us and have freed us from our sins by your Blood: Lord, have mercy.

Dismissal for Children's Liturgy of the Word

My dear children, God embraces the entire cosmos, and he knows each one of you by name. The love he has for you is greater than the universe and shines brighter than the sun. Jesus came to testify to this truth and to give you his life for it. Go and listen to his voice in today's readings and then come back to us so that we may celebrate his love with you.

Dismissal of Catechumens

Dear catechumens, Jesus Christ calls you to his Kingdom, which is not a kingdom of this world or any world in all of creation. His Kingdom is of heaven, of which his Church is a sign and foretaste. As you go to ponder this mystery, we eagerly await the day when you will join us in communion and in the banquet of Christ the King. Go in peace.

Dismissal of Extraordinary Ministers of Holy Communion

My dear friends, our humble and merciful King, Jesus Christ, has given us himself in the form of bread. The Bread of Life is now yours to take to our sisters and brothers who are sick and suffering. May Christ, the King of the universe, give them glory and everlasting life, and bring us, with them, into his heavenly Kingdom. Go in peace.

Universal Prayer

The Lord is King; let heaven and earth rejoice! Let us pray for the needs of this world so that God's Kingdom may reign here and now.

1. For the Church, that she may minister to all with integrity and truth, we pray:
2. For leaders of nations to understand that there is a greater power that does not belong to this earth, we pray:
3. For all those who, like Pilate, are afraid of the truth and do all they can to shirk the cross, we pray:
4. For the destruction of forces that animate terrorism, torture, narcissism, and disregard for the sacredness of human life, we pray:
5. For the triumph of God's perfect justice in the face of violence and hatred, we pray:
6. For our faith community, that we may be one in Christ's kingship and support one another in carrying his cross, we pray:
7. For hearts and voices that sing of and give witness to God's might and wonderful works, we pray:
8. For those who have died, that they may be welcomed into God's glorious Kingdom of light, happiness, and peace, we pray:

Lord Jesus Christ,
King of every nation under heaven,
you show us the truth that power resides
in the cross.
Continue Help us to reject our sinful lives.
May we come to share
in the fullness of your glory,
where you live and reign with the Father in the unity of the Holy Spirit,
one God, for ever and ever.
Amen.

Other Rites and Customs

- Encourage parishioners to attend the Thanksgiving Day Mass and to bring food for the poor.
- If there are baptized members of other Christian faiths who are ready to join the Catholic Church, receive them into the Church today or on one of the other Sundays of Ordinary Time when they are ready.

Liturgy and Life

Reflect on how you can honor God through compassionate encounter. Perhaps this means reaching out to an estranged friend or family member or direct service to the poor or needy.

Taking Place This Week . . .

Consider what can be done liturgically, catechetically, and ministerially to respond to these important needs.

- Today the special collection is for the Catholic Campaign for Human Development.
- World Day to Eliminate Violence Toward Women and US Thanksgiving Day (11/25)
- Native American Heritage Day (11/26)
- First Sunday of Advent (11/28)
- First Day of Chanukah (11/29)
- National Bible Week begins today.

MON 22 LM #503 or #681 / LMC #193–232 or #418 / red
Memorial of St. Cecilia, Virgin and Martyr

Today's Saint

According to legend, St. Cecilia (ca. third century) was beheaded because she would not forsake her vow of virginity and would not make sacrifices to the gods. She is the patron saint of musicians, singers, and poets.

Scripture Insights

We are called to love others, and to love others, we must give alms. The poor widow didn't skip giving because she was poor; she prioritized giving over her own self. We too are called to be generous; we must give according to the need of others.

Preaching Points

Parish Masses

- When the widow made her donation, she gave money that was not extra money; her money was from her own funds for her daily living.
- Other people made donations that were portions of their extra, or surplus, funds; these gifts were not felt by their pocketbooks. The poor widow's gift was valued because she gave of herself.

Masses with Children

- Extra money is the money people have after they pay for food, housing, and other bills. The widow didn't have extra money; she had only the money she would use for her living expenses, and she gave that money away.
- Some people made large donations of their extra money, but it was no sacrifice for them to give that money. The poor widow made a sacrifice to make her donation; she gave of herself.

Scripture Insights *(PS)*

Jesus is the bridegroom, and the Church is the bride, whom Christ loves and takes to his heart.

Preaching Points

Parish Masses

- St. Cecilia refused to marry, because she knew that Christ alone could be her spouse. Like the wise virgins in the parable, she did not allow anything to distract her but awaited Christ with eager hope.
- "I will lead her into the desert / and speak to her heart," says the beautiful prophesy of Hosea. In the desert—in quiet and stillness—God still speaks to our hearts. Is there enough silence in our lives? Do we take time to listen?

Masses with Children

- Use the same preaching points as those for parish Masses.

Missal Options

- The readings may also be from the CM or CV.
- The Collect is proper and found in the PS; the other prayers may be from the CM (For a Virgin Martyr) or from the CV (For One Virgin).
- Use EP-I (since Cecilia is named), and consider P-I or P-II of Saints, the Preface of Holy Martyrs, or the Preface of Holy Men and Women.

Song of the Day

"How Can I Keep From Singing?" (various publishers)

TUE 23 LM #504 / LMC #193–232 / green
Weekday

Optional Memorials of St. Clement I, Pope and Martyr / red; St. Columban, Abbot / white; and Bl. Miguel Agustín Pro, Priest and Martyr / red

Scripture Insights

The early Christians believed that they would see Jesus return to earth very soon; they were surprised when his return was not imminent. We still wait for Jesus' return, and we wait in trust of his promise.

Preaching Points

Parish Masses

- The dream in the reading from Daniel is an apocalyptic one and is about the political conquests that would change the land and affect God's people.
- Jesus spoke of the Temple being destroyed; the Temple had been destroyed in times past and would be destroyed again in the future. Jesus himself would be killed and would rise again.

Masses with Children

- The dream discussed in the Daniel reading is from a grouping of Scripture types that are "apocalyptic." This dream is about those who would conquer and rule the land of God's people.
- Jesus spoke of the Temple being destroyed, and it had been destroyed previously and rebuilt. Someday it would be destroyed again. Jesus himself would die and then would be resurrected.

Missal Options

- Consider using the prayers from the Second Sunday in OT.
- Use any of the three forms of the PA.
- Any of the eight Prefaces for OT or the six Common Prefaces may be used.
- You might use EPR-II.
- Any OT Collect may be used or adapted to conclude the UP. You might even look at the Collects in the Masses for Various Needs and Occasions for possible concluding prayers.

Song of the Day

"Glory and Praise to You" by Lucien Deiss (WLP)

Optional Memorials

Pope St. Clement I

Pope Clement I was the successor to St. Peter, leading the Church through an age of tumult and growth. He urged the Christian community to live in charity and unity. Like his predecessor, St. Clement was martyred in witness to his faith.

- The readings may be taken from the SW, PS #682, CM, CP (For a Pope), or LMC #419.
- Use the Collect from the PS; the other prayers may be taken from the CM (For One Martyr) or CP (For a Pope).
- Select from P-I or P-II of Saints, P-I or P-II of Holy Martyrs, or the Preface of Holy Pastors.
- Consider EP-I.

St. Columban

St. Columban, or Columbanus, was an Irish monk who left Ireland to establish monasteries in France and Germany, ending his life in Italy, where he founded a monastery that housed a great library and became a center of learning in Europe. St. Columban exhorted his monks to set aside temporary pleasures and remain focused on eternal things, a lesson he modeled in his own life of prayer and service.

- The readings may be taken from the SW, PS #683, CP (For Missionaries), CHMW/CS (For Religious), or LMC #420.
- Use the Collect from the PS; the other prayers may be taken from the CP (For Missionaries) or CHMW (For an Abbot).
- Select from P-I or P-II of Saints, the Preface of Holy Pastors, or the Preface of Holy Virgins and Religious.
- Consider EP-I.

Bl. Miguel Agustín Pro

Bl. Miguel Pro was a Jesuit priest who was martyred by anti-clericalists in Mexico. Bl. Miguel witnessed to his faith during his life with spiritual and corporal works of mercy: caring for the poor and hungry, offering the sacraments, and instructing the faithful.

- The readings may be taken from the SW, PS #683A, CM, CP, or LMC #421.
- Use the Collect from the PS; the other prayers may be taken from the CM (For One Martyr) or CP (For One Pastor).
- Select from P-I or P-II of Saints, P-I or P-II of Holy Martyrs, or the Preface of Holy Pastors.
- Consider EP-II.

WED **24** LM #505 or #683B (LS) / LMC #193–232 or #422 / red

Memorial of St. Andrew Dũng-Lạc, Priest, and Companions, Martyrs

Today's Saints

St. Andrew Dũng-Lạc was a Vietnamese priest and one of 117 martyrs who died practicing and preaching the Catholic faith in Vietnam between the sixteenth and nineteenth centuries.

Scripture Insights

This reading from Daniel tells of Daniel and King Belshazzar. It bears resemblance to the story of Moses and Pharaoh in that God's will is told to the leader by God's servant. God intervenes for his people and is with them even in their suffering.

Preaching Points

Parish Masses

- Loving and serving God does not guarantee a life free of persecution. The early Christians would face persecution, and it would spread the Gospel.
- The responsorial is actually from the Book of Daniel, and it calls on aspects of creation to praise and exalt the Lord. Even in times of difficulty, we too should praise the Lord.

Masses with Children

- Loving and serving God does not earn a person a life free of persecution; indeed, we are sometimes at the mercy of others' free will when they choose oppression. The early Christians faced persecution, and that persecution spread the Gospel.
- In the Responsorial Psalm, we hear that particular parts of creation are called to praise and exult the Lord. Even when we face difficulties in our lives, God is with us, and we too can praise him.

Scripture Insights *(PS)*

For the Church, persecution is inevitable, but patient endurance will bring salvation—and give witness.

Preaching Points

Parish Masses

- Jesus warns the disciples of what they have to expect: persecution, disgrace, even death. Our experience is very different from theirs. But we still need to ask God for the right words to speak when our faith is challenged or questioned, and the reward of perseverance will be the same for us as it was for them.
- For those who believe in the Resurrection, death is not the end. The martyrs who endured such torments are now in the hands of God and intercede for all of us. Do you know any Vietnamese Catholics? Their faith, the legacy of the Vietnamese martyrs, strengthens and enriches the Church in many parts of the United States.

Masses with Children

Jesus warns us that we could face hard times when we follow him. We need God to help us when we are challenged.

Missal Options

- The readings may also be from the CM.
- The prayers are proper and found in the PS.
- Use any of the three forms of the PA.
- Any of the OT Collects may conclude the UP.
- Select from P-I or P-II of Saints, P-I or P-II of Holy Martyrs, or the Preface of Holy Pastors.
- Consider EP-II.

Song of the Day

- "How Great Thou Art" (various publishers)

THU 25 LM #506 / LMC #193–232 / green
Weekday

Optional Proper Mass for Thanksgiving / white; Optional Memorial of St. Catherine of Alexandria, Virgin and Martyr / red

---

Scripture Insights

In the Old Testament reading, Daniel was unjustly thrown to lions, but they did not harm him, and the terrible ordeal served to bring people to know the Lord. We are called to faith without having such experiences and signs.

Preaching Points

Parish Masses

- Jesus asks us not to fear the coming of the Son of Man but to anticipate it and trust that he will come.
- We live in the present time and understand our history while anticipating our future. What do we do as we wait for Jesus' return? We live his teachings, practicing what he told us to do.

Masses with Children

- Jesus doesn't want us to fear his coming but tells us to anticipate it, trusting that he will come. We are happy that Jesus will return to us!
- We live in a time that is thousands of years after Jesus, and we do not know when he will return. How do we spend our time while we wait for him? We follow Jesus' teachings, and live how he taught us to live.

Missal Options

- Consider using the prayers from the MPVN-30/A/1.
- Use any of the three forms of the PA.
- Any of the eight Prefaces for OT or the six Common Prefaces may be used.
- You might use EP-II.
- Any OT Collect may be used or adapted to conclude the UP. You might even look at the Collects in the Masses for Various Needs and Occasions for possible concluding prayers.

Song of the Day

"Come, Ye Thankful People, Come" (various publishers)

Thanksgiving Day

- Any readings from LM #943–947 may be used.
- The Missal for the United States provides a set of prayers, including a Preface, at the end of the PS.
- The Gloria and Creed are not sung (or said).
- Consider EPVN-IV.
- The blessing of food is found in chapter 58 of the BB. It may take place within or outside Mass.

Optional Memorial

St. Catherine was an Egyptian Christian who was martyred by the Roman emperor Maxentius for refusing to renounce her faith. She is admired for her intelligence and wit, having defeated fifty of the emperor's pagan philosophers in debate with so much conviction and wisdom that, legend says, many of the philosophers converted to Christianity.

- The readings may be taken from the SW, PS #683C (LS), CM, or CV.
- Use the Collect from the PS; the other prayers may be taken from the CM (For a Virgin Martyr) or from the CM (For One Virgin).
- Use any of the three forms of the PA.
- Any of the OT Collects may conclude the UP.
- Consider EP-I.

FRI 26 LM #507 / LMC #193–232 / green **Weekday**

Scripture Insights

Jesus' words are eternal. Jesus is the Word of God, and he has brought us to the point of knowing the Kingdom of God. Through him we have the opportunity to participate in the Kingdom of God.

Preaching Points

Parish Masses

- Like the Gospel reading's fig tree that blossoms signaling summer, there will be signs that signal the coming of the Lord.

Masses with Children

- We know when seasons shift because we see changes in nature; Jesus says that we will anticipate his coming through changes too.

Missal Options

- Consider using the prayers from the MPVN-17/C.
- Use any of the three forms of the PA.
- Any of the eight Prefaces for OT or the six Common Prefaces may be used.
- You might use EP-IV with its proper Preface.
- Any OT Collect may be used or adapted to conclude the UP. You might even look at the Collects in the Masses for Various Needs and Occasions for possible concluding prayers.

Song of the Day

"Praise to You, O Christ Our Savior" by Bernadette Farrell (OCP)

SAT 27 LM #508 / LMC #193–232 / green **Weekday**

Optional Memorial of the Blessed Virgin Mary / white

Scripture Insights

God's people may experience persecution, hardship, and even worse, but in the end, they will triumph under Jesus, the King of the Universe. God loves and protects his people, and through Jesus, we are grafted onto the vine that is Israel.

Preaching Points

Parish Masses

- We must always be ready for our Lord to come back to us. We shouldn't grow lazy and neglect justice for the poor, neglect prayer, or stop following his Word.

Masses with Children

- We should always be ready for Jesus' return. This means that we must be Jesus' hands and feet on this earth, especially while he is in heaven.

Missal Options

- Consider using the prayers from the MPVN-47.
- Use any of the three forms of the PA.
- Any of the eight Prefaces for OT or the six Common Prefaces may be used.
- You might use EP-II.
- Any OT Collect may be used or adapted to conclude the UP. You might even look at the Collects in the Masses for Various Needs and Occasions for possible concluding prayers.

Song of the Day

"*Laudate, Laudate Dominum*"
by Christopher Walker (OCP)

Optional Memorial

- The readings may be taken from the SW, CBVM, or CMML.
- The prayer texts may be taken from the CBVM or CMMM. Any votive Mass for the BVM may be used.
- Use any of the three forms of the PA.
- Select from P-I or P-II of the BVM.
- Any of the OT Collects may conclude the UP.

Reception of the Holy Oils

Introduction

"The reception of the Holy Oils may take place in individual parishes either before the celebration of the Evening Mass of the Lord's Supper or at another time that seems more appropriate." (Roman Missal, Chrism Mass, no. 15)

In 1989, the Holy See confirmed a ritual text for the reception of the holy oils for optional use in the dioceses of the United States, allowing for the reception to take place during the procession of the gifts at the Holy Thursday Mass of the Lord's Supper or on another suitable day. *The Roman Missal*, Third Edition, implemented in 2011, introduces a new rubric at the conclusion of the Chrism Mass. The first option for the reception of the holy oils is before the Mass begins, but according to pastoral necessity and any guidelines of the diocesan Bishop, "another time that seems more appropriate" could also include the offertory procession (as in the original ritual) or perhaps before the Penitential Act.

The original text of the *Reception of the Holy Oils* is still in force as an optional rite in the United States. As indicated in its introduction, the text may be adapted as needed. Whether or not a formal reception of the oils is celebrated, the pastor may wish to acknowledge the presence of the newly received holy oils as a sign of unity with the Bishop and the diocesan Church.

Rubrics

1. It is appropriate that the Oil of the Sick, the Oil of Catechumens, and the holy Chrism, which are blessed by the Bishop during the Chrism Mass, be presented to and received by the local parish community.
2. The reception of the holy oils may take place at the Mass of the Lord's Supper on Holy Thursday or on another day after the celebration of the Chrism Mass.
3. The oils should be reserved in a suitable repository in the sanctuary or near the baptismal font.
4. The oils, in suitable vessels, are carried in the procession of the gifts, before the bread and wine, by members of the assembly.
5. The oils are received by the Priest and are then placed on a suitably prepared table in the sanctuary or in the repository where they will be reserved.
6. As each of the oils is presented, the following or other words may be used to explain the significance of the particular oil.
7. The people's response may be sung.

Reception of the Holy Oils

Presenter of the Oil of the Sick:

The Oil of the Sick.

Priest:

May the sick who are anointed with this oil experience the compassion of Christ and his saving love, in body and soul.

The people may respond:

Blessed be God for ever.

Presenter of the Oil of Catechumens:

The Oil of Catechumens.

Priest:

Through anointing with this oil, may our catechumens who are preparing to receive the saving waters of Baptism be strengthened by Christ to resist the power of Satan and reject evil in all its forms.

The people may respond:

Blessed be God for ever.

Presenter of the Holy Chrism:

The holy Chrism.

Priest:

Through anointing with this perfumed Chrism may children and adults, who are baptized and confirmed, and Priests, who are ordained, experience the gracious gift of the Holy Spirit.

The people may respond:

Blessed be God for ever.

The bread and wine for the Eucharist are then received and the Mass continues in the usual way.